Routledge Handbook
of Global Sport

The story of global sport is the story of expansion from local development to globalized industry, from recreational to marketized activity. Alongside that, each sport has its own distinctive history, sub-cultures, practices and structures.

This ambitious new volume offers state-of-the-art overviews of the development of every major sport or classification of sport, examining their history, socio-cultural significance, political economy and international reach, and suggesting directions for future research. Expert authors from around the world provide varied perspectives on the globalization of sport, highlighting diverse and often underrepresented voices. By putting sport itself in the foreground, this book represents the perfect companion to any social scientific course in sport studies, and the perfect jumping-off point for further study or research.

The *Routledge Handbook of Global Sport* is an essential reference for students and scholars of sport history, sport and society, the sociology of sport, sport development, sport and globalization, sports geography, international sports organizations, sports cultures, the governance of sport, sport studies, sport coaching or sport management.

John Nauright is Dean of the Stephen Poorman College of Business, Information Systems, and Human Services at Lock Haven University, USA. He is also Visiting Professor at Lomonosov Moscow State University in Russia; University of the West Indies in Barbados; and the University of Ghana. He edits an annual special issue of *Sport in Society* entitled "SportsWorld: Global Sports Business and Cultures".

Sarah Zipp is Lecturer in sport studies and management at the University of Stirling, UK. She has also taught in the USA, Netherlands, Singapore and Japan. Her work explores socio-cultural aspects of sport, including sport for development, gender equality, globalization, health and issues of social justice. Her research and sport for development field experiences have taken her to Zambia, Bosnia and Herzegovina, Barbados and St Lucia.

Routledge International Handbooks

For more information about this series, please visit: www.routledge.com/Routledge-International-Handbooks/book-series/RIHAND

Routledge Handbook of Global Sport

Edited by John Nauright and Sarah Zipp

LONDON AND NEW YORK

First published 2020 by Routledge

2 Park Square, Milton Park, Abingdon, Oxon OX14 4RN
605 Third Avenue, New York, NY 10017

Routledge is an imprint of the Taylor & Francis Group, an informa business

First issued in paperback 2022

British Library Cataloguing-in-Publication Data
A catalogue record for this book is available from the British Library

Library of Congress Cataloging-in-Publication Data
A catalog record for this book has been requested

ISBN: 978-1-138-88723-7 (hbk)
ISBN: 978-1-03-233723-4 (pbk)
DOI: 10.4324/9781315714264

Typeset in Bembo
by Apex CoVantage, LLC

This book is dedicated to the team of authors who contributed their time, expertise and diverse perspectives to this project. Special thanks to Zachary Beldon and Hongxin Li for their tireless efforts as research assistants. We are grateful to have such a truly global team working in collaboration, despite its challenges. They have given a vivid voice to each sport and sought to include the history of women, people of colour, people with disabilities and those who are often overlooked in sport history.

We also dedicate this book to our families – Jenni, Ashley and Lauren of Clan Nauright. To Aaron, Adelyn and Anna Gwenyth of Clan Zipp.

Contents

Contents

Contents

Contributors

Sergey Altukhov is Deputy Director of Sport Management at Lomonosov Moscow State University, Russia. He serves as the Chief Editor for the web portal sportdiploma.ru. Dr Altukhov is a member of the Expert Council for Physical Culture and Sport of the Council of Russian Federations. He is considered a leading figure in the management and business of ice hockey.

Christopher Atwater is Associate Professor of Sport Management at Pfeiffer University, USA and serves as the Director of Sport Management programs in the Division of Business.

Susan Barton is honorary Visiting Research Fellow in the International Centre for Sports History and Culture at De Montfort University, UK. She is an historian with a broad spectrum of research in social and cultural history with a particular interest in leisure and tourism.

Mikhail Batuev is Lecturer in Sport Management at Northumbria University, UK. His main research interests are organization of action sports, the sport program of the Olympic Games, and evolution of modern sports. He also has substantial practical experience in organizing and marketing international events in extreme and youth sports.

Zachary Beldon is PhD student in the Department of Kinesiology, Health Promotion and Recreation at the University of North Texas, USA. Zachary currently serves as a Research Assistant in the Recreation, Event and Sport Management program. Zachary's research interests include youth sport programming, sport for development, sport management and sport history.

David Black is Chair of Political Science and Lester B. Pearson Professor of International Development Studies at Dalhousie University in Halifax, Canada. His research interests have included Canada's involvement in Sub-Saharan Africa; sport, politics, and development; and post-apartheid South African foreign policies.

Gherardo Bonini is the Deputy Director of the Historical Archives of the European Union. He is a member of the European Committee for Sports History (CESH) and Co-founder of the Italian section of CESH. HI is a member of the Worldwide Society of Sport Historians (ISHPES). He has authored and co-authored more than 30 articles for the Journal of Serious Strength Athletes, made various contributions to encyclopaedias, journals and proceedings.

James Bowness is Lecturer in Sociology and Social Policy at Glasgow Caledonian University in Scotland, UK. His research interests include sporting communities, identities and Masters sport.

His PhD (2017) was titled "Physical Activity in Later Life: A Phenomenology of Ageing Men and Women in the Masters Highland Games".

Joe Bradley is Senior Lecturer in Sport Studies at the University of Stirling in Scotland, UK. His background is in political science, sociology and modern history. His research interests lie in sport's relationship with ethnicity, nationalism, identity, race, religion and politics.

Tim Breitbarth teaches in the Department of Management and Marketing at Swinburne University of Technology, Australia. Dr Breitbarth's has researched various aspects of management and marketing of sport, with particular focus on corporate social responsibility and sustainability in football. He serves on the editorial board of several journals, including the *Journal of Public Affairs*, *Sport & Entertainment Review*, *Managing Sport and Leisure*, *International Journal of Sport Management*, *Journal of Global Sport Management* and *Sports Business Management*.

Kipchumba Chelimo Byron is a Graduate Teaching Assistant in the Department of Kinesiology at the University of Georgia, USA. His research focus is on sport in Kenya.

Mike Callan is Principal Lecturer in Sport Development and Business at the University of Hertfordshire, UK. He is President of the International Association of Judo Researchers and Education Director of the Commonwealth Judo Association. Previously he was the International Federation Services Group Leader for Judo for the 2012 Olympic and Paralympic Games.

Mauro Cesar Gurgel Alencar de Carvalho is Lecturer at Universidad Católica del Maule, Chile. He is Physical Education teacher at Colégio Pedro II and International Program Coordinator of Euro American Network of Human Kinetics. He also has a judo black belt and works with school physical education, physical training of high-level athletes, judo, resistance training and physical evaluation.

Jepkorir (Rose) Chepyator-Thomson is Professor of sport management, Department of Kinesiology, University of Georgia, USA. Dr Chepyator-Thomson's research studies focus on issues of diversity in sport, women and sport, sport migration, and sport policy and African sport. Her current research centres on Kenyan runners and their athletic performances at the Olympics games.

Tsz Lun (Alan) Chu is Assistant Professor of Sport Psychology at the University of Wisconsin-Green Bay, USA. Dr Chu serves on the Coaching Committee of the National Collegiate Table Tennis Association. His research focuses on sport and exercise motivation.

Anne DeMartini is Associate Professor of Sport Management at Flagler College, Florida, USA. Ms. DeMartini teaches undergraduate students in sport law, sport sociology, sport ethics, and recreation and fitness management. Her research focuses on issues of discrimination in sport, legal consciousness and concussion protocol, and legal issues associated with CrossFit.

Marques R. Dexter is a Graduate Assistant in the Department of Kinesiology at the University of Georgia, USA. His research is on sport management and policy.

Geoff Dickson is Head of the Department of Management, Sport and Tourism within the La Trobe Business School, Australia. His research interests are expansive, including; inter-organizational relationship, sport governance, event impacts and legacies, volunteers, sponsorship, ambush marketing and consumer behaviour. He is a former president of the Sport Management Association of Australia and New Zealand and is also on the executive of the World Association of Sport Management.

Hunter Fujak is Lecturer in Sports Management at Deakin University in Melbourne, Australia. He is a Certified Practising Accountant. With a corporate background in market research and consultancy, he has published across sport marketing, media and management and researched across all four of Australia's football codes.

Gerald Gems is Professor Emeritus at North Central College in Naperville, Illinois, USA. He is a past President of the North American Society for Sport History and past Vice-President of the International Society for the History of Physical Education and Sport. He was named a Fulbright Scholar by the United States government in 2011–2012, and granted the Routledge Award for Scholarship in 2016.

Steve Greenfield is a Professor at the Westminster Law School, UK. He co-founded the Centre for Law, Society and Popular Culture. His research is focused on legal issues in sports and entertainment.

Luke Harris is Honorary Research Fellow in the Department of History at the University of Birmingham, UK. In 2016, his book won the International Society for Olympic Historians award for the outstanding book upon the Olympic movement.

Matthew G. Hawzen is Assistant Professor of Sports Administration in the School of Administrative Science at Fairleigh Dickinson University, USA. Matthew's research and teaching draw upon critical theory to develop understanding of the sociocultural and political economic dimensions of physical activity and sport management.

Susanna Hedenborg is Professor in Sport Sciences Malmö University, Sweden and President of the Swedish Research Council for Sport Science, has researched horse sports in various forms in history and today. Her main focus has been continuities and changes in gender relations intersected with social class, ethnicity and generation.

Steve Hendricks is Head Women's Volleyball Coach at Barry University in Florida, USA. He was selected as Sunshine State Conference Coach of the Year in 2018.

Jacob Hindin is a doctoral candidate in Sport Management at Florida State University, USA. His primary research interests are eSports and the politics and economics of stadium subsidization in the United States.

Dexter Zavalza Hough-Snee is an interdisciplinary cultural studies scholar whose research explores the intersections of sport, indigeneity and colonialities.

Mike Huggins is Emeritus Professor of Cultural History at the University of Cumbria, UK. He is on the editorial boards of five sports history journals. He has won awards for his work from the North American Society for Sport History and the International Society for the History of Sport and Physical Education.

Melly Karst is a retired teacher who has taught English, debate, speech, drama and English as a second language to secondary school students in public and private schools in Kansas and Texas, USA for more than 35 years. As a teacher, she has worked with student athletes from a variety of backgrounds and interests.

Ellyn Kestnbaum is an adult figure skater and a volunteer judge for singles, pairs and ice dance with US Figure Skating.

Jørgen B. Kjær is Researcher and Lecturer in the Sport Management Program at Towson University, USA. Dr Kjær's research focuses on professionalization processes in sport. His research experience includes involvement in a €600,000-funded qualitative research project on women's professional soccer in Scandinavia. Dr Kjær also conducts research related to effective coaching in youth sport and he serves as the boys' varsity soccer coach at Sidwell Friends School in Washington DC, USA.

Darlene Kluka has worked in academia, coaching, sport governance and consulting throughout her career. Amongst her many career highlights, she served as Dean of the School of Human Performance and Leisure Studies at Barry University, USA, worked with the United States Olympic Committee, served as Vice President of USA Volleyball, honoured with USA Volleyball Leader in Volleyball Award, and was inducted into the American Volleyball Coaches Association Hall of Fame.

Hongxin Li is a PhD student in the Department of Kinesiology, Health Promotion and Recreation at University of North Texas, USA where he serves as the Research Assistant in the Sport and Event Management Research Laboratory. Li's research interests include sport management, sport marketing, and sport pedagogy.

Cheryl Litman is an Economist with a focus on economic history, institutions and economic development. Her research is focused on the effectiveness of transparency as a form of regulation for non-profit institutions and the governance of sport. She serves as a volunteer official for US Figure Skating with judging and technical appointments in singles, pairs, dance and synchronized skating.

Charles Little is Senior Lecturer in Sports Management at St Mary's University Twickenham, UK. His research interests include sport and politics in Southeast Asia, sport and international relations, and sport, identities and colonial nationalisms within the British Empire.

Brandon Mastromartino is a PhD Candidate in Sport Management at the University of Georgia, USA. His research focuses on sports marketing, the globalization of sports, and sport fan psychology.

Leonardo José Mataruna-Dos-Santos is Assistant Professor, College of Business Administration, American University in the Emirates in Dubai, United Arab Emirates. He is also Associated Researcher at Coventry University – CTPSR and UFRJ-PACC. Part of the judo coaching team for Brazil at six Olympic and Paralympic Games, he is also PE Teacher and Journalist and worked as Consultant for UNESCO to promote Anti-Doping Orientation and Olympic Education.

Robert Matz is an Instructor at the Irvine Division of Continuing Education at the University of California Irvine, USA. He completed his doctoral degree in Kinesiology at the University of Georgia. His research focus is on sport management and policy.

Kieren McEwan is based within the Department of Sport and Exercise Science at the University of Portsmouth, UK, where he is the Program Coordinator for undergraduate courses in the fields of Sports Management and Sports Development. His research interests centre on the interplay between participant personality traits, resultant identities and their impacts on extreme sports markets.

Sarthak Mondal is a second-year PhD student of Sport Business Management in Sheffield Hallam University, UK. He currently works with the university to deliver the extra-curricular award to other students apart from academics and is a part of the Inclusion Advisory Group for the Sheffield and Hallamshire County Football Association, where he champions against discrimination of all forms on the football pitch. He is also a licensed football coach.

Chad Morgan is a graduate student in the Department of Kinesiology, Health Promotion and Recreation at the University of North Texas, USA. He is a ticket sales manager for the Allen Americans, a professional ice hockey club in Allen, Texas. Chad also serves as a Research Assistant in the Sport and Event Management Research Laboratory.

Joseph Muller is a PhD student at the University of Portsmouth, UK currently investigating the role that adventure and extreme sports play in mental well-being. He is a level 2 qualified coach in basketball.

Samuel Nabors is a graduate student in the Department of Kinesiology, Health Promotion and Recreation at the University of North Texas, USA where he serves as a Research Assistant in the Sport and Event Management Research Laboratory. Nabors's research interest is sports management with a focus on soccer and youth development.

John Nauright is Dean of the Stephen Poorman College of Business, Information Systems, and Human Services at Lock Haven University, USA. He is also Visiting Professor at Lomonosov Moscow State University in Russia; University of the West Indies in Barbados; and the University of Ghana. He edits an annual special issue of *Sport in Society* entitled "SportsWorld: Global Sports Business and Cultures".

Joshua Newman is Professor of Sport, Media, and Cultural Studies and Director of the Center for Sport, Health, and Equitable Development at Florida State University, USA.

Sandy Nguyen is a graduate student at the University of North Texas within the Recreation, Events, and Sport Management program, USA. She holds the position of Graduate Research Assistant for the Kinesiology Health Promotion and Recreation Department and is presenting research while completing her doctoral degree. Her research is focused on student athletics and their development.

Carol Osborne is Senior Lecturer in the School of Sport at Leeds Beckett University, UK, where she teaches on a range of social sciences modules. Her primary research and editing interest is women and gender relations in sport. She sat on the executive committee of the British Society of Sports History (BSSH) 2007–2017 and worked with the UK-based Sporting Heritage CIC on the Hockey Museum's 2016 scoping project, Investigating Hockey's International Heritage.

Charles Parrish is Assistant Professor of Sport Management in the College of Business at Western Carolina University, USA. His primary research interest is the management and utilization of sports stadiums as host venues for corporate and social events.

Gertrud Pfister is Professor Emeritus at the Department of Nutrition and Sport, University of Copenhagen, Denmark. Her areas of expertise are: Sport and gender, sport and leadership, sport and exercise in the context of ageing, ethnicity, migration and transnationalism; sport participation in various countries, physical activity and health, sport coaches, physical activity and sport - intercultural comparisons, media sport, women's soccer and fandom. In Germany and in Denmark, Pfister conducted several large national and international research projects, among others funded by the IOC, the German Ministry of Women and Youth, the Danish Agency of Science, Technology and Innovation and the EU.

Haozhou Pu is Assistant Professor in the Department of Health and Sport Science at University of Dayton, USA. His research interests focus on the political economy of mega-events, globalization, and consumer psychology of sport fandom. His most recent research involves a critical analysis of the legacy discourse related to the two Olympic Games in Beijing (the 2008 Summer Olympics and the 2022 Winter Olympics).

Anand Rampersad is Lecturer in sociology at the University of the West Indies, St Augustine, Trinidad and Tobago. He volunteers a weekly column "Sportification" for the Trinidad Guardian addressing different socio-economic and political issues related to sport. He is also a member of the management team of Trinidad and Tobago Women Cricket Association (TTWCA).

Leigh Robinson is Pro-Vice Chancellor and Executive Dean of the School of Sport and Health Sciences at Cardiff Metropolitan University, UK. Her research interests are in the area of sport governance and performance management in sport. She is a member of the editorial panels of *Managing Sport and Leisure*, *Sport Management Review*, *European Sport Management Quarterly* and the *Journal of Global Sport Management*.

Katja Sonkeng is a Graduate Teaching Assistant in the Department of Kinesiology at the University of Georgia. Her research includes areas of sport management, policy and physical activity.

Ryan Turcott is Assistant Professor at Adelphi University in New York City, USA. Dr Turcott's research and teaching revolve around sport media/public relations, sport marketing and sport labour migration.

Christina Villalon is a doctoral student at West Virginia University, USA. Her primary research interests include coach development, the coach–athlete relationship, and portrayal of females in sports.

Karen Weiller-Abels is an Associate Professor in the Department of Kinesiology, Health Promotion and Recreation at the University of North Texas (USA). She is also a member of the Women's and Gender Studies program. Her research and teaching is focused on sociology of sport and physical education.

Hanhan Xue is Assistant Professor of Department of Sport Management at Florida State University, USA. Her research and teaching focuses on the field of management of international business for professional sport organizations, particularly in the Chinese market, as well as e-sports. She is a fellow in the FSU Center for Sport, Health, and Equitable Development, where she conducts community needs assessments for urban redevelopment projects in Tallahassee, Florida.

Aaron Zipp is Lecturer in Sport Studies and Sport Management at the University of Stirling in Scotland, UK. His academic and practical interests include sporting heritage, sport event management and leadership. Aaron conducts Highland games heavy events for team building and leadership training. He has taught in the USA, Netherlands and the UK.

Sarah Zipp is Lecturer in sport studies and management at the University of Stirling, UK. She has also taught in the USA, Netherlands, Singapore and Japan. Her work explores socio-cultural aspects of sport, including sport for development, gender equality, globalization, health and issues of social justice. Her research and sport for development field experiences have taken her to Zambia, Bosnia and Herzegovina, Barbados and St Lucia.

Introduction

Developing our understanding of specific sports around the world

Sarah Zipp and John Nauright

The history and development of sport around the world reflects our own growth and evolution as people, societies and cultures. In this handbook, we share the stories of how more than 40 sports were created, developed and spread across the globe. Along the way, we explore the key people and movements that propelled each sport along its path. Authors from Europe, North America, Latin American and the Caribbean, Asia, the Middle East, Africa and Australia have contributed their knowledge and understanding to this collection. Within each chapter, we sought to include perspectives from women, people of colour, people with disabilities and people from the Global South, giving voice to those often written out of history.

Fundamentally, sport consists of a wide variety of physical activities designed to achieve a result, generate a physical feeling or better an opponent, in individual or team competition. Many sports are played almost everywhere around the world such as soccer or basketball, while many others have massive regional followings or have become synonymous with national identities. One can hardly think of Brazil without soccer, New Zealand without rugby, Canada without ice hockey or India without cricket, for example. Many cities and locales have become famous through their association with major sports events, such as the Old Course at St Andrews in Scotland, home of golf. In horse racing, the iconic Churchill Downs in the USA is the home of the Kentucky Derby.

Sports often take on unique socio-cultural variations and interpretations. For example, English test cricket, rooted in tradition and legacy, is vastly different from the fast-paced and commercialized Indian Premier League. "Calypso cricket" of the West Indies is yet another variation on this historic sport. Other sports develop differently for other reasons. In the USA, women's football (soccer) has become a global powerhouse, while the men's side struggles to qualify for international competitions. Understanding how and why sports follow these paths is key to understanding the role of sport in history and what the future holds.

Modern sports began to be commercialized in the 18th century though the period of "take-off" and global expansion dates from the latter 19th century. As sports became activities played and watched around the world, especially since the widespread advent of pay television from the 1980s onward, academic and popular literature on sports in general and individual sports in particular has blossomed. This volume seeks to bring together for the first time academic literature and understanding of individual sports played around the world. Books about specific sports have been around for decades. In the late 1800s the Badminton Library published books on specific sports, followed in the early 1900s by Spalding sporting goods company publishing annual guides to individual sports such as baseball, cricket, golf, tennis and soccer. The academic exploration of individual sports is a more recent phenomenon beginning with Harold Seymour's doctoral dissertation at Cornell University in 1956, which he developed into a three-volume history of baseball (Seymour, 1960, 1971, 1990). C.L.R. James, the great West Indian Marxist thinker, journalist, music critic and lover of the sport of cricket published *Beyond a Boundary* which examined the place of cricket in Caribbean identity during the twentieth century (James, 1962). In 1979, sociologists Eric Dunning and Kenneth Sheard published a historical account of the development of rugby football (Dunning & Sheard, 1979). In the early 1980s, Richard Cashman, one of the key figures in developing academic sports history, turned his attention to cricket in India and then to cricket crowds in Australia (Cashman, 1980, 1984). Janet Lever's *Soccer Madness* turned attention onto the rise and place of soccer in Brazilian society (Lever, 1983), while Tony Mason extended social history analysis to the rise of soccer in England (Mason, 1983) and Bill Murray examined the role of Glasgow soccer clubs Celtic and Rangers in the sectarian divide between Catholics and Protestants in Scotland (Murray, 1984).

Other books followed, and by the 1990s studies began to link individual sports with development of masculinities, markets, race, gender, class and colonialism. Some of the best examples of these include Rob Ruck's (1991) examination of baseball in the Dominican Republic; Beckles and Stoddart's (1995) exploration of cricket and liberation in the Caribbean; Nauright and Chandler's (1996) volume on rugby union football; Tony Collins's (1997) work on the split between in rugby that created the sport of rugby league; Bale and Sang's (1996) study of running in Kenya; Stoddart and Sandiford's (1998) study of cricket and the British Empire and Commonwealth; and Gruneau and Whitson's (1994) pioneering cultural study *Hockey Night in Canada*. In 1998, Bill Murray published the first of many global histories of soccer (Murray, 1998) while fellow Australian-based scholars Rob Hess and Bob Stewart published a wide-ranging history of Australian rules football (Hess & Stewart, 1998).

The primary focus of studies produced between the 1960s and the end of the 1990s sought to examine the historical development of individual sports and their role in shaping the societies and cultures where they were popular. Since 2000 literature on a handful of sports such as baseball, cricket, rugby, and soccer have mushroomed, with major presses publishing companions, handbooks and anthologies dedicated to that sport (cf. Hughson, Moore, Spaaj & Maguire, 2017; Parrish & Nauright, 2014). Yet, many other sports with global presence have received much less attention with some having vastly underdeveloped academic literature relative to their popularity such as volleyball and golf. Some individual sports clubs have had academic books published about them, such as Liverpool and Manchester United football (soccer) clubs and Collingwood Football Club (Australian rules football) (Stremski, 1986).

Many more studies have appeared with a specific sport as the focus since the pioneering works appearing before 2000. Since 2000, numerous new works have appeared that explore the business of specific sports and their major teams, competitions and events as well as squarely placing such sports in the political economies of the places where they are played. Additional works have examined the rise of corruption and match fixing, particularly in the sports of football and cricket. In this collection we touch on many of these works and introduce key points of development, controversy and understanding that surround specific sports around the world.

While our initial attempt was to be comprehensive, we realized quickly that, as this project was not meant to be an encyclopaedia (cf. Nauright & Parrish, 2012), we would not satisfy every reader. Unfortunately, not every sport of interest and importance was included. Rather, this book is designed to review many different types of sport, their backgrounds and literature as case studies and guides to how individual sports may be examined historically, sociologically, through marketing and business perspectives, or through focus on gender, race and class exclusion or inclusion. We know we have not covered every sport with important global or regional impact, but we hope this handbook proves useful to scholars and the general audience interesting in learning more about different sports around the world and how those sports have been studied and could be studied further in the future. As such, we expect others to take to their computers and begin writing additional examinations of sports, improving on ones already written, and pioneering new and innovative work where none yet exists.

References and selected further reading

Andrews, D.L., ed. (2004). *Manchester United: A Thematic Study*. London: Routledge.

Armstrong, G. & Giulianotti, eds. (1999). *Football, Cultures and Identities*. Basingstoke: Macmillan.

Bale, J. & Sang, J. (1996). *Kenyan Running*. London: Frank Cass (now Routledge).

Beckles, H.McD. & Stoddart, B., eds. (1995). *Liberation Cricket*. Manchester: Manchester University Press.

Black, D. & Nauright, J. (1998). *Rugby and the South African Nation*. Manchester: Manchester University Press.

Cashman, R. (1980). *Patrons, Players and the Crowd*. Andhra Pradesh: Orient Longman.

Cashman, R. (1984). *"Ave a Go Yer Mug!": Australian Cricket Crowds from Larrikan to Ocker*. Sydney: Harper Collins.

Chandler, T.J.L. & Nauright, J., eds. (1999). *Making the Rugby World: Race, Gender, Commerce*. London: Frank Cass (now Routledge).

Collins, T. (1997). *Rugby's Great Split: Class, Culture and the Origins of Rugby League Football*. London: Frank Cass (now Routledge).

Dunning, E. & Sheard, K. (1979). *Barbarians, Gentlemen and Players*. London: Routledge.

Gruneau, R. & Whitson, D. (1994). *Hockey Night in Canada: Sports, Identities and Cultural Politics*. Toronto: University of Toronto Press.

Hess, R. & Stewart, B. eds. (1998). *More Than a Game: An Unauthorised History of Australian Rules Football*. Melbourne: Melbourne University Press.

Hughson, J., Moore, K., Spaaj, R. & Maguire, J. (2017). *Routledge Handbook of Football Studies*. London: Routledge.

James, C.L.R. (1962). *Beyond a Boundary*. London: Stanley Paul/Hutchinson.

Lever, J. (1983). *Soccer Madness*. Chicago, IL: University of Chicago Press.

Mason, T. (1983). *Association Football and English Society, 1863–1915*. London: Harvester.

Murray, B. (1984). *The Old Firm: Sectarianism, Sport and Society in Scotland*. Edinburgh: John Donald.

Murray, B. (1998). *The World's Game: A History of Soccer*. Urbana, IL: University of Illinois Press.

Nauright, J. & Chandler, T.J.L., eds. (1996). *Making Men: Rugby and Masculine Identity*. London: Frank Cass (now Routledge).

Nauright, J. & Parrish, C., eds. (2012). *Sports around the World: History, Culture and Practice*. Santa Barbara, CA: ABC-CLIO.

Parrish, C. & Nauright, J. (2014). *Soccer Around the World: A Cultural Guide to the World's Favorite Game*. Santa Barbara, CA: ABC-CLIO.

Ruck, R. (1991). *The Tropic of Baseball: Baseball in the Dominican Republic*. Westport, CT: Mekler Publishing.

Seymour, H. (1960). *Baseball: The Early Years* (1st edition). New York: Oxford University Press.

Seymour, H. (1971). *Baseball: The Early Years* (2nd edition). New York: Oxford University Press.

Seymour, H. (1990). *Baseball: The People's Game*. New York: Oxford University Press.

Stoddart, B. & Sandiford, K.A.P., eds. (1998) *The Imperial Game: Cricket, Culture and Society*. Manchester: Manchester University Press.

Stremski, R. (1986). *Kill for Collingwood*. Crows Nest: Allen & Unwin.

Williams, J., Long, C. & Hopkins, S., eds. (2001). *Passing Rhythms: Liverpool FC and the Transformation of Football*. Oxford: Berg.

Part I
Invasion team sports

1

American football

Zachary Beldon, Karen Weiller-Abels and John Nauright

Early years

American football does not have one inventor, rather it was gradually developed from soccer to rugby to rugby football to football (Barron 1982). After the American Civil War concluded, in 1865, sports in the United States flourished with Americans fleeing the factories and going outdoors to participate in recreational sport (Barron 1982). Historically, American football has been recognized with two different dates of birth. The first ever recorded game of football took place at the collegiate level on November 6, 1869 and saw Rutgers University beat the College of New Jersey (later renamed Princeton University) by a score of 6–4, in a game that vaguely resembled the version of football that we see today (Dulles 1965: Barron 1982). After seeing a decrease in participation due to parental concerns regarding unnecessary roughness in the sport, American football was revived on November 13, 1875 when Harvard University won 4–0 against Yale University (Dulles 1965).

Since parents and participants were concerned with how rough the sport was, the Intercollegiate Football Association set out to modify the rules adopting several rules from the English Rugby Union (Dulles 1965). Among the rules that were enacted for this new sport was the reduction of players on the field at one time, from fifteen to eleven; new requirements for running, kicking and passing the ball; the replacement of the "scrummage" with the newer "scrimmage" line. By 1881, the Intercollegiate Football Association gave its approval of these rules, leaving very little left of English Rugby in American Colleges (Dulles 1965). Throughout the formative years of football, the rules were continuously evolving with colleges leading the way in implementing the rules of the game (Crepeau 2014).

From amateur to professional

American football was destined from the beginning to be a sport primarily for spectators (Dulles 1965). Perhaps one reason for the increase in fan adherence and the move toward what is today known as American football was/is the sport's connection with physical force which satisfies primitive instincts that can only be compared to a prize fight in boxing.

During the formative years of college football, the sport was dominated by the "Big Three" of the eastern colleges (Harvard, Princeton and Yale). The principal issue with American football has always been the fact that few adults are willing, or are able to, play football due to the highly aggressive nature of the sport (Dulles 1965). During the 1890s in eastern Ohio and western Pennsylvania, the semi-professional and professional level was easily recognized as the modern form of American football. The fields included no hash marks indicating individual yard lines, there were no end zones only goal posts that were located on the goal line 10 feet off the ground (Crepeau 2014).

On November 12, 1892 William Heffelfinger became the first documented case of pay for play when he reportedly earned $500 plus $25 in expense money to play for the Allegheny Athletic Association in their upcoming match versus the Pittsburgh Athletic Club; this game also saw three other players also receive payments for playing in the game, thus marking the first professional football game (Pro Football Hall of Fame undated). The move from college or amateur spectator sport had morphed into the pay for play mentality.

By the late 1890s there were at least five professional level clubs in Pennsylvania that were paying their players, as the sport spread across the country (Crepeau 2014). The rapid expansion of American football across the United States may be explained by the transition from amateur to professional football. The transition was driven by a key and critical desire to win, thus leading teams to begin the practice of paying for the best players to join their teams. Following the First World War and the influenza epidemic, teams became even more structured and organized with the expansion of professionalism and the pay for play mentality. During that time period, football games primarily attracted fans who worked in factories and mills in towns and in small cities. These workers typically worked six days per week, and had only one day for recreational activities, being drawn to the sport to help them relax by taking out their frustrations in a physical sporting event.

Professional football struggled to survive throughout the 1910s and the 1920s. Many teams struggled to survive on a weekly basis, due to the many costs associated with the infusion of professional football. Professional clubs began working with local sponsors to try and alleviate the increasing costs of fielding a professional team. With professional teams struggling to stay alive, attempts were made to reinvigorate the game with the field being altered to be one hundred yards, with ten additional yards to make the end zones. Some other fundamental rule changes were that the kickoff was moved back 10 yards (from mid-field to the forty-yard line), a requirement that seven players on offense must be on the line of scrimmage, teams had four downs to move the ball forward ten yards, while quarterback restrictions were removed and equipment remained minimal (Crepeau 2014).

Expansion of collegiate football

During the 1920s the power in football traversed in a western direction before turning towards the south in the 1930s. Oriard (2001) states that the 1920s and 1930s can be characterized as a time where football was broken up into distinct football regions where representatives of each region would face off annually thus mapping out the shift of power across the different regions (Oriard 2004). Newer teams in the Midwest, south and Far West became contenders to move the balance of power out of the Northeast. The 1920s saw college football divided into two geographic regions, the east and west, where the best teams from each region would face off in the Rose Bowl at the end of the season. When Alabama University made back-to-back trips to the Rose Bowl in 1926 and 1927 they established the south as a true football region (Oriard 2004). The southwest did not distinguish itself until the 1930s when Southern Methodist University began showing their "aerial circus" across the nation, giving the southwest a distinct difference between them and the general south (Oriard 2004).

Meanwhile, the Midwest (Nebraska, Kansas and Oklahoma) struggled to create their own identity in the shadow of the southwest (Oriard 2004). Towards the end of the 1930s the Rocky Mountain Region emerged on the heels of Byron "Whizzer" White who was the runner up for the Heisman Trophy Award (an award that is given annually to the most outstanding player in college football) in 1937 (Oriard 2004). Another Football region that appeared during the late 1930s was the Northwest region. This region was distinct in that it was only for internal pacific coast conference games (Oriard 2004). The creation of these distinct regions led to the creation of traditional college rivalries and ferocious intraregional games (Oriard 2004). The creation of regions also set the stage for national games for interregional competition, where the stakes for these games are much higher (Oriard 2004). The creation of rivalries and interregional competitions further promoted the sport throughout the country by expanding fan bases to areas that lack a collegiate football team.

Professional football in the 1920s

Compared to how college football defined the 1920s as a decade of glory, growth, and development, the 1920s may also be considered as the decade where professional American football laid its foundation. On August 20, 1920, seven representatives, of four teams, met in Canton, Ohio at Ralph Hay's Hupmobile Agency in hopes of establishing a professional football league (Crepeau 2014). At the conclusion of the meeting, the men had created the American Professional Football Association. One month later these men reconvened on September 17 and officially created the American Professional Football Association (APFA) (Crepeau 2014). The APFA began its first season a few weeks later on September 26, 1920 (PFRA Researchers 2015).

The 1920 season included 11 new teams with a majority of the clubs being located in Ohio, with Jim Thorpe being named league President. The season saw very little press action and essentially no fan interest outside league cities. The league struggled immensely to grow attendance throughout the season, compared to college football that managed to fill 100,000 seats in the larger stadiums. The league struggled to gain trust throughout the season, with fans and teams doubting the results of the games and championship, leading many to argue that the AFPA was a league in name only, without any credibility. Once the season concluded, club representatives met again to report on their discouraging finances. Despite the discouraging financial news, the league decided to move forward with a second season.

For the league's second season, the owners tried to sign up every professional football club in America by decreasing the cost of membership from $100 to $50 (Crepeau 2014). League owners also agreed that no player could sign with another club until they were declared a free agent. The intent was to limit clubs trying to outspend other teams and steal their player. Similarly, owners agreed that college players were ineligible to play professional football and any team that was caught violating this policy would be expelled from the league (Crepeau 2014). Jim Thorpe was replaced as President at the conclusion of the first season with Joe Carr.

The 1921 season saw 21 teams begin the season, with ten new franchises joining the league. However, only 13 survived the duration of the season (Crepeau 2014). The National Football League (NFL) states that the "Five teams that dropped out had their records stricken from [the] standings- Evansville, Hammond, Louisville, Minneapolis and Muncie" (PFRA Researchers undated a). According to the Professional Football Researchers Association, only Muncie actually had dropped out of the league, doing so after two games when their quarterback/coach broke his leg. The other teams played the entire duration of the season but did not compete in enough APFA competition to qualify for standings and the league championship (PFRA Researchers undated a). During the season, the Decatur Staleys owner, A.E. Staley, decided to leave the football industry and wrote a check to George Halas for $5,000 to ensure the team survived the season (Crepeau 2014; PFRA Researchers undated a). Staley suggested that Halas should move the team from Decatur to Chicago and asked only that Halas keep the nickname of Staley with the team (Crepeau 2014; PFRA Researchers undated a). Similarly to how the 1920 season ended, the 1921 season did not include an official championship game between the top teams in the league, instead the champion was self-claimed, by win-loss records, resulting in both the Decatur/Chicago Staleys and the Buffalo All-Americans claiming the championship (PFRA Researchers undated a).

In June 1922, the APFA met in Cleveland, Ohio and agreed to rebrand the league into the NFL. At that time, the league added more five more teams to bring the total to eighteen clubs. One of the teams to join the newly branded NFL was the Green Bay Packers (Crepeau 2014; PFRA Researchers undated b, c). The Green Bay Packers returned to the league after being expelled in 1921 for the use of college player. As previously noted, this practice had been banned in meetings prior to the season (Crepeau 2014; PFRA Researchers undated b). Upon returning to the league, the Packers struggled financially and were forced to take out a loan and sell shares of the team to the public for $5 a share. As a result the following year the team rebounded from their financial struggles and had in excess of $5,000 in the bank (Crepeau 2014). As a result of their strong financial base, the Green Bay Packers are the second oldest football team in America today, behind only the Chicago Bears (PFRA Researchers undated c).

Throughout the remainder of the 1920s the NFL consisted of around forty clubs that would come and go. Joe Carr remained as league president and focused his energies on moving the league out of small towns and into larger cities, balancing the league schedule and being able to determine a league champion (Crepeau 2014). The 1920s also saw the credibility of the NFL rise, thanks in part to Joe Carr's focus on reorganizing the league and the influx of college football stars, most notably Harold "Red" Grange, who managed to create considerable friction with the authorities of college football (Crepeau 2014; PFRA Researchers undated c).

Harold "Red" Grange is credited as being a catalyst for the growth and increase in popularity of the NFL, and eventually the American Football League (AFL) during the 1920s and into the 1930s (Carroll 1999). Grange was from Wheaton, Illinois where during his high school years, he scored 75 touchdowns, converted 82 extra points and lettered in four sports (PFRA Researchers undated c). Upon his high school graduation, Grange enrolled at the University of Illinois. During the twenty games of his collegiate career, Grange scored thirty-one touchdowns and gained over 3,300 yards (Crepeau 2014). Immediately following his final collegiate game, Grange announced that he would be turning professional and would be leaving the University, which was controversial because he had not yet graduated from college (Crepeau 2014). The next day, Grange obtained a manager and signed a contract with George Halas and the Chicago Bears, renamed from the Chicago Staleys (Crepeau 2014; PFRA Researchers undated c). After signing a contract with the Bears for the 1925 season, Grange attended the Bears game vs the Packers at Cubs Park. Upon his arrival at the game fans erupted in the stands leading police to be summoned to prevent the fans from mobbing Grange (PFRA Researchers undated c). Throughout the 1925 season, fans flocked to the stadium to get a chance to see Grange play, regardless if the team was home or away. At the conclusion of the season, Grange's manager began negotiations with Halas and the Bears to return for the 1926 season. George Halas believed that the contract for the 1925 season favored heavily towards Grange, but agreed that the club could afford the same agreement for the 1926 season (PFRA Researchers undated c). Grange's manager, C.C. Pyle, however wanted Grange also to have partial ownership in the Bears, an offer that the Bears refused, leading Pyle to declare that he would be forced to organize his own team that was built around Grange. Grange and Pyle set out to create a new league that Grange would be the star of, the AFL, which began play in 1926.

Professional struggles

When the American Football League began in 1926, the league consisted of franchises located in New York, Boston, Philadelphia, Cleveland, Chicago, and Brooklyn with two permanent road teams from Rock Island and Los Angeles (Crepeau 2014). After the AFL began competing, the NFL sought out to challenge the AFL for players and locations and rapidly began expansion into Los Angeles, Brooklyn and Hartford (Crepeau 2014). Both football leagues struggled throughout the 1926 season, especially in the NFL as the popularity of Red Grange had taken the AFL by storm (Crepeau 2014). Despite Grange's popularity, at the end of the 1926 season, only four AFL franchises survived, the Yankees, the Wildcats, the Philadelphia Quakers and the Chicago Bulls. AFL teams struggled to make payroll and create viable fan bases (Crepeau 2014; Barron 1982). It was difficult for AFL teams to gain fan bases thanks to the lackluster performances teams were putting on, as most teams only averaged one touchdown a game (Crepeau 2014). The following season professional football entered a depression as the combined number of active clubs decreased from 31 teams across two leagues to 12 teams in only one league, resulting in the AFL folding after just one season (Crepeau 2014; Barron 1982). In the third game of the 1927 season, Red Grange injured his right knee and was ruled out for the remainder of the season. The next season saw the NFL's two stars, Red Grange and Ernie Nevers both retire professional football (Crepeau 2014; Barron 1982).

The stock market crash in October 1929 punctuated the 1929–1930 NFL season (Crepeau 2014). While the NFL had managed to prosper and persevere during the 1920s, the league was struggling similarly to how the nation was struggling during the Great Depression (Crepeau 2014). In order to survive, the league was reshaped, while losing the weaker franchises and positioning itself to fully recover and grow during the 1930s (Crepeau 2014). Since the NFL operated at a lower cost than other professional sports leagues in America, the league did not suffer as much during the great depression (Crepeau 2014). The league revamped efforts towards effectively growing and utilizing clubs that were located in the larger markets and embraced the use of radio that proved to be very profitable for the league (Crepeau 2014). Throughout the 1930s the league saw franchises located in smaller markets fold, while franchises were being formed in the nation's larger markets and by 1937 the league was seen as stable with ten franchises (Crepeau 2014).

Segregation

In the early 1930s, the NFL implemented the unwritten rule of segregation which led to the end of African American participation, after having more than ten years of participation (Crepeau 2014). African Americans had been on NFL rosters since 1919, when Fritz Pollard became the first African American football player signed by a professional team (Crepeau 2014; Barron 1982). Between 1920 and 1933, there were thirteen total African American football players in the NFL and during the 1922, 1923 and 1926 seasons the league saw the most African American football players on active NFL rosters, with a total of five players throughout the league (Crepeau 2014; Barron 1982). These African American players faced harsh realities at the professional level. Despite Pollard being one of the stars of the team, he was never fully accepted as a member of the team. He was not allowed to use the team's locker room, stay at the team's hotel, nor eat with the team at local restaurants (Crepeau 2014). When the 1933 season concluded, NFL owners met and unofficially established color lines (Crepeau 2014). The league remained segregated until 1946, when Paul Brown signed Bill Willis from Ohio State University (Crepeau 2014; Barron 1982). Brown claims that he did not sign Willis to make a social statement, but that he did so because he wanted to improve his club's performance (Crepeau 2014). By the end of the 1940s, there were 26 African American players throughout all professional Football all of which were still subject to racism (Crepeau 2014).

Television

The first televised football game occurred at the collegiate level on September 30, 1939 and saw Fordham university play Waynesburg University (Vander 2015). The game is estimated to have drawn a television audience of anywhere from 500 to 5,000 viewers while another 9,000 watched in person (Vander 2015). The first televised professional football game occurred about one month later on October 22, 1939 between the Philadelphia Eagles and the Brooklyn Dodgers and saw an audience anywhere from 400 to 1,000 (Crepeau 2014). By 1946, there were approximately 12,000 television sets throughout the country. In 1947, the Chicago Bears began to televise all of their home games, which resulted in double the amount of ticket sales for each home game (Crepeau 2014). The following season, the Bears elected to only televise their final game of the season (Crepeau 2014). For the 1949 season, the Cleveland Browns sold their television rights to a local radio station (Crepeau 2014). In 1954, nearly two-thirds of the country had a television set and by 1956 every team had an affiliate agreement with CBS to broadcast their games, while NBC held the rights to the Championship game each season (Crepeau 2014).

The NFL championship game has been around since the 1933 season when the Chicago Bears beat the New York Giants 23–21 (Barron 1982). Despite the championship game being played since the 1933 season, the game was not televised until 1951 when Dumont Networks agreed to broadcast the game (Crepeau 2014). Thanks to the agreement between the NBC network and the NFL to broadcast the game annually, the competitiveness of these games, and the merger between the AFL and NFL, the annual championship game was rebranded in 1966 to be called the "Super Bowl." (Crepeau 2014) Today, the super bowl is the number one watched program worldwide and due to the massive popularity of the Super Bowl, youth around the globe grow up aspiring to play on the biggest stage of the sport.

While the super bowl is by far the most popular event of American football, playing football on Thanksgiving is one of the longest running traditions in American sports (Pope 2007). Football has been played on Thanksgiving day since 1876 when college football elected to play their championship game (Pope 2007). The annual game, rapidly became the most prominent nineteenth-century collegiate athletic competition and was key in legitimizing the role of intercollegiate football (Pope 2007). While early Thanksgiving games struggled to gain a large following, with only those who attend northeastern colleges or who live in New York really following the Thanksgiving games (Pope 2007). Thanksgiving games saw its popularity blossom in the late-1880s as it began to signal the start of the elite social competitions (Pope 2007). By 1890, press coverage of the games had rapidly expanded, proving that American football played on Thanksgiving had become a commercial success (Pope 2007).

Globalization

The commercial success of American football has led this sport to spread across the globe. In fact, the CEO of the NFL, Tod Leiweke (2015), said "We're not trying to replace soccer or cricket. What we're trying to do is take our rightful place in one of the most important global sports markets anywhere in the world" (Williams 2016). The NFL currently stakes its claim as the most popular and lucrative professional sport in America (Volpe 2007). Revenues reach into the billions (9.5 billion as of 2011–2012 season). The average NFL franchise in 2017 is worth $2.5 billion, up 8% from the total in 2016. All but five of the NFL's 32 teams are worth at least $2 billion dollars. Even with the variety of bad press and the "gladiator" nature associated with the sport, the NFL still remains a financial boom (Badenhausen 2017).

Sport as an entity, "has been the most significant cultural force associated with globalization since the late nineteenth century" (Gullainotti and Robertson 2007). The concept of globalization is a multidimensional phenomenon, including historical, cultural, economic, and social components and is quite a social phenomenon. Social scientists have equated globalization with neoliberal capitalism, as well as an increase in transnationalism (Bourdieu 1999). Both of these concepts will be purported here as a discussion of the expansion or globalization of the NFL is presented. As will be suggested and discussed in this section, an intent to globalize American football has served and we suggest, intends to serve as a means of expanding the local by intertwining with the global market. Bringing together the local with the global in a manner that promotes transnationalism is and will be key to greater acceptance and embracing of the NFL.

American sociologist, George Ritzer (2004) coined the term "grobalization" to describe cultural homogenization (Ritzer 2004). In Ritzer's view, three forces are at the heart of "grobalization." These forces, capitalism, corporate expansion, and Americanization support the idea of cultural homogenization. Americanization suggests major US corporations and cultural products/services such as McDonalds, CNN, Coca-Cola, and Disney are dominant in the promotion of American culture and values. Homogenization or cultural sameness, uniformity, and convergence would and will [in the future] bring individuals together across global markets.

An opposing view, heterogenization, suggests cultural differences and divergence exist in globalization. Fundamental rules and ethical differences in sport exist across the world. One aspect of heterogenization, hybridity promotes cultural mixing or blending of societies. One particular aspect of hybridity which applies to the globalization of the NFL relates to rules and game conditions and ethics of sport fitting with local conditions (Appadurai 1996). The term "glocalization" was put forward by Guilianotti and Robertson (2004) to particularly describe the intersection between the local and the global (Guillainotti and Robertson 2004).

In relation to the globalization of the NFL, the concept of hybridity explains how a sporting culture (e.g. the global NFL) can emerge from influences of varying societies. Dominant American value systems, lifestyles, products, and approaches across the world must come together. Though the American system of revenue sharing and the draft system have been said to be in opposition to the capitalist view, marketing techniques and a world economic perspective are what serve to support the expansion of the NFL (Szymanski and Zimbalist 2006). Global expansion and significant aspects of a global economy can be found in global sport (Guillainotti and Robertson 2004).

The NFL's European adventure

The NFL's first world expansion attempt ran from 1995 to 2007, with NFL Europe attempting to globalize the game. The intent was to further Europe's interest in the American sport. At the time, the league had six total teams, five in Germany and one in Amsterdam. NFL Europe was formed as an experiment, testing the possibility of a larger scale operation. The initial globalization attempt was to serve as a developmental league for the NFL's primary teams. There was a great deal of instability in the NFL Europe league (Volpe 2007). The fan base was low, with attendance rarely getting above 20,000 (Carlson 2006). There was little history of the actual sport being played in the regions where it was being promoted and little cultural association. The farm system approach was not received well as similarities in this developmental approach with the type supported by the NBA or MLB had been viewed to be unnecessary. Those who attended enjoyed the atmosphere created, however the fan base and the culture had not yet been aligned for success. Few names were recognizable as compared with the more popular soccer. Financially, the league lost approximately $30 million in its final season (NFL Europa 2007). The financial cost was greater than the result "it is the most complicated team sport on the planet . . . If we can create an understanding that will make a huge difference" (Volpe 2007). It is important to understand both the global and local perspectives. Donnelly (1996) notes sports from more powerful countries (US and NFL) cannot simply impose the meanings and culture upon those who are less powerful and who have little knowledge and background in that sport. So, how does the NFL begin its climb to international prominence?

A large portion of the American population grows up in a culture of football. This includes opportunities to watch endless games on television, stretching from Saturday college football to Sunday, Monday, and Thursday night professional football games, and Friday night high school games. Additional socialization includes video games featuring life-like games, fantasy football, and smartphone apps to catch the latest football news.

Succeeding in a greater global market means educating fans across the markets in which the NFL wishes to infiltrate. If potential fans cannot understand the game, it is less likely to be wholly supported. In 2007, the NFL created an online-based interactive seminar called Coach Stilo (Futterman 2008). The purpose of this was to be comical, rather than totally informative. The seminar featured kicking a field goal, with little set up. The kicking aspect was chosen to appeal to the similarity with rugby and soccer.

Bechta (2012) suggested an approach which would promote American football on a wide scale basis (Bechta 2012). Noting fans become so in one of three ways, Bechta suggested the appeal of American football would become more widespread by appealing to the fan base created as international students either attend college in America, live or work in the US, or watch NFL on European television with American friends (Bechta 2012). Although for some the appeal is gender based (watching the cheerleaders), the NFL hopes to go beyond this level. Bechta suggested the NFL should take advantage of these scenarios by making a concerted attempt to educate international students who have had these exposures to the sport during their time living in the US (Bechta 2012). Perhaps creating more online opportunities for potential fans to learn about the game, selling books in college bookstores on the topic, and putting an effort into an attempt to enhance a wider and younger fan base that can become ingrained into the European fabric of these potential fans as it is with American fans, would then expand the fan base into a more global market.

An extension of this movement into even younger fans is also suggested (Giulianotti 2013). The NFL holds clinics around the world for children in order to teach them about the sport. Continuing this movement would potentially allow for youth leagues to become popular in Europe, thus rivaling the choice of soccer as the sport of choice.

Aspects of the world economy are found in global sport. This is particularly true in male dominated sports such as the NFL. Transnational corporations, such as Nike, fast food chains such as McDonald's and other telecommunication companies not only have international divisions of labor, they also work to promote a hegemonic focus on sponsorship of elite sports. Guillanotti (2013) suggests the use of marketing promoting American practices and products may serve to additionally globalize this sport.

Sport and the NFL in particular, is one aspect of social life in which national identity is very relevant and quite prominent. Sport shows strong transnational aspects (Dosh 2012). Politically, sport is one institution where national identity and political prominence is strong. Promoting and offering a sporting national or international event affords nations an opportunity to promote their form of nationalism on a worldwide stage. National allegiance becomes significant in promotion of national identity. As noted above, building this national allegiance from a young age will serve to have potential fans become true fans and identify this new sport with their national affiliation.

Media consumption also contributes to the globalization of sport, as well as brand identity. Using a grassroots approach must also include a focus on marketing and brand identity. Use of powerful social media to enhance the branding of American football may help to cultivate a more long standing or lasting connection with this sport. Utilizing the NFL athletes' use of Twitter may enhance what the NFL wishes to achieve (Pegoraro 2010).

Challenges to expansion

A most pressing and challenging issue for the NFL is how to make this sport appeal to the masses of all ages, who do not grow up with this in their veins. How does the NFL gain global acceptance? The NFL proposes to field a team in London by the year 2022. Williams (2016) reported the league has plans to go from "a $10 billion dollar empire to a $25 billion dollar empire by 2027 and in order to do so he [Goodell] and the league feel it is necessary to expand into global markets such as Canada, Mexico, and England" (Williams 2016). The first stop will be in London as Goodell plans to continue to promote the International Series games.

Williams (2016) noted hindrances exist which Roger Goodell (NFL Commissioner) must address (Williams 2016). Obstacles such as where and when games will be held, immigration/work laws and tax laws need to be assessed and addressed (Gibbs 2015). Will a new stadium need to be built? Would tax payers be responsible for this cost? How would games be scheduled? How does the NFL continue to create and expand a fan base? When will games be held so fans in the US will be able to view them? Will the fan base remain and expand?

One of the biggest reasons for expansion is revenue increase. Tod Leiweke, NFL CEO, noted that "there is no reason why something like this cannot work" (Gibbs 2015). The NFL appears confident in addressing the possible difficulties. In an effort to co-exist with current global sports, and implementing a "global platform," to enhance viewership, fan base, talent pool, and market appeal, the NFL intends to harness the world wide sport globalization appeal (Williams 2016). Connecting with the fans via socialization, promoting the power and world- wide appeal of this sport, creating an international audience, and appealing to the nationalism and enthusiasm that sport (NFL) can create is all part of the vision as the NFL seeks to expand its global appeal.

As presented at the outset of this section, sport on a transnational platform is shaped by glocalization, the blending together of the local and global. Global sports represent a national identity, one which the NFL hopes to capture and market. Suggesting a socialization model that defines and promotes the NFL to fans of all ages in a widespread manner may critically engage and keep potential fans.

Conclusion

American football can be traced back to the American civil war, despite having some roots from early English sports. Despite the large roster sizes of football teams, the sport has always evolved with the spectators in mind. Throughout the early years of professional football, owners struggled to maintain the pay for play mentality and began to look for supplemental income to help stabilize franchises. Due to the overwhelming success of the Super Bowl and football on Thanksgiving, the NFL has sought out newer markets to further expand the sport globally.

References

Appadurai, A. (1996). *Modernity at Large: Cultural Dimensions of Globalization.* Minneapolis, MN: University of Minnesota Press.

Badenhausen, K. (2017). "New Balance Challenges Nike and Adidas With Entry Into Global Soccer Market." Retrieved from www.forbes.com/sites/kurtbadenhausen/2015/02/04/new-balance-enters-global-soccer-market/#337be3ab4ad2

Barron, B. (1982). *The Official NFL Encyclopedia of Pro Football.* New York: New American Library.

Bechta, Jack. (2012). "How NFL Can Expand Abroad." Retrieved from www.huffingtonpost.com/2012.10/25/how-nfl-can-expand-abroad-london_n_2016085.html

Bourdieu, P. (1999). *Acts of Resistance: Against the Tyranny of the Market.* Translated by R. Nice. New York: New Press.

Carlson, M. (2006). "NFL Europe Struggles with German Issue." Retrieved from www.nytimes.com/2006/04/25/sports/25iht-NFLE.html.

Carroll, J. M. (1999). *Red Grange and the Rise of Modern Football.* Urbana, IL: University of Illinois Press.

Crepeau, R. C. (2014). *NFL Football: A History of Americas New National Pastime.* Urbana, IL: University of Illinois Press.

Donnelly, P. (1996). "Proplympism: Sport Monoculture as Crisis and Opportunity." *Quest* 48(1): 25–42.

Dosh, K. (2012). "NFL Tries Home-Team Approach in Europe." Retrieved from http://espn.go.com/blog/playbook/dollars/post/_/id/262/nfl-tries-home-team-approach-in-europe-2

Dulles, F. (1965). *A History of Recreation: America Learns to Play* (2nd edn). New York: Appleton-Century-Crofts.

Futterman, Matthew. (2008) "Football Tries a New Play to Score Overseas." Retrieved from www.wsj.com/articles/SB122350239608216819

Gibbs, T. (2015). "NFL Expansion to London is 'Extraordinary', Says Leiweke." Retrieved from www.telegraph.co.uk/sport/othersports/americanfootball/11967718/NFLexpansiontoLondonisextraordinarysaysLeiweke.html

Giulianotti, R. (2013). "Playing Fields: Power, Practice, and Passion in Sport." In M. Vaczi (ed.), *Soccer, Culture and Society in Spain: An Ethnography of Basque Fandom.* Reno, NV: Center for Basque Studies, University of Nevada.

Guillainotti, R. & Robertson, R. (2004). "The Globalization of Football: A Study in the Glocalization of the Serious Life." *British Journal of Sociology* 55(4): 545–568.

Gullainotti, R. & Robertson, R. (2007). "Sport and Globalization: Transnational Dimensions." *Global Networks* 7(2): 107–112.

NFL Europa. (2007). "NFL Europa to Cease Operations." Retrieved from http://webarchive.org/web/20070703064828/www.nfl.com/news/story/10240829.

O'Reilly, N., Lyberger, M., Mccarthy, L., Séguin, B., & Nadeau, J. (2008). "Mega-Special-Event Promotions and Intent to Purchase: A Longitudinal Analysis of the Super Bowl." *Journal of Sport Management* 22(4): 392–409.

Oriard, M. (1998). *Reading Football: How the Popular Press Created an American Spectacle.* Chapel Hill: University of North Carolina Press.

Oriard, M. (2004). *King Football: Sport and Spectacle in the Golden Age of Radio and Newsreels, Movies and Magazines, the Weekly & the Daily Press.* Chapel Hill, NC: University of North Carolina Press.

Oriard. M. (2009). *Bowled Over: Big Time College Football from the Sixties to the BCS Era.* Chapel Hill: University of North Carolina Press.

Oriard, M. (2010). *Brand NFL: Making and Selling America's Favorite Sport.* Chapel Hill: University of North Carolina Press.

Pegoraro, A. (2010). "Look Who's Talking: Athletes on Twitter: A Case Study." *International Journal of Sport Communication* 3: 190–206.

PFRA Researchers. (2015). Associating in Obscurity. Professional Football Researchers Association.

PFRA Researchers. (undated a). *Once More, With Feeling 1921.* Professional Football Researchers Association.

PFRA Researchers. (undated b). *Birth and Rebirth 1922.* Professional Football Researchers Association.

PFRA Researchers. (undated c). *A Few More Loose Ends 1922.* Professional Football Researchers Association.

Pope, S. (2007). *Patriotic Games: Sporting Tradition in the American Imagination, 1876–1926.* Knoxville, TN: University of Tennessee Press.

Pro Football Hall of Fame. (n.d.). "Birth of Pro Football." Retrieved from www.profootballhof.com/football-history/birth-of-pro-football

Ritzer, G. (2004). *The Globalization of Nothing.* Thousand Oaks, CA: Pine Forge.

Szymanski & Zimbalist. Szymanski, S. & Zimbalist, A. S. (2006). *National Pastime: How Americans Play Baseball and the Rest of the World Plays Soccer.* Washington, DC: Brookings Institute.

Vander, E. (2015). "First Televised Football Game Featured Fordham, Waynesburg in 1939." Retrieved December 19, 2017, from www.ncaa.com/news/football/article/2014-09-28/first-televised-football-game-featured-fordham-waynesburg-1939

Volpe, N. (2007) "The NFL's Strategy for Globalization." *Kaleidoscope Journal* 5(1): 14–53.

Williams, C. (2016). "Globalization of the NFL." *American Football International*, February. Retrieved from www.americanfootballinternational.com/globalization-of-the-nfl

2

Association football

Charles Parrish, Hongxin Li and John Nauright

Ancient and folk football

Though the modern version of association football (soccer) originated in England during the mid-1800s, other games involving kicking a ball can be traced to earlier times. As framed by Uruguayan writer Eduardo Galeano, "In soccer, as in almost everything else, the Chinese were first."[1] Indeed, the ancient Chinese ball game *cuju* featured kicking as a way of advancing a ball towards an opponent's goals (there were multiple) at the opposite end of a defined field of play. First played during the fourth and third century BC, *cuju* rules became formalized during the Han dynasty (206 BC to 220 AD). It is believed the game initially served as a competitive form of military fitness training but later evolved into a leisure pursuit for the wealthy.[2] Citing the work of Hans Ulrich Vogel, Guttmann explains goalposts "through which the ball was kicked" were added during the Tang period (618–907) and women likely participated in *cuju* before the rise of Confucianism brought about its decline during the Qing dynasty.[3] Elsewhere in Asia the kick ball game *sepak raga* was practiced on the Malay Peninsula and *kemari*, similar to sepak raga in that participants tried to keep a ball aloft without using their hands or forearm, was an important activity for the Japanese high class during the medieval period.[4] In the Americas, natives practiced a variety of relay races, one of which required participants to kick a ball back and forth an established course over several days.[5] Likewise, Australian and Pacific Island natives also played kick ball games. Yet, as David Goldblatt asks with scepticism before embarking on his detailed global history of soccer, "Does that make these games and cultures the ancestors of football?"[6] Like Goldblatt, Alan Guttman acknowledged the similarities between association football and the ancient Chinese version but emphasizes modern football's "direct antecedents can be traced back to medieval Europe, where folk football . . . was played in one form or another …"[7]

During the Middle Ages, various forms of folk football were played throughout the British Isles and in parts of France (with the name *soule*). Bearing little resemblance to the modern game and in every way much more violent, some accounts suggest folk football was a derivative of the Roman ballgame *harpastum* (or *harpustum*).[8] Matches often coincided with holidays or festivals and were understandably chaotic given a lack of codified rules. There were no limits to the number of participants and on occasions entire neighbourhoods and villages were said to have competed in these contests. The playing field was also undefined and encompassed swaths of land between two villages, which were often situated several kilometres apart. The object of the game was to carry, kick or pass a ball (animal bladder) into the opponent's village and place it on a marked stone.[9] Though highly unstructured, "As a rule, the competitors in the games were men from the lower classes, such as farmers and craft apprentices."[10] Due to its violent nature and because it was viewed as a distraction from military training, folk football was banned on numerous occasions throughout the fourteenth century and beyond. Nevertheless, the game survived in areas of England and Scotland until the early twentieth century.[11] By then, a series of adaptations had occurred during the mid-1800s among practitioners of the elite English public schools. Dunning suggested these adaptations were part of a "temporally concentrated civilizing spurt" that facilitated the evolution of a modernized association football game.[12]

Folk football becomes modern football

As Britain evolved into an industrial society folk games, once played in the open countryside, also evolved in both structure and purpose. In the early nineteenth century football games were being played among students at a number of elite public schools in England. While each school developed their own set of rules they shared the overarching aim of instilling discipline, morals, and ethics through the spirt of masculine competition. At Rugby School, aggressive tackling and running with the ball in hand were permissible. Meanwhile, at Westminster and Charterhouse handling the ball was discouraged, and Eton and Harrow promoted a kicking game only. As Bill Murray notes, "As long as the boys of these schools played only among themselves, there was no problem about the rules of the game, which were based on tradition …"[13] However, with the growth of cities came an increase in social interaction, which led to football (among other activities) being played during times of leisure.

Eager to continue playing the game of football in adulthood, the "old boys" (alumni) of the public schools saw a need to establish a common set of rules so they could play together without confusion and disagreement over the laws of the game. In 1848 representatives who had played a version of football at several English public schools, including Eton, Harrow, Rugby, and Winchester among others, met in Cambridge to agree upon a common set of rules. Elsewhere, in 1857 Sheffield Football Club was established and featured a large contingent of alumni from Sheffield Collegiate School. A year later, the Sheffield Rules became the first published modern rules for football and would serve as the foundation for the laws that would govern the future Sheffield Association (formed in 1867) in northern England. In 1863, fifteen years after the meeting in Cambridge, representatives from several of the London area "old boys" clubs held a series of meetings at the Freemason's Tavern to once and for all establish the laws of the game. At the heart of the dispute was disagreement over the elimination of "hacking" (deliberately kicking an opponent's shins) and handling the ball. The Blackheath club refused to join and eventually helped to establish what became the Rugby Football Union (1871), which allowed handling and running with the ball. As a result of the meetings, the London Football Association was established along with the first published and distributed rules of association football (the name a derivative of the Football Association name). Several years later the Sheffield and London Football Associations reconciled their rules differences, culminating in Sheffield joining the London association in 1877. Eventually the London geographic identifier was dropped and the organization became simply the Football Association as it set about establishing agreements with local and regional associations in England, the United Kingdom, and beyond while promoting its national FA Challenge Cup as the flagship championship. The growth of the FA in the last two decades of the nineteenth century was remarkable. As Koller and Brandle note, "In the 1880s, what had been an association of London clubs became a national umbrella organization …

In 1867, the FA had only ten member clubs. There were fifty by 1871, one thousand by 1888, and ten thousand by 1905."[14]

As football gained in popularity the "old boys" grip on exclusivity waned as the sport quickly spread across societal class divisions. As Matthew Taylor notes, school teachers, members of religious institutions, and employees of various companies formed teams, which provided a point of entry for a variety of participants from diverse social backgrounds.[15] After years of tension brought on by a desire to maintain amateurism, in 1888 and 1893 respectively, the directors of the Football Association and Scottish Football Association reluctantly yielded to the wave of professionalism and began recognizing clubs openly fielding professional players. This process not only brought about a class balance on the field of play, but also in the stands. Working class spectators came to the football grounds by the multitude. At the turn of the century large stadiums were being erected and quickly became "cathedrals" with topophilic value for the clubs' dedicated supporters.[16] By the first decades of the twentieth century, spectators were paying dues and entry fees, club directors had instituted a "retain and transfer" system to control player movements and restrict wages, and players had unionized to gain better leverage during labour disputes. In other words, British football had clearly evolved from a folk game with ritual connotations into a structured commercial institution.

Global diffusion

This momentum and growth, however, was not isolated to the British Isles. While the FA was focused on extending its geographical influence, promoting the FA Challenge Cup as the pinnacle of achievement, and treating the women's game with ambivalence,[17] football was quickly becoming a global sport practiced around the world. The process of diffusion was complex and included contributions from British functionaries across the empire and beyond, as well as efforts that stemmed from global migration and cultural exchange.

With respect to continental Europe, historical accounts on the diffusion of modern football suggest a strong British influence in various countries between the 1860s and 1880s. In Switzerland, it appears the game developed due to educational exchanges. Specifically, the first organized football clubs in Switzerland emerged in Geneva (1869), St Gallen (1879), and Zurich (1886) thanks to the efforts of English pupils studying in Switzerland and Swiss alumni of English universities who had returned home. Likewise, in Denmark, Sweden, Belgium, and the Netherlands, a combination of efforts from British expatriates and residents returning home from stints in England began forming clubs in the late 1870s and 1880s.[18] Football's diffusion in Spain was the result of commercial relationship rather than education. British miners and railway employees working near the port city of Huelva in Andalusia began playing the game as early as the 1870s and founded the first formal club, Recreativo de Huelva, in 1889. In the north, strong economic links with Britain in the Basque Country port of Bilbao brought English migrants and Basque students who had returned from their studies in England together on the pitch in the early 1890s, leading to the creation of Bilbao Football Club (1898) and later Athletic Bilbao (1901). As participants across much of Europe took to football with enthusiasm, the sport's emergence in Germany and France in the 1870s was met with opposition. The game was first played in France in 1872 in Le Havre but it wasn't until clubs were established in Paris by Scottish and English expatriates in the 1890s that the sport really began to flourish. In Germany, football was introduced to schoolboys in Braunschweig in 1874 but support for the sport was isolated and temporal. The first football clubs were formed in 1880 in Hanover and Bremen, yet they proved unsustainable. It wasn't until the late 1880s and early 1890s that interest was sustained when clubs that would withstand the test of time and criticism were established in Hamburg and Berlin. At the heart of the critique in Germany was a preference for and commitment to the tenets of Turnen gymnastics and a general disdain for football by those in positions of influence, including churches and advocates such as Friedrich Ludwig Jahn and Otto Heinrich Jager. In France, cycling had captivated the populace following significant improvements to the Penny Farthing and the later mass production of the modern bicycle. Nevertheless, football persisted. In 1900 Germany's national football association (Deutscher Fussball-Bund) was founded to provide much needed organization for the steady increase in the number of clubs throughout the country and in 1904 the Fédération Internationale de Football Association (FIFA) was established in the French football hotbed of Paris. Similar narratives featuring British expatriates and cautious acceptance by locals have been written to describe football's arrival and development in Russia. Though accounts indicate the game was being played by British sailors in Odessa in the early 1860s, it was English, Scottish, German, and French expatriates in the city of St Petersburg that provided the support the first organized clubs in the mid to late 1890s. At about the same time, in Moscow, British factory employees formed the first club near the Moscow suburb of Orekhovo. Thanks to the expansion of rail lines outward from Moscow, additional teams sprung up in the suburbs. This growth, however, was stymied in the first decade of the twentieth century by a genuine mistrust towards autonomous organizations which, as it was rationalized, could become cradles of resistance to authority with football serving as a cover for covert militant training. But as was the case in Germany, ideological barriers would not extinguish the public's enjoyment of the game. By the second decade of the twentieth century, football had spread well beyond the urban centres of St. Petersburg and Moscow. In January of 1912 the All-Russia Football Union (VFS) was established in St Petersburg and in June the organization became affiliated with FIFA.[19]

Across the Atlantic, in Buenos Aires, British migrants (notably from England and Scotland) looking to reap the benefits of Argentina's strong export economy and the firm trade partnership between the two countries established enclave communities. They also developed a network of private schools as well as the country's first athletic clubs in support of a growing number of expatriates. In 1867 the Buenos Aires Football Club was founded by the sons of Scottish immigrant Thomas Hogg (Tómas and James), along with William Head. Though the growth of the game suffered a setback several years later when the club opted to focus on rugby, the arrival of Scottish school teacher Alexander Watson Hutton in 1881 proved to be a catalyst for momentum. After three years at St Andrews College, Hutton founded the Buenos Aires English High School, which featured football as an important physical activity within the curriculum. Over the next several years other schools introduced football and in 1893, Hutton launched the Argentine Association Football League. Lomas Athletic Club was the class of the league up until the turn of the century but it was Alumni, a football club comprised of former students of the English High School, that would come to dominate the Argentine championship up until about the time of the First World War. Though the organization has changed its name over the years it remained intact and is recognized as one of the longest continuously running football leagues outside the British Isles.[20] Across the Rio de la Plata, Scottish physical educator William Poole was able to harness the enthusiasm for the sport at the English High School in Montevideo and founded the first football club in Uruguay. Due to a lack of competition there, the club took advantage of its proximity to Buenos Aires and competed against some of the early Argentine clubs. Elsewhere in Latin America, English migrants were responsible for the early development and promotion of football in Chile, with Valparasio FC being founded in 1889 as the first Chilean football club. In Brazil the legend of Charles Miller, born to English parents, dominates the diffusion narrative despite the fact that football was played in São Paulo, Porto Alegre, and Recife before his birth. As the story goes, Miller returned to São Paulo from his studies in England in 1894 with soccer balls and a set of rules in tow. He soon set out to recruit players from the São Paulo Railway and organized a match against a side from Mackenzie College on the grounds of the local cricket club. By 1902, enough interest had been generated to form several local clubs, leading to the formation the Sao Paulo league.[21] In Mexico, British miners established teams in the 1880s and later founded the country's first football club in 1901, Pachuca Athletic. In 1902 the first league was organized and by 1910 teams were comprised of other European expatriates, namely French and German. Interestingly, the onset of the First World War may have actually benefited the development of football in Mexico as "Many English, French, and German players returned to Europe to fight …"[22] The void created by their departure meant additional opportunities for the increasing number of Mexican players who were taking to the game, as well as an influx of Spanish immigrants. This allowed the sport to develop beyond the niche expatriate communities in and around Mexico City. Regional and national tournaments soon followed.

As Bill Murray notes, football was established throughout the British Empire by the turn of the twentieth century but "it had failed to take root in the lands that had once been under British colonial control".[23] The slow and reluctant development of football in the United States is well documented. With the exception of industrial New England and New Jersey, the Midwest gateway cities of St Louis and Chicago, and isolated pockets in the Pacific Northwest, early attempts at organizing and sustaining the sport for mass participation failed. Rather than emulate British physical culture, Americans opted to sever ties and instead demonstrated a preference for baseball, American gridiron football, and basketball. The first attempt at a professional association football league occurred in 1894 but was abandoned within months. In the first decade of the twentieth century the sport appeared poised to benefit from a crisis that threatened the survival of collegiate gridiron football but nationalist rhetoric created an ideological barrier by framing the association game as un-American. In 1921, just eight years after the US federation had become affiliated with FIFA, another attempt at a professional league was launched and enjoyed some success throughout the decade. Some of Europe's top clubs routinely toured the country and played in front of large crowds; the league also attracted players from Europe seeking higher wages. Governance disputes, the effects of the Great Depression, and an increase in xenophobic banter appear to have pushed the league itself and football in general into the margins once again.[24]

The Canadian experience was both similar and different. Like their counterpart to the south, Canadians demonstrated a preference for their own version of gridiron football but ice hockey was clearly the national passion. Support for association football initially came from elite private schools and universities in the middle of the nineteenth century. By the late 1800s participants primarily came from various pockets of working class British immigrants across the vast Canadian landscape.[25] Though the game did eventually spread from east to west, thanks to the development of an expansive railway network, association football in the early twentieth century existed as a comparatively niche cultural activity in Canada. The first national governing body was formed in 1912 when previously established provincial associations from Alberta, Manitoba, New Ontario, Ontario, Quebec and Saskatchewan formed the Dominion of Canadian Football Association. This organization later became the Canadian Soccer Association.

In Australia, New Zealand and South Africa football became an important element of culture and identify formation by the early twentieth century. However, the football codes that captured the attention of the masses at this time were not the association game. In Australia, the localized Australian Rules game became representative of an emerging culture distinct from Britain while in New Zealand rugby was the preferred code among the indigenous Maori and British expatriates. South Africa established its national association football governing body in 1892 however the sport evolved in the margins given rugby benefited from a particular social hierarchy. As Murray notes, "After New Zealand and Wales, the most fanatical rugby country is South Africa, but only among the white population ... the more popular soccer became with the nonwhites the more the whites looked down on it."[26] Over time association football gained traction among white and black South Africans yet racial connotations remain.

Though the periodization was similar to other world regions, the diffusion of football in Asia was a comparatively slow and fickle process. This is not surprising given its 17.2 million square miles is the largest land mass among the world regions. Perhaps equally important, Asia was and remains highly complex in terms of culture (e.g. religion, language), which made international cultural exchanges, such as football, even more difficult. In China, football was played as early as the 1870s and some of the first teams were expansions of early athletic clubs established by British and other European prospectors and functionaries. Specifically, Hong Kong, Shanghai, and Beijing were particularly influential cities with respect to the game's development. In 1886 Hong Kong FC was established and a year later Shanghai FC began as an extension of an existing athletic club. Up until the first decade of the twentieth century, the Chinese generally viewed elements of Western culture, football included, with scepticism as the populace remained committed to traditional ways centred on Confucianism and Taoism. However, Western sports gained some acceptance as tools to achieve modernization, which Chinese officials felt was necessary in defence against impending hostilities in the region.[27] The creation of YMCA affiliates and a variety athletic associations before the outbreak of the First World War allowed for marginal levels of development. However, unlike in Japan, football was not integrated into Chinese schools. This severely restricted its growth and continues to be a barrier today as the Chinese government implements plans to develop its football industry in the twenty-first century.[28] In Japan, football was being played in the port of Kobe as early as 1871 and was later introduced to students at a navy school near Tokyo in 1873. Though the game remained confined to British expatriates until about 1900, Japanese students at Tokyo University began playing football in the first decade of the twentieth century. Soon after, the sport was taught in middle and high schools across Japan. The Ministry of Education, through its subsidiary Japanese Amateur Sports Association, organized a men's national team during the First World War. In 1921 the Japanese Football Association was established and later affiliated with FIFA in 1929.

Early women's football

Women participated in the ancient Chinese football game *cuju* as well as folk football in England. However, the development of the modern association game in Britain excluded women on the grounds their participation not only violated the very Victorian tenets of masculinity the sport was supposed to help foster, but also, sport in general was viewed as a threat to feminine ideals and to a woman's physical wellbeing. Further, the very contexts in which the game developed were not institutions readily accessible to women (e.g. the military, elite public schools, and "old boys" clubs). Despite ideological and institutional barriers, women's association football matches have been organized since the late nineteenth century. In 1892 women participated in a formal match arranged by the Scottish football association.[29] Two years later a British Ladies Football Club was founded and played its first match under FA rules in front of 7,000 spectators in 1895.[30] Women's football gained significant momentum during and after the First World War in several countries, notably France and England, yet a series of bans by national football governing bodies hindered growth. Before the FA barred women from using affiliated clubs' football grounds at the end of 1921, the Dick, Kerr Ladies had emerged as a powerful and popular team in England. In 1920, "The team played some 30 matches ... including four against a French representative side in front of a total of 61,000 spectators . . . The acknowledged high point, however, was the 1920 Boxing Day charity match at Goodison Park against St Helen's, which attracted more than 53,000 (with many thousands more locked out)."[31] In 1921 the English Ladies Football Association, comprised of approximately 25 teams, was launched at about the same time as women's teams were forced out of proper stadium grounds by the FA ban. The league appears to have folded after contesting one championship, which was awarded to Stoke Ladies FC in the summer of 1922. The following year, in 1922, the Dick, Kerr team arrived in North America to contest a series of exhibition matches. The tour was supposed to feature fixtures against North American women's teams but a ban on women's football by the Canadian association and a general lack women's teams in the United States forced changes to the original plan. Nevertheless, the abbreviated tour pressed forward and the Dick, Kerr Ladies lined up opposite primarily nascent men's teams in the United States in front of thousands of curious spectators. In the years that followed English women's football teams attempted persevere in the face of the FA ban and heightened public criticism. However, their relegation to municipal parks and other green spaces coupled with the aforementioned structural and societal barriers negatively impacted their legitimacy and ultimately their appeal among spectators.[32]

Elsewhere in Europe, similar bans were issued in the Netherlands and Germany. In addition to this type of structural prohibition, critical media accounts and growing social pressure in opposition to women's participation effectively stunted the development of women's football. For example, in Germany, popular media outlets framed women's participation as unsuitable, unaesthetical and unnatural. In at least one published account in 1930, the formation of a women's club was reported as a "scandal" and the "many of the players yielded to the pressure from both their families and the general public and left the club ..."[33] In Sweden, the implementation of the FA ban in England provided the justification for curtailing women's participation in the early 1920s. Towards the end of the First World War women's football in France had gained significant momentum, particularly in and around Paris. Yet, like in other European countries, interest waned after the war as normalcy returned and the French association abandoned the women's championship in 1932.[34] Around the world, women's football was nudged into the margins and continued primarily as a participatory based subculture. It took nearly half a century of increasing criticism and pressure for governing institutions (e.g. FIFA, national associations) to address blatant gender discrimination in football. Though independent leagues for women certainly existed they operated primarily as recreational pursuits until women's football was formally integrated into national governing bodies' purview. This movement was further aided by FIFA's push towards developing the women's game in time to stage the first Women's World Cup in 1991.

Emergence of FIFA and the status of modern football

As the preceding paragraphs indicate, football evolved in various parts of the world at different points in time as a component of rituals, ceremonies, and celebrations, a physical pursuit with targeted social and political outcomes, and a leisure activity with health benefits. Of course, the sport also became a global enterprise governed by a complex institutional structure with the Fédération Internationale de Football Association (FIFA) at the apex. By the end of the nineteenth century football associations existed in countries around the world. These associations, as well as prominent clubs acting as de facto authorities in countries lacking national associations (e.g. Real Madrid football club in Spain), had begun staging international matches and exhibitions while also providing an administrative or organizational structure for the sport within their own borders. The need for an international governing body in order to facilitate future growth of the game while maintaining some form of standardization across national borders was increasingly becoming apparent. In 1903 French engineer and newspaper editor Robert Guérin moved forward with his idea of establishing an international federation and began by seeking administrative guidance from the well-established and respected British football authorities. That year he met twice with Frederick Wall, then secretary of the English FA, as well as with FA president Lord Kinnaird to discuss the formation of an international governing body yet it was apparent from the outset the English administrators perceived such an organization as unnecessary. Nevertheless, Guérin pushed forward and invited delegates from Belgium, Denmark, Netherlands, Spain, Sweden and Switzerland to meet in Paris in 1904 to establish FIFA as the prominent international governing body for football. A year later, after his efforts to create an international competition failed and amidst strategic politicking by the English FA, Guérin resigned from the helm of FIFA. In 1906 Daniel Woolfall, treasurer of the English FA, was elected as the second FIFA President. By the start of the First World War, FIFA's membership had expanded to 24 members and featured associations well beyond continental Europe. Interestingly, in several instances, the formation and growth of FIFA served as a catalyst that led to the creation of national associations in countries lacking a legitimate national governing body. For example, the French are generally credited as a driving force for and one of the original founding members of FIFA. Yet the French Football Federation (FFF) wasn't established until 1919, fifteen years after the creation of FIFA.[35]

The growth of FIFA in the early twentieth century was a contentious process requiring resolutions to several matters that threatened the legitimacy and sustainability of the organization. Among the most pressing issues involved the eligibility of players and the inclusion (or exclusion) of certain national associations. With respect to the former, the dispute centred on whether to adhere to a conservative view of amateurism across member national associations while at the same time balancing each national associations' right to regulate the sport within their own borders as granted in FIFA's bylaws. The latter issue stemmed from geopolitical disputes over which national associations could be admitted into FIFA. As Tomlinson points out, "At the Vienna Congress in 1908, Scotland and Ireland were rejected as members. Should Scotland and Ireland have been accepted, Austria and Germany had planned to request membership for their confederate states, numbering 26 and 12 respectively."[36] Ultimately both disputes resulted in the English FA leaving and then re-joining FIFA on multiple occasions throughout the first half of the twentieth century. Additionally, these issues culminated in the creation of a (short lived) rival international governing body in Europe (Union Internationale de Amateur de Football Association) as well as numerous un-sanctioned ("rogue") football leagues in countries around the world whose directors and member clubs chose to operate in a manner inconsistent with FIFA's statutes restricting payments to players.

The expansion of FIFA

Currently, there are 209 national associations which have the FIFA membership. The expansion of its membership in the past years demonstrated FIFA's remarkable impact on international sport.[37] In 1904, it has only seven members. However, by 1914, the number of associations in FIFA had grown to 24 before the First World War, including South Africa, Argentina, Chile, and the USA. After the war, Brazil, Paraguay, and Uruguay became the members of FIFA. However, the British associates withdrew from FIFA because FIFA kept authorizing matches against defeated nations.[38] In spite of the British withdrawals, FIFA continued to expand into other continents: the Egyptian FA was the first African association to join FIFA in 1923, while the Thailand FA joined FIFA as the first Asian member in 1925, and Cuba and Costa Rica joined in 1927.[39] By the first World Cup in 1930, 74% of the affiliated associations were from the European nations and there were 41 members in total. After the Second World War, the number of FIFA's membership had boosted to 95.[40] Since the 1950s, with the establishment of the continental governing bodies for FIFA, the number of the members has been skyrocketed.

By now, FIFA has six continental governing bodies, and they are:

1   The South American Football Confederation (CONMEBOL), founded in 1916, and it has 10 members now.
2   The Union of European Football Associations (UEFA), founded in 1954, and it has 53 members from Europe and Israel.
3   The Asian Football Confederation (AFC), founded in 1954, and it has 46 members from Asia and Australia.
4   The Confederation of African Football (CAF), founded in 1957, and it has 54 members now.
5   The Confederation of North, Central American and Caribbean Association Football (CONCACAF), founded in 1961, and it has 35 members.
6   Oceania, the confederation for the South Pacific region, founded in 1966, and it has 11 members from New Zealand and the Pacific islands.[41]

FIFA World Cup

FIFA World Cup, which usually refers to Men's World Cup, is one of the most popular sporting events in the world. Every four years, 32 teams from different continents enter the final tournament with a total number of 64 matches in one month. During that month, hundreds of millions of people around the world attentively watch the most talented players competing in the tournament on behalf of their countries. However, in the first World Cup, there were only 13 teams in the tournament of 13–30 July 1930. Among the 13 teams, seven teams were from South America, four teams were from Europe and two teams were from North America. Many European countries did not send teams to the first world cup due to the boycott caused by Italy's failure on bidding to host the game. Other countries in Europe, such as Germany, Austria, and Switzerland declined because they thought it was worthless to take a two-week boat journey to South America. In the final game, 93,000 people watched the game live and witnessed Uruguay winning the first World Cup.[42]

The second World Cup was hosted by Italy, which added a qualification phase where national association teams competed to qualify for the World Cup Finals, and the number of the teams playing in the final tournament expanded to 16, which maintained the same until 1982. Finally, Italy won the 1934 World Cup, becoming the first European World Cup winner. Four years later, Italy defended the championship in France.

FIFA canceled the World Cup tournament in 1942 and 1946 because of the Second World War. In 1950, the World Cup returned, hosted by Brazil, and continued its development around the world with tournaments between 1950 and 1986 rotating between Latin America and Europe. In 1982, the number of the teams in the World Cup Finals had enlarged from 16 to 24, which expanded to 32 in 1998. In 1990 the USA hosted the tournament, with subsequent expansion to other regions including Asia (Japan and South Korea) in 2002, Africa (South Africa) in 2010 and the Middle East (Qatar) in 2022. Furthermore, on 10 January 2017, FIFA announced that for the 2026 World Cup, which will be joint hosted by the USA, Mexico and Canada, there, would be 48 teams in the tournament.[43] Brazil has won the most World Cup titles with five (1958, 1962, 1970, 1994, 2002), while Germany has won four times (1954, 1974,

1990, 2014), as has Italy (1934, 1938, 1982, 2006). Germany has also lost in four other finals (1966, 1982, 1986, 2002). Argentina (1978, 1986), France (1998, 2018) and Uruguay (1930, 1950) have all won the World Cup twice. The only other winners have been England (1966) and Spain (2010).

The Women's World Cup has a relatively short history. Like Men's World Cup, FIFA governs the Women's World Cup that also takes place every four years. In 1991, the first FIFA Women's World Cup was held in China, featuring 12 teams. The United States won the inaugural tournament. In 1999, there were 16 teams in Women's World Cup final tournament and in 2015, the number expanded to 24.[44] The most successful team at the Women's World Cup has been the USA, winning four titles in 1991, 1999, 2015 and 2019, and never finishing worse than third. Germany won twice in 2003 and 2007, while Japan (2011) and Norway (1995) have also been victorious.

World Cup finals attract hundreds of millions of television audience all around the world. In the 1970s, on João Havelange's election to the president of FIFA, expanding broadcast market has become FIFA's major business plan. In 1987, Havelange recognized the importance of television in his editorial in FIFA News and announced FIFA's long-term partnership with the television industry. Then, FIFA sold its broadcasting rights to the European Broadcasting Union for the following three World Cups (1990, 1994, and 1998 World Cups) with 95 million Swiss francs, 115 million, and 130 million respectively.[45] In the twenty-first century, the prices for the broadcasting rights of World Cups went up dramatically. For the 2014 World Cup, FIFA made $2.4 billion in TV rights payments and $1.6 billion in sponsorships,[46] whereas in 2018, FIFA benefited more than $3 billion from broadcasting revenues.[47]

With the World Cup and major leagues in Europe, North America and Asia now holding major television and online platform contracts, the sport has become the most important commercial sporting enterprise in the world. Billions of dollars are bet on the outcome of soccer matches all over the world and transfer fees for the top players now exceed $100 million. With the rise of the Chinese Super League, major investment from the Middle East, China and North American capital in leading clubs, the place of football atop the global sporting landscape does not looking like ending anytime in the foreseeable future.

Notes

1 E. Galeano, *Soccer in Sun and Shadow* (London: Verso, 1998), 22.
2 D. Goldblatt, *The Ball is Round: A Global History of Soccer* (New York: Riverhead Books, 2006), 4–6; M. Speak, "Recreation and Sport in Ancient China: Primitive Society to AD 960", in J. Riordan and R. Jones, *Sport and Physical Education in China* (London: Routledge, 1999), 20–44.
3 A. Guttmann, *Sports: The First Five Millennia* (Amherst, MA: University of Massachusetts, 2004), 41.
4 D. Goldblatt, *The Ball is Round*, 6–8; A. Guttmann, *Sports: The First Five Millennia*, 237; A. Leibs, *Sports and Games of the Renaissance* (Westport, CT: Greenwood Press, 2004), 31–33.
5 A. Guttmann, *Sports: The First Five Millennia*, 8.
6 D. Goldblatt, *The Ball is Round*, 8.
7 A. Guttmann, *Games & Empires: Modern Sports and Cultural Imperialism* (New York: Columbia University Press, 1994), 41–42.
8 C. Koller and F. Brandle, *Goal!: A Cultural and Social History of the Modern Game* (Washington D.C.: The American University Press, 2015), 9.
9 C. Wagner, "Association Football in England and Wales", in J. Nauright and C. Parrish, *Sports Around the World: History, Culture, and Practice* (Santa Barbara, CA: ABC-Clio, 2012), 19–26.
10 C. Koller and F. Brandle, *Goal!*, 9.
11 A. Guttmann, *Games & Empires*, 43.
12 E. Dunning, *Sport Matters: Sociological Studies of Sport, Violence, and Civilization* (London: Routledge, 1999), 62.

13 B. Murray, *The World's Game: A History of Soccer* (Urbana, IL: University of Chicago, 1996), 3.

14 C. Koller and F. Brandle, *Goal!*, 18.

15 M. Taylor, *The Association Game: A history of British football* (Harlow: Pearson, 2008), 34–37.

16 A. Guttman, *Sports*, 106–111.

17 C. Dunn and J. Welford, *Football and the FA Women's Super League: Structure, Governance, and Impact* (New York: Palgrave Macmillan, 2015), 9. See also J. Williams, *A Beautiful Game: International Perspectives on Women's Football* (New York: Berg, 2007) and J. Williams, *A Game for Rough Girls?: A History of Women's Football in Britain* (London: Routledge, 2003).

18 A. Guttman, *Sports*, 180–182.

19 D. Goldblatt, *The Ball is Round*, 146–168.

20 E. P. Archetti, *Masculinities: Football, Polo and the Tango in Argentina*, 47–49; D. Goldblatt, *The Ball is Round*, 126–128; A. Guttmann, *Sports*, 168–169; T. Mason, *Passion of the People?: Football in South America* (London: Verso, 1995), 2–3.

21 A. Bellos, *Futebol: The Brazilian Way of Life* (New York: Bloomsbury Publishing, 2002); C. Gaffney, "Association Football in Brazil", in J. Nauright and C. Parrish, *Sports Around the World: History, Culture, and Practice* (Santa Barbara, CA: ABC-Clio, 2012), 25–32; A. Guttmann, *Sports*, 171; C. Parrish and J. Nauright, *Soccer Around the World: A Cultural Guide to the World's Favorite Sport* (Santa Barbara, CA: ABC-Clio, 2014), 27.

22 J. Nadel, *Fútbol: Why Soccer Matters in Latin America* (Gainesville, FL: University of Florida Press, 2014), 179.

23 B. Murray, *The World's Game*, 15.

24 D. Wangerin, *Soccer in a Football World: The Story of America's Forgotten Game* (Philadelphia, PA: Temple University Press, 2006), 64–69; C. Parrish and J. Nauright, *Soccer Around the World*, 279–280.

25 D. Goldblatt, *The Ball is Round*, 88–89.

26 B. Murray, *The World's Game*, 18.

27 Ibid, 19.

28 R. Jones, "Football in the People's Republic of China", in W. Manzenreiter and J. Horne, *Football Goes East: Business, Culture, and the People's Game in China, Japan and South Korea* (London: Routledge, 2004), 59–60.

29 D. Goldblatt, *The Ball is Round*, 179–180.

30 C. Dunn and J. Welford, *Football and the FA Women's Super League*, 9.

31 M. Taylor, *The Association Game*, 135.

32 D. Goldblatt, *The Ball is Round*, 180–181. For an account of Dick, Kerr Ladies in the United States see G. Czubinski, "Kick, Kerr Ladies in Washington, DC, 1922", *Society for American Soccer History*, 2015. Retrieved from www.ussoccerhistory.org/dick-kerr-ladies-in-washington-dc-1922.

33 G. Pfister, K. Fasting, S. Scraton, and B. Vázquez, "Women and Football – a Contradiction? The beginnings of women's football in four European countries", in S. Scraton and A. Flintoff, Gender and Sport: A Reader (London: Routledge, 2002), 68.

34 C. Dunn and J. Welford, *Football and the FA Women's Super League*, 10–11.

35 A. Tomlinson, "FIFA and the Men Who Made it", in J. Garland, D. Malcolm, and M. Rowe, *The Future of Football: Challenges for the Twenty-First Century* (London: Frank Cass, 2000), 55–71; A. Tomlinson, *FIFA: The Men, the Myths, and the Money* (London: Routledge, 2014), 12–14.

36 A. Tomlinson, *FIFA: The Men, the Myths, and the Money*, 15.

37 Ibid, 17.

38 Ibid, 19.

39 P. Dietschy, "Making Football Global? FIFA, Europe, and the Non-European Football World, 1912–74", *Journal of Global History* 8 (2013): 279–298.

40 A. Tomlinson, *FIFA: The Men, the Myths, and the Money*, 17.

41 Ibid, 26.

42 C. Lisi, *A History of the World Cup: 1930–2014* (London: Rowman & Littlefield, 2015), 130.

43 P. MacInnes, "How Will a 48-team World Cup Work? FIFA's Plan for 2026 Explained", *The Guardian*, www.theguardian.com/football/2017/jan/10/48-team-world-cup-fifa-plan-2026 (10 January 2017).

44 J. Molinaro, "Canada Gets 2015 Women's World Cup of Soccer", www.cbc.ca/sports/soccer/canada-gets-2015-women-s-world-cup-of-soccer-1.988843 (3 March 2011).

45 A. Tomlinson, *FIFA: The Men, the Myths, and the Money*, 59.

46 T. Manfred, "FIFA Made an Insane Amount of Money Off of Brazil's $15 Billion World Cup", *Business Insider*, www.businessinsider.com/fifa-brazil-world-cup-revenue-2015-3 (20 March 2015).

47 K. Badenhausen, "FIFA World Cup 2018: The Money Behind The Biggest Event In Sports", *Forbes*, www.forbes.com/sites/kurtbadenhausen/2018/06/14/world-cup-2018-the-money-behind-the-biggest-event-in-sports/#7859bbed6973 (14 June 2018).

3

Australian football

John Nauright

Origins

Melbourne was a city built on the riches of an 1850s gold rush. Forms of football playing occurred in the colony of Victoria in Australia from the 1840s. Australian football (commonly known as Australian rules football, or simply "Aussie rules") first appeared in 1858 and provided local men with a sport to play in the off season of cricket. As with other areas of British settlement during the 19th century, cricket emerged as the primary summer sport. Concerned about off-season fitness, cricketer Thomas Wentworth Wills (1835–1980), who was born in Australia but educated at Rugby School in England – where he captained the cricket team and excelled in football – believed that a football club should be formed to keep his teammates fit during winter. The Melbourne Cricket Club agreed with Wills's suggestion and, as there were no standardized football codes at that time, appointed a committee to devise a set of rules. The Melbourne and Geelong football clubs were established in 1858 and 1859, respectively, and are two of the oldest football clubs in the world. The rules agreed to by the committee on 17 May 1859, were a compromise between those of several English public schools, notably Winchester, Harrow, and Rugby. Players were allowed to handle the ball but not to run farther than necessary to kick it. In 1866 H.C.A. Harrison (1836–1929), a cousin of Wills, rewrote the rules. These rules imposed no limit on the number of players, though in the 1880s, 20 men per team became standard. Several works have explored the foundations of Australian football as there was much debate over the years as to whether the sport was descended from observations of Aboriginal Australian leisure practices, related to Gaelic football (which was only codified in 1884 many years after Australian football) and whether the over-abundance of Cambridge men in southern Australia as compared to New South Wales and New Zealand led to a sport very different from the dominant rugby union football that emerged there (Blainey, 2003; Collins, 2018; deMoore, 2008; Hess et al., 2008).

Concerned about the possibility of injury on the hard Australian grounds, players were reluctant to commit to the tackling and hacking (kicking or tripping an opponent) rules of the Rugby School game, and hacking was banned. Distinctive aspects of Australian football rapidly appeared. At the outset, a provision was made that players who caught (or "marked") a ball cleanly in the air were allowed a free kick. Players could also retain possession of the ball while running, but after some dispute it was agreed in 1865 that the player with the ball had touch or bounce it off the turf at least every 10 metres. Most crucial, and what makes Australian football unique compared other football sports, there was no offside rule, which meant that players from each team were located behind and in front of the ball during play. By 1874 players no longer scored by carrying the ball between goal posts but scored by kicking the ball through them (Hess & Stewart, 1998).

Australian football also developed a unique set of goalposts with two large goalposts flanked by two shorter "behind" posts. The centre bounce used by umpires to start games and to restart play after a goal was instituted in 1891 and also remains unique to Australian football. Goal umpires were first mentioned in 1874 in accounts of the game. The practice of the goal umpire's waving a flag to signal a goal began in Tasmania in 1884 and was adopted in Victoria in 1886.

The game expanded rapidly during the 1870s and 1880s. In the1870s, matches between the Melbourne and Carlton football clubs attracted as many as 10,000 spectators, who at that time watched for free. Spectators often spilled onto the playing surface, and this led to the enclosure of grounds for ease of play. The first facility built specifically for Australian football use appeared in 1876 on land leased by Carlton from Melbourne University. The first Carlton–Melbourne game at the ground attracted 5,000 spectators. By the mid-1880s crowds approaching 34,000 were attending matches between leading clubs (Hess & Stewart, 1998; Hess et al., 2008).

With clubs appearing across the region of southern Victoria, a league was needed to ensure regular competition. On 7 May 1877, representatives of the Albert Park, Carlton, East Melbourne, Essendon, Geelong, Hotham, Melbourne, and St Kilda football clubs met to form the Victorian Football Association (VFA). During the 1870s over 125 clubs appeared in Melbourne, and another 60 senior clubs were established elsewhere in Victoria. A regular schedule of matches was developed; additional grounds were enclosed; and VFA clubs were able to charge admission.

The game continued to spread throughout the Australian colonies. In 1877 the South Australian Football Association was formed in Adelaide. Tasmania accepted VFA rules in 1882, and in 1885 the Western Australian Football Association was established in Perth. Despite these successes, the game struggled to gain a foothold in the northeastern parts of Australia. The first game in Sydney took place in 1877, but rugby union, with its imperial connections, was favoured by the 1890s. A similar process occurred in Queensland and across the Tasman Sea in New Zealand. The great distances that separated colonies and the capital cities meant that regular competition between clubs from different areas was not possible, and indeed the first participation of an interstate team in the main Victorian competition did not occur until 1982. However, because road games between Victorian teams were often only a tram ride away, many fans could go to all of their team's games in any given season at little expense and this helped solidify the sport in Melbourne.

The depression of 1893–1895 caused attendance at games in Melbourne to decline, and the VFA proposed a revenue-sharing scheme to assist struggling clubs. Leading clubs, which wanted more control over the game, opposed the scheme. In 1896 those eight leading clubs – Melbourne, Essendon, Geelong, Collingwood (Stremski, 1987), South Melbourne, Fitzroy, Carlton, and St Kilda – came together to form the Victorian Football League (VFL). The VFL allowed open payment of players and reduced the number of competitors on the field from 20 per side to 18. With economic improvement, VFL clubs were able to pay most players by 1899. A national body, the Australasian Football Council, was formed in 1906 to regulate interstate player movement and develop contests on the national level, though it remained under the control of the VFL. As the council's name suggests, efforts to keep the game alive in New Zealand as well as in Australia were part of its mission.

While the VFL moved into the 20th century as the leading competition, the VFA remained nearly as strong into the 1920s. In 1925 the VFL added VFA clubs Footscray, Hawthorn, and North Melbourne, giving the league 12 teams and solidified the VFL as the premier football competition in Victoria (Hess & Stewart, 1998; Hess et al., 2008).

After South Melbourne football club relocated to Sydney in 1982, the VFL sought further national expansion, founding teams in Queensland, Western Australia and South Australia from the mid-1980s to the late 1990s. In 1990 the VFL changed its name to the Australian Football League (AFL) to reflect its new national focus. In 2005 the AFL comprised 16 teams: the Adelaide (South Australia) Crows, Brisbane (Queensland) Lions, Carlton Blues, Collingwood Magpies, Essendon Bombers, Fremantle (Western Australia) Dockers, Geelong Cats, Hawthorn Hawks, (North Melbourne) Kangaroos, Melbourne Demons, Port Adelaide (South Australia) Power, Richmond Tigers, St Kilda Saints, Sydney Swans, West Coast (Perth, Western Australia) Eagles, and Western (Footscray) Bulldogs. Two additional teams were added on the Gold Coast (Suns) in 2011 and in Western Sydney (Greater Western Sydney Giants) in 2012.

National expansion has not been easy, with large interstate clubs seen by Melbournians as a threat to their clubs and supporters of interstate teams arguing that the league is still too focused on Melbourne. Despite these problems, Australian football is the most popular spectator sport in Australia, and, with championships having been won by West Coast, Adelaide, and Brisbane by 2001, the AFL began the millennium its strongest ever. Australian football is also being played in leagues as far afield as Denmark, England, the Netherlands, and the United States, and AFL preseason matches have been played in Canada, New Zealand, and South Africa.

Women have a long history of playing Australian football (Lenkic & Hess, 2016). In recognition of this, the AFL undertook a national study of the game in 2013 with a view of possibly sponsoring a competition. In February 2017 the Australian Football League began a competition for women linked to existing men's team brands. By 2020, fourteen clubs will have teams in the League. The first Grand Final was won by the Adelaide Crows.

Football and its fans

Australian football is woven deeply into the fabric of Australian society, particularly outside the rugby zones in the states of New South Wales and Queensland. Until 1983 competitions remained state-based, with clubs largely forming in suburban areas that matched parliamentary electorates. Unlike American professional sports franchises, AFL teams are (and always have been) membership-based clubs rather than private franchises, which means that members ostensibly control their club. When clubs have been threatened with mergers, as Footscray and Hawthorn were in 1989 and 1995, respectively, members were able to save their clubs from amalgamation. Melbourne-based club Fitzroy chose to merge with Brisbane to create a strong and sustainable fan base in two cities rather than see Fitzroy die. A brief flirtation with private ownership in the 1980s failed. In 1995, in order to prevent hostile takeovers, which had occurred in rugby league that year, the AFL amended its constitution to ban any one interest from controlling more than 5 per cent of a club.

Early VFL teams developed loyal fans, known as "barrackers", many of whom were club members. Unique among football sports, Australian football has always had a large number of female supporters who attend matches, and by 1900 women formed one-third or more of audiences. By the 1930s each team had theme songs, some derived from popular American tunes.

The league's championship, known as the Grand Final, began in 1898 and starting in 1904 was held at the Melbourne Cricket Ground (MCG), the spiritual home of Aussie Rules. It became, after the Melbourne Cup horse race, the most significant sporting and cultural event on Victoria's annual calendar. The league's popularity continued to rise, particularly with the advent of radio broadcasts of matches in 1925. Live broadcasts of Grand Finals began only in 1946, owing to reluctance of the cricket officials, who controlled the MCG, to allow them. After the Second World War, radio coverage expanded, and live match attendance also boomed as nearly all workers were given Saturday afternoons free by 1946. With the arrival of television coverage in 1957, radio stations intensified their range of broadcasts in order to compete. Seven stations covered matches that season. For many years television coverage was allowed for only the final quarter of a game or on delay as the VFL felt it would hurt attendance if full game broadcasts were allowed. Today all AFL games can be seen via pay or free to air television or streamed online, though for many years the coverage of Friday night games were shown in the small hours of the morning in Queensland and New South Wales where rugby codes have been more popular (Nauright, 1997).

In 1957 a record 2.5 million fans attended VFL matches (Melbourne's population at the time was only 1.7 million), and 100,324 fans attended the Grand Final between Melbourne and Essendon. Final attendance peaked in 1970, when 121,696 fans showed up at the MCG to see Carlton defeat Collingwood. Concerns over the Melbourne Cricket Club's control of the main stadium, the MCG, however, had led the VFL to buy land for its own ground in 1962. The league built a 70,000-seat stadium (an original plan called for 157,000 seats) in central Melbourne, which opened as VFL Park in 1970. The stadium proved unpopular with fans and was abandoned by 2001 for a new inner-city stadium. While most teams played at their own grounds before the mid-1960s, between 1965 and 2001 a process of stadium rationalization took place, with all games in Melbourne eventually held at two stadiums, the MCG and the Telstra Dome (Hess & Stewart, 1998; Hess et al., 2008).

A striking feature of the AFL is every team has a team theme or fight song reminiscent of US College football. Many of the songs of Melbourne teams and the Sydney Swans show links to US songs popular in the 1920s and 1930s. The Sydney Swans song is to the same tune as the Notre Dame University fight song. The St Kilda Saints song is, not surprisingly, "When the Saints Go Marching in." Melbourne Demons chose "It's a Grand Ole Flag". Geelong chose a more high culture route with its song written to the tune of the main chorus in Bizet's opera "Carmen".

In 2017 the AFL launched a women's competition with 10 clubs linked to AFL men's clubs building on the dramatic growth of female participation in the sport over the past two decades. The first match was played on 3 February 2017 at Princes Park in Melbourne. The match was watched by a capacity crowd of 24,568 with many spectators turned away. The game was televised as well attracting a national TV audience estimated at 896,000. Adelaide defeated Brisbane to win the first title in March 2017.

Rules of play

Australian football is played with an oval ball that weighs between 450 and 480 grams (16 and 17 ounces) and has a short circumference of 545–555 mm (21.5–22 inches) and a wide one of 720–730 mm (28–29 inches). Australian football is one of the few field sports that does not use a uniform-sized ground; it is played on an oval field that can vary in width between 110 and 155 metres (120 and 170 yards) and in length between 135 and 185 metres (145 and 200 yards). Two goalposts not less than 6 metres (20 feet) in height are placed 6.4 metres (21 feet) apart at each end of the ground. Two shorter posts, called behind posts, rise to a minimum height of 3 metres (10 feet), with each one placed at the side of a goalpost at a distance of 6.4 metres. The line between the goalposts is called the goal line, and this line's extension from each goalpost to its behind post is called the behind line.

A team consists of 18 players on the field. Players may run with the ball but must bounce or touch it on the ground at least once every 15 metres, a change from the sport's early rules, which required the ball to be bounced once every 10 metres. A player may hold the ball and run with it until he is held by an opponent, when which he must dispose of the ball immediately. Players pass the ball to teammates either by punt-kicking it or by handballing, the latter in which a player holds the ball in one hand and hits it with the clenched fist of the other hand. Throwing the ball is illegal, and there is no offside rule.

A major difference from other types of football is the awarding of a set kick, or mark, when a player manages to catch the ball directly from the kick of another player who is not less than 15 metres away. The player who makes the mark is allowed a free kick at the goal from anywhere behind where he marked. The game's finest spectacle is the high mark, in which three or four competing players leap, sometimes riding on the back or shoulder of an opponent, in order to catch the ball and receive the resultant mark.

Each match is controlled by one field umpire, a goal umpire at each end, and boundary umpires on each side. The game begins with the field umpire bouncing the football in the centre of the field and players leaping in order to knock it down to a teammate. After a goal, the ball is bounced again at the centre of the playing field. After a behind is scored, the scored-upon team kicks the ball into play from its own goal area. A match consists of four 20-minute quarters.

Australian football entails more body contact than association football (soccer) but less than rugby, American or Canadian football. A player may be "shepherded", or checked, by an opponent by the use of a hip, shoulder, chest, arms, or open hand, provided the ball is not more than 5 metres away. Players who tackle opponents above the shoulders, below the knees, or in the back are penalized with opponents winning a free kick. Free kicks are also awarded to the defending team when an attacking player is deemed by the umpire to have held the ball too long or to have run with the ball without bouncing or touching it on the ground. Dissent or flagrant offenses are penalized with the opposition gaining 50 metres plus a free kick.

A goal is scored when the ball is kicked clearly through the goalposts by a member of the attacking team; a goal registers 6 points. A "behind" is scored when the ball crosses a behind line in any event or when the ball crosses the goal line without meeting all the required conditions for a goal to be scored (e.g., when the ball touches a goalpost). A behind is worth one point. The four posts are distinctive of Australian football. Scores are written in the format of goals followed by behinds followed by total points; for example, 20.11.131.

Academic study and popular culture

There is now a robust literature on Australian football primarily from sports studies scholars based in Australia particularly those based in the primary Aussie Rules playing states of Victoria, South Australia, Western Australia and Tasmania. Some thirty articles have appeared since the late 1980s in the journal *Sporting Traditions*, the journal of the Australian Society for Sports History. Many of these articles can be found online via the LA 84 Library collection. The *International Journal of the History of Sport* has also published several articles on the sport, while key academic books on the origins and history of the game have also appeared over the past 25 years.

In 1977, playwright David Williamson's play *The Club* was first staged in Melbourne, later made into a movie starring Jack Thompson and directed by Bruce Beresford. Williamson also wrote the screenplay for *Gallipoli*. In 1979, Mike Brady's song "Up There Cazaly", memorializing 1910s and 1920s legend Roy Cazaly, became the modern anthem for the sport, originally written for the Channel 7 television coverage. "Up There Cazaly" was also a battle cry for Australian troops during the Second World War and the phrase captured Cazaly's reputation for taking high-flying marks during his career which ended in 1927. Brady was still performing the song to audiences across Australia in 2018 including a live performance in front of 100,000 spectators at the AFL Grand Final between the West Coast Eagles and the Collingwood Magpies. *The Footy Show* began weekly analysis of the sport in 1994 hosted through 2018 by journalist Eddie Maguire, former player Sam Newman and comedian Trevor Marmalade (Brooks, 2000). *The Footy Show* theme song "More Than a Game" added to the musical lexicon of the game and is also the title of the first wide ranging history of the sport by historians Rob Hess and Bob Stewart, also former VFA (Victorian Football Association) and VFL players respectively published in 1998.

Though only a truly national competition since the later 1980s, the Australian Football League's competition is the most watched by live and television viewers in Australia. While the sport lags behind soccer in total national participation, it has remained resilient in the face of global sporting challenges and competitions. The AFL has sponsored competitions in other countries where the sport retains a small, but committed following. Aussie Rules remains the single sport that defines Australian uniqueness and is a key component of contemporary national and regional identities. When other sports such as rugby league and rugby union faced turmoil in the 1990s as media interests invaded ownership structures, the AFL banned any entity from owning more than a five per cent stake in a club. To 2020, Australian football clubs are membership driven entities where those who buy memberships in their club have a direct voice in major club decisions. Fan groups of Footscray (now Western Bulldogs) and Hawthorne successfully prevented mergers of their clubs in 1989 and 1996 respectively through voting down the propositions at their annual general meeting (Nauright & Phillips, 1997; Phillips & Nauright, 1999). Unlike many sports today, where identities are more and more malleable and younger fans often follow star players, AFL fans in cities like Melbourne, Adelaide and Perth will tell you that there are two rules to a successful life there: first, you must have a footy team; and second, you never change your footy team. The club remains the most significant form of identity in Australian football and the sport continues to hold a strong place in Australia, while growing around the world since the 1980s with competitions affiliated with the AFL in 20 countries (Alomes, 1997). The Australian Football International Cup is played every three years and is the pinnacle of international amateur competition in the sport. There have been close links to Ireland over the years as skill sets useful in Gaelic football and Australian football are similar. An International Rules competition which modifies the rules of each sport has been played between teams from Australia and Ireland. While Australian football is growing globally, it remains uniquely and identifiably Australian every bit as much as gridiron or American football is identified with the United States of America.

References

Alomes, S. (1997). Australian football the international game? The Danish Australian Football League and the internationalisation of Australian football, 1989–1996. *Sporting Traditions* 13(2), 3–17.

Blainey, G. (2003). *A Game of Our Own: The Origins of Australian Football*. Melbourne: Black Inc.

Brooks, K. (2000). "More than a game": The Footy Show, fandom and the construction of football celebrities. *Football Studies* 3(1), 27–48.

Collins, T. (2018). *How Football Began: A Global History of How the World's Football Codes Were Born*. London: Routledge.

deMoore, G. (2008). *Tom Wills: His Spectacular Rise and Fall*. Sydney: Allen and Unwin.

Hess, R. & Stewart, B. (1998). *More Than a Game: An Unauthorised History of Australian Rules Football*. Melbourne: Melbourne University Press.

Hess, R., Nicholson, M., Stewart, B. & DeMore, G. (2008). *A National Game: The History of Australian Rules Football*.

Lenkic, B. & Hess, R. (2016). *Play On! The Hidden History of Women's Australian Rules Football*. Melbourne: Echo Publishing.

Nauright, J. (1997). Early Saturday morning's not a great morning for football: Critiquing Australian football coverage in Queensland and the marketing of the Australian Football League. *Sporting Traditions*, 13(2), 171–174.

Nauright, J. & Phillips, M.G. (1997). Us and them: Australian professional sport and resistance to North American ownership and marketing models. *Sport Marketing Quarterly*, 6(1), 33–39.

Phillips, M.G. & Nauright, J. (1999). Sports fan movements to save suburban-based teams threatened with amalgamation in different football codes in Australia. *International Sports Studies*, 17(1), 23–38. Copy available online at www.la84.com.

Stremski, R. (1987). *Kill for Collingwood*. Melbourne: Allen & Unwin.

4

Basketball

Zachary Beldon

Origin

The game of basketball was invented in 1891 at Springfield College in Springfield, Massachu-setts by Dr. James Naismith.[1] Dr. Naismith was a physical education teacher who needed to reinvigorate the time between the football and baseball seasons to satisfy students' desires for physical activity.[2] The original version of basketball used Peach baskets as hoops and soccer balls. After a team scored a basket, a ladder would be brought out and a player would have to climb the ladder to remove the ball from the basket. Eventually the bottom was removed in order to increase the speed of the game. The rules were simple and the number of players allowed on the court was dictated by the size of the court. For example, there was no dribbling of the basketball, only passing and shooting and players ranged from 4–6 per team on the court.

Basketball turned out to be well-received by participants from the start and it did not take long for colleges and local Young Men's Christian Association, YMCAs, to form teams. The first ever recorded public basketball game occurred on March 11, 1892 between the teachers of the International Young Men's Christian Association (YMCA) training school and the students.[3] Following the turn of the century, basketball saw amazing growth, including in female participa-tion. Basketball spread rapidly from the colleges and YMCAs to the American school system and playgrounds throughout the country. Today, basketball is played by people of all genders in every region across the United States and the world.

Rules of the game

The game has evolved drastically since its founding in 1891. For example, from 1891 until the 1930s after each made basket, the game required a new jump ball at center court, which resulted in a slow paced and low-scoring game that was not of interest to many spectators. In order to speed up the game, three time-limit rules were implemented. The first being the "ten-second" rule that requires the ball be advanced into the front court within ten-seconds, thus preventing a team from withholding the ball on the opposite end of the court.[4] The second time-limiting rule was the "three-second" rule, whereby an offensive player cannot remain inside the free-throw lane for longer than three-seconds, thus limiting a tall-players effectiveness inside the lane.[5] The third time-limiting rule that was implemented was the adoption of a shot-clock, thus putting a limit on the amount of time that the offensive team can hold on to the ball without shooting.[6] The shot-clock varies based on gender and competition level; international teams, college women and high school girls' teams use a thirty-second clock while college men use a thirty-five-second clock.[7]

Prior to 1950, all shots had to have been taken with at least one foot down on the court, however it was later realized that players could still accurately shoot the ball from the highest point in their jump, thus making it far more difficult for the defense to defend against a shot. Then in 1954, basketball added the "bonus" free-throw.[8] This free-throw gave the player who was fouled prior to shooting the ball a second free-throw shot if they made the first free-throw attempt. This rule was criticized heavily and was later altered so that the "bonus" shot would only occur after the seventh foul of the half at the college-level or the fifth foul in high-school. A couple of years later basketball again tried to limit the effectiveness of the taller players by expanding the free-throw lane from six feet wide to twelve feet wide.[9] Since no offensive player can stand inside the lane for longer than three-seconds this opened up the middle area for drives to the basket. It is important to note that the size of the lane varies based on the competition level with the NBA having the widest lane and International competition using a trapezoid shape that is twelve feet wide at the free-throw line and nineteen feet wide on the baseline.[10]

The 1970s and 1980s was a time period that involved major rule changes. The most significant change in the rules for women's basketball occurred in 1971 when the game went from having six players per team on the court at once to five players at once.[11] Prior to 1971, women's basketball was played with three forwards and three guards, none of which were able to cross mid-court at any point. With the elimination of one player, the game evolved into being played fully across the length of the court. A few years later, in 1976, the College Rules Committee voted to legalize "dunking" on the basket, becoming effective for the 1976–1977 college season.[12] Then in the spring of 1986, the three-point field goal was added by the College Rules Committee to college basketball.[13] The following year, the three-point jump shot was implemented at the High School level by the National Federation of High School Athletic Associations. The implementation of the three-point field goal into basketball has had as much, if not more, effect on the game as any other rule change in the sports history due to the newfound complexities of offensive and defensive schemes.

Collegiate basketball

The history of basketball at the collegiate level is a debated topic by historians. The National Collegiate Athletic Association (NCAA), published a story in 2014 about the first collegiate basketball game and the first teams. According to the NCAA, "the first intercollegiate game was played between the Minnesota State School of Agriculture and Hamline College" with this game taking place on February 9, 1895.[14] However, both Vanderbilt University and Geneva College claim to have been fielding basketball teams since 1893.[15] Vanderbilt University claims that they played the first collegiate basketball game on February 7, 1893 against the YMCA, a game that they won 9 to 6. However, Geneva College claims on their basketball webpage that they are the "Birthplace of College Basketball."[16] Geneva claims that the first ever college basketball game was organized as an intramural activity by the students in February of 1892.[17] To add to the case further for Geneva College, in 2010 Ian Naismith, one of the grandsons of James Naismith, visited the college claiming that "he wanted to see the birthplace of college basketball for himself."[18] Both colleges have many publications referring to their institution as the birthplace of college basketball, unfortunately however, the Naismith Memorial Basketball Hall of Fame does not confirm or deny either sides claim only stating that the "first team" is recognized as the YMCA team that played in 1891 in Springfield, Mass.[19]

In 1927, collegiate basketball coaches joined together to form the National Association of Basketball Coaches (aka NABC) in Kansas City, MO.[20] The organization was formed as an emergency response, to present a united opinion on the Joint Basketball Rules Committee, who was the governing body over collegiate basketball, who changed the rules to virtually eliminate dribbling from the game.[21] The NABC states that their central purpose is to further the game of basketballs best interests.[22] A decade after being formed, the former NABC president Harold Olsen, envisioned the concept of a national championship event for college basketball.[23] In 1940, following the second championship tournament, and a profit of $9,500, the NABC approached the NCAA to take administrative control over the tournament, so that coaches can focus on coaching, in exchange NABC members would be included on the tournament selection committee and be given complimentary tickets to the finals.[24] Until 1975, the tournament was limited to one team per conference, however after multiple high ranking teams across the country were denied participation in the tournament, the NCAA started to place at-large teams in the tournament, instead of just conference champions.[25] Prior to the at-large teams receiving invitations to join the tournament, these teams participated in the NIT tournament, which was competing for prestige with the NCAA Tournament.[26] In 1970, the NCAA forbade teams from playing in any other championship tournament after rejecting an invitation to participate in a different tournament.[27] Currently, the NCAA tournament consists of the 32 Division I conference champions, who receive automatic bids, and 36 reams that are referred to as "at-large" teams that are selected via the NCAA selection committee.[28] Since the first NCAA Tournament, five institutions have won the tournament at least five times, led by the University of California Los Angeles winning 11 championships.[29]

Recently, college basketball has been filled with corruption. These issues of corruption have ranged from academic corruption[30] to financial corruption.[31] Most recently, it was revealed that the University of North Carolina at Chapel Hill was sponsoring fake courses for two decades, in order for athletes to receive credit for courses that were never actually taught.[32] Following the three-and-a-half-year investigation, the NCAA stated that it could not definitively conclude that the courses of interest were offered solely to benefit student-athletes and not non-athletes, therefore limiting the NCAA's ability to discipline, despite the institution acknowledging their wrong-doing in the situation.[33] On September 26, 2018 the Federal Bureau of Investigation, FBI, and the United States Attorney for the Southern District of New York revealed the arrests of 10 men involved heavily in collegiate basketball, that were in connection with fraud and corruption schemes, under investigation since 2015.[34] The officials stated that these 10 men accepted bribes from business managers and financial advisers in exchange for them to influence their players towards specific brands and companies once the players reached the NBA.[35] Likewise, an Adidas senior executive was accused of working with these advisors to funnel payments to high school athletes and their families, in exchange for the players' commitment to attend schools that were sponsored by Adidas.[36] On October 16, 2017 Rick Pitino, the head men's basketball coach at the University of Louisville, was fired for the institutions role in the case.[37] However, Rick Pitino was also heavily scrutinized earlier in 2017 due to revelations that the men's basketball team was providing improper sexual benefits to recruits and players.[38] The sex scandal resulted in the University of Louisville being stripped of 123 wins between the 2011–2012 season through the 2014–2015 season and Louisville became the first institution to have their NCAA Tournament Championship title revoked by the NCAA.[39]

Professional basketball in America

Professional basketball has also evolved throughout the life of the sport. At the beginning, the professional level was struggling due to two rival leagues battling for star players. In 1946 the Basketball Association of America (BAA) was formed and was immediately seen as the main challenger of the National Basketball League (NBL) which was founded in 1937, due to the BAA establishing teams in larger cities than the NBL which focused on smaller Midwestern cities.[40] Since, the BAA was established in larger cities, teams played in larger arenas than their counterparts in the NBL, thus attracting bigger stars. The attraction of so many stars to the BAA also convinced some of the NBL teams to switch leagues.[41] After a destructive three-year battle between the BAA and the NBL, the two leagues each sent representatives to meet on August 3, 1949 to finalize a merger that would create the National Basketball Association (NBA).[42] Upon completion of the merger between the BAA and the NBL, the NBA began in 1949, with a total of 17 teams that represented a mixture of both small towns and big cities across the nation.[43] Despite the merger occurring in 1949, according to NBA's website, the first season for the NBA occurred between 1946 and 1947, the same year that the BAA was established.

During the NBA's first decade, the league struggled immensely with fan support, leading to the number of active teams to be diminished and by the 1954–1955 season, only eight teams remained.[44] That same year is when the NBA decided to add the 24-second shot clock to increase the speed of the game, it also led the games to be more exciting and fun to watch for fans. With the NBA struggling to keep a fan base, another professional league was developed on October 13, 1967 called the American Basketball Association (ABA).[45] During the first season of the ABA, the league consisted of eleven teams that were located throughout the country. Throughout the leagues ten year history, fans saw the new ABA as a looser kind of atmosphere where fans could do a lot of things that the NBA didn't allow them to do.[46] Some of the defining differences between the NBA and the ABA is that players fighting on the court was seen as normal, the ABA used a 30-second shot clock (as opposed to the 24-second shot clock in the NBA), even the ball colors were different with the ABA using red, white and blue colored balls compared to the traditional orange balls that the NBA was using.[47] However, the biggest difference between the two leagues was that the ABA began implementing the three-point line prior to the NBA implementing it into their games.[48]

The NBA did its best to avoid acknowledging that there was a rivalry between the two-leagues, but the NBA could not ignore the talent level of some of the ABA stars.[49] ABA teams struggled to sell enough tickets to games to stay afloat and without a national television contract, the league struggled to assist teams that were financially unstable.[50] By the start of the 1976 season, the league dwindled down to just nine remaining teams, but before the season ended two more teams' ceased operations. During the season, the league hosted the first ever slam dunk competition as part of the all-star game, an event that is still played during the annual NBA All-Star Weekend.[51] At the conclusion of the 1976 season, the league was bankrupt and it was decided that they would merge with the NBA.[52] Four ABA teams remained intact during the merger, while the other clubs crumbled, resulting in the players becoming free agents in the NBA.

Since the merger between the NBA and the remaining ABA teams, the newly formed NBA has grown drastically in popularity due to engaging rivalries and star players. The oldest rivalry in the sport has pitted the Boston Celtics vs the Los Angeles Lakers. These teams have faced each other 12 times in the NBA Finals with the first appearance in 1959, with the Celtics winning the series nine times.[53] The rivalry has also fostered rivalries amongst players, whether it be Bill Russell vs Wilt Chamberlain, Larry Bird vs Magic Johnson, Celtics "Big 3" (Paul Pierce, Kevin

Garnett, and Ray Allen) vs Lakers "Big 3" (Kobe Bryant, Pau Gasol, and Ron Artest). The Celtics and the Lakers have historically dominated the NBA, combining for 33 of the 77 NBA Titles (43%), however the 1990s brought a new team into the spotlight.[54]

Out of the ten NBA championships throughout the 1990s, the Chicago Bulls claimed six of them. Led by Michael Jordan, whom they drafted with the third-overall pick in the 1984 NBA draft, the Chicago Bulls finally claimed an NBA championship at the end of the 1990–1991 season, the team then followed their first championship with two more championships the following seasons.[55] Following three-years of championship-less seasons, Michael Jordan "unretired" and resumed playing for the Chicago Bulls, where he led the team to another three NBA titles in consecutive seasons, before ultimately retiring again and watching the Bulls rebuild with younger players.

WNBA

On April 24, 1996 the Women's National Basketball Association was founded and approved by the NBA Board of Governors, becoming the first professional women's basketball league to gain the full support of the NBA.[56] Following the 1996 USA Women's National Basketball Team's Gold medal at the Summer Olympics the WNBA began league play in 1997 with eight teams.[57] The WNBA season would run opposite of the NBA season, beginning in May and ending in late-September or early October, so that there would be less sports competitions and thus could be easily broadcasted live on NBC, ESPN and Lifetime Television.[58] The WNBA has since doubled in expansion from the original eight teams to 16 teams.[59] Compared to the NBA, the WNBA has a six-second longer shot clock (30 seconds), is played in two 20-minute halves, and uses an "orange-and-oatmeal" colored ball that is one inch smaller (28.5 inches) in circumference than the NBA's regulation ball.[60] Unlike the NBA, there are not two teams that consist of nearly half of the championships, in fact no team has won five titles, the most titles won be a single team is four (Houston Comets and Minnesota Lynx).[61]

FIBA

The sport of basketball saw a rapid expansion across the globe. In 1930, basketball was officially recognized as a sport by the International Olympic Committee, IOC.[62] Two years later, in 1932, the International Basketball Federation was founded in Geneva and was originally named the "Fédération Internationale de Basketball Amateur" (FIBA).[63] FIBA was founded by eight members: Argentina, Czechoslovakia, Greece, Italy, Latvia, Portugal, Romania and Switzerland.[64] During the 1936 Summer Olympic Games, FIBA honored Dr. James Naismith, the founder of basketball, as their honorary President.[65] Since 1950, FIBA has been responsible for organizing both the Basketball World Cup and the Women's Basketball World Cup, which alternate with the Olympic competition every four years.[66] Until 1988, FIBA competition was only available for those athletes who were considered amateurs, athletes who play a sport without any payment. In 1989, for the first time FIBA allowed Professional basketball players to participate in the Olympic Games, thus leading FIBA to rebrand as the "Fédération Internationale de Basketball" but retaining the FIBA acronym.[67]

Global expansion

Basketball is one of the most played sports across the globe. The expansion of basketball can be largely attributed to the 1992 Olympic Games, where the world got to see basketball played at its finest. The United States, being one of the powerhouses of basketball in the world, managed to show its superiority by forming what is now known as the "Dream Team."[68] The 1992 Dream Team was special in many ways. For one, it was the first Olympic team from the United States to include professional NBA players rather than amateurs.[69] Up until the 1992 Olympics, the United States had always formed their Olympic basketball teams from college athletes. However, due to the loss in the 1988 Olympics, the United States felt embarrassed and was forced to make some drastic changes to the team if they wanted to show their dominance once again.[70] Although the idea of having professional players play in the Olympics was not fully supported by all, the International Basketball Federation (FIBA) passed the motion to allow professional players to play internationally.

Even though the NBA was not on board with this notion, they would soon find out the benefits of having their players play in the Olympics. At first many thought it would be difficult to get professional players to play during the summer Olympics because it was their off season. Lots of players enjoyed their downtime after a vigorous season. But after word got around that professional players could play in the Olympics, many jumped at the opportunity to be on the team.[71] This new rule by FIBA expanded the game of basketball domestically and internationally. Before when only college players were picked for the team, it excluded many young, talented ballplayers who made the decision to leave school early and follow their dreams to play in the NBA. Therefore players such as Larry Bird and Magic Johnson missed the opportunity to represent the United States in any international competitions.[72] This impacted the game tremendously by allowing players more options to finish school or join the league whenever they pleased. With the expansion of eligible players to make the team, the United States greatly raised their chances to win the next Olympic Games.

The United States revamped their system for the 1992 Olympics. They did not hold tryouts like previous years. Instead, four NCAA representatives and two at large representatives formed a committee that would review professional players performances during the 1990–1991 and 1991–1992 basketball seasons.[73] The process was tedious as there were many talented professional players wanting and capable of making the team. Due to the exclusiveness of being chosen and creating this feeling of desire and need, many professional players wanted to be on the team.[74] After some time a roster of 12 was finally picked. Starting with the core of the team Michael Jordan, Magic Johnson and Larry Bird were the top three mentioned throughout the committee. Then players such as Charles Barkley, Clyde Drexler, Patrick Ewing, Christian Laettner, Karl Malone, Chris Mullin, Scottie Pippen, David Robinson and John Stockton filled the remaining spots on the roster.[75] This all-star team was led by head coach Chuck Daly, who was the head of the Detroit Pistons during that time.

This team had the biggest unforeseen impact on the game of basketball than anyone could have known. During the Olympic Games, the Dream Team dominated each game scoring more than 100 points and not allowing a team to score more than 85 points.[76] They won by an average of 44 points throughout the entire tournament, beating teams such as Spain, Germany and Croatia. The effort and success of this team turned this American sport into a global phenomenon. Many viewers from all over the world were highly impressed with the ball movement and tenacity with which this team dominated the Olympic Games. The Dream Team's style of play expanded the game to show a more creative, team-supported style of play rather than a hard, drive to the hoop style that most thought was the game of basketball.[77] With their dominant performance, many teams knew they were playing the best and did not care if they lost. They took it more as an honor to say that they played against some of the best players in the world.[78] The way the Dream Team played opened up many views and interest for the game of basketball around the world.

To better understand the global expansion of basketball we must look prior to the 1992 Olympic Games. Before the 1992 Olympics, basketball was still a young, new sport in other countries. It wasn't until the boycotts of the Olympics in the 1980s that other countries began to raise their level of play. In 1980, the United States boycotted the Olympics in Moscow due to political reasons.[79] President Carter boycotted the 1980 Olympics as a protest against the Soviets invading Afghanistan in 1979.[80] Although devastating to many athletes that had been training for the Olympics, it was a power statement that the Americans committed to against the Soviet Union.[81] This political feud led to a total of 66 countries boycotting the Olympics of 1980. In retaliation for this act, the Soviet Union then decided to boycott the 1984 Olympics held in Los Angeles. The soviets reasoning behind the boycott referred to the safety of their athletes.[82] The Soviet government felt as if their athletes would not be safe competing in the United States given the prior hostility held from the United States boycott in 1980.[83] About 15 other countries such as East Germany, Angola, Cuba and Poland followed the Soviets actions and also boycotted the 1984 Olympics.[84] The impact the feud had on the games was tremendous. The United States and the USSR were the two powerhouses of basketball in the world.[85] After not attending the 1980 and 1984 Olympics, it allowed for other countries to practice and play at a level closer to that of the United States and USSR teams.

After both teams rejoined the Olympics in 1988, the loss the United States endured made the coaches and staffs rethink and re-evaluate their options for a better team. Thus, the 1992 Olympics opened the door for lots of people internationally.[86] Once players from other nations saw the talent the United States team had, they soon realized how attainable and accessible that type of play was. The 1992 Olympic Games sparked other countries to better their basketball athletes in hopes of competing with the United States Dream Team.[87] Young, international players idolized the 1992 Dream Team and sought to play in the best league, the NBA. Exploits of the Dream Team drew an influx of international players to the United States.

By the next Olympics in 1996, there were more than thirty international players in the NBA.[88] Many of these players thought this was their way to escape poverty. Due to the global media coverage the Dream Team received, many of the players were seen as famous, wealthy role models that international player's desired.[89] Thus, the expansion of international players in the NBA greatly affected the sport into what it is now. The increase of international players playing in the United States helped change the style of play in the NBA. International players knew how to spread the floor and were good shooters around the perimeter, giving more options than just hard style dribbling to the basket.[90] A lot of this style of play can be seen from international players in the league now such as Tony Parker, Dirk Nowitzki and Pau Gasol.[91] Being able to compete in the best basketball league in the world allowed not only international players to get better, but also made the United States players elevate their game as well. From the creation of the Dream Team in 1992, the global expansion for basketball has noticeably increased the number of interests and views around the world.

Global leagues

Today, there is a big divide in opportunities for both men and female basketball players to play professionally, with there being over 50 professional men's basketball leagues around the world and only 24 women's leagues worldwide.[92]

The oldest European basketball league is Italy's "Lega Basket Serie A" (LBA), which was formed in 1920.[93] The teams of the LBA have two roster formulas that they can use; one in which teams can have five players from outside the European Union and five Italian players, the other in which teams can have three players from outside the European Union, four players from the European Union and five Italian players.[94] The Euro League, also known as Turkish Airlines EuroLeague, is the basketball equivalent of the European soccer's Champions League, where the top European clubs qualify each year.[95] Teams that participate in the EuroLeague compete against other EuroLeague teams during the week and spend the weekends playing teams within their own country.[96] The league was introduced in 2000 to replace the FIBA EuroLeague, which was run by FIBA since the late 1950s. The EuroLeague is one of the most popular indoor sports leagues globally. Beginning in the 2016–2017 season, the league restructured the season format to include a regular season round-robin format, with each team facing each other twice, and the best eight-teams advancing to the playoffs. Spain's Liga ACB (Asociacion de Clubs de Baloncesto) was formed in 1957 and has consistently been dominated by FC Barcelona and Real Madrid who have won 85% (51/60) titles.[97] Similar to most leagues outside of the United States, Spain's Liga ACB has a relegation system whereby the bottom two teams are relegated to the lower leagues.[98] Despite basketball being played in Turkey since the early 1900s, the Turkish Basketball Super League (BSL) wasn't founded until 1966.[99] Germany's BBL (Basketball Bundesliga) is believed to be the best basketball market in Europe, due to the league being a consistent pipeline to the German National Team.[100] In 1964, the German Basketball Federation decided to form a split West German federal league, which consisted of one division in the north and one division in the south, each with 10 teams. In 1975, the league was restructured to a relegation style league with a top division and a bottom division each consisting of ten teams that could be relegated or elevated to the other league after each season. One of the newest and fastest growing basketball markets is in Lithuania, where basketball is commonly seen as the second largest religion amongst the country's 3 million residents.[101] Lithuania gained their independence from Russia in 1993 and formed the Lietuvos krepsinio lyga (LKL) later that year.[102]

The Australian National Basketball League is the pre-eminent basketball league in Australia, with seven of the eight teams being located within Australia and the remaining team being located in New Zealand.[103] The league was formed in 1979 and plays their season from October to April, in an attempt to avoid the busy Australian Winter Sports Season. In 2013, after years of struggles, the NBL de-merged from Basketball Australia, which is the governing body over the sport within the country, and since then the league has grown in popularity.[104]

The Chinese Basketball Association, CBA, is Asia's preeminent basketball league, being formed in 1955.[105] The league has some of the strictest regulations when it comes to foreign players, with teams only being allowed to carry two foreign players and they can only play a total of six quarters combined.[106] With the CBA relying so heavily on Chinese players, the quality of competition is far below the leagues in Europe and with the league season wrapping up in February, it gives the players the chance to jump to an NBA team prior to the playoffs beginning in the United States.[107] Outside of the United States, China is the largest consumer of basketball.[108] China specifically is the largest market outside of the United States for the NBA leading the league to announce in 2007 that they are pursuing a Chinese subsidiary that will be headed by Timothy Chen from Microsoft.[109] In 2016, Adam Silver, the NBA Commissioner, was quoted about his desire to expand the NBA's presence in China by saying "Nothing can be No. 1 at anything in the world unless it is No. 1 in China."[110] Under Adam Silver, the NBA has refocused their efforts towards player developments and brand expansion.[111] Silver, in 2017, addressed the difficulty of consistently playing games abroad: "We can play games in China and Europe, or occasional preseason games as a one-off, but under existing airline technology, the planes aren't fast enough to at least play in the current framework of our regular season."[112]

Conclusion

The NBA is the most global US Sport Brand and as a result, the sport of basketball has continued to grow and develop around the world. This is partly due to other nations striving to defeat the NBA to keep their premiere athletes' home. Despite the NBA having their eyes set on expansion in China, the NBA should also further develop and invest into their European outreach, as the European market has recently been one of the largest markets for NBA broadcasts. Lately, the NBA has furthered their commercial footprint, with the allowance of sponsorships on NBA team official uniforms.[113] Recently, NBA has also partnered with the Walt Disney Company and plans to open up "The NBA Experience" at Disney Springs in Orlando, Florida.[114] With the NBA growing their commercial footprint and with the formation of new partnerships with companies around the world, the expansion of the NBA and of basketball will continue for the foreseeable future.

Notes

1 G. Wilkes (1998) *Basketball* (7th edition), New York: McGraw-Hill.
2 Ibid.
3 "1st Ever Public Basketball Game Played …" (undated), retrieved from www.rarenewspapers.com/view/206238.
4 Wilkes, *Basketball*.
5 Ibid.
6 Ibid.
7 Ibid.
8 Ibid.
9 Ibid.
10 Ibid.
11 Ibid.
12 Ibid.
13 Ibid.
14 Lauren Kirschman (2014) "Vanderbilt Lays Claim as the True 'Birthplace of College Basketball'," *The Beaver Times*, 29 November, retrieved from www.ncaa.com/news/basketball-men/article/2014-11-29/vanderbilt-lays-claim-true-birthplace-college-basketball.
15 Ibid.
16 "Geneva Basketball" (undated), retrieved from http://athletics.geneva.edu/documents/2017/7/13/mbb_2016.pdf.
17 Kirschman, "Vanderbilt Lays Claim."
18 Ibid.
19 "CHC: VU First College to Play Basketball" (undated), retrieved from www.vucommodores.com/sports/m-baskbl/spec-rel/031208aaa.html.
20 "Key Dates in NABC History" (undated), retrieved from www.nabc.org/about/history/index.
21 Ibid.
22 Ibid.
23 Ibid.
24 Ibid.
25 Ibid.
26 J. McPhee (1999) *A Sense of Where You Are: Bill Bradley at Princeton*, New York: Farrar, Straus and Giroux, pp. 114–115.
27 Ibid.
28 "March Madness Bracket: How the 68 Teams are Selected for the Division I Men's Basketball Tournament" (2018), retrieved from www.ncaa.com/news/basketball-men/article/2017-03-12/march-madness-bracket-how-68-teams-are-selected-division-i.
29 "NCAA basketball champions from 2017 to 1939" (2018), retrieved from www.ncaa.com/history/basketball-men/d1.

30 "Breaking: NCAA Finds No Academic Fraud by UNC" (undated), retrieved from www.insidehigh-ered.com/news/2017/10/16/breaking-ncaa-finds-no-academic-fraud-unc.

31 M. Sherman (2018) "Everything You Need to Know about the College Basketball Scandal," retrieved from www.espn.com/mens-college-basketball/story/_/id/22555512/explaining-ncaa-college-basketball-scandal-players-coaches-agents.

32 "Breaking: NCAA Finds No Academic Fraud by UNC."

33 Ibid.

34 Sherman, "Everything You Need."

35 Ibid.

36 Ibid.

37 Ibid.

38 M. Tracy (2018) "Louisville Must Forfeit Basketball Championship Over Sex Scandal," retrieved from www.nytimes.com/2018/02/20/sports/ncaabasketball/louisville-ncaa-title.html.

39 Ibid.

40 "NBA is Born" (undated), retrieved from www.history.com/this-day-in-history/nba-is-born.

41 Ibid.

42 Ibid.

43 Ibid.

44 Ibid.

45 "American Basketball Association Debuts" (undated), retrieved from www.history.com/this-day-in-history/american-basketball-association-debuts.

46 Ibid.

47 Ibid.

48 Ibid.

49 Ibid.

50 Ibid.

51 Ibid.

52 Ibid.

53 "NBA Season Recaps: 1946–2017" (2017), retrieved from www.nba.com/history/season-recap-index#.

54 Ibid.

55 Ibid.

56 "History of the WNBA" (undated), retrieved from www.wnba.com/archive/wnba/about_us/historyof_wnba.html.

57 Ibid.

58 Ibid.

59 Ibid.

60 Wilkes, *Basketball*

61 "History of the WNBA."

62 "History" (undated), retrieved from www.fiba.basketball/history.

63 Ibid.

64 Ibid.

65 Ibid.

66 Ibid.

67 Ibid.

68 "Dream Team, Barcelona Games Continue to Impact NBA" (2014), retrieved from www.usatoday.com/story/sports/nba/2014/09/15/dream-team-barcelona-games-continue-to-impact-nba/15654271.

69 Ibid.

70 "The 1992 Dream Team: Basketball's Greatest Legends Lived Up to the Hype" (undated), retrieved from www.offtheball.com/The-1992-Dream-Team-USA-Basketball.

71 Ibid.

72 "Paying Homage to Greatest Basketball Ever Assembled: The Dream Team" (2017), retrieved from www.nba.com/article/2017/07/31/morning-tip-remembering-dream-team-michael-jordan-magic-johnson-larry-bird-1992#.

73 "Men's Teams" (undated), Retrieved from www.usab.com/history/usa-basketball.aspx.

74 "Paying Homage to Greatest Basketball Ever Assembled."

75 "1992 United States Men's Olympic Basketball" (undated), retrieved from www.basketballreference.com/olympics/teams/USA/1992.

76 Ibid.
77 "The Lasting Impact of the Dream-Team on Professional Basketball" (undated), retrieved from www.basketballforum.com/nba-forum/472742-lasting-impact-dream-team-professional-basketball.html.
78 Ibid.
79 "Carter announces Olympic Boycott" (undated), retrieved from www.history.com/this-day-in-history/carter-announces-olympic-boycott.
80 Ibid.
81 Ibid.
82 "Soviets Announce Boycott of 1984 Olympics" (undated), retrieved from www.history.com/this-day-in-history/soviets-announce-boycott-of-1984-olympics.
83 Ibid.
84 Ibid.
85 "Guided History" (undated), retrieved from http://blogs.bu.edu/guidedhistory/russia-and-its-empires/guy-mcfall.
86 "NBA is Born."
87 "March Madness Bracket."
88 "The Lasting Impact of the Dream-Team on Professional Basketball."
89 Ibid.
90 "Dream Team, Barcelona Games Continue to Impact NBA."
91 Ibid.
92 "List of Basketball Leagues around the World" (undated), retrieved from www.allaboutbasketball.us/basketball-leagues/list-of-basketball-leagues-around-the-world.html.
93 "Top 12 Basketball Leagues in the World Outside the NBA" (undated), retrieved from http://abcnews.go.com/Sports/top-12-basketball-leagues-world-nba/story?id=44826666.
94 Ibid.
95 Ibid.
96 Ibid.
97 Ibid.
98 Ibid.
99 Ibid.
100 Ibid.
101 Ibid.
102 Ibid.
103 "The Official Website of the National Basketball League" (undated), retrieved from https://web.archive.org/web/20140311195933/www.nbl.com.au/article/id/q6ujg582svk91sq2lkcg7cs0c.
104 Ibid.
105 "Top 12 Basketball Leagues in the World Outside the NBA."
106 Ibid.
107 Ibid.
108 K. Bradsher (2007) "New Push into China by NBA," retrieved from www.nytimes.com/2007/09/19/business/worldbusiness/19hoops.html.
109 Ibid.
110 "The NBA Begins Global Takeover in China" (undated), retrieved from www.theshadowleague.com/story/the-nba-begins-global-takeover-in-china.
111 Ibid.
112 Amick, S. (2017, October 8). "As NBA Shoots for the Stars in Growing Game, China and Europe are a 'One-Off' – for Now," retrieved from www.usatoday.com/story/sports/nba/columnist/samamick/2017/10/05/nba-overseas-china-europe-regular-season-technology/734611001.
113 Z. Glover (2017) "Here Are the 14 NBA Teams That Now Have Jersey Sponsorship Deals," retrieved from www.forbes.com/sites/zacglover/2017/09/12/here-are-the-14-nba-teams-that-now-have-jersey-sponsorship-deals.
114 "A First Look at The NBA Experience at Walt Disney World Resort Coming to Disney Springs in Summer 2019" (undated), retrieved from https://disneyparks.disney.go.com/blog/2017/10/a-first-look-at-the-nba-experience-at-walt-disney-world-resort-coming-to-disney-springs-in-summer-2019.

5

Field Hockey

Carol Osborne

Origins of the modern game and developments before 1914

The modern game of field hockey – now more accurately described as outdoor hockey due to the introduction of artificial playing surfaces – is a stick and ball game played 11-a-side. Games with teams of 5-, 6- or 7-a-side are also played, as is indoor hockey, a derivative of the field game which emerged during the 1950s in Germany to counter inclement weather conditions and allow for year-round play.

Players enthusiastic about the history and heritage of the modern outdoor game take pride in identifying the origins as residing in antiquity. Games organised around the striking of a ball with a hooked stick are routinely traced back by internal historians to a bas-relief at Athens dating from around 500 BC, which depicts two men holding hooked sticks, posturing over a spherical object, sticks in hand apparently ready to 'bully-off' – a renowned feature of hockey, but no longer retained. Although various forms of the game have been identified, evidence otherwise for consistency between such games, that is as occurring across diverse geographical locations is lacking. As player-historian M.K. Howells observed of hockey-like games 'they were intermittent, unrelated, localised and sporadic affairs ... Thus romantic accounts of the antiquity of the game should be regarded in proper perspective.'[1]

In keeping with a number of sports institutionalised in the late nineteenth century, the emergence of modern field hockey is largely attributed to the increasing enthusiasm for team games adopted by boys' public schools in England from the mid-nineteenth century onwards. Early exponent of the game Philip A. Robson recalled meeting men who played the game before 1840. Brief coverage of hockey's origins, foundation and associated developments can also be found in academic texts. Notably, Derek Birley pays attention to 'the hockey group of games ... played with the bent or knobbled stick' (i.e. bandy, shinty, hurling and camogie) and identifies the 'threat' hockey respectively constituted to football at Cambridge University, England during the late 1840s and to hurley in Ireland in the early 1880s. The latter development apparently incited founder of the Gaelic Athletic Association (1884), Michael Cusack, to revive and elevate the native game of hurling, that is, as distinct from hurley (identified with English hockey).[2] Indeed, the playing of field hockey among other 'British' sports was prevented on GAA grounds to abate the exertion of 'foreign' influence on Irish culture. Although an Irish Hockey Union was ultimately founded (1893), the game never attained the levels of attraction identified for cricket, rugby and soccer.[3]

However, it is Lowerson who provides a sense of the internal politics which played – out until the 1890s, referencing 'the Evangelicals' who preferred playing hockey to rugby, the 'isolationist' Teddington club, a short-lived National Hockey Union and, perhaps more significantly for the game's future, the (English) Hockey Association's refusal to accept women into their fold – thereby compelling the foundation of the All England Women's Hockey Association (AEWHA) in 1895.[4] As far as the Evangelicals' dedication to the game is concerned, they made an active choice within a context where the football codes and cricket dominated and sport was beginning to hold more sway generally in the educational life of boys and the social/professional life of men.[5]

While the game of hockey germinated in the public schools, was accepted by them and, ultimately, cultivated by Old Boys who went up to the universities of Oxford and Cambridge, codification occurred *beyond* institutions in sports clubs. The playing of team games continued to be valued by adult men, not only for the corporeal buzz secured through vigorous outdoor exercise, but for the sociability as product of club life. Blackheath can be considered significant in this respect. Founded by the Old Boys of Blackheath Proprietary School, this club still claims itself to be the oldest in the world today.[6] Located in south east London, the 1861 minute book titled 'Football and Hockey' Club testifies to the fact that hockey was not the only interest among members. Notably, just one year after the codification of football (soccer) in 1863 a separate hockey club was established. But it was not via Blackheath that the game now identifiable as modern hockey came: rather, it was the Teddington Cricket Club in seeking a winter activity to complement the gentleman's favoured summer game. This probably explains why Teddington also identifies itself as being 'the oldest hockey club in the world'.[7]

Reminiscent of the wrangles associated with the early codification of football in 1863 (evolving as either a kicking game or kicking and handling game). Blackheath's hockey was akin to rugby football in allowing catching, marking and scrimmaging – tactics dictated by use of a rubber cube in play. In contrast, Teddington hockey was more identifiable with Association football – including playing on a ground of similar size and limitation of players to eleven per side; this game prevailed. By co-opting the club's old cricket balls for play, the Teddington men enjoyed a free-running game and, according to M.K. Howells, the club continued to refine it until the nearby Surbiton and Richmond clubs joined the evolving hockey fold in 1874. Among other critical developments originating with Teddington in the 1870s was the striking circle (the 'D') to avert long shots at goal for the purpose of goal shooting. Other features generally acknowledged as consolidating the features of the modern game – not stopping the ball with hands or raising the stick about the shoulder, not shooting recklessly but only from the 'D' circle in front of the goal – came via Middlesex.[8]

The logical progression from the emergence of self-styled clubs – in the case of field hockey located in the southern English counties of Middlesex and Surrey – was to form an association between those known to each other. On 24 April 1875 the *Richmond and Twickenham Times* briefly reported the 'Formation of a Hockey Association' at Canon-street hotel. Aside from the Blackheath representatives – who still insisted that a more robust approach to play should prevail – all others present (Richmond, Teddington, Surbiton, Sutton, East Surrey, Upper Tooting and The Strollers) adopted the Teddington rules.[9] Although this first association struggled to survive into the 1890s, Teddington tried again in 1896. The meeting between representatives of Surbiton, Wimbledon, Trinity College Cambridge, Molesey and Ealing at the Holborn Restaurant, London inaugurated the first known Hockey Association. Blackheath tried again to resist the new 'Association' rules and stridently responded by forming an albeit short-lived National Hockey Union (1887–1895).[10]

The underpinning principle of the association was to organise friendly games between affiliated clubs, rather than develop a more competitive league system. Thus conceived (and typical of the time), field hockey was unequivocally a game developed by and for gentleman amateurs. There was a definite reluctance to see hockey go the same way as Association Football: indeed, a column in *C. B. Fry's Magazine* (1904) noted:

> One of the chief causes of the popularity of the game, apart from its intrinsic merits, is the total absence of professionalism from its ranks. At the present time it comes to the aid of a large number of 'Soccer' players who, after they leave the Universities, have met the difficulty of getting good football matches. Thus, they take to hockey, and swell the ranks of the London clubs.[11]

But the take up was neither simply confined to London and the home counties of England, nor the male professional classes who played in these locations. In Britain the geographical spread of hockey is best indicated by the foundations of national representative associations: in Ireland (1893), Wales (1897) and Scotland (1901).[12] Moreover, during the same decade organisation in Europe can be pinpointed to the oldest club on the mainland – the Amsterdam Hockey and Bandy Club (1892).[13] Jan Feith identifies the origin of the Dutch game as residing with the ice game of bandy, whereby 'ordinary land hockey' was instigated for training purposes. Inconsistent weather allowed the latter to flourish as an alternative, leading to the foundation of The Netherlands Hockey and Bandy Club (1898, NHBB). Notably, English rules were not adopted which precluded play at formal international level until the 1920s.[14]

It was also during the 1890s that the women's game came to the fore in Britain. Sanctioned by independent girl's schools if played in appropriate dress and manner, hockey quickly disseminated via educational institutions as an acceptable field game for middle class girls. After leaving school the adult women's game progressed through the university system and, more importantly, via physical education training colleges.[15] The impetus for stronger organisation of the women's game in England actually came via the Irish Ladies Hockey Union (1894). A friendly match was played between teams from Newnham College, Cambridge and Alexandra College, Dublin. Another quickly followed and by November 1895 the first meeting of the Ladies Hockey Association in London had taken place. An approach was made to join the men's Hockey Association, but it was firmly rejected. On the one hand, as coming in a period when men's and women's participation in sporting activities was strongly divided along sex lines, on the other the rejection came at an interesting juncture. This is because Shinobu Akimoto has convincingly shown that the phenomenon of mixed hockey was emerging during the 1890s. Mixed hockey was not only played privately, but increasingly within club contexts where ladies 'sections' existed.[16] Even so, while separatism ultimately prevailed at governance level in Britain, attitudes in Europe remained more flexible because accommodation of female participation was considered in some quarters to 'alter' the game.

The men's Hockey Association did not see how this would cement the determination of the women to make game of hockey their own and, in doing so, significantly impact its character, both at home and abroad. The intent was made clear by the re-naming of their organisation to the All England Women's Hockey Association (AEWHA) – sealed by an official international match played between England and Ireland, in Dublin. No aspect of the game thereafter fell beyond the AEWHA's sight; administrative functions ranged from pronouncements on rules, to selection of the England team and production of a periodical *The Hockey Field* (1901) dedicated to the promotion and progress of the women's game wherever it was played – and progress it did. Further take up across the home nations validates McCrone's view that by 1914 field hockey was 'the paramount winter team game for adult middle class women'.[17]

While these origins and the nature of the evolving associational culture points to a wholesale amateur monopoly of the game in Britain, Halpin identifies how the women's game in particular placed the ethos under strain before 1914. This was due to the foundation of the Ladies Lancashire and Cheshire Hockey League (LHL) in 1910 and the subsequent rash of organised competitions which spread to the Midlands and North of England. For the originators and administrators of the 'English' game, the significance of these initiatives can be viewed as lying more within the introduction of a socially diverse participation base, that is, as coming from welfare, education and workplace teams,[18] rather than truly undoing what Williams has called the 'high amateurism' insisted upon by AEWHA (and for that matter its male counterpart, the Hockey Association). Either way the authority within it rested with an educated elite keen to disseminate it as an ideal game for girls and women an enthusiasm which extended to the international scene. Indeed, on the eve of the First World War an AEWHA coordinated England team embarked on a first invitational tour beyond Europe – to New Zealand, with Australia (Sydney) smartly taken in *en route*.

Field hockey's development as institutionalised sport was product of settler colonialism in both these nations: in New Zealand it gained traction through school play in the late 1880s, progressing to club-based interprovincial matches, then tournaments from 1900 onwards. The New Zealand Hockey Association and the New Zealand Ladies Hockey Association were established in 1902 and 1908 respectively, however, Watson's research highlights the importance of local conditions and values as bringing nuance to the culture of the game there: the social mix was more varied than in England with players drawn from churches, workplaces and technical colleges. Moreover, while administration was held firmly in the hands of the middle and upper classes, male umpires and administrators were accepted in the women's game.[19] In Australia, British Naval Officers are explicitly credited as teaching 'the locals' in the late nineteenth century, thereby laying the foundations for further development. However, the spread was secured via private schools and clubs whereby it was women who excelled again – evidenced by the foundation of the Australia Women's Hockey Association in 1910. The latter initiative inaugurated an interstate tournament and Australia's status of colony saw it simultaneously affiliate to the AEWHA.[20]

The game was therefore well enough established to justify the tour in terms of time and money personally spent by the tourists; they played 26 matches (including four internationals) between July and October 1914 and, according to Watson, were afforded 'the same rites, rituals and venues as visiting men's [sports] teams'.[21] The tour also ensured that the AEWHA retained its weight as the authority behind the women's game – not least due to the acknowledged superiority of England's play. More generally, in addition to play international fixtures presented opportunities for women to socialise and cannot be discounted as influential in the enthusiasm for a more concerted governance of the women's international game. The context and motivation for the development of men's international play beyond the essential value of participating for the love of the game can be discerned as somewhat different.

International developments: Olympic hockey, the FIH and IFWHA

In men's hockey scheduled international matches were variously played between England, Ireland, Scotland, Wales and France from the mid-1890s onwards and continued well into the 1920s.[22] Turned as explicitly 'friendly' encounters firmly in keeping with the amateur ideal, these nevertheless demanded that rules be consistent, understood and enforceable across international events. Thus, in 1900 a common code (which for the first time gave umpires status within the game) was agreed by representatives of the English, Irish and Welsh associations. The initiative to take hold of the rules can be viewed as a pragmatic, directed towards achieving efficiency of play between nations; there was no taste to instate an administrative machinery, but in holding copyright over them by default the board (notably led by the English Hockey Association) came to wield influence over the nature of the international game until after the Second World War.[23]

In attracting a showing of only six playing nations (England, Ireland, Wales, Scotland – entered collectively as Great Britain – France and Germany) hockey's Olympic debut at the London Games (1908) did not provide an especially convincing testing ground for the pre-scribed international rules, at least not through engagement of a wider constituency of hockey playing nations beyond Britain. Rather, by securing the gold medal England consolidated its authority as the 'home' of hockey. It did so again at Antwerp, although the opportunity to play at all at the 1920 Olympiad had been won by Belgian advocates who petitioned the Olympic authorities to include hockey on their home ground. A further threat of omission from the 1924 Paris Olympics finally secured the formation of the Fédération Internationale de Hockey sur Gazon (FIH). It was Frenchman (and duly first President) Paul Léautey who rallied the National Federations of Austria, Belgium, Czechoslovakia, France, Hungary, Spain and Switzerland to form the required governing body, although not in time for participation on his home ground.

In the short term, the foundation of the FIH not only secured Hockey re-entry into the 1928 Amsterdam Olympic Games, but encouraged formation of national associations in Den-mark, Holland, Germany and India – all willing to affiliate and thereby attain access to the Olympic stage. The formation of the FIH can therefore be considered equally pragmatic as the formation of the Rules Board in progressing the good of the international game and, if Howells' brief comments on the matter are anything to go by, this was precisely the spirit in which the British home nations perceived it, that is, to the point of *not* affiliating to the FIH at all, but paradoxically retaining control over the codes until forced to concede FIH input ahead of the London Olympiad in 1948.[24] The politics of Britain's detached attitude to the FIH is not fully addressed within existing histories, but the Hockey Association's pre-existing sense of owner-ship, coupled with a commitment to high amateurism (also shared by the home nations) could explain the reluctance to affiliate, despite the FIH's explicit declaration of commitment to it in the Official Report of 1928.

Even so, the move into regular Olympic participation under the auspices of a federation arguably shifted the founding ethos of hockey away from 'friendly' matches as played annually between nations by mutual agreement, to a more competitive framing of such encounters: chas-ing medals in the context of a formalised competition perhaps came too close to 'pot hunting and prizes'. Indeed, Olympic tournaments quickly assumed the mantle of a world champion-ship for field hockey where none had previously existed, in much the same way as it had done for Association football. The latter entered the Olympics in 1924 under the auspices of FIFA its international governing, however, unlike FIFA, which mobilised quickly to establish its own World Cup tournament in 1930, the FIH took many more decades to stage a world champion-ship on its own terms.

Until the first Hockey World Cup in 1971, the FIH essentially existed to oversee the co-ordination of men's field hockey at Olympic level. In doing so it became the conduit for existing and newly-formed national associations as the game's geographical reach extended. In operating as the international governing body, it would be easy to assume that the FIH held the future of hockey in its hands, but given the strength and autonomy residing within the women's game, nothing could have been further from the truth.

Equally important as the FIH for the future of hockey's governance was the foundation of the International Federation of Women's Hockey Associations (IFWHA) in 1927. IFWHA was founded to further the best interests of the game among women of all nations; to promote friendly intercourse among players; to work for uniformity of rules (as agreed on its terms) and to promote international matches. The ethos of IFWHA turned on it being a fully fledged women-only organisation, one that unequivocally refused interference by men or their associations at the level of governance and strategy. This is best illustrated by the exclusion of women from Germany, France, Belgium and the Netherlands because they were aligned to their respective national associations as sections and, by default, the male administrated FIH. Consequently, the founding nations of IFWHA were Australia, Denmark, England, Ireland, Scotland, South Africa, the USA and Wales. At the time of IFWHA's foundation, the robust game of women's field hockey was barred from the Olympic Games. IFWHA's reply was to establish a triennial Conference. Beginning primarily as a decision-making event at Geneva in 1930, the USA Women's Field Hockey Association suggested these occasions should become a tournament *and* touring opportunity for those nations able to send teams. Given that women were not admitted to the Olympic Games until 1980, this initiative provided an antidote to that exclusion. The influence of the USA from the outset is noteworthy, not only because the game had been introduced to the elite women's colleges on the east coast of America by influential English practitioner, Constance M.K. Applebee, but because the game would not achieve traction – let alone respect – within male sporting culture until the late twentieth century.[25]

By establishing IFWHA, administrators and players further cultivated an international community based on a shared love of the game, but it is fair to say that much ground had already been laid by English touring teams which found spectator and dignitary enthusiasm for their matches abroad, as well as opportunities to coach players in host nations willing to learn from the innovators turned practitioners.[26] It is not therefore unreasonable to suggest that the women's game progressed on a model spearheaded by English innovators, although this had implications for hockey's evolving culture as one that eschewed overt competitiveness (especially in the guise of knock out competitions) in favour of welcoming all comers into the fold. The attitude ultimately softened with the inauguration of the 'internationals' played at Wembley Stadium from 1951 onwards. As the venue suggests, these occasions not only attracted huge spectatorships, but were also deemed important enough in the sporting calendar to be televised by the British Broadcasting Corporation (BBC).[27]

India: innovation, independence and icons

Whereas the coming of the FIH and IFWHA have received relatively little attention in sports history, the emergence of India as the preeminent playing nation during the same period and beyond is better documented, both in academic and popular texts. It is likely that stick and ball games akin to hockey were enjoyed in India (just as elsewhere) before codification, but again the British military is typically credited with disseminating field hockey in India as by-product of its imperial mission.[28] The first clubs in Calcutta (Kolkata) are written as predating the foundation of the English Hockey Association by a year (1885) and during the following decade the Beighton Cup (1895) and the Aga Khan Tournament (1896) came into being – despite the British home nations' aversion to 'pot hunting'.

In addition to sport being a staple part of military life and integral to the experiences of boys and young men educated under the British Raj, the states of Punjab, Kerala and Goa provided a glut of talented players who fuelled grassroots growth, popularity and success of the game in India. Alikhan is especially forthright about the contribution which Anglo-Indians made to the national team's success,[29] as is Megan Mills, who identifies a not especially wealthy and 'relatively minuscule community' which suffered disadvantage due to social and economic discrimination based on their status as mixed-heritage. This, she argues necessitated a 'compensatory culture' cultivated through English-medium schools, church and community activities which, unsurprisingly, appreciated the values of athleticism and character building of which sport became an important part. Hockey also became 'the preferred sport' of female Anglo-Indians who formed the majority of India's national and international players. Moreover, after the partition of India in 1947 Anglo-Indian migrants are credited with taking their talent and coaching skills to Western Australia, thereby contributing to the elevation of hockey as a favoured national sport there.[30]

The ability to exercise developmental influence over the Australian game specifically, but also more generally was grounded in a protracted period of success on the Olympic stage. Quick to affiliate to the FIH in 1925, India rapidly asserted its authority as the premier playing nation by not only winning gold in the 1928 Olympic Games, but in successive games until 1956. The figure of Major Dhyan Chand has become synonymous with this achievement; he is routinely identified as probably the 'best' player ever and has become a sporting icon in India. Although cricket has displaced hockey in the nation's affections, not least due to the burgeoning commercial success of the Indian Premier League (IPL), in 2012 hockey was assured a lasting prominence in the public psyche by the identification of Chand's birth date (29 August) with the foundation of India's National Sport Day.[31]

The persistent elevation of Chand over time – almost to the exclusion of other star players integral to India's ongoing success – has not, however, gone unchallenged. Notably, Balbir Singh Sr. who played for India after the Second World War was, like Chand, a triple Olympic gold medal winner (1948, 1952, 1956) and has also been called 'a legend in his own right'.[32] Unlike Chand, who took his gold medals before the war (1928, 1932, 1938), Singh's playing career intersected with the politically charged event of India's partition and independence from Britain – recently subject of a Bollywood feature film *Gold: The Dream That United Our Nation* (2018). Released to coincide with Independence Day (15 August), the film forthrightly marked the 70th anniversary of India's emphatic (4–0) defeat of Britain at the 1948 London Olympiad. The film's trailer 'Winners Under British India' . . . 'Legends Under Free India' encapsulates the experiential tensions of those players who had grown up and played hockey under British rule and went on to embody the promise of its liberation in front of a predominantly British crowd and on British soil. Welcoming the film, Balbir Singh observed 'It was something special to beat our former rulers, in their country, on their playground . . . I felt that even I was flying with our national flag that day.'[33]

In terms of state and popular celebration, India's victory over Britain at Wembley Stadium in 1948 was an outcome perhaps only matched in nationalistic overtones and reaction by Pakistan's post-partition defeat of India at the Rome Olympics (1960). This marked the end of India's phenomenal Olympic gold run, however, the team reasserted itself by regaining 'their' Olympic title at Tokyo in 1964 – only for it to be taken again by Pakistan in 1968.[34] The dominance of India in hockey – and latterly Pakistan as a post-partition nation – was underpinned by a distinctive playing style, facilitated by local conditions of climate, pitches and stick technology. In writing about sport and the military, Mason and Riedi note that hockey 'was far more prevalent in India, where the hard, dry grounds made it a faster and more skillful game'.[35] The 'Indian head' stick was handcrafted in mulberry wood with a discernibly shorter striking 'toe' (curved end) which allowed better ball control, characterised by close passing and zone marking – as opposed to the extended curve of the 'English head' stick and a discernible 'hit and run' style of play.[36] Although the Indian stick came into general use during the 1950s, it is not this which enabled other hockey-playing nations to begin beating India at what had effectively become its own game. Rather, it was the decision to introduce artificial pitches within top flight competition. The innovation in AstroTurf accepted and tried out at the Montreal Olympics (1976) ultimately changed the character of the elite game from 'field' hockey to 'outdoor' hockey.

Interviewed in 2016, Brenda Read (Secretary of the FIH Equipment Committee, 1982–2002) identified the protracted processes involved with making the change. Objectively, artificial surfaces ensured 'true' conditions for play, injecting pace and preciseness of technique into the game. The FIH were aware that installation would be costly, maintenance challenging and changes to equipment (notably sticks) necessary.[37] In principle, this should not have disadvantaged talented teams from India (or Pakistan), but for the associated financial costs in a nation where, Mujumdar has shown, ownership of the game had become contested between politically ascendant southern states and the northern states. As earlier noted, Punjab, Kerala and Goa were effectively the heartlands of Indian hockey, but by 1975 the president of the Indian Hockey Federation was a southern politician, close to the President of the FIH, Rene Frank. Thus, in complex political circumstances India fell into line with the proposed Astro-Turf strategy.[38]

Unsurprisingly, the beneficiaries of this step-change were economically buoyant nations, particularly those with relatively well-established and supportive sports systems. In particular, the AstroTurf era saw Germany, the Netherlands and Australia not only prosper, but ultimately become dominant forces in the global game due to a willingness to invest in the new playing surface. In having also developed indoor hockey (*Hallenhockey*) as a derivative of the field game during the 1950s, West German players were especially accustomed to working on smooth, uniform surfaces – as were those more generally in Europe where clubs adopted the indoor game as a welcome alternative to muddy pitches when weather conditions were poor.

Liberating the game: developments post-1970

The FIH decision to make artificial surfaces mandatory for international tournaments was literally a game changer for all nations invested in top flight hockey. It was not, however, the only significant decision to impact the character of the game during the 1970s. In 1970 the English Hockey Association finally became a member of the FIH and with it came the absorption of the International Rules Board into the FIH framework. Thus, for the first time since the game's inception *men's* hockey throughout the world finally became united. Howells interprets this as the FIH acquiring 'world control of the game except for the IFWHA whose absorption was only a matter of time.'[39] As written, the observation somewhat glosses over the tensions between the two controlling bodies because, firstly, over time the men's and women's games were played under different rules and, secondly, women were either affiliated to the FIH *or* the IFWHA in significant numbers.

The statement in 1973 that the FIH 'would go its own way about women's hockey without any longer taking into consideration the IFWHA'[40] therefore constituted a very real threat to IFWHA's longstanding authority – not only within the women's game, but for the game itself should the future of hockey end up governed by two attitudinally divided authorities. Ultimately, in 1975 representatives of IFWHA – affiliated nations moved in favour of the two Federations forming a Supreme Council. Almost immediately a more competitive face for the women's game was articulated through the first IFWHA World Championship held in Edinburgh the same year, played for a trophy presented by the Royal Bank of Scotland. At the associated championship conference, IFWHA representatives voted for women's hockey to be included at the Olympic Games – this could never have happened had governance of the men's and women's game remained separate because the International Olympic Committee (IOC) would only recognise one international body. IFWHA therefore had no choice but to fully merge with the FIH if women were to attain equal opportunities to play hockey at Olympic level.

As it turned out, for those women who played for the leading hockey nations, the promise of appearing on the world stage alongside their male counterparts was frustrated due to a controversial boycott of the Moscow Olympics in 1980. An invasion of Afghanistan by the Soviet Union in 1979 provoked the United States to spearhead a strident political protest through the games – it was effective in leading many nations to either totally withdraw or partially withdraw from them.[41] Hockey was adversely affected on both counts; of the leading nations at the time Argentina, Pakistan, West Germany, the Netherlands and Great Britain did not go. The tournament went ahead, but diminished in the number of nations competing and supplemented by reserve teams. Ultimately, Zimbabwe triumphed over Czechoslovakia and India prevailed over Spain in the women's and men's tournaments respectively.[42]

Looking back to look forward: developing the global game

By 1980 the game of hockey had emerged through significant changes in the context of play and governance, but fundamentally it remained an amateur game. Nearly thirty years later in 2009, opinions expressed by player-enthusiasts in Britain bemoaned the fact that hockey still was 'not professional'.[43] These commentators recognised the differences between the ways in which the culture of their game had evolved, as compared to other modern team sports originating from the nineteenth century: they rightly observed that, unlike soccer, hockey had never cultivated an audience of casual and non-playing fans willing to pay to watch play. With hindsight, the subtext of that predicament can be explained by hockey being a product of middle and upper – class recreational sociability, grounded in club culture across nations which thrived on friendly play, rather than the rivalries needed to fuel league and cup competitions that worked so well for business. Moreover, where the game of rugby union had succeeded, hockey had failed: 'Why is hockey not pro? . . . [It] is the total lack of crowds. Look at Rugby Union – before turning pro it had sustained spectator interest: something we lack!'[44]

But it is not quite true to say that hockey lacked crowds; Olympic competitions drew them, the aforementioned women's annual internationals at Wembley Stadium (1951–1991) secured incredible turnouts, and a cursory look at illustrated texts show outdoor and indoor hockey as well-attended in Europe too. Hockey's success over time turned upon it being an *internally* self-serving family of generally supportive players, clubs and associations; to all intents and purposes the game evolved by operating on its own terms, surviving happily with sponsorship arrangements which did not entail pressure to fundamentally change the culture of the game. The latter allowed an enduring resistance to paying players – and keeping the club game at the heart. Since the late nineteenth century a spirit of voluntarism all over the world witnessed innumerable well-educated practitioners step up to secure the greater good of the game, whether through the writing of instructional publications, self-organised tours or by undertaking other activities such as coaching (often aligned to teaching positions), umpiring and administration at club and association levels. Indeed, Gavin Featherstone has noted that it was the professional (middle) class – rising on the back of industrial, commercial and administrative regeneration after the Second World War – which facilitated the circumstances whereby the Netherlands would emerge as the dominant force in the global game. Not least, Dutch innovation and enterprise in the development of synthetic surfaces made for mutually beneficial sponsorship opportunities. In addition, local authorities funded the laying of pitches for 'public' use which included contracts of adoption by local hockey clubs.[45] Thus, from the 1970s India's circumstantial misfortune became the Netherlands gain: outdoor hockey did not only thrive there, it began to flourish from grassroots to elite level – as evidenced by the ongoing success of both men's and women's teams on the international stage.

The rewards of becoming a professional hockey player in the Netherlands have been noted as 'substantial'. Bleichrodt et al. observe that 'the game has a high status . . . and the players are public figures. Consequently, businesses are keen to hire the players either during (for promotional activities) or after their career.'[46] Unsurprisingly, the Netherlands has become a magnate for the best players in the world seeking to immerse themselves within a sporting culture where hockey uniquely commands comparable respect with professional soccer. Otherwise, definitive declaration that hockey 'is' a fully fledged professional team sport is not easy to find. Moreover, the idea that it should 'turn pro' is not yet universally endorsed; for example, Heino Knuf, high performance director of the German Hockey Federation (Deutscher Hockey-Bund) has asserted 'we do not here in Deutschland want to see the game go professional. We value the family of hockey too much. As soon as money, agents and contracts start to dominate, we will lose the social dimension in the game with its unique set of networking which we all currently enjoy.'[47] Historically and in the present, clubs remain at the heart of hockey, so conditions in the Netherlands merely demonstrate that opportunity to play exclusively as a paid professional is highly dependent upon both the material conditions of, and supportive attitudes within, national sports systems.

For the majority of other hockey playing nations, broader public visibility has been dependent upon the game's presence at the Olympic Games, although since 2010 the FIH has been increasingly active with regard to its aspirations for raising hockey's public profile. First, after successfully hosting the World Cup in New Delhi (2010), India's desire 'to rejuvenate' the game at home found substance via a partnership between headline sponsors Hero MotoCorp and the FIH. Significantly, this led to the formation of a self-contained professional hockey league in 2013. Following a model akin to the IPL (India Premier League in cricket), the *Hero Hockey India League* brought top players from around the world to five city-based franchises. Apparently building on the Hero league success, in 2014 the FIH announced its intention to extend the reach of hockey via the launch of a comprehensive ten-year strategy focused on professionalising the game. A work in progress, the 'Hockey Revolution' essentially aims to cement a commercial culture for hockey by 2024 – the FIH's centenary year.[48]

In addition to the Olympics which the FIH acknowledges as 'Quite simply the most prestigious tournament in hockey . . . for players and fans',[49] the lynchpin of the revolution is a portfolio of events spread across each calendar year, the associated matches played internationally and distributed globally via television broadcasts and online.[50] Beginning in 2019, the Hockey Pro League is the touchstone event – it locks nine top tier playing nations into a competition which also serves as the qualifier for the men's and women's Hockey World Cups *and* the Olympic Games. It remains to be seen as to whether hockey can generate and sustain the kind of year-round mass spectator support like that enjoyed by other well-established team sports. It should not be forgotten that soccer and rugby (in various codes across the world) have evolved overtime to accommodate business initiatives and commercial imperatives which now enable them to identify as 'professional', that is, in a way not yet seen in hockey. The prospect of hockey becoming so is not without its critics; ex-player, coach and pundit Todd Williams noted how the pressure of travelling and playing across the globe means 'The sport's elite will be entering new territory on the body and mind.[51] Also writing in *The Hockey Paper*, Rod Gilmour noted how those elite players – upon whom the FIH and many national associations – depend to generate income and funding, are without international or domestic unions to protect their welfare.[52]

Conclusion

While England is generally acknowledged as the 'home' of modern hockey on account of codifying the game, it is clear that other nations have been integral to making hockey the global sport it is today. International developments in the men's game could not have happened without the French motivation to establish the Fédération Internationale de Hockey sur Gazon (FIH) in 1924, bringing the game to the Olympic stage. Similarly, co-operation between several women's associations enabled the International Federation of Women's Hockey Associations (IFWHA) to thrive from 1927 to 1983, when full amalgamation with the FIH occurred. Technology and styles of play as influential in the changing fortunes of Asian and European teams during the twentieth century have also been important, however, the future success of hockey resides not so much with the amateur game as now played across every continent, but with the FIH's management of the 'hockey revolution' which seeks to raise the public profile and status of the sport.

Notes

1 M.K. Howells, *A Centenary of Modern Hockey 1871–1971* (London: M.K Howells/The Oyez Press, 1971), 5; 7.
2 D. Birley, *Sport and the Making of Britain* (Manchester: Manchester University Press, 1993), 36; Paul Rouse, *Sport & Ireland: A History* (Oxford: Oxford University Press), 13.
3 The main sporting threats to cultural nationalism in Ireland were identified as rugby, cricket and Association football, hurling constituted a successful antidote to field hockey. See Rouse, *Sport & Ireland*, 164–176.
4 J. Lowerson, *Sport and the English Middle Classes 1870–1914* (Manchester: Manchester University Press, 1993), 85–86, 212–213. Each of these aspects deserves more detailed research than currently exists.
5 See J.A. Magan, *Athleticism in the Victorian and Edwardian Public School* (Cambridge: Cambridge University Press, 1981) the seminal work in this respect.
6 Blackheath & Elthamians Hockey Club, 'History', www.blackheath.co.uk/a/history-32741.html (accessed January 2018).
7 Teddington Hockey Club's website states 'We are the oldest hockey club in the world and one of the best hockey clubs in London'; see www.teddingtonhockey.club (accessed January 2018).
8 Howells, *A Centenary of Modern Hockey 1871–1971*, 9–17.
9 Reproduced in Howells, ibid., 14.
10 Ibid., 17.
11 'Hockey Advances', *C.B. Fry's Magazine of Sports and Outdoor Life*, 1(1) (April 1904), 61.
12 N. Miroy, *The History of Hockey* (Staines: Lifeline, 1986), 157–188 provides detailed accounts.
13 The Amsterdam Hockey & Bandy Club, 'History', www.ahbc.nl/site/default.asp?option=2502&stc name=declub_historie&menu=1 (accessed February 2018).
14 J. Jan Feith, *Sport in the Netherlands* (Leiden: Eduard Ydo, 1915), 20–22. Thanks to Dr Nick Piercy for recommending this source.
15 Not entirely uncontested, see K.E. McCrone, *Sport and The Physical Emancipation of English Women 1870–1914* (Abingdon: Routledge, 2014 orig. 1988), 130–135.
16 S. Akimoto, 'A Very Serious Part of Hockey'? Mixed Hockey in England before 1914 (Research Presentation), www.hockeymuseum.net/index.php/study-topic/mixed-hockey (accessed January 2018).
17 McCrone, 129–130 (quote 134).
18 J. Halpin, 'Thus FAR and NO FARTHER': THE RISE of WOMEN'S HOCKEY LEAGUES in England from 1910 to 1939, *Sport in History*, 37(2) (2017), 146–163, 149–150. The complete article is important for understanding the deep associational politics related to the initiatives outlined.
19 G. Watson '"See These Brilliant Exponents of the Game": The England Women's Hockey Team Tour of Australia and New Zealand, 1914', *The International Journal of the History of Sport*, 33(17) (2016), 2105–2122. Available research does not allow for a more comprehensive explanation of early dissemination of the game across nations.

20 Hockey Australia, 'History of Hockey in Australia', www.hockey.org.au/Governance/History/History-of-Hockey-in-Australia (accessed September 2018). The men's Australian Hockey Association was formed 1925.

21 Watson, 'See These Brilliant Exponents of the Game', 2112.

22 E. A. C. Thomson, *Hockey: Historical and Practical* (London: George G. Harrap & Company, 1925), 111–124. One official game occurred between England and Germany in 1913. Oxbridge matches, English trials (instituted 1920), Inter-Divisional (English regions) and Inter-Services matches are also listed demonstrating widespread take-up of the game.

23 Application for the International Rules by overseas playing nations went to the Hockey Association (England) which maintained a controlling vote on the Board. See M.K. Howells, *The Romance of Hockey's History* (Surrey: M.K. Howells/Teddington Hockey Club, n.d.), 83–84; Miroy, *The History of Hockey*, 143–147.

24 Howells, *The Romance of Hockey's History*, 83–84. The true extent of the context and politics surrounding the formation of the FIH and the ongoing relationship with the Rules Board has yet to be comprehensively detailed within existing internal histories.

25 See Steve Wulf, 'Who Are These Guys?' *Sports Illustrated: Special Preview the 1984 Olympics* (17 July 1984), 402–418. The by-line is telling: 'And why aren't they wearing skirts? After all, everyone in the US knows that field hockey is a girls' sport.' Available at www.si.com/vault/issue/44475/toc.

26 N. Tomkins and P. Ward, *The Century Makers: A History of the All England Women's Hockey Association 1895–1995* (Shrewsbury: AEWHA, 1995), 97–102.

27 The Hockey Museum, 'International Hockey at Wembley Stadium, 1951–1991' www.hockeymuseum.net/index.php/study-topic/international-hockey-at-wembley-stadium (accessed March 2018). See also Nan Williams and Christabel Russell Vick, *The magic of Wembley: Women's Hockey Internationals 1951–1991* (Woking: The Hockey Museum, 2018).

28 See R. Sen, *Nation at Play: A History of Sport in India* (New York: Columbia University Press, 2015), esp. ch. 7, 'The Early Olympics: India's Hockey Triumphs', 137–164.

29 A. Alikhan, 'How the Anglo-Indian Community Created Two No 1 Hockey Teams' *The Times of India* (14 August 2016), https://timesofindia.indiatimes.com/home/sunday-times/How-the-Anglo-Indian-community-created-two-No-1-hockey-teams/articleshow/53690148.cms

30 M. S. Mills 'A Most Remarkable Community: Anglo-Indian Contributions to Sport in India', *Contemporary South Asia*, 10(2), 223–236.

31 DD News, 'India's National Sports Day', report at www.youtube.com/watch?v=QB4goLNyeh8 Accessed June 2018. Chand was born 29 August 1905.

32 The Hindu, www.thehindu.com/sport/hockey/1948-olympics-record-fourth-gold-medal-for-india/article3620679.ece (accessed June 2018).

33 'Gold' (Trailer) published 24 June 2018 at www.youtube.com/watch?v=Pcv0aoOlsLM. Balbir Singh Sr testimony available at 'Balbir Singh, India's Legendary Hockey Player Who Inspired Gold', *The Quint* (18 August 2018), www.thequint.com/sports/hockey/balbir-singh-on-1948-london-olympics-gold-akshay-kumar (accessed August 2018). Sources generally indicate that it was the victory in itself which inspired the film with aspects of Singh's experiences represented.

34 N. Raheel, 'Olympic Champions: When Pakistan Claimed its First Gold Medal', *The Express Tribune Pakistan* (9 August 2014), https://tribune.com.pk/story/746264/olympic-champions-when-pakistan-claimed-its-first-gold-medal (accessed August 2018).

35 T. Mason and E. Riedi, *Sport and the Military: The British Armed Forces, 1880–1960* (Cambridge: Cambridge University Press, 2010), 34.

36 Miroy, *The History of Hockey*, 68–69 speculates as to the reasons for the shorter 'crook' size (i.e. whether by accident or design).

37 The Peter Savage Oral History Collection, interview with Brenda Read, 15 March 2016, available at http://hockeymuseum.net/index.php/oral-histories (accessed July 2018).

38 B. Majumdar, 'When North-South Fight, the Nation Is Out of Sight: The Politics of Olympic Sport in Postcolonial India', *International Journal of the History of Sport*, (23)7: 1217–1231.

39 Howells, *The Romance of Hockey's History*, 109.

40 Tomkins and Ward, *The Century Makers*, 179.

41 K. Jefferys, 'Britain and the Boycott of the 1980 Moscow Olympics', *Sport in History*, 32(2) (2012), 279–301 provides context and illustrative case study of the complex politics associated with the boycott.

42 FIH, 'Events Page', www.fih.ch/events/olympic-games (accessed October 2018).

43 Field Hockey Forum, 'Why is Hockey Not Professional' thread 23 May–11 September 2009, archived at www.fieldhockeyforum.com/threads/why-is-hockey-not-professional.7714 (accessed July 2018).

44 Ibid.

45 G. Featherstone, *The Hockey Dynamic: Examining the Forces That Shaped the Modern Game* (Spring City, PA: Reedswain Publishing, 2015), 173–178.

46 H. Bleichrodt, O. L' Haridon and D. Van Ass, 'The Risk Attitudes of Professional Athletes: Optimism and Success Are Related', *Decision*, 5(2) (2018), 96.

47 Quoted in Featherstone, *Hockey Dynamic*, 179.

48 Hockey Revolution, www.fih.ch/inside-fih/our-strategy.

49 FIH Olympic Games, www.fih.ch/events/olympic-games (accessed October 2018).

50 Hockey Revolution, www.fih.ch/inside-fih/our-strategy.

51 T. Williams, 'International Hockey Players Heading into Pressured Waters Ahead of Pro League', *The Hockey Paper* (6 April 2018), www.thehockeypaper.co.uk/articles/2018/04/06/international-hockey-players-heading-into-pressured-waters-ahead-of-pro-league (accessed October 2018).

52 R. Gilmour, 'Maddie Hinch's International Break Highlights Hockey Pro League Pitfall', *The Hockey Paper* (19 September 2018), www.thehockeypaper.co.uk/articles/2018/09/19/maddie-hinchs-international-break-highlights-hockey-pro-league-pitfalls?utm_source=newsletter&utm_medium=email&utm_campaign=why_the_pro_league_has_its_pitfalls&utm_term=2018–09–19 Accessed October 2018

6

Ice hockey

John Nauright and Sergey Altukhov

The sport of ice hockey is governed by the International Ice Hockey Federation (IIHF) based in Switzerland. Major professional leagues exist in North America (National Hockey League – NHL), Russia, eastern Europe and Asia (Kontinental Hockey League – KHL), with other smaller-scale professional leagues in Sweden, Switzerland, Germany, France, Czech Republic, Finland and the United Kingdom. Ice hockey is the flagship team sport of the Winter Olympic Games with many famous Olympic battles including the "Miracle on Ice" win of the USA over the Soviet Union in 1980, the Canada overtime win over the USA in Vancouver 2010 in the men's competition, and epic battles between the Canadian and USA women's teams in the 2000s. While the NHL is regarded as the best hockey league in the world, the KHL is close behind and includes the Kunlun Red Star franchise in Beijing, China. At the Pyeongchang Winter Olympics in 2018, North and South Korea combined for a unified Korean team. While largely still confined to countries in colder climates, hockey continues to expand throughout the world and into new markets.

While soccer is the dominant sport in most countries, ice hockey can lay claim to being the most popular sport in Canada, Russia, Finland, Sweden, the Czech Republic and Slovakia, though soccer in strong in most of these countries as well. In Switzerland, hockey is not far behind soccer and the leading Swiss league team, Servette in Geneva, draws more spectators per match than any club outside the NHL. The most famous professional hockey players of all time come from these countries. The Montreal Canadiens hold the record for most NHL Stanley Cup wins, the Red Army team of the former Soviet Union dominated hockey there during the period before 1990 as well. From the 1920s until 1967, the NHL consisted of the "original six" teams of Montreal Canadiens, Toronto Maple Leafs, Boston Bruins, New York Rangers, Detroit Red Wings and Chicago Black Hawks. In the latter 1900s and early 2000s the NHL expanded across North America placing teams in the south and west in the USA including notoriously hot cities of Phoenix and Dallas.

After using the mid-1920s as a decade for the expansion of the NHL, the late 1920s through the early 1940s can be described as an era of trial and error for the NHL. Complicated by the great depression and North America's entrance into the Second World War, the NHL franchises struggled to stay in operation (Klein, 2016). By 1942, the league was down to six teams, the "original six". The NHL expanded for the 1967 season, which is commonly viewed as the largest expansion of any professional sports league in sports history (Klein, 2016). The NHL added the California Seals, the Los Angeles Kings, the Minnesota North Stars (now Dallas Stars), Philadelphia Flyers, Pittsburgh Penguins and St. Louis Blues, doubling the NHL from six teams to twelve (Klein, 2016). Throughout the 1970s the NHL continued to expand throughout the United States and Canada (Klein, 2016). Despite the majority of hockey clubs being located in the United States, an overwhelming majority of players were from Canada.

With the NHL consisting mostly of teams located in the United States, it is surprising to note that for the most part throughout the history of NHL expansion, there was a drastic difference in where teams were located, with a majority of the teams being located in the heavily populated northern and eastern half of the United states, only two teams located west of Minnesota and no teams located in the southern part of the nation. One of the reasons why the NHL did not expand to the West during the 1970s is due to the formation of the World Hockey Association which was active from 1972–1979 ("WHA-Teams," n.d.). When the World Hockey Association ceased operations after the 1979 season, the two leagues merged, resulting in the NHL starting the 1980 season with three new clubs located west of Minnesota ("WHA-Teams," n.d.). In recent times, debates over the soul of hockey versus the economics of hockey have plagued the NHL and the sport, With several new teams located in the southern USA such as Arizona, Texas and Florida, the percentage of NHL teams in the USA is at an all-time high with only Montreal, Ottawa, Toronto, Winnipeg, Calgary, Edmonton and Vancouver in Canada having teams. The Winnipeg team was initially lost to Arizona (Nauright & White, 1996; Silver 1995), before being restored a decade later. Large arenas exist in Saskatoon, Hamilton and Halifax, but the markets have been deemed too small for the NHL. The Quebec Nordiques were highly successful in attracting local and regional fans but were relocated to Colorado. It is most likely that any new Canadian team will be based there in future.

While Canada pioneered the early development of ice hockey in the 1870s and 1880s, the game also expanded internationally by 1900 especially to colder countries in northern Europe and into the USA. The first organized hockey competitions in Russia began in St. Petersburg in 1898. After 1900 hockey began to develop in Moscow as well. The special requirements for standardized arenas did not exist yet, so hockey could be played anywhere a clean sheet of ice could be found. Snowdrifts acted like a board area, ice hockey sticks were made of tree branches bent at a right angle and dried over fire to fix the shapes, sizes, hockey goals were similar to the size of football goals, and player equipment was very primitive. In 1907 the Saint-Petersburg Hockey League was created and moves towards standardization began (Altukhov & Nauright, 2018).

Early games in Canada and Russia were amateur with many early club members coming from middle and upper classes. Increasing competition led to regular competitions and moves towards commercialization. The development of hockey coincided with the emergence of new indoor sporting arenas such as Madison Square Garden in New York City. Early sporting entrepreneurs who built and operated ice rinks and new arenas in both Canada and the Northern United States recognized the value of hosting games to be watched by many spectators. As experts on hockey history have pointed out, this phenomenon quickly left large cities such as Montreal, Toronto and Detroit spreading the game to more remote towns where local business leaders attracted players with increasingly large sums of money to play for local teams such as those in Cobalt and Renfrew, Ontario, and Houghton and Calumet, Michigan (Cosentino, 1990; Mason & Schrodt, 1996; Mason, 2018). As hockey scholar Dan Mason states: "The local arena thus became a focal point of local communities where spectators could gather on cold winter nights to watch their teams play" (Mason, 2018).

Cold War hockey

The sporting events that were by far the most symbolic during the Cold War were nearly all hockey matches. The 1972 "Summit on Ice" series between Canada and the Soviet Union, the 1975 Montreal Canadiens versus Red Army game and the 1980 "Miracle on Ice" matchup between the USA and the Soviets, all were significant moments during the Cold War. The Red Army match against the Montreal Canadiens at the Montreal Forum which ended in a 3–3 tie on 31 December 1975 is considered by many to be the greatest hockey match in history. The game featured superstar goaltenders Vladislav Tretiak for the Red Army and Ken Dryden for the Canadiens. Tretiak is credited with single-handedly keeping the Red Army in the game as the Canadiens dominated the play (Denault, 2010). Leading NHL and Soviet teams continued to play against each other during the late 1970s and early 1980s paving the way for Soviet players to come to play in the NHL by the late 1980s.

Hockey in popular culture

The success of hockey stars and their increasingly celebrity as role models for communities has consistently expanded in the post-Second World War era. While hockey competitions remain central to the success of the sport, in countries where hockey is the dominant sport, hockey stars achieve tremendous fame and adulation as well as serving as focal points for identity. Most Canadians born before 1970 can tell you where they were "when Henderson scored for Canada" in the final game of the 1972 Summit on Ice series against the Soviet Union. In the Province of Quebec, the province of Canada that is predominantly French speaking, the Montreal Canadiens have served as a key focal point for identity. For many decades most of the Canadiens' players were raised in Quebec and many of them were French-speakers such as Maurice and Henri Richard, Jean Beliveau, Jacques Lamaire, Guy Lapointe, Bernie "Boom Boom" Geoffrion, Yvan Cournoyer, Guy LaFleur and goalies such as Jacques Plante and Patrick Roy (Ransom, 2014).

In the case of Maurice Richard, he became symbolic of the struggle of the Quebecois in the face of Anglo-centrism. Richard was clearly denied assists that would have gone to him had he been an English-speaking player and he was ejected for the end of the 1955 season which cost him the scoring title. This prompted a series of riots in Montreal which were called the Richard Riots. Many attribute as the starting point of Quebec nationalist activism which led to two referenda on separation from Canada that narrowly failed, but did lead to a nationalist government in the Province (Bélanger, 2013; Salutin, 1977; Ransom, 2014). Quebecois cultural scholar, Benoît Melançon produced one of the best cultural biographies ever written on the legacy and cultural meaning of Richard in his *The Rocket: A Cultural History of Maurice Richard* (Melançon, 2009). A movie by the same name portrayed the career of Richard up through the time of the Richard Riots. In the famous Canadian cartoon movie and children's book *The Hockey Sweater*, all the boys in a small town wear Richard jerseys (Melançon, 2009; Ransom, 2014). Canadian playwright Rick Salutin placed the Richard Riots and other key events in Quebec history together with that of the Montreal Canadiens in his 1977 play *Les Canadiens* which culminates in the first referendum on Quebec independence from Canada.

While hockey is a national sport in Sweden, Finland, Russia, the Czech Republic and Slovakia as well in Canada, the politics of hockey and nationalist identity have been most pronounced in Canada and Quebec. Other hockey players have achieved iconic status in wider culture, most notably Wayne Gretzky, known as "The Great One", who is the all-time leading scorer in the National Hockey League and holds 61 NHL records. Gretzky created a moment of national angst when he was traded by the Edmonton Oilers to the Los Angeles Kings in 1988.

Many Canadians blamed his American wife who worked in Hollywood and viewed the loss of Gretzky to an American team as momentous for Canadian identity (Jackson, 1988). Indeed, the Disneyfication of hockey reached its peak with the *Mighty Ducks* 1992 movie (and its sequel *D2*) which was linked directly to the NHL through Disney's investment and creation of the Mighty Ducks of Anaheim (1993–2006), though now the team is back to being styled the Anaheim Ducks. The *Mighty Ducks* movies grossed nearly $100 million between them.

Gordie Howe became known as "Mr. Hockey" playing competitively well into his 50s, while Boston Bruins defenseman Bobby Orr was thought to be the best pure talent in the history of the sport. In a strikingly similar storyline to *The Rocket*, Russian star Valeri Kharmalov, who died tragically at age 33 in 1981, had his life story told in *Legend No. 17*, released in 2013. The following year *Red Army*, a documentary about the great Soviet teams of the 1970s and 1980s appeared. Several movies and documentaries have appeared examining the Summit on Ice series between Canada and the Soviet Union that took place in 1972. However, the movie *Miracle* released by Disney in 2004, which grossed over $64 million became the most watched hockey movie of all-time. Starring Kurt Russell as US coach Herb Brooks, the movie follows the USA men's hockey team of 1980 which miraculously defeated the multiple defending Olympic and World Champion Soviet Union in an epic semi-final game in Lake Placid, New York.

Globalizing ice hockey

The Swedish Ice Hockey Federation is a member of the Swedish Sport Confederation which was established 1903. The Swedish Sport Confederation today consists totally of 71 sport federations, with 20,000 sport clubs and over three million members in a country of eight million. Initially hockey fell under the auspices of football (soccer) with the Swedish Football Association becoming a member of the International Ice Hockey Federation in 1912. As ice hockey grew in popularity the Swedish Ice Hockey Federation was founded in 1922 (Backman, 2018; Stark, 2010). The Swedish Ice Hockey Federation has since been the governing body for all Swedish ice hockey. In Finland, hockey first appeared in 1899 or the 1920s depending on the source. Regardless, the sport was organized in 1927 under the Finnish Skating Federation, which also released the first rules, based on the IIHF rules for ice hockey. The Finnish Skating Federation joined the IIHF in 1928 (Backman, 2018). Sweden and Finland began a long rivalry in the sport in 1928 first playing on 29 January. Not surprisingly Sweden, with a longer history of organization, won the first match easily prompting the formation of a separate ice hockey federation in Finland in 1929. Sweden and Finland both have professional leagues, with Sweden having a promotion-relegation system and Finland have a closed league structure. The largest Finnish team, Jokerit, now plays in the Russian-dominated Kontinental Hockey League (KHL). Top players from both countries since the 1980s have aspired to success in the NHL, however.

Since the 1980s, the number of non-Canadian players achieving stardom in the NHL has increased dramatically. Before that time up to 90% of NHL players had been born in Canada with most of the rest being from the USA. Players from the former Soviet Union, particularly Russia have had a significant impact on the NHL. Alex Ovetchkin, who has played his entire career with the Washington Capitals leads all Russian point scorers in NHL history. Other great Russian players have included Sergey Fedorov, Viacheslav Fetisov, Evgeni Malkin (entire career with the Pittsburgh Penguins), Pavel Datsyuk (Detroit Red Wings). Finnish star Jari Kurri won several Stanley Cups partnering Wayne Gretzky scoring 601 goals in his NHL career. His scoring total of 1,398 points was later passed by Temu Selanne, second all-time European scorer and leading Finn with 1,457 total NHL points including 684 goals. Swedish star Peter Forsberg has only been surpassed in assists per game by Gretzky, Mario Lemieux and Bobby Orr. Nine

Swedish players have now won the "Triple Gold" (Olympic Gold, World Championship Gold, and a Stanley Cup title), only trailing Canada with ten as of 2019. Russian star Pavel Bure, "The Russian Rocket" was perhaps the fastest of all players and stands fourth all-time in goals per game. Bure began a Legends of Hockey series pitting star former players from European countries in competition in 2016. Czech player Jaromír Jágr played 24 seasons in the NHL and six seasons in the KHL before returning to the Czech Republic in 2018 to finish his long career. Jágr was one of only three players to lead the NHL in scoring between 1981 and 2001 (with Wayne Gretzky and Mario Lemieux being the other two). He is the third all-time leading scorer in NHL history and leading European scorer in history with 1,921 points including 766 goals (third all-time behind Gretzky and Gordie Howe).

With the advent of the KHL in 2008, leading Russian and European players have been able to earn substantial incomes without coming to North America. Several star players with NHL experience have chosen to play in the KHL including Pavel Datsyuk and Ila Kovalchuk, both of whom play for SKA in St. Petersburg. KHL teams compete for the Gregarin Cup and the league now boasts teams in several European and Asian countries including Kulun Red Star in Beijing, China. The League pays the highest salaries and attracts the most total spectators of any league outside the NHL.

The World Championships and Olympic competitions remain the pinnacle for national hockey teams with the Soviet Union and Russia being the most successful over the latter four decades of the 20th century and into the 21st. NHL players on teams in the Stanley Cup play-offs routinely miss the World Championships while most Olympic competitions have occurred without NHL players. One exception was at the 2010 Vancouver Olympics when Canadian superstar Sidney Crosby scored a goal in overtime to defeat the USA. In the women's game, Canada and the United States have regularly contested world and Olympic titles, though in 2019, Finland defeated Canada in the semi-finals before losing in a shoot-out to the USA. In the USA, intercollegiate hockey has gained in strength with the "Frozen Four' emulating the "Final Four" in basketball. Teams from New England and the upper Midwest have dominated NCAA competition and college players have formed the bulk of US national teams including the "Miracle" gold medal winning team in the 1980s Olympics.

With tiered international competition the sport of hockey continues to expand around the world with teams such as the New Zealand "Ice Blacks" competing for championships and opportunities to move to the next level of competition. With the Winter Olympic Games coming to Beijing, China in 2022, there has been massive investment in Chinese hockey with the best players joining Russians in Kunlun Red Star. The club also is home of the best women's players placing two teams in the Canadian professional women's league which sadly folded in 2019 (Li & Nauright, 2018). In the Pyeonchang Winter Games the two Koreas fielded unified teams in the men's and women's competitions with Seoul being mentioned as a potential leading candidate for further KHL expansion in Asia (Kim, 2018).

Expanding ice hockey research

Ice hockey has been well served by scholars internationally with much of the English-language literature produced by scholars based in Canada and the USA. In 1991, the Society for International Hockey Research was created by a group of 17 scholars in Canada. Since that time several academic conferences and international forums have been held in Canada and Russia to expand the impact of ice hockey research on the history and contemporary issues facing the sport. Ten conferences beginning in 2001 have been organized in Canada and the northern USA, known as "The Hockey Conference." Since 2017, the International Ice Hockey Federation and Russian

Hockey Federation working in conjunction with academic scholars, journalists and hockey officials have held the World Hockey Forum annually each December in Moscow, Russia. In 2018,
the first major academic global history of hockey was written, by Stephen Hardy and Andrew
Holman, long-time scholars of the sport, simply titled *Hockey: A Global History*. Also that year,
feature panels on ice hockey appeared at the European Association for Sport Management Congress held in Sweden. While there have been clear advances in research on the history, culture,
science, business and political economy aspects of hockey around the world, much remains to
be done particularly outside of core hockey regions of North America and northern Europe.

References

Althukov, S. & Nauright, J. (2018). *World Hockey Forum 2017: Innovation for the Future of Ice Hockey Around
the World*. Moscow: М: Спорт.

Backman, J. (2018). Hockey Organization and Innovation in Sweden and Finland. In S. Althukov & J. Nauright (eds), *World Hockey Forum 2017: Innovation for the Future of Ice Hockey Around the World*. Moscow:
М. Спорт.

Bélanger, A. (2013). Le hockey au Québec, bien plus qu'un jeu: Analyse sociologique de la place centrale
du hockey dans le projet identitaire des Québécois. *Loisir et Societe* 19(2), 539–557.

Cosentino, F. (1990). *Renfrew Millionaires: The Valley Boys of Winter 1910*. Burnstown: General Store Publishing House.

Denault, T. (2010). *The Greatest Game: The Montreal Canadiens, the Red Army, and the Night That Saved
Hockey*. Toronto: McClelland & Stewart.

Kim, 2018

Klein, 2016

Li, H. & Nauright, J. (2018). The Kunlun Red Star Phenomenon as a case study for hockey growth in Asia.
In S. Althukov & J. Nauright (eds), *World Hockey Forum II: New Technologies, New Markets, New Opportunities for Global Ice Hockey*. Moscow: М. Спорт.

Mason, D., (1998). The International Hockey League and the professionalization of ice hockey, 1904–1907.
Journal of Sport History, 25(1).

Mason, D., & Schrodt, B. (1996). Hockey's first professional team: the Portage Lakes Hockey Club of
Houghton, Michigan. *Sport History Review*, 27(1), 49–71.

Melançon, B. (2009). *The Rocket: A Cultural History of Maurice Richard*. Toronto: Greystone Books.

Nauright, J. & White, P. (1996). "Save our Jets": professional sport, nostalgia, community and nation in
Canada. *Avante*, 2(3), 24–41.

Ransom, A. (2014). *Hockey PQ: Canada's Game in Quebec's Popular Culture*. Toronto: University of Toronto
Press.

Salutin, R. (1977). *Les Canadiens*. Montreal: Talon Books.

Silver, J. (1995). *Thin Ice: Money, Politics and the Demise of an NHL Franchise*. Halifax, Nova Scotia: Fernwood
Books.

Stark, T. (2010). Folkhemmet på is: Ishockey, modernisering och nationell identitet i Sverige 1920–1972
[Ice hockey, modernization and national identity in Sweden 1920–1972]. PhD dissertation, Linnéuni-
versitetet, Sweden.

7

Lacrosse

Ryan Turcott

Initial rules and equipment

Long before lacrosse became a competitive sports enterprise at the international, professional, collegiate and youth levels, this sport was rooted in Native American history and spiritual traditions across different regions of North America. The name of the game as well as the rules varied by tribe. The number of players on each side as well as the size of the field would also change depending on tribe. Even the name of the game was different from one tribe to another such as *baggataway* by the Algonquian, *kabocha-toli* by the Choctaw or *tewaarathon* by the Mohawk.[1] Recognized as the oldest team sport in North America, the game was invented and played by the Six Nations of the Iroquois and was much more physical than the sport of lacrosse is played today.

The structure was rather informal at first as participation sometimes involved thousands of men with playing fields that stretched kilometers long. The game seemed to rise from the very land itself as the equipment for playing came directly from the nature or habitation of North America.[2] The Native Americans used balls carved from wood, or deerskin stuffed with hair, and the sticks were hickory (a sacred wood) and strung with deerskin or groundhog leather. The purpose was for each player to disable as many opponents as possible with their stick and then attempt to score a goal.[3] There was no set time to the games as competitions would often last several days. The two teams would agree on a set amount of points and would play from sunrise to sunset until the amount of points was achieved.[4] Violence and injuries were very common, and players would often walk away with minor cuts, broken bones and head injuries. Occasionally a death would occur. Men were the only participants in the matches; women were spectators.

The creators game and "little brothers of war"

Broadly known across Native American tribes as the *creators game* for its spiritual and religious significance, the game helped tribes put their lives into perspective and teach lessons, such importance of friends and allies or how to survive hardship.[5] Complex rituals and spiritual dancing often preceded competitions of the creator's game. When competitions started, each team had a medicine man who would chant incantations to strengthen their team and weaken the other.[6] The sport was played to bring honor and amusement to the creator, as well to thank the Creator for allowing the medicine people to continue to stay with the tribe.[7] When a tribe member fell ill, the sport would also be played in hopes that the creator would look favorably the individual and spare them.[8] According to Fisher, the game also "reinforced each [native] nation's unique relationship with the creator and embodied Man's relationship with nature," and thus maintained a strong spiritual connotation.[9] The physicality of the game caused players to face serious injuries and even die while playing. Native Americans used the sport as a way of training young men to be combat ready as well as to settle disputes between tribes and thus avoiding war. Thus, the sport was initially coined as "little brother of war."[10] The similarities of the sport to war led to growth of appeal from spectators. In the end, players were even buried with their lacrosse sticks as they believed they would need them for playing once awakening in the afterlife.[11]

Colonizing the creators game

It wasn't until 1637 when French missionaries living among the Huron-Wendat tribe first witnessed the game and coined the term "la crosse."[12] Although some historians believe the game was given this name because the stick resembled a bishop's "crosier," others note French colonizers used the phrase *jouer à la crosse* in reference to all games played with a curved stick and ball.[13] As European immigration and colonization increased across the 18th century and into the 19th, the new immigrants were drawn to the Native American game. Native American connection of the sport to the Creator had also begun to diminish when members of the Mohawk tribe converted to Christianity and purposes were much more sport-driven in place of the spiritual connections.[14] In terms of the immigrants, French speaking regions of Canada, specifically Montréal, were among the most enthused, as European sportsmen learned basic skills and rules of the game from the nearby Mohawk Tribe. It was also during this time period where European influence was beginning to morph the medicine healing activity into a full-on sport. In 1834, a group of European immigrant businessmen were able to first lure the games into an urban setting and a sporting spectator environment at the racetrack at Ville Saint-Pierre between different tribes such as the Kahnawake versus the Akwesasne.[15] Historically this was an important event as prior to this time period, games were exclusively played by large groups in open fields and forests previously set out by ancestors and elders of North American and First Nation peoples.

William George Beers, lacrosse and Canadian nationalism

While interest from Europeans grew, a teenaged European-Canadian named William George Beers became particularly captivated by the sport. Beers was introduced to the game from the Kahnawake Mohawk Tribe and would go on to participate in a competitive match between First Nation and Anglo-Canadian players for the visiting Prince of Wales titled the "Grand Display of Indian Games."[16] Beers would go on to publish some written materials which entailed basic rules such as field size and the number of players allowed per side.[17] Although Beers was not the first white man to play the sport, he is often referred to as the "father of modern lacrosse" for creating a written record of the rules that first standardized men's lacrosse in 1860.[18] In 1867, Beers helped establish the National Lacrosse Association (NLA) and pushed strongly for lacrosse to be declared the official sport of Canada. His campaign failed but his efforts helped grow the number of clubs from six to 80 after a national convention Beers organized in Kingston, Ontario.[19] At this time period, white, middle-class, protestant men experienced a crisis in masculinity. Canada found itself in a conundrum trying to figure out ways to boost national pride while also helping male citizens (particularly lacrosse players) develop masculinity.[20] The church had become increasingly populated by supposedly effeminate men whose interests focused on scholarly pursuits more so than physical endeavors; middle-management-level positions in corporations required less physical than mental engagement.[21] Beers felt the sport would help mold strong Canadian men and would be unique to Canada as opposed to the British imperialist sport of cricket.[22] In 1869, Beers published a complete rule book for the modern version of the sport lacrosse entitled *Lacrosse: The National Game of Canada*. While Beers continues to be recognized as the father of modern lacrosse, it is also important to note the colonial role he played in dehumanizing First Nations people, perhaps no better depicted when he noted in his book: "Just as we claim as Canadian the rivers and lakes and land once owned exclusively by Indians, so we now claim their field game as the national field game of our Dominion."[23]

Racism and discrimination of Native American players

Manipulation of eligibility requirements and changing of the rules in regards to the actual game allowed white Canadians to unofficially exclude Native Americans. The idea of amateurism emerged in England; the amateur concept was used as a way to establish participation in a sport predicated on social class.[24] Using amateurism as a prerequisite for lacrosse competition turn deemed the majority of Native Americans ineligible. This was a way for whites to essentially exclude the Native Americans, to categorize them as "other" and unequal to the amateur white players and unworthy of participation in the sport created by their ancestors. In an odd display of flexing their imperial might, European-Canadians were keen on converting Native American traditions and practices into their own, in order to distinguish their own unique national identity. Importantly, Historian Robidoux points out this decision was more about proving colonial mastery over an indigenous sport rather than as Canadians attempting to unite themselves with First Nations tribes.[25] In this sense, lacrosse was seen as an apparatus to leverage both masculinity and colonial control prowess, as later reflected by the NLA policies built on the principles of Native America exclusion.[26] Historians have since classified NLA's amateurism application as racially motivated and one the major decisions that formally excluded Native Americans from organized lacrosse in Canada.[27]

In terms of the actual rules of the game, Beers felt further compelled to adjust the rules of the creator's game in order to accommodate the white players. This was done most notably by vastly shortening the playing field. When the goals were placed a half mile apart in the traditional sense, the white players were unable to compete, let alone touch the ball.[28] According to Wiser, changing the rule of play was also a way to Beers to make a statement and project white supremacy and Canadian nationalism by directly changing the way the game was played.[29] Beers hoped to "turn the Native American version into a rationalised sport that would distinguish the white Canadian participants from the native ones."[30] Beers viewed lacrosse as a "symbolic torch passed from the noble savages of primitive Canada to modern progressive gentlemen of a nation-state."[31] First Nations people did not give up on their game despite it becoming a white man's version of what their ancestors had created. Many native players continued to participate and when opportunities arose to compete against the white players, it served as one of the spaces where Native Americans could challenge colonial ideologies and racial discrimination. Or as Fisher described, "it furnished an opportunity to prevent total racial subordination."[32]

Native American participation in lacrosse has diminished but still remains popular in Native American communities. According to the *NCAA Race and Gender Demographics Database*, the number of American Indian/Alaska Native student-athletes has grown on the men's side from

20 to 63 and on the women's side from 13 to 63 respectively in comparing the 2008 and 2018 seasons.[33] However, tension and mistreatment towards Native American lacrosse players continues to persist in North America and continues to represent a battle ground of different cultures. In 2018 the Dakota Premier Lacrosse League made national headlines for banning three majority-Native American youth teams from participating in the only league in the Dakotas. The Native American players were taunted by fans, opponents, and even coaches with racist terms including, "savages," "dirty Indians," "prairie niggers," "bunch of drunks," and others.[34] While US Lacrosse has ordered an investigation into the matter, this incident is concerning given the historical relations and treatment of Native Americans by white Americans both on and off the lacrosse terrain.

Modern lacrosse and overseas dissemination

Beers also played an important role in first promoting lacrosse abroad and led Canadian teams to England in 1876 and 1883 to showcase and grow the game to new audiences. Additionally, the sport was utilized as part of a larger strategy of promoting immigration to Canada as hundreds of thousands of brochures promoting immigration were distributed during these events.[35] With Beers involvement, these tours included teams made up of amateur players from the Montreal Lacrosse Club, Toronto Lacrosse Club, and non-amateur players from the Kahnawake tribe. The overseas lacrosse tour in 1883 took Canadian players to the United Kingdom for 62 games in 41 cities through Scotland, Ireland, Wales and England in just over two months.[36] Around this same time period, lacrosse was first brought to the United States by Native Americans in upstate New York. The Mohawk Lacrosse Club in the city of Troy, NY, is recognized as the first official lacrosse club in the US. Canadian immigrants would also have a role in disseminating the game as they formed and helped assemble clubs in bustling urban areas such as New York City and Boston.[37] Today, lacrosse is played primarily in the United States and Canada, Great Britain and Australia. Recently, the sport has begun to grow internationally with its arrival in many new countries in Europe, East Asia and Sub-Saharan Africa.

Men's intercollegiate field lacrosse

While intercollegiate men's and women's field lacrosse is arguably most recognizable in the United States' NCAA system, Japan, Canada, and the United Kingdom also sponsor the sport at the university level. However, it was the US intercollegiate field lacrosse system that fueled the growth and development of the modern game into what it is today during the early stages of the twentieth century. Oddly enough, it was the elite universities, such as Yale, Harvard, Princeton and NYU, that would take up a hankering for the sport on their respective campuses and begin the first organized intercollegiate lacrosse competitions.[38] This small group of institutions eventually formed the US Intercollegiate Lacrosse League (USILL) in 1906. Combining school with men's lacrosse was pushed for aggressively by elite private schools in the northeastern US. By doing so, upper class lacrosse enthusiasts viewed lacrosse as an "activity through which men of class could learn school spirit and develop a classed, masculine character."[39] Due to the stigmatization and discrimination of Native Americans as "savages" becoming the white American status quo, leveraging lacrosse as a sport for the working man or for different societal classes never surfaced on the path to an elitist activity in the United States. This type of racist and classist environment solidified lacrosse in the early years of development in the US for "well-to-do sportsmen who felt secure enough about the alleged superiority of their race and class to associate themselves with Native Americans in any way."[40] Aligning lacrosse with socio-economically elite institutions such as preparatory high schools was another way to drive this message home as well as devising feeder programs for college and university teams.

Exemplifying the important role of US universities in developing the sport, the US lacrosse Olympic teams in 1928 and 1932 were represented respectively by the intercollegiate teams from Johns Hopkins University and Rensselaer Polytechnic Institute for the 1928 and 1932 Summer Olympics as a demonstration (non-medal) sport.[41] It wasn't until 1970 when lacrosse would join forces with the National Collegiate Athletic Association when at this point more than 500 universities participated in intercollegiate lacrosse.[42] The NCAA's decision to bring in lacrosse was indicative of the popularity and growth of the sport up to this point not just along the US Eastern Seaboard but into regions such as the South and Midwest. Today, upstate New York and the Baltimore metropolitan area are still considered to be the lacrosse hotbeds, much due to the early introduction of lacrosse relatively in comparison to other regions of the United States. Currently there are 368 men's teams competing at the NCAA level, the largest association and governing body of US collegiate athletics, across Divisions I, II, and III.[43] The majority of teams compete under the Division III affiliation, which does not offer athletic scholarships to their student-athletes (NCAA). A notable change to the college game was the implementation of the shot clock (20 seconds to get over midfield and 60 seconds once the player has crossed midfield) in 2015.[44] Club lacrosse is offered to non-NCAA men's lacrosse programs as Men's Collegiate Lacrosse Association was established by US Lacrosse in 2006 and currently sponsors national championships for approximately 180 teams.[45]

Women's lacrosse

Women's lacrosse was first popular in Scotland and later expanding into the USA. Historians have pointed to female physical education teachers from St. Leonard's School who attended a men's game in Montreal, Canada in 1884 and brought the game across the Atlantic to their female students in Scotland.[46] Women were not socially permitted to participate in sport at this time, especially a physical sport as lacrosse. In the early 1900s, the women's game, which was modified as less strenuous than the men's, began to gain popularity as it was more socially acceptable in Great Britain. Still existing today, the modifications to the newly found women's game included: a smaller field, shorter halves, no body contact or checking, ban on shooting within crease, and a rule against guarding one's own crosse.[47] Once the women's game was established, an additional barrier was facing the wrath of field hockey supporters who felt their game was not only superior but also more suitable for females. In rebuttal, women's lacrosse advocates claimed their sport was more beneficial for women because it improved their "upright posture."[48]

At the intercollegiate level in the United States, women's lacrosse is most commonly represented by the NCAA. As opposed to the men's game, women's intercollegiate lacrosse was not offered until 1978 when the US Women's Lacrosse Association was founded under the Intercollegiate Athletics for Women (AIAW).[49] This governing body would lead the women's game and provide championships until 1982 when the NCAA took over the governing responsibilities. NCAA women's lacrosse has since blossomed into 375 teams across three separate divisions. Similar to the men's game, the majority of the women's teams compete under the Division III affiliation and feature universities and colleges in the northeast and mid-Atlantic regions of the US. The National Association of Intercollegiate Athletics (NAIA) as well as the National Junior College Athletic Association (NJCAA) both sponsor men's and women's lacrosse on much smaller scales than the NCAA with only a handful of teams represented under each association. At the university club level, women's intercollegiate lacrosse is offered at the club level under the Women's Collegiate Lacrosse Associates (WCLA), featuring over 260 college club teams.[50] The women's game is still on the rise and in no way has it yet reached its potential. According to a US Lacrosse survey in 2016, participation numbers for female players is growing across multiple different age demographics. Girls aged 14 and under have doubled in the number of participants from has nearly doubled from 81,609 players in 2006 to 161,832 in 2016. Similar growth rates are also evident at the high school and college levels for female participants in the US Lacrosse report.[51]

Box (indoor) lacrosse and professional men's field lacrosse

Mostly in part to the cold winters, an indoor version of the game emerged in Canada during the 1920s. The availability of ice hockey arenas in the summer months gave way for the lacrosse to flourish indoors. Reversibly, indoor lacrosse was a popular alternative to ice hockey during the winter months when the weather was too frigid for field lacrosse. The indoor version was played with fewer players (five players plus one goalie per team) and was officially named box lacrosse due to the playing area forming the shape of a box, as opposed to the open playing surface in field lacrosse. Box lacrosse grew quickly in Canada, becoming more popular than field lacrosse. Today it is recognized as Canada's official national summer sport. The FIL sponsored the World Indoor Lacrosse Championships inaugurally in 2003 and has continued to do so quadrennially. Canada hosted the first two tournaments, followed by the Czech Republic in 2011 and the Onodaga Nation in 2015. However, box lacrosse still lags behind field lacrosse on a global participation and popularity scale. This is exemplified by the low participation of countries involved, as only 15 of the 65 member nations recognized by the FIL have ever competed in a WILC.

Professional lacrosse

The first competitive post-collegiate professional lacrosse league for women, the United Women's Lacrosse League (UWLX) was founded in Boston, Massachusetts and held its inaugural season in 2016. The UWLX was co-founded by Play It Forward Sports Foundation's (PIFS), under the ownership of United Women's Sports LLC in a strategic partnership with STX.[52] The UWLX has also tweaked some of the women's lacrosse rules, instituting more contact, reducing the number of penalties called and allowing for more movement on free position chances. The league is composed of four teams: the Baltimore Ride, Boston Storm, Long Island Sound and Philadelphia Force. An additional women's lacrosse league in the United States began play in 2018.

The Women's Professional Lacrosse League (WPLL) is composed of five teams: the Baltimore Brave, New England Command, New York Fight, Philadelphia Fire, and Upstate Pride. Further complicating this matter, WPLL founder Michele DeJuliis is the former commissioner or the UWLX who departed to create her own league. In turn, this has led to some uncertainty from lacrosse enthusiast about how the two new women's professional lacrosse leagues will coexist. Contrarily, the most recognized professional men's field lacrosse league is the Major League Lacrosse (MLL). Founded in 2001, the MLL currently has nine teams play a 14-game regular season and thus far has found success growing the game outside of the lacrosse hotbeds with franchises already established in Florida, Georgia, Texas, and Colorado.

The most prominent men's professional box lacrosse league is the National Lacrosse League (NLL) in North America with its inaugural season in 1987. Currently the NLL has seven teams in the United States and four teams in Canada with agreements already in place for expansion teams in the upcoming seasons. New teams are set to be established in San Diego and Phila-delphia for the 2019 season, as well as Halifax, Nova Scotia and Long Island, New York the fol-lowing year. Historically, box lacrosse has been exclusively a men's sport Women who played the sport of lacrosse typically played the women's field lacrosse version.[53] However, in 2003, New Jersey Storm goaltender Ginny Capicchioni became the first woman to compete in the NLL, after appearing in three different games. Similar to the men's side, box lacrosse among Canadian women is becoming more popular as leagues have already been established for female players in Ontario, Alberta, Nova Scotia and British Columbia.

International governance, World Championships and Olympics

In terms of international governance, lacrosse is represented by the Federation of International Lacrosse (FIL), which was founded in 1974 following the Men's World Championships. The FIL is responsible for the men's, women's, and indoor versions of the sport. Initially, this federation was founded solely for male teams, and did not sponsor events for women. The first Lacrosse World Championship happened in 1967 with only United States, England, Canada, and Aus-tralia represented with their respective national teams.[54] The tournament would take place again in 1974 and occurring quadrennially ever since. The tournament would rotate between the previously mentioned countries (three times in each country) until Israel broke the trend when they hosted in 2018. The Women's Lacrosse World Cup was first sponsored by the IFWLA beginning in 1982 and continued until 2007. Men's lacrosse first featured as an Olympic medal sport at the 1904 games in St. Louis, Missouri (USA) and again at the 1908 games in London, England. However only Canada, England, and the United States fielded lacrosse teams in these inaugural Olympic Games. Given the low level of countries involved, men's field lacrosse would not make another appearance in the Olympics until 1928 when it was held as a demonstra-tion event. It was again recognized at the demonstration level for the 1932 and 1948 Summer Olympics.

The year 2008 marked the merger of men's and women's international lacrosse governing bodies, creating the present-day international governance structure. Currently, after the addition of Ecuador and Ukraine in 2018, the FIL consists of 62 member nations and has made signifi-cant progress in getting the men's and women's field lacrosse recognized by the International Olympic Committee as a full-on medal sport.[55] An important milestone in achieving this mile-stone was the FIL's formal acceptance into the informal group of Olympic and non-Olympic international sport federations in 2012 known as *SportAccord*. This umbrella organization offers a commercial platform sporting experts and practitioners to collaborate and strategize with the world governing bodies of sport and their key decision-makers.[56] This acceptance helped push the IOC's Executive Board to push the sport towards full recognition at a November 2018 meeting in Tokyo, Japan. Lacrosse being back in the Olympics would mark several important milestones, most notably women's lacrosse having never been represented at an Olympic Games.

The Iroquois and Haudenosaunee Nationals

Perhaps the unique characteristic of lacrosse on the international level is the presence and rec-ognition of the men's and women's national teams recognized under the First Nations Lacrosse Association in present day upstate New York and Ontario. The Iroquois Nationals represent the men's team and the Haudenosaunee Nationals make up the women's team.

In 2008, the Haudenosaunee women's national lacrosse team became a full member of the Federation of International Lacrosse and have since participated in the 2009, 2013 and 2017

Women's Lacrosse World Cups. The Iroquois men's national lacrosse team received FIL recognition in 1987 and first competed in the 1990 World Lacrosse Championship. However, the Iroquois Nationals were forced to forfeit all of their games at the 2010 World Lacrosse Championship after United Kingdom government officials did not accept their Iroquois passports.[57] Another notable milestone occurred in 2006 when the Iroquois Nationals signed a partnership with Nike, Inc. in providing apparel and assisting with implementing programs in Native American communities that "promote wellness-and-fitness activities in Native American communities throughout the region."[58] Another milestone occurred when the 2015 WILC was hosted by the Onondaga Nation, south of Syracuse, New York. The opening ceremonies took place in the sold-out War Memorial Arena, and featured a spectacular show that honored and told the Haudenosaunee origin story of the creator's game in the form of light shows and traditional dancing.[59]

Notes

1 Marshall, T. and Calder, J., "Lacrosse: From Creator's Game to Modern Sport," *The Canadian Encyclopedia*, retrieved from www.thecanadianencyclopedia.ca/en/article/lacrosse-from-creators-game-to-modern-sport (accessed 1 December 2018).
2 Ibid.
3 *Encyclopedia Britannica*, "Lacrosse," retrieved from www.britannica.com/sports/lacrosse (accessed 1 December 2018).
4 Haman, Z. *The Creator's Game: Native American Culture and Lacrosse*, SMU History Media, 2017.
5 *Encyclopedia Britannica*, "Lacrosse."
6 Haman, *The Creator's Game*.
7 *Encyclopedia Britannica*, "Lacrosse."
8 Wiser, Melissa C., "Lacrosse History, a History of One Sport or Two? A Comparative Analysis of Men's Lacrosse and Women's Lacrosse in the United States," *The International Journal of the History of Sport* 31, no. 13 (2014): 1656–1676.
9 Fisher, Donald M., *Lacrosse: A History of the Game*, JHU Press, 2002.
10 Vennum, T., "American Indian Lacrosse of War. American, Little Brother" [book review], *Anthropologist*, 98(1) (1996): 204–205.
11 Fisher, *Lacrosse: A History of the Game*.
12 Marshall and Calder, "Lacrosse: From Creator's Game to Modern Sport."
13 Ibid.
14 Wiser, "Lacrosse History, a History of One Sport or Two?"
15 Marshall and Calder, "Lacrosse: From Creator's Game to Modern Sport."
16 Ibid.
17 Fisher, *Lacrosse: A History of the Game*.
18 Ibid.
19 Ibid.
20 Wiser, "Lacrosse History, a History of One Sport or Two?"
21 Ibid.
22 Fisher, *Lacrosse: A History of the Game*.
23 Beers, William George, *Lacrosse: The National Game of Canada*, New York: Townsend & Adams, 1869.
24 Menzel, Benjamin A., "Heading down the Wrong Road: Why Deregulating Amateurism May Cause Future Legal Problems for the NCAA," *Marq. Sports L. Rev.* 12 (2001): 857.
25 Robidoux, Michael A., "Imagining a Canadian Identity through Sport: A Historical Interpretation of Lacrosse and Hockey," *Journal of American Folklore* (2002): 209–225.
26 Morrow, D., "The Institutionalization of Sport: A Case Study of Canadian Lacrosse, 1844–1914," *The International Journal of the History of Sport*, 9(2) (1992): 236–251.
27 Wiser, "Lacrosse History, a History of One Sport or Two?"
28 Fisher, *Lacrosse: A History of the Game*.
29 Wiser, "Lacrosse History, a History of One Sport or Two?"
30 Beers, *Lacrosse: The National Game of Canada*.

31 Ibid.

32 Fisher, *Lacrosse: A History of the Game.*

33 "NCAA Race and Gender Demographics Database," retrieved from www.ncaa.org/about/resources/research/diversity-research (accessed 5 December 2018).

34 "Native American Lacrosse Teams Reported Racial Abuse. Then Their League Expelled Them," retrieved from https://deadspin.com/native-american-lacrosse-teams-reported-racial-abuse-t-1824292659 (accessed 2 December 2018).

35 Marshall and Calder, "Lacrosse: From Creator's Game to Modern Sport."

36 Ibid.

37 Ibid.

38 *Encyclopedia Britannica,* "Lacrosse."

39 Fisher, *Lacrosse: A History of the Game.*

40 Ibid.

41 Marshall and Calder, "Lacrosse: From Creator's Game to Modern Sport."

42 Ibid.

43 Delsahut, Fabrice, "From Baggataway to Lacrosse: An Example of the Sportization of Native American Games," *The International Journal of the History of Sport* 32, no. 7 (2015): 923–938.

44 Ibid.

45 Ibid.

46 Wiser, "Lacrosse History, a History of One Sport or Two?"

47 Ibid.

48 McCrone, Kathleen, *Sport and the Physical Emancipation of English Women (RLE Sports Studies): 1870–1914,* Routledge, 2014.

49 US Women's Lacrosse Association was founded under the Intercollegiate Athletics for Women (AIAW).

50 Wiser, "Lacrosse History, a History of One Sport or Two?"

51 US Lacrosse, "Participation Survey," www.uslacrosse.org/sites/default/files/public/documents/about-us-lacrosse/participation-survey-2016.pdf (accessed 13 October 2019).

52 Delsahut, "From Baggataway to Lacrosse."

53 Fisher, *Lacrosse: A History of the Game.*

54 Delsahut, "From Baggataway to Lacrosse."

55 See https://filacrosse.com (accessed 3 December 2018).

56 "FIL Becomes Newest Member of SportAccord," retrieved from https://filacrosse.com/fil-becomes-newest-member-of-sportaccord (accessed 4 December 2018).

57 Delsahut, "From Baggataway to Lacrosse."

58 Fryling, Kevin, "Nike Deal Promotes Native American Wellness, Lacrosse," retrieved from www.buffalo.edu/ubreporter/archive/vol37/vol37n43/articles/BrayLyonsLacrosse.html (accessed 7 December 2018).

59 Marshall and Calder, "Lacrosse: From Creator's Game to Modern Sport."

8

Netball

John Nauright

Netball is the leading sport for women and girls in the former colonies of the United Kingdom in the Caribbean, Africa and the Pacific. It is played by significant numbers of girls and women in the British Isles and Canada. Netball is the national sport of the Cook Islands in the Pacific. The importance of participation from so many different countries helped instigate the creation of the International Federation of Women's Basketball and Netball in 1960 with founding nations all being members of the Commonwealth.

Despite women gaining the vote in the late nineteenth century ahead of other countries, restrictions on women in public life remained very rigid in Australia and New Zealand in the late nineteenth and early twentieth centuries. Women had to carve out their own public spaces which were largely confined to education, health and sports. While middle class women took control of women's sports, they largely accepted that public society was male dominated and that women should behave in certain ways which were different from male behaviour. As a result, middle class women supported restrictions on female participation in those sports which were thought to be too masculine for women (Burroughs & Nauright, 2000; Taylor 2001). Nevertheless, these women also actively encouraged participation in sports such as hockey, tennis, and especially netball. Australia and New Zealand have dominated world netball since the beginning of international tournaments in the 1960s and in both countries netball is played by huge numbers of women. Netball in New Zealand receives coverage as one of the nation's four major sports, including the airing of live test matches on prime time television and live coverage of national league games on Saturday and Sunday afternoons. The largest netball playing nation in total numbers is Australia. In the period from October 2015 to September 2016, the Australian Sports Commission collected data that showed there were 562,698 adult women participating in the sport.

Under the International Netball Federation, the standard set of rules has drastically changed from the 1901 adaptation of basketball. Logistically, the game has been moved indoors to a rectangular court and uses a ball the equivalent to a soccer ball. Similar to the early adaptations made in 1901, the court is split into three zones; however, the numbers of players have decreased from nine to seven. Each player has a designated zone and must stay in their zone throughout the game. Although there is still no dribbling or contact, to keep the ball moving, the INF has restricted players to holding the ball for three seconds and only allowing players to take one step with the ball. The biggest change from earlier days of netball to today is the attire. Women today do not have to dress as conservatively as those in the 1900s. The attire has transformed from pleated tunics below the knees, stiff cotton shirts, and dark stockings to shorts, or pleated skirts, with a tank top showing the initials of what position the players are playing, and tennis shoes. This drastic difference not only portrays how much society has changed, but also shows how much the game of netball has improved from a sporting standpoint.

The INF, like any other governing body in sport, sets the standards for the game and makes sure the rules of netball are maintained. The INF updates the world rankings for netball and is responsible for organising the World Netball Championships. Based out of Manchester, England, the organisation has over seventy members across five regional areas. The five regional areas are Confederation of African Netball Association, Americas Federation of Netball Associations, Netball Asia, Netball Europe, and Oceania Netball Federation. Even though the INF governs netball globally, it is each regional area's responsibility to govern netball for their region and report all standings to the INF for national recognition.

Netball prospered in the first half of the Twentieth Century partly because of restrictions on women in sport. Netball became the sport for women because it embodied female attributes and was viewed by doctors, reformers, politicians, the media and middle class women as the best team sport for women and girls to play. In addition, netball prospered because women controlled it as their game outside of male influence. A female sporting culture developed in Australia and New Zealand through netball. Towns and cities facilities which provided thousands of women and girls the chance to participate in a cultural activity in spaces dominated by women rather than by men.

Case study

While rugby is the 'national sport' for men in New Zealand, then netball is the national women's sport. As early as 1929 the media referred to netball as the 'national game . . . for women' (*Wanganui Herald*, 19 May 1929). Since the 1930s, netball has been the dominant woman's team sport in New Zealand. It succeeded despite numerous male attempts to limit female physicality and control public displays of the female body. Despite male hostility to women's sports, some men supported netball as they viewed it an acceptable sport for young women. Some men also initiated netball in schools and towns and served as referees and administrators. By 1948 netball had the largest number of players in any sport except for rugby. In 1991–1992 there were more netball clubs than in any other sport, with 10,928 registered teams affiliated with Netball New Zealand (NNZ), the game's governing body. An estimated 155,600 women and school girls played the game in 1988, nearly ten per cent of all females in the country (Hume, 1994). By 2018 the number of registered players exceeded 140,000 and total participants in the sport was 300,000. Only Australia has greater numbers of participants than New Zealand. In addition, major international netball matches involving the national team, the 'Silver Ferns', now draw large television audiences approaching levels of support for major rugby, rugby league and cricket matches.

In New Zealand, women netball players and administrators successfully developed a female centred culture and identity in public spaces where they exerted power and control with little male interference. By the 1980s, new challenges in the form of sponsorship, media images and the conformity to sponsor and media demands, threatened to change the sport and culture surrounding it, however this is the subject of another article. Between the late 1920s and 1970s, many women experienced an identity around netball organised in local, provincial and national associations and competitions. Although not all women play netball, a majority played in schools and a relatively high percentage of playing age women participate in the game each year. No other organised women's social activity in New Zealand approaches netball's numbers of participants.

The expansion of the sport in New Zealand has received the most academic attention (Nauright & Broomhall, 1994; Nauright, 1995). The most common version of the origins of netball in New Zealand asserts that the Presbyterian Rev. J.C. Jamieson first introduced the game in Auckland in 1906, although Fry suggests that netball was first played at Otago Girls' High School in 1902 (Fry, 1986). In 1907 several teams formed in Auckland under the auspices of the YWCA with seven players a side, baskets for goals and three bounces allowed by each player in possession. The Wellington Technical College organised the first team in Wellington in 1914 with the first match played the following year. Also in 1914, Wellington High School became the first school to recognise netball as an organised girls' activity (Archer, 1984). The game also began to expand in the South Island. Each area played by its own set of rules, however. By 1914 Otago teams played seven-a-side while Canterbury teams played nine-a-side. In 1916 W. Lloyd Phillips formed a secondary schools league in Dunedin with five teams from Otago Girls' High School, Columba College and St Hilda's Collegiate School (all girls only schools) Rena Mackenzie, long-time secretary, president and national delegate of the Otago Association, recalls the enjoyment and physical freedom netball offered young women in Dunedin in the early 1910s:

> When I played first of all we played on grass, and we had then got the use of some asphalt courts . . . When it was [on] grass we played down in Woodhaugh Gardens . . . we'd go and play ball and we . . . had lots of lovely fun sliding over on wet [grass] when it had been raining.
>
> *(Quoted in Nauright & Broomhall, 1994)*

Netball grew rapidly in the four largest cities and provincial associations formed in Auckland, Canterbury (Christchurch), Otago (Dunedin) and Wellington between 1911 and 1920. Netball developed equally as fast in other areas, and in 1922, the Auckland Association wrote to the Otago, Canterbury and Wellington Associations proposing the formation of a national body. Two years later in May 1924 a meeting of netball officials from Auckland, Wellington and Canterbury founded the New Zealand Basketball Association (NZBA). By this time, most teams played the nine-a-side version of the game which the NZBA adopted. The NZBA decided in the late 1930s that shortage of courts prohibited changing to the seven-a-side game played in Australia (*Auckland Star*, 18 September 1948). New Zealand only adopted the seven-a-side game played in other countries in 1959, after long debate during the 1950s, to allow for easier international competition.

Slowly netball began to adopt competitive tournaments and competitions. The first National Tournament was organised and played in Dunedin in 1926 as part of the Empire Exhibition. Teams travelled from five main centres to compete. Press coverage was minimal at this stage, but the *Otago Daily Times* carried news of the tournament. The paper supported the tournament and netball as a 'game eminently suitable for every girl, especially the business and industrial girl, who gets practically no exercise during the week'. The article also reported that netball was played in every primary school and most secondary schools throughout New Zealand with 2,000 registered senior players (*Otago Daily Times*, 8 April 1926).

Middle class reformers felt young working women needed organised activities to keep them healthy and on the high moral path until they fulfilled their ultimate destiny of marriage followed by motherhood. Groups like the YWCA actively promoted team sports for young working women to teach them fitness and cooperation. Netball benefited from the new focus on female health and sporting activity. Many sports were still 'off-limits' to women, but most thought netball the sport most suitable for women. During the 1930s and 1940s officials included net-ball within the girls' school physical education curriculum. The majority of primary schools adopted netball as the winter sport for girls once the medical profession recommended it. In reporting on the establishment of the Wanganui Basketball Association, the local press reported that 'Basketball is regarded by the medical profession as a very suitable game for young women'. In addition, the organisers echoed broader concerns about the health of young women waged-workers, 'The aim . . . is to provide a game for young ladies in shops and offices, who at present take part in no winter sport. The game is inexpensive, and at the same time provides very good exercise' (*Wanganui Herald*, 8 May 1929).

Although netball expanded in the 1920s and 1930s, few women played after marriage. For-mer national coach, Lois Muir, recalls that people expected her to quit playing when she mar-ried at age nineteen in 1954:

> People tended to get married a lot younger then, but very few managed to keep up their sport afterwards. I did and found it difficult; the longer I kept playing, the more certain it was every year that I'd end up at the Nationals. Surprised officials and players would ask what I was doing back there. As soon as you were married they expected you to stay at home, have children, and rock the cradle.
>
> *(Stratford, 1988: 160)*

As this quote suggests, those active in sport and social reform for women concentrated on young working women who ultimately were expected to marry and focus attention on their families. By 1920, a little over twenty per cent of women were in paid employment. Most of these were unmarried and formed the bulk of netball's adult playing constituency. Despite nearly all mar-ried women giving up playing netball, some became very active in administration and coaching. About half of delegates to the national Council meetings in the 1930s and 1940s were married.

The NZBA grew slowly but steadily during its first few years of existence. During the 1920s and into the 1930s, the game's strength was in the South Island and in the North Island cit-ies of Wellington and Auckland. Annual tournaments rotated between cities and the executive and national headquarters was located in the home city of the NZBA president, Wellington, in 1924–1929, Invercargill in 1929–1932, again in Wellington for 1933–1949, Christchurch from 1949 to 1968, and Wellington once more until the 1989 move to Auckland. The NZBA admin-istered the game through an Executive Committee which met monthly during the season and a National Council which met annually in conjunction with the New Zealand Tournament. Each provincial association was allocated a number of votes based on team numbers under their jurisdiction, although each had two delegates to Council. Provincial associations organised local competitions and arranged for inter-provincial matches. In several cases men were instrumental in establishing local competitions and associations, but women soon took the lead.

A number of men initially held positions of authority in New Zealand women's sports, although women were in the majority from the establishment of the NZBA. By 1935 only three of the 31 delegates to the annual national council meeting were male. The Otago Association passed a resolution in the late 1920s which stated that only women could hold positions on their Executive. Rena Mackenzie recalls that men were initially helpful but, 'we decided in the end that women should control their own game . . . [the] constitution in Otago . . . cut all the men out . . . no male would be appointed to an office' (quoted in Nauright & Broomhall, 1994). Mackenzie felt very strongly that women should control their own game rather than letting men have any power. Former YWCA Sports Officer and netball referee and administrator, Barbara

Marchant, states that at national level 'and others, we worked very hard to get [men] out at one stage, fortunately [because] they were beginning to take over . . . We couldn't stop clubs using them, but we stopped them being on the executive' (quoted in Nauright & Broomhall, 1994). The exclusion of men from decision making positions meant that women made their own decisions about the organisation and operation of netball.

As late as the 1990s some women active in netball administration were wary of male coaches and administrators taking too much of an interest in women's netball. They argue that men have enough scope for involvement in male sports and should leave women's sports to women administrators and coaches. Controversially, men have been allowed to coach club and representative teams in some areas in recent years, but were not initially allowed to take part at the national tournament level. Almost all those with direct involvement in the sport historically were women which greatly aided the development of a women-centred culture around the sport. This point should not be underestimated as netball gave women time and space free from males who held nearly all positions of public power and defined norms of behaviour and culture throughout the rest of New Zealand society. As Barbara Marchant relates in reference to men and sport: '[Netball] was very definitely a women's sport and you notice the sport that men take over because of our pakeha and western men [who] have always been brought up as the dominant thing' (quoted in Nauright & Broomhall, 1994).

Netball's development has also been assisted by a stable core of officials at both regional and national levels. At both levels, administrators and coaches frequently hold positions for many years. From 1930 to 1971, Catherine Vautier, for example, was president or vice-president of the Manawatu Association, Rena Mackenzie held similar positions in the Otago Association for nearly fifty years from the 1920s to 1975, being president from 1955 to 1975. At national level, Myrtle Muir held the office of president from 1934 to 1949 and Eileen Lane from 1949 to 1968. These are just a few of the many examples of administrators' longevity. In addition, Lois Muir coached the national team from 1974 to 1989 when she retired and was replaced by Lyn Parker. Long-serving officials enabled the game to prosper and grow through efforts over many years.

Despite the hard work of the NZBA and provincial officials to promote the game, some provincial associations initially struggled to establish netball competitions and financial security. In 1930 and 1931 the Wanganui Association withdrew from the NZBA as they could not get enough teams to sustain local competitions. Rotorua and Nelson also had to withdraw in 1931 after forming provincial associations and running local competitions. It appears that associations which were not well established by 1931 suffered from the effects of the Depression which forced many women out of work during 1931 and after. Larger associations were able to sustain competitions and did not lose many teams, while new teams were also formed in the largest cities.

The Second World War caused tremendous disruption to netball. The NZBA cancelled annual tournaments and council meetings between 1942 and 1945. The Wellington Association, among other provincial bodies, struggled to keep netball alive. Many supporters of the game served in the armed forces, Auxiliary Units and many worked long hours supporting the war effort.

Netball regained its popularity and continued to grow after the interruption of the Second World War. Netball, however, suffered from a lack of resources and wider popularity in the New Zealand community. National tournaments still received the bulk of the year's press coverage, but reports reflected how much women administrators and players had to work to maintain and develop the game. New Plymouth hosted the Nineteenth Tournament in 1948 and the media dubbed it the 'City of Women' as 500 players descended on the town. Players could not stay in hotels, however, as horse racing fans has taken most of the town's accommodation. Players had to be billeted out to local families as was the practice each year. Provincial teams continued to hold special events to raise enough money to send teams to the national tournament after the war. The NZBA's financial position was so poor in 1950 that it laid a special levy on associations to bring in an additional £140. In addition, the NZBA cancelled a planned tour of Australia in 1951 due to shortage of funds (Nauright & Broomhall, 1994).

Despite struggles, netball continued to expand reaching 35 provincial associations and 2,180 teams affiliated to the NZBA in 1951. Provincial associations and the NZBA succeeded in creating female communities through weekly competitions, provincial matches and the national tournament. Similar growth appeared in Australia. In the late 1940s, 1950s and 1960s, most provincial associations succeeded in establishing their own facilities for local netball competitions. The provision of a city-wide venue strengthened a community identity around netball. Numbers of teams grew dramatically in the post-war period and many associations were forced to start matches earlier and earlier on Saturdays. Netball courts and facilities provided a space for hundreds of women and girls to meet each week throughout the winter in most New Zealand towns.

Associations also created new leagues in the 1970s and 1980s. Mid-week games have attracted many married women who had quit playing. Women organised child care and many players previously lost to netball returned to the game. The Waikato Association started mid-week matches in 1971 with some grandmothers being drawn back to the game. In response to the development of men's netball in recent years, some officials argue that men's and women's netball should never merge and that women should always keep a separate association. As former NZNA President Joyce McCann puts it: 'I don't see it [netball] would ever be mixed . . . it would just lose something if it ever did become that way, we'd lose our identity' (quoted in Nauright & Broomhall, 1994). Netball leagues and tournaments have provided a space for women which has been largely free of male influence and control in a wider society in which men hold the most of the reins of power. While all women have not experienced this space of cultural freedom, netball activities have drawn more women together throughout New Zealand than any other single social activity. Certainly, the focus for this identity has been local, but through the links to provincial representative teams and the national tournament and national team, many women have been drawn into a wider identity shaped in part by their sporting experiences. As former players and administrators attest, the success of netball in the past was due to women controlling their own game.

A global game?

Netball in New Zealand and Australia is part of the national sporting pantheon and the Trans-Tasman Super League with teams from the two countries and the two competing in nearly every major final for the past several decades has led to television and spectator followings unmatched in other parts of the world. Recent investment in netball performance in England has led to rapid improvement in the national game there. South Africa, now that it has emerged from the vestiges of apartheid, has also improved while several nations in the Caribbean continue to perform well, particularly Jamaica and Trinidad & Tobago. In the Cook Islands netball has been the most popular sport. While netball is played in many nations, the primarily location of the sport in the Oceania, the British Isles, the Caribbean and parts of Africa have limited its global impact beyond many Commonwealth nations. With growing numbers of international participants, a world championship and regular international competitions, however, the sport continues to expand and is one of the most significant sports played primarily by women around the world, while mixed netball and men's netball has also expanded over the past two decades (cf. Tagg,

2008). Research on the history and social context of netball beyond Australia and New Zealand is underdeveloped and more work should be done on the core areas of netball strength as well.

References

Archer, C. (1984). 'Betty Armstrong: New Zealand Netball Pioneer'. *Netball* (May 1984), 6.

Burroughs, A. & Nauright, J. (2000). 'Women, Sport and Embodiment in Australia and New Zealand'. *International Journal of the History of Sport*, 17(2/3), 188–205.

Fry, R. (1986). 'Don't Let Down the Side'. In B. Brookes, C. Macdonald and M. Tennant (eds), *Women in History: Essays on European Women in New Zealand*. Wellington: Allen & Unwin.

Hume, P. (1993). *Sports Injuries in New Zealand*. Otago: University of Otago.

Nauright, J. (1995). 'Netball, Media Representation of Women and Crises of Male Hegemony in New Zealand'. In J. Nauright (ed.), *Sport, Power and Society in New Zealand*. Sydney: The Australian Society for Sports History.

Nauright, J. and Broomhall, J. (1994). 'A Woman's Game: The Development of Netball and a Female Sporting Culture in New Zealand, 1906–70,' *International Journal of the History of Sport* 11 (3), 387–407.

Stratford, T. (1988). *Guts, Tears and Glory: Champion New Zealand Sports Women Talk to Trish Stratford*. Auckland: self-published.

Tagg, B. (2008). '"Imagine, a Man Playing Netball!"': Masculinities and Sport in New Zealand'. *International Review for the Sociology of Sport*, 43(4), 409–430.

Taylor, T. (2001). 'Gendering Sport: The Development of Netball in Australia'. *Sporting Traditions* 18(1), 57–74.

9

Rugby league

Charles Little and Hunter Fujak

The roots of rugby league grew out of the diffusion of rugby football into the north of England in the later nineteenth century. The Rugby Football Union (RFU) had been formed in London in 1871 and was controlled by men of the upper-middle classes with strong ties to the Public Schools. Established football clubs in the north of England like Huddersfield (1864), Hull (1865) and Rochdale Hornets (1866) soon joined the RFU, and rugby football became popular across the north. Initially these new clubs did not upset the status quo, as their players and administrators were drawn from the same social strata as in the south.[1]

The rapid growth of rugby in the north meant that it quickly outgrew its middle-class roots and was embraced by men from the growing industrial working classes. Hundreds of new clubs were formed in the 1870s and 1880s, and working-class players and clubs quickly came to dominate the sport. These changes brought tensions and a clash of values, particularly around the issue of financial rewards for playing the game. Besides this, it was also clear that many of the former public schoolboys resented being defeated by men they considered their social lessers. These tensions were exacerbated by the growing popularity of rugby as a spectator sport in Yorkshire and Lancashire, stimulated by inter-country representative matches and the establishment of the Yorkshire Cup knock out competition in 1877. Five-figure crowds soon become commonplace, creating the necessary financial conditions for commercial sport. The RFU's reaction to all of these developments was to assert that amateurism must be the fundamental principle of the sport.[2]

For almost a century, the split in rugby and the emergence of rugby league was largely portrayed as solely a dispute over payment for players between adherents of amateurism, schooled in the ideology of athleticism, and those who favoured professionalism. The reality, however, was far more nuanced and amateurism was effectively 'weaponized' by middle class administrators in order to assert their control over the sport. As Tony Collins, the foremost historian of rugby league, has noted, 'the real cause of the 1895 split was the coming of the working class player to rugby in the 1870s and 1880s and the reluctance of the middle class leadership of rugby union to allow his participation in the sport on an equal footing'.[3]

The culmination of these tensions came on 29 August 1895. Representatives of 21 of the leading clubs in Yorkshire and Lancashire met at the George Hotel in Huddersfield and broke away from the RFU to form the Northern Rugby Football Union (commonly referred to as the Northern Union).[4] The new organisation allowed the payment of 'broken time' payments (essentially compensation for lost wages) but initially resisted outright professionalism and even required all players to be in full-time employment. The restrictions against full professionalism were lifted in 1898.[5]

The RFU sought to crush the breakaway competition, targeting any player who associated with the rival code. Playing a single match of rugby league, even without payment, was deemed to have 'professionalised' a player, earning them a lifetime ban from rugby union. The determination of rugby union's authorities to punish any player who dabbled with the rival code is reflected in reports from as far afield as Bulawayo (Zimbabwe), Kaitangata (New Zealand) and Perak (Malaysia) of players being banned from local rugby union competitions for the sin of having played rugby league in their past.[6] Rugby Union also used its influence in positions of power within society to ensure that rugby league was excluded from most educational institutions and the armed forces – the Armed Forces ban was only overturned in 1994.[7]

Aside from the on-going ideological opposition and social prejudice from the Rugby Football Union, rugby league was also facing a commercial challenge from association football in the guise of the Football League, which sought to expand the presence of professional association football into rugby league's northern heartlands. Dave Russell notes that 'the politically astute and highly expansionist Football League rarely missed an opportunity of encouraging the game in rugby's heartlands'. Hull City and Leeds City were admitted to the Football League despite short histories and modest on-field achievements, while, most strikingly, the Manningham rugby league club (who had been the Northern Union's first champions in 1895) were enticed to switch wholesale to the round-ball code and were given a place in the Football League (under the new title of Bradford City) despite never having played a single match of association football.[8]

Partially in response to this challenge from association football, but also reflecting long-standing debates about how rugby football should best be played, significant rule changes were introduced by the Northern Union in 1906. Minor changes had been adopted in 1897 (reducing the value of goals and abolishing lineouts), but the sport essentially remained a variant of rugby union. The 1906 changes firmly broke this mould – the number of players on the field was reduced from 15 to 13, and the play-the-ball (which would become the distinguishing feature of rugby league) was introduced to replace rucks and mauls. These changes marked the transition of rugby league from a variant of rugby union governed by a breakaway governing body into a unique and distinctive new sport.[9]

Rugby league gained an international dimension a year later (1907), when Albert Baskerville and 1905 All Black George Smith organised a New Zealand professional rugby team to tour the United Kingdom. This team, dubbed the *All Golds* (although later New Zealand teams would be known as the *Kiwis*), played against teams belonging to the Northern Union (now Rugby Football League). Upon their return to New Zealand in 1908, these players established rugby league in their homeland. This proved a challenging task, particularly in the face of fierce resistance by the rugby union establishment. Despite this, rugby league gained a foothold in some parts of the country, particularly in Auckland, Christchurch and more latterly the Waikato and the West Coast, although efforts to develop the game in other regions proved less successful.[10]

As well as laying the foundations of rugby league in New Zealand, the All Golds tour was also a significant catalyst for the establishment of rugby league in Australia (which would eventually grow to become the sport's dominant power). The New Zealand tourists transited in Sydney en route to Britain and played three matches against local players who defected from rugby union. This group of players spearheaded the formation of the New South Wales Rugby League (NSWRL) in August 1907. Unlike the situation in Britain, it was individual players who switched to the new code rather than entire clubs. The historiography of the split in Australia had initially positioned it as similar to that it Britain, being rooted issues of social class and ideology, although more recent accounts have highlighted more practical disagreements about the management and direction of rugby union in Sydney as being equally important.[11] Eventually, nine clubs took part in the NSWRL's inaugural championship in 1908, which was won by the South Sydney club. Despite the optimism surrounding the establishment of rugby league in Australia, the new competition struggled to attract public support and a subsequent tour of Britain by the national team (dubbed the Kangaroos) at the end of the season turned into a major financial disaster.[12]

The code's future in Australia was only secured following the intervention of newspaper owner and entrepreneur James Joynton Smith, who enticed key members of the national rugby union team (the Wallabies) to play a series of matches against the Kangaroos. Although Smith's intervention proved controversial, it meant that rugby league now had the services of Australia's best rugby players. With the players came the fans, and the following season saw the fortunes of the two codes reversed – rugby league saw crowds for club matches rise from as low as a few hundred to up 17,000, while rugby union suffered a precipitous decline. Although the 'rugby war', as it has been billed, would last a few more seasons, rugby league had already secured what would prove to be the decisive victory, establishing itself as the leading football code in Sydney.[13]

While Sydney was the birthplace of the sport in Australia, the game soon spread to other regions. A club from the northern New South Wales city of Newcastle played in the inaugural Sydney competition, before leaving to establish its own competition in 1910. Rugby League also spread quickly throughout other parts of regional New South Wales.[14] In 1909, the Queensland Amateur Rugby Football League (later becoming the Queensland Rugby League) was also established. Although its scale was comparatively modest to its NSW counterpart, the league was successful in establishing itself as the premier football code of Queensland.[15] The formative successes of rugby league in NSW and Queensland was not, however, replicated in the four remaining southwestern states, in which Australian Rules football remained fervently entrenched instead. This geographic division in football preferences between the rugby codes and Australian Rules football is colloquially referred to as the Barassi Line, and remains embedded in Australia's sporting preferences today.[16]

Rugby league's development in the Southern Hemisphere was not matched by geographical expansion in Britain. The Northern Union made efforts to popularise the sport by playing international matches in such far-flung locations as London, Cheltenham, Birmingham, Newcastle and Edinburgh, but lacked any long-term strategy to develop the sport in these or any other regions and the efforts proved fruitless. Moreover, there were on-going tensions within the sport between those who sought to expand the geographical scope of the sport and those favoured consolidation in its existing heartlands, and this battle would remain unresolved through the next century. Furthermore, despite being seen as a 'northern' sport, rugby league struggled to gain a substantial foothold in most of the major northern cities such as Manchester, Liverpool, Sheffield and Newcastle – only Leeds and Bradford of the major northern metropolises became strongholds of the games, and the British game remains rooted in towns and smaller cities along what would later be dubbed the 'M62 Corridor'.[17]

A particular frustration for rugby league was its inability to gain a foothold in Wales. Given its strong level of working class involvement in rugby union, especially in the mining towns of the Valleys, Wales appeared to be a strong candidate to embrace rugby league. The Northern Union made a concerted effort to grow the sport there, and club sides were formed at Ebbw Vale and Merthyr Tydfil in 1907, and soon there were six Welsh clubs. Despite hopes to develop this outpost, all of these had folded by 1912, and further attempts throughout the twentieth century were equally fruitless. Rugby league's 'failure' in working-class Wales was largely the result of the Welsh Rugby Union taking a more lenient approach to amateurism than their English counterparts. International success in rugby union played an important role in Welsh national identity, and for the Principality's administrators pragmatic nationalism trumped strict amateurism. Despite the failure to develop sustainable club sides in Wales, large numbers of Welsh players, including many international rugby union caps, went on to sign contracts with professional rugby league clubs in the north of England (a process widely referred to as 'going north') throughout the 20th century. This steady stream of rugby union converts allowed Wales to field a competitive national rugby league team for most of the twentieth century.[18]

Among those Welsh players who switched codes were a significant number of black players, who had encountered entrenched racial prejudice in rugby union. By contrast, perhaps as a consequence of its own struggles, rugby league stood out as a relatively progressive sport in terms of racial equality. George Bennett was selected for Wales in 1935 (53 years before a black player would be capped for the Welsh rugby union team) and Jimmy Cumberbatch for England in 1937 (more than 40 years before Viv Anderson became the first black player in the national association football team). They would be followed by players like Cec Thompson, Billy Boston, Clive Sullivan, and more latterly Martin Offiah and Ellery Hanley, who became both legends of the sport and folk heroes in their adopted northern communities. Rugby league also offered other opportunities far in advance of other football codes – Clive Sullivan became the first black captain of a major British sports team when he led Great Britain to victory in the 1972 World Cup, Roy Francis coached at club level in both the United Kingdom and Australia the 1950s and 1960s, and in 1995 Ellery Hanley became the first black coach of a major British national sporting team.[19]

Inclusiveness was also a feature of rugby league in the southern hemisphere, particularly in New Zealand where there was a strong Maori presence within the code from its very origins. A Maori representative team toured Australia in 1908, the first year of the sport in the Southern hemisphere. As Greg Ryan and Geoff Watson note 'rugby league had a constituency among Maori from its inception in New Zealand and during the interwar period there were a number of marae-based teams, particularly in the Waikato, where Kingitanga leaders lent their support'.[20] Significant Aboriginal involvement was somewhat slower to develop in Australia, although there were a handful of indigenous pioneers during the early years of the sport. Aboriginal clubs such as La Perouse and the Redfern All Blacks began to emerge in the 1930s and 1940s, and Dick Johnson's selection for New South Wales in 1938 marked the first time that an indigenous player received representative honours. The number and influence of Aboriginal players grew rapidly through the 1950s and 1960s, capped by Arthur Beetson captaining Australia in 1973 (the first occasion that an indigenous player had captained Australia in any major sport) and then coaching the national team in 1983.[21]

However, the sport's inclusiveness did not extend to women. This became apparent in the 1920s when efforts were made to establish women's rugby league, paralleling the boom in women's association football at this time. The most concerted effort came in Sydney, Australia, in 1921 where, despite increasingly hysterical opposition from the NSWRL, a number of women declared, 'we are going to play football – as men play it'. Two women's rugby league matches were played, the first drawing an attendance estimated at 20,000–30,000 spectators, but the NSWRL rallied to block their access to grounds and resources and prevent a planned competition from being launched. Nor was the situation any more tolerant in Britain, where in February 1922 the RFL (UK) banned women's football from all grounds under its control. Despite the eagerness of women to play the sport, the response of its administrators showed that they believed that it was 'no game for girls'.[22]

One explanation for this exclusion of women as active participants was that rugby league was seen by its male players and administrators as vital to inculcating and expressing working-class masculine identity, which would be threatened and undermined by female players. Rugby league was steeped in a tough working-class masculine ethos, and Tony Collins has noted that 'the attitudes of rugby league players were . . . shaped and defined by the world of industrial labour, which was intensely physical, often aggressively oppositional to management and, above all, almost absolutely masculine' and that 'the masculinity of manual labour, with its emphasis on strength, endurance and intimidation (and the ability to stand up against it) . . . was reflected strongly in rugby league'.[23] Writing in the Australian context, Andrew Moore, has similarly noted that '[i]n urban life before the advent of machines made work easier, physical prowess was widely revered. In a society greatly concerned with potency and virility, rugby league became an important ritual of working-class Australian manhood. It expressed a set of values to do with masculinity, authority and strength.'[24]

Rugby League's international dimension was boosted in the 1930s by divisions within rugby union. In 1931 France was excommunicated from international rugby union and the Five Nations championship due to a number of grievances held by the four British rugby unions. Seizing upon this Anglo-French split, rugby league's administrators were uncharacteristically pragmatic in seeking to promote their own sport into the resulting vacuum. A demonstration match between the British and Australian national teams was staged in Paris in 1933, and the Ligue Française de Rugby à Treize (LFRT) was formed the following year. The new code grew most strongly in the traditional rugby heartlands of the South-West (such as Carcassonne, Perpignan and Villeneuve), but also developed into largely untapped territories like Paris and Nantes. After just five years rugby league boasted 434 clubs, while the number of rugby union clubs dropped precipitously from 784 in 1930 to only 473 in 1939. In 1939 the national rugby league team defeated both Wales and England [the latter a feat that the rugby union team had never achieved] to be crowned European champions.[25]

The Second World War abruptly halted this momentum. Not only did the outbreak of conflict cause the expected disruption to sporting activities, it allowed darker forces to seize upon the chaos to crush the new code. In June 1940 France had surrendered to its German invaders, and a collaborationist government under Marshall Petain was established in the spa town of Vichy. Among the measures soon taken under Petain's right-wing 'National Revolution' was the prohibition of rugby league. Although ostensibly prohibiting all professional sport, in reality rugby league was specifically targeted by these measures – the LFRT was forcibly dissolved, the assets of it and its clubs were expropriated, and playing the sport was banned. Vichy's ban of rugby league was partially rooted in the wider political situation in France, with the sport being perceived as too closely aligned with the leftist Popular Front government of the late 1930s, but there was also the clear hand of rugby union sympathisers who exploited the opportunity to crush their rival sport.[26]

Despite these setbacks, the French game initially appeared to bounce back undiminished from the Vichy ban. The national team was the dominant force on the world stage, highlighted by two successful tours of Australia in the early 1950s. In 1954 the French also organised and hosted the first Rugby League World Cup – a concept that they had initially proposed nineteen years earlier. Great Britain (the RFL having adopted this name for its national team, rather than England, in 1947) won the inaugural edition, triumphing over runners-up France, Australia and New Zealand who were still the only countries where the game was played.[27]

While the inaugural World Cup was contested by only four nations, rugby league's international isolation looked likely to change, as the late 1950s saw serious initiatives to establish rugby league in Italy, Yugoslavia, South Africa and the United States.[28] Despite this flurry of activity, none of these initiatives were successful in laying down permanent roots in these countries. The old bugbear of obstruction and discrimination by rugby union's authorities and their supporters in positions of political authority played a part, particularly in Italy and South Africa.[29] Just as often, however, it was rugby league's own administrators who were to blame. The sport had always been troubled by fractious relations within its own administrative ranks and splits and counter splits were a common occurrence,[30] and such disputes put paid to the initiatives in South Africa and the United States. As Tony Collins has noted, rugby league's administrators frequently 'demonstrated their ability to never miss an opportunity to miss an opportunity'.[31]

This paucity of vision by rugby league's administrators was best illustrated by the spectacular growth of the sport in one virgin territory, Papua New Guinea. The sport arrived among the cultural baggage of Australian colonists in the then separate territories of Papua and New Guinea, and the first matches were played in New Guinea in 1934. Local leagues were established in both New Guinea (initially at Wau and Bulola, and later incorporating Rabaul, Goroka and the Western Highlands) in 1948 and Papua (based around Port Moresby) in 1949, and an inter-territory representative fixture was inaugurated the following year (1950). No active efforts were made to spread the sport to the indigenous population, and indeed a 'colour bar' actively prevented their participation until after 1960, yet by the time that the newly united Papua New Guinea attained independence in 1975, rugby league was the dominant sporting preoccupation of the country. The PNGRL was established in 1974, the country played its first test match the following year, and Papua New Guinea is the only country where rugby league is the nation's most popular sport.[32]

At the club level, the Sydney-based NSWRL premiership evolved into the sport's highest-profile club competition. Commencing with eight Sydney based clubs and a ninth Northern New South Wales, the competition was largely Sydney-centric in the century that has followed. Between 1908 and 1987 all nine new additions to the competition were either Sydney (7) or regional New South Wales (2) based. This begun to change towards the end of the 1980s with two significant events. First, in 1988, the Gold Coast Giants and Brisbane Broncos were the first non-New South Wales teams to be admitted into the NSWRL competition. Secondly, in 1992, an organisational review titled *A Blueprint for the Expansion of Rugby League* set the strategic framework for the expansion and reorganisation of the competition.[33] This resulted in the NSWRL ceding governance of the competition to the Australian Rugby League, who despite being founded in 1924, had only served the purpose of administering the national team. Soon afterwards, in 1995, four new teams were added from New Zealand, Western Australia and Queensland (2) in an attempt to nationalise the league.

Undoubtedly the most seminal moment in the progress of rugby league in Australia came in the late 1990's, when News Corporation launched a rebel league that resulted in a brief but highly damaging period referred to as the Super League war. The antecedents of the Super League war lay firmly in the introduction of pay television in Australia in 1995, resulting in competitive tension for broadcast rights between Australia's two prominent media moguls: incumbent Kerry Packer and new entrant Rupert Murdoch.[34] The battle lines however were also reflective of a deeper philosophical division between those who were supportive of moving toward a more commercial/strategic orientation (Super League) and those who were loyal to the existing structures and governance (Australian Rugby League).

Despite only two years of parallel competing leagues, the war would cost over half a billion dollars before a peace treaty was reached. This resulted in a unified competition in 1998 that was jointly owned by the Australian Rugby League and News Corporation. However, the damage caused to the sport from a fan perspective would take more than a decade to overcome.[35] As noted by Moore: 'Rugby league churned many fans. Many supporters of the North Sydney

Bears have never watched another game of rugby league since the demise of their club at the first grade level in 1999.'[36] Despite the adoption of the word 'National' in their moniker, the process of club rationalisation during reunification resulted in rugby league becoming (and since remaining) less national than it was in the period prior to Super League in 1996. News Corporation surrendered their share of the NRL to the ARL in 2012, resulting in the formation of the Australian Rugby League Commission as the single controlling body and administrators of the game henceforth.

The sport's centenary in 1995 also saw British rugby league undergo radical changes. The catalyst for these changes was the Australian 'Super League War', during which News Limited sought to partner with other national governing bodies to consolidate power against the Australia Rugby League. Although some such proposals were already under discussion, News Corporation's changes attempted to rapidly commercialise the British league. The competition season was switched from winter to summer to avoid scheduling clashes with Britain's most popular sport (association football) and the championship was rebranded as Super League. The composition and branding of clubs also commercialised. A French club was added to the all-English competition, although further plans to rationalise the competition through mergers (often of traditional local rivals) did not succeed after fierce community resistance. Nonetheless, many existing clubs adopted new Americanised nicknames that displaced old historical monikers that often reflected team locality and industry (thus in Warrington 'the Wire' became the Wolves, and Bradford Northern became Bradford Bulls).[37]

The current club composition of both the Australian NRL and European Super League display remarkable parallels despite antithetical competition structures. The NRL utilises a North American style franchise/license structure that has meant the composition of the league has stayed relatively consistent since unification in 1998. From the 22 teams that operated at the time of the Super League war, mergers and expulsions resulted in a 20 team NRL in 1998, before stabilising to 15 by 2002 and adding an extra team in 2007. While this stability was vital for financial recovery of the league, it has resulted in Sydney remaining stubbornly over-crowded with no structural mechanism to redistribute teams. Simultaneously, other highly populated regions of strategic value have yet to regain teams lost during the unification of the competitions. Presently, 9 of 16 NRL teams are Sydney based and only one team operates in a non-heartland market. The European Super League similarly has but one successful expansion team within Super League (in 2018) to show for their strategic efforts since 1996. Rather, the remaining 11 teams of Super League are congested within the traditional northern British heartland. In contrast to the NRL however, Super League adopts a promotion and relegation structure that provides mobility to aspirational teams. It is therefore within these second and third divisions of English rugby league where there appears to be glimpses of growth occurring. The second division of English rugby league currently features not only a French team, but also the first professional transatlantic sports team, the Canadian based Toronto Wolfpack.

The history of contemporary women's rugby league is poorly researched, although it is clear that numerous barriers remained for women seeking to play the sport. Even as late as 1993 the General Manager of the NSWRL stated that 'we support women coaching and refereeing, but it is not in our charter to support them playing'. In spite of this opposition, the Women's Amateur Rugby League Association was formed in the UK in 1985, which by 2015 had grown to over 40 clubs, and competitions in Australia followed suit in the mid-1990s. At international level, the first women's rugby league World Cup was staged in 2000, with New Zealand defeating Great Britain in the final. Subsequent tournaments have been held in parallel with each men's World Cup, with New Zealand and Australia sharing the honours. Further signs of progress came with the launch of the Women's Super League in England in 2017 and the semi-professional NRL

Women's Premiership in Australia the following year, although rugby league still trails most other football code in offering opportunities for female participation.[38]

Among the most significant changes within the recent history of rugby league has been in respect to the composition of its athlete base, in particular the adoption of the game by Pasifika people. The Pasifika is said to encapsulate peoples from the Cook Islands, Maori, Niuean, Fijian, Tongan, Samoan and other South Pacific nations. At a junior development level, Lakisa, Adair and Taylor observe that the representation of Pasifika players in the pinnacle junior Australian Schoolboys side has grown from 4% to 25% over the past quarter century.[39] This has cascaded into the elite competition, with players of Pasifika heritage now accounting for 45% of NRL players, a remarkably large increase from 30% in 2011.[40] The influence of Pasifika rugby has however extended beyond the NRL, with their global migration filtering to representation within the European Super League.[41] The growing significance of Pasifika reached a recent crescendo, with several of the game's most high profile players leading a defection from the Australian and New Zealand national teams to represent Tonga in the 2017 Rugby League World Cup. Predicated upon a commitment to family and culture over financial reward, these defections led to a groundswell of support that has reinvigorated international rugby league and provided a rare source of viable growth moving forward.[42]

Tonga's near overnight development into an international force provided a rare moment of enthusiasm toward international rugby league, which has largely been subdued during Australia's extended dominance of the sport. International rugby league provides an exemplar case of Neale's Louis-Schmeling Paradox,[43] with the vibrancy of international rugby league largely diminishing as a correlate to Australia's absolute dominance of the international domain. Figure 9.1 provides a summary of the comparative win rate between Australia, New Zealand and England/Great Britain by decade, showing the seismic change in landscape that commenced in the 1950s, culminating with Great Britain's last major tournament victories against Australia in 1970 before winning the 1972 World Cup. Australia would then go on to win nine of the next ten World Cups that have since followed from 1975. Given New Zealand has achieved some successes with a World Cup (2008) and tournament victories in 2010 and 2014, Australia's dominance has largely come at the expense of Great Britain.[44]

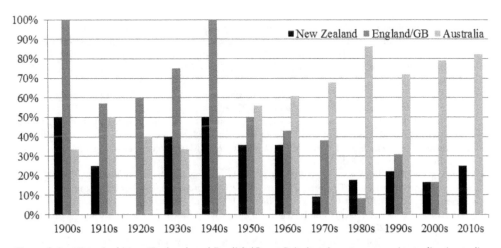

Figure 9.1   Historical New Zealand and English/Great Britain win rate versus Australia. Australia win rate combined against both competitors. Excludes draws.

Although international rugby league contests between Australia, New Zealand and England occur frequently, the global organisation of the sport more broadly remains a work in progress. Rugby League in fact only received international recognition as a sport in 2018, when it was granted observer status by the Global Association of International Sports Federations (formerly Sport Accord) after years of lobbying.[45] The sport is governed globally by the Rugby League International Federation (RLIF), of which there are four classes of membership. There are currently three Tier 1 Full Members, 15 Tier 2 Full Members, eight Affiliate Members and 35 Observers. Notably, there is no specific standard which defines a Tier 1 from a Tier 2 member, despite significant implications in terms of both athlete eligibility and voting rights within the RLIF. These 18 Full Members also sit within two recognised confederations: Rugby League European Federation (RLEF) and Asian Pacific Rugby League Confederation (APRLC), which implement regional competition structures in alignment to RLIF objectives.[46]

Notes

1   T. Collins, *A Social History of English Rugby Union* (London: Routledge, 2009), pp. 22–30.
2   H. Richards, *A Game for Hooligans: The History of Rugby Union* (Edinburgh: Mainstream Publishing, 2007), pp. 57–78.
3   T. Collins, *1895 and All That: Inside Rugby League's Hidden History* (Leeds: Scratching Shed, 2009), p. 38.
4   The clubs present at the meeting were Batley, Bradford, Dewsbury, Halifax, Huddersfield, Hull, Hunslet, Leeds, Leigh, Oldham, Rochdale Hornets, St Helens, Wakefield Trinity, Warrington, Widnes, Wigan (all of whom are still in existence as senior rugby league clubs) and Brighouse Rangers, Broughton Rangers, Liversedge, Manningham, and Tyldesley (which are now defunct).
5   T. Collins, *Rugby's Great Split: Class, Culture and the Origins of Rugby League Football* (London: Routledge, 1998).
6   C. Little and J. Nauright, 'Rugby League, Great Britain, in J. Nauright & C. Parrish (eds), *Sports Around the World: History Culture and Practice* (Santa Barbara, CA: ABC-Clio, 2012); C. Little, 'Football, Place and Community in a New Zealand Mining Town, 1877–1939', *International Journal of the History of Sport*, 34:10 (2017), pp. 915–934; *Straits Times*, 5 September 1925, p. 10.
7   T. Collins, *Rugby League in Twentieth Century Britain: A Social and Cultural History* (London: Routledge, 2006), p. 139.
8   D. Russell, '"Sporadic and Curious": the Emergence of Rugby and Soccer Zones in Yorkshire and Lancashire, c.1860–1914', *International Journal of the History of Sport*, 5, 2 (1988), pp. 185–205.
9   T. Collins, *How Football Began: A Global History of How the World's Football Codes Were Born* (London: Routledge, 2019).
10 J. Haynes, *All Blacks to All Golds: The Remarkable Story of Rugby League's International Pioneers* (Brighouse: League Publications Limited, 2007); M. Falcous, 'Rugby League in the National Imagination of New Zealand Aotearoa', *Sport in History*, 27:3 (2007), pp. 423–446; C. Little 'Rugby League (New Zealand)' in J. Nauright & C. Parrish (eds), *Sports Around the World: History Culture and Practice* (Santa Barbara: ABC-Clio, 2012).
11 C. Little, 'The "Hidden" History of the Birth of Rugby League in Australia: The Significance of "Local" Factors in Sydney's Rugby Split', *Sport in History*, 27:3 (2007), pp. 364–379.
12 The foundation clubs were South Sydney, Eastern Suburbs, Glebe, North Sydney, Balmain, Cumberland, Newtown, and Western Suburbs (all from inner-city Sydney) and one club from Newcastle.
13 M. Howell, '1909: The Great Defection', in D. Headon & L. Marinos (eds), *League of a Nation* (Sydney: ABC Books, 1996), pp. 29–38.
14 I. Heads, *True Blue: The Story of the NSW Rugby League* (Sydney: Ironbark, 1992).
15 H. Irvine and M. Fortune 'The First 25 years of the Queensland Rugby Football League: Claims to Legitimacy in Annual Reports', *Accounting History*, 21:1 (2016), pp. 48–74.
16 H. Fujak and S. Frawley (2013). 'The Barassi Line: Quantifying Australia's Great Sporting Divide', *Sporting Traditions*, 30:2 (2013), p. 93.
17 This takes its name from the M62 motorway, which stretches between Hull on the East Coast and the outskirts of Liverpool in the West. K. Spracklen, 'Dreams of Parkside and Barley Mow', in P. Bramham & S. Wagg (eds), *Sport, Leisure and Culture in the Postmodern City* (London: Routledge, 2016), pp. 153–170.

18 P. Lush & D. Farrar, *Tries in the Valleys: A History of Rugby League in Wales* (London: London League Publications, 1998).

19 T. Collins, 'Racial Minorities in a Marginalized Sport: Race Discrimination and Integration in British Rugby League Football', in M. Cronin & D. Mayall (eds), *Sporting Nationalisms: Identity, Immigration and Assimilation* (London: Frank Cass, 1998), pp. 154–173.

20 J. Coffey & B. Wood, *100 Years of Maori Rugby League, 1908–2008* (Wellington: Huia, 2008); G. Ryan & G. Watson, *Sport and the New Zealanders: A History* (Auckland: Auckland University Press, 2018), p. 469.

21 C. Little, 'Rugby League's Indigenous Pioneers: Aboriginal Sportsmen in South Sydney before World War II', in A. Moore & A. Carr (eds), *Centenary Reflections: 100 Years of Rugby League in Australia* (Sydney: ASSH, 2008), pp. 95–109; C. Little, *Through Thick and Thin: The South Sydney Rabbitohs and their Community* (Sydney: Walla Walla Press, 2009); J. Hartley, 'Black, White . . . and Red? The Redfern All Blacks Club in the Early 1960s', *Labour History* 83 (2002), pp. 149–171.

22 C. Little, '"What a Freak Show They Made!" Women's Rugby League in 1920s Sydney', *Football Studies* 4:3 (2001), pp. 25–40; V. Dawson, 'Women and Rugby League: Gender, Class and Community in the North of England, 1880–1970' (PhD Thesis, De Montford University, 2017), pp. 140–170.

23 T. Collins, *Rugby League in Twentieth Century Britain: A Social and Cultural History* (London: Routledge, 2006), pp. 149–150; A. Moore, *The Mighty Bears: A Social History of North Sydney Rugby League* (Sydney: Macmillan, 2006), p. 21

24 Collins, *Rugby League in Twentieth Century Britain*, pp. 149–150; Moore, *The Mighty Bears*, p. 21.

25 P. Dine, *French Rugby Football: A Cultural History* (Oxford: Berg, 2001), pp. 79–91.

26 M. Rylance, *The Forbidden Game: The Untold Story of French Rugby League* (Brighouse: League Publication Limited, 1999).

27 Ibid.

28 T. Collins, *The Oval World: A Global History of Rugby* (London: Bloomsbury, 2015), pp. 308–309, 313–314.

29 H. Snyders, 'Preventing Huddersfield: The Rise and Decline of Rugby League in South Africa, c.1957–1965', *International Journal of the History of Sport* 28:1 (2011), pp. 9–31; Collins, *The Oval World*, pp. 313–315.

30 See for example, S. Fagan, *The Rugby Rebellion: The Divide of League and Union in Australasia* (London: London League Publications, 2005), pp. 258–263; C. Little, 'More Green than Red: Sectarianism and Rugby League in Otago, 1924–34', *Sporting Traditions*, 21:1 (2004), pp. 33–51.

31 T. Collins, *Rugby League in Twentieth Century Britain*, p. 67; G. Willacy, *No Helmets Required: The Remarkable Story of the American All Stars* (Brighton: Pitch Publishing, 2003); Snyders, 'Preventing Huddersfield', pp. 16–23, 25.

32 *Daily Telegraph* [Sydney] 19 March 1934, p. 4; Jim Huxley, *New Guinea Experience: Gold, War and Peace 1940–1966* (Loftus: Australian Military History Publications, 2007), pp. 355–369;

33 H. Fujak And S. Frawley, 'The Barassi line', p. 93.

34 D. Rowe, 'Rugby League in Australia: The Super League Saga', *Journal of Sport and Social Issues*, 21:2 (1997), pp. 221–226.

35 D. Rowe, *The Stuff of Dreams, or the Dream Stuffed? Rugby League, Media Empires, Sex Scandals, and Global Plays* (Sydney: Australian Society for Sports History, 2007).

36 A. Moore, 'Interpreting 100 Years of Rugby League', in A. Moore & A. Carr (eds), *Centenary Reflections: 100 Years of Rugby League in Australia* (Sydney: ASSH, 2008), p. 4.

37 M. Falcous, 'Global Struggles, Local Impacts: Rugby League, Rupert Murdoch's "Global Vision" and Cultural Identities', in J. Nauright & K. Schimmel (eds), *Sport and Political Economy* (London: Palgrave Macmillan, 2005), pp. 57–84.

38 J. Hargreaves, *Sporting Females: Critical Issues in the History and Sociology of Women's Sport*, (London: Routledge, 1994) p. 273; C. Little, *Through Thick and Thin: The South Sydney Rabbitohs and their Community* (Sydney: Walla Walla Press, 2009).

39 D. Lakisa, D. Adair, and T. Taylor, 'Pasifika Diaspora and the Changing Face of Australian Rugby League', *The Contemporary Pacific*, 26:2 (2014), pp. 347–367.

40 NRL, 'Multicultural Fact Sheet', retrieved from www.nrl.com/siteassets/community/nrl—multicultural-fact-sheet-v7.pdf (accessed 21 November 2018).

41 P. Horton, 'Pacific Islanders in Global Rugby: The Changing Currents of Sports Migration', *The International Journal of the History of Sport*, 29:17 (2012), pp. 2388–2404.

42 RLIF, 'New Era for Rugby League in the Pacific', retrieved from www.rlif.com/article/8493/new-era-for-rugby-league-in-the-pacific- (accessed 21 November 2018).

43 W. Neale, 'The Peculiar Economics of Professional Sports', *The Quarterly Journal of Economics*, 78:1 (1964), pp. 1–14.

44 Rowe, *The Stuff of Dreams, or the Dream Stuffed?*, p. 14.

45 GAISF, 'Observers', retrieved from https://gaisf.sport/about/observers (accessed 21 November 2018).

46 RFIL, 'RLIF Manual', retrieved from www.rlif.com/ignite_docs/RLIF%20Manual%20(Final%20Version).pdf (accessed 21 November 2018); RLIF, 'RLIF Strategic Plan', retrieved from www.rlif.com/ignite_docs/RLIF-Strategic%20Plan%202015-2025%2018pp%20LR.pdf (accessed 21 November 2018).

10

Rugby union

Steve Greenfield

The history and development of the game: amateurs and professionals

The emergence of the game is located within a broader context of the historical development of football and the English class system. As Young notes:

> The era which saw the transformation of the ancient football game, and its bifurcation into Rugby and Association, also saw the emergence of a new professional class, comprising scholars, physicians, surgeons, the Established clergy, the armed forces, lawyers, and civil servants.[1]

With historical roots in the English public school system, rugby union developed naturally through the empire in those countries with a suitable climate spreading to Australia, South Africa and New Zealand. There was some rugby played in India, most notably at the Calcutta Football Club, but rugby was overtaken by football. The Calcutta Football Club was established in 1872 to play rugby but by 1894 had switched to football.[2] The original split with the Northern Union enshrined the concept of rugby union as an amateur sport that was to create further divisions and hostility.[3]

The formal shift from the stated position of amateurism to the professional era was the most significant event for rugby union since the original split over the same issue in 1895. Ironically a game founded on the amateur ethos had long since been operating what was described as 'shamateurism'. The seemingly inexorable move towards legitimizing payment for playing became irresistible following the 1995 World Cup in South Africa. There had been longstanding concerns in the Northern hemisphere that the rules seemingly being strictly enforced by the RFU were not so rigorously followed elsewhere. Williams argues that the first World Cup in 1987 was a turning point in the debate; 'Evidence that the southern hemisphere nations were well ahead of the game in providing an environment which, by paying lip service to official guidelines, allowed their players to dedicate themselves to the game, was there for all who chose to see in the World Cup.[4] Rob Andrew, one of the senior England players at the 1995 tournament, described an environment where discussions over the potential for a professional breakaway overshadowed the events on the field. The apparent precedent for the rumoured new venture (World Rugby Corporation) was Kerry Packer's disruption of the international cricket establishment in 1976–1977 with the birth of World Series Cricket. Rugby players should be an even easier target, than the cricketers, for an entrepreneur with a new blueprint as there weren't any existing contractual relationships to overturn. Furthermore relationships between players and some of the national unions had become strained by the lack of progress towards resolving the financial arrangements. When the dust settled a new competition was in place funded, as with World Series Cricket, by a broadcaster but in this case Rupert Murdoch's News Corporation organization.[5] Once the national unions had been given huge sums of money for broadcasting rights it was inevitable that players would expect to receive their share of the revenue they were generating. The context was an IRB motivated by a fear of losing control of the game and a potential exodus of players to the new rugby league competition in Australia. League has historically provided a route for players to switch codes and be paid. The most significant switch was that of Jonathan Davies, who had captained Wales at rugby union and joined Widnes from Llanelli in 1989. Davies had a successful 6-year league career playing in both England and Australia and represented both Wales and Great Britain. Davies returned to union joining Cardiff in 1995 after the game became open. Since the union game became open in 1995 players have moved in the other direction into union from league perhaps most notably Jason Robinson who won the World Cup with England in 2003. Sonny Bill Williams started in League representing New Zealand and transferred into Union with Toulon. He represented New Zealand at rugby union, winning two World Cups. Williams also returned to League for a year with the Sydney Roosters but also had seven fights as a heavyweight professional boxer.[6]

Once the principle, of permitting payment for playing, had been established there were huge practical implications least not who would contracts be between. It became necessary after 1995 to set up new contractual arrangements for players (and coaches and others) with their clubs. This now had the potential to create friction with the national associations who wanted the players for international matches yet they now had contractual obligations elsewhere. As with football and cricket, there is an inevitable tension between 'club and country' based around player availability. The authorities have sought to reach agreements on player release. The issue of centrally issued contracts with a national union for international rather than with a club or region to provide greater control over players is still a core issue in both the men's and women's professional game.[7]

Governance, laws and regulations

> It is through discipline, control and mutual respect that the spirit of the game flourishes and, in the context of a game as physically challenging as rugby, these are the qualities which forge the fellowship and sense of fair play so essential to the game's ongoing success and survival.
>
> Old-fashioned traditions and virtues they may be, but they have stood the test of time and, at all levels at which the game is played, they remain as important to rugby's future as they have been throughout its long and distinguished past. The principles of rugby are the fundamental elements upon which the game is based and they enable participants to immediately identify the game's character and what makes it distinctive as a sport.[8]

Each rugby playing country is represented by a national association whether a board, federation or union. This national organization is ordinarily affiliated to World Rugby, the international governing body, as either a member union or associate union. National governing bodies are also affiliated to one of the 6 regional union providing a federation structure comparable with association football.[9]

The comprehensive Objectives and Functions of World Rugby are set out in Bye-Law 3:

(a) Promoting, fostering, developing, extending and governing the Game.

(b) Framing and interpreting the Bye-Laws, the Regulations and the Laws of the Game.

(c) Deciding and/or settling all matters or disputes relating to or arising out of the playing of or the proposed playing of the Game or a Match or any dispute between two or more Unions relating to the application of the Regulations.

(d) To regulate and co-ordinate arrangements to ensure that there is a fair and equitable programme of matches, tours and tournaments for Senior National Representative Teams of all Council Member Unions.

(e) Controlling all other matters of an international character affecting the Game.

(f) To prevent discrimination of any kind against a country, private person or groups of people on account of ethnic origin, gender, language, religion, politics or any other reason.[10]

The history of World Rugby (and its predecessor bodies) is of an organization rooted in the British Isles with the game originally governed by the four home nations. The organization was set up as the International Rugby Football Board (IRFB) in 1886 by Scotland, Wales and Ireland with England joining in 1890. The organization of the Board followed a number of acrimonious disputes between England and Scotland, over the rules by which the game was being played, and the English union declined to join originally for fear of losing its dominant position.[11] A parallel model was Association football, which had established an international governing body, the International Football Association Board in 1886.[12] The IRFB became the International Rugby Board (IRB) in 1998 before adopting the World Rugby Board title in 2014 and locating in Dublin. World Rugby has responsibility for the laws of the game, regulations and a number of international competitions most notably the Rugby World Cup (RWC) that commenced in 1987.[13] The laws of the game are subject to review as the game itself changes especially in relationship to a greater understanding of the cause of injuries. A notable example is the change made to law 19, the scrum, to prevent collapses and the potential for catastrophic spinal injuries. The initial change was to how the scrum was refereed introducing a crouch–touch–pause–engage sequence to prevent charging and this was subsequently altered to a more simplified to the current crouch–bind–set which is detailed in law 19. The World Rugby regulations cover some 24 issues setting out a broad swathe of issues and specifications. The interaction between the laws and the regulations can be seen with respect to pitches which is governed by law 1 (The Ground) and under 1(2) 'The permitted surface types are grass, sand, clay, snow or artificial turf (conforming to World Rugby Regulation 22).' Regulation 22 sets out in detail the specificities of artificial turf which is permitted. A full sized adult pitch must be rectangular in shape and a maximum of 100 meters long and 70 meters wide. The fundamental issue with artificial surfaces is any impact on injury types or rates in comparison to grass pitches and research is ongoing. Ranson and colleagues examined three seasons from two UK clubs who played all home games on an artificial surface:

Overall rugby union match injury risk is comparable between grass and artificial playing surfaces. However, there was a higher risk of concussion and chest injuries on grass, and higher incidence of thigh haematoma and foot injuries on artificial surfaces. There was also a higher injury incidence within forwards playing on grass surfaces.[14]

There must be an in goal area behind the posts which is the part of the field where the ball can be touched down for a 'try' to be awarded.[15] Historically scoring a try did not carry any points in itself but permitted the scoring team a chance to kick a goal and be awarded one point. Over time a try has itself become a means of scoring and allocated at various times 1, 2, 3, 4 and (from 1992) 5 points. The scoring of a try still permits a kick at goal (conversion) which is worth two further points. The other means of scoring are through a successful penalty kick or a drop goal that are each worth 3 points. Increasingly to promote attacking rugby many competitions award bonus points based on scoring a certain number of tries.

One fundamental difference, between league and union, is the number of players on the pitch; 13 players in league 6 forwards and seven backs and 15 players in union, 8 forwards and 7 backs. In international matches up to 8 substitutes may be named with a squad size of 23. For other matches it is the organizing body who decides the permitted number of substitutes up to a maximum of 8. Players may be substituted for a number of reasons. Some substitutions are permanent for tactical reasons while others are temporary while a player is assessed for a head injury or there is a blood injury being treated. In response to the growing fears of concussive injury players who receive a blow to the head are required to leave the field for a head injury assessment (HIA) before either passing and returning to play or being permanently replaced. A number of high-profile players have been forced to retire early due to persistent concussion for example; Ben John, Jonathan Thomas, Reggie Goodes, James Broadhurst and Alistair Hargreaves In the union game the ball can be contested in open play as well as during the two set pieces the scrummage and line out. Rugby league is possession based, centred on six tackles hereafter the ball is overturned and presented to the other team. In union the side in possession play until an offence by either side is committed or the ball is lost; if the opposing team win control of the ball legally the game continues. The ball may be kicked and passed but passes cannot be forwards. There is a distinction drawn between an infringement of the laws such as a 'knock on' where possession of the ball is then contested by both teams through either a line out or scrum and the more serious penalty and lesser free kick offences where control of the ball is transferred directly to the other team. The team awarded a penalty can elect to kick at goal for 3 points. Improved quality of pitches and an increased understanding of kicking techniques has permitted greater accuracy and an ability to kick from long distances. Some kickers are able to successfully score penalties from inside their own half on the pitch, over 50 metres.

The global game

As of 2016 there were 121 countries affiliated to World Rugby comprising 103 Member Unions and 18 Associate Unions. There are over 8 million male players spread throughout the six federations, with England dominating statistically with more than 2 million players. Arguably given its resources England has underperformed on the World stage with only one World Cup win in 2003. Of course the same charge can be levelled at England's Football side with only one World Cup win back in 1966. Its professional structure has a Premiership with 12 sides. Within the British Isles the other major competition is the Pro 14 that encompasses teams from Scotland, Wales, Ireland, Italy and two South African franchises. For the 2018–2019 season the 14 sides comprised four Irish provinces, four Welsh teams, two Scottish teams, two Italian sides and the two South African teams split into two conferences.

The premier club tournament in the Southern Hemisphere is Super Rugby with teams from Argentina, Australia, Japan, New Zealand and South Africa organized in 2018 into three geographical conferences. In total there were five New Zealand teams, four each from South Africa and Australia and one each from Japan and Argentina. A further expansion of the game has developed through the promotion of seven-a-side rugby, 'Sevens'. As the title indicates it is played with seven players on each side, three forwards and four backs. Remarkably played on a full size pitch game time is heavily reduced. The incorporation of rugby Sevens into the Olympics in 2016 provided an opportunity to showcase the game and attract a new audience. 15-a-side rugby was part of the Olympic programme sporadically from 1900 to 1920. Significant efforts commenced in the 1990s to have rugby considered as an Olympic sport and inclusion of the shorter version was accepted in 2009 to start in 2016. Rugby Sevens is a far better fit for the Olympics, than 15-a-side rugby with its requirements for player rest and the length of games. The numbers of countries playing Sevens is over 100 with established tournaments to permit qualification.[16] Both the men's and women's tournament consisted of 12 teams with Australia winning the women's tournament and Fiji the men's.[17] Wheelchair rugby known colloquially as 'murderball' due to its physicality has increased in popularity and became an Olympic Sport in 2000 after being designated a demonstration sport in 1996.[18] It is the subject matter of the 2005 film *Murderball*.

Rugby was one of the two key team sports at the heart of the political battles over the apartheid system in South Africa. South Africa occupied a key position in both rugby and cricket and had long provided national touring teams and hosted foreign tours. As political and economic pressure grew on the South African regime sport and rugby became an arena of direct protest notably in Britain and New Zealand. In 1969 a protest organization, Halt All Racist Tours (HART) was created in New Zealand while in Britain the 'Stop the 70's Tour' was the banner under which disruptions to the 1969–70 tour were carried out. Sporting tours could be used as a focus to galvanize national anti-apartheid movements more generally. As with cricket there were also unofficial or rebel tours such as the New Zealand Cavaliers tour to South Africa in 1986 for which the players were paid.[19]

The rise of women's rugby

Women's rugby has a significant if sketchily documented history but has risen in popularity importance with a growing player base across the world. There are over 2 million players worldwide. While noting the increase in player numbers in New Zealand, Curtin charts the history of women playing rugby in New Zealand.[20] One of the stated barriers to the participation of women in rugby has been the hyper masculinity of the game with the increasing emphasis on strength and physical power. The masculinity dimension to rugby has been a source of academic interest.[21] Other forms of the game such as tag rugby or sevens provides an attractive alternative that encompass some of the required skillset although there are significant differences in the playing rules and shape of the game. World Rugby has sort to promote the women's game:

> By 2025, rugby will be a global leader in sport, where women involved in rugby have equity on and off the field, are reflected in all strategy, plans and structures, making highly valued contributions to participation, performance, leadership and investment in the global game of rugby.[22]

A fundamental challenge is to build a national infrastructure in those countries with a sufficient player base and develop international tournaments. The Women's Rugby World Cup has a history only just shorter than the men's tournament, first held in 1991 rather than 1987. However the original tournaments were organized outside of the governance of the IRB but were retrospectively recognized. The winners have been; the United States (1991) in Wales; England (1994) in Scotland; Netherlands (1998) in Wales; New Zealand (2002) in Spain; New Zealand (2006) in

Canada, New Zealand (2010) in England; England (2014) in France and New Zealand (2017) in Ireland. The 2021 tournament is to be held in New Zealand. In total some 20 nations have participated. In Europe the Women's Six Nations has emerged in line with the men's tournament and is now played in parallel. As with the men's tournament it started life as the 4 Home Nations and became aligned in 2007 when Italy replaced Spain. Unsurprisingly, given its level of resources, England have dominated, winning 13 Grand Slams between 1996 and 2018, with Wales achieving a 2019 grand slam.

The Six Nations, the Rugby Championship and the Rugby World Cup

In addition to the World Cup there are several key competitions at both national, international and intra national level. In the British Isles the original competition, the Home Nations Championship was inaugurated in 1883 between England, Ireland, Scotland and Wales. Unlike football Rugby Union in Ireland is all Ireland based.[23] Prior to the formation of the Championship friendly matches had been played and the only formal competition was the Calcutta Cup between England and Scotland from 1879. Its history was an 1872 match in Calcutta between two sides of English and Scottish origin. When Rugby ceased to be played by the Calcutta Football Club the remaining funds were used to provide the trophy that was presented to the RFU to be contested between England and Scotland. As Collins, notes the split over professionalism in 1895 greatly weakened the English national side who had a reduced player pool to select from: 'in the five seasons following the split, England won just four, and drew two, out of 15 matches, as clubs in the north abandoned the RFU for the NU'.[24] Results got worse with a link to the consequences of the split: 'The continual defeats suffered by England in the 1900s became a testimony to the RFU's sacrifice and steel in upholding the amateur banner'.[25] The Four Nations championship was expanded in 1910 to include France and in 2000 adding Italy to create the contemporary format of Six Nations. In 2017 bonus points were introduced and the continuing struggle of Italy has led to arguments that Georgia ought be given the opportunity to participate either in their own right or through the introduction of promotion/relegation. Italy won their first game in 2000 but had to wait until 2003 before winning their second beating Wales who were whitewashed. Given the demands of club rugby and the need to shorten the playing year to protect players it is unlikely that the tournament will be expanded with the current calendar. In the Southern Hemisphere the equivalent of the Home Nations Championship was slower to be established although friendly internationals were played intermittently between Australia, New Zealand and South Africa. Following the 1995 World Cup and the advent of professionalism a formal Tri Nations tournament, on a home and away basis, was initiated. In 2012 the tournament was extended to include Argentina following its progression as a competitive rugby country and renamed the Rugby Championship. Both tournaments have been dominated by New Zealand. In the Tri Nations held between 1996 and 2011 New Zealand won 10 tournaments, Australia three and South Africa three. Since 2012 New Zealand have won six and Australia one. There are concerns that this domination has led to diminishing interest in the tournament particularly in Australia.

The first Rugby World Cup (RWC) took place in Australian and New Zealand in1987 and was won by New Zealand beating France in the final. The 1991 tournament took place in Europe (it was hosted across Europe by 5 Nations, England, France, Ireland, Scotland and Wales) and was notable for the first time a non-seeded nation beat a seeded nation with Western Samoa stunning one of the hosts Wales 16–13. The 1995 RWC was in many ways the most iconic given the readmittance of South African into the world game and the appropriation of the Springbok jersey by Nelson Mandela. The historic events were transformed into the sports drama film 2009 *Invictus* based on the book by John Carlin.[26] Since 1995 the trophy has been won by Australia (1999) in Wales; England (2003) in Australia; South Africa (2007) in France; New Zealand (2011) in New Zealand and New Zealand (2015) in England. The 2019 tournament is located for the first time in Japan. In March 2019 World Rugby proposed a new controversial international tournament, the Nations Championship bringing together the leading nations in a ten team tournament.

Player, coaches and great teams

There have been numerous outstanding individual players who have performed at the highest level and innovative coaches who have developed the game. However, rugby is known for teams who are cherished for either a ground-breaking performance, tour or period of longevity. This reflects the essential value of rugby as a team sport, available to all 'shapes and sizes'. In 2006 the International Rugby Board (IRB) instigated a Hall of Fame, now the World Rugby Hall of Fame. The first two inducted in 2006 were William Web Ellis and Rugby School itself.[27] There is a broad mixture of players, coaches, administrators, teams, clubs and broadcasters with a combination of both historical and contemporary figures. It is an eclectic mix including for example the 1888–1889 New Zealand Native football team, the Romanian Olympic team of and contemporary players from the men's and women's game. The recent New Zealand side has won consecutive World Cups in 2011 and 2015 and are considered the finest team of the professional era with a number of notable players including Richie McCaw and Dan Carter. McCaw and Carter have each won World Rugby Player of the Year a record three times. McCaw won 148 caps becoming the most capped rugby union player and captaining the side on 110 occasions. Carter won 112 caps and is the record international points scorer with 1598 points. Alongside the great players within this New Zealand side was coach Steve Hanson who took over from Graham Henry after the 2011 World Cup win and presided over the development of the team that went on to claim the 2015 tournament.

An iconic playing link between the Southern and Northern hemispheres is provided by the touring British and Irish Lions. There is a long history of British sides touring overseas though in the earliest days these were private arrangements.[28] The Lions now tour every four years to one of three nations – Australia, New Zealand or South Africa in turn – and thus there is a 12-year gap between tours to the same country. Two matches have been played by the Lions outside of the country the side was touring. First which was played under the Lions badge but was unconnected to any tour was a 1990 charity fixture with a Four Home Unions XV versus Rest of Europe XV played to raise money to contribute to the rebuilding of Romania. The second match was played in 2005 at the Millennium Stadium Cardiff immediately before the start of the tour to New Zealand. The match ended in a 25–25 draw and was the first match against Argentina since the 1936 tour.[29] The first 'official' representative tour took place to South Africa in 1910 and the most recent to New Zealand in 2017. The 2017 Lions Tour to New Zealand ended in an epic series with each side winning one Test and the third Test drawn. The British Lions squad is selected from the 4 Home Nations though there is no requirement that the head coach be a national from any of the countries. In 2001 a New Zealander, Graham Henry, coached the team that toured Australia while in 2013 and 2017 Another Kiwi, Warren Gatland, coached the touring party to Australia and then his own native New Zealand. A key part of the Lions philosophy has been the concept of unity between the players from the four different nations who would ordinarily be playing in opposition for the national side. However, in a rousing speech at the start of the 1971 Tour to New Zealand coach Carwyn James stressed the importance of national identity to the common cause:

> You each have a singular and ultimate quality to give in abundance to this team of ours, and you must only express it, both on the field and off it, in your own special, God-given way. And if you do, there will not be remote shadow of doubt that we shall prevail in the huge endeavour we have set ourselves.
>
> I demand only that you be uncliquey, that in our glorious fusion of national differences and differing temperaments we shall make our whole a vastly more potent force than the sum of our parts.
>
> You Irish must continue to be the supreme ideologists off the field, and on it, fighters like Kilkenny cats. Let you English stiffen those upper lips and simply continue to be superior. And the conservative traditionalism of you Scots – strong, dour, humourless in phoney caricature – let it be seen as colourfully fired up these next 90 days by the oil of your country's new-found radicalism. As well, I demand that all of you make sure you let us Welsh continue to be bloody-minded and swaggeringly over-cocky in our triple-clowning, triple-crowning arrogance.[30]

James's 1971 Lions beat the Kiwis 2–1; the first and only team to win a series in New Zealand. Changes to the international calendar have to take into account the Lions' touring commitment that is still highly valued.

Contemporary issues: player movement and injuries

A key issue for nations, especially South Africa and some of the smaller Pacific Island nations has been the movement of players. In the case of South Africa it was an exodus of young players moving to ply their professional trade abroad notably in England and France. The concern was that this weakened the domestic professional sides and consequently the national side. The right to move to Europe was based around the Cotonou agreement and the *Kolpak* decision of the ECJ that has seriously impacted on County Cricket in the same way.[31] There are two broad categories of players who move abroad. First the older established or ex international players who are moving for largely financial reasons and younger players who are giving up their international aspirations. The professional clubs in England, France and to a lesser extent the Scottish clubs and the Irish provinces have recruited international players and indeed overseas coaches. South Africa had originally instituted a policy in 2011 of not selecting overseas players for the national side unless there were 'exceptional circumstances'. A similar domestic players only policy was also adopted by the RFU after the 2011 World Cup that led to the European Rugby Player of the Year in both 2014 (Steffon Armitage at Toulon) and 2015 (Nick Abendanon at Clermont) eligible but not picked by England due to this criteria. With its large player base England is better able to absorb the problem of overseas players and it is those nations who have fewer players and a less financially powerful home league that inevitably lose more players and are less well equipped to not select such players. It is not clear how the post Brexit political landscape will impact on player movement.

The most serious problem facing rugby at all levels concerns the physicality of the game and propensity for players to suffer serious injury. For professional players and clubs this is an employment issue and requires clubs to maintain large squads to cover player absence. The high profile catastrophic spinal injuries appear to have lessened and this may be due to a combination of factors including improved grounds and referring and changes to the Laws relating to front row engagement though the results may be tragic. A poignant example is the case of 23-year-old Dan James, who was paralysed in a training session and ended his life at Dignitas, the youngest Britain to do so.[32] The greater medical knowledge of concussion and especially second impact syndrome and the publicity relating to the NFL litigation in the USA has caused enormous concern throughout world rugby. Policy has developed and concussion protocols in place but it is an ongoing problem. At junior level there are wider issues around the differences in size and weight of children of the same school age playing against each other and moves to classify children using measures other than age. In England a mismatch in age and subsequent injury led to a claim in negligence against the school master. Similarly an amateur referee was successfully sued over his handling of a game in which a player suffered serious injury.[33]

In a controversially received 2014 book, Professor Allyson Pollock argued the case for wider monitoring of injuries and greater parental knowledge: 'We need to have an urgent debate about whether the rules of children's rugby should be radically changed, and whether it should remain a compulsory sport in some schools.'[34]

Rugby has undoubtedly become more physical at a professional level as players have become much fitter and stronger and this has filtered down through junior rugby. Grounds have improved and the game is quicker and the hits bigger. The masculine culture of rugby relishes these collisions which are integral to the game whatever the level and present a dichotomy for all those involved in the game.

Notes

1 Percy M. Young (1968) *A History of British Football* (Stanley Paul and Co, London), 2.
2 Paul Dimeo (2001) Football and Politics in Bengal: Colonialism, Nationalism, Communalism, *Soccer and Society*, 2:2, 57–74.
3 James W. Martens (1993) 'They Stooped to Conquer': Rugby Union Football, 1895–1914, *Journal of Sport History*, 20:1, 25–41.
4 Peter Wiliams (2008) Cycle of Conflict: A Decade of Strife in English Professional Rugby, *The International Journal of the History of Sport*, 25:1, 66.
5 P. FitzSimons (2003) *The Rugby War* (Harper Sports, London).
6 See www.allblacks.com/Player/AllBlacks?id=2039.
7 In January 2019 the RFU announced that 28 central contracts had been awarded for Women 15 a side players (see www.englandrugby.com/news/england-women-contracts-red-roses-and-squad).
8 See https://laws.worldrugby.org/?charter=all.
9 Rugby Europe is the regional body for European Rugby (www.rugbyeurope.eu) and does have several members who are not affiliated to World Rugby.
10 See www.world.rugby/handbook/bye-laws/bye-law-3.
11 T. Collins (2009) *A Social History of English Rugby Union* (Routledge, London), 158.
12 T. Mason (ed.) (1989) *Sport in Britain: A Social History* (Cambridge University Press, Cambridge).
13 L. Peatey (2015) *A Complete History of the Rugby World Cup* (New Holland Publishers, London).
14 C. Ranson, J. George, J. Rafferty, J. Miles and I. Moore (2018) Playing Surface and UK Professional Rugby Union Injury Risk, *Journal of Sports Sciences*, 36:21, 2397.
15 See https://laws.worldrugby.org/?law=1&language=EN.
16 See https://library.olympic.org/Default/doc/SYRACUSE/171150.
17 See www.olympic.org/rugby.
18 K. Lindemann and J.L. Cherney (2008) Communicating In and Through 'Murderball': Masculinity and Disability in Wheelchair Rugby, *Western Journal of Communication*, 72:2, 107–125.
19 See https://nzhistory.govt.nz/media/photo/cavaliers-rugby-tour-1985.
20 Jennifer Curtin (2016) Before the 'Black Ferns': Tracing the Beginnings of Women's Rugby in New Zealand, *The International Journal of the History of Sport*, 33:17, 2071–2085.
21 J. Nauright and T.J.L. Chandler (eds) (1996) *Making Men: Rugby and Masculine Identity* (Frank Cass, London).
22 See www.world.rugby/womens-rugby/development-plan.

23 J. Tuck (2003) Making Sense of Emerald Commotion: Rugby Union, National Identity and Ireland, *Identities: Global Studies in Culture and Power*, 10:4, 495–515.

24 Collins, *A Social History of English Rugby Union*, 391.

25 Ibid.

26 J. Carlin (2008) *Playing the Enemy: Nelson Mandela and the Game that Made a Nation*, (Penguin London).

27 See www.world.rugby/halloffame.

28 C. Thomas and G. Thomas (2016) *The British and Irish Lions: The Official History* (Vision Sports Publishing).

29 Ibid.

30 See www.lionsrugby.com/2012/04/16/the-power-of-speech-iii.

31 See S. Greenfield, G. Osborn and J. P. Rossouw (2016) Beyond Kolpak: European Union Law's Unforeseen Contribution to the Movement of African Cricketers, *The International Journal of the History of Sport*, 33:15, 1748–1766.

32 See www.telegraph.co.uk/news/uknews/3216838/Rugby-player-takes-own-life-at-suicide-clinic-after-being-paralysed-in-training-accident.html.

33 S. Greenfield (2013) Law's Impact on Youth Sport: Should Coaches Be 'Concerned about Litigation'? *Sports Coaching Review*, 2:2, 114–123.

34 A. Pollock (2014) *Tackling Rugby* (Verso, London) 2.

11

Volleyball

Darlene A. Kluka and Steve Hendricks

By its nature, the game of volleyball requires cooperation and communication. A team's success not only depends upon individual skill and effort but also upon the total contribution of an individual's effort to overall team performance. A true team is composed of individuals who ultimately understand the language of the game and can perform in rhythm.

An indoor volleyball team consists of six players. They are arranged in a rotational order at the time of service (serving order), with three players in the back court and three in the front court. The three players in the front court are considered potential spikers (hitters or attackers on offence – left, middle, right – or blockers on defence); the three back court players are referred to as backs (left, middle, right). There is also a position designated as a setter. Depending upon the offensive system played and the rotational order before the serve, the setter can be in the front court prior to the serve or come from the back court into the front court once the ball is served.[1]

Special qualities of the game

Many team sports played in the world are possession sports. Football, field and ice hockey, rugby, and basketball have rules and strategies that allow each player to control the ball for extended periods of time. One statistic kept for those sports is "time of possession" of the ball for each team.

Volleyball, however, is a sport of rebound and movement. The ball is never motionless from the time it is served until it contacts the floor or is whistled dead by an official. Winning in volleyball is determined by points, and a set must be won by a margin of two or more points.

The size of the court is relatively small for the number of players, creating a congested playing area. Because of this, the game has evolved into one of efficiency, accuracy and supportive movements. Each team has a maximum of three contacts with which to accomplish the objective: to return the ball and have it contact the floor on the opponent's side of the net within the boundaries of the court. One player is not allowed to contact the ball twice in a row. The outcome of the rally, set and match becomes a summation of each player's efforts. This is the ultimate in individual contribution and team effort.[2]

Substitutions are limited, encouraging versatility among players. Because player rotation is a mandatory part of the game, each player experiences up to six different orientations, three in the back court and three in the front court. Timeouts are brief, creating the potential for dramatic shifts in momentum. These shifts in momentum help make the sport of volleyball constantly dynamic and continuously intriguing.

Volleyball is a team sport which uses a net to create no intentional physical contact between opposing teams. Reaching over the net into the opponent's court is permitted during the follow through motion of the attacker's arm after the ball has been hit, or in the act of blocking after the hitter has contacted the ball.[3]

The individual techniques of the game are quite different from those of most team sports. Because the essence of the game requires the body to move through all zones of movement (air-borne, high, medium, low), the ball can be played at the highest point of a jump or just a centimetre above the floor. The forearm pass is one technique used uniquely in the game. No other team sport fosters ball-to-forearm contact as an accurate, efficient and effective skill.

Techniques have evolved as a direct result of the rules that govern the game. The quality of the administrator of those rules, the referee, may determine the level of skill acceptable to play a successful match (generally three out of five sets). The acceptability of each contact is interpreted by a referee. Volleyball technique, or how the ball is contacted, is a primary ingredient of the game. Court size, number of players, number of contacts permitted, and ball speeds (ranging from less than 1 m per second to in excess of 180 km per hour) contribute to the excitement and popularity of the game for both players and spectators.[4]

Volleyball has evolved into three types for the purposes of this chapter: six-player indoor; two-player beach; and six-player sitting. A brief history is presented about each type.

Indoor volleyball

William G. Morgan was physical director of the Holyoke, Massachusetts, United States of America (USA) Young Men's Christian Association (YMCA), and created a game called Mintonette in 1895. It was initially devised as a less strenuous activity than basketball for middle-aged businessmen who attended YMCA classes. The game incorporated baseball, handball, and tennis-related skills. The objective was to hit the ball back and forth with the hands. Each team, having any number of players, was permitted three outs (similar to baseball), whereby the ball contacted the floor, before the team forfeited the ball.[5]

Because the basic idea of play was to bat the ball with the hands back and forth over a net, the game was renamed "volleyball" in 1896. Earliest rules mandated the game be played in 9 innings on a 25 × 50 feet (7.62 × 15.24 metres) court. The serve was hit over a 6.5 feet high (1.982 metres) net and could be assisted by any offensive player. The bladder for a basketball was originally used for the ball, but it proved to be too light. A basketball was too heavy. A.G. Spalding (later Spalding Sporting Goods Company) constructed a ball expressly for the game.[6]

Touching the net during a point attempt was illegal. The ball could be dribbled within 4 feet of the net. By 1900, the concepts of innings and dribbling were eliminated; nets were 7 feet (2.134 metres) high, substantially shorter than the ones used in men's and women's volleyball today. Twelve years later, the YMCA formed a special committee which developed major rule modifications and standardized ball handling. The court was enlarged to 30 × 60 feet (10.668 × 18.288 metres); the net was raised to 7.5 feet (2.286 metres); serve rotation of players was incorporated, and the two-out-of-three game match was established. The YMCA used the new rules in the first Open Invitational Tournament held in Germantown, Pennsylvania USA. Players called their own fouls. In 1916, the YMCA, in conjunction with the National Collegiate

Athletic Association (NCAA), published men's rules. The net was elevated to 8 feet (2.438 metres); the game was concluded at 15 points.[7]

During the early 1900s, the YMCA exerted the greatest influence upon the growth and development of the sport. The sport was introduced in Canada, Central and South America by YMCA missionaries as well as in Southeast Asia. By 1912, the YMCA had taken volleyball to Cuba, Puerto Rico, and Uruguay. In 1913, it was included in the Far Eastern Games in Manila, Philippines; by 1914, it was being played in England and Europe. By 1916, an offensive style of setting the ball to another player was invented in the Philippines. During the First World War, American Expeditionary Forces distributed over 16,000 volleyballs to their troops and allies in Western Europe. Immediately after the Great War, several Eastern European nations adopted the sport and rapidly began national competitions. In 1916, the NCAA was invited to assist in the editing of YMCA volleyball rules in an attempt to promote the sport in the USA. It was added to school and college physical education curricula throughout the country.[8]

The physical education directors of the YMCA, encouraged particularly by two professional schools of physical education, Springfield College in Massachusetts and George Williams College in Chicago, adopted volleyball in all its societies throughout the United States, Canada and also in many other countries: Japan (1908), China (1909), Philippines (1910), Burma (1911), India (1940s), and others in Mexico and South American, European (1917) and African (1940s) countries.[9]

By 1913 the development of volleyball on the Asian continent was assured as, in that year, the game was included in the programme of the first Far-Eastern Games, organized in Manila. It should be noted that, for a long time, Volleyball was played in Asia according to the "Brown" rules (named after Elwood S. Brown who brought the game via the Philippines) which, among other things, used 16 players (to enable a greater participation in matches).[10]

An indication of the growth of volleyball in the United States was presented in the 1916 *Spalding Volleyball Guide*. It was estimated that the number of players had reached a total of 200,000 people subdivided into the YMCA (boys, young men, and older men) 70,000, the YWCA (girls and women) 50,000, schools (boys and girls) 25,000 and colleges (young men) 10,000.

By 1916, the YMCA managed to induce the National Collegiate Athletic Association (NCAA) to publish its rules and a series of articles, contributing to the rapid growth of volleyball among young college students. In 1918 the number of players per team was limited to six and, in 1922, the maximum number of authorized contacts with the ball was fixed at three.[11]

The 1920s was the decade of most rapid change for volleyball in the USA. Three hits per side and back row attack were implemented. Each game was changed from 21 points to 15 points. Points were scored only when a team initiated the serve. The men's first YMCA National Championships were held in 1922 at the Brooklyn Central (New York) YMCA. The National Amateur Athletic Federation (NAAF) – later the Amateur Athletic Union (AAU) sanctioned volleyball as an official national activity in 1923. By 1924, the first intramural volleyball programme was instituted at the University of Illinois in the USA. That same year, the first interscholastic (high school) volleyball programme was founded in Pittsburgh, Pennsylvania USA.[12]

Special rules were published for girls and women in the Red Cover Series of the *Spalding Athletic Library*.[13] Additionally, in 1926, the National Section on Women's Athletics (NSWA), a division of the American Physical Education Association (APEA), created a totally independent set of rules for females. Court dimensions were restructured to 30 × 60 feet (9.144 × 18.288 metres), the ball could be contacted legally above the waist only, and no more than three contacts per side were permitted.

In 1928, to regulate rules nationally and create a national open championship, the United States Volleyball Association (USVBA) was formed. National championships were contested in a joint USVBA/YMCA tournament in three men's divisions: open, veterans (now called senior), and YMCA.

Until the early 1930s volleyball was a game of leisure and recreation, with a few international activities and competitions. There were different rules of the game in the various parts of the world; however, national championships were played in many countries. Volleyball thus became more and more a competitive sport with high physical and technical performance.

During the 1930s, NSWA had changed to the National Section for Girls' and Women's Sports (NSGWS) and had published a separate rules book for girls and women. The rules were used at the high school and college levels in volleyball classes and intramural competitions. By 1934, the importance of having qualified referees was heightened, and national volleyball referees were approved and recognized. Three years later, 1937, the AAU officially recognized the United States Volleyball Association (USVBA) as the official national governing body of the sport in the USA.[14]

The ten years prior to the Second World War were relatively stable ones for volleyball, with few changes in rules or play. The University of Washington (USA) formed the first men's varsity volleyball programme with awards in 1934. The State of Pennsylvania sanctioned the first boys' high school championships in 1938. Net height for men was adjusted to 8 feet (2.43 metres) and 7 feet 4 inches (2.24 metres) for women.

American armed forces stationed in the South Pacific during the Second World War found the game of volleyball a relaxing alternative to fervent fighting in the jungles and on the beaches. A rope, strewn with seaweed, was strung between two trees to serve as a net. The game spread among the people of the islands occupied by American troops. The Japanese, in particular, developed a keen sense for the game.[15]

During the five years after the war, several advancements occurred internationally in the sport. In 1946, college club teams developed all over the USA as war veterans, who had played during the war, returned to college. The Federation Internationale de Volleyball (FIVB) was established in 1947 with 14 charter member nations to serve as the official international governing body for the sport. In 1948, the first European Championships were held in Rome, and the first world championships were held in Prague, Czechoslovakia in 1949. Men's European Championships were long dominated by Czechoslovakia, Poland, Hungary, Bulgaria, Romania, and the Soviet Union (later Russia). The Soviet men's and women's teams have won more titles than any other European country.[16]

The first college in the USA to offer men's scholarships in volleyball and have a full-time coach was Florida State University in 1949. The USVBA, in the same year, added a women's division to its national Open Championships. By 1951, volleyball was played by over 50,000,000 people annually in 60 countries and, in 1955, the sport was included in the Pan-American Games. Two years later, in 1957, the International Olympic Committee (IOC) determined that volleyball was to be part of the Olympic programme in the 1964 Olympic Games in Tokyo. A major breakthrough for the sport also came when the International University Sports Federation (FISU) held the first University Games that included volleyball as one of eight sports.[17]

NSGWS became the Division for Girls' and Women's Sports (DGWS) in 1958. The Division published guides that included rules which were recognized as official for girls and women. Each guide included rules, standards, officiating instructions, and professional written teaching/coaching articles.

During the two decades following the Korean conflict, the USVBA began its surge of national leadership in the amateur sport of volleyball. In 1952 and 1953, the USVBA sponsored a men's team at the first and second World Championships; it instituted the men's National Collegiate Championships and was involved with them until 1969; it helped sponsor a men's team to the first Pan-American Championships in 1955; and it assisted in sending men's and women's teams to the Olympic Games in 1964. In the 1960s, new techniques were added to the sport: soft spike (dink), forearm pass (bump), blocking across the net, and defensive diving and rolling.[18]

Although volleyball had its roots in the USA, it was not played as competitively in the USA as in Japan, Cuba, or the former Soviet Union. When the 1964 Olympic Games were held in Tokyo, volleyball was initiated as an Olympic sport for men and women. The Japanese style of play revolutionized and helped develop the game into one of power, agility, endurance, and finesse. The Japanese women, particularly, reflected the introduction of private corporations in the training of athletes. Women, working at the same company, invested their free time to team practice and competition with fulltime professional coaches. As a result of intensive training and flexible working conditions, the women won the World Championship in 1962, 1966 and 1967, as well as the gold medal at the 1964 Tokyo Olympic Games. Additionally, the texture and size of the ball were altered to make it faster and more difficult to manipulate. Ball handling interpretations by officials were also adapted to assist the style of play.

Women's involvement in the sport rapidly increased after the Second World War. The war provided opportunities for women to work outside of the home in many areas of the world as a result of millions of men being drafted into their country's armed forces. This different perspective of women in the workforce prompted increased participation in sport outside the home. After the first women's USVBA National Championship (1949) and the first World Championships for women (1952), the Women's Athletic Division (DGWS) of the American Association for Health, Physical Education, and Recreation (AAHPER) revised its rules to coincide with the women's rules of the USVBA.[19]

Women served as head coaches for the USA women's Olympic volleyball team in the 1964 Olympic Games in the form of W. P. "Doc" Burroughs, and 1968 Olympic Games in Jane Ward. Ward served as the last female head coach for any USA team until 2008 when Lang "Jenny" Ping, of China, served as the head coach. Males have served as head coaches for every USA men's Olympic volleyball team to date.[20]

The FIVB, in 1969, devised a four-year rotational cycle for international volleyball events. The World Championships were held in 1969, one year after the Olympic Games. Two years after the Olympic Games, regional competition began (Pan-American, All-Africa, Asian, European Games).

Volleyball gained enough popularity by the early 1970s to justify the development of the first professional volleyball competition in the western USA. An organization known as the International Professional Volleyball League was also formed. Although athletic abilities were substantial to make the league exciting, professional volleyball disappeared within a few years because of lack of sufficient funding. A decade later, another effort to start a professional men's volleyball league was initiated in the USA.

The National Collegiate Athletic Association (NCAA) continued the men's collegiate championship series by sponsoring the first NCAA Championship in 1970. The Association of Intercollegiate Athletics for Women (AIAW) sponsored its first women's national championship in 1970 and continued until 1981. As a result of the NCAA sponsorship of a women's national championship in 1982 with expenses paid to participating teams, the AIAW lost participants and, ultimately, dropped its own championships.[21]

In 1975, women's volleyball was the first national Olympic programme to develop a fulltime residency training programme, centred in Texas. Players selected for the national team lived, worked, and trained together for the first time.

Internationally today, the sport is controlled and regulated by the FIVB. The federation currently has 210 member countries. International headquarters are located in Lausanne, Switzerland.

Games called "doubles" and "triples" were variations that were added to the indoor game. A doubles team consisted of two players; a triples team was composed of three. Each team's court was slightly shorter than the six-player court. Individual techniques differed slightly because of varying zones of responsibility on the court.[22]

Coed play (males and females on the same team) gained popularity in the 1970s. Its roots branched from the West Coast of the USA eastward in the country and then into Europe, South America and Europe. Serving order alternated one female and one male on the court. If the ball was played more than once per side, at least one contact had to be made by a female. Other rule modifications were incorporated to make the game challenging and exciting for players. Mixed Six National Championships were established in the USA in 1993.

Olympic volleyball originally participated in a round robin format where each team played against each other and then were ranked by wins, set average, and point average. The number of teams grew exponentially since 1964. Since 1996, both men's and women's events were comprised of 12 qualified countries. Multiple men's gold medal victories in Olympic competition is shared by three teams: former Soviet Union (Russia) earned three gold medals; United States of America earned three; and Brazil earned three to date. The women's gold medal victories appear to be dominated by five different teams: Brazil, China, Cuba, Japan and the former Soviet Union (USSR – now Russia) in fourteen Olympic Games since 1964.[23]

The 2000 Olympic Games provided opportunities for substantive rules changes in international competition. The libero, a player who is a back row defensive specialist and wears a differently coloured jersey, was added. Another rule change involved the concept of rally scoring, whereby a point could be scored by the defence *or* the serving team each time the ball was served. Each set became 25 points, winning by 2. Each match was the best 3 out of 5 sets.[24]

As volleyball has grown, so has its strategies of attack:

1   Backcourt attack – an attack by a backrow player. The player must take off from behind the 3m line before contacting the ball, but may land in front of the line after the contact.
2   Line and crosscourt attack – a line attack follows a trajectory parallel to the sideline; a cross court attack has a trajectory that crosses through the court at an angle. An extreme angle cross court attack hits the floor in front of the 3 metre line of the opponent and is referred to as a cut shot.
3   Dip/dink/tip/cheat/dump – player touches the ball with just enough force so that it falls into an area of the opposite court that is not being covered by the defence.
4   Tool/wipe/block – players hit the ball only hard enough to use the block to create an out-of-bounds play.
5   Off-speed hit – players hit the ball softly, providing less speed and more confusion for the opponent.
6   Quick hit/"one" – an attack usually in the middle with approach and jump initiated before setter releases the ball. The quick set is positioning the ball only slightly above the net for the hitter who leaves the floor almost simultaneously when the ball leaves the setter's hands.
7   Slide – a variation of the quick attack that uses a low back set. The middle hitter goes around the setter and hits from behind him/her.
8   Double quick attack/stack/tandem – a variation of the quick attack using two hitters, one in front of the setter and one behind or both in front of the setter, jumping to perform a

quick attack simultaneously. The idea is to stress opposing blockers and free a fourth hitter attacking from the backcourt, with no block.

As the popularity of volleyball continues to grow throughout the world, its media coverage continues to be a major catalyst. Two factors have contributed to the sport becoming mainstream in many areas of the world: the introduction of cable television stations and the willingness of volleyball-related organizations to initially buy airtime to broadcast events, particularly in the USA. In free societies where governments do not own or financially support television stations, broadcasts must be paid for. Commercials are solicited to pay for airtime. In the early 1990s, the American Volleyball Coaches Association (AVCA) initially paid for NCAA Division I women's volleyball to be broadcast on a cable television station in the USA. Today the sport is broadcast on several cable stations globally involving both men's and women's teams, high school volleyball, match of the week, and conference and national championships as well as club play.

Beach volleyball

The initiation of volleyball outdoors was developed on Waikiki Beach in Hawaii, at the Outrigger Canoe Club in 1915. This game became known as beach volleyball. The Outrigger Canoe Club became a place where men and women could commune with the sand, sea and sun, along with the *Aloha spirit*. The first recorded match occurred in 1915, organized by George David "Dad" Center, a member of the club.[25]

By 1920, the City of Santa Monica, California USA created new jetties with sandy areas for public enjoyment. The first permanent nets with erected for beach volleyball, and people began to participate recreationally on public portions of beach. Eleven beach clubs appeared in the Santa Monica area, beginning in 1922. The first inter-club competitions occurred in 1924. The beach game appeared in Europe by the 1930s on beaches of Portugal, Spain, England, and Scotland.

With its origination, beach volleyball was played with at least six players per team, similar to the indoor game. The concept of two-person beach volleyball was initiated by Paul "Pablo" Johnson, an indoor player from the Santa Monica Athletic Club. It began as a result of only two players appearing for a match. Johnson decided to play two against six, thereby changing the beach volleyball team size forever. Although players continue to play recreationally with six per team, official beach volleyball matches are played with two per side. By the 1940s, beach tournaments were played for trophies in Santa Monica. The first tournament to offer a prize of a case of Pepsi was held in Los Angeles, California USA. In France, however, the prize for winning the tournament was 30,000 francs. The Manhattan Beach Open in Southern California was held in 1960. The Open grew to become the Wimbledon of Beach Volleyball. In the 1960s, there was an unsuccessful attempt to begin a professional volleyball league for men in Santa Monica.[26]

The first professional beach volleyball tournament was the Olympic World Championship of Beach Volleyball in the summer of 1976 in Pacific Palisades, California USA, later referred to as the Pacific Palisades Tournament. The first world championship had a total prize purse of US$5000. *Volleyball Magazine* hosted the event the following year at the same location and was sponsored by Schlitz Light Beer. A sport promotion company, Event Concepts, was begun in 1978 that moved the World Championship of Beach Volleyball to Redondo Beach, California USA. Jose Cuervo tequila became the sponsor and funded a prize purse of US$50,000. The successful event led to Jose Cuervo sponsoring an additional three tournaments the following year. The California Pro Beach Tour was founded with events in Laguna Beach, Santa Barbara and the World Championship in Redondo Beach.[27]

In the next decade, the tour continued to expand and was retitled as the Pro Beach Volleyball Tour. The newly established tour spread from California to Florida, Colorado and Chicago. The best players in the world were Karch Kiraly, Randy Stoklos and Sinjin Smith, among others. By 1984, the Pro Beach Tour included 16 events with a total prize purse of US$300,000. By 1985, Event Concepts, the original sport promotion group, left the tour because of a players' strike at the World Championship. This opened the path for the initiation of the Association of Volleyball Professionals (AVP).[28]

By the mid-1980s, this professional sport began to produce outstanding players that gave greater popularity to the sport. Kiraly and Kent Steffes were the first to win an Olympic Gold Medal in beach volleyball at the first appearance of the sport in 1996. Kiraly was also part of two Olympic Gold Medals as part of the USA men's indoor team as well as winning 142 beach titles. At the first FIVB World Beach Volleyball Championships in Rio de Janeiro, Brazil, Sinjin Smith and Randy Stoklos won gold and US$22,000 in prize money. By 1996, there were 27 FIVB beach tournaments (including World Championships and Olympic Games), with US$4,300,000 total prize money.[29]

Despite gaining popularity in the two decades following the 1984 Olympic Games in Los Angeles, difficulty with sustainability of the pro beach tour concept was unsettling. In 1998, the American women's profession tour (WPVA) filed for bankruptcy, as well as the AVP professional men's tour.

In 2001, the AVP was resurrected as a publicly traded company that included both men's and women's tours with equal prize money. In 2010, the AVP again filed for bankruptcy.

Meanwhile, beach volleyball entered the Olympic Games for the first time officially in 1996, as its 1992 debut was as an International Olympic Committee demonstration sport. More than 60 countries qualified through the SWATCH FIVB World Tour. Over 10,000 spectators watched competition daily on site for 12 days. By the 2012 Olympic Games in London, 96 of the best beach volleyball players participated. Approximately 425,000 fans shared in the revelry at the venue.[30]

In the 2010–2011 season, the NCAA began beach volleyball, originally calling the sport "sand volleyball". It was also referred to as an emerging women's sport. NCAA Division II began the first competitions; NCAA Division I was added the following year. Following standard beach volleyball rules, five doubles teams from each institution compete. Sand volleyball, changed to beach volleyball in 2015, became a fully sanctioned NCAA championship sport during the 2015–2016 season and launched a single all-divisions (NCAA Divisions I, II and III) championship.[31]

Contemporary skills of beach volleyball include serving, passing, setting, attacking, blocking and digging, the same used in the indoor and sitting games. The team is composed of two players, and no substitutions are permitted. At the time of service, there are no predetermined positions on the court. The players can change at any time. Using a rally system of scoring (introduced in 1999), the first team to reach 21 points with a two-point advantage wins the set. The first team to win two sets out of three wins the match. A third set equals 15 points. Unlike indoor and sitting, teams change sides of the court after every 7 points in the first two sets. If a third set is needed, the change occurs at 5 points played.

The sport of volleyball has produced a number outstanding characters: Karch Kiraly, Gene Selznick, Harry Wilson, Doug Beal, Sinjin Smith, Flo Hyman, Mary Jo Peppler, Jenny Lang Ping and Kerri Walsh-Jennings, to list a few. The USA Volleyball Hall of Fame has honoured them as superb athletes, coaches or administrators and remarkable individuals.

Karch Kiraly (USA), a former student athlete at UCLA, won three Olympic gold medals. With a phenomenal ability to focus and work incessantly, he became the world's top indoor player as well as the best on the beach. He was also the consummate professional by providing class to a sport that has come from laid back and recreational images. Karaly was voted the World's Best Volleyball Male Player in the first one hundred years of the game by the FIVB in 1996. He helped propel the USA women's Olympic team, as an assistant, to the silver medal in 2012. He has served as the head coach and earned a bronze medal in the 2016 Olympic Games in Rio de Janeiro.

Gene Selznick (USA) has been referred to as volleyball's "problem child". As a multi-talented player whose Maverick charisma endeared him to spectators, he was selected as an All-World player in Paris in 1956 and provided the world with the most advanced system of play and international rules to American volleyball. With his flamboyant attitude, he frequently found himself engaged in disputes with Harry Wilson, the czar of USVBA. Selznick was the first to introduce Wilt Chamberlain to the sport and created a four-person tour in the 1970s across the nation.[32]

Mary Jo Peppler (USA), an all-around player, a coach, innovator, visionary and proponent, was arguably the best female player in the history of the game. She won television's first Superstars Competition, an Olympian at the age of 19 (1964) and was the only female player-coach in the professional International Volleyball Association (IVA). She was also the catalyst behind the first USA national team programme that began in Pasadena, Texas USA in 1973. Prior to Title IX, she began two collegiate programmes from infancy: Sul Ross State University; Utah State University. Both captured national championships. She also coached the all-time great women's beach team in the world – Karolyn Kirby and Liz Masakayan. Peppler and her indoor and outdoor teammates have carried the torch for women's volleyball that laid the groundwork for success of the women's game.[33]

Sinjin Smith (USA) was the winningest player in the history of beach volleyball at 135. Being the first player to actually pursue the media, sponsors, fans and FIVB President, Ruben Acosta, Smith succeeded in revaluing beach volleyball to the world. He and Randy Stoklos laid the groundwork by playing in FIVB tournaments to get beach volleyball into the Olympic Games in 1996.[34]

The first czar of volleyball, **Harry Wilson** (USA) was a player, a coach and an administrator during the 1930s. He established the *International Volleyball Review*, the first printed volleyball news magazine. As a coach, his teams won 12 USVBA national championships which opened the way for him to be named the 1964 USA Olympic team coach. Although his coaching style remained locked into an antiquated American system, his contributions to organization and administration of the sport poised it for the next level of excellence.[35]

Doug Beal (USA) was one of the most innovative coaches of the game during the 1980s. Beal and his assistants devised a two-passer system that changed serve reception for the entire game. The USA 1984 Olympic team, under his direction, won gold. But he contributed much more to the sport. He spearheaded the establishment of the first men's training centre in Dayton, Ohio USA, and later facilitated the move to Southern California, where most of the players resided. He has served for over 25 years as CEO of USA Volleyball and provided continuous leadership at national and international levels for over forty.[36]

Flo Hyman (USA) has been touted as one of the all-time great indoor attackers in women's volleyball in the 20th century. At 6 feet 5 inches (1.96 metres) tall, Hyman joined the USA national team in 1976. By 1977 the team finished fifth at the World Championships. Her contribution to offensive play involved a powerful attack that traveled frequently at 110 mph (180 km/h). Planning to play in the 1980 Olympic Games in Moscow, her dreams were dashed when the USA boycotted the event. By the 1984 Olympic Games in Los Angeles, the team had earned a bronze medal in the 1982 World Championships. In Los Angeles, the women finished with a silver medal, losing to China in the finals. After the 1984 Olympic Games, Hyman moved to Japan and joined the Daiei women's team in the Japanese Volleyball League. Identified as the best hitter at the World Cup Competition (1981), she was ranked #69 on the greatest women athletes of the 20th century *Sports Illustrated* list. On January 24, 1986, Hyman's life ended while playing volleyball. She had asked the coach to make a substitution for her, told the team to play on, sat down on the bench, and shortly thereafter collapsed to the floor. The cause of her death was Marfan syndrome, a disorder from birth that created a weakness in the aortic artery, producing a fatal aortic dissection and instantaneous death. Interestingly, her younger brother was shortly thereafter checked for the disorder. It was found that he too had Marfan syndrome, and had emergency surgery to correct the defect. In essence, her death saved her brother's life.[37]

(Jenny) Lang Ping (China) has been referred to as one of the most eminent and admired person in the history of volleyball globally. Referred to as *the Iron Hammer* because of her impressive attack, Ping went on to become one of the most outstanding international coaches in the world. Her performances throughout her career culminated regularly in being the best – as a player, she won a World Championship (1982) and an Olympic gold (1984), and as a coach she led China to silver at the 1996 Olympic Games in Atlanta and the World Championships (1998). By 2005, she was asked to become the head coach of USA Volleyball's women's national team and, by 2008, she had coached the team to a silver medal in the Olympic Games in Beijing, China. The USA beat China in the preliminary round but lost to Brazil for the gold medal. After 2008, Ping was named coach of the Chinese women's national team again. By 2016, the Chinese women had won a gold medal in Rio at the Olympic Games, bringing Lang Ping from gold medallist as a player in 1984 to gold medallist as a coach in 2016.[38]

Kerri Walsh-Jennings (USA) has had one of the most impressive and prestigious careers in volleyball. She continues to be *the* premiere professional beach volleyball athlete in the world. A four-time Olympic medallist, she leads in career wins at the end of 2016 with 133 wins and in excess of US$2.5 million in prize money. She and her teammate, Misty May-Treanor, have been called "the greatest beach volleyball team of all time", having won Olympic gold medals in 2004, 2008 and 2012. For most of her volleyball career, Walsh-Jennings played with May-Treanor from 2001 to 2012. After May's retirement, Walsh-Jennings has played with April Ross and has become the most winning professional volleyball athlete in the world, male or female. Her accolades have been many: the holder of four Olympic medals, the most in Olympic history; FIVB Best Blocker, 2005–2008, 2011, 2012, 2014; FIVB Best Hitter, 2005–2007, 2012, 2014; FIVB Most Outstanding, 2007, 2012–2014.[39]

Sitting volleyball

In 1956, the Dutch Sports Committee presented the game of Sitting Volleyball to the world. It is a combination of Sitzball, begun in Germany in 1953, and volleyball. Played in more than 60 countries, sitting volleyball has evolved to be a highly competitive game for those with and without physical disabilities. Double leg amputees, spinal injuries below the waist, and those with limited abilities involving the lower extremities can become elite players. Played on a smaller court and reduced net height, sitting volleyball closely resembles the spirit of the game invented in 1895. The major difference in the contemporary game from that of indoor volleyball is that players must remain seated while playing the ball. In 1976 Sitting Volleyball was entered as a demonstration sport in the Paralympic Games in Toronto. It was not until 1978, however, that the International Sports Organization for the Disabled (ISOD) placed sitting volleyball for men on the official programme. By 1980, it was accepted as a Paralympic sport for men in Arnhem, Netherlands. In 1993, championships for women were established.[40]

Unintended consequences from war frequently result in loss of appendages in battles or IEDs in the late 20th and early 21st centuries. Additionally, explosive mine fields in a variety of former war zones in Iraq, Iran, Afghanistan, Vietnam, and Mozambique have also caused loss of appendages to boys and girls. These events have generated additional need and demand for Paralympic volleyball.

The sport of volleyball has developed and embraced opportunities for many people throughout the world. Its popularity continues to increase, particularly involving populations with diverse needs. With gaining sponsorship of professional indoor and beach and increased visibility through cable television, the game continues to elevate in exposure as an exciting spectator sport as well as one providing joy and excitement for its participants.

Notes

1 Kluka, Darlene, and Dunn, Peter. *Volleyball* (4th ed.). New York: McGraw-Hill Company, 2000.
2 Ibid.
3 Beal, Douglas. *Spike*. Berkeley, CA: Avant Books, 1985.
4 Ibid.
5 Donnelly, Steven. *A Concise History of Volleyball*. Digital Publications, 2014.
6 Ibid.
7 Ibid.
8 Odeneal, William. *A Summary of Seventy-five years of Rules: 1970 Annual Official Volleyball Rules and Reference Guide of the United States Volleyball Association*. Colorado Springs, CO: USVBA, 1970.
9 Ibid.
10 Ibid.
11 Davies, Glenn. *USVBA Diamond Jubilee Celebration*. Colorado Springs, CO: USVBA, 1970.
12 Ibid.
13 Ibid.
14 Ibid.
15 Ibid.
16 *FIVB Fortieth Anniversary: 1947–1987*. Lausanne: FIVB, 1988.
17 Ibid.
18 Ibid.
19 Karen Johnson PhD (USA Volleyball Executive Committee member) in discussion with the author, January 15, 2003.
20 Ibid.
21 Ibid.
22 Shewman, B., *Volleyball Centennial: First 100 Years*. Louisville, KY: Masters Press, 1996.
23 Beal, *Spike*.
24 Ibid.
25 Couvillon, A. *Sands of Time: 1895–1969*. Information Guides, 2002. Couvillon, A. *Sands of Time: 1970–1989*. Information Guides, 2003. Couvillon, A. *Sands of Time: 1990–2004*. Information Guides, 2004.
26 Ibid.
27 Ibid.
28 Ibid.
29 Ibid.
30 Ibid.
31 Ibid.
32 USA Volleyball, "Eugene Selznick", www.volleyhall.org/eugene-selznick.html (accessed 20 March 2016).
33 USA Volleyball, "Mary Jo Peppler", www.volleyhall.org/mary-jo-peppler.html (accessed 20 March 2016).

34 USA Volleyball, "Sinjin Smith", www.volleyhall.org/Sinjin-smith.html (accessed 20 March 2016).
35 USA Volleyball, "Harry Wilson", www.volleyhall.org/harry-wilson.html (accessed 20 March 2016).
36 USA Volleyball, "Douglas Beal", www.volleyhall.org/douglas-beal.html (accessed 20 March 2016).
37 USA Volleyball, "Flo Hyman", www.volleyhall.org/flo-hyman.html (accessed 20 March 2016).
38 USA Volleyball, "Lang Ping", www.volleyhall.org/lang-ping.html (accessed 20 March 2016).
39 "Kerri Walsh Jennings", Beach Volleyball Database, www.bvbinfo.com/player.asp?ID=1923 (accessed 20 March 2016); Branch, John, "Kerri Walsh Jennings Seeks Olympic Success With a New Partner", *New York Times*, 8 July 2016.
40 Ng, Kwok. (2015). *When Sitting is Not Resting: Sitting Volleyball.* www.alibris.com.

Part II
Combat sports

12

Boxing

Gerald Gems

Individual combat inevitably started at the dawn of time, but by 1700 BCE more formal boxing became a part of military training in China. There is evidence of boxing as an Olympic sporting event as early as 688 BCE.[1] Greek influence spread throughout the Mediterranean for centuries thereafter, and Etruscans adopted the sport by the sixth century BCE. Their successors, the Romans, added an additional measure of ferocity by inserting spikes in the caestus (gloves), which made the contest 'more like a knife fight than a boxing match.'[2] African fighters may have adopted the caestus as early as the second century BCE, and a similar form of boxing is still practiced in Sudan, Chad, Nigeria, Cameroon, Niger, and Angola, while bare knuckle bouts have endured in South Africa for centuries. An alternative form, kickboxing, has been practiced in Southeast Asia since at least the thirteenth century.[3]

Boxing did not reach global proportions until the early twentieth century. Allen Guttmann's framework of modern sport characteristics include a governing body that sets rules and regulations for the activity, specialized roles and sites, and professionalism, all of which the Greeks displayed in varied measures. They lacked the characteristics of quantification, the quest for records, and commercialized events, which began to appear in early modern England.[4]

Initial forms of dueling with cudgels and swords had transitioned into fistic encounters by the early eighteenth century and James Figg, adept at all three forms of combat, was acknowledged as the English boxing champion by 1719. Social class has always been a factor in boxing and men of the lower rank often fought for the amusement and largesse of wealthy patrons of the sport. The sanctions of upper class males protected the sport from undue interference by those who questioned its morality and legality. Boxing also crossed gender lines as a female bout was recorded by 1722 and others continued throughout the decade with Elizabeth Stokes declaring herself to be the female champion of London. James Figg, acknowledged as the male champion of England opened an amphitheater that sponsored both male and female bouts. In 1743 Jack Broughton, a boxer and promoter, refined the rough and tumble, free for all rules to eliminate gouging and low blows, and established parameters for the boxing ring, as well as judgments for knockdowns and decisions. Additional regulations, known as the Marquis of Queensberry rules, were further defined to establish timed rounds and the use of padded gloves in 1867 as the sport moved toward greater regulation.[5]

In what might be termed the linguistic period boxing spread through parts of the English speaking empire during the remainder of the eighteenth century. By mid-century Irish boxers traveled to England to engage in matches and Peter Corcoran, an Irishman, claimed the Hibernian championship from 1769 to 1776. By the end of the century Scottish boxers also contended for honors and the great Anglo-Jewish fighter, Daniel Mendoza, embarked on a tour of Ireland in 1791, while another Englishman defeated a French pugilist in London that same year. As the British rationalized their colonial successes by superior intelligence, culture, morality, and physicality racial comparisons became more prominent in the head to head combat of boxers. Mendoza tested himself against Irish and English foes, and both Welsh and black boxers challenged the British specimens in prize fights for lucre and honor. Boxing appeared in the British colony in South Africa soon after the imperial navy gained control in 1795. British settlers in America also brought their sporting interests across the Atlantic, and southern plantation owners matched their slaves against one another or wagered against the champions of other slavekeepers. A former slave, Bill Richmond, became the valet of British general Hugh Percy and returned to England with him during the American Revolution, where he gained prominence as a boxer. Richmond unsuccessfully challenged Tom Cribb, the British champion in 1805, but won his last bout at the age of 55.[6]

Richmond served as the trainer for another American black, Tom Molyneaux, who had honed his pugilistic skills on the New York docks; but sought greater fortune in England, where he, too, challenged Tom Cribb in 1810. Molyneaux lost a disputed decision, and the rematch a year later fostered ardent nationalism. 'No pugilist . . . offered a challenge to Molineaux [sic], nor could he get a battle on until Tom Cribb, who had publicly announced his retirement from the ring, was called upon to "prevent the championship of England from being held by a foreigner" . . .'[7] An estimated 20,000 spectators turned out to view the spectacle, and a reporter claimed that 'for twenty miles within the seat of the action not a bed could be obtained on the preceding night; and by six o'clock the next morning, hundreds were in motion to get a good place near the stage, which even at that early period proved a difficult task.' Once again, Cribb triumphed. Molyneaux toured Ireland thereafter, where he died in 1818.[8]

Boxing assumed greater development within the English speaking world concurrently. The first recorded match in Australia took place in 1814, with international bouts occurring by 1824. The first recognized bout for the championship of the United States occurred when Jacob Hyer defeated Tom Beasley in a New York match in 1816. By that time the confrontations within the British Isles between English, Irish, Welsh, Scots, and American contenders extended to France, as English fighters sparred in Paris exhibitions for dignitaries from several countries, including Prussians, Russians, and Austrians. In 1818 three Englishmen again traveled throughout France performing for Russian, Prussian, and German princes as well as assorted other nobility and military officers. The first Australian fighter, Izaac Gorrick (aka 'Bungaree'), arrived in England in 1842 and by mid-century technological advances allowed for greater ease of travel as clipper ships plied international waters.[9]

The invention of the telegraph would eventually speed the news of athletic results to international audiences, further enhancing nationalistic challenges. In 1849 Tom Hyer, the son of Jacob Hyer, defeated 'Yankee' Sullivan, an Irish immigrant, for the American championship in a battle that symbolized the conflict between nativists and ethnic newcomers, duly reported by the print media.[10] In 1860 John C. Heenan traveled to England to match his skills against Tom Sayers, the British champion. The hotly contested battle, declared a draw, generated more publicity than any other sporting event of the period, resulting in recriminations on both sides of the Atlantic. Heenan returned to England for an 1863 bout with then British champ Tom King. By 1870 English heavyweights arrived in New Orleans in a transatlantic exchange and Canadian

George Godfrey invaded Boston as the British Commonwealth sought to demonstrate its global preeminence in comparison to the growing power of the United States. [11]

The years after 1880 might be termed the age of media as first print journalism and then radio fostered the construction and promotion of racial, ethnic, and national boxing heroes. Richard Kyle Fox, an Irish immigrant to the United States, gained control of the *National Police Gazette*, a weekly newspaper that became the sporting bible of the bachelor subculture. Fox featured boxing matches and promoted the sport by offering opulent championship belts as trophies to the best boxers in each designated weight class, which allowed for more equitable competition and a measure of specialization. The *Gazette* extolled the bare knuckle championship bouts of the 1880s, creating media spectacles and heroic figures, soon followed by the mainstream press that envied Fox's circulation figures. Paddy Ryan took 87 rounds to knockout the English heavyweight Joe Goss in 1880. Two years later Ryan lost his title to the upstart John L. Sullivan, whose enmity with Fox was played out in the *Gazette* and only increased the popularity of the sport. Sullivan's celebrity earned him acknowledgement as the first great American sports star over the next decade and the media celebration of the sport and its practitioners reached international proportions by the 1890s, greatly aided by the transatlantic telegraph cable that allowed for the transmission of sports results. [12]

Imperialism and the testing of Social Darwinian beliefs in the survival of the fittest provided greater impetus to the sport as colonizers and the colonized pitted themselves against one another throughout the later nineteenth century. As nations met in war on the world's battlefields, boxing provided the ultimate test of man to man combat without the benefit of technology or industrialized weaponry. A public display of one's masculinity took on even greater importance as a rising tide of feminism threatened male power. Boxing offered regular ritualized demonstrations of male hegemony in response.

But women, too, challenged the prescribed gender boundaries of Victorian culture by boxing. In England women appeared as boxers, taking on men in tents at county fairs, where spectators paid to watch and bet on such spectacles. In the United States female vaudevillians put on boxing exhibitions, but graduated to full competition with national championships at stake, promoted by Richard Kyle Fox's *Police Gazette*. By the 1890s Hattie Leslie, Hattie Stewart, and Cecil Richards were all acknowledged as female world champions. Richards had defeated Hattie Moore, the female champion of Australia, in 1896 and even challenged the male champions of the era, who refused to put their masculinity on the line. [13]

Boxing held substantial interest throughout the British Empire by the 1880s, as a Scotsmen, James Robertson Couper, claimed the South African championship after defeating Joe Coverwell, the Malay favorite, in 1883. Australians adopted the Marquis of Queensberry rules a year later. Billy Palmer, a former Australian boxer turned trainer, became famous for his defensive techniques and both Peter Jackson, the black heavyweight who traveled to Australia from the West Indies in 1879, and Bob Fitzsimmons, born in England and raised in New Zealand, were among his pupils. Jackson won the Australian championship in 1886 and fought in the United States, England, and France thereafter. He defeated Jem Mace, the British champion in England in a non-title fight and earned a draw with James J. Corbett in the United States in 1891. Corbett subsequently defeated John L. Sullivan to become the American champion, but denied Jackson a rematch. Fitzsimmons also embarked for the United States and conquered Corbett to gain the world championship in 1897. Boxing had become a global enterprise by the late nineteenth century as boxing took root in China, Singapore, and Hawaii during the 1890s and would continue to attract new practitioners and new audiences after 1900. The martial arts had a long tradition in Asian countries and the British occupation of territories as well as the Spanish–American War of 1898 brought soldiers and American entrepreneurs to the Philippines, where the military taught boxing to the indigenous peoples. Promoter Frank Churchill initiated weekly bouts in Manila by 1910.[14]

The United States had become an international center for boxing by the end of the nineteenth century as the perceived feminization of culture and consequent crisis of masculinity spurred a reactionary attraction to the martial sports of football and boxing. The upper classes took instruction in the art of self-defense, and even President Teddy Roosevelt had such a tutor while in the White House. Lower class males, more assured of their physicality, engaged in commercialized spectacles in which promoters offered large purses to combatants. To earn ever greater cash prizes fighters needed a string of victories against lesser opponents in order to market themselves as local, regional, or national champions. [15]

An Australian, Albert Griffiths, who fought under the name of Young Griffo, beat New Zealander 'Torpedo' Billy Murphy for the featherweight crown in 1890, but sought greater fortune in the USA in 1893, where he lost to Solly Garcia-Smith, a Mexican-American from California, and George Dixon, a black Canadian, who reigned over the bantamweights and featherweights of the era. As a nineteen-year-old, Dixon had traveled to England in 1890, where he won the bantamweight crown of the British champion, Nunc Wallace. In 1891 Dixon returned to the United States, where he gained the undisputed featherweight title against another Australian, Abe Willis.[16]

Both Dixon and Garcia-Smith represented a host of racial and ethnic migrants who learned and bettered their craft in the United States. Swiss born Frank Erne captured the lightweight championship, Jack Root hailed from Czechoslovakia, Battling Nelson left Denmark, and Stanley Ketchel, from Poland, was considered an all-time great as a middleweight. Barbados Joe Walcott arrived in the United States in 1897, while American stars Joe Gans fought in Australia, and lightweight champ Kid Lavigne and heavyweight Jim Jeffries travelled to England. Another black fighter, Bobby Dobbs, opened boxing schools in France and Germany between 1898 and 1901 and a year later Erne traveled to London and then trained French boxers in Paris as boxing increasingly extended across transnational markets. Throughout the era the American military and American influence fostered the growth of the sport in the Philippines, the Caribbean, Central and South America. Boxing films, developed in the 1890s, made the sport increasingly popular in Europe and American fighters quickly realized the entrepreneurial opportunities.[17]

Kid Mc Coy (Norman Selby), the colorful American middleweight, embarked on a tour to South Africa in 1896, where he claimed that country's championship, and proceeded on to Australia and the Pacific region. In 1901 he traveled to England, where he scored three knockouts over British fighters. Aaron Brown (aka 'Dixie Kid'), an African American, and welterweight champ from 1904–1908, gained his greatest fame fighting in Europe, as did Andrew Jeptha, a South African welterweight.[18]

The Social Darwinian presumptions of the era as well as the nationalistic fervor that preceded the First World War gave great impetus to the individual confrontations inherent in the sport of boxing. In 1904 the American organizers of the Olympic Games added boxing to the program. The United States increasingly served as the core market for boxing spectacles, while other regions offered contests on the periphery of the global marketplace. When Canadian Tommy Burns (Noah Brusso) gained the heavyweight championship in 1906 he took on all comers and defended the title in a global tour that took him to London, Dublin, Paris, and Sydney, Australia. In Sydney in 1908 Burns lost his title to the African American Jack Johnson, which engendered a search for any 'Great White Hope' who might return the championship to the presumably superior Caucasian race. Johnson's flamboyant lifestyle and his marriages to white women so antagonized the white authorities that they generated a legal crusade to imprison him and wrest his laurels from him. Johnson's consequent exile and his peregrinations only enhanced his fame and the interest in black fighters.[19]

The racial oppression prevalent in the United States at that time caused many blacks to seek their fortune elsewhere, and France held a particular appeal. Top fighters such as Sam McVey headed to Paris in 1907, followed by Jack Johnson, Joe Jennette, and Sam Langford. Langford, a Canadian by birth, claimed the heavyweight championship of England, Australia, Canada, and Mexico during his career. McVey's travels took him to England, France, Belgium, Australia, Argentina, and Panama. Both McVey and Jennette became fan favorites in Paris, where French men and women developed a fascination with the black body.[20]

Historian Theresa Runstedtler has termed the American blacks as 'figures of fear and desire' during their French sojourn, and the 1909 bout between McVey and Jennette (that lasted 49 rounds) brought ticket requests from 'London, Brussels, Liege, Anvers, Geneva, Roubaix, Lille, Troyes, Rouen, Reims, Orleans, and even Bordeaux,' with thousands turned away.[21] Bobby Dobbs enjoyed similar acclaim in Denmark the following year, where he easily defeated the local heroes and opened a boxing school in Copenhagen. In Berlin he conquered both German and other American boxers while providing pugilistic instruction to Kaiser Wilhelm's family, and then took his talents to Austria and Hungary.[22] The cultural flow that originated in England was thus reversed by the twentieth century as Americans cultivated the sport in Europe.

In Europe race became an exotic, erotic commodity that could be sold in the boxing arena; but the sport held additional significance for the French, with the ever present and increasing danger of war with Germany. Georges Carpentier rose from a circus performer to a European champion, traversing the European continent and traveling to the United States in his quest for a world title. His post-First World War bout with Jack Dempsey in 1921, promoted by Tex Rickard, brought the first million dollar gate in boxing history, and only engendered even larger spectacles and foreign challengers. In 1922 Carpentier lost his European light heavyweight title to Battling Siki, who was born in Senegal, a French colony in Africa. Dempsey would then take on the Argentinian Angel Luis Firpo in 1923, the wildest fight on record, which produced another million-dollar till. The United States became a mecca for all Argentinian fighters thereafter.[23] The Spanish speaking Firpo became a hero in Mexico, which soon spawned its own stars.

Boxing had reached such global proportions by 1913 that representatives from France, England, Belgium, and Switzerland, with approval of the New York commission, formed the International Boxing Union (IBU); but it ceased to function when the First World War erupted. The organization resumed operations in Paris in 1920; but the International Sporting Club, a British association operating in New York, made an unsuccessful attempt to regulate the sport. Despite the failure of governing bodies and reformers' efforts to ban boxing, the sport flourished. Boxing films and new medium of radio created athletic celebrities. Promoters and sportswriters heightened public interest by portraying nationalistic and racialized images of foreign or non-white fighters as a Social Darwinian contest for supremacy. African Americans were cast in the Sambo image, Firpo became the 'Wild Bull of the Pampas,' and Siki was likened to a chimpanzee, as entrepreneurs sought exotic warriors throughout the globalizing marketplace.[24]

In the United States and Great Britain a variety of ethnic, racial, and religious groups contended for greater inclusion in the mainstream society. Sport provided one means for greater visibility and acceptance. In the boxing ring, Jews replaced Irish champions, and Benny Leonard (Benjamin Leiner) ruled the lightweight ranks from 1917 to 1925 while wearing the Star of David on his boxing trunks and refusing to fight on Jewish holidays. Jews were then supplanted by a host of Italian champions, who wore the laurels for a generation.[25]

In the Pacific a nexus of Asian boxing developed between the Philippines, Japan, Hawaii, and the west coast of the United States as upstarts sought greater recognition and bigger paydays and over the hill professionals sought to prolong their careers. Francisco Guilledo, a Filipino better known as Pancho Villa, became the most famous as the world flyweight champion from 1923 to 1925. American sportswriters characterized Villa's conquests of white opponents as the work of an inhuman demon or a monkey; but Filipinos idolized him as a hero who negated Anglos' perceptions of racial superiority in a counter-hegemonic response to colonialism. Authorities in the Philippines instituted collegiate boxing programs in 1923 with the intent of molding their charges into models of American civilization. Governor General Leonard Wood reasoned that 'Boxing develops every muscle in the human body, quickens the brain, sharpens the wits, imparts force, and, above all, it teaches self-control.'[26]

In South Africa both the black working classes as well as the upper classes began to pursue boxing as a means of social uplift by the 1920s. Boxing clubs in Johannesburg offered to teach lessons in 'civility, discipline, respectability, independence, and self-defence.' Indian and other 'colored' fighters centered in Cape Town and Durban, where Joe Louis, an African American, would become a heroic symbol for the racially oppressed in the 1930s.[27] In neighboring Rhodesia (now Zimbabwe) historian Terence Ranger claimed that 'boxing . . . had sprung up and become enormously popular without any direct European instigation, patronage, or influence at all.' Government-sponsored bouts served as a means of social control and transferred more deadly tribal rivalries to a surrogate form of warfare.[28]

Throughout the 1920s and early 1930s Paulino Uzcudun, a Basque heavyweight, carried the flag for Spain as he challenged American supremacy. Uzcudun's brawling style left him susceptible to negative stereotypes, and he lost to the Fascist strongman, Primo Carnera of Italy, twice (1930, 1933), who was also racialized by sportswriters. Race continued to factor into boxing comparisons as Max Schmeling, a German, attained the championship. Each fought Joe Louis in the 1930s as race meshed with politics to produce symbolic clashes between democracy and fascism that only heightened the interest in boxing as Europe moved closer to real carnage throughout the decade. [29]

By that time Panama Al Brown had emerged as the world bantamweight champion (1929–1935, 1938) and Mexican and Caribbean fighters entered the fray at lower weight classes. A Cuban, Kid Chocolate (Eligio Sardinias Montalvo), entered the pro ranks in 1927 as a seventeen-year-old and claimed both the light welterweight (1931–1933) and featherweight titles (1932–1934) by 1932. Sixto Escobar, the first Puerto Rican champion, succeeded Brown as bantamweight champ by beating the Mexican Baby Casanova, who had won 42 of his 43 fights by knockouts. Puerto Ricans feted Escobar upon his return to the islands and named a stadium after him to commemorate his triumph. His 1937 title defense in San Juan was the first to be contested on the island and it was claimed that he 'brought the game of boxing at [sic] Puerto Rico from nothing more than club-fighting to international spotlight, and spawned a whole new generation of fight fans and boxers.' [30]

Boxing held such widespread appeal that even amateurs engaged in transcontinental matches. Both the New York *Daily News* and the *Chicago Tribune* offered amateur tournaments as promotional ventures, which became intercity contests known as the Golden Gloves in 1928. A combined all-star team from the two cities fought a French contingent in Chicago's Soldier Field stadium in 1931. Bernard Sheil, the Catholic bishop of Chicago, initiated a comprehensive athletic program throughout all Chicago parishes in 1930 as a means of social control aimed at male youths. Boxing remained the core of the Catholic Youth Organization (CYO) and it shared fighters with the Golden Gloves and provided athletes to the 1936 US Olympic team. The best boxers competed on the CYO's international boxing squad that traveled across the world, competing in Hawaii, Panama, and against opponents from France, Ireland, Poland, Italy, Germany, and South America.[31]

In the post-Second World War era television spurred great interest in boxing as Rocky Marciano supplanted a host of black fighters as the only undefeated heavyweight champion. Another African American, however, was widely acclaimed as the greatest fighter of all time, as Sugar Ray Robinson's (Walker Smith, Jr.) career lasted twenty-five years in which he accumulated six world championships in the welterweight and middleweight classes against top contenders. His six encounters with Jake La Motta were among the most brutal in boxing history.[32]

Robinson's long tenure ushered in the civil rights movement of the mid-twentieth century and its most prominent athletic activist, Muhammad Ali. Ali not only fought some of the most memorable battles in the ring against Sonny Liston, Joe Frazier, and George Foreman; but took on the United States government as well. Ali contended that his Black Muslim religion forbid his participation in the Vietnam War, for which his title was revoked, as he fought only in the courts for nearly four years. Ali eventually won on both counts, forcing the government to honor his constitutional rights of freedom of speech and freedom of religion, and regaining his heavyweight championship in a series of international fights that made him a global icon for Muslims around the world and African nations engaged in their own struggles for independence.[33]

Ali's ascendance also marked the rise of not only black, but Hispanic and Asian boxers across all weight classes. Thais, Koreans, and Japanese claimed the titles in the lower weight classes throughout the remainder of the century; while Hispanics vied largely with African Americans for supremacy in other ranks. Julio Cesar Chavez, a Mexican fighter. Went undefeated for fourteen straight years and claimed the championship in three weight divisions. A Mexican-American, Oscar De La Hoya, won titles across several weight classes from 1993 to 2007, while parlaying his fame and celebrity into entrepreneurial ventures as a promoter. A Nicaraguan, Alexis Arguello, and Panamanian Roberto Duran won multiple titles while engaging in some of the greatest fistic encounters in boxing history. At the turn of the twenty-first century Filipino Manny Pacquiao was deemed by many to be the greatest pound for pound boxer in the world. He held eight titles in four weight divisions (due to the proliferation of competing governing bodies), to become one of the highest paid athletes in the world. His success fostered greater opportunities to extend his brand, resulting in multiple vocations as a singer, actor, professional basketball team owner, and politician.[34]

Women's boxing, too, has gradually reached international proportions with the establishment of the International Women's Boxing Federation in 1992. The first televised bout occurred in 1996 featured American Christy Martin and Ireland's Deirdre Gogarty and world championships followed in 2001, producing such stars as the German Regina Halmich, the Netherlands, Lucia Rijker, and Laila Ali, daughter of Muhammad Ali. With the inclusion of Olympic competition for women in 2012 female boxers surmounted another long standing gender barrier.[35]

Although the sport of boxing has largely given way to mixed martial arts (MMA) events in America and Europe, it still enjoys a good deal of popularity in other regions of the world. Poverty supplies a continuous labor force as the working class chases dreams in a quest for celebrity, a measure of fame, and at least a temporary social mobility that has continued as a premodern vestige in modern times.

Notes

1 S.G. Miller, *Ancient Greek Athletics* (New Haven, CVT: Yale University Press, 2004), 22–3.
2 T.F. Scanlon quoted in S.R. Murray, 'Boxing Gloves of the Ancient World', *Journal of Combat Sport* (July 2010); http://ejmas.com/jcs/jcsframe.htm (12 June 2012).
3 G.R. Gems, *Boxing: A Concise History of the Sweet Science* (Lanham, MD: Rowman & Littlefield, 2014), 5–8.

4 A. Guttmann, *From Ritual to Record* (New York: Columbia University Press, 1978). D. Terry, 'Boxing: Some Early British History,' *Annual of CESH* (2003), 41–50, traces the evolution of boxing in England from the fifteenth to the eighteenth centuries.

5 P. Egan, *Boxiana* (London: Smeeton 1812), 10–22, 43–4, 258–59 (Toronto: Nicol Island Pub., 1997 ed.); H.D. Miles, *Pugilistica: the History of British Boxing* (Edinburgh: John Grant, 1906), 9–61; R.J. Park, 'Contesting the Norm: Women and Professional Sports in Late Nineteenth-Century America,' *International Journal of the History of Sport*, 29,5 (April 2012), 730–49; Terry, 'Boxing.' B. Heiskanen, 'Boxing,' in S.A. Riess, ed., *Sports in America: From Colonial Times to the Twenty-First Century* (Armonk, NY: M.E. Sharpe, 2011), 188–97, offers a good, succinct rendition of the rules and boxing history in the United States.

6 Egan, *Boxiana*, 60–61, 216–41, 392–403; Miles, *Pugilistica*, 79–140, 372–88; T.J. Desch Obi, 'Black Terror: Bill Richmond's Revolutionary Boxing,' *Journal of Sport History*, 36,1 (Spring 2009), 99–114; D.K. Wiggins, 'Good Times on the Old Plantation: Popular Recreations of the Black Slave in the Antebellum South, 1810–1860,' *Journal of Sport History*, 4 (1977), 260–84; S. Lussana, 'To See Who Was the Best on the Plantation: Enslaved Fighting Contests and Masculinity in the Antebellum Plantation South,' *Journal of Southern History*, 76,4 (November 2010), 901–22. See R. Jackson, 'The origins of boxing in SA,' www.supersport.com/boxing/blogs/ron-jackson/The origins of boxing in SA (July 8, 2011), on South Africa.

7 Miles, *Pugilistica*, 363 (quote); Egan, *Boxiana*, 354–62.

8 Egan, *Boxiana*, 363 (quote), 362–75 provides a full account of the fight and its aftermath.

9 See www.aussiebox.com/australian-boxing-history.php (July 8, 2011); M. L. Adelman, 'Pedestrianism, Billiards, Boxing and Animal Sports,' in D.K. Wiggins, ed., *Sport in America: From Colonial Leisure to Celebrity Figures and Globalization* (Champaign, IL: Human Kinetics, 2010), 45–83; Miles, *Pugilistica*, 386, 393, 601–02.

10 *Spirit of the Times*, February 17, 1849, 618–19, in G.B. Kirsch, ed., *Sports in North America: A Documentary History, vol. 3: The Rise of Modern Sports, 1840–1860* (Gulf Breeze, FL: Academic International, 1992), 121–29; Adelman, 'Pedestrianism, Billiards, Boxing and Animal Sports,' 63–70.

11 Kirsch, ed., *Sports in North America*, vol. 3, 115–16, 141–54; Adelman, 'Pedestrianism, Billiards, Boxing and Animal Sports,' 64–66, 71. See *Winnipeg Free Press*, June 6, 1879, 1, March 18, 1881, 4, and March 22, 1882, 8, on early boxing in Canada.

12 G. Reel, *The National Police Gazette and the Making of the Modern American Man, 1879–1906* (New York: Palgrave Macmillan, 2006); E.J. Gorn and W. Goldstein, *A Brief History of American Sports* (New York: Hill & Wang, 1993), 115–24; D. Welky, 'National Police Gazette,' in Riess, *Sports in America*, 654–56; G.R. Gems, *Sports in North America; A Documentary History, vol. 5, Sports Organized, 1880–1900* (Gulf Breeze, FL: Academic International, 1996), 199.

13 Gems, *Boxing*, 209–38; M. Smith, *A History of Women's Boxing* (Lanham, MD: Rowman & Littlefield, 2014); G. Gems and G. Pfister 'Women Boxers: Actresses to Athletes – The Role of Vaudeville in Early Women's Boxing in the USA,' *International Journal of the History of Sport*, 31,15 (2014), 1909–24.

14 See *North China Herald* (Shanghai), Jan. 16, 1891, 15, March 18, 1892, 3, for early matches in China and Singapore. www.aussiebox.com/australian-boxing-history.php (July 7, 2011); D.K. Wiggins, 'Peter Jackson and the Elusive Heavyweight Championship: A Black Athlete's Struggle against the Late Nineteenth Century Color Line,' *Journal of Sport History*, 12 (Summer 1985), 143–68; B. Petersen, 'Peter Jackson: Heavyweight Champion of Australia,' in C. Aycock and M. Scott, *The First Black Boxing Champions* (Jefferson, NC: Mc Farland, 2011), 32–47; www.fitzsimmons.co.nz/main.html (October18, 2011). See G.R. Gems, *The Athletic Crusade: Sport and American Cultural Imperialism* (Lincoln: University of Nebraska Press, 2006), 56; and J. R. Svinth, 'The Origins of Philippines Boxing, 1899–1926,' *Journal of Combative Sport* (July 2001) at http://ejmas.com/jcs/jcsart_svinth_0701.htm (July 8, 2011); D. Stradley, 'A look at the history of boxing in the Philippines,' http://sports.espn.go.com/sports/boxing/news/story?id=3458707 (July 8, 2011).

15 E.A. Rotundo, *American Manhood: Transformations in Masculinity from the Revolution to the Modern Era* (New York: Basic Books, 1993); A. Douglas, *The Feminization of American Culture* (New York: Anchor Books, 1977; and G. R. Gems, *For Pride, Profit, and Patriarchy: Football and the Incorporation of American Cultural Values* (Lanham, MD: Scarecrow Press, 2000), 46–70. See D. Fridman and D. Sheinin, 'Wild Bulls, Discarded Foreigners, and Brash Champions: US Empire and the Cultural Constructions of Argentine Boxers,' *Left History* 12,1 (Spring/Summer 2007), 52–77, on the globalization of the boxing labor market.

16 See http://cyberboxingzone.com/boxing/griffo-young.htm (October 18, 2011); http://cyberboxing-zone.com/boxing/smith-s.htm (October 18, 2011); M. Glenn, 'George Dixon: World Bantamweight and Featherweight Champion,' in C. Aycock and M. Scott, *The First Black Boxing Champions*, 48–59.

17 C. Aycock and M. Scott, *Joe Gans: A Biography of the First African American World Boxing Champ* (Jefferson, NC: McFarland & Co., 2008), 46, 53–4, 66, 96, 131, 133; R. V. McGehee, 'Boxing in Latin America from the Bull of the Pampas to Julius Caesar,' presentation delivered at the North American Society for Sport History Conference, Austin, Texas, May 30, 2011.

18 *The Day*, March 10, 1914, 2; 'Kid McCoy, Once Greatest Scrapper, Tells How He Used to Get the Coin in the Olden Days,' *Milwaukee Sentinel*, August 1, 1915, 10. C. van Ingen, '"Dixie Kid" Aaron Brown: World Welterweight Champ,' in Aycock and Scott, *The First Black Boxing Champions*, 129–43. See http://boxrec.com/list_bouts.php?human_id=45977&cat=boxer on Jeptha.

19 G. R. Gems, 'Jack Johnson and the Quest for Racial Respect,' in D. K. Wiggins, ed., *Out of the Shadows: A Biographical History of African American Athletes* (Fayetteville, AK: University of Arkansas Press, 2006), 59–77. See *Illustr. Osterr Sportblatt*, (January 7, 1911– December 9, 1911) on European coverage and boxing films in Germany.

20 C. Moyle, 'Sam Langford: Heavyweight Champion of Australia, Canada, England, and Mexico,' in Aycock and Scott, *The First Black Boxing Champions*, 158–70; http://boxrec.com/list_bouts. php?human_id=011023&cat=boxer&pageID=3 (Nov. 26, 2011); and A. Pierpaoli, 'Joe Jennette and Sam McVey: Colored Heavyweight Champions,' in Aycock and Scott, *The First Black Boxing Champions*, 171–99; http://boxrec.com/list_bouts.php?human_id=011631&cat=boxer&pageID=3.

21 T. Runstedtler, 'African American Boxers, the New Negro, and the Global Color Line,' *Radical History Review*, 103 (Winter 2009), 59–81, (quotes, 61, 66, respectively).

22 Aycock and Scott, *The First Black Boxing Champions*, 72–5.

23 Runstedtler, 'African American Boxers, the New Negro, and the Global Color Line,' 63, 67; http://boxrec.com/media/index.php/Battling_Siki (Nov. 29, 2011); J. Waltzer, *The Battle of the Century: Dempsey, Carpentier, and the Birth of Modern Promotion* (Santa Barbara: Praeger, 2011); Fridman and Sheinin, 'Wild Bulls, Discarded Foreigners, and Brash Champions'.

24 See http://boxrec.com/media/index.php/International_Boxing_Union (Nov. 29, 2011); see *The Perry (Iowa) Daily Chief*, Dec. 28, 1920, 7, the *Sandusky, Ohio Register*, Jan. 13, 1921, 8, and the *Joplin, Missouri Globe*, Jan. 13, 1921, 5, on failed attempts to form regulating bodies. R. Roberts, *Papa Jack: Jack Johnson and the Era of White Hopes* (New York: Free Press, 1983); http://boxrec.com/media/index.php/Battling_Siki (Nov. 29, 2011); see 'Frank Klaus Sees Firpo in Action,' *New York Times*, September 2, 1923, 18; *Uniontown, PA. Morning Herald*, July 16, 1923, 6, and *Oakland Tribune*, September 14, 1923, 34; 'Firpo Had The Title Within His Grasp,' *New York Times*, September 15, 1923, 1; and Sid Sutherland, 'Latin Lacks Ring Wit to Cope with Yank, the Experienced,' *E*, September 15, 1923, 11. See G. Early, 'Battling Siki as 'Other': the Boxer as Natural Man,' *Massachusetts Review*, 29,3 (Fall 1988), 451–72.

25 Gems, *Boxing*, 137–88; G. R. Gems, *Sport and the Shaping of Italian-American Identity* (Syracuse, NY: Syracuse University Press, 2013).

26 Oriental and Pacific Boxing Federation: History, at www.opbf.jp/info/history.html (July 8, 2011); Gems, *The Athletic Crusade*, 60–1, 77; Svinth, 'The Origins of Filipino Boxing,' 6 (quote).

27 T. Fleming, '"Now the African reigns supreme': The rise of African boxing on the Witwatersrand, 1924– 1959,' *International Journal of the History of Sport*, 28,1 (January 2011), 47–62, (quote, 47).

28 T. Ranger, 'Pugilism and Pathology: African Boxing and the Black Urban Experience in Southern Rhodesia,' in W. J. Baker and J. A. Mangan, eds. *Sport in Africa: Essays in Social History* (New York: Africana Pub. Co., 1987), 196–213 (quote, 199).

29 J. S. Page, *Primo Carnera: The Life and Career of the Heavyweight Boxing Champion* (Jefferson, NC: McFarland, 2011); www.boxinginsider.com/history/men-of-iron-paulino-uzcudun (Nov.29, 2011); D. Margolick, *Beyond Glory: Joe Louis, Max Schmeling, and the World on the Brink* (New York: Alfred A. Knopf, 2005).

30 See http://boxrec.com/media/index.php/Panama-Al_Brown (July 8, 2011); http://cyberboxingzone. com/boxing/kidchoc.htm; http://boxrec.com/media/index.php/Sixto_Escobar (Nov. 29, 2011); http://boxrec.com/media/index.php/Sixto_Escobar_vs._Rodolfo_(Baby)_Casanova (Nov. 29, 2011); J. J. Mac Aloon, 'La Pitada Olimpica,' 326, cited in Gems, *Athletic Crusade*, 105; Sixto Escobar file, International Boxing Hall of Fame. See J. Iber, S. O. Regalado, J. M. Alamillo, and A. De Leon, *Latinos in U.S. Sport: A History of Isolation, Cultural Identity, and Acceptance* (Champaign, IL: Human Kinetics, 2011), 101–42, on the rise of Mexican and Caribbean boxers.

31 G.R. Gems, 'Sport, Religion and Americanization: Bishop Sheil and the Catholic Youth Organization,' *International Journal of the History of Sport*, 10,2 (August 1993), 233–41; G.R. Gems, 'The Politics of Boxing: Resistance, Religion, and Working Class Assimilation,' *International Sports Journal*, 8,1 (Winter 2004), 89–103.
32 Gems, *Boxing*, 114–17.
33 Ibid, 118–23.
34 Ibid, 129–35, 177–88.
35 Ibid, 230–38.

13

Mixed martial arts

Hongxin Li and Samuel Nabors

Mixed martial arts (MMA) is a relatively new sport. Also known as cage fighting or ultimate fighting, MMA is a full-contact sport, allowing fighters with various background to use different techniques of judo, karate, taekwondo, kickboxing, and other types of martial arts to compete against each other. Usually, in MMA, there are few rules and protective gear, and fighters can use striking, kicking, wrestling, locking, choking and grappling techniques while they are either standing or on the ground.

The history of MMA

The origin of MMA can be traced back to 6000 years ago in ancient China. Han Chinese military generals and solders invented shuai jiao, which is an ancient style of martial arts combined kung-fu and wrestling, also recognized as the earliest form of MMA (Matuszak, 2015). They used Shuai Jiao techniques to kill enemy soldiers on the battlefield. Those techniques included kicking, punching, throwing, joint locks, finger locks, leg locks, leg sweeps, and close range trapping techniques, most of which are the key elements of grappling techniques of modern judo and jiu-jitsu ("Mixed Martial Arts," n.d., para. 5).

Hieroglyphics and paintings showing that Egyptian soldiers in Mesopotamia and Sumer (3000 BC to 2300 BC) were training with empty hand fighting techniques. For example, engraved hieroglyphic inscriptions of ancient Egyptians fighting and practicing martial arts were found on the Great Pyramids, and along the Nile River, there are some mural paintings in the ancient Egyptian's tombs showing the same ("History of MMA," n.d., para. 4).

About 3000 years ago, there were three empty-hand combat sports practiced in ancient Greece: wrestling, boxing and pankration. Pankration was known as a sport has ever come to no rules to combat. As the word "pankration" shown, it is composited with two Greek words: "pan" and "kratos," where "pan" means "all," and "kratos" means "powers" (Liddell, 1894). Gradually, pankration, which was an athletic event that combined techniques of wrestling and boxing, as well as other additional elements, became the most popular and it was introduced into the 33rd Olympiads in 648 BC because it filled a niche of "total contest" that neither boxing nor wrestling could (Poliakoff, 1987). Pankration was an event in Olympic Games for around 1000 years.

The techniques of pankration are very similar to techniques in today's MMA competitions, which includes using of takedowns, chokes and locks on the ground, joint locks, and strikes with the legs. According to Georgiou (2008), "pankration" was an empty-hand submission sport with few rules, and only biting and gouging out the opponent's eyes are not acceptable. Later on, pankration was passed on to the Romans as a combat sport (Little & Wong, 2000).

Records also showed that in Siam (Thailand) in 200 BC, muay (a martial art, early form of muay thai) was popular and used to be an important part of local festivals and celebrations. At first, it was used for warfare. Gradually, it became a spectator sport. Different from the modern muay thai, muay had very few rules, which was similar to the MMA matches in these days. To this day, although muay thai is the most popular combat in Thailand, underground MMA matches have continued with few or no rules ("History of MMA," n.d., para. 6).

Dating back to the early 1700s, there were American street fight matches that had no rules, allowed different combat techniques such as boxing, grappling, groin strikes, hair pulling, and even eye gouging. Usually, the brutal bouts, often called as "boxing matches" would not finish unless there was a knockout or a submission ("History of MMA," n.d.).

In the mid of 19th century, a new format of combat, savate, was popular in France. There were matches between French savateurs and English bare-knuckle boxers to find out which type of martial arts is better. Finally, the French fighter Rambaud alias la Resistance beat English fighter Dickinson by using his kicks. Since then, more similar contest occurred because many fighters of other combat styles came to challenge French savateurs (Green, 2010).

Another early example of MMA was "no-holds-barred" fighting. In 1880s, came to prominence throughout the Europe. Wrestlers and other martial arts masters participated in the tournaments and music-hall challenge matches. Similar to the "no-holds-barred" fighting, later in the United States, there were combat matches and fighters could use different types of martial arts. The first game was between a boxer and a wrestler in 1887 (Kent, 1968).

Bartitsu was founded by Edward William Barton-Wright in 1899. In bartitsu, Barton-Wright combined the martial arts of Asian and European fighting styles including catch wrestling, judo, boxing, savate, jiu-jutsu and "canne de combat" (aka French stick fighting) (Noble, 2001). It was reported that Barton could defeat seven larger men within three minutes. Moreover, in order to further developing this martial art, he even invited three Japanese Judo practitioners to his club to serve as instructors. However, the hand injury stopped Barton showing bartitsu to the Prince (*Nugent, 1901*).

In the end of 19th century, there were several forms of martial arts in the Philippines such as boxing, grappling, foot fighting, and weapon-based arts, and people preferred to use swords to settle their differences with duels. Until 1930s, they started to use the full-contact bouts with rattan sticks instead of swords. When the fighters were at close range, they could strike with the butt of the weapon, punches, elbows, knees and kicks, and use the techniques of grappling, submissions, sweeps, and throws, which looked much like the modern MMA. One major difference was that combatant could hold a stick in the right hand and used their left hand to strike or punch the opponent. The match would not stop until one of the combatants was killed or not able to continue. Later on, Filipinos brought this type of combat to Hawaii and California, where some of them became boxers and making a living by boxing ("History of MMA," n.d.).

As for the modern MMA fighting as seen today in the US, it can be traced back to Brazil in the early 20th century and in particular the Gracie family. At the beginning of the 1900s, a judo master, Mitsuyo Maeda, went to Brazil in 1914 for further the work of the Japanese in the colony of Brazil. He met a Brazilian businessman, Gastao Gracie in Belem. In appreciation of the Brazilian businessman's help with business dealings, Maeda taught the skills of judo to his son, Carlos Gracie and his brother, Helio Gracie even though teaching judo to non-Japanese was forbidden at that time. Gracie brothers modified the judo, making it as practical as possible, and rely less on strength and more on leverage. At the beginning, it was hard for Helio to adopt those Judo techniques due to his small statue. For beneficing smaller players, Helio practiced different leverage skills so that he could maximize the efficiency of a technique and have an equal advantage when fighting with a much stronger opponent. Ultimately, employing the techniques of joint locks and chokeholds, the new judo form evolved into a new martial arts form, known as Brazilian jiu-jitsu (Bledsoe, 2009).

In 1920s, with Helio's continuous improvement on jiu-jitsu, Carlos attempted to promote Jiu-jitsu by offering a challenge allowing any man using any martial art request a fight. They named those matches as "vale tudo," which means, "anything goes" in Portuguese. Because of Helio's high winning rate in those "no holds barred" matches, the Gracie brothers enjoyed a widespread reputation in Brazil (Bledsoe, 2009). Until 1950s, vale tudo became well known in Brazil due to a television show in Rio called "Heroes of the Ring." Gracie family was one of the founders and hosted the show. Fighters participated in the "style-versus-style" bouts, including two members from Gracie family, Carlson Gracie and Carley Gracie. However, due to the rules of the vale tudo, one fighter did not submit even though he was caught by his opponent in an armbar, and his arm was broken. Therefore, the show was cancelled and replaced by a wrestling game show. From then on, vale tudo existed as a subculture in south and north region of Brazil ("Vale Tudo," n.d.).

In the late 1960s and early 1970s, Bruce Lee developed jeet kune do in the US, which was a mixed martial art based on Chinese kung fu, boxing, muay thai, wrestling and other types of combats. Bruce Lee's philosophies on jeet kune do, emphasizing the importance of learning advantages from different types of martial arts, were considered as a significant influence on the modern MMA ("Mixed Martial Arts," n.d.). "The best fighter is not a boxer, karate or judo man," Lee once said. "The best fighter is someone who can adapt to any style. He kicks too good for a boxer, throws too good for a karate man, and punches too good for a judo man." Lee's description ultimately became the sport of MMA. Dana White, the president of Ultimate Fighting Championship (UFC), called Bruce Lee as "the father of modern MMA" (Lole, 2012).

In February 12, 1963, there were "muay thai versus karate" fights in Thailand. Three Japanese Karate fighters went to Thailand to challenge three muay thai fighters with three matches. Finally, Karate fighters won by two winnings. Later in June of the same year, another match was hold between the top Thai fighter, Samarn Sor Adisorn and one of the Japanese karate fighters, Tadashi Sawamura. After Sawamura's loss of the game, he would incorporate the skill in the evolving kick boxing tournaments (Duuglas-Ittu, 2015).

In 1983, a Japanese famous pro wrestler, Satoru Sayama created a Shoot Wrestling called "Japanese Shooto." This combat sports derived from Japanese Sambo, Wrestling, Muay Thai, Judo and Jiu-jitsu, highly resembled modern MMA with the techniques of striking and grappling ("History of MMA," n.d.).

In 1970s, Rorion Gracie, one of the sons of Helio Gracie, immigrated to the United States and later he began to introduce jiu-jitsu to the American market. Along with his brothers, Rickson, Royce and Royler, Rorion held up the "Grace Challenge" and offered $100,000 to any challengers who could defeat him or any one of his brothers in the Jiu-jitsu match. Gradually, the Gracies were noticed by the martial arts community in the America ("History of MMA," n.d.).

Although the Gracies was becoming famous in American martial arts community, Rorion was not satisfied with what they had achieved. In 1993, he founded Ultimate Fighting Championship (UFC) as the MMA promotion organization in Las Vegas, Nevada. The purpose of the early UFC was to identify which was the most effective among competitors with different kinds of martial arts. It was promoted as "no-holds-barred" events with no weight classes, no time limits, and few rules in the championship for pay-per-view television. In the first championship tournament (later called UFC 1), Royce Grace beat three challengers in a total of five minutes, which marked a revolution for martial arts ("Ultimate Fighting Championship," n.d.).

In fact, the first event was planned as a one-off. However, the first event of UFC was extremely successful, and it attracted 86,592 television subscribers on the pay-per-view television ("Ultimate Fighting Championship," n.d.). Therefore, those UFC events started to become a continuing series of fighting tournaments. By 1995, eight UFC events had been held ("List of UFC Events," n.d.).

Although the UFC became a successful fight program, it drew many criticisms. Many states in America banned UFC on TV because of the tag line "There are no rules!" and the brutality of the sport (Plotz, 1999). A US senator, John McCain, even called the UFC events "human cockfighting." Banned from pay-per-view in 36 states, UFC came near to bankruptcy. In the late 1990s, many fighters went to Japan to continue their career (Re, 2013).

In 2001, the Station Casinos executives, Frank and Lorenzo Fertitta, along with their business partner, Dana White, purchased the UFC for $2 million. Then they created Zuffa, LLC as the parent entity to control the UFC. From then on, Zuffa began to institute a set body of new rules and work with both the New Jersey State Athletic Control Board, so that the sport could become a sanctioned event in those states and land back on pay-per-view television ("History of MMA," n.d.). After Zuffa's purchase, UFC's pay-per-view clients increased tremendously. For example, UFC 40 event had 150,000 pay-per-view subscribers, which was marked as the "turning point" for the MMA to survive in America ("Ultimate Fighting Championship," n.d.).

In order to promote the UFC, Zuffa created a series called The Ultimate Fighter (TUF), which is a reality television show. From 2005 to 2012, under the leadership of Dana White, TUF made a big success outside the bounds of pay-per-view by cooperating with Spike TV. Since August 2012, starting from TUF's 15th season, the television network has been changed into FOX, so that the TUF's episodes could be edited and broadcast within a week instead of several months (Martin, 2011).

The increased visibility helped the UFC's pay-per-view buy numbers sky rocketed to 620,000 for UFC 60, 775,000 for UFC 61, and more than 1 million for UFC 66 in 2006. At the end of 2006, UFC generated over $222,766,000 in revenue, which broke the record for a single year's business of pay-per-view, and surpassed both WWE and boxing ("Ultimate Fighting Championship," n.d.).

Since 2006, Zuffa started to acquire other MMA programs, including the northern California-based promotion World Extreme Cagefighting (WEC) and Las Vegas rival World Fighting Alliance (WFA). Later, both WEC and WFA were merged into UFC. Another momentous purchase was Zuffa's purchasing Strikeforce. Under Zuffa's ownership, UFC signed many of Strikeforce's top fighters and made some changes. In 2013, after the last Strikeforce show, Zuffa dissolved the promotion for Strikeforce and all the fighters' contracts were either ended or transferred into the UFC ("Ultimate Fighting Championship," n.d.).

In 2016, Zuffa was sold to William Morris Endeavor (WME-IMG) for $4 billion (Rooney, 2016). Currently, 50 states in the USA have sanctioned the sport of MMA, and people can watch UFC on TV in 150 countries and 22 different languages ("Ultimate Fighting Championship," n.d.).

Women's MMA competition has been documented in Japan since the mid -1990s. In 2001, the Smackgirl competition was formed in Japan, and it became the first major all-female organization in mixed martial arts ("Mixed Martial Arts," n.d.). In the United States, prior to the success of UFC, some early organizations invited women fighters in their MMA competitions.

From the mid-2000s, more organizations started to invite women to compete in their MMA competitions. In 2011, UFC began to promote women's MMA competitions since Zuffa's acquisition of Strike force. One year later, Dana White confirmed to feature women's MMA with signing the contract with the first female fighter, Ronda Rousey (Gross, 2012).

Rules of MMA

Since the early days of MMA, the rules have changed significantly. Even within UFC, the rules have changed dramatically. The original events were recognized as "no-hold-barred" events, whereas the current MMA matches keep some regulations, which focus on the safety of the fighters and the recognition of a legitimate sport.

The Unified Rules of Mixed Martial Arts divide fighters into nine different weight classes: flyweight up to 125 lb, bantamweight 125–135 lb, featherweight 135–145 lb, lightweight 145–155 lb, welterweight 155–170 lb, middleweight 170–185 lb, light heavyweight 185–205 lb, heavyweight 205–265 lb, and super heavyweight over 265 lb ("Unified Rules and Other Regulations," n.d.).

According to the "Unified Rules and Other MMA Regulations," the MMA contests should be held in a ring or in a fence area, which is between 20 feet square and 32 feet square. In non-championship MMA matches, there are 3 rounds of 5 minutes each, with a rest period of 1 minute between each round, whereas in the championship MMA contest, there are five rounds in each match, and each round has no more than 5 minutes duration. Fighters can have one-minute rest time between each round (New Jersey Athletic Control Board, 2002).

In MMA matches, all the fighters are required to wear glove during the competition. The gloves are used to protect their fists and reduce the occurrence of cuts. Usually the promoter will supply small, open-fingered gloves with the commission's approval. In addition, fighters are also required to wear a mouthpiece. For the clothing, male fighters are required to wear shorts, and they are allowed to wear a groin protector of their own selection, whereas female fighters should wear shorts and a chest protector. Shoes and any type of padding on the foot are not allowed in MMA (New Jersey Athletic Control Board, 2002).

MMA matches have five possible outcomes: judge's decision, knockout (KO), technical knockout (TKO), tap out (TO), and choke. In the judge's decision, if fighters finish the entire time of the match without decisive victory, a panel of three judges will make the decision on the winner based on the fighters' scoring. Knockout is defined as one of the fighters is unable to continue due to legal strikes, then the opponent is declared to win. Technical knockout usually happens when the fight is ended in one of the three ways when the fighter is not able to continue. First, the referee will call for the stoppage when the fighter cannot intelligently defend himself. Second, the referee will call for a time out when the ringside doctor feels a fighter is unable to continue fighting safely. Third, a fighter's corner man could signal a defeat by throwing a towel into the ring. A tap out is unique in MMA and it happens when one fighter taps on the mat or on his opponent for three times when he was caught and cannot free himself. Choke occurs when a fighter gets choked unconscious before tapping out.

For the fouls of MMA Matches, the UFC list 31 acts that may result in penalties:

- butting with the head;
- eye gouging of any kind;
- biting;
- spitting at an opponent;
- hair pulling;

- fish hooking;
- groin attacks of any kind;
- putting a finger into any orifice or any cut or laceration of an opponent;
- small joint manipulation;
- striking downward using the point of the elbow;
- striking to the spine or the back of the head;
- kicking to the kidney with a heel;
- throat strikes of any kind, including, without limitation, grabbing the trachea;
- clawing, pinching or twisting the flesh;
- grabbing the clavicle;
- kicking the head of a grounded opponent;
- kneeing the head of a grounded opponent;
- stomping a grounded opponent;
- holding the fence;
- holding the shorts or gloves of an opponent;
- using abusive language in fenced ring/fighting area;
- engaging in any unsportsmanlike conduct that causes injury to an opponent;
- attacking an opponent on or during the break;
- attacking an opponent who is under the care of the referee;
- attacking an opponent after the bell has sounded the end of the round;
- timidity, including, without limitation, avoiding contact with an opponent, intentionally or consistently dropping the mouthpiece or faking an injury;
- throwing opponent out of ring/fighting area;
- flagrantly disregarding the instructions of the referee;
- spiking an opponent to the canvas on his head or neck;
- interference by the corner; and
- applying any foreign substance to the hair or body to gain an advantage.

("Unified Rules and Other Regulations," n.d.)

Global expansion

Like the globalization of many other sports, MMA has been growing fast around the world. Twenty five countries and regions have legalized MMA competitions. UFC has visited 20 countries all over the world, including North America, South America, Europe, Asia, and Oceania.

Pride Fighting Championship (Pride FC) was a famous mixed martial arts promotion company in Japan. It was founded by Nobuyuki Sakakibara and Nobuhiko Takada, and the first event was held on October 11, 1997. In March 2007, Pride FC was sold to the UFC owner, Zuffa. At the beginning, UFC and Pride FC had the plan to cooperate with each other. However, the cooperation was not successful. On October 4, 2007, Pride FC laid off their staff in Japan, marking the end of this organization ("Pride Fighting Championships," n.d.).

Canada has hosted 24 UFC events, starting with UFC 83 in 2008 and most recent event was UFC 215 in September 2017. Within the 24 UFC events in Canada, UFC 129 was UFC's biggest event that attracted more than 55,000 attendance at Rogers Centre. Mexico has held 5 UFC events since 2014, starting with UFC 180 and the recent event was UFC Fight Night: Pettis vs. Moreno ("List of UFC Events," n.d.).

Brazil has been home for 30 UFC events. The first UFC event in Brazil, UFC Brazil: Ultimate Brazil was held in Sao Paulo in 1998. After the first UFC event, Brazil did not hold any

UFC events until 2011 for UFC 134. Since then, the promotion in Brazil developed rapidly. Until October 2017, Brazil has hosted 30 events ("List of UFC Events," n.d.).

With the UFC 38 in London, 2002, UFC made its debut in Europe. Since then, 21 UFC events have taken place in the United Kingdom. The most recent event was UFC Fight Night: Nelson vs. Ponzinibbio in Glasgow, Scotland in October 2017. Five UFC events have been held in Germany, beginning with UFC 99 in 2009, and the latest was UFC Fight Night: Arlovski vs. Barnett in 2016. Since 2012, Sweden has held five UFC events in 5 years, starting with UFC on Fuel TV: Gustafsson vs. Silva in 2012, and recently with UFC Fight Night: Gustafsson vs. Teixeira in 2017. Poland has held 2 UFC Fight Night events since 2015, and Netherlands has held two UFC Fight Night events since 2016. In addition, there are also UFC Fight Night events in Croatia ("List of UFC Events," n.d.).

To date, UFC has visited 6 countries in Asia. The first UFC event in Asia was UFC Japan: Ultimate Japan in 1997. Since then, Japan has held 9 UFC events, and the most recent event was UFC Fight Night: Saint Preux vs. Okami in 2017. China has held 3 UFC events in Macau, beginning with the UFC on Fuel TV: Franklin vs. Le, and the last event was the Ultimate Fighter China Finale: Kim vs. Hathaway in 2014. In other Asian countries, United Arab Emirates has held 2 UFC events since 2010, Singapore has held 2 events since 2014, Philippines held 1 event in 2016, and one UFC event was held in South Korea in 2017 ("List of UFC Events," n.d.).

Besides UFC, there are regional and national promotions around the world, such as Konfrontacja Sztuk Walki (KSW) in Poland, ONE Fighting Championship (One FC) in Singapore, Super Fighter League (SFL) in India, Inoki Genome Federation (IGF) in Japan, Extreme Fighting Championship (EFC) in South Africa, etc. Together with UFC, these promoters made MMA's global expansion going stronger (Anderson, 2015).

Important figures

Jeff Blatnick was a wrestler, UFC commentator and former UFC commissioner. After a distinguished wrestling career, in which he won the Olympic gold medal in Greco-Roman wrestling in 1984, Blatnick became a commentator for UFC in 1994 for UFC 4 and continued commentating until 2001 and UFC 32. During UFC 17, he was named as the official commissioner of the UFC. As commissioner he helped develop the modern rules of sport, creating policies, procedures and rules, many of which are still in use today (Meltzer, 2012).

Joe Silva was the UFC's Vice President of Talent Relations, or matchmaker as it is more informally known. He started working with the company in the early days in 1993 and helped develop the judging criteria, rules and regulations for the fledgling sport along with Jeff Blatnick (Meltzer, 2012). As a matchmaker for the majority of the UFC's history, he was instrumental in the growth and development of the sport. He developed the idea for the long-running television show "The Ultimate Fighter," which helped the UFC became more of a household name as opposed to a pay-per-view spectacle (Meltzer, 2016).

John McCarthy is a UFC referee and has served as a UFC referee since UFC 2. From UFC 2 to UFC 77 he served as a head referee for nearly every fight. Known as "Big John," he has become ubiquitous with the UFC and his call of "Let's get it on!" has become his trademark similar to Michael Buffer's "Let's get ready to rumble!" ("Refereed by John McCarthy," n.d.). As the UFC's earliest peacemaker, he also helped codify and establish the rules of the octagon along with Jeff Blatnick and Joe Silva.

Dave Meltzer is a journalist who covers both mixed martial arts and professional wrestling. Though he is most renowned for his coverage of professional wrestling and his introduction of the star ratings, he has covered the UFC since the very first UFC bout. He has been considered an "insider's insider" and is often the first to break major news in the sport. He has focused on the business side of the sport and has written for a wide range of publications including Fox Sports, the *Los Angeles Times* and Yahoo! Sports. In addition he has served as a UFC judge and radio host (Virgilio, n.d.).

Dana White is the president of the UFC. After working as a manager for high-profile fighters Tito Ortiz and Chuck Liddell, he became the president of the company in 2001 when the UFC was purchased by the Fertitta brothers, of whom he was a childhood friend (Wickert, 2004). Under White's leadership the UFC has grown into a multi-billion dollar enterprise. He oversaw the sale of the UFC to investors led by WWE-IMG for $4 billion in 2016 and remains the president of the company and the public face of the company (O'Reilly, 2016).

Joe Rogan is a stand-up comedian, podcast host and color commentator for the UFC. He has become the famous "voice" of the UFC. His career with UFC began as a back-stage interviewer and after becoming friends with UFC president Dana White, was offered the job of color commentator for UFC matches ("Exclusive Interview: Joe Rogan," n.d.). He has been named "MMA Personality of the Year" four times by the World MMA Awards. His energetic and enthusiastic commentary style has become ubiquitous with UFC.

Royce Gracie is a Brazilian mixed martial artist who is considered to be one of the most influential fighters of all time. He and his brothers were instrumental in popularizing Brazilian jiu-jitsu and revolutionizing the sport as a whole (Hodges, 2010). The introduction of Brazilian jiu-jitsu to the fledgling UFC would have a resounding impact on the organization and the sport as a whole. The stark difference in Gracie and Art Jimmerson at UFC 1 was apparent as Gracie easily handled Jimmerson, a light heavyweight boxer who was hopelessly mismatched. His early dominance in UFC helped pave the path for future Brazilians and others of various ethnicities and nationalities who brought their own unique fighting styles to the table over time and diversify UFC and MMA as a whole (Braun, 2012). Gracie was involved in the UFC from the start and was the tournament winner in UFC 1, 2 and 4 and fought to a draw in UFC 5. Gracie was the first inductee into the UFC Hall of Fame and still holds the record for most tournament wins in UFC history. Gracie retired from the UFC in 2013 but continues to fight in other competitions.

Lorenzo Fertitta and Frank Fertitta, III, also known as the Fertitta brothers, were business partners who acquired the UFC in 2001. After making their money in the casino industry in the 1990s, Lorenzo and Frank established Zuffa, LLC and purchased the UFC for $2 million in 2001 ("Company Overview," n.d.). Lorenzo became chairman and CEO of the company following the purchase and placed his childhood friend Dana White in the role of president. The Fertitta brothers put large amounts of money into the UFC and helped facilitate the massive growth throughout the early part of the 21st century. In 2016, Zuffa, LLC sold the UFC to WWE-IMG for $4 billion and Lorenzo stepped down from his role as chairman and CEO (Schwartzel & Nagesh, 2016).

Ronda Rousey is a mixed martial artist and judoka and is renowned as a pioneer for women in the UFC and MMA as a whole. Rousey's career began in judo and was the youngest judoka in the 2004 Olympics in Athens at age 17. She competed in the 2008 Olympics in Beijing and won the bronze medal, becoming the first American to win an Olympic medal in women's judo (Mihoces, 2008). She retired from judo following the Olympics and pursued a career in MMA. She got her start in Strikeforce in 2011 and became bantamweight champion in 2012 (Martin, 2015). She became the first woman signed by the UFC in 2012 and proceeded to win six straight fights, mostly winning extremely quickly. She finally lost her title to Holly Holm in 2015 and lost again in her return to the sport in 2016 but she had already paved the way for women fighters in the UFC.

Anderson Silva is a Brazilian fighter who is widely considered to be one of the greatest fighters in the history of the sport. Silva's career outside of Brazil began in Japan fighting with Pride FC but he quickly made the jump to the United States, signing with the UFC in 2006 (Gerbasi, 2006). He quickly established himself in the UFC, winning his first 16 fights and defending his middleweight title ten times. He still holds the record for longest title streak in the history of the UFC. He has been called the one of the greatest fighters of all time by the likes of Dana White and Joe Rogan (Erickson, 2012). Although by the time Silva came to dominate the UFC there had been a long history of Brazilian fighters dating back to the Gracies and UFC 1, Silva was notable as an Afro-Brazilian. The sight of black faces in UFC was nothing new when Silva signed with UFC in 2006 but the sheer dominance of a black fighter had not been seen in UFC to that point. Along with Quinton "Rampage" Jackson, Demetrious Johnson and Rashad Evans, Silva made the sight of successful black fighters a regularity in the late 2000s and early 2010s and this has not changed as the decade comes to a close.

Georges St. Pierre is a Canadian fighter and three-time UFC welterweight champion. He has amassed a 19–2 record in his UFC career and successfully defended his title on nine occasions. He has been named as one of the greatest fighters of all time and is renowned for his grappling ability ("Georges St. Pierre," n.d.). Many of St. Pierre's fights throughout his career have gone to decision as opposed to being ended by knockout. He retired in 2013 after voluntarily vacating his title, however he announced his return to the sport in 2016 (Al-Shatti, 2016). As of the time this has been written, he has not lost a fight in over a decade.

Chuck Liddell is a retired fighter and former UFC light heavyweight champion. Liddell successfully defended his title four times before giving it up. Liddell was primarily known for his defensive wrestling and counter punching but was not a pioneer in either technique. However, he was the face of the UFC when it exploded into the mainstream in the mid-2000s and his signature Mohawk, tattoos and fighting style made him a source of inspiration for a generation of fighters (Wyman, 2015). Liddell was inducted into the UFC Hall of Fame in 2009 and retired from the sport in 2010.

Urijah Faber is an American retired mixed martial artist who is widely regarded for bringing attention to the lighter weight classes in MMA (Doyle, 2013). He was the first lightweight fighter to gain stardom in the UFC and was a major contributor to technical developments in combining grappling, striking and wrestling (Wyman, 2015). Faber was known for the fluidity he was able to switch between styles. In addition to his contributions and his successes in the ring, Faber has been an influential trainer, teaching fighters such as TJ Dillashaw and Chad Mendes in his Team Alpha Male. Faber is a member of the UFC Hall of Fame and retired from the sport in 2016.

Pat Miletich is an American retired mixed martial artist and current works as a commentator. Miletich was the first ever welterweight champion in the UFC and defended his title on four occasions. He is renowned for being one of the first American fighters to pursue a well-rounded fighting style, combining boxing, jiu-jitsu and wrestling (Wyman, 2015). Similar to Urijah Faber, his gym, Miletich Fighting Systems, taught his approach to successful and famous fighters such as Matt Hughes, Jeremy Horn and Robbie Lawler. Miletich retired from fighting in 2008 and was inducted into the UFC Hall of Fame in 2014 (Thang, 2014).

Frank Shamrock is a retired American mixed martial artist. Shamrock started his career fighting in the Pancrase organization and was an accomplished fighter by the time his UFC career began. He became the first middleweight champion in UFC history and retired from the UFC having never lost a fight (Snowden, 2010). Like Miletich and Faber, Shamrock had an influential and diverse skill set and would go on to be an influential coach, training the likes of BJ Penn (Wyman, 2015). Shamrock retired from fighting in 2010 and continues to work as a coach and broadcaster.

Maurice Smith is a retired American mixed martial artist who most famously founded the "sprawl-and-brawl" style of fighting (Wyman, 2015). Smith was primarily a striker but showed the MMA world that if a striker could learn enough about handling takedowns and ground fighting, striking could be a viable option in the world of MMA, which to that point was dominated by ground fighting and takedowns. Smith was not an overly successful fighter, he only defended his UFC heavyweight title one time, but he blazed a trail for fighters who were not focused on fighting on the ground. Smith retired from fighting in 2013 and was inducted into the UFC Hall of Fame in 2017 (Gerbasi, 2017).

Randy Couture is an American retired mixed martial artist who has competed in the most title fights in UFC history at 16. Couture got his start in Greco-Roman wrestling and was an Olympic alternate two times before his MMA career ever began (Wyman, 2015). He became known for his "dirty boxing" technique in which he would tie up his opponent in a clinch and unleash a flurry of knees and punches to inflict damage. His skills in Greco-Roman wrestling allowed him to counter opponents who had adapted sprawl-and-brawling pioneered by Maurice Smith. Similar to Frank Shamrock, Pat Miletich and Urijah Faber, his gyms would go on to train an array of successful MMA fighters such as Forrest Griffin and his techniques were widely influential across the sport (Wyman, 2015). Couture was inducted into the UFC Hall of Fame in 2006 and was the fourth member of the Hall of Fame. He retired from fighting in 2011 and continues to coach and do commentary.

Mark Coleman is a retired American mixed martial artist who is known as "the godfather of ground-and-pound." Prior to his MMA career, Coleman was an accomplished wrestler who competed at the 1992 Olympic Games. Coleman turned his wrestling skills into the ability to end fights with a flurry of incredibly hard punches on the ground (Wyman, 2015). Coleman won multiple UFC tournaments and was also an accomplished fighter for Pride FC. Coleman's ground-and-pound is an influence on virtually all MMA fighters and has become an integral part of the sport itself. Coleman was inducted into the UFC Hall of Fame in 2008 and retired from fighting in 2010.

Satoru Sayama is a Japanese professional wrestler and MMA promoter who founded shooto. Shooto is a fighting system based around shoot wrestling. Sayama trained famous shooto practioners like Rumina Sato and Yuki Natai and also hosted the Vale Tudo Japan event, which introduced Brazilian jiu-jitsu to the country (Breen, 2008). After originating in Japan, shooto events are now seen in Brazil as well.

Masakatsu Funaki and Minoru Suzuki are the founders of pancrase, an MMA promotion company that based its rules on professional wrestling. Funaki and Suzuki left their previous company and established pancrase around shoot wrestling with no predetermined outcomes. Pancrase continues to be a major company in the Japanese MMA scene with fights also aired in the UK and Canada.

Nobuyuki Sakakibara and Nobuhiko Takada are the founders of Japanese MMA promotion company Pride Fighting Championships, better known as Pride FC. Pride FC began in 1997 to support a fight between Rickson Gracie and Nobuhiko Takada (Grant, 2013). It would go on to grow into one of the most popular MMA companies, particularly in Japan, and still holds the record for largest live audience for an MMA event with just over 91,000 turning out to the Japanese National Stadium in Tokyo in 2002 ("Total Attendance," n.d.). Pride was purchased by Zuffa, LLC in 2007 and absorbed into in the UFC.

Rumina Sato is a Japanese retired mixed martial artist. Sato got his start in shoot wrestling and fought with shooto. He was a well-rounded fighter who integrated a wide variety of fighting styles and components. He was particularly renowned for his unorthodox and creative submissions and still holds the record for the fastest tap out in professional MMA history at six seconds (Wyman, 2015). He was praised by renowned fighters such as Rickson Gracie ("Rickson Gracie Interview," n.d.). Sato is known as an idol for multiple generations of Japanese fighters and is still active in the sport as a coach and trainer.

Kazushi Sakuraba is a Japanese mixed martial artist and professional wrestling who became known as "The Gracie Hunter." Sakuraba got his start in wrestling and was a professional wrestler in Japan prior to the start of his professional MMA career. Sakuraba became renowned for defeating four members of the Gracie family, who were seen as invincible at the time. Most notably he defeated Royce Gracie in the longest bout in modern MMA history at 90 minutes (Wyman, 2015). Sakuraba's wrestling and catch wrestling skills were highly influential on the technical development of the sport and his legacy can still be seen in modern mixed martial artists. Owing to his background in professional wrestling, Sakuraba also showed that showmanship and flair had a place not only in pro wrestling but in mixed martial arts as well (Wyman, 2015). Sakuraba is still an active fighter and wrestler in Japan and was inducted into the UFC Hall of Fame in 2017 (Okamoto, 2017).

Conclusion

MMA has seen monumental growth within the past few decades, growing from a truly underground and little-known sport to a global phenomenon and multi-billion-dollar enterprise. Fighters have gone from specialization to building outward from a foundation and incorporating other styles. Now, mixed martial artists are beginning to be trained in a variety of styles from the very start of their careers (Juul, 2017). This development will lead to even more skilled fighters and a generation of fighters who can expertly utilize the entire gamut of fighting styles and martial arts. This, coupled with increasing investment and attention paid to MMA, will make the coming years and decades incredibly important in the development of the sport and the culture surrounding it.

References

Al-Shatti, S. (2016). "Georges St. Pierre Announces He is Ready to Return to Fighting." Retrieved from www.mmafighting.com/2016/6/20/11982548/georges-st-pierre-announces-he-is-ready-to-return-to-fighting

Anderson, J. (2015, June 1). "MMA's Global Expansion Going Strong, Questions Arise." *The MMACORNER*. Retrieved from http://themmacorner.com/2015/06/01/mmas-globall-expansion-going-strong-questions-arise/

Bledsoe, G. H. (2009). "Mixed Martial Arts." In Kordi, R., Maffulli, N., Wroble, R. R., & Wallace, W. A. (Eds.), *Combat sports medicine* (pp. 323–330). London: Springer.

Braun, D. (2012). "UFC's Diversity has Driven Expansion." Retrieved from www.theventureonline.com/2012/01/ufcs-diversity-has-driven-expansion/

Breen, J. (2008). "Changes Come to Shooto, Fighters React." Retrieved from www.sherdog.com/news/news/Changes-Come-to-Shooto-Fighters-React-13082

"Company Overview of Zuffa, LLC." (2017). Retrieved from www.bloomberg.com/research/stocks/private/person.asp?personId=656262&privcapId=31207841

Doyle, D. (2013). "A Pioneer for Smaller Fighters, Faber Not Ready to Call it Quits Just Yet." *Sports Illustrated*. Retrieved from www.si.com/mma/2013/02/07/urijah-faber-ivan-menjivar

Duuglas-Ittu, S., (2015, December 28). "Origins of Japanese Kickboxing – the Karate vs Muay Thai Fight that Started it All." *8LimbsUs*. Retrieved from http://8limbs.us/muay-thai-thailand/the-origins-of-japanese-kickboxing-the-karate-muay-thai-fight-that-started-it-all

Erickson, M. (2012). "Greatest Fighter Ever? Anderson Silva Making Strong Case." *USA Today*. Retrieved from https://usatoday30.usatoday.com/sports/mma/post/2012-07-05/greatest-fighter-ever-anderson-silva-making-strong-case/797716/1

"Exclusive Interview: Joe Rogan." (2012). Retrieved from www.cagepotato.com/exclusive-interview-joe-rogan/

"Georges St. Pierre." (n.d.) Retrieved from www.tapology.com/fightcenter/fighters/georges-st-pierre-rush

Georgiou, A.V. (2008). "Pankration: A Historical Look at the Original Mixed-Martial Arts Competition." *Black Belt, 2008* (4), 92–97.

Gerbasi, T. (2006). "A New Contender Arrives in the UFC." Retrieved from https://web.archive.org/web/20080103153339/www.ufc.com/index.cfm?fa=news.detail&gid=2521&pid=440

Gerbasi, T. (2017). "Maurice Smith Gets UFC Hall of Fame Nod." Retrieved from www.ufc.com/news/Maurice-Smith-joins-2017-UFC-Hall-of-Fame-class-042217?id=

Grant, T.P. (2013). "MMA origins: Fighting for Pride." Retrieved from www.bloodyelbow.com/2013/5/2/4220042/ufc-mma-history-origins-pride-fc-rickson-gracie-Nobuhiko-Takada

Green, T.A. (2010). *Martial arts of the world: An encyclopedia of history and innovation.* Santa Barbara, CA: ABC-CLIO Corporate.

Gross, J. (2012, November 16). "Ronda Rousey Signs Landmark Deal." *ESPN.* Retrieved from www.espn.com/mma/story/_/id/8639858/ronda-rousey-becomes-first-female-sign-ufc-deal.

"History of MMA." (n.d.). In *Wikipedia.* Retrieved from https://ockickboxing.com/blog/mma/history-of-mma-mixed-martial-arts/

Hodges, M. (2010). "The 10 Most Influential Figures in MMA." Retrieved from http://bleacherreport.com/articles/422132-top-10-influential-figures-in-mma#page/11

Juul, M. (2017). "The Future of MMA: Why the Sport is about to Enter a New Era in Fighters." Retrieved from http://bleacherreport.com/articles/1054474-the-future-of-mma-why-the-sport-is-about-to-enter-a-new-era-in-fighters

Kent, G. (1968). *A Pictorial History of Wrestling.* Middlesex: Spring Books.

Liddell, H. G. (1894). *A Greek–English Lexicon.* New York: Harper & Brothers.

"List of UFC Events." (n.d.). In *Wikipedia.* Retrieved from https://en.wikipedia.org/wiki/List_of_UFC_events

Little, J. R., & Wong, C. F., (2000). *Ultimate Martial Arts Encyclopedia.* New York, NY: McGraw-Hill.

Lole, K., (2012, November 5). "Bruce Lee's Impact on Mixed Martial Arts Felt Nearly 40 Years after his Death." *Yahoo! Sports.* Retrieved from www.yahoo.com/news/mma--bruce-lee-impact-on-mixed-martial-arts-ufc-felt-nearly-40-years-after-his-death.html

Martin, B. (2015). "Ronda Rousey: Pro Fight no. 5 – Defeated Miesha Tate via Submission (Armbar), 4:27, First Round." *Los Angeles Daily News.* Retrieved from www.dailynews.com/2015/07/29/ronda-rousey-pro-fight-no-5-defeated-miesha-tate-via-submission-armbar-427-first-round/

Martin, D. (2011). "Spike TV Announces Partnership with the UFC has Ended, TUF 14 Will be the Last on the Network." *MMAWEEKLY.* Retrieved from www.mmaweekly.com/spike-tv-announces-partnership-with-the-ufc-has-ended-tuf-14-will-be-the-last-on-the-network

Matuszak, S. (2015, March 12). "Shuai Jiao: China's Indigenous Wrestling Style." *Fightland.* Retrieved from http://fightland.vice.com/blog/shuai-jiao-chinas-indigenous-wrestling-style

Meltzer, D. (2012). "Whenever You Hear the Term Mixed Martial Arts, You Should Think of Jeff Blatnick." Retrieved from www.mmafighting.com/2012/10/24/3550680/whenever-you-hear-the-term-mixed-martial-arts-you-jeff-blatnick

Meltzer, D. (2016). "The Unlikely Story of Joe Silva, a Guy Working at an Arcade Who Changed the History of MMA." Retrieved from www.mmafighting.com/2016/9/4/12746572/the-unlikely-story-of-joe-silva-a-guy-working-at-an-arcade-who

Mihoces, G. (2008). "Rousey's Bronze Makes U.S. History in Women's Judo." *USA Today.* Retrieved from http://usatoday30.usatoday.com/sports/olympics/beijing/fight/2008-08-13-womensjudo_N.htm

"Mixed Martial Arts." (n.d.). In *Wikipedia.* Retrived from https://en.wikipedia.org/wiki/Mixed_martial_arts#cite_note-10

New Jersey State Athletic Control Board. (2002, November 2). "Mixed Martial Arts Unified Rules of Conduct Additional Mixed Martial Arts Rules." *The State of New Jersey Department of Law & Public Safety.* Retrieved from www.state.nj.us/lps/sacb/docs/martial.html

Noble, G. (1999). "An Introduction to EW Barton-Wright (1860–1951) and the Eclectic Art of Bartitsu." *Journal of Asian Martial Arts*, 8(2), 50–61.

Nugent, M. (1901). "Barton-Wright and his Japanese Wrestlers: A Man and his Method." *Health and Strength*, 3, 336–341.

Okamoto, B. (2017). "Urijah Faber, Kazushi Sakuraba Headling UFC Hall of Fame '17 Class." Retrieved from www.espn.com/mma/story/_/id/19881394/ufc-2017-hall-fame-include-urijah-faber-kazushi-sakuraba-maurice-smith-joe-silva

O'Reilly, L. (2016). "The Hugely Popular Mixed Martial Arts League UFC has Been Sold for $4 Billion." *Business Insider.* Retrieved from www.businessinsider.com/mixed-martial-arts-league-ufc-sold-for-4-billion-to-wme-img-2016-7?r=UK&IR=T

Plotz, D. (1999, November 17). "Fight Clubbed." *Slate.* Retrieved from www.slate.com/articles/briefing/articles/1999/11/fight_clubbed.html

Poliakoff, M. B. (1987). *Combat Sports in the Ancient World: Competition, Violence, and Culture.* New Haven, CT: Yale University Press.

"Pride Fighting Championship." (n.d.). In *Wikipedia.* Retrieved from https://en.wikipedia.org/wiki/Pride_Fighting_Championships#cite_note-4

Re, G. (2013). "Mixed Martial Arts." *On The Risk*, 29(2), 63–67.

"Refereed by John McCarthy." (n.d.). Retrieved from www.tapology.com/search/mma-fights-by-referee/big-john-mccarthy

"Rickson Gracie Interview." (2006). Retrieved from http://onthemat.com/rickson-gracie-interview-2/

Rooney, Kyle. (2016, July 11). "UFC Confirms $4 Billion Sale Of The Company." *Hnhh.* Retrieved from www.hotnewhiphop.com/ufc-confirms-s4-billion-sale-of-the-company-news.22773.html

Schwartzel, E. & Nagesh, G. (2016). "Investors Pay $4 Billion for Mixed-Martial Arts Group UFC." *Wall Street Journal.* Retrieved from www.wsj.com/articles/ufc-sells-for-approximately-4-billion-to-talent-agency-wme-img-1468238282

Snowden, J. (2010). "The Kingpin: Best Fighters in MMA History." Retrieved from www.bloodyelbow.com/2010/7/13/1567110/the-kingpin-the-best-fighters-in

Thang, K. (2014). "Pat Miletich Inducted into the UFC Hall of Fame." Retrieved from https://cagepages.com/2014/07/06/pat-miletich-inducted-ufc-hall-fame/

"Total Attendance." (n.d.) Retrieved from www.tapology.com/search/mma-event-figures/total-attendance

"Ultimate Fighting Championship." (n.d.). In *Wikipedia.* Retrieved from https://en.wikipedia.org/wiki/Ultimate_Fighting_Championship

"Unified Rules and Other Regulations." (n.d.). In *UFC.* Retrieved from www.ufc.com/discover/sport/rules-and-regulations

"Vale Tudo." (n.d.). In *Wikipedia.* Retrieved from https://en.wikipedia.org/wiki/Vale_tudo

Virgilio, D. (n.d.) "Dave Meltzer." Retrieved from http://mmahalloffame.com/world/judgeprofile/46/dave-meltzer

Wickert, M. (2004). "Dana White and the Future of UFC." Retrieved from https://magazine.fighttimes.com/dana-white-and-the-future-of-ufc/

Wyman, P. (2015). "Sherdog's Top 10: Most Influential Fighters." Retrieved from www.sherdog.com/news/articles/2/Sherdogs-Top-10-Most-Influential-Fighters-82005

14
Wrestling

Dexter Zavalza Hough-Snee

Wrestling: the oldest global sport

Wrestling's global character might be considered almost as old as humanity. Across the world, diverse forms of wrestling or grappling preceded the rise of the two, predominant modern, internationally contested wrestling styles, Greco-Roman and Freestyle. Though these styles have prevailed as the contemporary forms of global wrestling since the nineteenth century, wrestling crossed borders long before organized international competition. The three wrestling categories dating to antiquity include belt-and-jacket, catch-hold, and loose styles. Belt-and-jacket wrestling styles require special clothing that provides a means for opponents to grip each other. Catch-hold requires wrestlers to take and sustain a prescribed hold at the match's beginning. Loose styles, such as modern Greco-Roman and Freestyle, begin with wrestlers separated. Far from existing in isolation, these wrestling forms unite distinct geopolitical and ethnic groups from antiquity through wrestling's international institutionalization.

While wrestling only became a modern, internationally regulated sport during the early twentieth century, from antiquity to the industrial revolution wrestling's worldwide folkstyles had diverse forms of governance (ranging from the political to the religious), and training and competition were held in specialized sites. Social hierarchies surrounding wrestling often demarcated cultural roles. Likewise, professionalism existed in certain cultures and loose quantification (the number of falls for a victory, for example) characterizes some of the oldest wrestling traditions. Wrestling served numerous functions prior to its modern manifestations – military training, court entertainment, diplomacy, and philosophical and spiritual practice. When public spectacle, pre-modern wrestling was even commercialized in the form of entry fees or tribute, even if modern record keeping was lacking.

Connecting early, highly localized forms of wrestling to modern international (amateur) wrestling is the fact that most folkstyle wrestling disciplines share the objective of match termination by fall. Four primary types of fall categorize global folk wrestling: break-stance, or fall by forcing an opponent out of a determined competition area or out of position (as in Japanese *sumo* and Senegalese *laamb*);[1] toppling, or fall by throwing an opponent or forcing them to the ground (as in ancient Greek *palé*, whose objective was to throw an opponent to the ground from a standing position);[2] touch-fall and pin-fall, restraining an opponent in a certain position (as in the shoulder fall common to many wrestling traditions); and submission. Some variation or combination of these fall criteria were common to veritably all pre-modern wrestling contests, and modern scoring criteria – in the form of a point system awarding takedowns, back exposures, reversals, and escapes – only evolved in the mid-twentieth century to determine winners in contests not decided by fall.[3]

Having existed in remarkably similar forms across the world since antiquity, wrestling distinguishes itself from most modern sports for its pre-modern popularity among diverse cultures on all continents. Many early grappling disciplines never attained global prominence, though adjacent wrestling cultures often competed across ethnic or community groups.[4] From antiquity through the nineteenth century, the expansion and standardization of wrestling styles often accompanied political and military expansion.[5] And though wrestling's was only standardized as a competitive sport during the nineteenth century with professional wrestling and Olympic revitalization,[6] wrestling's circulation between antiquity and industrialization is essential for understanding the sport's modern global character.

Wrestling from antiquity to 1800

The ancient Sumerians (3000 BCE) were one of the first cultures to practice wrestling. Within the literary record, references to belt wrestling appear in the *Epic of Gilgamesh*, a Mesopotamian poem written in cuneiform circa 2100 BCE. Throughout the region, sculptures and low reliefs document wrestling's prominence. In Egypt, the archaeological record places wrestling around the same period. Most notably, the tomb of Egyptian official Baqet III in the Beni-Hasan cemetery – dating to 2100 BCE – depicts some 400 pairs of wrestlers demonstrating diverse techniques.[7] Such elaborate depictions have been taken as evidence of the sport's regional codification around formal rules and established techniques.

Wrestling is also a tradition in South Asia, dating to 1500 BCE.[8] The earliest textual references in the region are found in the foundational Hindu epics known as the *Ramayana* (*c.*450 BCE) and the *Mahabharata* (900–400 BCE). Chinese wrestling was recorded circa 2500 BCE, evolving into *jiao li* (角力), a form of jacket wrestling used for military training, during the Zhou Dynasty (1122–256 BCE).[9] During the Qin Dynasty (221–207 BCE), *jiao li* doubled as a throwing sport for court amusement and imperial bodyguards were selected from the best wrestlers. Renamed *shuaijiao* (摔跤 or 摔角; "wrestling" in Mandarin) in modern times, Chinese wrestling includes several centuries-old regional jacket and loose styles.

The ancient Greek Olympics were inaugurated from 708 BCE, with wrestling already established in many regions of the world. In the Greek games wrestling was not a single event but served as the decisive discipline to designate the winner of the pentathlon, the only crowned athlete of the games. The most famous Greek wrestler was Milon of Croton, an associate of the philosopher Pythagoras. A constant presence at all four of the Pan-Hellenic Games held in ancient Greece, Milon was six-time Olympic champion (540–516 BCE), ten-time winner of the Isthmian Games, nine-time champion of the Nemean Games, and seven-time victor of the Pythian Games.

Wrestling continued after the Roman conquest of Greece (146 BCE), retaining importance in the Olympic tradition under Augustus. Grappling had always been central to Roman military training and the palestra was associated with military success, as mentioned in Lucius Cassius Dio's *Roman History* (211–233 CE). Competitors came from throughout Eurasia, and in 281 CE, Armenian King Tiridates III (286–342 CE) won the 265th Olympiad, foreshadowing Armenia's popularization of *kokh* folkstyle. After Christian Roman Emperor Theodisius I prohibited pagan sports in 393CE, formal wrestling competition declined across Roman territories. While losing official importance during the early Middle Ages, wrestling continued across the former Western Roman Empire. Wrestling was also practiced in the Byzantine Empire, and Basil I (811–886) allegedly gained the favor of predecessor Michael III by defeating a Bulgarian wrestling champion.[10] However, after such prominence in Greece and Rome, wrestling became peripheral in much of medieval Europe.

Outside of Europe, wrestling was practiced continuously from antiquity through the early modern period. In South Asia, the encyclopedic twelfth-century *Manasollasa* and thirteenth-century treatise *Malla Purana* ("book of grappling") explored techniques of ancient *malla-yuddha* ("wrestling combat").[11] Similar wrestling took place in modern-day Thailand, Malaysia, and Java as Indian culture spread to Southeast Asia. *Malla-yuddha* remained a vital practice on the Indian sub-continent until Central Asian Mughals conquered northern India in the sixteenth century, infusing *malla-yuddha* with groundwork common to Turkic styles and creating *pehlwani/kusti*, a linguistic borrowing from the Persian *koshti pahlevani* ("heroic wrestling") common to Turkic wrestling cultures. *Malla-yuddha* was displaced by *pehlwani/kusti*, and today the ancient Indian form is relegated largely to Southern India. The Jain poet Ratnakara Varni's *Bharatesa Vaibhava* (1557) describes challenges among wrestlers. Portuguese explorer Domingo Paes visited the Vijayanagara Empire, describing how *malla-yuddha* wrestlers from across the empire congregated at the Navaratri Festival in his *Chronica dos reis de Bisnaga* (1520). Maratha (17th–19th centuries) rulers supported *pehlwani/kusti* by organizing tournaments with large prize purses while Rajput princes (6th–20th centuries) sponsored wrestlers who competed for entertainment. Local princes supported wrestlers throughout British colonization.

In Turkey, the folkstyle *karakucak* was popularized after the conquest of Anatolia by Seljuk Turks between 1037 and 1194. Among its variants, today's *köprülü karakucak* style practiced around Çukurova follows rules similar to Freestyle. *Yağlı güreş*, or Turkish oil wrestling, is the Turkish national sport, similar to *karakucak* rules but with traditional dress and oil. Oil wrestling was common in ancient Egypt, Assyria, and Babylonia, arriving to Turkey and Iran during Persian imperial occupation of Egypt (550–330 BCE). In addition to lexical parentage in the Persian *koshti* ("wrestling"), the word *güreş* (Turkish) or *keriš* (Old Turkic), meaning "wrestling," has cognate forms across the Turkic world (Kazakh *kuresh*, Uzbek *kurash*, Tatar *köräş*, Tuvan *khuresh*, etc.), testament to the tremendous historical popularity of wrestling throughout Eurasia.

The Sabantuy festival founded during the Volga Bulgaria state (7th–13th centuries) and celebrated today by Turkic peoples across Eurasia, features *kurash* as the main event. The Turkish Kirkpinar oil wrestling tournament, established during the Ottoman Empire and held annually since approximately 1360, is one of the world's oldest continually sanctioned sporting events, held in Edirne, near the Turkish borders with Greece and Bulgaria. The Balkan Peninsula reinforced strong local wrestling traditions under Ottoman rule, where wrestling was an official pastime.

Wrestling became European court entertainment during the late Middle Ages and the social elite arranged, contested, and wagered on wrestling matches into the Renaissance. Grappling also served as military training alongside other weapons disciplines, and nobles wrestled as part of their education. In 1520, Francis I of France famously threw Henry VIII of England in a wrestling bout at the Field of the Cloth of Gold festival.[12]

Early modern European wrestling is documented in dozens of fifteenth- and sixteenth-century combat manuals known in German as *fechtbücher*. Austrian *ringen* (German: "grappling") specialist Ott Jud's fifteenth-century wrestling system was printed in *fechtbücher* throughout the region. Artists from across Europe depicted wrestlers, including Caravaggio, Poussin, and Rembrandt. In Nuremberg circa 1512, Albrecht Dürer produced an incomplete *fechtbuch* manuscript featuring 120 illustrations of *ringen*, perhaps based on the 1470 Codex Wallerstein.

In 1539, German noble Fabian von Auerswald published the seminal *Die Ringer Kunst* (*The Art of Wrestling*), adorned with 85 woodcuts by Lucas Cranach the Younger depicting wrestling technique. Auerswald called wrestling a "knightly and noble art"[13] and his training manual depicts techniques still used today. In 1602, Sir Richard Carew's *Survey of Cornwall* discussed Cornish wrestling at great length, associating the practice with Cornish foundation narratives of Brute and Corineus.[14] Carew further noted that the Cornish were wrestling fanatics comparable to the ancient Greeks and Ottoman Turks.

Isolated to the Celtic British Isles, collar-and-elbow is another folkstyle practiced through the Middle Ages. Purported to have originated in the Tailteann Games of ancient Ireland,[15] it was practiced in Celtic territories from 500–800, evidenced by a series of Irish and Scottish carvings of collar-and-elbow grappling pre-dating Norse invasion.[16] The discipline slowed after the Norman invasion (*c.*1170) but was rejuvenated by the construction of a wrestling gymnasium by Scottish Lord of the Isles Domhnuil Gruamach circa 1400, and reemerged as organized sport in the seventeenth century.[17] A commoner's pastime in Ireland, collar-and-elbow reemerged as a gentleman's practice in colonial America, later practiced by American presidents from George Washington to William H. Taft.[18]

To the north in Scandinavia, *glíma* folkstyles flourished during the ninth century, mentioned in Viking poetry by Norwegian court poet Bragi Boddason (790–850) and Kveldúlfr Bjálfason (820–878). Like their contemporaries, these authors narrate mythological wrestling matches between deities, in this case, Norse god Thor's defeat to Elli. *Glíma* also appears in the Icelandic *Prose Edda* of 1220. Such mythological and literary foundations accompanied vibrant wrestling traditions during the Viking Age (ninth–twelfth centuries), where men, women, and children practiced grappling across Scandinavia for sport and military training.

Throughout the Americas, West Africa, and the Pacific, indigenous wrestling traditions were observed during European colonial expansion. In North America, Inuit break-stance wrestling was first observed in 1741 by Danish Christian missionary Hans Egede in Greenland. Colonial British and Dutch accounts cite wrestling among the Woodland and Plains Indians during the seventeenth century. Among the Six Nation Iroquois Confederacy, wrestling was sacred and diplomatic, handed down from the Great Peace Maker Deganawida and used to settle political disputes. Wrestling was also recorded among the Blackfoot (1801), Winnebago (1870s), Choctaw First Nations, Cherokee, and Cree.

In Latin America, several forms of wrestling existed that incorporated ancient mythologies, some with costumed combatants embodying deities. The Tarahumara people of Chihuahua, Mexico's Sierra Madre practiced belt wrestling known as *najarapuame*. The states of Oaxaca and Guerrero also feature forms of wrestling. In Peru, *takanakuy* wrestling was practiced in Chumbivilcas, Cuzco during the Inca Empire, where competitions were judged by top political officials. The 1560 Taki Unqoy revolt in colonial Peru organized no-holds-barred wrestling matches to interrupt Spanish Christmas festivities. The Yaghan people of Tierra del Fuego (Chile) practiced *kulaka mulaka*, first observed by German priest Martin Gusinde circa 1917. *Tinku* fighting among the Aymara of Bolivia, *huka huka* knee wrestling in south-central Brazil, and pan-Brazilian *luta corporal* are other South American styles documented during colonization.

Folk wrestling from the circus to the stadium: the birth of Greco-Roman and Freestyle

Amid this vibrant matrix of folk wrestling, professional wrestling[19] emerged in France circa 1830 as a spectacle of strength and bravado. Showmen promoted French strongmen such as "Edward, the Steel Eater" and "Gustave d'Avignon, the Bone Wrecker," who "would challenge members of the public to knock them down for 500 francs."[20] A former Napoleonic soldier-turned-showman, Jean Exbroyat, formed the first modern wrestling circus troupe in 1848, prohibiting holds below the waist. Initially termed "Flat Hand" wrestling and prohibiting striking, the French style spread throughout Europe as a carnival pastime, gaining strong followings in the Austro-Hungarian Empire, Prussia, Russia, Denmark, and Italy, eventually taking the name of Greco-Roman wrestling.[21]

Through the mid-nineteenth century, troupes traveled Europe, the British Isles, North America, and Latin America, organizing matches between predetermined opponents and encouraging challengers from the public. Performing in barrooms, fairs, and circuses, wrestling was more a loose-knit, niche entertainment circuit than a modern sport. Wagers were common among spectators and prizes were offered to incentivize challengers. As sport-entertainment syndicates traveled from town to town, staying in one place as long as they could hold interest and make a profit, wrestling served as a spectacle to encourage betting and sell tickets alongside other attractions. Accompanying strongman acts and other folk pastimes, rules were determined by promoters, lacking institutional oversight although certain rules (prohibitions against eye-gouging, low-blows, leg holds, etc.) quickly became commonplace.[22]

The cases of Rafael "the Italian Hercules" Scalli and Pablo Raffeto, both Italian wrestler-entertainers active in mid-nineteenth-century South America, exemplify wrestling's global reach as circus entertainment.[23] In 1863, Scalli set up a tent for a month in front of the Teatro Solís in Montevideo, Uruguay. His multi-faceted show included demonstrations of strength, including weightlifting and equestrian feats, culminating in wrestling matches against his companions and, later, challengers from the public.[24] The Italian Raffeto arrived to Buenos Aires, Argentina, in 1869, where he garnered fame for "challenging audience members to wrestling matches and always winning," also giving grappling demonstrations with a bear.[25] Raffeto, known as "the Genoese Barnum" for his circus promotions, later recruited wrestlers from three continents (both Americas and Europe), and wrestling figured somewhere between magic, swordplay, music, and dance in his shows.[26]

World Greco-Roman Champion, Frenchman Thiebaud Bauer, introduced Greco-Roman wrestling to the United States in 1875 after an illustrious career as "The Masked Wrestler of Paris," a take-all-comers wrestler who threw Parisian challengers in the carnival style popularized by Exbroyat. After traveling to San Francisco via New York, Bauer defeated storied Californian wrestler Louis Gerichten, throwing him in two consecutive falls. He matched the feat against Australian World Champion, "Professor" William Miller.[27] Interest in the sport followed as American cities trained and offered up challengers, including William "The Iron Duke" Muldoon, the US Greco-Roman champion.[28] Muldoon would prove triumphant in later matchups with Bauer (1880 and 1884), wresting the world title from his French opponent before initiating a short-lived business partnership and lifelong rivalry with fellow American Clarence Whistler, who won multiple American and World Greco-Roman and Catch-as-Catch-Can titles.

As countless high-profile Greco-Roman matches featuring international opponents took place in theaters across the United States, Greco-Roman gained a legitimate American following. Beginning in 1875, American promoters billed high-profile matches as "World Championships" in spite of no unified governance across continents.[29] Muldoon faced a slew of international opponents, including English émigré Edwin Bibby, Englishman Tom Cannon, Scotland's Don Dinnie, Japan's Sorakichi Matsuda, and "the German Oak" Karl Abs.

While Matsuda and Bibby stayed in the US after building their careers, Cannon, Dinnie, and Abs each returned home. Matsuda tried, unsuccessfully, to export Greco-Roman and Catch-as-Catch-Can wrestling to Japan. In 1885, Miller would challenge Whistler to a match in Australia, which Whistler won in Melbourne, tragically dying in the months after his victory. Abs's strength attracted circus promoters' attention circa 1880, leading him to tour Germany as a wrestler and strongman, touring America in 1885–1886. Upon returning to Germany, he traveled with European circuses, defeating Frenchman Pierre Rigal, Austrian Cheri Robinet, and Italian Antonio Pierri, winning the European Greco-Roman Heavyweight Championship over Cannon in 1891.[30] Muldoon pioneered professional combat sports by promoting the sport beyond carnival audiences and recruiting opponents for his act, including German-born American Ernst Roeber, who defeated a slew of foreign opponents under Muldoon's promotion.

Havana and Mexico City figured as Latin American professional wrestling epicenters. In 1909 Cuban promoters brought an international Greco-Roman troupe to Havana's Teatro Molino Rojo, featuring French, Italian, American, Turkish, Spanish, and Cuban wrestlers. Japanese judo expert Mitsuyo Maeda, who wrestled in New York (1905–1906) and Europe (1907–1908), spent several months in Havana in 1908–1909.[31] He then went to Mexico City in July 1909, eventually booking the Principal Theater where his standing offer was 100 pesos (US$50) to anyone he failed to throw and 500 pesos (US$250) to anyone who could throw him.[32] January 1910 saw Maeda wrestle the Swede Hjalmar Lundin in a tournament in Mexico City.[33] Maeda returned to Cuba in July 1910, promoting wrestling and martial arts with a troupe of mostly Japanese collaborators, including Soishiro Satake. Departing Cuba in 1913, Maeda's troupe toured much of Latin America before arriving to Brazil in 1914, where they stayed until early 1916. After retiring and settling in Brazil, Maeda taught Brazilian Jiu Jitsu pioneer Carlos Gracie, contributing wrestling and judo techniques to the emerging sport.[34]

Alongside Greco-Roman's popularization in the Americas, two additional styles were practiced on the global carnival circuit: Collar-and-Elbow and Catch-as-Catch-Can. A modified form of the standing, loose wrestling styles practiced in Ireland and the UK, Collar-and-Elbow was introduced to America by Irish immigrants circa 1830 and spread among soldiers during the American Civil War (1861–1865). The style was named for its starting position in which opponents grasped one another by the collar and elbow to eliminate striking and rushing. The objective was to register a fall by throwing one's opponent to the ground, decided when one wrestler touched the ground with both hips and one shoulder or one hip and both shoulders. The style was short-lived, displaced by the Olympic-adopted Greco-Roman and professionalized Catch-as-Catch-Can by the nineteenth century's close.

Catch wrestling is a loose classical-folkstyle hybrid that originally had the goal of winning by submission or pinning the opponent's shoulders to the ground. Catch wrestling formally developed in the British Isles as a hybrid of the three prevailing English styles known by their geographic origins – Cumberland and Westmorland style, Cornwall and Devon style, and Lancashire style.[35] Popularized in England by sports promoters J.G. Chambers circa 1871 and subsequently by J. Wannop,[36] Catch wrestling evolved simultaneously through travelling professionals and newfound amateur clubs, such as the Cumberland and Westmorland Amateur Wrestling Society.[37] Its namesake refers to the technical and strategic freedom of wrestlers to take their opponents to the ground and leverage the fall without a predetermined starting position. The discipline evolved to include groundwork, known as *par terre* in Catch's descendant, modern Freestyle.

Briton "Limey" Joe Acton was named the first Catch Heavyweight World Champion in 1881, touring America later that year where he popularized the discipline with bouts against Bibby, Whistler, and Sorakichi. Other notable Catch world champions include the American Martin "Farmer" Burns, who defeated Evan "Strangler" Lewis. More than anyone from the professional era, Iowan Frank Gotch further popularized the sport in the American interior, reigning as World Heavyweight Champion from 1908 to 1913, winning marquis victories over Austro-Hungarian Stanislaus Zbyszko and defeating Russian Georg Hackenschmidt for a

Chicago crowd of 30,000 and a record gate of $87,000.[38] Gotch's retirement is seen to coincide with an era of rampant corruption in professional wrestling.[39]

Catch wrestling's sustained popularity in Europe brought together influences from around the globe, including the Indian *pehlwani* style. Tom Cannon visited India in 1892, where he was defeated by 21-year-old Kareem Buksh. Indian champions "Great Gama" Ghulam Muhammad, and Imam Baksh Pahlawan wrestled out of London. *Pehlwani* champ Gulam (not to be confused with Ghulam Muhammad) defeated Turkish star Cour-Derelli in Paris in 1900. Bulgarian-born Yusuf "The Terrible Turk" Ismail and other eastern European and Turkish wrestlers were recruited by French promoter Joseph Doublier to wrestle in Paris (1894) and New York (1898). Doublier had previously promoted Turkish wrestlers Kartanci Mehmet Pehlivan and Kurtdereli Mehmet Pehlivan in Paris. Bulgarian Doncho Kolev Danev, who launched his career by defeating strongman Jeff Lawrence as an audience challenger at Circus "Victoria" in 1914, claimed multiple titles in Europe, Japan, Brazil, and America, introducing Balkan folkstyle techniques to international wrestling.

North American folkstyle, Freestyle, and mixed martial arts (MMA) each partially evolved from Catch wrestling, which purported to be the "most rational style of wrestling, as the competitors are not restricted by any rules as to taking and retaining a particular hold, but are at liberty to catch each other as they please, as in a natural struggle."[40] Indeed, many nineteenth-century Catch techniques depicted in wrestling manuals came into use in Freestyle and American folkstyle.[41] However, though the English-speaking world tends to see Freestyle as descendant exclusively of Catch wrestling for its popularity in Britain and the US, many worldwide folkstyles long evinced techniques, rules, and objectives common to today's Freestyle.[42]

Beginning with Alexander II, Russian Czars were some of the earliest state promoters of wrestling, paying wrestlers 500 francs to compete in annual Greco-Roman tournaments and offering 5,000 francs to the champion, a tradition lasting into the twentieth century.[43] Many European cities held Greco-Roman tournaments in the late-nineteenth century and folkstyles and Catch wrestling prevailed in the UK and North America. In the US, state and national championships were organized by local sporting associations, paving the way for international governance.

Wrestling quits the circus: 1896–1952

Early-twentieth-century professional wrestling quickly accumulated detractors, who alleged that untimed matches, unlimited weight classes, win-by-fall criteria, and promoter rules enabled fraud. Countless famous bouts were allegedly fixed, including Gotch and Hackenschmidt's Comiskey Park scuffle. Arbitrarily titled world championship matches were meant to ensure the financial success of promoters, not structure inclusive international tournaments.[44] As professional wrestling became more theatrical and boxing's integrity also proved suspect,[45] wrestling's competitive legitimacy was preserved by the sport's amateur institutionalization, first by local associations such as the American Athletic Union, which recognized Greco-Roman in 1888, and later in the modern Olympics.

As professional wrestling continued to fill circus tents and theaters throughout Europe and America, Greco-Roman appeared at the 1896 Athens Summer Olympics. Given wrestling's coexistence in such diverse venues, turn-of-the-century wrestling muddled the boundaries of amateur sport, profession, and spectacle, allowing the 1896 Games to retain characteristics of folk wrestling. In fact, the French rules used for the 1893 World Championships were not yet commonplace in England or the US, two nations essential to the 1896 Olympic revival.[46] There were no weight classes among the five-man field and three entrants had competed in other events. German entrant Carl Schuhmann – the gymnastics champion – defeated British Launceston Elliott – the weightlifting champion – in the semifinals. While the rules resembled modern Greco-Roman wrestling, some leg contact and holds were permitted. As in professional wrestling of the era, there was no time limit or point system, so matches had to be terminated by fall, judged simply by throwing one's opponent to the ground. In the final, Schuhmann prevailed over Greek competitor Georgios Tsitas in a match that had to recess overnight due to darkness before resuming in the morning.[47] The event was so marginal to the larger wrestling world, which already had several major international meets, that the 1900 Olympics dropped wrestling.

Freestyle replaced Greco-Roman to first appear at the St. Louis Olympics in 1904, which doubled as the AAU championships. Boxing weight classes were adopted, an Olympic first. The event was hardly international, though, as only Americans were allowed to compete in AAU events.[48] By the 1908 London Games, both Greco-Roman and Freestyle were contested by an international field of 115 wrestlers from 15 nations, featuring mostly Europeans and Americans. This reflected the constituent nations of the International Federation, founded by the Deutsche Athleten-Verband in 1905 to organize world championships in strength sports, including wrestling.

The 1912 Stockholm Games reflected a prevailing lack of consensus about the dominant international style. The newfound International Wrestlers' Union (IWU; Internationaler Ring Verband), convened by the Swedish Athletics Federation prior to Stockholm, dropped Freestyle, restructuring Greco-Roman to resemble Scandinavian *glíma* folkstyles. This was also because of a proliferation of European Greco-Roman meets considered world championships between 1910 and 1911 with stronger competition than Stockholm.

In 1913, delegates from Germany, Finland, Denmark, Sweden, Russia, Hungary, Austria, Bohemia, and Great Britain attended the IWU First Congress, renaming the organization the International Union of Heavy Athletics (Internationaler Amateur Verban für Schwerathletik), declaring German its official language, and setting out to develop Greco-Roman, boxing, and weight sports.

By 1920, both "French" Greco-Roman and "Catch-as-Catch-Can" Freestyle would be permanent fixtures in Antwerp, with five weight classes each (featherweight, lightweight, middleweight, light-heavyweight, and heavyweight). This would also be the first Olympics to contest wrestling indoors. In Antwerp, the IOC mandate that every sport have its own independent federation led to the 1921 creation of the International Amateur Wrestling Federation (IAWF), which modified existing rules and match structures and regulated international wrestling until 1952.[49] Testament to heightened American and UK participation, the IAWF adopted English as its official language. In 1921, Catch-as-Catch-Can rules were modified in the IAWF's "Rules of the Game" to eliminate submissions and overt violence, christening the sport "Freestyle," a translation of the French *lutte libre*.[50] The AAU would follow suit, formally abandoning Catch-as-Catch-Can in favor of Freestyle in 1922. This also divorced international competition from the by-then scandalous world of professional wrestling, which championed Catch-as-Catch-Can until mid-century.

Sanctioned World Championships accompanied early Olympic wrestling, first held in Greco-Roman in 1904. Contested through 1913, the event was canceled during World War I. Extra-Olympic wrestling resumed at the Inter-Allied Games of 1919 (Paris) and in 1920 the World Championships were contested in Vienna, with only one Antwerp Olympian participating. Hungary, Austria, and Germany made up all but one competitor in Vienna, their athletes excluded from the Antwerp Games for their role as aggressors during World War I. After the IAWF held championships in Helsinki (1921) and Stockholm (1922), the event was postponed until reinstatement in 1951.

The 1932 Los Angeles Olympics marked the first time when a nation could enter only one wrestler per weight class, now standard in Olympic competition. This drastically cut the field from earlier games: in 1932, 79 wrestlers from 18 countries contested seven weight classes in each style, compared to several hundred competitors in previous years.

The sport's rules were in constant flux between the London Games of 1908 and 1948. Additional weight classes were added and ground wrestling (*par terre*) was introduced. Time limits (first set in 1920) and overtime criteria were revised, and a three-judge panel was appointed to award decisions in the absence of a fall (after 1912). These changes rendered the sport less exhausting for organizers, spectators, and competitors alike.

With pin-fall as the only means of terminating a match, early Olympic bouts were contested as best of one fall or two out of three falls (as in the medal matches in 1904 and 1908) with no set time limit. Subsequent tournaments featured rounds ranging from 10 to 30 minutes apiece, with infinite rounds possible prior to a fall. In Stockholm 1912, the 75-kilogram Greco-Roman semifinal between Estonian Martin Klein (representing Russia) and Finland's Alppo Asikainen lasted 11 hours and 40 minutes, when Klein won by pin-fall. Too exhausted to wrestle the final, Klein defaulted to silver. Rules to promote greater action were also established, and one or both competitors could be disqualified for passivity. The latter occurred in the 1912 light heavyweight final when Finland's Ivar Böhling and Sweden's Andres Ahlgren were both disqualified for passivity after a nine-hour bout failed to yield a pin-fall. From these marathon bouts, match times steadily decreased, decisions became as commonplace as falls, and new rules placed an emphasis on wrestler activity and aggression instead of stamina.

Through 1948, Greco-Roman was dominated by Scandinavian countries, most notably Finland and Sweden, who won the most Olympic medals four and three times, respectively, by mid-century. Iconic Swede Carl Westergren competed in four Olympics (1920–1932), winning three gold medals, each in different weight classes (1920, middleweight; 1924, light heavyweight; 1932, heavyweight), as well as the world middleweight title in 1922. Countryman Ivar Johansson won Greco-Roman welterweight and Freestyle middleweight gold in 1932, also winning the Greco-Roman middleweight title in 1936. Johansson, also a nine-time European champion (1931–1939), is matched only by Estonian heavyweight Kristjan Palusalu, who won double-gold in 1936. Finnish Kalle Anttila also won gold in both styles across two Olympics, in Freestyle as a lightweight in 1920 and in Greco-Roman as a featherweight in 1924, when the Finns took a record sixteen medals across both styles.

Early Freestyle saw the US and Great Britain rival Scandinavian Greco-Roman prominence, the US winning multiple medals in all but the 1912 Stockholm Games. Great Britain's best Olympic result was in 1908, when they garnered 11 of 27 medals. Though Europe dominated, wrestling quickly afforded Asia and Africa their first Olympic medals, with featherweight Katsutoshi Naito earning a bronze for Japan in 1924 and Egypt's Ibrahim Moustafa winning the 1928 Greco-Roman gold in the light heavyweight division (shared with Sayed Nosseir, who won weightlifting gold in 1928).

In 1936, Hungary won two Freestyle golds and a Greco-Roman gold after earning medals in 1908, 1912, 1924, and 1928. 1936 was also Germany's banner year in wrestling, winning seven medals but no golds. Turkey's Yaşar Erkan won featherweight gold in Greco-Roman, and Ahmet Kireçci tallied a bronze in middleweight Freestyle, announcing the traditional wrestling powerhouse's arrival to the international and Olympic circuit. By 1948, Turkey would win eleven medals, including four Freestyle and two Greco-Roman golds, second only to Sweden's continued dominance, winning thirteen medals and five Greco-Roman golds.

Early US Freestyle success was partially attributable to early-century wrestling between Ivy League universities, including the first intercollegiate meet between Yale and Columbia in 1903 and the inauguration of the Eastern Intercollegiate Wrestling Association (EIWA) in 1905. The 1922 institutionalization of American folkstyle wrestling under the National Collegiate Athletic Association (NCAA) would see the NCAA become a feeder system for American international wrestlers, and many an early American Olympian was an EIWA or NCAA champion. Perhaps the biggest US contribution to international wrestling, though, was the point system, devised by Oklahoma State University coach Art Griffith and implemented in collegiate wrestling in 1941. Though popular in the United States, a similar point system would take two more decades to arrive to international wrestling.

The FILA era, Olympic demotion and the UWW: 1952–2016

After the 1948 Olympics, the Greco-Roman World Championships were reinstated by the IAWF in 1950, held annually on non-Olympic years since 1961. The IAWF's inaugural Free-style World Championships were held in Helsinki in 1951, featuring fields significantly more inclusive of longtime wrestling nations in the Middle East and Asia. Turkey, in fact, won the first three Freestyle events (1951, 1954, 1957), and Iran quickly tallied Freestyle titles (1961, 1965). In 1952, Frenchman Roger Coulon was elected IAWF President, renaming the organization the Fédération Internationale des Luttes Associées (FILA; International Federation of Associated Wrestling Styles). French became the organization's official language in response to Cold War politics. Organizing world championships in both styles and overseeing Olympic qualification, FILA streamlined competition across regions to render wrestling a truly global affair. With FILA's rise, boxing weight class terminology disappeared in favor of simple weight limits and Catch-as-Catch-Can was fully replaced by Freestyle.[51]

The Freestyle championships also signaled a turn in the hosting practices of international wrestling: instead of holding championships exclusively in Europe as predecessor organizations had, early FILA governance saw events in Eurasia (Turkey, 1957; Bulgaria, 1963), the Middle East (Iran, 1959), East Asia (Japan, 1954, 1961), South Asia (India, 1967), and Latin America (Argentina, 1969; Mexico, 1978). After being held solely in Europe between 1904 and 1960, Japan hosted the Greco-Roman championships alongside the Freestyle event in 1961. While the two events often coincided in the same city, both championships have only been held simultaneously – and alongside the Women's Freestyle championships – at a single venue since 2005.

The most significant change to international wrestling under FILA was the introduction of an open, visible scoring system to determine decisions. Since the 1920 Games, international wrestling panels of three judges scored bouts in secret, holding up paddles to indicate their decision for matches not culminating in pin-fall. Criteria were hypothetically standardized to reward the aggressor, but specific criteria were vague, leaving occasion for many an arbitrary 2–1 judges' decision. Prior to the 1960 Olympics, FILA Vice President Dr. Albert de Ferrari advocated for an NCAA-styled open, visible scoring system rewarding points for takedowns, counterattacks, escapes, and back exposures, as well as a "controlled fall" rule, meaning that a fall was only determined when an offensive wrestler had initiated the action.

The scoring system saw the addition of decision by technical fall (superiority) in 1968, a mercy rule ending the match when a competitor gained a significant advantage, most recently calibrated at eight points in Greco-Roman and ten points in Freestyle for the 2016 Rio Olympics. While international rules have long been modified between each Olympic cycle, often to the confusion of spectators and wrestlers alike, they have consistently attempted to encourage greater competitor action, risk, and scoring while improving judging transparency and eliminating judges' decision (last used as tie-breaker criteria in 1996). This trend demanded reduced match times, leading to the system in place for the 2016 Olympic cycle, featuring two three-minute periods with a thirty-second break between periods.

The landscape of international wrestling shifted greatly at mid-century with the Soviet Union's debut at the 1952 Olympics. The USSR won the most medals in each Olympics between 1952 and 1980 before boycotting Los Angeles, dominated by the United States in 1984. The USSR, with 48 team world championships and 415 individual medals, won all but one Greco-Roman World Championship between 1953 and 1991, conceding the 1971 contest to Bulgaria in Sofia. Between 1959 and 1991, the USSR's streak at the Freestyle World Championships was interrupted only three times, when Iran won in 1961 and 1965, and Turkey in 1966. Freestyler Aleksandr Medved smashed world records for the USSR, winning the 1964, 1968, and 1972 Olympics, also accruing seven World Championships. Medved is surpassed only by countryman Aleksandr Karelin, who competed in Greco-Roman for the USSR, the Unified Team and Russia, winning three Olympic golds and nine World Championships from 1988 to 1999.

In spite of the USSR's dominance, other nations with longstanding local wrestling traditions also registered significant medal counts during the Cold War era. Bulgaria, Japan, Turkey, Hungary, and Iran all crowned multiple Olympic champions and medalists between Rome and Montreal. Iran's rapid mid-century transition from *koshti pahlavani* to Freestyle between 1948 and 1952, indicative of many legacy folkstyle nations' institutionalization of Olympic wrestling, saw their strongest Olympic run between 1952 and 1968, winning seventeen medals. On the backs of their own wrestling traditions, India tallied a Freestyle bronze in 1952 (adding additional medals in 2008, 2012 and 2016 via Sushil Kumar, Yogeshwar Dutt and Women's freestyle 58 kg Sakshi Malik) and Mongolia accrued eight of its nine all-time medals between 1968 and 1980. Freestyler Valentin Yordanov anchored Bulgaria, winning Olympic gold and bronze and seven world championships between 1983 and 1996.

The Americans held their ground in Freestyle against the USSR, anchored by American folkstyle legend and Olympic gold medalist Dan Gable (1972) and heavyweight Bruce Baumgartner, who won two Olympic golds, a silver, and a bronze, as well as three World Championships between 1984 and 1996. The United States has also had a gold medalist in every non-boycotted Olympics since 1968 and leads the overall Freestyle medal count with 112, including 48 golds. South Korea, far dominant over Soviet allies China and North Korea, has also excelled in recent decades, amassing 36 medals across both styles, most after 1980.

While Russia remains a powerhouse – tallying 25 team titles, 244 individual world championship medals, and 63 Olympic medals – their dominance has been challenged in recent decades. The collapse of the Soviet Union in 1991 led former Soviet states and allies to excel in the Olympics, most notably Azerbaijan (22 medals), Georgia (18), Kazakhstan (15), and Ukraine (13). Cuba, having cultivated a strong wrestling tradition under Soviet guidance, continues to be visible on the world stage (24 Olympic medals), led by Mijaín López, a three-time Greco-Roman Olympic gold medalist and five-time world champion. Talented Cuban defectors also regularly compete for other nations, such as Frank Chamizo, who has won world (2015, 2017) and European (2016) titles and Olympic bronze for Italy.

In 1987, FILA established the Women's Freestyle World Championships, adding four women's categories to the 2004 Olympics. This was expanded to six weights in 2016. With its strong martial arts and women's sporting traditions, Japan has proven unstoppable, winning twenty of twenty-seven Women's Freestyle World Championships and claiming many of women's wrestling's all-time greats. Saori Yoshida has won veritably every major event, highlighted by three Olympic golds and thirteen world championships. Teammate Kaori Icho has won four Olympics and ten world championships, holding the world's longest undefeated streak (189–0) between

2003 and 2016. Hitomi Obara, who competed at a non-Olympic weight for much of her career, won eight world championships before taking Olympic gold in 2012. Eri Tosaka has continued the legacy of Japanese Women's Freestyle success, winning three world championships before claiming her first gold in the Rio Olympics. Yoshida and Icho are the most decorated wrestlers ever among men and women, Yoshida's sixteen and Icho's thirteen international titles far outpacing Medved's ten and Karelin's twelve golds. With 11 golds and 16 Olympic medals, Japan has medaled in all but two brackets since Women's Freestyle was first included in the games.

While FILA grew the sport greatly through expanded international competition,[52] officials had long faced allegations of corruption. Swedish two-time world champion (1970–1971) and Olympic silver medalist (1964) Pelle Svensson described the organization as inherently corrupt, citing a case of referee bias during the 84 kg Greco-Roman finals at the 2004 Athens games.[53] Allegedly, the Russian federation had bribed the Romanian referee over one-million Swedish Krona to tilt the match in favor of Russian Alexei Michine over Sweden's Ara Abrahamian.

Svensson also denounced controversial rulings in favor of Italian Andrea Minguzzi during the 2008 Greco-Roman tournament. FILA referee Jean-Marc Petoud, a first cousin of then-FILA President Raphaël Martinetti, assessed Abrahamian with a penalty after the match, advancing Minguzzi by decision. The judging panel and FILA administrators then denied Abrahamian's coach an appeal. The Court of Arbitration for Sport ruled that FILA had broken the Olympic Charter and its own rules by denying Abrahamian an appeal.[54] FILA officials refused to attend the hearing and later disputed the CAS and IOC rulings.

Such allegations against FILA were accompanied by dubious anti-doping and weigh-in procedures, culminating in the IOC Executive Board's 2013 recommendation to drop wrestling from the 2020 Tokyo Olympics. In February 2013, FILA held an emergency meeting where President Raphaël Martinetti was put to a vote of confidence after a group of Eastern delegates alleged his responsibility for the sport's Olympic demotion. Receiving support from only half of the FILA Board, Martinetti was forced to resign.[55] Serbian businessman Nenad Lalovic was named acting president and a campaign was launched to petition the IOC and assert upcoming changes to the sport, led by 2000 Olympic Freestyle champion Nigerian-Canadian Daniel Igali and Canadian 2008 Women's gold medalist Carol Huynh. On September 8, 2013, the IOC restored wrestling's inclusion in the 2020 Olympics after negotiating a series of demands, including shorter matchtimes, fewer men's weight classes, and more women's weight classes (six, as of Rio).

In response to IOC pressures, FILA changed its name to United World Wrestling (UWW) in September 2014, and undertook major reforms. Since transitioning from FILA to UWW leadership, international wrestling has taken a zero tolerance approach to PED use among its athletes, a response to allegations of lax enforcement against FILA during the sport's temporary Olympic demotion in 2013. Their position has been tested between London and Rio. After the widespread Russian doping scandal in the Sochi Winter Games, all seventeen Olympic-qualified Russian wrestlers were cleared to compete in Rio. Indian 74kg Freestyle qualifier Narsingh Yadav tested positive for a banned substance in July 2016 after a hard-fought battle against two-time Olympic medalist Sushil Kumar to represent India in Rio. Yadav alleged a conspiracy by Kumar's circle to spike his food with methandionene and disqualify him from competition. By August, the Indian Wrestling Federation and UWW reinstated Yadav, who traveled to Rio.

Wrestling for a living? MMA and professional wrestling's shortcomings

Even with its centrality to the Olympics and folkstyle wrestling's canonization as a national sport in several countries (Senegal, Turkey, Mongolia, Iran and Iceland), wrestling has remained something of a cult sport in Europe (outside of the former Soviet Union) and the West more generally. This is, in part, due to the limited financial potential for wrestlers, who are compensated significantly less than their professional boxing and MMA counterparts. Attempts to establish professional wrestling around local folkstyle or Olympic rules has had limited success in Europe and America. The American Real Pro Wrestling League, founded in 2002, pitted American Olympic and collegiate stars against each other in a modified Freestyle format, garnering some broadcast success. The franchise, however, failed to compete with MMA's rising popularity and folded after one season (2005–2006). Several successor organizations were founded between 2013 and 2015, each disbanding by 2016.[56]

Since the 1950s, Senegal has organized professional wrestling based on their nationally contested folkstyle, *laamb*. Earning hundreds of thousands of dollars for a single match, Senegal is one of the few nations where professional wrestlers are well-compensated, often figuring as celebrities throughout West Africa. Numerous countries of Eastern Europe, Central Asia, and the Middle East have annual professional folkstyle events, including Turkey's Kirkpinar Oil Wrestling Festival, which pays over US$100,000 to its winner.

In 2015, the UWW- and IOC-recognized Wrestling Federation of India founded the Pro Wrestling League with a prize purse of $3.3 million and $1.8 million in salaries. Promoting the league around Indian stars Kumar, Yadav, and Olympic-medalist Yogeshwar Dutt and attracting fans through India's longstanding wrestling traditions, the PWL consists of six franchises with nine wrestlers (five Indians and four foreign, five men and four women) who wrestle a series of dual meets under UWW Freestyle rules. The league, which claims "the richest ever event in the sport" seeks to afford athletes lucrative financial opportunities through legitimate professional wrestling in internationally sanctioned styles.[57]

Still, MMA remains the dominant draw for international wrestlers seeking to make careers as professional athletes. With the popularity of MMA, wrestling has gained a greater worldwide following among spectators and practitioners who acknowledge its value for MMA training. As MMA remains infinitely more lucrative than wrestling, countless MMA notables have emerged from national amateur wrestling programs.

Notes

1 Known as *lute sénégalaise* in French and *njom* in Serer, the sport is referred to as *laamb in* Wolof, Senegal's most widely spoken language.

2 On the fall in ancient wrestling, see M. Poliakoff, *Combat Sports in the Ancient World: Competition, Violence, and Culture* (New Haven, CT: Yale University Press, 1987), 23–24.

3 The precursor to international scoring was devised in US collegiate wrestling circa 1941: J. Hammond, *The History of Collegiate Wrestling: A Century of Wrestling Excellence* (Stillwater: NWHFM, 2006), 133.

4 For example, in 1826, Devon wrestler Abraham Cann faced Cornish wrestler James Polkinghorne in Morice Town (Plymouth) for a crowd of 17,000. Similar challenges frequently took place between wrestlers expert in divergent disciplines, and rivalries were common across ethnic borders in the UK, Balkans, Middle East, Scandinavia, and central and south Asia.

5 Early examples include Egyptian oil wrestling's arrival to Iran during the Persian Empire; the installation of Turkic wrestling across the Ottoman Empire, and the expansion of Mughal wrestling to India during the sixteenth century. Collar-and-elbow spread during the American Civil War and the base for "French" Greco-Roman wrestling was born of the Napoleonic Wars.

6 Alan Guttmann, *From Ritual to Record: the Nature of Modern Sports* (New York: Columbia University Press, 1978), 60. Guttmann states, "Modern sport ... took shape over a period of approximately 150 years, from the early eighteenth to the late nineteenth centuries. ... Modern sports were born in England and spread from their birthplace to the United States, to Western Europe and the world beyond" (60). Also, see Stefan Szymanski, "A Theory of the Evolution of Modern Sport," *Journal of Sport*

History 35 no. 1 (2008): 1–32. Szymanski notes, "a fixed set of rules is one of the principal characteristics of a modern sport as defined by Guttmann" (15).

7 The tomb of the Vizier Ptah-hotep (2300 BCE) displays six pairs of wrestlers and an additional frieze at Medinet Habu, Egypt (1200 BCE) depicts wrestling before spectators. See H. Wilsdorf, *Ringkampf in Alten Aegypten* (Wurzburg: Triltsch, 1939).

8 J. Alter, *The Wrestler's Body: Identity and Ideology in North India* (Berkeley, CA: University of California Press, 1992).

9 T. Zhongyi and T. Cartmell, *The Method of Chinese Wrestling* (Berkeley, CA: North Atlantic Books, 2005), 21.

10 The feat is recounted in the *Codex Græcus Matritensis Ioannis Skyllitzes* (fol. 85v), an illuminated manuscript narrating the Byzantine Empire from 811 to 1057.

11 J. Alter, "The *Sannyasi* and the Indian Wrestler: The Anatomy of a Relationship," *American Ethnologist* 19.2 (1992): 317–336.

12 M. Poliakoff, "Freestyle Wrestling," in D. Levinson and K. Christensen, *Encyclopedia of World Sport: From Ancient Times to the Present* (Santa Barbara, CA: ABC, 1996), 461.

13 F. Auerswald, *Die Ringer Kunst* (Wittemberg: Hans Lufft, 1539), 4.

14 R. Carew, *Survey of Cornwall* (London: Bensley, 1811 [1602]), 199–200.

15 The games were purportedly inaugurated in 1829 BCE to commemorate the death of Queen Tailte.

16 V. Williams, *Weird Sports and Wacky Games from Around the World* (Santa Barbara, CA: Greenwood, 2015), 52–54.

17 Ibid.

18 Ibid.

19 I use the term "professional wrestling" to refer to wrestlers paid to compete in legitimate contests, this in opposition to the modern entertainment form of professional wrestling centered around choreographed theatrical combat.

20 T. Corvin, *Pioneers of Professional Wrestling, 1860–1899* (Bloomington, IN: Archway, 2014), 1.

21 Ibid, 2. Bartolo Bartoletti is credited with coining the term "Greco-Roman" to highlight the style's ancient origins.

22 Corvin, *Pioneers of Professional Wrestling*, 2.

23 W. Acree, "Hemispheric Travelers on the Rioplatense Stage," *Latin American Theatre Review* 47.2 (2014): 5–24.

24 Ibid., 12–13.

25 Ibid., 19–20.

26 Ibid.

27 Corvin, *Pioneers of Professional Wrestling*, 24–25.

28 Ibid., 45.

29 Inaugurated in the late 1870s, the American "World Championship" took precedence over the European "World Championship" (1886–1905) before the titles were united in 1905. Several wrestlers were billed as American, European, and World Greco-Roman Champions, many at the same time, and the title was more a promotional designation than a sporting title.

30 *Carl Abs: Der unbesiegte Meisterschaftsringer: Sein Leben und seine Thaten [Carl Abs: the Undefeated Championship wrestler: His Life and Deeds]* (Frankfurt: Stoltze, 1895), 8–12.

31 T. Green and J. Svinth, "The Circle and the Octagon: Maeda's Judo and Gracie's Jiu-jitsu," in *Martial Arts in the Modern World*, eds. T. Green and J. Svinth (London: Praeger, 2003), 61–70.

32 *Mexican Herald*, July 14, 1909.

33 *Mexican Herald*, January 23, 1910.

34 Green and Svinth, "The Circle and the Octagon," 61–70.

35 W. Armstrong, *Wrestling* (New York: Frederick A. Stokes, 1890), xiv.

36 Ibid.

37 On the CWAWS, ibid.

38 N. Fleischer, *From Milo to Londos. The Story of Wrestling Through the Ages* (New York: King Athletic Library, 1936), 121.

39 Ibid.

40 Ibid., 34.

41 Ibid., 34–42.

42 Icelandic *glíma* (lausatök), Swedish *kragkast*, Swiss *calegon*, Turkish *carakucak*, and Indian *kushti*, among other loose folkstyles, greatly resemble Freestyle.

43 On the Czar's Tournament: M. Poliakoff, "Wrestling, Greco-Roman," in *Encyclopedia of World Sport: From Ancient Times to the Present*, Vol. 3, eds. D. Levinson and K. Christensen (Santa Barbara: ABC-CLIO, 1996), 1194; G. Morton and G. O'Brien, *Wrestling to Rasslin': Ancient Sport to American Spectacle*, (Bowling Green, OH: BGSU Press, 1985), 34.

44 For examples of journalist Al Spink's 1919 indictment "that the entire game of wrestling was rotten," see Corvin, *Pioneers of Professional Wrestling*, 24.

45 See G. Gems, "Boxing," Chapter 12, this volume.

46 P. Coubertin, *Les Jeux Olympiques d'Athenes 1896* (Athens: Beck, 1896).

47 P. Lambros and N. Politis, *Die Olympischen Spiele: 776 v. Chr.–1896 n. Chr.* (Athens: Beck, 1896), 93.

48 Some competitors did, however, retain foreign citizenship: Charles Ericksen and Bernhoff Hansen, welterweight and heavyweight champions, respectively, were Norwegians resident in the US while German-born heavyweight silver medalist Frank Kugler only became a US citizen in 1913.

49 "Creation of IAWF," *UnitedWorldWrestling.org*. Retrieved from https://unitedworldwrestling.org/organization/united-world-wrestling (accessed August 1, 2016).

50 J. Nash, "The Martial Chronicles: The Forgotten Olympic History of Catch-as-Catch-Can Wrestling," *BloodyElbow.com* August 13, 2012. Retrieved from www.bloodyelbow.com/2012/8/13/3238285/martial-chronicles-olympics-history-catch-wrestling (accessed August 1, 2016).

51 In 1950, American government publications still referred to Freestyle alternately as Catch-as-Catch-Can. See *Wrestling* (Annapolis: US Naval Institute, 1950). By 1961, later editions of the same publication only reference Freestyle.

52 Wrestling has been featured at the Pan-American Games since 1951; Asian Games since 1954; and African Games since 1965. The European Championships were inaugurated in 1911, combining both styles at the same venue since 2005. The Wrestling World Cup, a team dual meet competition, was inaugurated in 1973. Wrestling has also appeared at the Commonwealth Games, excluding 1990, 1998, and 2008.

53 "Pelle Svensson: Jag blev mordhotad," *Afton Bladet*, August 14, 2008. Retrieved from www.aftonbladet.se/sportbladet/os2008/article11486183.ab (accessed August 1, 2016).

54 "Arbitration CAS ad hoc Division (OG Beijing) 08/007 Swedish National Olympic Committee (SNOC) and Ara Abrahamian v. Fédération Internationale des Luttes Associées (FILA) & others, award of 23 August 2008." Retrieved from http://jurisprudence.tas-cas.org/Shared%20Documents/OG%2008-007.pdf (accessed August 1, 2016).

55 "Wrestling Chief Resigns after Olympic Snub," *AlJazeera.com* February 13, 2013. Retrieved from www.aljazeera.com/sport/olympics/2013/02/2013216154419722800.html (accessed August 1, 2016).

56 The Association of Career Wrestlers was founded in 2013, folding in 2015. The Global Wrestling Championships were held in Ithaca, New York in 2014, staging freestyle championships. The Flo Premier League also held semi-regular promotions between American Olympians competing in a freestyle–folkstyle hybrid between 2014 and 2015.

57 "About," *Prowrestlingleague.com*. Retrieved from www.prowrestlingleague.com/about.php (accessed August 01, 2016).

15

Martial arts

Leonardo José Mataruna-Dos-Santos, Mauro Cesar Gurgel Alencar de Carvalho, Mike Callan and John Nauright

Basic elements of judo and Brazilian jiu-jitsu

A significant number of combat sports, such as judo and Brazilian jiu-jitsu, have their origins in the ancient martial arts (IJF, 2019; Gracie 2019). These martial arts may be described as groups of stereotyped movements, philosophical and moral concepts and values, exercises, behaviors and social roles (Farrer and Whalen–Bridge, 2011). Both ancient martial arts and modern combat sports aim to shape the character and the way citizens should think, believe, move, act, react, and conduct themselves in society (Wargo, Spirrison and Henley, 2007). So, this is an important aspect of these activities, due to the large spectrum of influence on dynamics of practitioners' social relations and quality of life (Matsumoto and Konno, 2005; Borba-Pinheiro et al., 2010; DiMare et al., 2016).

Green (2001) and Green and Svinth (2003), reminds us that the definition of martial arts is not universal, and inevitably, is focused by time, place, philosophy, politics, worldview, popular culture, and other cross-cultural variables by the person who defines, explains and presents the historical aspects of certain physical cultural activities. Papakitsos (2017) emphasizes three important aspects regarding terminology in martial arts and combat sports for understanding and conceptualizing them. The first aspect mentioned is military training which is focused on preparing the individual soldier for the battlefield for damaging the enemy using the appropriate tools and weapons. In this primary manifestation the training methodology emphasizes team-work, and valorizes the collective. In the second aspect, it presents the combative sports, while the athlete has to function within certain rules or set of regulations. The individual component is venerated and an external person or people, nominated referee, mediates the action or combat. The most important element is the security of the practitioner, which aims at ensuring physical safety and integrity of the contestants. The usage of weaponry is restricted to certain categories (namely those of the various sport-fencing arts). And the third manifestation is the civilian arts, commonly labeled as self-defense activities. It is possible to present based on a code of ethics and regulations, but basically used the principle to save and protect the integrity of the people attacked for someone else. The representation combines individual and collective actions under different circumstances.

Channan and Jennings (2014) highlight that although 'martial arts' or 'combat sports' differing in types, both emphasize the need to deal with the issues related to physical violence and human combat that includes sporting, military or civilian circumstances. Both could be used to improve human behavior as they can promote the better understanding of controlling aggression. In some cases traditional martial arts concentrate on the patterns of movement, while globalized forms increasingly emphasize combat elements (Deaton, Kim and Nauright, 2020; Lawton and Nauright, 2019; Ueda, 2017).

The International Judo Federation defines judo as the educational method created by Professor Jigoro Kano in 1882, derived from the martial arts, which became an official Olympic sport at the 1964 Tokyo Olympic Games. They explain that judo is a highly codified sport where the mind controls the body and contributes to education (Kodokan Institute, 2019). Nowadays, much attention has been drawn to the Olympic Sport, sponsorship and television broadcasts. Stakeholders of globalized judo have prompted alterations in values and rules of the sport (Ueda, 2017). Changes in the colors of the clothes (one fighter uses blue and the other white *judogui* – a *kimono*), time of combat, and the dynamic of the sport (Ebell, 2008; Ueda, 2017). Nonetheless, in Japan traditional competitions, avoid the global tendencies and continuing use of the traditional aspects of rules, colors and dynamic of the judo (Ebell, 2008).

Jigoro Kano suggested that judo can be thought of in the wide sense and in the narrow sense (IJF, 2018). Judo in the narrow sense can be thought of as that which developed from the ancient martial art of ju-jutsu. However, Kano was keen to stress that unlike ju-jutsu, Kodokan judo is based on physical education principles, and particularly the principle of maximum efficient use of mind and body. He described this as a great principle of humanity, a moral doctrine. This is judo in the wider sense (Hayashi, 1972).

The modern Olympic sport element of judo is manifest through international matches managed by the International Judo Federation as part of the IJF World Tour, culminating annually with either the World Championships or the Olympic Games. Currently judo matches last four minutes, and judoka aim to score ippon using throws (*nage-waza*), holds (*osaekomi-waza*), armlocks (*kansetsu-waza*) or strangles (*shime-waza*). Judo matches (shiai) are one way to learn judo, the other ways are free practice (*randori, yaku-soku-geiko, kakari-geiko, tandoku-renshu*) prearranged forms (*kata, keashi-waza, renraku-renka-waza, uchi-komi, nage-ai*), lectures (*kogi*) and question and answer (*mondo*).

The application of judo relies on yielding in order to break the balance of the opponent (*kuzushi*). This is the principle of JU. To apply techniques, a judoka uses the principle of maximum efficient use of mind and body (*Seiryoku-Zenyo*). IJF (2018) presented the words of Kano regarding the philosophy of education: 'the utmost use of one's energy or, in short, the maximum of efficiency. What Kano called energy did not simply imply physiological energy or physical vigor, it connoted the 'living force' including both the spiritual and physical aspects of life' (Maekawa and Hasegawa, 1963).

When judoka apply this principle to society, for mutual welfare and benefit, this is known as *jita-kyoei*. Jigoro Kano thought in the global perspective to designed the principles of Judo and his education project based on the *jita-kyoei*. IJF (2018) acknowledges Kano speech: 'In order to perfect myself, I do not for a moment forget to be of service to the world . . . I will dedicate my future activities to the service of society and for this purpose I shall strive to build up my character and form a firm foundation for my life' (Maekawa and Hasegawa, 1963).

Kano created values for the sport close to the Olympic Values, such as: respect, friendship and collaboration (IOC, 2017a). Del Vecchio and Mataruna (2004) advocate the values created simultaneously are not connected in the sport developed by Jigoro Kano and Pierre de Coubertin, the founder of the modern Olympics. They were promoted in isolation without connection.

Sanada (2019) holds the view that de Coubertin, was also keen on educational reform based on sports realized in Japan, so he was eager to surround himself with people like Kano. The author comments that upon joining the IOC, Jigoro Kano became actively involved in the Olympic Movement and the relationship of Judo and Games started to become possible. It was expected to happen in the 1940 Olympic Games, when Japan was expected to host the first Games in Asia, but the Second World War forced cancellation of the Games (Collins, 2007). The campaign promoted by the organizer for the 1940 Tokyo games considered the Olympics as an event to combine internationalism and heightened nationalism to support the Japanese state's vision of its role in creating a new order in Asia. Judo made its first appearance on the Olympic program at the Games of the XVIII Olympiad when the Olympics finally came to Tokyo in 1964 (IOC, 2017b).

Ohlenkamp (2019) comments that Judo is not only an Olympic Sport. According to IJF (2019), 'Judo is a tremendous and dynamic combat sport that demands both physical prowess and great mental discipline'. Considering the individual skills and limitations of every person, to practice judo means an opportunity for training different potentials of movements. Surprisingly, the 'gentle way' remains a remarkably effective self-defense training even when practiced as a sport. Since, other modern 'combat' methods appeared, judo continue with the same essence and traditional principles (Ohlenkamp, 2019). 'Jigoro Kano applied modern sport training methodology to the traditional koryu ju-jutsu and found that it produced a better combat art, which has proven itself again and again over the last 120 years' (Ohlenkamp, 2019). As self-defense system, judo has the Kodokan goshin-jutsu, an exercise program formally established in 1956 to teach the principles and techniques of defense against armed and unarmed attacks, and to meet contemporary lifestyle needs (Jones, Savage and Gatting, 2016).

At the beginning of the 20th century, one of the Jigoro Kano instructors began to travel internationally promoting Judo in the United States (Yoshinori, 2002). He stayed for short period of time in the USA and moved to Brazil in 1914. For some reason, historically not identified until this moment, the Japanese man rejected using the Judo name in the South American country. One of the hypothesis is based on the usage of the terminology 'Kano ju-jutsu' instead of judo, that caused confusion to the lay people.

This informational gap requires further and proper historical investigation for understanding the reasons of the break relations with Kodokan traditions. He start to fight to promote the combat sport, renamed as jiu-jitsu, different of the *ju-jutsu* from Japan, because it was developed upon the Judo Techniques, focusing the fight on the floor and less on throws. A number of Japanese migrants entered Brazil in the south and southeast escaping from the War to work with agriculture and, improved the opportunity for teaching *Kodokan judo*, based on throw techniques (Yoshinori, 2002). Green (2001: 52) comments that the parent system of Brazilian jiu-jitsu is Kodokan judo. The author also mentions that Brazilian jiu-jitsu is a virtually synonymous with the Gracie family, through whose lineage the system was passed and whose members modified the original Japanese art into its present state.

Key highlights of the history and development of judo and Brazilian jiu-jitsu

These ways of self-defense are still engaged to their historical, geographical contexts and biological capability, while attacking and defending themselves to survive. The biological or phylogenetic capability relies on our 'reptilian brain', according to the triune brain theory (MacLean and Kral, 1973). It is the most ancient part of human cerebrum and has phylogenetic structure that responsible for the attack and defend relationship and comprehension of this dynamics.

Therefore, humans do not need special teaching or training sessions to learn the basic movements, derived emotions and dynamics to fight, because they are natural movements, feelings and strategies supported by the reptilian brain or R-complex comprehend the brainstem and basal ganglia (Santos et al., 2012). So, fighting skills are based upon natural movement structure that everyone has in their natural motor vocabulary such as pushing, pulling, crawling, rolling, holding balance walking, running, hitting, kicking, etc.

Actual Martial Arts fighting skills are more complex. They are still based on the R-complex structure, but also on other regions of the brain, because they are not so simple as natural movements. They are socially acquired skills (ontogenetic abilities) that demand more processing of the nervous system to follow a specific kinetic chain. So, they are supported by the basic movement structures such as organic hardware (reptile brain), other superior parts of the brain structure and software, which means neurons-neurons and neuron-muscle synapse, RNA processing, and specific protein production are required for movement planning and execution. They depend also on specific teaching to be acquired also on other superior brain structures.

These fighting skills also added clothes and implements which were available in nature, such as animals' leather, bones teeth, sticks etc. Later, they were changed to become *Samurais'* armor, judo kimono, javelin, bow and arrow, sword and knife, for example. The applied strategies to fight also changed and improved according to the intellectual development as time goes by, showing the historical influence on this matter. So, the amount of knowledge about fighting is also restricted to its historical time and context.

While looking to Middle Ages until the Early Modern Japan periods, the adopted political system, *Shogunate*, illustrates the importance of *samurai* in that society. These periods embraced the Kamakura, Ashikaga and Tokugawa Shogunates (1192–1868). *Samurai* were the most important social caste and their leader, the *Shogun*, was the supreme governor, who had more power than the emperor himself. *Samurai* were involved in many other activities and functions beyond the military aspects, but they ought to follow a very strict hierarchy and code of conduct, called *Bushido* (Ueda, 2017).

'The Takeuchi style of jujitsu, under Hisamori Takeuchi, is the oldest known form of jujitsu. This particular school specialized in immobilizing the aggressor. Around 1598 other styles became popular among the samurai warriors. About 1650 in the Wakayama Prefecture, Jushin Sekiguchi taught what became known as *yawara*, and developed the principles of break falls (*ukemi*). Free-fighting (*randori*) was introduced in the 17th century. During this time jujitsu was still the identified primarily as a battlefield art' (Matsumoto, 1996).

For 200 years, during the *Shogunate* days, Japan have closed their harbors to Europeans with only the Portuguese Jesuits and the Spanish Franciscans monks allowed to develop limited commercial relations with Japanese archipelago. Geographical, political and social isolation led to strengthening cultural values, crystallization of behavioral patterns and lack of social flexibility to deal with different ideas, cultures and behaviors. Forced contact with the American Commodore Perry opened a new commercial route with the Japanese that brought new military weapons and human resources. A subsequent '*coup d'etat*' ended with the *Shogunate* system of governance, to start the *Meiji* dynasty, as romantically shown in both *Shogun* and the *Last Samurai* movies. In the following years, the *samurai* lost their power, respect and jobs. American and European cultures overcame the old one and *samurai* were socially marginalized. But somehow, they still had to survive, so they started selling part of their knowledge about Martial Arts. Many schools of Martial Arts (*ryu*) were opened and they started teaching the Japanese style of archery (*kyūdō*), or how to fight throwing punches and kicks (*karate*), or their kind of wrestling (*ju-jutsu*), or how to fight with a bamboo sword (*kendo*), because they should never teach the whole knowledge on fighting together to common people, who did not follow the *bushido*.

According to Matsumoto (1996) there were over 160 ju-jutsu schools, teaching different styles, including the kito-style, which began in 1795. The Kito-style and kyushin-style specialized in free-fighting (*randori*) while the Yoshin-style and Tenjin Shinyo-style focused on joint bending techniques (*kansetsu-waza*), striking techniques (*atemi-waza*) and patterns of movement (*kata*).

Jigoro Kano was born at the beginning of the Mejii period, a time of great social change in Japan, when the country was opening up to external influences for the first time in over two centuries. As a young man in his early twenties, he drew on his influences from two different *ju-jutsu ryu* to form the emergent Kodokan judo form in 1882. However the name of Kodokan judo was created later. First, it was known as Kano jiu jitsu.

Global spread of judo and Brazilian jiu-jitsu

Judo (gentle way) and Brazilian jiu-jitsu (gentle art) present strong similarities regarding the motricity and also in the sport global perspective. Both are based on the Japanese culture, while Judo uses more throwing techniques and floor control, Brazilian jiu-jitsu (BJJ) essentially uses levers, torque and pressure in order to take one's opponent to the ground and dominate them (CBJ, 2019; Gracie, 2019).

The Japanese philosophy associated with a program of physical education, eliminated the strong and risk techniques from Judo. Using the representation of feudal martial arts called ju-jutsu, a pedagogical professor named Jigoro Kano, created the judo that means gentle way. Kano learned different types of ju-jutsu and decided to create his own method with an educational perspective. His intention was to internationalize Judo sending instructors that he prepared to present and challenge people around the world. Kano had a motto to promote his sport, to use 'maximum efficiency with minimum effort'.

According to IJF (2019), Kano created The Kodokan Institute in 1882 and became the first Asian member of the International Olympic Committee (IOC). In 1912 he helped to establish the Japan Amateur Athletic Association and was a Japanese representative at the Olympic Games of 1928 in Amsterdam, 1932 in Los Angeles and 1936 in Berlin. Kano died while travelling back from Europe, in 1938, at the age of 77, on board NYK Line motor ship Hikawa Maru.

The archives of the Brazilian Judo Federation show that Japanese immigration was the most important factor in the emergence of judo in Brazil. The influence exerted by professional wrestlers representing various ju-jutsu Japanese schools also contributed to the development of Judo. Eisei Mitsuyo Maeda, a direct student of Jigoro Kano, was also called conde koma. He arrived in Brazil on November 14, 1914 entering the country through Porto Alegre. On December 18, 1915 along with other Japanese fighters he went to Manaus in the interior. However, before that, he toured the whole of Brazil demonstrating the challenges of fights. Conde Koma settled in Belém do Pará in 1921. Maeda founded his first judo academy in Brazil in the Rowing Club, a neighborhood of the old city (CBJ, 2019).

The contribution of Japanese immigrants who spread judo seems to have been more important than the contribution of Count Koma and his fellow fighters. From the arrival of Kasato Maru to Brazil (1908) until the Second World War, names and practices were confused. One finds in the literature judo, jiu-do, ju-jutsu, jiu-jitsu and also jiu-jitsu Kano, often designating the same practice (CBJ, 2019). For a better understanding it is necessary to observe the figure 15.1, where it is possible to clarify the influences suffered for different schools of ju-jutsu.

The Kodokan Institute (2019) explains that Kodokan judo directly received influences of classical ju-jutsu styles (tenjin shinyo-ryu and kyto-ryo). Maeda was directly student of Jigoro Kano at Kodokan, but he also received influences of ju-jutsu takenouchi-ryu, that presented more combats on the floor.

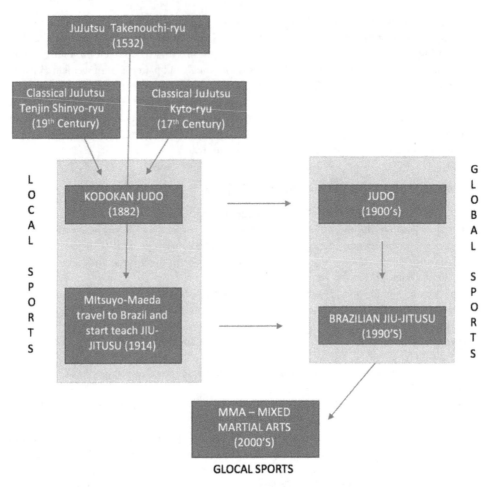

Figure 15.1 Development of the martial arts in the local, global and glocal perspectives.

Giulianotti and Robertson (2007), state that the globalization of sport 'took off' from the 1870s onwards, such as the 'games revolution' colonized British imperial outposts (e.g. cricket in Asia and Australasia), the 'global game' of football underwent mass diffusion along British trading and educational routes (e.g. in Europe, South America), and distinctive indigenous sports were forged as part of the invention of national traditions in emerging modern societies. Petersen-Wagner and Mataruna (2015), comment on transnational contexts from a global sport perspective, mentioning the case of Jigoro Kano Kodokan judo in Brazil to Gracie Family Brazilian jiu-jitsu in Japan. Judo comes from Japan to Brazil and in the new country developed as another movement, going back to Japan as a recycled product with new values, new philosophy and new techniques to be relearned. Giulianotti and Robertson (2007) reveal that transnational processes impact upon individual sports, and regional and national dimensions, reinforce the theory of the Petersen–Wagner and Mataruna (2015).

While judo experienced a 'boom' as a result of the Olympics, jiu-jitsu developed the concept of sport internally. To become a global sport, judo passed through important sportisation stages as can be seen in Table 15.1. Nonetheless, Cruz (2018) remembers that Carlos and Helio Gracie would later turn that martial art into a global phenomenon as the primary developers of modern

Table 15.1 Global development of judo.

Entry in the Olympic Games 1940 cancelled to the proper start in 1964	1960: At the 58th IOC Session held in Rome in August, it was decided to recognize the International Judo Federation and to integrate this sport into the program of the Games of the XVIII Olympiad in Tokyo in 1964.
Mexico City 1968	1963: At the 61st IOC Session held in Baden-Baden in October, it was recalled that a decision had been taken in 1962 (at the 60th Session in Moscow) to accept a maximum of 18 sports on the 1968 program. A vote was held to eliminate certain sports, and this included judo.
Munich 1972	1965: At the 64th IOC Session held in Madrid in October, it was decided to increase the number of sports on the program to 21 for the Games of the XX Olympiad in Munich in 1972. Judo was on this new list.
Women's inclusion 1992	1985: At the 90th IOC Session held in Berlin in June, it was decided to include women's judo on the program of the Games of the XXV Olympiad in Barcelona in 1992, subject to certain pending issues being settled by the Federation.
Entry in the Paralympic Games 1988 and 2004	1988: Judo for blind and impaired vision people made its Paralympic debut at Seoul Games and has been contested at every Games since.
	2004: Women's events were added at Athens 2004. The sport was the only martial art on the Paralympic program per 32 years from 1988 to 2020. Before Judo, the program had Wrestling per just two games successively (Arnhem 1980 and New York 1984) for people with visual disability. In the Tokyo 2020 Games will start the Taekwondo.
Mixed team event 2020	2017: A decision was taken during the IOC Executive Board meeting held in Lausanne in June to include a mixed team event at Tokyo in 2020.

Source: adapted from IOC (2017b) and IPC (2019)

Brazilian jiu-jitsu, and the name Gracie would live on for decades as one of the most formidable families in the world of sport.

Jiu-jitsu expanded further globally during the last two decades of the 20th century. Using a commercialisation strategy the sport moved to the USA with the Gracie family starting the Ultimate Fight Championship (UFC). The fight challenge received rules and the name of Mixed Martial Arts (MMA). Jiu-jitsu itself received the new name of Brazilian jiu-jitsu (BJJ).

Jigoro Kano sent many of his students overseas to help spread globally the growth of judo. Famously these students included Yamashita Yoshitagu who travelled to the USA and became the teacher of President Theodore Roosevelt. Whilst not originally a Kodokan student, Gunji Koizumi was heavily influenced by Kano and founded the Budokwai in London in 1918. A very influential organisation, the Budokwai had many famous members including Mikonosuke Kai-waishi, Trevor Leggett and Moshe Feldenkrais, and was instrumental in the development of the European Judo Union (1948), and the International Judo Federation (1951). Earlier efforts to form a European organisation in the 1930s did not survive the conflict during the Second World War. And a new sport called Brazilian Jiu-Jitsu comes from Kano's global initiatives.

With MMA achieving so much global acclaim, in 2007, in Rio de Janeiro, the IJF Presidency passed to the naturalized Austrian judoka and businessman Marius Vizer. Vizer had a clear vision for the sport and set about a strategic plan to take the sport into the 21st century. So many developments have followed, most noticeably the introduction of the IJF World Tour, the World Ranking List, significant levels of prize money, live streaming of events and the broadcast contract with CNN. Additionally he has overseen other developments that demonstrate the educational nature of judo including the Judo for Peace initiative, Judo for the World series, the first Gender Equity conference and the World Kata Championships. He developed a new moment of global sport for Judo (IJF, 2017).

Final considerations

The emergence and popularity of mixed martial arts events (e.g. K-1 and Ultimate Fighting Championship) created a market demand for new forms of entertainment value in martial arts. The increased number of martial arts practitioners, products, organizations and events reflects that martial arts have become global cultural products (Ko, 2007; Ueda, 2017).

The growth of martial arts as global cultural products can be best illustrated in the cases of Judo and Taekwondo, both Olympic sports. Today, the International Judo Federation (IJF) lists about 180 member nations, and the number of Judo practitioners in the world is over 8 million (IJF, 2017). The World Taekwondo Federation (WTF) is made up of 185 national governing bodies, and the number of Taekwondo practitioners in the world is estimated to be 70 million (Deaton et al., 2020). The increased popularity of Judo and Taekwondo and their addition to the Olympics clearly indicates that martial arts have become popular cultural products (Ko, 2007).

Judo was introduced to the Olympic program at the 1964 Tokyo Games and since 1972 has featured in every Olympiad. Judo became more popular in the five continents after the Olympic Games. In Japan, Brazil and France is inserted in the primary and secondary schools, and universities as part of the syllabus of Physical Education classes. Militaries academies or schools used judo as part of self-defense or for discipline. Money prizes started in the judo competitions in the International Judo Federation events. The intention is to make the sport more attractive for spectators and athletes. To enhance the dimension of sport and develop it globally, Marius Viser every year launches new tournaments in different countries.

During the Rio 2016 Olympic Games, the #Judo was the number one trending topic in the World on the Twitter platform on five days out of seven days of competition (IJF, 2017). As the most cited sport in this edition of Summer Olympics than any other sport in social media, it demonstrates not only the popularity of judo but also the potential to engage with different audiences. Through social media, the public have an opportunity to share, post, discuss and be more involved with the sport's content. Therefore, social media has been actively used as an important tool that impacts the way that sport can be seen and communicated.

Judo and ju-jitsu, along with taekwondo and karate, demonstrate the multi-faceted ways in which globalization has impacted sports as they expand from traditional locations and cultures to others. In some cases like taekwondo it has led to multiple international organizations with one being linked to the Olympics and another promoting competition along traditional lines (Deaton et al., 2020). Karate's globalization has followed similar patterns to tae kwon do (Lawton and Nauright, 2019) In the case of judo and ju-jitsu it has led to new sport forms resulting in today's MMA. Martial arts is thus one of the most fertile grounds for examining globalization, sportization and conflict and compromise that is necessary as a result.

References

Borba-Pinheiro, C.J., Carvalho, M.C.G.A., Lima da Silva, N.S., Drigo, A.J., Bezerra, J.C.P. and Dantas, E.H.M. (2010). Bone Density, Balance and Quality of Life of Postmenopausal Women Taking

Alendronate Participating in Different Physical Activity Programs. *Therapeutic Advances in Musculoskeletal Disease*, 2(4).

CBJ (2019, January 21). CBJ. Retrieved from www.cbj.com.br

Channon, A. and Jennings, G. (2014) Exploring Embodiment through Martial Arts and Combat Sports: a Review of Empirical Research, *Sport in Society: Cultures, Commerce, Media, Politics*, 17(6), 773–789.

Collins, S. (2007) The Rise of Japanese Militarism. *The International Journal of the History of Sport*, 24(8), 1097–1130.

Cruz, G. (2018, February 3). Belem Back in the Spotlight 101 Years after a Historical Meeting. Retrieved from: www.mmafighting.com/2018/2/3/16874482/belem- spotlight-101-years-after-historical-meeting-ufc

Deaton, C., Kim, Y. and Nauright, J. (2020). Globalization Impacts on Taekwondo. *Sport in Society*, forthcoming.

Del Vecchio, F.B. and Mataruna, L. (2004, January 10). Jigoro Kano e Barão De Coubertin: Nuances de um pré Olimpismo no Oriente. Retrieved from www.efdeportes.com.

DiMare, M.,Vechio, F.B. and Xavier, B.E.B. (2016). Handgrip Strength, Physical Activity Level and Quality of Life of Judo Master Competitors. Revista Brasileira de Educação Física e Esporte, (São Paulo) 2016. *Out-Dez*; 30(4):847–855.

Ebell, S.B. (2008). Competition versus Traditional in Kodokan Judo. *Journal of Asian Martial Arts*, 17(1).

Farrer, D.S. and Whalen-Bridge, J. (2011). *Introduction Martial Arts, Transnationalism, and Embodied Knowledge in Martial Arts as Embodied Knowledge: Asian Traditions in a Transnational World*. New York: Suny Press.

Giulianotti, R. and Robertson, R. (2007). Sport and Globalization: Transnational Dimensions. *Global Networks*, 7(2), 107–112.

Gracie, R. (2019, January 5). The History of Jiu-Jitsu: A Brief History of the Gentle Art, from the Samurai to the UFC Champions and IBJJF Gold Medalists. Retrieved from www.graciemag.com/en/ the-saga-of-jiu-jitsu.

Green, T.A. (2001). *Martial Arts of the World: An Encyclopedia*, vol.1. Santa Barbara, CA: ABC Clio.

Green, T.A. and Svinth, J.R. (2003). *Martial Arts in the Modern World*. Westport, CT: Greenwood Publishing.

Hayashi, N. (1972). Judo. *Journal of Health, Physical Education, Recreation*, 43(7), 50–55.

IJF (2017, May 7). IJF Media Commission Report. Retrieved from http://99e89a50309ad79ff91d-082b8fd5551e97bc65e327988b444396.r14.cf3.rackcdn.com/up/2018/01/Report_of_the_Medias_Commissio-1516701103.pdf

IJF (2018, December 18). Kano and the Beginning of the Judo Movement. Retrieved from www.ijf.org/ history/judo-corner

IJF (2019). *IJF Manager Course*. Budapest: IJF Academy.

IOC (2017a, July 31). Friendship and Courage are Key in the Chase for Tokyo 2020 Mixed Team Gold. Retrieved from www.olympic.org/news/friendship-and-courage-are-key- in-the-chase-for-tokyo-2020-mixed-team-gold.

IOC (2017b, November 10). Judo: History of Judo at the Olympic Games. Retrieved from https://stillmed. olympic.org/media/Document%20Library/OlympicOrg/Factsheets-Reference-Documents/Games/ OG/History-of-sports/Reference-document-Judo-History-at-the-OG.pdf

IPC (2019, March 13). Judo. Retrieved from www.paralympic.org/judo.

Jones, L.C., Savage, M.P. and Gatting, W.L. (2016). Kodokan Judo's Self-Defense System: Kodokan Goshin-jutsu. *Journal of Asian Martial Arts*, 25(1).

Ko, Y. and Kim, Y. (2010). Martial Arts Participation: Consumer Motivation. *International Journal of Sports Marketing and Sponsorship*, 11(2), 2–20.

Kodokan Institute (2019, February 26). History of Kodokan Judo. Retrieved from http://kodokanjudoin-stitute.org/en/doctrine/history

Lawton, B. and Nauright, J. (2019). The Globalization of the Traditional Okinawan art of Shotokan Karate. *Sport in Society*.

MacLean, P.D. and Kral, V.A. (1973). *A Triune Concept of the Brain and Behaviour*. Ontario Mental Health Foundation.

Maekawa, M. and Hasegawa, Y. (1963). Studies on Jigoro Kano, Significance of His Ideals of Physical Education and Judo. *Bulletin of the Association for the Scientific Studies of Judo*, Kodokan, 1963.

Matsumoto, D. (1996) *An Introduction to Kodokan Judo: History and Philosophy*. Tokyo: Hon-no-Tomosha.

Matsumoto, D. and Konno, J. (2005). The Relationship between Adolescents' Participation in Judo, Quality of Life, and Life Satisfaction. *Research Journal of Budo*, 38(1), 15–25.

Ohlenkamp, N. (2019). Martial Art vs Sport. Retrieved from https://judoinfo.com/sport.

Papakitsos, E.C. (2017, November 23). A Brief Essay about the Traditions of the Occidental Martial Arts. *International Journal of Martial Arts*, 3, 32–51. Retrieved from http://injoma.com/gnuboard4/bbs/board.php?bo_table=injoma_searchandwr_id=12.

Petersen-Wagner, R. and Mataruna, L. (2015) *A Return Trip to Japan: From Jigoro Kano Kodokan Judo in Brazil to Gracie Family Brazilian Jiu-Jitsu in Japan*. Zurich: Sport in Society in Transnational Contexts.

Sanada, H. (2019, April 1). The Olympic Movement and Kano Jigoro. Retrieved from wwww.joc.or.jp/english/historyjapan/kano_jigoro.html.

Santos, L.M., Boschena, S.L., Bortolanza, M., Oliveira, W.F., Furigo, I.C., Mota-Ortiz, S.R., Cunha, C., Newton, C.C., Boschen, S.L., Bortolanza, M., Oliveira, W.F., Furigo, I.C., Mota-Ortiz, S.R., Cunha, C. and Canteras, S. (2012). The Role of the Ventrolateral Caudoputamen in Predatory Hunting. *Physiology and Behavior*, 105(3), 893–898.

Udea, Y. (2017). Political Economy and Judo: The Globalization of a Traditional Japanese Sport. *Sport in Society*, 20(12), 1852–1860.

Wargo, M., Spirrison, C. and Henley, T. (2007). Personality Characteristics of Martial Artists. *Social Behavior and Personality: An International Journal*, 35, 399–408.

Yoshinori, N. (2002, May 1) Helio Gracie Reveals the True Story behind his EPIC Battle with Kimura Masahiko. Interviewed by Nishi Yoshinori, From Kakutou Striking SpiritRetrieved from www.global-training-report.com/helio.htm

Part III
Racquet, bat and club sports

16

Badminton

Jørgen Bagger Kjær

A sport does not come into being overnight. It takes years if not decades of rules modification before it becomes the game we know. Badminton, as we know it, resembles a game played by British officers in India around the beginning of the 19th century.[1] At the same time, there are many games around the world in which players hit a shuttlecock with a racket, foot or the palm of a hand. This chapter begins with an introduction to the early versions of badminton as it was played in ancient China (from 206 BC to AD 907), Europe and North America. In so doing, it gives a history of the game and its cultural meanings in different part of the world. The chapter will then describe the sportification process of the modern game, including a discussion of its Olympic history.

Badminton was developed to include women in the game from the very beginning. This is what makes badminton unique, as compared to other sports. Hence, a section of the chapter is devoted to contextualize the long history of women's access to the game. Lastly, this chapter will discuss the recent development, including the increased professionalization of the game, doping cases in badminton and a player scandal, where athletes lost on purpose at the 2012 Olympics in London.

Early development

The first evidence of a game that uses a shuttlecock is found in China. A game called Ti-jian-zi was developed during the Hang and Tang dynasties (from 206 BC to AD 907). The game consists of kicking the shuttlecock with toe, heel, foot or bouncing it off the knee. The game was developed to improve soldiers' skills. Players who returned the shuttlecock from a stationary position and with one foot only were called "little warriors." Players who were able to jump and kick the shuttlecock were called "big warriors." Gradually, the game lost its military connection and becomes a game for children who played it in winter to keep warm.[2]

In the 13th century, after the Sung dynasty, the game was renamed Chien-tsu from the Chinese word for "arrow", which rhymes with the word for "shuttlecock".[3] From China, the game found its way to other Asian countries. In Taiwan the shuttlecock-kicking game took root around the Han dynasty (206 BC–AD 220). In Korea, the game was called Jeigi-Chagi; the shuttlecock was made from a flattened cotton ball and filled with ashes or clay with a pheasant feather stuck in the top. As in China the game was a popular winter pastime. Shopkeepers would play it to keep their feet warm. The game also spread to Thailand and Malaysia. The Miao people who lived between China and Thailand use a wooden bat to hit a bamboo shuttlecock (called *nbî*) into which are inserted three feathers.[4]

It is at this point the game began to resemble badminton as wooden rackets was used. In Japan the game was called Hagoita. In 1544, Ichijo Furuya called it "the game of the little barbaric demons." People in Japan said that the game chased away evil spirits. There is also evidence of shuttlecock games being played in North and South America. It was popular among many Native American tribes. The game and the materials used varied. Some players used their palms; others used either round or square bats. In South America the game was played in northern Peru before the Inca kingdom was established. Sometimes the game was part of a ceremony. The ancient culture of Moche in Peru used the game of shuttlecock as a ceremonial activity to help crops to grow. From there the game spread to Amazonia, eastern Brazil and the Gran Chaco.[5]

In all cultures in which the game was played, the shuttlecock was never to touch the ground. Outside of Europe, the ritual and ceremonial aspect of the game was empathized. In France and England, shuttlecock was more a recreational and social activity beginning in 13th century. It was not played on a regular basis until the Renaissance. Francois I of France (r. 1515–1547) was reputed to be a master of the game. In England the game was called "battledore", but the term "badminton" most likely derives from the Duke of Beaufort's Badminton House in Gloucestershire. Because children were known to play battledore in the Badminton House, it is plausible that this is how the game acquired its modern name.[6] However the beginning of the modern game now takes us to India.

Birth of modern badminton

Modern badminton seems to have been invented by British imperial officers in the late 19th century. A photo taken in 1867 shows several Englishmen playing shuttlecock with a net. Although there is evidence of badminton being played in various parts of India, Poona seems to have been the centre.[7] At first the game was simply known as Poonai.[8] It was played with balls of wool because it withstood humidity and wind better than cotton. Poonai was played mostly by the upper classes, most notably by the Prince of Tanjore's family, thus contributing to its popularity. In October 1873, Major Forbes sent to *The Field* a short rulebook, titled *A Handbook of Badminton*. The Great Eastern Hotel Company published the book in Calcutta. The rules were written so that the game would be as fair as possible when women played against men.[9]

The game develops in England

By 1875, returning officers had started a badminton club in Folkestone, Kent. It was quickly established that contests between two or four competitors were preferably. The shuttlecocks were coated with India rubber and sometimes weighted with lead. One of the members of the club was Lieutenant Seymour S.C. Dolby, future founder of the Badminton Association. A series of rules books was published over the next few years. The number of players, how many points it takes to win and whether the net should go all the way down to the ground were matters of debate. However in 1876, J. Buchanan, a maker of sport and leisure equipment, wrote in *Lawn Tennis and Badminton* that badminton had at least one advantage over cricket: fewer players and female participation.[10]

Sportification and the birth of the All-England Championship tournament

To facilitate inter-club play, the rules of badminton were standardized. On 13 September 1893 the Badminton Association was established with Lieutenant Dolby as elected honorary secretary and treasurer. Badminton spread into Ireland and Scotland over the next seven years.[11]

On 10 March 1898 the Guildford Badminton Club held the first badminton tournament. Twenty players registered for the mixed doubles, six for ladies' and seven for the men's. The tournament was played on an hourglass-shaped court in order to make the game as fair as possible for women when playing with men in mixed doubles. The tournament was so popular that the Badminton Association held its own tournament a year later. The first shuttlecocks used in competition were called "barrel shuttles" due to their shape. Chicken feathers were inserted into a cork with the flat side of the quill facing outwards. Goose feathers later replaced the chicken feathers, giving the shuttlecock a straighter shape and improving its flight and speed. The rackets were made in Sealkoy, India. As the shuttlecocks were hit harder, the rackets had to become stronger. English equipment makers – Prosser, Jefferies and Slazenger's – competed for the market. In 1900, the Badminton Association had 45 clubs registered and the first singles tournament was played to 15 points.[12]

In 1901 the rectangular court was adopted. In 1902 the Badminton Association tournament is called the All England Open Badminton Championships (later shortened to All-England). It served as the unofficial World Badminton Championships until 1977 when IBF launched its official championships. The All England Championships were suspended because of the World Wars, from 1915 to 1919 and from 1940 to 1946.[13]

More tournaments, a badminton magazine, the building of halls and attempts to spread the game to other countries, especially in northern Europe, marked the beginning of the 20th century. Danish badminton was born on September 10, 1925. The club, Skovshoved IF, already offered tennis, shooting and football but was looking for a winter sport to offer its members. The club had just bought a hall from the Danish Institute of Gymnastics, but it was not suited for tennis. Badminton was perfect and a match was scheduled. Denmark quickly dominated the sport. The country had a strong tradition of gymnastics, in part to help farmers get some exercise over the winter. Denmark therefore had a good infrastructure of small halls that were too small for tennis but perfect for badminton. Within a decade, Denmark had produced its first All England Champion. Tage Madsen won the men's singles, and Ruth Dalsgaard and Tonny Olson won the ladies' doubles. Over the years Denmark has won 87 All-England titles.[14]

In Canada, the Canadian Badminton Association was created in December 1921. The new badminton association is the result of rising interest in badminton in Canada. The Ladies' Montreal Tennis and Badminton Club had been founded in 1907 and the first open tournament began play in 1914. When Dorothy Walton won the ladies' singles in All-England in 1939, Canada claimed its first All England title.[15]

New Yorkers introduced badminton to the United States. In 1878, Bayard Clake returned from India and E. Langdon from England. Along with their friend Oakley Rhinelander, they founded the New York Badminton Club. Initially a social pastime, regular badminton matches were played at the New York and Boston clubs, the latter established in 1908.[16] Badminton's popularity boomed in the 1930s as schools, YMCAs, and hundreds of newly formed clubs offered instruction. Also fuelling the sport's popularity in the 1930s was the avid play by celebrities such as James Cagney, Bette Davis, Boris Karloff, Dick Powell, Ginger Rogers, Joan Crawford, and Douglas Fairbanks. The American Badminton Association (ABA) was established in

1936, when Donald Wilbur, Robert McMillan, and twins Donald and Phillip Richardson, all of Brookline, Massachusetts, decided to unite the badminton groups across the country. Programs from New York, Massachusetts, Chicago and the West Coast came together to standardize the rules of the game. The ABA held its first National Championships in 1937, and joined IBF in 1938.[17]

The year 1949 brought the United States its first All-England champions when David Freeman of Pasadena, California, won the men's singles. Americans Clinton and Patsy Stevens won the All England mixed doubles title the same year. Between 1949 and 1967, the United States won 23 All England championships (one men's singles, twelve women's singles, one men's doubles, eight women's doubles, and one mixed doubles) and three women's world team championships. *Sports Illustrated* acknowledged the United States' badminton success by featuring top male player Joe Alston on the cover of its 7 March 1955 issue. The number of US clubs declined in the 1970s and badminton became more a backyard and beach game although high school and collegiate play did expand in pockets around the country.[18]

India was a pioneer in the development of the game. However the first tournament was not organized until 1929 in Punjab. The Badminton Association of India (BAI), formed in 1934, is the country's governing body for badminton. It has been holding nationwide tournaments since 1936. Shri Prakash Padukone became the first Indian to win the All England in men's singles in 1980. The Malayan states benefited from the experience of the English military and East India Company, as well as the importance placed on the game from missionaries who saw badminton as way to develop a sound body and spirit. The Penang Badminton Association was created in 1925. In 1934, Penang, Selangor, Johore and Singapore established the Malayan Badminton Association. A year later, 25,000 Malayans were reported to be playing badminton. In the 1950s Malayan won eight All-England titles due to Wong Peng Soon (four AEC singles titles) and Chong Ewe Beng "Eddy" (four titles). The speed and dexterity of the players impressed the spectators.[19]

In Australasia, the growth of badminton extended to New Zealand. The Auckland Badminton club was founded in 1900.[20] The New Zealand Championship followed in 1927 in Wanganui, the same year that the New Zealand Association was founded. In 1938 the first international match was played between Australia and New Zealand; the winner won the Whyte Trophy.[21]

Creation of an international badminton federation

On Thursday 5 July 1934, at Bush House, Aldwych, London, representatives of the Badminton Association met representatives of all known badminton associations in the world to form the International Badminton Federation (IBF). The Badminton Association wanted to pass on the rules of the game to an international body given badminton's international popularity. The IBF would be responsible for any amendment of the laws. The Association proposed:

> That this meeting, consisting of duly authorised representatives of National Badminton Organisations, shall and hereby does form an International Badminton Federation; and that the Draft Rules already circulated to each National Organisation by the Badminton Association be and hereby are adopted as the Constitution of the Federation.[22]

After a short discussion, this Resolution was then put to the meeting and carried unanimously. At that point, the Badminton Association ceased to exist, and the Badminton Association of England became responsible for badminton in England.[23]

Thomas Cup and Uber Cup

The Thomas Cup story began in England when an English nobleman, having derived much pleasure from badminton, decided to leave something for posterity. That man was the baronet of Yapton, Sir George Alan Thomas. A leading player of the English badminton scene for more than two decades, between 1903 and 1927 Sir Thomas had won 21 All-England championships, including the singles titles for four successive years. Sir Thomas envisaged a World Cup for badminton similar to that for football. His proposal was well received by the IBF.[24]

In 1939, Sir George presented to the IBF the 28-inch gold-plated trophy hammered in silver. The Second World War delayed the first Thomas Cup competition until 1948. The Thomas Cup was played every three years until 1982. Since then, the tournament has been played every two years with a format of three singles and two doubles.[25]

The final phase of the tournament involves 12 teams competing and coincides with the final phase of the world women's team championships, the Uber Cup (first held in 1956–1957). Since 1984 the two competitions have been held jointly. Of the 28 Thomas Cup tournaments held since 1948–1949, only five countries have won the title. Indonesia is the most successful team, having won the tournament 13 times. China, which did not begin to compete until 1982, follows Indonesia with nine, and Malaysia has won five. Japan and Denmark each have one.[26] The Thomas Cup and, to a lesser extent, Uber Cup are for some the world's most prestigious regularly held badminton events. For many they are more noteworthy than the venerable All-England Championships, the BWF World Championships, and even the badminton competitions at the Olympic Games.

Women have often struggled to be accepted in sports (e.g., cricket, football), with many sports only granting women access in the early 1970s (e.g., football). The argument typically made by male leaders was that it was not healthy for women to participate in sport. Women had to demand access and equal treatment to participate. Many women resisted and refused to be socially discriminated against based on biological arguments. This was not the case in badminton. In 1899, *Lawn & Tennis Magazine* wrote: "The growing popularity of Badminton is due, in great measure, to its intrinsic merits as a game giving scope for a high degree of skill, and providing hard and healthy exercise for both sexes."[27] Women have been evenly matched with men in badminton since the beginning. More specifically, during the first badminton tournament, held in 1898 in Guildford, men and women played side by side as mixed doubles teams; ladies doubles teams were added before men's singles. Therefore it was only natural that women play in a tournament equivalent to the Thomas Cup. Betty Uber – one of the first female superstars in Badminton – used her fame to propose a team tournament for women in 1950. She found a supporter in New Zealand's Nancy Fleming. Due to lack of financial resources the first tournament was not played until 1955 when Uber presented a trophy and IBF hosted the event. Uber also made the draw for the 1956–1957 inaugural tournament, which took place at Lytham St Annes in Lancashire, England. Eleven countries registered for the first Uber Cup. Denmark was dominating ladies badminton in the 1950s until two young American players and Margaret Vaner won All-England titles. The USA wins the first Uber Cup, beating Denmark 6–1. The USA would win the next two Uber Cups as well. By the 2016 tournament, China had won 14 times. Japan was second, having won five times, followed by Indonesia and United States, each with three Cups.[28]

With the arrival of the World Championships we see several women badminton players receiving national idol status in their respective home countries. In Denmark, Lene Køppen became very popular when she won the women's singles title at the first World Championship in 1977 (she also won the mixed doubles title with Steen Skovgaard). Køppen is one of very few athletes to have won both the World Championship and All England. In a very traditional Danish way, Køppen was able to combine elite sport with higher education, as she managed to attend university to become a dentist. She was not the most skilful player, but was admired for her work effort, mental toughness and ability to concentrate during the big moments[29].

In the 1950s, the Chinese government laid the foundation for high-level performances by women in sports. Chinese athletes, including women, started to compete internationally in sports in the 1970s. Badminton, together with other sports, helped create an image of the strong sporting women in China, as Chinese women fared better in international competitions than Chinese men. According to Brownell, this "led to a heated public debate about why 'the yin waxes and the yang wanes'. In some ways, the success of the sportswomen confirmed the stereotype of the 'sick man of East Asia' and made Chinese people wonder: 'What's wrong with our men?'"[30] From the very beginning, Chinese women did not have to break through the traditional barriers of the right to participate in sports. In the communist regime, success in women's sport was seen as proof that China was becoming a powerful nation, thanks to its communist leadership.[31] Women that were successful in sports (e.g. Han Eiping, Le Lingwei) were called women warriors. In the 1980s, Han Eiping and Le Lingwei received great praise when they won the World Championship singles title for China. Sadly, the fame came with backlash. By the end of her career, Le Lingwei was physically drained and no longer performed well, resulting in a great deal of criticism in China. This is a testimony to the importance of China's interest in women's success in sports. That being said, Lingwei's long successful career helped her into a leadership role in sport, after retiring as a player. Despite not having participated in the Olympics herself, she became one of a few female sports leaders that became an International Olympic Committee (IOC) member in 2012. She was also honoured by being one of five retired athletes to carry the flag at the 2008 Olympics in Beijing.[32]

The Indian badminton player, Saina Nehwa, is another female who has overcome traditional gender barriers in sports. She has become a national representative for India and an idol. This is especially important, as a woman's role in Indian society is typically to focus on being a housewife and a mother first[33]. Nehwa is the first Indian player to have won at least one medal in every major individual international federation event: the Junior World Championship, the World Championship and the Olympics. She was ranked as the number 1 player in 2015. She captained her team in the 2015 Uber Cup, helping the team win its first ever Uber Cup medal (bronze). Also in 2015, the Indian Government presented her with the third highest civilian award, the Padma Bhusman award. Consequently, she has served as a role model for many young players, both females and males.[34]

China takes centre court and divides world badminton

The victories by Asians in the Thomas Cup, the Uber Cup and the All-England, led to two important initiatives. In 1959, the Asian Badminton Confederation (ABC) was created at the initiative of the Malayan federation. Three years later, the first Asian tournament was held in Kuala Lumpur and in 1962 the game was introduced at the Asian games. However, one major country was conspicuously absent: China.

On 11 September 1958 the Chinese Badminton Association was founded in Wuhan. However, the organization cannot be part of IBF because Taiwan is already a member and therefore cannot partake in international competition, despite that China had already produced world-class players. In 1965, China played in Denmark and won all 24 of its singles matches. Strict training based on running and jumping and supple wrist technique seems to have been a factor in China's wins. China will be able to compete in Asia through ABC and the Asian games. At the Asian games in Teheran in 1974, the Chinese team defeated Indonesia who had won the Thomas Cup the previous two times.[35]

In the mid-1960s, efforts were made to add badminton to the Olympic program. Badminton was a demonstration sport at the Munich Olympics in 1972, and it was expected that it became a regular sport soon.[36] Twenty-five players from 11 member associations participated; Indonesia's Rudy Hartono and Japan's Noriko Nakayama (née Takagi) won the singles titles, while Ade Chandra/Christian Hadinata (Indonesia – men's doubles) and Derek Talbot/Gillian Gilks (England) won the mixed doubles. There was no women's doubles.[37]

From then on, however, progress stalled as a sensitive political issue rose to the forefront. The World Badminton Federation (WBF) was formed on 24 February 1978 on a request by the Malaysian, Teh Gin Sooi. Thirteen Asian and six African associations became part of the breakaway group who left IBF. There are several reasons for this break. The WBF objected to the IBF's decision not to expel Taiwan in order to have China become a member. Second, they favour the principle of "one nation, one vote" for the decision-making process and they refuse to ratify the existence of several British associations (England, Scotland, Ireland and Wales). Finally they opposed the inclusion of South Africa because of the apartheid government. The new group created an alternative World Championship and boycotted the All-England and the Thomas Cup. The split in the IBF shattered its hope of seeing badminton in the Olympics.[38]

The World Championship

The tournament started in 1977 and was held once every three years until 1983. However, IBF faced difficulty in hosting the first two events because of competition from the WBF. The two federations tried to reach a rapprochement. On 26 May 1981 they signed a Deed of Unification in Tokyo. They settled most of the differences that coursed the split, by reaching compromises on the voting issues and integrating China. The reunification of the world body revived its Olympic hopes. Juan Antonio Samaranch, President of IOC, attended the IBF World Championships in 1983; the event produced some exhilarating badminton and convinced Samaranch that badminton deserved a place in the Olympic program.[39] Starting in 1985, the World Championship tournament was played once every two years until 2005. Starting in 2006, the tournament was changed to an annual event on the BWF calendar to give more chances for the players to be crowned world champions. However, the tournament will not be held once every four years to give way to the summer Olympic Games.

The long-awaited moment came on 5 June 1985 at the 90th IOC session. Badminton was unanimously added to the 1992 Barcelona Olympics and would be played as an exhibition sport in the 1988 Seoul Olympic games. The IOC flag was presented to the IBF at the World Championships in Calgary.[40]

Just before this recognition, a new world competition was created. The Sudirman Cup is the world mixed-team badminton championship and takes place every two years. There are five matches in every round: men and women's singles, men and women's doubles and mixed doubles. The Cup is named after Dick Sudirman, a former Indonesian badminton player and the founder of the Badminton Association of Indonesia (PBSI). The first Sudirman Cup tournament took place in Bung Karno Stadium, Central Jakarta, Indonesia on 24–29 May 1989.[41]

The arrival of professionalism

Like in many other sports, the debate between professionalism and amateurism existed in badminton. The world's first open badminton tournament was played in the Royal Albert Hall in

London in September of 1979. This was the first open tournament, where both professionals and amateurs could compete in the same tournament. The 1979 tournament marked the arrival of Open Badminton and gave players an opportunity to receive prize money for playing in tournaments. The total prize money distributed to the Men's Singles and Ladies' Singles champions was £7,500, where the winner received £3,000. In the Men's and Ladies' Doubles competition, the prize money totalled £2,850, with the winning pair sharing £1,500. In May of 1979, the IBF's annual general meeting was held and badminton rules were revised and adopted. This would not harm the aspirations for badminton to become an Olympic sport, but did allow for the concept of professionalism in badminton[42]

Badminton at the Olympic Games

On 28 July 1992 the long-cherished dream of millions of badminton fans came true. Foo Kok Keong of Malaysia struck the first shuttlecock in Olympic badminton history, in the new Pavella de la Mar Bella. Barcelona saw 178 players from 37 countries take part. The on-court action justified all the hard work that had gone into bringing badminton to the Olympics. An early-round women's doubles match between Gill Clark/Julie Bradbury (England) and Rosiana Tendean/Erma Sulistianingsih (Indonesia) was so compelling that TV viewership reportedly reached 150 million.

Over the next few days, all four categories – men's singles, women's singles, men's doubles and women's doubles – produced matches of the highest class. That Indonesian off-court couple Allan Budi Kusuma and Susi Susanti won the singles medals in a picture-perfect moment for decades to come. Indonesia's wait for an Olympic gold medal had ended. Korea earned the other two gold medals, through Park Joo Bong/Kim Moon Soo (men's doubles) and Hwang Hye Young/Chung So Young. Badminton had come of age.[43]

Subsequent development of the Olympics

Over the course of the next five Olympics – Atlanta (1996), Sydney (2000), Athens (2004), Beijing (2008) and London (2012) – badminton's impact at the Olympics only grew, with viewership consistently breaking records.[44] In 2005, the International Badminton Federation was renamed the Badminton World Federation (BWF).[45]

In Atlanta 1996, mixed doubles was introduced – making badminton one of the few sports in which men and women shared the field of play. Another major change was the playoff for bronze.

London 2012 saw the introduction of group competition followed by knockout. The same format was followed for Rio 2016, but with a draw after the group stage to prevent players from anticipating their opponents. Although badminton is attributed to England, Asian countries have dominated the sport in all the major badminton events, including Olympics. The Asian countries have bagged almost all the medals in the Olympic competition with China, Republic of Korea and Indonesia being the dominant countries followed by Denmark and Great Britain. These nations have consistently produced the most talented players. In fact, China has become a force to reckon with. Badminton has become more organized worldwide, with almost all countries having associations to organize and develop the sport.[46]

Recent developments

In 2006, BWF launched a new series of elite badminton tournaments. The series contained elements of the American sports corporate model. This was especially evident when BWF, in

2011, divided the super series up into two levels. One season of the Super Series features twelve tournaments around the world. Five of these tournaments are classified as Super Series Premier or major tournaments: All-England, Malaysia Open, China Open, Danish Open and Indonesia Open. The Super Series Premier Tournament offers higher-ranking points for the overall rankings, as well as a higher minimum total amount of prize money. The top eight players/pairs in each discipline in the Super Series are invited back to the Super Series Finals, held at the end of the season.[47] This format is similar to the tennis ATP/ WTA season finale, which also invites back the eight best ranked players.

As stated previously, the super series increased the amount of prize money to players. Beginning with the 2008 season, men and women were earning the same amount of money. The Super Series premier has a minimum prize of $600,000, while the regular Super Series has a minimum prize of $325,000. The Super Series Final has a prize of $500,000. Often the prize exceeds the minimum amount. The finals held in Dubai in 2017 offered $1,000,000 as a prize. Currently, the number one ranked gentlemen, and 2017 world champion is Victor Axelsen from Denmark. His career prize earnings are $447,077 at the age of 23. The number one ranked woman is Tai Tzu Ying, from Taiwan. To date, she has earned $712,305 in prize money. It is rare that a female athlete has earned almost twice the amount in prize money as her male counterpart. Hence, this is yet more testimony that women and men are treated equally in the game of badminton[48].

The modern game of badminton has had to deal with some controversial issues. During the 2012 Olympic games in London, four pairs of doubles on the women's side were thrown out of the tournament for violating the code of player's conduct, which states that players should make their best effort to win games. During the group stage of the women's doubles matches, four women doubles were thrown out of the tournament because they were losing on purpose to get a better draw for the knockout stage. The Chinese top seeds, Yu Yang and Wang Xiaoli, and their South Korean rivals, Jung Kyung-eun and Kim Ha-na, did not want to win the match. The referee intervened several times to warn the players about their actions. A similar situation occurred in the next game between the South Korean duo, Ha Jung-eun and Kim Min-jung, and their Indonesian opponents, Meiliana Jauhari and Greysia Polii, as they did what they could to lose by hitting the shuttlecock into the net or very wide.[49]

Despite the early encouragement of women to play the game, badminton did get its own case of sexism when the WBF made it mandatory for all women players to wear a skirt during matches. The objective of the WBF was "to ensure the attractive presentation" of the players. Several countries (e.g. China, India, Malaysia, Indonesia) protested. This rule did not make it any easier for Muslim women to step onto the court. After a year of debate, the WBF finally withdrew the proposal, before the 2012 Olympics in London, so it did not stir up controversy during the games.[50]

Badminton has also witnessed doping cases. In 2015, the former men's number one player in the world, Lee Chong Wei from Malaysia, was given an 8-month back dated ban for using an illegal drug. The WFB imposed a rather mild penalty, as they believed Wei did not intend to cheat, but did act rather negligently.[51] In 2016, the Chinese women doubles player, Yu Xiaohan, tested positive for the use of the illegal drug sibutramin. The WFB decided to take another mild approach by giving her a 7-month backdated ban. They decided to believe Xiaohan's story that she did not take the drug to enhance her performance.[52]

The two doping cases illustrate that the sport has decided to take a more preventive approach to doping, perhaps because it is yet to be a major problem, as in other sports (e.g., cycling, track and field/athletics). To illustrate this point, during the 2017 Premier series finale, the BWF ran an integrity campaign for a clean sport, where the top players campaign with the slogan "I am clean. I am honest. I am badminton."[53]

Game, set, match

The first shuttlecock was hit in China centuries ago and it is still China that leads international competition with a handful of other countries trying to catch up. Today the sport is played in many parts of the world. The many team tournament (Thomas, Surdiman and Uber Cups) and individual tournaments like All-England, the World Championship as well as its accession to the Olympic Games has made it a sport with a wide following. However, it is still not a big-time global TV sport despite efforts from governing bodies to make it more appealing for TV viewers and fans, including changing the rule for counting the score in 2006. The main change from the traditional counting system was to adopt rally point scoring, in which the winner of a rally scores a point regardless of who served. Furthermore, games were lengthened to 21 points, with ladies' singles matches now using the same rules as men's singles. There must be at least a two-point difference between scores to win a set. However, the change in scoring did not make the games any shorter. Badminton's fame still needs to be spread to regions such as Southern Europe, the Middle East, Africa and Latin America in order to be a true global sport. Those regions have little interest in the sport today. Badminton as a sport is more than a century old and one can only hope that its longevity will match that of the traditional games of shuttlecock and battledore as those games are still played around the world despite being thousands of years old.

Notes

1 P. H. Lim & M. S. Aman, "The History of Modern Organized Badminton and the Men's Team Thomas Cup Tournaments, 1948–1979", *The International Journal of the History of Sport*, 3, 7–8 (2017).
2 J. Guillain, *Badminton: An Illustrated History* (Paris, France: Publibook, 2004), pp. 15–31.
3 See www.badminton-information.com/history-of-badminton.html
4 Guillain, *Badminton*.
5 Ibid.
6 P.M. Parker: *Badminton: Webster's Timeline History 1521–2007* (San Diego, CA: Icon Group International, 2009); Guillain, *Badminton*.
7 Lim & Aman, "History".
8 See www.britannica.com/sports/badminton; Parker: *Badminton*.
9 Guillain, *Badminton*; Lim & Aman, "History"; www.badmintonindia.org/organization/history
10 Guillain, *Badminton*.
11 See www.badmintonengland.co.uk/text.asp?section=2647&sectionTitle=Col+S+S+C+Dolby#.Wkrx JoVvdFU
12 Guillain, *Badminton*; Lim & Aman, "History".
13 See www.allenglandbadminton.com/championship-info; Guillain, *Badminton*.
14 L. Barnekow, T. Holst-Christensen & N. Rasmussen, *Fra Fjerbold til Badminton: Danmarks Badminton Forbund gennem 75 år* (Brondby, Danmark: Dansk Badminton Forbund, 2005).
15 Guillain, *Badminton*.
16 P. Welch & B. Ericson, "Badminton: A New Olympic Sport", Journal of Physical Education, Recreation & Dance, 62:9, 38–40, (1991); Lim & Aman, "History".
17 See www.teamusa.org/USA-Badminton/USAB/History/Badminton-in-the-US
18 See www.athleticscholarships.net/history-of-badminton.htm; Lim & Aman, "History".
19 Guillain, *Badminton*.
20 Lim & Aman, "History".
21 Guillain, *Badminton*.
22 See www.badmintonengland.co.uk/text.asp?section=1711&sectionTitle=1934%2C+Formation+of+ IBF#.WkucgCMrIdU
23 Ibid.
24 Lim & Aman, "History"; Barnekow et al., *Fra Fjerbold til Badminton*.
25 See http://bwfcorporate.com/events/thomas-and-uber-cups
26 See www.malaysiakini.com/letters/343834; Lim & Aman, "History".

27 The Badminton Association produced the first magazine devoted entirely to badminton in 1907; *Lawn Tennis*, 6 December 1899, p. 439, retrieved from www.badmintonengland.co.uk/text.asp?section=252 7&sectionTitle=Early+magazine+pages%2C+1899%2C+part+1#.WkKvO4VvdFU

28 Barnekow et al., *Fra Fjerbold til Badminton*.

29 See http://badmintonbladet.dk/tidl-badmintondronning-lene-koppen-fylder-60-ar

30 S. Brownell, "Challenged America: China and America – Women and Sport, Past, Present and Future", *The International Journal of the History of Sport*, 22:6, 1173–1193, here 1183.

31 Ibid.

32 See www.scmp.com/article/1007825/badminton-legend-li-lingwei-wins-ioc-seat

33 V. Kadhiravan, "Status and Recognition of Sportswomen in Indian Society", *British Journal of Sports Medicine*, 44:62 (2010).

34 Ibid

35 Guillain, *Badminton*.

36 Welch & Ericson, "Badminton".

37 See www.olympic.org/munich-1972/badminton/singles-women

38 Guillain, *Badminton*.

39 Ibid.

40 Welch & Ericson, "Badminton".

41 See http://bwfsudirmancup.com/the-historic-journey

42 Lim & Aman, "History".

43 See http://olympics.bwfbadminton.com/history

44 See http://bwfcorporate.com/events/olympic-games

45 See http://bwfcorporate.com/about

46 See http://olympics.bwfbadminton.com/history

47 See www.badmintonengland.co.uk/landingpage.asp?section=5444&sectionTitle=The+Majors&prev iew=1#.VZFJl_lVhBc

48 See http://bwfbadminton.com/rankings/2/bwf-world-rankings/7/women-s-singles/2017/51/?rows= 25&page_no=1

49 P. Walker & T. Branigan, "Badminton's World Governing Body Apologises after Players are Disqualified", *The Guardian*, 1 August 2012, retrieved from *The Guardian*. www.theguardian.com/sport/2012/aug/01/badminton-body-apologises-players-disqualified

50 R. Gilmour, "World Badminton Ditches Controversial Women's Skirts Ruling Ahead of London Olympics", *The Telegraph*, 28 May 2012, retrieved from www.telegraph.co.uk/sport/olympics/bad minton/9294626/World-badminton-ditches-controversial-womens-skirts-ruling-ahead-of-London-Olympics.html

51 Reuters, "Badminton Player Lee Chong Wei Given Backdated Eight-Month Doping Ban", *The Guardian*, 27 April 2015, retrieved from www.theguardian.com/sport/2015/apr/27/lee-chong-wei-badminton-malaysia-backdated-eight-month-ban-doping

52 See http://badmintonbladet.dk/doping-kineser-faar-dom

53 See http://bwfcorporate.com/integrity/anti-doping

17

Baseball and softball

Christina Villalon

Baseball

Abner Doubleday is widely believed to have invented baseball in the US, yet historical evidence suggests it may have been invented earlier in England.[1] In 1905 a commission was appointed to determine where and when baseball began. However, commission members had conflicting views. British born Henry Chadwick believed baseball evolved from the English game of rounders while American nationalist Albert Spalding supported the invention of baseball in America, by an American. Officially, the commission decided in 1908 that Abner Doubleday invented baseball at Cooperstown, New York in 1839. Yet the evidence the commission used in this decision is not backed by fact. Versions of baseball rules have also been found published prior to the claimed invention in 1839 and Robert Henderson, historian of bat and ball games, has documented origins to games played in England. Therefore, the birthplace of baseball is unknown. Despite lacking a singular place of birth, the United States largely contributed to its growth, both nationally and internationally. The game itself is a fundamental part of American culture. "Whoever wants to know the heart and mind of America had better learn baseball," said cultural historian Jacques Barzun.[2]

Growth in the United States

Before it ever became a business, a career, or a way to pay for college, it was a game. Americans begin playing in the 1840s. In 1871, the first league was created in which teams were paid to play.[3] However, this league only lasted about five years. In 1876, the National League of Professional Baseball Clubs was created, an enterprise better known today as the National League (NL). In 1889 the National League decided to cap player's salaries with top pay of $2,500. This cap upset the players and a minor league manager, Byron Bancroft Johnson, chose to capitalize on the situation and encouraged the owners of minor league teams to sign major leaguers and move their franchises to larger cities. These teams renamed themselves as members of the American League (AL). AL teams begin pulling in larger crowds than their NL counterparts, but after a "peace meeting" in 1903 Major League Baseball was born.

While the AL and the NL remained the dominant leagues over the years, early history of baseball in America included a variety of leagues, distinguished by gender and ethnicity. Additionally, technological advances and social decisions have played a role in the development of the current state of baseball in America. The following will discuss some of the major socio-cultural events throughout American baseball history.

"Black Sox" scandal

In 1919, Major League Baseball became shrouded in scandal after it came to light that gambling bookies had paid a sum of $100,000 to several Chicago White Sox players to intentionally lose their World Series against the Cincinnati Reds.[4] The White Sox were a heavy favorite over the Reds that season and while there were suspicions of a controversy by sports writers at the time, it was not until August of 1920 that the World Series was examined. A grand jury began to investigate and by October 1920, eight of the so-called "Black Sox" were indicted on nine counts of conspiracy.[5] However, all of the paper records relating to their confessions vanished before trial and thus the eight were found not guilty. Yet, Judge Kenesaw Mountain Landis, the newly appointed first commissioner of baseball, permanently banned all eight from baseball for life.

The scandal "marks a crucial milestone in US socio-history. Before the scandal, baseball's contamination by business and gambling were regarded as minor but necessary evils in a supposedly free-market economy. Afterwards, the painfully disillusioned public could no longer keep up the pretense of the sport's arcadian purity."[6] When scandal touched baseball, it touched a national nerve.[7] The Black Sox have become "to baseball history what Benedict Arnold is to American history."[8]

All-American Girls Professional Baseball League

Women and girls begin participating in baseball in the late 1800s on teams referred to as bloomer girls.[9] These teams helped to lay the groundwork for the All-American Girls Professional Baseball League (AAGPBL) in the 1940s and 1950s. Anticipating a potential shutdown of the major leagues due to the Second World War, Phillip Knight Wrigley had the idea to create a league of female ball players.[10]

The All-American Girls Softball League in 1943 changed to the All-American Girls Ball League in 1944, before finally adopting the name the All-American Girls Professional Baseball League (AAGPBL) in 1945.[11] The League existed between 1943 and 1954 and games were played in mid-sized war production cities in the Midwest.[12] Initially there were only four teams, but the league grew as large as 10 teams and 545 women played in this league during its existence. The name of the league, rules and size of the ball evolved over the years from a softball/baseball hybrid into essentially "baseball, plus or minus a few feet."[13] Salaries offered by the League ranged from $55–150 per week, higher than the salary of the average American in the United States at that time. Also notable, is that about 10 percent of the players in this league were Canadian, mainly from Manitoba and Saskatchewan,[14] but not a single African American played in the league.[15]

Scouts were instructed to recruit feminine players.[16] Most of the players for this league were converted softball players. Previously, softball players had about the same social standing as prostitutes. Therefore, Wrigley was intent on rebranding the perception of softball players and making these girls into ideal All-American girls. After making the team, the players would practice during the day, and then attend Charm School at night. Female players were expected to abide by a rigid code of conduct; otherwise, any "inappropriate" behavior on or off the field resulted in a fine.[17] Uniforms were belted tunics with elastic shorts underneath.[18] The players saw this style as impractical, as it was the talent and the excitement of the games that kept the fans coming back not the uniform.

The League was very popular with magazine articles claiming that "some towns draw four times their population every season"[19] and "there are nights when you have to stand in the back to see what is going on at the plate."[20] The League had a profound effect on how the people of the 1940s look at something that was supposedly "a man's game."[21] In 1948, at the League's peak, the season drew over a million fans to the games. The argument was made by some that the women ballplayers were as good as men, and some of the women ended up receiving contracts for men's minor league teams.[22] However, these effects did not appear to permeate societal beliefs for long. Major League Baseball formally banned the signing of contracts with female professional baseball players on June 21, 1952. Eventually, listless promotion of the League, televised Major League Baseball games, and the lack of a farm system to develop new players for the league to replace retirees contributed to the demise of the league in 1954.[23]

Negro Leagues and Jackie Robinson

Baseball prides itself on having been ahead of the nation on desegregation by bringing Jackie Robinson to the majors seven years before the mandated desegregation by *Brown v. Board of Education*. However, baseball was also ahead of the nation in the institutionalization of the color line. More than two decades before Plessy v. Ferguson's "separate but equal," blacks were admitted to play in some leagues, but not others. Then, baseball was purged from the top down. The Major Leagues never formally banned blacks, but since the way to the majors was through the minor leagues, they never had to; the minors were closed to men of color.[24]

The unwritten rules that barred African-Americans from playing in the professional leagues led to blacks beginning to develop their own independent and semi-pro teams, however, they remained unorganized and the teams struggled until about 1920.[25] In 1920, Rube Foster, created the first successful baseball league for African-American players, the Negro National League. This league was comprised of eight independent teams. From this league, such innovations as the batting helmet, shin guards, and night baseball were produced. However, this league was not prepared to adapt to integration of African Americans into the professional leagues and therefore was caught off-guard and unprepared when Jackie Robinson was signed by the Brooklyn Dodgers.

Jackie Robinson, a player for the Kansas City Monarchs broke the color barrier when he debuted with the Brooklyn Dodgers in 1947 to become the first African-American professional baseball player in America. His journey was not easy, and he was met with lots of resistance, but he went on to become a league MVP and win a World Series. His actions helped pave the way for not only other athletes of color, but also international athletes to play in the Major Leagues.

It was difficult for the Negro Leagues to compete with the powerful symbolism of Robinson in the Majors. Additionally, the Majors begin to scout from the Negro Leagues signing the top performers, thereby decreasing the level of play in the Negro Leagues. So, while Robinson playing professional baseball was an accomplishment for the African Americans of the nation, it largely contributed to the end of African-American baseball leagues.

Televised baseball

While major league baseball was first broadcasted on August 26, 1939, very few individuals owned a television set at that time and regular programming did not yet exist.[26] It was not until the mid-1950s that television sets were more common in the American household. Games were shown in black and white and from only two camera angles. Since then, the coverage of sporting events has evolved into a multi-billion-dollar industry.

Televised baseball helped to raise the sport's profile. It also influenced changes to the game, such as night games and the designated hitter (DH).[27] For example, more night games were added because more people were not working at that time and therefore available to watch TV. The designated hitter allowed for increased offense and more offense brings in more viewers. Every change made to the game weighs the decision of the impact on its TV ratings and the resulting broadcast revenue.

Astrodome

The Astrodome was built in 1965 with the specific purpose of being an indoor professional baseball facility in order to attract patrons who otherwise would not want to sit outside in the sticky Houston weather surrounded by mosquitoes.[28] The Astrodome was the world's first multi-purpose, domed sports stadium. While it no longer plays host to Houston's professional teams, the development of the Astrodome changed many things about both the spectator experience, by including box suites and interactive scoreboards, and the way in which sport is played, due to the game being played indoors and on AstroTurf.

Development of the Astrodome also changed the way in which the game was presented. The Astrodome incorporated suites for season rental as well as video scoreboards. The suites allowed for a higher quality, unique experience in which to watch games, and were especially popular with companies and corporations. Additionally, these interactive scoreboards helped to lead cheers and get the audience involved the game using various animations. By the 1990s almost every big league stadium had similar scoreboards. As technology has increased over the years, these have turned into video scoreboards and jumbotrons. However, the way the fans experienced the game was not the only thing that changed; the way the athletes experienced the game changed as well.

The building of the Astrodome brought changes to the sport for the athletes such as being indoors, and artificial turf. By playing indoors, players no longer had to fight, or be able to benefit from, the natural elements of the wind, the sun, or even the dirt. Artificial Turf, coined AstroTurf, allows for "perfect bounces." While artificial turf is easier in terms of upkeep, it may result in more serious injuries than those on grass.

Ball Four

Ball Four was a book published in 1970 written by Jim Bouton, a professional baseball pitcher that had previously pitched for the New York Yankees.[29] This book created a lot of controversy at its release because it broke the code of silence in terms of keeping what happened off of the field off-limits to those outside the professional sport world. This book exposed stories about what it was really like to be a professional ball player. However, it has since been lauded as being one of the most influential sport books ever written.[30] Additionally, it has been attributed with changing sports literature and journalism, and honored as one of the greatest books of its century.

Steroid Era

The Steroid Era has no specific start or end, but is generally considered to have run from the late 1980s to the late 2000s. This Era refers to a period of time in Major League Baseball (MLB) when drug testing for Performance Enhancing Drugs (PED) was not routinely performed.[31]

Jose Canseco, a former major leaguer, estimated 50–85% of MLB were using steroids during this period.[32] Although steroids were banned by MLB in 1991, league-wide testing was not implemented until 2003.

The increased offensive power and the home run record chase that resulted from use of PEDs caught the attention of the nation and helped regain popularity for the league. Players alleged that baseball administration turned a blind eye to the steroid use in the 1990s because the power increase helped baseball to recover from the strike in 1994. Significantly more players hit over 40 home runs in a single season during the steroid era compared to before and after this time period. However, six of the ten players who reached baseball's 500 home run club between 1998 and 2009, have been linked to PEDs.

In 2006, United States Senator George Mitchell began investigating steroid use by major league players. The resulting report, referred to as the Mitchell Report, linked 89 major leaguers with the use of illegal PEDs. The report also proposed 20 ways in which to strengthen the MLB drug policy because the use of such drugs severely threatens the integrity of the game. As a result, the drug policy for MLB has been adjusted multiple times.

Modern Era

Baseball in America today consists of the Major Leagues, farm leagues, Independent Leagues, and a variety of amateur Leagues. The various leagues allow for individuals of all ages to compete, from senior leagues with a 55+ category, to toddler "pamper leagues" at 3 or 4 years old.

Major League Baseball

Major League Baseball (MLB) refers to the collective organization of the professional baseball leagues in America when the two leagues merged in 2000. MLB includes the Major League teams and their 240 minor league clubs, and is led by the Commissioner of Baseball.

Major Leagues

The Major Leagues in the United States are made up of two leagues, the National League (NL) and the American League (AL). There are a total of 30 teams in the two leagues, 15 teams in each League. American cities host 29 teams, and one team, the Toronto Blue Jays, is housed in Canada. Each team plays 162 games per season. The All-Star Game is in the middle of the season and the players that participate are voted on by the fans. In the All-Star Game, players from the NL compete against players from the AL in the one game series. The league that wins the All-Star Game is awarded home field advantage during the World Series. The World Series is a seven-game series played by the winner of the National League Championship against the winner of the American League Championship resulting from the post-season Playoffs during the month of October. Yet, this competition was not always known as the "World Series," but rather "the Championship of the United States." Then in 1884, the Providence Grays of the National League beat the New York Metropolitan Club of the American Association, and many newspapers described the Grays as "World Champions."[33]

Farm Leagues

Farm Leagues collectively refer to the minor leagues or the farm system developed for each Major League club. These farm leagues compete at three different levels, increasing in skill, A,

AA, and AAA. Major League teams are able to "farm" or work to develop talent and see which players might be ready to play in the Majors. The leagues also provide an opportunity to send Major League players down to the minors to rehab, or continue to work on their skills.

Independent Leagues

Independent Leagues have no affiliation with the MLB. These leagues tend to struggle to compete with Minor League team markets. Many of the teams in these leagues struggle to remain in business every year. The quality of play also tends to be lesser than that of farm leagues.

Colleges/Universities & High Schools

Collegiate programs and high school teams compete in interscholastic competitions, with the epitome being the College World Series and State Championships, respectively. Scouts for professional baseball teams in America tend to watch collegiate players, most commonly at the NCAA DI or junior college level, as well as high school players. These players, at both the high school and collegiate level, have the opportunity to be "drafted" by Major League team. Those drafted then tend to try to work their way up through the minor leagues until they reach the Majors, are released, or do not have their contract renewed.

Women in baseball

Although the AAGPBL women were banned from professional baseball until 1992, this did not keep women from playing baseball. The American Women's Baseball Association (AWBA) was founded in July 1988 in Illinois.[34] The league was centered in the Chicago area from 1988 to 2004. In 1992, the American Women's Baseball League was created to help promote women's baseball in the United States and around the world, and in 2003, women's baseball became the thirty-ninth sanctioned sport in the Amateur Athletic Union.

In 2015, Melissa Mayeux, a French baseball player became the first women ever to be added to the MLB international registration list, thereby making her eligible to be signed by any MLB team. Additionally, in 2016, two women, Kelsie Whitmore and Stacy Piagno, were signed to the independent Sonoma Stompers baseball team.[35] In that same year Justine Siegal was hired by the Oakland A's becoming the first female coach in the Major Leagues. Despite the lack of women in the MLB, the United States does field a National Women's Baseball Team.

The United States Women's National Team was founded in 2004.[36] They compete each year in the Women's Baseball World Cup Tournament, winning in 2004 and 2006. In 2013 and 2014 the US team only lost to Japan, a team with its own women's professional league.[37] Members of the national team have to have other jobs in order to support themselves, and a number of players play either collegiate baseball, collegiate softball, or are still in high school.[38]

Youth baseball

Hundreds of thousands of leagues around the United States have youth baseball leagues. The baseball organization that oversees the league determines the specific rules. One of the more popular leagues over the years has been those that abide by the Little League Organization's rules. The Little League Organization hosts the Little League World Series (LLWS), an annual international competition of 11–1-year-olds that take places in South Williamsport, Pennsylvania. Most of these youth leagues do not discriminate based on gender at the younger levels, for example Mo'ne Davis pitched as a thirteen year old female at the LLWS. However, as female players increase in age, they tend to be faced with pressure and encouragement to play softball which is usually considered the Title IX equivalent to baseball.[39]

There has also been a growth in youth sports, outside of the seasonal leagues, referred to as select/club/travel teams. These teams tend to play year-round, while leagues only tend to host games during the spring season, and occasionally the fall season, depending on the demand. The growth and emphasis on specializing in one sport at such a young age, for example, playing baseball year-round as opposed to only during the spring season, can lead to increased overuse injuries.

The youth development of baseball has led to continued talent for the MLB. America remains to have the professional league for baseball with the highest quality of players with the greatest players in other countries striving for a chance to play in MLB. However, there are a number of other professional leagues for baseball players to compete in outside of the United States. Although the globalization of baseball tends to be associated with America, many countries have taken the sport and made it their own.

International growth

The way baseball is played in many countries worldwide looks very similar to the way in which the game is played in the United States, but while the players use the same equipment, similar uniforms, and follow the same basic rules, different history and culture in each of the countries influences the nuances of the sport differently.[40] International competitions in which the countries compete against each other include, most notably, the Olympics, the World Baseball Classic (WBC), and the World Cup of Baseball.

International competitions

Baseball was first played in the Olympics in 1992. However, the IOC voted the sport out in 2005 along with softball, thus becoming the first sports voted out of the Olympics since polo was removed from the 1936 Olympics. However, in 2016 it was voted back in for the 2020 Olympics in Tokyo.

One week after the International Olympic Committee (IOC) announced that baseball was dropped from the Olympics, the MLB organization announced the funding of the WBC. The WBC was another example of MLB's control over baseball globalization, and a way in which the globalization of baseball has acted as a surrogate for US foreign policy. The first WBC was played in 2006. The competition is arranged as a sixteen-nation tournament divided into four pools in four cities, quarterfinals, semi-finals, and finals. However the United States teams were argued by other countries to have received unfair advantages and the competition was run according to MLB rules. Yet, 2006 saw a WBC final in which Japan and Cuba fought for the title, demonstrating the international nature of the sport.[41]

Prior to the WBC, the International Baseball Federation (IBAF), hosted the World Cup of Baseball. It was held 38 times, with the first occurring in 1938, but was discontinued in 2011 in favor of the WBC. However, the Women's Baseball World Cup continues. The Women's Baseball World Cup begin in 2004, so it has not existed for as long as their male counterparts, but has most recently included 12 teams in 2016, with the Japanese winning the last five competitions.

Most countries were introduced to baseball either through American troops occupation in their country, Americans working in their country, of natives of the country visiting America and bringing knowledge of the sport back when returning home. One way of increasing popularity of the sport of baseball occurred when any American team played exhibition games in other countries around the world. Outside of the United States, the most foreign-born players come from the Dominican Republic, Venezuela, and Puerto Rico, but more than eighteen different countries have supplied the MLB with Major Leaguers.[42] The MLB begin recruiting from these countries as early as the 1940s, and has since to slow down.[43] The following will briefly describe the countries in which baseball has been the most prominent.

Canada

Most Canadians tend to consider baseball as an extension of America, yet Canadian baseball appears to be prospering at the youth, amateur, semiprofessional, and professional level. Canada was crucial in the implementation of Jackie Robinson to the MLB.[44] It was believed that Robinson would be able to get his feet wet with the Montreal Royals without having to deal with racial taunting. While this event largely influenced the MLB in America, Canadian baseball was greatly influenced years later when they were awarded a MLB franchise. Canada is the only country besides the United States to have a team that is part of MLB. There used to be two teams in Canada, the Montreal Expos and the Toronto Blue Jays, but after the work stoppage in 1994 the Expos never really recovered. After the 2004 season the Expos franchise was moved to become the Washington Nationals. A weak Canadian dollar made it difficult for the Blue Jays to compete with wealthier organizations for a number of years, but recent seasons have found the Blue Jays in contention for the American League Championship Series.

Mexico

It is unknown exactly who first introduced baseball to Mexico. Some claim the Cubans brought it to the Yucatan Pennisula, some claim US sailors introduced it when they arrived at the Ports of Mazatlan and Guaymas, and other claim US railroad employees played the first game in Northern Mexico.[45] Regardless, Mexico's embracing of the Western sport signaled movement to modernity and success at the international level reflected favorably on social and governmental efforts. The 1957 LLWS victory by a team from Monterrey boosted national pride and led to the development of the Mexican League Baseball Academy. Since then, Mexican teams went on to win three more LLWS titles, and were named the runner-up in three more. Yet, after being the dominant sport for nearly a century, in 1980 baseball interest and support begin to wane. Although futbol became the game of the masses, Mexican leagues have remained fairly stable over the last 30 years with sixteen teams in the main league, and eight teams in the winter league.[46] Over 100 Mexican players have competed in the US, and the Mexican national team has experienced success in the World Cup of Baseball, the Pan American Games, and the Central American and Caribbean Games. However, Mexico has not competed in Olympic baseball, or medaled in the World Baseball Classic.[47]

Caribbean

DOMINICAN REPUBLIC

The Dominican Republic (DR) ties to baseball run deep. While baseball became the national sport of the DR during occupation by the United States, the DR patterned their game after the Cubans. It is believed that two Cuban brothers, Ignacio and Ubaldo Aloma, introduced the island nation to baseball in 1891.[48] Due to the racial restrictions of the MLB, scouts largely ignored the DR until the early 1950s. Since then, the DR has supplied the MLB with more talent per capita than anywhere else in the world. Not only did Dominicans comprise a tenth of major leaguers and a third of minor leaguers in the early 21st century, but they have also won many of the highest honors awarded by the MLB in recent years. The island also hosts a couple of leagues. The most notable is the Dominican Summer League, the largest professional baseball league in the world, and the winter league, which plays from October to February. Baseball in the DR is now a significant contributor to the economy.

This hotbed of talent has led every major league team to open and operate a baseball academy on the island to train young recruits. Young baseball prospects from the DR, other Caribbean countries and South American countries like Venezuela are trained and housed in these academies. However, rampant corruption and exploitation of young players has been a major issue. A range of concerns erupted over these academies in the early 2000s and many still plague the academy system today. Complaints over unsafe and unclean housing conditions were common, with young players crammed into small rooms to sleep. Dangerous on-field conditions and lack of medical staff have also been a problem, with players suffering injuries and, in at least one case, death. Furthermore, unregulated agents called "buscones" often claim large signing fees and exploit players desperate to make it into the "big leagues" of the MLB. Players who enter the academies generally dropped out of school to devote themselves full time to baseball, leaving them precariously uneducated if they failed to make the MLB or suffered a career-ending injury.[49]

Despite these serious concerns, the MLB has failed to adequately address these problems and maintains a double standard of regulations for DR prospects. MLB recruits from within the US are protected from dangerous conditions and agent exploitation, but not international recruits. The league did enforce a spending limit on international agent fees, with the intention of reducing the amount buscones claimed in signing bonuses. Additionally, individual teams, notably the Pittsburgh Pirates and San Diego Padres, have invested in upgraded training facilities and offer education opportunities along-side training so that players can earn high school diplomas.[50]

PUERTO RICO

Baseball clubs first appeared in Puerto Rico in 1897 when the Cubans introduced it to the island, and by about 1900 baseball was taught in schools and Puerto Rican towns established their own teams. While the middle class initially played the game, soon everyone was playing. For years, Puerto Rican players were smaller and less muscular than the American players, and tended to only play middle infield and outfield positions at the higher levels. However after introduction of successful social and educational programs like Head Start, nutrition and health care improved and players are now of size to compete for any position on the field.[51] Puerto Rico also provided a winter league, from October to March, for many black players in the American Negro Leagues. Another incredible development in Puerto Rico was the creation of the Puerto Rico Baseball Academy High School in 1999, partially funded by grants from the MLB.[52] The purpose of this school was to develop the students' academic, baseball, and social development relative to succeeding in American professional baseball. Incredibly, twelve of the students were drafted from the academy in 2004, the most players ever from one high school. As with many other countries, success at the international level has helped to increase the popularity of the game at the lower levels.

CUBA

The cultural significance of baseball is perhaps greater in Cuba than in any other nation. While this may be surprising due to the labeling of "American national pastime" and the strained relationships between the nations, baseball was tied to the new cultural identity of independence by a new nation free of Spanish rule. Unlike the introduction of many other countries that were introduced to baseball through US military occupation, baseball was brought to Havana by native Cuban brothers, Nemesio and Ernest Guillo, in 1864. Early in the 1900s the Cuban professional league was developed and adapted. Rebellions and poor attendance tended to shorten and cancel the professional season. The economically driven, racially integrated league provided Negro ballplayers a place to play in a winter league between 1900 and 1950. The 1960s saw rapid expansion of the professional league across the island. While these professional players are paid much less their American or Japanese counterparts, the National Series Cuban League no longer qualifies as amateur. Additionally, players in the league are not traded from team to team, nor do they qualify for "free agency." Instead, the ball players play only for their native province, thus increasing athletes and fans loyalty to the team. Games are also televised across the island, or fans can pay about $1 to watch a game. But not all Cubans want to play in the league of their native country, for many, the American professional league is very appealing and offers a life without control by a communist government. Therefore, a number of Cuban players have defected by escaping Cuba. Rene Arocha became the first baseball star to do so and opened the door for others to do as well.[53]

For the Cubans, baseball is also an opportunity to beat the Americans. Cuba has been very successful at the international level, making the Olympic final in all five Olympics that baseball has been played, winning three golds. Cuba has also won 18 of 22 International Baseball Federation (IBAF) World Cups. Nine of these were in a row. Additionally over the course of ten years, Cuba won 151 consecutive tournament games and their overall winning percentage holds at over 90%.

South America

Baseball in less popular in South American than it is in North America and the Caribbean. Like many other countries, US occupation accelerated the spread of baseball from 1912 to 1933, but Nicaragua's governmental influence and lack of publically funded amateur baseball in the 1980s led to the decline of baseball in the country.[54] However, interest in the sport came back around following the civil war in the 1980s and remains one of the more popular sports in the country.[55]

VENEZUELA

The Franklin brothers formed the first baseball club, the Caracas Baseball Club, in Venezuela in 1895.[56] But, it was the discovery of oil in the 1920 that caused baseball to spread across the country.[57] The Venezuelan Professional Baseball League was initially established in 1945 with four teams. The League has since grown to eight teams who play a sixty-three game season from October through December. For many young men, baseball is an opportunity to escape political and economic turmoil in an uncertain country. Like the DR, major league clubs opened baseball academies in the early 2000s. MLB clubs were signing about 2000 Venezuelans to Minor League contracts every year because they offered cheaper labor whilst free-agency costs rose.

BRAZIL

In Brazil, it is hard for any sport to compete with the popularity with the futbol. Baseball largely exists in Brazil due to the popularity of the game among Japanese communities.[58] Baseball first appeared in Brazil in the early 1900s around the same time as it showed up in Mexico and the

Dominican Republic. The game was played by US employees who were in the country to work on short-term projects. However, the game was also popular among the wave of Japanese immigrants who arrived about the same time to work on coffee farms. Yet, Brazilian baseball looks different from both American baseball and Japanese baseball. It was not until the mid-1980s that a national body was formed to govern baseball and softball and attempt to include non-Japanese in the game. Loss of funding in recent years led to a decrease in interest in the sport. However, that is when the MLB began to become more involved in the growth of the sport in Brazil.

Europe

While baseball has been played in Europe almost as long as in the United States, it has been slow to catch on. This has been due to fans being more interested in watching soccer, cricket, and rugby.[59] It is still considered to be a minority sport in Europe, and the only countries to win a European Championship besides the Dutch and Italian teams are Spain and Belgium. However, in recent years the sport appears to be experiencing growth in participants in Great Britain, Austria, Czech Republic, and Germany.

The Netherlands were the first European country to begin a league, and a league champion has been awarded every year since 1922.[60] In order to improve the quality of play, league organizers toured US facilities, hired US coaches, and sent their players to US spring training camps. One major difference from the American game is the size of the playing field; the Dutch fields are much smaller, likely due to the limited available space in the small country. Yet, despite the development at the national level, there are no interscholastic or intercollegiate games, and soccer is a dominant sport, thus creating a small pool of baseball players. However, in terms of international competition, the Dutch West Indies also compete for the kingdom of the Netherlands. It is believed that Venezuela political refugees and oil refinery workers from Venezuela brought baseball to the Dutch West Indies in 1930. This inclusion of the Dutch West Indies (Aruba, Buracao, Bonaire, Sint Maarten, Sint Eustatius & Saba) has helped the Netherlands to win 20 European Championships since 1954. US scouts have considered this area as a hot bed of talent since the 1990s.[61]

The Netherlands biggest European rival is Italy, but the sport was very slow in gaining popularity. Especially when Benito Mussolini prohibited the sport due to its US roots. Yet, during US occupation after the Second World War, the sport was reintroduced to a country whose youth looked up to the Italian American professional major leaguers like the DiMaggio brothers.[62] The country unified two professional leagues into one in 1950 and has featured a national championship every year since.

While some of the countries play similar versions of American baseball. Other countries versions are less similar. The Finnish version of baseball is called pesapallo, and is considered the national game of Finland.[63] However there are a number of differences between the American version and the Finnish version. The most significant difference is the vertical pitching. In pesapallo, the pitcher and batter face each other and the pitcher pitches by throwing the ball at least 1 meter over their head over the home plate. The first official pesapallo game were played in 1921, and was featured as a demonstration sport during the 1952 Helsinki Summer Olympics.

Africa

American immigrants during the gold rush in 1895 brought baseball to South Africa.[64] An official league commenced in 1899 and teams from America and Europe were invited to tour the country. However, growth of South African sport was limited for years. By 1970 more than twenty sports, including baseball, experienced boycotts preventing them from being allowed to participate in international competitions due to the apartheid of the South African government. However, by 1990 the apartheid had lost political control, and South African sports teams were reintegrated into the global sporting world. These teams have since made enormous strides. For example, in 2000 South Africa beat the Holland team in the Olympics, and also had a positive showing against Canada during the 2006 WBC. Lack of sponsorship of baseball by corporate America has placed a heavy financial burden on players, hampering the number of individuals that can afford to play the sport. There are about 70,000 registered baseball players in the country, but most tend to play at a social level.[65]

Middle East

Like South American and Africa, baseball in the Middle East region is not very popular. However, baseball is Israel is promoted as having many cultural ties and teaching important life skills. The Israel Association of Baseball (IAB) started in 1980 but is very poorly funded and existed with almost no equipment or facilities to play or practice.[66] A professional baseball league began and folded in 2007. Yet, participation in the World Baseball Classic drew more people to baseball in Israel, and thus with the increase in publicity and popularity, new role models and donors appeared for promoting play at the youth levels.

Pacific

The Pacific area has demonstrated the greatest talent outside of the United States and the Caribbean region. Some of the strongest countries in baseball include Japan, China, Taiwan, Korea, Australia, and New Zealand. Success at all levels have been seen from this region, however, athletes from these countries are not as common in MLB because cheaper labor can be signed from the Caribbean region.

Japan

Horace Wilson, an American professor, is attributed with introducing baseball to Japan in 1872.[67] The first professional Japanese team was created in 1878 and from then on the Japanese changed the American game to make it their own. However, after the Second World War, the Japanese professional league, or the Nippon Professional Baseball League (NPB), needed American players to peak Japanese interest in the sport. However, only four non-Japanese players are allowed on any one professional team. The NPB consists of two divisions that have six teams apiece. The season is 144 games long and runs from April to October. The winner of each league meets in a best of seven series. Unlike the MLB, each professional team also only has one farm team. The Japanese have experienced success at many different levels of play including the Little League World Series, winning seven LLWS Championships, six medals at the Baseball World Cup, and four at the Women's Baseball World Cup. Japan has also won multiple World Baseball Classics and three Olympic medals.

However, there are other major differences related to the culture of baseball in Japan.[68] The Japanese implemented a smaller ballpark, bigger strike zone, and utilize different training methods compared to their American counterparts. Yet, perhaps most notably, Japanese teams put team over the individual. Part of this concept includes this idea that players are unaware of their salary. An additional aspect of the culture is that the team considers themselves a big family, so much so that once an athletes' playing career is over, they typically are asked to work in the front office of the team they played for.

Historically, the Japanese work ethic when it came to competitive sports could be described as somewhat obsessive and perfectionistic. However, in 2013, after complaints of abuse at the national level and an athlete suicide, a societal changed occurred. In the following year, the number of coaches suspended for corporal punishment in high school baseball doubled with increased severity in punishments.

China

Baseball games were played for at least a decade in China before they were played in Japan. At times, part of the stated purpose of promoting baseball was the belief that teaching baseball to young men would give them quality practice similar to that of throwing hand grenades.[69] The MLB opened China development centers in Changzhou, Wuxi, and Nanjing that provides scholarships to student-athletes across the country.[70] More than 5 million Chinese children have been exposed to school programs since 2008. The China Baseball League begin in 2002, making it the newest of the major leagues in Asia. The league is made up of six teams.

Taiwan

Unlike most other countries, the Japanese introduced Taiwan to baseball in 1897. The game served as a way to challenge Japanese rule and Chinese Nationalist hegemony.[71] Despite being under Chinese control, Taiwan's style of play is more similar to the Japanese than the Chinese.[72] Taiwan has demonstrated years of success in the Little League World Series, winning 17 championships over a course of 25 years, the most of any country. However, the success at the youth level has not translated well to the international level. Taiwan won the silver medal at the 1992 Olympic Games, but has not experienced much success since. Additionally, the development of a Taiwan professional league has also been unsuccessful due to the ability to watch American and Japanese professional games on Taiwanese television and because the best players also tend to leave Taiwan to play in American and Japanese leagues.

South Korea

Baseball was first played in Korea in 1905 when it was introduced by American missionary Phillip Gillett.[73] However, during Japan's occupation of the country, the Japanese used the game as propagation and acculturation, banning any Korean-organized tournaments and requiring that the Japanese rules be followed. Thus, the South Korean baseball style more closely resembles the Japanese style of play than the American style of play, but the South Korean game tends to be associated with anti-Japanese sentiments and American modernisms and affluence.[74] Like Taiwan, the game gained in popularity, both as a result from the American soldiers that were stationed in South Korea and from the games' ability to offer the South Korean people a peaceful avenue in which to challenge oppressive rules. The first professional league was organized in South Korea in 1982. South Korea won its first baseball Olympic medal, bronze, in 2000, and medaled again in 2008, this time in gold.

Oceania

Baseball first begin in Australia in 1857 in Melbourne.[75] In 1934 a state-based competition called the Claxton-Shield was introduced, and to this day remains the main avenue in which Australian players are discovered for professional contracts. Australia has had limited success in international events, winning Olympic Silver in 2004, but has never finished higher than 12th in the WBC.[76] Australia's sister nation, New Zealand does not share quite the same skill level. Softball tends to be more popular than baseball on New Zealand and it remains unlikely that baseball will become a major sport in the area with a passionate fan base.[77] However, independent associations, such as the Wellington Baseball Association are working to hold camps and increase interest in the sport.

With the success of professional leagues in other countries, and the United States failing to win international competitions, it can be argued that baseball has very much become an international sport. However, the MLB still remains the premier league in terms of level of competition, despite the sometimes questionable approaches the organizations may take in terms of recruiting talent. With players entering the league from countries that have not previously produced a major leaguer every year, growth of the sport is likely to continue. However, with a decrease in the popularity of watching baseball, compared to other professional sports, such as the National Football League (NFL) and National Basketball Association (NBA), the MLB will likely continue looking for ways in which to expand their market.

Softball

History

Softball is proposed to have begun on Thanksgiving Day 1887 in Chicago, Illinois with Yale and Harvard alumni at the Farragut Boat Club.[78] Over the next week, a Chicago reporter, George Hancock, and members of the Farragut Boat Club established a few rules. In 1889 Hancock distributed the first softball rule book, which at the time was called "indoor baseball." The game was wildly popular, but each league took to fashioning their own unique rules. For example, some leagues preferred slowpitch, while others preferred fastpitch; some used a fourth outfielder for a total of ten fielders, while others stuck with the traditional nine fielders. In 1933 the first amateur softball tournament was held in Chicago as part of Chicago's World Fair. There was a women's division, and two men's divisions- fastpitch and slowpitch. The Amateur Softball Association (ASA) was founded later that year. ASA standardized the rules so that they were consistent across leagues and tournaments, facilitating the growth of the sport. It is estimated that as many as five million people around the globe were playing organized softball by the end of the 1930s. Softball continued to be spread worldwide during the Second World War with soldiers introducing and teaching the game to the inhabitants where they were stationed. By the end of the 20th century, more than 100 countries were playing softball. World Championships at both the Junior and Adult levels continued to increase popularity in the sport, but it was not until the introduction of women's fastpitch into the Olympic Games in Atlanta in 1995 that the sport really took off. While the United States and Canada have a long history with the game, international competition is challenging, especially Pacific Rim powers like Japan, China, New Zealand, and Australia.

National growth

Softball was the most popular sport in America in 1943.[79] Both men and women played the sport. However, at the time, female softball players tended to have similar reputations to that of prostitutes. While fastpitch tends to be more competitive, slowpitch tends to be more synonymous with concepts of recreational play.

Slowpitch was more popular than fastpitch prior to the implementation of Title IX. However, since softball was seen as the female equivalent to baseball, many schools at the high school and collegiate level added fastpitch softball as an interscholastic sport in order to comply with Title IX. The passage of Title IX contributed largely to increasing female participation in sport, and contributing to the growth of softball in America. The implementation of Title IX led to the perception of fastpitch softball as only being played by girls. However, men's teams competed until the competition was restricted to women only in 2003 (the US still fields a men's national slowpitch team). Prior to 2003, the US men won five World Cup titles, and US women have won seven World Cup titles. By 2009, softball was the third-most popular female high school sport, and second-most popular NCAA female sport with nearly 23,000 athletes in 2008. Outside of interscholastic competition, in 2009 the American Softball Association (ASA) registered more than 3.5 million players.

Despite this popularity at the amateur level, the popularity of the professional level has struggled. In 1976 the first women's professional league was established. The International Women's Professional Softball Association featured 13 United States teams and 1 Canadian team. However, the league bottomed out in 1979. The Women's Pro Softball League (WPSL) ran from 1997 to 2001. Again, success was short lived, but remaining assets were used to create a new league, National Pro Fastpitch (NPF). This league began in 2004 with six teams and is still in existence, recently adding a Chinese-based team to the league. However, there are many more professional leagues overseas in Europe and Japan.

International growth

Internationally, there have been multiple competitions, and fastpitch has proven more popular than slowpitch, with the USA only fielding their first women's national slowpitch team in 2017. In 1965 Australia hosted and won the first women's softball World Championship and Mexico hosted the first men's softball World Championship the following year. Men's teams competed until the competition was restricted to women only in 2003. Women's softball was first played in the Olympics in 1996. The United States won the first 3 competitions, but fell to the Japanese in 2008. However, the IOC voted the sport out for the 2012 and 2016 Olympics, but has since reinstated it for the 2020 Olympics. Despite exclusion from the Olympics, the World Cup of Softball is an annual national competition first held in 2005. The format is round robin. The United States holds the most titles, making the championship final all twelve years. The only other champion at the World Cup and the Olympics has been the Japanese team.

Japan, Taiwan, and various European countries have professional leagues for women's fastpitch that are played during the spring and/or fall seasons. The Japanese professional league features 12 teams, but each team is only allowed two foreigners. Several American NPF players play in this league when the NPF is not in season. The Taiwanese league began play in June 2016 with four teams in hopes to solidify themselves as a contender in the 2020 Olympics. In Europe, the Netherlands and Italy tend to have the most prominent leagues. However the NPF and the Japanese league tend to feature the best talent. As mentioned earlier, in 2017 NPF announced that a Chinese team, Beijing Shougang, would join the league as the first international team in the league.[80] Additionally, this comes after the expansion move of allowing eight Australian players to sign American contracts for the 2017 season.

However, the lack of professional leagues in other countries does not represent a lack of the sport in those other countries. In Canada the Canada Amateur Softball Association (Softball Canada) registers more than 300,000 players annually and sponsors eight fast-pitch tournaments and two slow-pitch tournaments for 140 teams, involving more than 75,000 players. While softball in Latin America does not draw quite the interest that soccer, baseball, and boxing does in terms of numbers of participants, the sport is played in more than 30 countries in Latin America.

Two-thirds of these countries field national teams, including the Puerto Rico, Venezuela and Cuba powerhouses.[81]

Australia also produces tough teams at the national level for both men's and women's competitions. Competitive softball was first played in Australia during the Second World War before being incorporated as a national fitness program in the New South Wales school system. Australia has won multiple international titles.[82] However, much of the men's success in this sport have been overlooked due to the perception of it being a women's sport, and as such considered to be less important. So, unlike the baseball version in which international success tends to promote growth in the sport in the country, the success from elite Australia men's softball teams has not grown the participation numbers in the sport. Some of the best men's fastpitch softball players end up seeking employment coaching women's teams in the US.

Initially when the IOC dropped softball from the Olympics, one of the arguments was that the United States was too dominant. While the US teams have been very dominant at the international level, likely due in large part to Title IX giving them the opportunity to compete at the high school and collegiate level, simply removing the sport from the program does not help other countries to improve their own programs. Growth in recent years, especially the development of the professional league in Taiwan, the incorporation of Australian players into the NPF, and the inclusion of a Chinese professional team into the NPF league will likely continue to grow the sport both in size and skill, particularly outside of the United States. The decision to include softball in the 2020 Olympics, may also help ignite a spark in countries that had not previously devoted national funding to softball programs and competitions.

Notes

1 Anderson, D. W., Gumpert, B., & Gumpert, E. "Abner Doubleday." Society for American Baseball Research. Assessed October 9, 2017. https://sabr.org/node/37301.
2 McDaniel, D. "Jacques Barzun, 'Baseball's Best Cultural Critic,' Turns His Back on the Game." Bleacher Report. July 6, 2009. https://bleacherreport.com/articles/212819-when-baseballs-best-cultural-critic-turned-his-back-on-the-game
3 Helyar, J. Lords of the Realm: The Real History of Baseball. New York: Villard Books, 1994.
4 Andrews, E. "The Black Sox Baseball Scandal, 95 Years Ago." History, 2014. www.history.com/news/the-black-sox-baseball-scandal-95–years-ago.
5 Nathan, D.A. Saying It's So: A Cultural History of the Black Sox Scandal. Chicago: University of Illinois Press, 2010.
6 Candelaria, C. Seeking the Perfect Game: Baseball in American Literature. Westport: Greenwood, 1989.
7 Will, G. F. Bunts. New York: Simon and Schuster, 1999.
8 Honig, D. The American League: An Illustrated History. New York: Crown, 1983.
9 Heaphy, L.A., & M.A. May, M.A. Encyclopedia of Women and Baseball. Jefferson: McFarland, 2016.
10 Browne, L. Girls of Summer: In Their Own League. Toronto: HarperCollins Publishers, 1992.
11 Provance, G. "All-American Girls Professional Baseball League." In Encyclopedia of Women and Baseball, edited by L.A. Heaphy & M.A. May. Jefferson: McFarland, 2016.
12 Roepke, S. Diamond Gals: The Story of the All-American Girls Professional Baseball League. Cooperstown: The National Baseball Hall of Fame & A.A.G.P.B.L. Cards, 1986.
13 Randle, N. 1992. "Their Time At Bat: A Women's Professional League That Made Baseball History." Chicago Tribune, July 5.
14 Howell, C. "Canada: Internationalizing America's National Pastime." In Baseball Beyond Our Borders: An International Pastime, edited by G. Gmelch and D.A. Nathan. Lincoln: University of Nebraska Press, 2017.
15 Schweinbenz, A. "All-American Girls Professional Baseball League." In Baseball Beyond Our Borders: An International Pastime, edited by G. Gmelch and D.A. Nathan, 163. Lincoln: University of Nebraska Press, 2017.
16 Fincher, J. 1989. "The Belles of the Ball Game Were a Hit with their Fans." Smithsonian, July; Weiller, K. H., & Higgs, C. T. "The All American Girls Professional Baseball League, 1943–1954: Gender Conflict in Sport?" Sociology of Sport Journal, 11, (1994): 289–297.
17 Provance, Encyclopedia of Women and Baseball.

18 Browne, *Girls of Summer.*

19 Fay, B. 1949. "Bells of the Ball Game." *Collier's,* August 13.

20 Gordon, J. 1945. "Beauty at the Bat." *American Magazine,* June, 24–25.

21 Turner, J. R. "AAGPBL History: Diamonds are a Girl's Best Friend." *All-American Girls Professional Baseball League Players Association.* Accessed October 12, 2017. www.aagpbl.org/index.cfm/articles/diamonds-are-a-girl-s-best-friend/31.

22 Fincher, "The Belles of the Ball Game Were a Hit with their Fans."

23 Roepke, *Diamond Gals.*

24 Goldman, S. "Segregated Baseball: A Kaleidoscopic Review." MLB.com. Accessed October 10, 2017. www.mlb.com/mlb/history/mlb_negro_leagues_story.jsp?story=kaleidoscopic

25 Lanctot, N. *Negro League Baseball: The Rise and Ruin of a Black Institution.* Philadelphia: University of Pennsylvania Press, 2008.

26 History. "1939: First Televised Major League Baseball Game." *History.* Accessed October 12, 2017. www.history.com/this-day-in-history/first-televised-major-league-baseball-game

27 Gruen, S. 2014. "Lights, Camera, Acrimony: Baseball's First Televised Game Changed Everything." *Rolling Stone,* August 26. www.rollingstone.com/culture/news/lights-camera-acrimony-baseballs-first-televised-game-changed-everything-20140826

28 Helyar, *Lords of the Realm.*

29 Bouton, J. *Ball Four.* New York: Midpoint Trade Books, 1970.

30 NPR. 2012. "'Ball Four': The Book That Changed Baseball." *NPR,* April 26. www.npr.org/2012/04/26/151457344/ball-four-the-book-that-changed-baseball.

31 Erickson, B.J., Yanke, A., Monson, B., Romeo, A. "The Effect of the Steroid era on Major League Baseball Hitters: Did It Enhance Hitting?" *Sports Medicine and Doping Studies* 5, no. 3 (2015).

32 Canseco, J. *Juiced: Wild Times, Rampant 'Roids, Smash Hits and How Baseball Got Big.* New York: Harper Collins, 2005.

33 Beneteau, A. "World Series (United States)." In *Sports Around the World: History, Culture, and Practice,* edited by J. Nauright & C. Parrish, 428–429. Santa Barbara: ABC-CLIO, 2012.

34 Heaphy, L.A. & M.A. May, eds. *Encyclopedia of Women and Baseball.* Jefferson: McFarland, 2016.

35 Slonksnis, C. 2016. "Sonoma Stompers Make History by Signing 2 Women to Professional Baseball Team." *SB Nation,* June 29. www.sbnation.com/2016/6/29/12061936/kelsie-whitmore-stacy-piagno-sonoma-stompers-indie-league

36 Karmelek, M. 2015. "Does Women's Baseball Have a Future in the US?" *Newsweek,* July 30. www.newsweek.com/american-womens-baseball-looks-ahead-358386

37 Krieger, D. 2012. "For Some Women, the Name of the Game is Baseball." *NYTimes,* March 19. www.nytimes.com/2012/03/20/sports/baseball/20iht-baseball20.html?_r=0

38 Karmelek, "Does Women's Baseball Have a Future in the US?"

39 Puzey, B.K. "Title IX and Baseball: How the Contact Sports Exemption Denies Women Equal Opportunity to America's Pastime." *Nevada Law Journal,* (2014): 1000–1017.

40 Gmelch, G. and D.A. Nathan, eds. *Baseball Beyond Our Borders: An International Pastime.* Lincoln: University of Nebraska Press, 2017.

41 Bjarkman, P.C. "Baseball, Cuba." In *Sports Around the World: History, Culture, and Practice,* edited by J. Nauright & C. Parrish. Santa Barbara: ABC-CLIO, 2012.

42 Azzoni, C., Azzoni, T. & Paterson, W. "Brazil: Baseball Is Popular, and Players Are (Mainly) Japanese!" In *Baseball Beyond Our Borders: An International Pastime,* edited by G. Gmelch and D.A. Nathan. Lincoln: University of Nebraska Press, 2017.

43 Ryan, E. "Baseball, Central and South America." In *Sports Around the World: History, Culture, and Practice,* edited by J. Nauright & C. Parrish, 55–57. Santa Barbara: ABC-CLIO, 2012.

44 Howell, "Canada: Internationalizing America's National Pastime."

45 McGehee, R.V. "Baseball, Mexico." In *Sports Around the World: History, Culture, and Practice,* edited by J. Nauright & C. Parrish, 65–66. Santa Barbara: ABC-CLIO, 2012.

46 Iber, J. "Mexico: Baseball's humble Beginnings to Budding Competitor." In *Baseball Beyond Our Borders: An International Pastime,* edited by G. Gmelch and D.A. Nathan. Lincoln: University of Nebraska Press, 2017.

47 McGehee, "Baseball, Mexico," 66.

48 Klein, A. "Dominican Republic: From Paternalism to Parity." In *Baseball Beyond Our Borders: An International Pastime,* edited by G. Gmelch and D.A. Nathan. Lincoln: University of Nebraska Press, 2017.

49 Emily B. Ottenson, *The Social Cost of Baseball: Addressing the Effects of Major League Baseball Recruitment in Latin America and the Caribbean*. Washington University Global Studies Law Review. 13(4) 767–800. 2014; Gordon, I. *Inside Major League Baseball's Dominican Sweatshop System*. Mother Jones. 2013.

50 Ottenson, *The Social Cost of Baseball*; Gordon, *Inside Major League Baseball's Dominican Sweatshop System*.

51 Ryan, E. "Baseball, Puerto Rico." In *Sports Around the World: History, Culture, and Practice*, edited by J. Nauright & C. Parrish, 66–68. Santa Barbara: ABC-CLIO, 2012.

52 Otto, F. & Van Hyning, T.E. "Puerto Rico: A Major League Stepping-Stone." In *Baseball Beyond Our Borders: An International Pastime*, edited by G. Gmelch and D.A. Nathan. Lincoln: University of Nebraska Press, 2017.

53 Wendel, T. "Cuba: The Curtain Begins to Fall." In *Baseball Beyond Our Borders: An International Pastime*, edited by G. Gmelch and D.A. Nathan. Lincoln: University of Nebraska Press, 2017.

54 Gordon, D. "Nicaragua: In Search of Diamonds." In *Baseball Beyond Our Borders: An International Pastime*, edited by G. Gmelch and D.A. Nathan. Lincoln: University of Nebraska Press, 2017.

55 Ryan, E. "Baseball, Central and South America," 55–57.

56 Ruck, R. "Baseball, Dominican Republic." In *Sports Around the World: History, Culture, and Practice*, edited by J. Nauright & C. Parrish, 60–64. Santa Barbara: ABC-CLIO, 2012.

57 Marcano, A.J. & Fidler, D.P. "Venezuela: The Passion and Politics of Baseball." In *Baseball Beyond Our Borders: An International Pastime*, edited by G. Gmelch and D.A. Nathan. Lincoln: University of Nebraska Press, 2017.

58 Azzoni, C., Azzoni, T. & Paterson, W. "Brazil: Baseball Is Popular, and Players Are (Mainly) Japanese!"

59 Chetwynd, J. "Great Britain: Baseball's Battle for Respect in the Land of Cricket, Rugby, and Soccer." In *Baseball Beyond Our Borders: An International Pastime*, edited by G. Gmelch and D.A. Nathan. Lincoln: University of Nebraska Press, 2017.

60 Shapiro, H. "Holland: An American Coaching Honkbal." In *Baseball Beyond Our Borders: An International Pastime*, edited by G. Gmelch and D.A. Nathan. Lincoln: University of Nebraska Press, 2017.

61 Zipp, S. "Baseball, Dutch West Indies." In *Sports Around the World: History, Culture, and Practice*, edited by J. Nauright & C. Parrish, 64. Santa Barbara: ABC-CLIO, 2012.

62 Carino, P. "Italy: No Hot Dogs in the Bleachers." In *Baseball Beyond Our Borders: An International Pastime*, edited by G. Gmelch and D.A. Nathan. Lincoln: University of Nebraska Press, 2017.

63 Hyvarinen, M. "Finland: Pesapallo, Baseball Finnish Style." In *Baseball Beyond Our Borders: An International Pastime*, edited by G. Gmelch and D.A. Nathan. Lincoln: University of Nebraska Press, 2017.

64 Rademeyer, C. "Baseball, South Africa." In *Sports Around the World: History, Culture, and Practice*, edited by J. Nauright & C. Parrish, 108–109. Santa Barbara: ABC-CLIO, 2012; Grundlingh, M. "South Africa: The Battle for Baseball." In *Baseball Beyond Our Borders: An International Pastime*, edited by G. Gmelch and D.A. Nathan. Lincoln: University of Nebraska Press, 2017.

65 Rademeyer, C. "Baseball, South Africa," 108–109.

66 Ressler, W. "Israel: From the Desert to Jupiter . . . and Beyond." In *Baseball Beyond Our Borders: An International Pastime*, edited by G. Gmelch and D.A. Nathan. Lincoln: University of Nebraska Press, 2017.

67 Stockstill, J. "Baseball, Japan." In *Sports Around the World: History, Culture, and Practice*, edited by J. Nauright & C. Parrish, 197–200. Santa Barbara: ABC-CLIO, 2012.

68 Gordon, D. "Japan: "No Matter What Happens, Stand Up."" In *Baseball Beyond Our Borders: An International Pastime*, edited by G. Gmelch and D.A. Nathan. Lincoln: University of Nebraska Press, 2017.

69 Reaves, J.A. "China: A Century and a Half of Bat Ball." In *Baseball Beyond Our Borders: An International Pastime*, edited by G. Gmelch and D.A. Nathan. Lincoln: University of Nebraska Press, 2017.

70 Caple, J. 2017. "China, Where Baseball is on the Rise, Hopes to Show Progress at WBC." *ESPN*, March 3. www.espn.com/mlb/story/_/id/18790735/china-country-where-baseball-rise-hopes-show-progress-world-baseball-classic

71 Morris, A.D. "Taiwan: Baseball, Colonialism, Nationalism, and Other Inconceivable Things." In *Baseball Beyond Our Borders: An International Pastime*, edited by G. Gmelch and D.A. Nathan. Lincoln: University of Nebraska Press, 2017.

72 Little, C. "Baseball, Taiwan." In *Sports Around the World: History, Culture, and Practice*, edited by J. Nauright & C. Parrish, 202–203. Santa Barbara: ABC-CLIO, 2012.

73 Reaves, J.A. "Korea: Straw Sandals and Strong Arms." In *Baseball Beyond Our Borders: An International Pastime*, edited by G. Gmelch and D.A. Nathan. Lincoln: University of Nebraska Press, 2017.

74 Cho, Y. "Baseball, Korea." In *Sports Around the World: History, Culture, and Practice*, edited by J. Nauright & C. Parrish, 200–202. Santa Barbara: ABC-CLIO, 2012.

75 Neal, H. "Baseball, Australia." In *Sports Around the World: History, Culture, and Practice*, edited by J. Nauright & C. Parrish, 360. Santa Barbara: ABC-CLIO, 2012.

76 Burton, R. "Australia: Baseball's Curious Journey." In *Baseball Beyond Our Borders: An International Pastime*, edited by G. Gmelch and D.A. Nathan. Lincoln: University of Nebraska Press, 2017.

77 Ryan, G. "New Zealand: Baseball Between British Traditions." In *Baseball Beyond Our Borders: An International Pastime*, edited by G. Gmelch and D.A. Nathan. Lincoln: University of Nebraska Press, 2017.

78 Baker, J. & Hofstetter, A.B. *An Insider's Guide to Softball*. New York: The Rosen Publishing Group, Inc, 2015.

79 Turner, *All-American Girls Professional Baseball League Players Association*.

80 Lombardo, K. 2017. "American Pro Softball is Going Global. Here's What It Means for the Future of the Sport." *Excelle Sports*, May 3. www.excellesports.com/news/npf-softball-china-australia-tokyo.

81 Silvestrini, V. & Parrish, C. "Softball, Latin America." In *Sports Around the World: History, Culture, and Practice*, edited by J. Nauright & C. Parrish, 137–138. Santa Barbara: ABC-CLIO, 2012.

82 "Softball, Australia." In *Sports Around the World: History, Culture, and Practice*, edited by J. Nauright & C. Parrish, 137–138. Santa Barbara: ABC-CLIO, 2012.

18

Cricket

Sarthak Mondal and Anand Rampersad

The use of the word cricket can be traced back to 1598 as Florio's Italian-English dictionary[1] defines the term *sgrillare* as 'to play cricket-a-wicket and be merry'. On the basis of the explanation, it can be assumed that cricket initially started as an individual sport, later developing into a team sport as it is played in the modern era. The 1611 Randle Cotgrave's French-English dictionary[2] translates the term *croffer* to 'play cricket' which raises speculations if the game was first played in France as paintings from the medieval stained-glass windows show people playing bat and ball games.

Like other sports, the origin of the game is buried in myth and speculations. Bat and ball games were developed with different names in different parts of the world with rules varying from place to place.[3] However, it is unknown when the game developed into one where the hitter defended a target against the thrower. Historians and academics agree on the fact that the bat and ball game was established in many parts of Kent, Sussex and Surrey in the sixteenth century and became a feature of leisure time in many schools.[4]

Cricket evolved from being a rural leisure event into an activity that was cherished and appreciated by the landed gentry.[5] In the nineteenth century the Victorians began extolling the game as the manifestation of the English way of life accentuating Anglo-Saxon manners, ethics and morals[6]. The growth of cricket was given impetus by key institutions such as the church and the school system as it was believed to represent desirable cultural value.[7] Significantly, the cultural elites – the aristocrats and landed gentry – incorporated the social value of cricket into hegemonic cultural power which became the desired norm for all social strata.[8]

The education system through public schools and headmasters encouraged cricket as it was believed to have inculcated values that resulted in disciplined and well-mannered students and civic minded citizens.[9] Cricket became part of the public school curriculum in 1830 and many cultural elite graduate played cricket at the MCC but also into the civil service and politics.[10] The impact of the education system was reinforced by the church as many clergymen served as headmasters and emphasised the importance of muscular Christianity.[11] In essence the Victorian saw cricket as social act which embodied gentility of morals, ethics, manners, religion and life.[12]

Unlike football and rugby, the popularity of cricket is confined to the residents of the nation-states of the former British Empire.[13] It is believed that cricket was introduced in the Caribbean Islands in 1652 by the British colonies based there but there are no relevant sources to establish it. The first instance of cricket being played outside Britain was in 1676 as a diary entry records at least 40 British residents engaging in pastime activities such as fishing, shooting, handball and *krickett* among others. By the start of 18th century, matches were recorded, and articles of agreement were put in place to govern their conduct. In the year 1744, the first laws of the game were devised, formalising the pitch[14] or surface of play as 22 yards long. The first recorded women's match[15] was reported in *The Reading Mercury* on 26 July 1745 in which 'eleven maids of Bramley and eleven maids of Hambledon, all dressed in white'. The leg before laws[16] were introduced in 1774, and by 1787 members of White Conduit Club formed the Marylebone Cricket Club,[17] following the match against Middlesex at the Thomas Lord's ground, which is recognised as the sole authority on the Laws of Cricket since its foundation.

By the start of the 19th century, the popularity of the game started gathering pace in Britain in in 1806, the first Gentlemen vs Players[18] match was played at Lord's. The first recorded women's county match was played in 1811 between Surrey and Hampshire at Ball's pond in London and in 1828, MCC revised the laws to allow bowlers to raise *his*[19] hand level with the elbow. The first recorded international cricket match[20] was played in 1844 between USA and Canada at St George's Club Ground on September 24 and 25 with players mostly from New York and Toronto.

Cricket playing in the colonies was impacted upon by different strategic and economic factors the colonies had toward the British Empire.[21] The diffusion, appropriation and development of cricket in the colonies was dependent upon local elites embracing the game, its promotion by cultural entrepreneurs and the role of the educational system.[22] The objective of the Victorians was to 'civilise' the colonies with the ethos of the Anglo-Saxon values and ethics.

The imperialist relationship between England and Australia epitomised by cricket as it was seen as the essence of 'Englishness'.[23] It was introduced into Australia as a test to ascertain whether the English culture could exist and thrive in distant places away from home.[24] It also became the gauge of the changing relationship between the colony and England.[25]

Cricket in Australia started with a visit by cricketers from Victoria to Tasmania in February 1851. The first officially recognised Test match was played between England and Australia from 15 to 19 March 1877 at the Melbourne Cricket Ground in Victoria, Australia and it was the start of private cricket tours between the two nations. In 1882, Australia defeated England at The Oval in London and following riots where wickets and bails were burned down, The Ashes was born. It is still the oldest existing rivalry in cricket.

As cricketed evolved, the relationship between the colony and the motherland began to reflect agitation of nationhood and nationalism.[26] Defeating the motherland was seen not only as a growing sense of nationalism but equally important a weakening of imperialism on the society.[27] Australian administrators unlike the British counterparts were more willing to encourage greater participation of the working class.[28] Whereas the late 19th century nationalist reinforced pro-imperial links, by the 1970's a more pragmatic and business approach was taken to structure and organise the game.[29] These changes were reflected by Kerry Packer's market driven World Series Cricket which involved day-night one day internationals, the introduction of coloured clothing and huge spectator turn-out and television audiences through Channel 9.[30] By the end of the 20th century and the start of the 21st century Cricket Australia have fashioned its own style of cricket with its own identity and ethos very much different when the game was first introduced in the colony.

Cricket was introduced into South Africa by the military, administrators and settlers from Britain.[31] Cricket in South Africa grew as the British settlers' encouraged segregated play among middle class blacks and Asians.[32] Sport missionaries used sport inclusive of cricket as a means of instilling 'respectability' among the emerging black middle class as well as providing an example for the less 'respectable' blacks.[33] Although, blacks were excluded from white cricket clubs as well as playing for the national team; they were allowed to play and view the games.[34] Since the end of apartheid 27 April 1994, the South African team have been readmitted to the ICC. Additionally, the government policy of ensuring that a percentage of non-white players must comprise every national team has seen transformation of the team's ethnic makeup.

The introduction of sport in India was not a priority of the colonisers; in fact organised sport remained exclusive to the colonisers.[35] As a result, although cricket was played from 1721, it was over 100 years before the Indians were encouraged to play the game.[36] Cricket started with the Parsi community in India establishing the Oriental Cricket Club in 1848. They were a wealthy entrepreneurial group who appropriate the game of cricket to demonstrate to the British that they were fit to be brokers between the British and the Indian.[37] The British Anglicisation policy of 1835 focusing on the English-educated Indian elite indirectly pointed to the important cultural value of cricket.[38]

Cricket was introduced into the West Indies by the British military at the beginning of the 19th century.[39] Cricket was used to concretise the rigid class and race structure and divide. Although blacks and Indians were encouraged to play the game, clubs were organised according to class and race. Therefore, the system that operated in the West Indies was one that integrated but maintained separateness.[40] The Anglo-centric colonial system shaped the structure and power dimensions of the West Indies team and the West Indies Cricket Board of Control (WICBC) as it related to leadership. Captains and vice-captains from 1900 to 1960 and the presidency of the WICBC 1927 to 1990 were always white.[41] The post 1960 period saw the rise of the first black captain, Sir Frank Worrell. The cultural practice of the British that was introduced to civilise the non-white population was now being appropriated and just as their Australian counterparts, used cricket as a powerful social tool for establishing their own self-identity through nationhood development and achieving self-governance and whittling the pro-imperial influence and clout.[42]

Following objections from board members in Australia and support from the president of MCC, Lord Chesterfield and Lord Harris, the Imperial Cricket Conference was formed in 1909 to overlook the game across the Commonwealth, with the President of the MCC installed as the chair of the body. Membership was initially limited to test-playing nations but in 1964, a consensus was reached to grant membership to non-test playing nations and the governing body was renamed to International Cricket Conference. Under its aegis, the first men's cricket World Cup was organised in 1975 with 8 teams taking part.[43] With the game rapidly spreading globally, the ICC renamed itself to the International Cricket Council and the trend of the MCC President automatically becoming the Chairman of ICC was terminated.[44]

With ICC as the governing body and MCC as the guardians of the game, the rules of cricket have changed slightly from time to time to accommodate the use of technology, keeping the values in place and annual meetings take place every year to ratify those changes and keep up with pace. The current rules of the game can be found on the MCC website[45] consisting of 42 laws to govern the game uniformly.

It was in 1996 when former Blackcaps opener, Martin Crowe came up with a truncated format of the game, where a side would bat twice, but it was not a test and each of them would have a total of 20 overs to bat, but it was not a Twenty20 (T20).[46] The rationale behind the new format was to provide great entertainment and an exciting result in 3 hours of cricket while keeping some old traditions of the game. New rules such as last man stands, no leg before wicket, 4 stumps instead of 3 and free hit on a no-ball (batsman cannot be dismissed unless he is run out) were introduced and fast-tracked into the international scene as the Blackcaps took on an English Lions side in a 3-match series in October 1997.[47] However, the propaganda was short lived as the new format failed to generate enthusiasm and was relegated to a pre-season tournament by 2000,[48] with the last Cricket Max played between a touring Indian side and the Black Caps on 4 December 2002 in Christchurch.[49]

A research commission by the England and Wales Cricket Board in 2000 to examine the falling domestic attendances and decline in participation figures revealed that long games and matches being played at inconvenient times were acting as a barrier to participation and spectating. It also recognised that if the management could develop a product that delivered value and entertainment, there is a significant market potential.[50] In April 2002 with English counties scheduled to vote for or against the introduction of a new 20-over championship, the then English Chairman, Lord MacLaurin made multiple phone calls on his way to Lords' Cricket Ground hoping to sway the five or six counties who were on the fence. It was voted 11–7 in favour of the introduction of the 20-over championship and is probably one of the biggest moments of the game played out in a car.[51]

The product focused on two target groups: sporting public aged between 16 and 34 years who were general sports fans and women, members of the office crowd and children. There was a notion that if these groups were attracted, the event provided the best odds to be developed over long term. A year after the crucial vote, the first set of T20 games were played in England. A total of 360,000 fans turned up the watch the tournament with most of them being families with kids and the county grounds were not used to this kind of crowds in terms of both numbers and demographics. Martin Williamson reported for ESPNCricinfo on that the counties played their part in drawing crowd, as Nottinghamshire got their more toned players to pose topless on posters as they billed games as Girls' Nights Out. Worcestershire placed a Jacuzzi on the boundary edge; Gloucestershire warned their committee that if any of them turned up wearing a tie they would be kicked out; Yorkshire sold tickets at £2; Glamorgan asked fans to turn up in pyjamas.[52] On 19 July 2003, Surrey was crowned the first T20 champions and it was the birth of a new format which changed the way the game is played forever.

On 17 February 2005, New Zealand took on Australia in the first ever men's T20 International at Eden Park in Auckland and the players dressed up in 1980s retro gear. With no guaranteed future at the international level, the game was looked off as an one-off evening's entertainment, but 13 years down the line, 706 matches has been played at the international level[53] (an average of 54 matches per year) and six World Cups[54] has been held in this short span with five different teams winning the tournament (West Indies[55] are the only team to win it twice). Women were ahead of men in this format like the Cricket World Cup, as England women took on New Zealand women in the first ever T20 International match[56] in mid-2004 in Brighton. It is quite fitting that the match involved the Blackcaps as it was Martin Crowe who can be seen as the pioneer of the modern T20 game with his vision about Cricket Max.

Following India's successful campaign in the inaugural World T20 in 2007, the BCCI launched the Indian Premier League,[57] which can be described as an amalgamation of global cricket superstars and the Indian film industry, Bollywood. 8 franchisees went head to head in a home and away fixture before the top four culminated for the play-offs and the final for over 2 months and Gautam Bhattacharya, an Indian sports journalist described it as a cocktail of mega-entertainment for an average Indian.[58]

However, it should be noted that Indian Premier League did not revolutionise Twenty20 cricket in India. If we go back a year, Kapil Dev along with Kiran More, with the backing of Zee Entertainment Enterprises founded the franchisee and city based Indian Cricket League to take cricket to smaller venues. The only caviar to the league was the lack of support from the BCCI and the ICC and with the advent of Indian Premier League in 2008, commercial partners started backing out from the Indian Cricket League leaving it in the middle of nowhere and leading to subsequently being defunct in 2009.

One of the major impacts that the Indian Premier League had on Twenty20 cricket is the increase in the viewership of the game. With a format, which is 410 overs shorter than the longest version of the game and marketed to all age groups, and no shortage of innovations such as time-outs, the Indian Premier League was well received by the general public with over 100 million viewers watching the tournament.[59] Currently the Indian Premier League attracts players from all over the world with many players from West Indies and New Zealand refusing to sign central contracts to participate in the tournament. This has led to the creation of a competitive imbalance in overall International Cricket as more often than not, some countries field potentially second-string sides in the international matches which take place alongside the Indian Premier League season.

Following the footsteps of BCCI, other cricket boards have come up with their own Twenty20 domestic leagues such as the Big Bash League in Australia, Pakistan Super League in Pakistan, Caribbean Premier League in the West Indies and T20 Blast in England. Sri Lanka and South Africa have a love-hate affair with domestic Twenty20 leagues as time and again they have tried to chop and change their existing system without success. With the popularity of the condensed format of the game ever increasing, it can be emphasised that T20 cricket has completely changed the way cricket is played and made it a truly global game.

Cricket was seen as an expression of masculinity in England and in the colonies.[60] The masculine qualities of a cricketer were seen as courage determination, endurance, strength, energy and fitness. This view of masculinity and the assumption that women required protection from men reinforced the cricket gender ideology while at the same justifying female exclusion on the basis female weakness.[61] The situation represented a strong sense of 'blokeism,' where sport provides a social space for men to define themselves and engage in unfettered male bonding and in cricket this 'blokeism' was evident as the home of British cricket, the MCC, was an all-male club.[62] The social exclusion was also seen in the absence of female umpires and the non-admittance to the pavilions of some county grounds.[63]

Despite the challenges of social exclusion the first recorded women's cricket match was between eleven maids each from Bramley and Hambledon.[64] Two of the early famous women's clubs were the White Heather Club from Yorkshire and Original English Lady Cricketers,[65] in England the Women Cricket Association (WCA) was formed in 1926. (Williams). The WCA main focus was the development of women's cricket and emphasised the formation of clubs throughout the country to increase participation.[66] As in the men's game, those who controlled the WCA belonged to the privileged social classes and organised the women's game along the values and principles of the men's cricket clubs for those who belong to the south of England.[67] The class division was also reflected in the school system as cricket as highly restricted to private and selected secondary schools to which working-class children rarely attended.[68] The Australian Women's Cricket Council was established in 1931 and the New Zealand Women's Cricket Council was formed in 1934.[69] In 1934–1935, England travelled to Australia to play three test matches and one in New Zealand; a reciprocal tour by Australia for three matches took place in 1937.[70]

Women's cricket in the subcontinent was slower to develop compared to England and Australia.[71] India's first international match took place in 1975, forty years after England and Australia played the first women test series.[72] In 1997, representative teams for Pakistan and Sri Lanka played in their first major international event the 1997 World Cup.[73] A number of factors including religion and playing apparel such as wearing culottes (divided skirt) as was done by Australia, England and New Zealand as opposed to trouser accounted for the slow development of the women's game in the subcontinent.[74]

As in England, Australia and the subcontinent, the gender structure of cricket was reinforced in the West Indies along the lines of masculinity and patriarchy.[75] Additionally, there was no vested interest on the part of the colonialist nor the nationalist movement in the Caribbean to challenge the prevailing culture of dominant patriarchy.[76] As much as the institution of cricket provided a space to expose and challenge the prevailing social class and racial inequalities, it was very stoic and unwavering when addressing the issue of gender.[77] Both the African and Indian males viewed cricket as symbolic of their accomplishments and executed a gender ideology that only served to marginalise women cricketers claims for legitimacy.[78]

The development of women's cricket in the West Indies gained momentum in the post-Second World War period that coincided with the period of political success of nationalist and socialist movements against the imperialist movements such as attaining black leadership of the West Indies team.[79] The Jamaica Women's Cricket Association (JWCA) was formed in 1966 as the first established body for women's cricket in the region; similar organisations were also developed in other territories such as Trinidad and Tobago, Barbados, St Lucia, St Vincent, Grenada and Guyana.[80] Jamaica played England three two-day 'test' matches in 1970. In 1973, Jamaica and Trinidad and Tobago became members of the International Women's Cricket Council (IWCC) and participated in the first Women's World Cup.[81] In 1975, the Caribbean Women's Cricket Federation (CWCF) was formed with the Jamaican Monica Taylor at the helm.[82]

The International Women's Cricket Council (IWCC) was formed in 1958 to replace the English Women's Cricket Association (WCA) as the coordinator of the women's game. In 2005, the IWCC merged with the International Cricket Council (ICC) with the intended purpose of enhancing the development of both the men and women's game. Test cricket has been mainly been played by England, Australia and New Zealand. As in the men's game, Ashes test match between England and Australia is the most famous women's test match. One of the popular forms of the game since the merging of the IWCC and the ICC have been the One Day International (ODI) Championship which culminates in a World Cup every four years. The first World Cup was played in 1973 in England with the support of businessman Sir Jack Hayward who contributed forty thousand pounds and a major role was played by Rachel Hayhoe-Flint, the former English captain in roping the sponsorship. The ODI World Cup have been dominated by Australia with six wins England was the 2017 champions defeating India; the next World Cup is scheduled for New Zealand in 2021.

Women's T20 cricket started in 2004 and since then there have been six T20 World Cups since 2009. Australia has been crowned world champions on four occasions with the most recent in the West Indies in 2018 where they defeated arch rivals England. The ICC has applied to the Commonwealth Games Committee for women T20 to be included in the Birmingham 2022 games. The development of T20 cricket internationally and the move by both the ICC and respective cricket boards to encourage greater participation of women in cricket as well as create a career of cricket have seen the establishment of two women's franchise tournaments. The Kia Super League (KSL) in England and the Women's Big Bash League (WBBL) has provided players from both England and Australia and from other countries with an opportunity to display their skills and earn financial rewards. The fourth edition of the BBL, 2018 is scheduled to have twenty three matches broadcast live by Fox Sports and the Seven Network. There have been a call for women's Indian Premier League (IPL) and the signs are encouraging as there was an exhibition at the 2018 edition of the tournament which involved top players from across the world. At the end of the 2018 T20 World Cup in the Caribbean, the owners of the Caribbean Premier League (CPL) have indicated interest of a women's CPL. In 2017, the Trinidad and Tobago Women's Cricket Association (TTWCA) started T20 franchise competition for players from Trinidad and Tobago and the other regional players who represent the West Indies.

Cricket may have gained popularity and support in 19th century England as embodying the Victorian ethos of manner, ethics and morals and diffused to the British empire as a powerful cultural agent of 'civilising' but by the 21st century the ethos of capitalism and the market has been dictating its global trend. The growth of T20 leagues across the cricketing world have resulted in the disruption of the status quo of test cricket especially in those territories where the national boards are unable to retain their best players throughout the year. There has been a shift in the economic and political power of cricket away from the motherland to India. With new formats such as 100-ball cricket being authorised by the England Cricket Board and the emergence of T10, it remains to be seen how shorter formats impact on the future of the cricket.

Notes

1 J. Florio, *A Worlde of Words 1598* (New York: Georg Olms Verlag, 1972).
2 R. Cotgrave, *A Dictionarie of the French and English Tongues 1611* (New York: Georg Olms Verlag, 1970).
3 D. Underdown, 'The History of Cricket', *History Compass*, 4, 1 (2006), 43–53.
4 ESPNCricinfo, *Origins and Development: A Brief History of Cricket*. Retrieved from www.espncricinfo.com/ci/content/story/239757.html (accessed 3 November 2018).
5 F. Mustafa, 'Cricket and Globalisation: Global Process and the Imperial Game', *Journal of Global History*, (2013), 318–341.
6 K.A.P. Sandiford, 'England', in B. Stoddart and K.A.P. Sandiford, *The Imperial Game: Cricket, Culture and Society* (Manchester: Manchester University Press, 1998), 9–33.
7 O. Patterson and J. Kaufmann, 'Cross-National Cultural Diffusion: The Global Spread of Cricket', *American Sociological Review* (Feb 2005), 70, 82–110; Mustafa, 'Cricket and Globalisation'.
8 Sandiford, 'England'.
9 Ibid.
10 Ibid.; Patterson and Kaufmann, 'Cross-National Cultural Diffusion'; Mustafa, 'Cricket and Globalisation'.
11 Sandiford, 'England'.
12 Ibid.; Patterson and Kaufmann, 'Cross-National Cultural Diffusion'; Mustafa, 'Cricket and Globalisation'.
13 D. Malcolm, J. Gemmell and N. Mehta, 'Cricket and Modernity: International and Interdisciplinary Perspectives on the Study of the Imperial Game', in D. Malcolm, J. Gemmell and N. Mehta (eds) *The Changing Face of cricket: From Imperial to Global Game* (Abingdon: Routledge 2010), 1–16.
14 For more details, read Law 6 – The Pitch.
15 G. Buckley, *Fresh Light on 18th Century Cricket: A Collection of 1000 Cricket Notices from 1697 to 1800 AD Arranged in Chronological Order* (Birmingham: Cotterell, 1935).
16 For more details, read Law 36 – Leg Before Wicket.
17 Lord's, 'What is MCC?', retrieved from www.lords.org/mcc/the-club/what-is-mcc/ (Accessed 3 November 2018).
18 Read C. Barnett, *The Pride and the Fall: The Dream and Illusion of Britain as a Great Nation* (New York: The Free Press, 1987).
19 It is quite fascinating how MCC used male pronouns to describe the laws of the game.
20 ESPNCricinfo, 'The Oldest International Contest of Them All', retrieved from www.espncricinfo.com/magazine/content/story/141170.html (accessed 3 November 2018).
21 Mustafa, 'Cricket and Globalisation'.
22 Patterson and Kaufmann, 'Cross-National Cultural Diffusion'; Mustafa, 'Cricket and Globalisation'.
23 Sandiford, 'England'; Patterson and Kaufmann, 'Cross-National Cultural Diffusion'; Mustafa, 'Cricket and Globalisation'.
24 R. Cashman, 'Australia', in B. Stoddart and K.A.P. Sandiford, *The Imperial Game: Cricket, Culture and Society* (Manchester: Manchester University Press, 1998), 34–54.
25 Ibid.; Mustafa, 'Cricket and Globalisation'.
26 Cashman, 'Australia'; Mustafa, 'Cricket and Globalisation'; Patterson and Kaufmann, 'Cross-National Cultural Diffusion'.
27 Cashman, 'Australia'.
28 Ibid.
29 Ibid.; Patterson and Kaufmann, 'Cross-National Cultural Diffusion'
30 Cashman, 'Australia'.

31 Ibid.
32 C. Merret and J. Nauright, 'South Africa', in B. Stoddart and K.A.P. Sandiford, *The Imperial Game: Cricket, Culture and Society* (Manchester: Manchester University Press, 1998), 55–78.
33 Patterson and Kaufmann, 'Cross-National Cultural Diffusion'.
34 Merret and Nauright, 'South Africa'; Patterson and Kaufmann, 'Cross-National Cultural Diffusion'; Mustafa, 'Cricket and Globalisation'.
35 Patterson and Kaufmann, 'Cross-National Cultural Diffusion'.
36 R. Cashman, 'The Subcontinent', in B. Stoddart and K.A.P. Sandiford, *The Imperial Game: Cricket, Culture and Society* (Manchester: Manchester University Press, 1998), 116–134; Patterson and Kaufmann, 'Cross-National Cultural Diffusion'.
37 Cashman, 'The Subcontinent'; Patterson and Kaufmann, 'Cross-National Cultural Diffusion'.
38 Patterson and Kaufmann, 'Cross-National Cultural Diffusion'.
39 Cashman, 'The Subcontinent'.
40 H. Beckles, *The Development of West Indies Cricket, Vol. 1: Age of Nationalism* (London: Pluto Press); F. Birbalsingh, *The Rise of West Indian Cricket: From Colony to Nation* (Antigua: Hansib Publishing; 1996); B. Stoddart, *Sport, Culture and History: Region, Nation and Globe* (New York: Routledge, 2008).
41 Birbalsingh, *The Rise of West Indian Cricket*.
42 Beckles, *Development of West Indies Cricket, Vol. 1*; Birbalsingh, *The Rise of West Indian Cricket*; Stoddart, *Sport, Culture and History*.
43 Details about the Women's World Cup and the women's game has been discussed in a separate section.
44 For details about the governing body of the game: International Cricket Council, 'History of ICC', retrieved from www.icc-cricket.com/about/the-icc/history-of-icc (accessed on 3 November 2018).
45 Lord's, 'Laws of Cricket', retrieved from www.lords.org/mcc/laws-of-cricket/laws (accessed on 3 November 2018).
46 ESPNCricinfo, 'Cricket Max – The Game Invented By Martin Crowe', retrieved from www.espn-cricinfo.com/ci/content/story/67577.html (accessed 3 November 2018).
47 J. Bell, 'Cricket to the Max, NZ Cricket Museum', retrieved from http://nzcricketmuseum.co.nz/cricket-max (accessed on 3 November 2018).
48 G. Ryan, 'Amateurs in a Professional Game: Player Payments in New Zealand Cricket, c.1977–2002', *Sport in History*, 25, 1 (2006), 116–137.
49 ESPNCricinfo, 'India tour of New Zealand at Christchurch', retrieved from www.espncricinfo.com/series/15259/scorecard/112812/new-zealand-vs-india-india-tour-of-new-zealand-2002-03 (accessed 3 November 2018).
50 P. Kitchin, 'Twenty-20 and English Domestic Cricket', in S. Chadwick & D. Arthur (eds) *International Cases in the Business of Sport* (Amsterdam: Butterworth-Heinemann, 2008), 101–113.
51 ESPNCricinfo [ESPNCricinfo]. 'How did the First T20 Season Change Cricket (7/25)' [Video file], 22 September 2018, retrieved from www.youtube.com/watch?v=jGEPr1gGuEk (accessed on 3 November 2018).
52 M. Williamson, Crash, bang and Pandora's box is opened, *ESPNCricinfo*, 25 August 2012. Retrieved from www.espncricinfo.com/magazine/content/story/579245.html (Accessed on 3 November 2018).
53 ESPNCricinfo, 'Statsguru', retrieved from http://stats.espncricinfo.com (accessed 3 November 2018).
54 The ICC World T20 was held on 6 occasions so far (2007, 2009, 2010, 2012, 2014, 2016). The next event is scheduled to be hosted in 2020 in Australia. The ICC Women's World T20 2018 to be held in West Indies is the first standalone version of the women's tournament. It has been held alongside men's tournament until the last edition.
55 West Indies men's cricket team won the World T20 in 2012 in Sri Lanka and 2016 in India. They are the first side to win the tournament on two occasions. West Indies is also the first side to win 2 ODI Cricket World Cups in 1975 and 1979.
56 A. Miller, 'Revolution at the Seaside', ESPNCricinfo, 6 August 2004, retrieved from www.espncricinfo.com/story/_/id/23142298/revolution-seaside (accessed on 3 November 2018). New Zealand cricket holds the distinct record of playing the first T20 International match in both men's and women's game.
57 H. Khondker, R. Robertson, R. Giulianotti and D. Numerato, 'Glocalization, Consumption, and Cricket: The Indian Premier League', *Journal of Consumer Culture*, 18, 2 (2018), 279–297.
58 J. Kimber, S. Collins and J. Hotten (Directors), *Death of a Gentleman* [Documentary], 2015. Sheffield: Dartworth Films, Two Chucks, Wellington Films. The documentary reviews the existence of the game and compares Test cricket with T20.

59 Lalit Modi, 'IPL Facts', retrieved from www.lalitmodi.com/IPL-Fact.php (accessed on 3 November 2018). Lalit Modi is the brain behind the foundation of the Indian Premier League.

60 J. Williams, *Cricket and England: A cultural and Social History of the Inter-war Years* (London: Frank Cass, 1999); B. Stoddart and K. Sandiford, *The Imperial Game: Cricket, Culture and Society* (Manchester: Manchester University Press, 1998); Beckles, *Development of West Indies Cricket, Vol. 1*.

61 J. Williams, *Cricket and England: A Cultural and Social History of the Inter-war Years* (London: Frank Cass, 1999).

62 Ibid.

63 Ibid.

64 Ibid.

65 Ibid.

66 Ibid.

67 Ibid.

68 Ibid.

69 Beckles, *Development of West Indies Cricket, Vol. 1*.

70 Williams, *Cricket and England*.

71 Cashman, 'Australia'.

72 Ibid.

73 Ibid.

74 Ibid.

75 Beckles, *Development of West Indies Cricket, Vol. 1*.

76 Ibid.

77 Ibid.

78 Ibid.

79 Ibid.

80 Ibid.

81 Ibid.

82 Ibid.

19

Darts

Luke J. Harris

Introduction

Darts is a sport where two or more players throw a 'dart' at a board that contains twenty numbered sections that score between one and twenty, with the highest score of 60 possible from a single 'throw'. Darts is most commonly associated with the British Isles, although it is also popular across the former Dominions of the British Empire in particular. In the twenty-first century it has become increasingly popular on television across the world and this has been a factor in its globalisation, with an increasing number of players and events taking place overseas. Darts is now a sport popular in the Netherlands, as well as having a passionate following in North America and Australia, and a growing Asian market.

Current rules dictate that the distance between the board and the 'oche' (the place where throwers throw their darts from) should measure 7 feet 9.25 inches. The object of the game is to reach zero from a score of 501, with players throwing three throws at a time. These rules are certainly not the only way that darts has been played, and historians differ in perspectives regarding the origins of the sport. The modern day rules of darts were first established in 1924, and prior to this they had been different depending upon region and sometimes venues, making it perhaps the last sport established within Britain to have formalised national and international rules.

The origins of modern darts comes primarily from within the public houses and social clubs which existed mainly in England during the early part of the twentieth century. From these largely working-class origins came the first professional players in the 1930s. It was the advent of colour television in the 1970s which revolutionised darts and brought about the first professionals that played the game on a full-time basis, turning the leading protagonists into household names and darts forever.

From a historiography perspective, academic writing on the sports is limited, but growing. The seminal work on the sport is Patrick Chaplin's *Darts in England, 1900–1939: A Social History*. Despite current interest in the sport, there still remains plentiful work to be done on the sport from a historical perspective, particularly surrounding the circumstances of its emergence as a popular television sport in the late 1970s and development towards a global sport in the twenty-first century.

Origins and early modern development

In one form or another, the game has been played in England (not Britain), since the sixteenth century, primarily within public houses. Although there is some debate about the sports origins and darts historian, Patrick Chaplin acknowledges that there have been various forms of darts played in other countries in Western Europe at the start of the twentieth century and even in China 'touhu' could be considered a distant cousin.[1] These were in some cases, quite different to the English game 'as they were existing folk games which involved throwing projectiles or employed darts as a toy'.[2]

Richard Holt states that the modern form of darts 'with the clock-board and flighted cylindrical darts'[3] dates from the turn of the twentieth century, a point supported by Julian Norridge argues that it was being played in the public house from the 1890s.[4] Holt explains that a 'curious legal case' from 1908 did much to help the game and transform it into popular recreation activity:

> 'Foot' Anakin, a northern publican with huge feet, threw three double-twenties twice in succession at a Leeds Magistrates Court after a junior clerk, who had never played the game, was instructed by the bench to have a go and missed the board entirely with two of his first three throws. The magistrates swiftly pronounced darts to be 'skilful' and therefore a legal pub activity. This in practice allowed men to back themselves or others for a pint or a few bob during an evening at the pub dartboard.[5]

It is instances such as this, that helped transform the game 'into one of the most popular forms of recreation in the country'[6] in the period 1919–1939. Patrick Chaplin makes the case that it was the fact that darts was the 'most sociable and most adaptable of all'[7] pub games that ensured it became so popular. The change in allowing betting on darts helped to revolutionise the popularity of the sport by the end of the First World War: by 1918 darts pervaded many aspects of popular culture, the public house, the club, the summer fete, the fairground and the home as a pleasurable diversion or recreation, one not restricted to the working class. In addition, even though there were a few indicators that darts had the potential to grow, such as the introduction of the first organised brewers' leagues, darts remained unencumbered by national rules and regulations.[8]

Based upon these arguments, the focus for this chapter will begin in this period. Prior to the inter-war years, there is little evidence of darts being played in a pub for fun, with no record of leagues. Typically darts was just one of many 'indoor sports' options for social clubs such as at Birmingham firm 'Blackstones' which within its Social club offered 'darts, dominoes, cribbage and pool'[9] in addition to the main outdoor sports. During the 1920s the sport remained the preserve of the pub and this led to the involvement of breweries who established competitions within public houses, which in turn helped their returns via increased consumption of alcohol. The first notable association with a brewery occurred in 1924 when Barclays Perkins Brewery became the first to support a league.

In 1925 another significant event for the development of darts, with the formation of the first national governing body for darts: the National Darts Association (NDA). This occurred on 12 February 1925 in the offices of the Morning Advertiser, where a group of professional men met to 'discuss the establishment of an English darts association for the 'control of the game of darts and of unifying the rules'.[10] This was the organisation which helped to transform darts into a 'cultural phenomenon'[11] during the 1930s and was required because prior to this darts had been developing with many different rules, including variations on almost all aspects of the game.

It was the 'pub' or social club, a leisure site for the working classes where the focus of darts remained initially before expanding, allowing the game to develop. Chaplin states that while the during the first two decades of the twentieth century darts was 'restricted to working-class pub going males, this situation significantly changed from the mid-1930s when the upper classes, particularly in the London area were attracted by the novelty of the game'.[12] The consequence of the new-found organisation and national interest in darts was a boom during the 1930s, resulting in the first professional players emerging. These professionals almost exclusively came from working class routes, were small in number and generally played for small amounts of money which prevented them from becoming full-time professionals.

The continued work of the National Darts Association enabled darts to take off during the latter part of the 1930s as an organised sport. Other important developments included the production of darts equipment, with companies such as Birmingham toy maker Chad Valley mass producing darts sets in the late 1930s and inclusion of darts competitions within the press.[13] Pivotal to the development of organised darts was the interest of the written press, whom both wrote about and sponsored many events in the late 1930s. Particularly significant was the formation of the first publication exclusively dedicated to darts: *Darts Weekly News*, which was first published in September 1937. Although it only lasted until February 1939, it provided a detailed yet naturally biased account of the success of darts during the latter part of the decade and provided some evidence of the threat posed by the NDA by an alternative darts organisation, the British Darts Council (BDC), detail that was not available from any other source.[14]

Another significant breakthrough for the sport was its first broadcast on BBC radio in 1936, when BBC Regional Service broadcast a match on 28 May at 8.15 p.m. Chaplin states that 'a 'descriptive commentary' was featured from The Horns public house, Kennington, on the finals of the 'Team Championship of London'.[15] In total, the broadcast lasted for 15 minutes and helped darts to become an 'occasional feature' on the BBC's regional network, along with broadcast of some notable events where features which demonstrated the new found popularity. For example, in November 1937, F.H. Wallis, the winner of the 1936/7 *News of the World* London and Home Counties Individual Darts Competition, played 'all listeners', where 'Wallis threw three darts; there was a pause while the listeners threw their three darts at home, registering scores against the champion'.[16] Darts was undoubtedly on the rise during the period during the two world wars.

Second World War

During the Second World War, darts joined the host of sports which proved a popular means of raising money for wartime charities on the long 'blacked out' evenings that Britain endured throughout the conflict. The ease of playing darts and availability of equipment ensured that it became a major part of the fundraising undertaken for the Red Cross and St John Fund, which had been formed shortly after the outbreak of war, in October 1939. The Red Cross helped to organise exhibition for leading players, along with producing and selling a booklet entitled '25 ideas for Red Cross Darts Contests', which sold 6,000 copies.[17] The BBC continued its broadcasting of darts, through commentaries of 'several contests', beginning with a slightly bizarre contest between Air Raid Wardens and Firemen on 11 October 1939.

The popularity of darts within pubs and clubs during the war proved significant for the globalisation of the game, as Servicemen, from the allied countries who had been based in Britain experienced the games in public houses and mess halls took the game home with them. This witnessed a new interest in darts from Australia, Canada, New Zealand and the United States of

America. Post-war, the number of British expatriates settling across the world helped to further disseminate it, such as in the Netherlands, which was aided by British Legion Clubs being established here, resulting in clubs and leagues being set up.

One casualty of war was the National Darts Association, although it was survived through the rules which it had established in 1924. It took until 1954 for a new organisation to take hold of the game and between 1954 and the early 1970s, darts was governed by the National Darts Association of Great Britain. This organisation was formed in London, through local darts organisations and *The People* newspaper.

Chaplin states that during its period of governance this association 'darts remained very much a low-profile pub game of little or no national significance in terms of media coverage, except for the People team and the News of the World individual championship'.[18] The lack of progress made during this period encouraged others to take an interest in administrating the sport. This led to the establishment of the British Darts Organisation (BDO) in 1973, formed by entrepreneur Olly Croft, whose tenacity ensured the game grew in terms of sponsorship and television coverage in the years following.

Crofts crusade did not stop here, as the following year he formed the World Darts Federation, which became the official world governing body for darts. At its inception, 15 nations joined, a number that has continually grown and it now boasts 70 members. Its actions have been an important cog in the establishment of darts as a 'global organised sport'.[19]

Darts as a television sport

Darts had been firstly broadcast on television in 1962 on the Independent Television Services (ITV) channel and produced by the south-western Westward Television Company in a tournament which bore their name. The first broadcast didn't bring an immediate plethora of events and darts certainly wasn't a regular on British television and it took until the advent of colour television to it made its breakthrough.

The combination of the commercially aware BDO and colour television that helped to propel darts forward. Along with using revolutionary split-screen technology that allowed both the thrower and the board to be seen close up on a single shot, the sport became a hit on television. Now 'almost overnight amateur dart players were transformed into highly paid professional players'. In his research into the professionalisation of darts between 1970 to 1977, Leon Davis explains the impact of colour television for darts during the 1970s:

the introduction of the colour television in 1968, traditional pub games such as darts and snooker had a platform on which to promote and develop their product. The landscape of the darts world began to change irreversibly in the 1970s through a process of professionalisation, which brought darts into the wider sporting stratosphere.[20]

The first event broadcast in the coloured age was the 1970 News of the World Championship, giving darts a totally new perspective. The sport of snooker also enjoyed a similar revolution in its popularity thanks to colour television. Prior to colour television, like darts it had been broadcast on television, but the problems of determining the lie of the table proved a major issue for television companies and audiences alike. Colour television enabled the viewer to easily determine the location of every ball, and consequently from the late 1960s it became a hit on television. Both sports also proved popular with broadcasters, as they were cheap and easy sports to produce compared to others, which required multiple cameras and were also at risk to the elements. This helped to encourage frequent coverage of both sports, resulting in greater public interest, more sponsorship, more tournaments and more players becoming full-time professionals.

One player who embraced this new professionalism was Welshman Leighton Rees, who gave his full-time job working in an industrial components factory in 1976 in order to devote his time fully to darts. This proved a major dilemma as he stated 'I was perfectly happy (at work) and who needs fame, fortune and flashiness if you're happy and healthy enough not to have a hangover after a night out with your mates.'[21] The move to focus on darts exclusively proved a catalyst, helping him to win both the team and individual World Cup's in December 1977, although not the World Championship he craved.

The pinnacle of the darts year from 1978 was the World Championship, a competition formed on the recommendation of the players, whom desired to mirror the Snooker World Championship, which had first been broadcast and been an instant hit.[22] In 1979, the World Championship darts final between John Lowe of England and Leighton Rees at Stoke-on-Trent and attracted 8 million viewers, an event which signalled its true arrival as a professional sport.

By the early 1980's, darts was one of the most broadcast sports upon British television, with 10 to 15 tournaments given coverage between the BBC and ITV. The result of this was that the prominent players became household names. This enabled players such as Bobby George, Eric Bristow and Jocky Wilson to earn sufficient money both at the oche and via sponsorship. Much of their popularity surrounded their somewhat larger than life personalities, an attribute particularly applicable to George, who made his entrance wearing a crown, cloak and large amounts of jewellery, boasting the name the 'King of Darts'. This accepted, despite his failure to win the World Championship and winning only two major titles during the course of his career. George's defeat to Bristow in the 1980 World Championship final is in George's words an event that 'changed darts' and undoubtedly is a significant event, further propelling the event into the spotlight.

The biggest contributor to darts (and snooker) sponsorship during the 1970s came via tobacco companies, such as Embassy, who sponsored the World Championships in both sports. Davis believes this is an indication of both sports 'were perceived by the sponsors to have an appeal to working-class identity'.[23] Historian Thomas Reilly made the suggestion about the high concentration of alcohol within many professional darts players:

> As the bar-room sport of darts has moved to a larger stage, the technique that has developed among the more successful players is one of regular small 'topping up' doses of alcohol so as to avoid fluctuating blood alcohol concentrations.[24]

Wray Vamplew states that this might be undertaken for the benefit of players, arguing that in 'aiming' sports such as darts, 'the sedative effect of alcohol can be useful where a firm stance and a reduced heart rate could be important'.[25] Whether helpful or not, the consequence of being allowed to drink alcohol and smoke tobacco on stage, (which undoubtedly linked it back to its routes in the public-house), was a factor in the downfall of darts in the mid-1980s, damaging its perception with the television companies or the media. This came at a low-point in the image of British sport, damaged by the actions of alcohol fuelled 'football hooligans'.

Prior to this, the popularity of darts had been further increased through two television programmes – *Indoor League* and *Bullseye* – where it played a prominent part. *Indoor League* was first broadcast on 5 April 1973 and ran for five seasons. It was produced by Yorkshire television, part of the ITV network and was hosted by Yorkshire and England cricketing legend Fred Truman, who presented with a pipe and pint of ale in hand. Along with pool, billiards, skittles, table football, wrestling and others, darts was included and initially played upon a Yorkshire dartboard (which fails feature any opportunity to score a 'treble'), but as the programme became more popular, it took the form of a regular board, and the players came from across the country (initially only

Yorkshire region players had been invited). The winner of the competition received £100 and the runner-up £50, the first competition won by the relatively unknown Colin Minton, who beat Charles Ellis 2–0.

Bullseye had darts very much at its centre. Hosted by the comedian Jim Bowen, professional players teamed up with members of the public, with contests combining the talents of the darts player and the general knowledge skills of the contestant, in order to win prizes. Like *Indoor League*, it was shown on ITV and it was screened during primetime television, running from 1981 until 1995.

Indoor League also did much to help popularise women's darts, a sport which is frequently marginalised upon television up to the present day, with a women's event running alongside the male tournament from the first series in 1972. From 1973 onwards, a mixed darts competition also took place. This is not to say that women's darts was not popular, and Tony Collins and Wray Vamplew state that 'women's darts became possibly the most popular participation sport in the years following the end of the Second World War'.[26] This they describe as because for women in provided one of the rare occasions when they could venture into the public house unaccompanied by a man and subsequently women's darts established a bridgehead within the 'masculine republic' of the public house.

The split

By the late 1980s, *Bullseye* presented one of the few opportunities where darts appeared on television. In 1988, the only tournament on television was the World Championship, meaning that its attractiveness for sponsorship decreased and this had a major impact for the professional players, who no longer gained the required exposure and so struggled to make a living from the sport.

The degradation of the sport on television brought about tensions between the ruling British Darts Organisation and the leading darts players. In 1992, the players decided they could no longer stick with the BDO, and 16 professional players, including all the previous world champions, created a breakaway body the 'World Darts Council' (WDC). The players' motivation for this move was that they felt they could no longer make a living from the game and that commercial opportunities. Davis explains that new broadcaster 'Sky Sports had expressed an interest in running a tournament with the players, which would generate exposure and income'.[27] Croft did not appear to be interested in this and consequently many players began a breakaway movement.

On 7 January 1993, the leading players stated that they would only compete in the forthcoming World Championship if it came under the control of the WDC, a motion dismissed by the BDO, which suspended the players from participating in any BDO tournaments.

The division between the BDO and the players of the WDC continued for many years and ended up in court, with the legal battle which was solved in 1997 by a Tomlin order (which is designed as a form of consent order). This forced by the BDO to recognise the WDC, which in term recognised the World Darts Federation as the games governing body, which was it rename itself as the Professional Darts Corporation (PDC). The consequence was the formation of two separate professional circuits, with two sets of players who have to choose between one organisation or the other.

The split between the BDO and PDC continues to the present day. The two organisations have their own pool of players which compete within their tournaments and their own World Championships. Upon its formation, the PDC established a television rights deal with British subscription television provider, Sky, a deal which enabled it to establish it as the leading darts organisers, with all of its tournaments broadcast on its dedicated sports channels. The consequence is that all of the leading players compete in PDC events, many of whom have started in the BDO circuit before 'progressing' to the more lucrative PDC. It is the combination of the PDC and Sky's marketing of the sport which has enabled it to become popular in Britain and for its sale across the world to various television companies, with growth areas of interest in North America and Australia. The success of the PDC owes to ability of creating its own identity. Davis explains how it has sold darts

> as a live carnival event that fans would want to consume and create a seductive atmosphere, which would hopefully entice television views into attending 'live' darts events. Attracting a larger fan base through a sporting spectacle would in turn become attractive to broadcasters (such as Sky Sports) and a multitude of prospective sponsors, who would embrace darts once again.[28]

The most significant player in the history of the PDC is Englishman Phil Taylor, who was one of the 16 'rebels' to breakaway in 1993. It is his prominence, with a record 16 World Championship victories, including eight consecutive wins between 1995 and 2002 that helped the sport to gain attention within the mainstream sports media. Taylor's prominence has seen him shortlisted for the prestigious BBC Sports Personality of the Year in 2006 and 2010, where he was to finish as runner-up. Prior to his retirement in 2018, it was Taylor's ability, along with his charisma and image as a 'nice guy', that has helped to promote darts beyond its regular audience.

Despite the split, and the money encouraging many of the leading players to be part of the PDC, the BDO has continued to have a popular circuit, with an ever increasing number of tournaments broadcast upon various broadcasters. Its World Championships, held every January have remained on free to air television in Britain, and regularly attracts viewing figures around the 3 million mark on an annual basis.

In the twenty-first century, despite the prominence of British players such as Taylor, there has been a number of prominent players who have come overseas. One particular hot-bed for darts has been the Netherlands, which has contributed several of the modern leading players, beginning with Raymond Van Barneveld, whose success initially with the BDO in the late 1990s helped to popularise the sport in his home country. Van Barneveld won the BDO World Championship for the first of four times in 1998, before switching allegiance to the PDC in 2006. Despite only winning the PDC's premier event, the World Championship once in 2007, his success resulting in him winning all of the major titles and the rivalry he forged with Taylor did much to promote the sport beyond its traditional markets. Both within the BDO and PDC, darts remains primarily British. Only John Part (Canada), Simon Whitlock (Australia) and Michael van Gerwen (Netherlands) along with Van Barneveld have reached the PDC World Championship Final since its conception in 1994 and only the two Dutch 'throwers' have been successful.

The British centric nature of darts is also represented in the location of many of the top events, which have remained within the Isles. The growth in markets for the sport have witnessed tournaments being held in locations including Australia, the Netherlands and Austria. Perhaps the most significant event held outside of Britain was that held in Las Vegas during 2017, part of the PDC's desire to break into the potentially lucrative North American market.

Neither the modern–day darts boom nor that which occurred in the 1970s and 1980s have produced any interest in female professional darts. Both the BDO and PDC boast women's circuits, although they attract little attention from sponsors and the media alike. The lack of exposure has ensured that there have been few full-time professionals and the standard somewhat lower than the men's game. Some of the problems that women's darts players are explored in the autobiography of ten-times women's world champion Trina Gulliver's autobiography *Golden Girl*, published in 2007, giving detailed coverage of many of the key matches from her career.[29] At a social level, there is evidence that snooker is a popular activity among women.[30]

The outlook for both men's and women's darts does look promising thanks to its status as a sport by the British sporting bodies. Debates about darts as a sport has been longstanding, and the controversy around this owes much to its origins as a pastime in the pub, the physicality involved, and excludes the skill required to be successful. After extensive debate, Sport England recognised darts as a sport on 25 March 2005, and this move was followed by both Sport Scotland and Wales. This move was important move, as the new status enabled it receive funding from the bodies previously mentioned and gives it the potential to be considered for multi-sports events such as the Commonwealth and Olympic Games.

Sport England chief executive Roger Draper explained that the acceptance as darts as a sport came from its prominence of being played 'by many millions of people across the country in locations ranging from schools to village halls, social clubs and sports centres',[31] and that its positive sporting and social values also made a significant part. Chairman of the PDC, Barry Hearn explains the significance for darts: 'It's great news for our players that they are now officially seen as proper sportsmen, which is what they deserve for the hard work and dedication that they show week-in and week-out. This will help us continue to take darts to the next level . . .'[32] Since 2005, there is evidence that participation levels in darts is in decline. Sport England's 2015/16 statistics indicate that 67,400 participated in the sport, a decline from 2005/06 where 119,800 had participated (defined as partaking at least once a week). A worrying statistic, but one replicated across sport in England.[33]

Conclusions

In 2018, darts has a growing following worldwide, with players idolised and tournaments a big hit with paying spectators and television companies. Both the booms of the 1970s and modern day owe much to television, initially the introduction of colour and subsequently subscription satellite services. The atmosphere generated at events, which often resembles as a party, along with the ability of the leading players has also done much to promote the game, particularly at PDC events, where the perfect '9 dart finish' is a common but still exciting spectacle.

From its inception to the modern day, darts has been the preserve of Britain, chiefly as an activity enjoyed within public houses. Its association with the public house has done much to popularise the game, but also hold its back in terms of acceptance. In the 1980s, its association with alcohol did much to damage its image, while in the twenty-first century it was part of the reason why some believe that darts isn't a sport.

There is much to promote darts as a sport, as its one on one nature, with close matches played in front of sell-out crowds ensure that it is popular with television, sponsors and most significantly the public. There can be little doubt that darts has a potentially bright future and its evolution will undoubtedly be of curiosity to historians and sociologists with an interest in sport.

Notes

1 Tony Hwang and Grant Jarvie, 'Sport, Nationalism and the Early Chinese Republic, 1912–1927'. *Sports Historian* Vol 21, No 2, (2001) p. 10.

2 Patrick Chaplin, *Darts in England, 1900–39: A Social History* (Manchester, Manchester University Press, 2012).

3 Richard Holt, *Sport and the British* (Bristol, Clarendon Press, 1989), p. 192.

4 Julian Norridge, *Can We Have Our Balls Back Please? How the British Invented Sport (and Then Almost Forgot How to Play it)* (London, Penguin, 2008), p. 377, cited in Leon Davis, 'From a Pub Game to a Sporting Spectacle: The Professionalisation of British Darts, 1970–1997', *Sport in History*, 38(4) (2018), p. 512.

5 Holt, *Sport and the British*, p. 192.

6 Chaplin, *Darts in England*, p. 217.

7 Ibid., p. 7.

8 Ibid., p. 68.

9 John Bromhead, 'George Cadbury's Contribution to Sport', *Sports Historian*, 20(1), p. 110.

10 Chaplin, *Darts in England*, p. 103.

11 Ibid., p. 169.

12 Ibid., p. 197.

13 Steve Beauchampe and Simon Inglis, *Played in Birmingham*, (Croatia, English Heritage, 2006), p. 107.

14 Ibid., p. 24.

15 Chaplin, *Darts in England*, p. 186.

16 Ibid., p. 187.

17 Tony McCarthy, *War Games: The Story of Sport in World War Two* (Queen Anne Press, 2014), p. 85.

18 Ibid.

19 Chaplin, *Darts in England*, p. 223.

20 Davis, 'From a Pub Game to a Sporting Spectacle', p. 516.

21 Patrick Chaplin, 'Rees, Leighton Thomas', *Oxford Dictionary of National Biography*, accessed on 28 November 2018.

22 Davis, 'From a Pub Game to a Sporting Spectacle', p. 518.

23 Ibid., p. 517.

24 Thomas Reilly, 'Alcohol, Anti-anxiety Drugs and Sport', in David R. Mottram, ed., *Drugs in Sport* (London, 1996), p. 155.

25 Wray Vamplew, 'Alcohol and the Sportsperson: An Anomalous Alliance', *Sport in History*, 25(3) (2005), p. 395.

26 T. Collins and W. Vamplew, *Mud, Sweat and Beers: A Cultural History of Sport and Alcohol* (Oxford: Berg Publishers, 2002).

27 Davis, 'From a Pub Game to a Sporting Spectacle', p. 523.

28 Ibid., p. 526.

29 Trina Gulliver, *Golden Girl: The Autobiography of the Greatest Ever Ladies' Darts Play* (London, John Blake Publishing, 2008).

30 Simon Inglis, *Played in London* (Frome, English Heritage, 2014), P120.

31 'At Last! Darts is an Official Sport', retrieved from http://www.patrickchaplin.com/Dartsisasport.htm, accessed on 26 November 2018.

32 Patrick Chaplin, 'Darts is a Sport', www.patrickchaplin.com/Dartsisasport.htm, accessed on 27 November 2018.

33 'Number of People Participating in Darts in England from 2006/2007 to 2015/2016', *Sport in England: Public Funding and Participation in the UK*, 10 (October 2015–September 2016).

20

Golf

Geoff Dickson and Tim Breitbarth

Introduction

Historical overview

The origin of golf as we know it today goes back to the 15th century, when people in the Kingdom of Fife used sticks to hit pebbles around the sand dunes of eastern Scottish coast (Golf Europe, n.d.; Lane, n.d.). While golf was banned for some time in the mid and late 15th century, support from the British royal family would lift golf's status and popularity throughout the 16th century. Importantly, golf was first codified in 1744 when *The Gentlemen Golfers of Leith* drafted a set of 13 rules for a competition endorsed by the City of Edinburgh. The oldest golf club still operating today is located at the clubhouse of the Royal & Ancient Golf Club of St. Andrews, originally erected in 1854. The Open, the first major national championship and today one of the four "majors", was first held in 1860 at Prestwick Golf Club.

Golf became further codified, organized and institutionalized in an industrially based 19th-century Victorian Britain that left a cultural legacy that still exists today – and could well be seen as challenges for the modern development of the game and as barriers to foster participation (Rankin, Bakir & Bullock, 2018). However, with different speed and routes, the game was exported via the British colonies: for example, the India's Royal Calcutta Golf Club was founded in 1829; the Australia's Royal Melbourne Golf Club founded in 1891; and elsewhere the British established Japan's first golf club, Kobe Golf Club, in 1903. In America, some favourable dynamics allowed the game to go from "nothing to something" within only a few years (Moss, 2013). These dynamics included affluent men such as John Rockefeller and Andrew Carnegie who funded the development of golf courses and made the sport both fashionable, aspirational and the game to be played by business leaders. Generally, the capitalism that gave rise to industrialization and the birth of the consumer society enabled the global spread of both British and Western culture (Ferguson, 2012).

Today, golf is experiencing considerable pressure to change, perhaps more than any other sport (Breitbarth, Kaiser-Jovy & Dickson, 2018). Obviously, the game has come a long way since its origins and, for example, is a £1 billion industry with one in every 125 jobs dependent on golf alone in Scotland, the "Home of Golf" (Golf 20/20, 2013). Interestingly, golf may well have been the trailblazer and blueprint for modern sport business and marketing. The historic "hand-shake deal" between Mark McCormack (founder of IMG) and American golfer Arnold Palmer ushered in a new era of commercialized sport and celebrity endorsements. In the early 1960s McCormack packaged and marketed Palmer and his fellow players Jack Nicklaus (US) and Gary Player (South Africa) as the "Big Three", created the idea of an athlete as a global brand and negotiated lucrative television and endorsement deals. He envisioned sport as an ideal marketing platform due to its high visibility, positive image and international scope.

Global diffusion

The global supply of golf courses is highly centralized. The vast majority (89%) of that supply is located in the top 20 golfing countries. There are far more countries with only one golf course compared to nations that have more than 100, and even fewer are home to 500 or more (R&A, 2015). Though worldwide golf supply contains a large proportion of private clubs, golf resorts and golf-centric real estate developments, the sport remains largely accessible. Of the 33,161 facilities, 75% are open to the public.

Africa

With 885 golf facilities, Africa accounts for only 3% of all golf facilities in the world. Fifty of the 59 African countries have golf courses, but more than half are in South Africa. The five countries with the most golf courses in Africa are South Africa (484), Nigeria (51), Kenya (42), Morocco (40) and Zimbabwe (39) (R&A, 2017). Throughout Africa, oil companies built western-style leisure communities with private golf courses to house their employees. The development of large resort communities is another trend in golf course construction in Africa, especially in the north (R&A, 2015).

Asia

The five countries with the most golf courses in Asia are Japan ($n = 2290$), South Korea ($n = 444$), China ($n = 383$), India ($n = 267$) and Thailand (240) (R&A, 2017). Growth in Japan is greatly constrained by the lack of developable land (R&A, 2015). Golf maintains an uneasy relationship with the Chinese government (Washburn, 2014). Asia is responsible for most of the global golf growth. Increased economic prosperity and an emergent new middle class underpin this growth (Dickson, Zheng & Chen, 2017).

Europe

Golf courses are in 40 of the 50 European countries, accounting for 22% of the global supply. The five countries with the most golf courses in Europe are England ($n = 1991$), Germany ($n = 747$), France ($n = 637$), Scotland ($n = 540$) and Sweden ($n = 485$). Golf is weakest in central and southeastern Europe (R&A, 2017).

North America, Central America and the Caribbean

The number of golf facilities in the U.S. and Canada has declined since the early 2000s, following a significant increase in new course construction in the 1990s and early 2000s. The five countries/regions with the most golf courses in North America are USA ($n = 15047$), Canada

(n = 2295), Mexico (n = 239), Dominican Republic (n = 27) and Puerto Rica (n = 17) (R&A, 2017). All golf development projects in the Caribbean are connected to resorts intended for destination golfers and vacationers (R&A, 2015).

Oceania

The five countries with the most golf courses in Oceania are Australia (n = 1591), New Zealand (n = 410), Fiji (n = 17), Papua New Guinea (n = 15) and Guam (n = 9) (R&A, 2017). Resort courses account for less than 4% of the region's existing golf supply. However, more than 70% of new golf projects are linked to a resort and/or real estate development (R&A, 2015).

South America

With 658 golf facilities, South America comprises roughly 2% of the world's total golf supply. All 14 countries in the region have at least one golf course. The five countries with the most golf courses in South America are Argentina (n = 316), Brazil (n = 122), Chile (n = 77), Colombia (n = 60) and Venezuela (n = 23) (R&A, 2017). Most new course developments are associated with luxury living communities and lifestyles (R&A, 2015).

Governance

The governance of golf is characterized by a complex networks of organisations (Shilbury, 2018). Internationally, the three key organizations are the International Golf Federation (IGF), the R&A and the United States Golf Association (USGA).

International Golf Federation

Formed in 1958, the IGF is recognized by the International Olympic Committee (IOC) as the world governing body for golf. The need to coordinate major international events that were beyond the purview of either the USGA or Royal and Ancient Golf Club of St Andrews was the impetus for its establishment. Originally known as the World Amateur Golf Council (WAGC), the WAGC rebranded itself as the IGF. The vision of the IGF is "to ignite global excitement about golf and to grow the game". The objects of International Golf Federation are to (a) encourage the international development of the sport of golf, (b) foster friendship and sportsmanship among the peoples of the world by organizing biennially amateur team championships for the Eisenhower Trophy (for men) and the Espirito Santo Trophy (for women), (c) promote golf as an Olympic sport, and (d) act as the international federation for golf in the Olympic Games and thereby to establish and enforce, in accordance with the Olympic spirit, the rules concerning the playing of golf in the Olympic Games and to fulfil in respect of the sport of golf the mission and role of an international federation within the Olympic movement. Unlike most other international federations, the IGF is not responsible for developing the rules of golf.

There are two classes of members of International Golf Federation. In 2017, the IGF had 149 National Federation Members (e.g. Golf Australian, Indian Golf Union) from 144 countries. The Professional Members of International Golf Federation are the Asian Tour, the Australian Ladies Professional Golf Tour, the Canadian Professional Golf Tour, the Japan Golf Tour Organisation, the Korea Ladies Professional Golf Association, the Korea Professional Golf Association, the Ladies Asian Golf Tour, the Ladies European Tour, the Ladies Professional Golfers Association of Japan, the LPGA, the PGAA, the Professional Golf Tour of India, the PGA European

Tour, the PGA Tour, the PGA TOUR of Australasia, The R&A, the Sunshine Tour, the Tour de las Americas, and the USGA. An organization may be a member of more than one class of IGF membership.

The R&A

In 2004, The Royal and Ancient Golf Club of St Andrews (RAGCSA) relinquished control of the rules to a newly formed group, known as "The R&A" (R&A, 2016). The R&A is a separate entity from RAGCSA. The R&A and the USGA provide a single code for the Rules of Golf, Rules of Amateur Status and Equipment Standards. The R&A governs worldwide, outside of the United States and Mexico. The R&A has national affiliated organizations in 138 countries and territories and 12 transnational affiliated organizations (i.e. Africa Golf Confederation, Asia-Pacific Golf Confederation, Caribbean Golf Association Council of National Golf Unions, European Golf Association, Ladies European Tour, Ladies' Golf Union, Oceania Golf Union, PGA European Tour, Professional Golfers' Association, Professional Golfers' Associations of Europe, and the South American Golf Federation).

USGA

The United States Golf Association (USGA) is the United States' national association of golf courses, clubs and facilities and the governing body for golf in the US and Mexico. The USGA has international relevance because, together with The R&A, the USGA produces and interprets the rules of golf.

Elite competitions – men

A professional golf tour is governed by a PGA (Professional Golfers' Association) or tour organization which is responsible for arranging events, finding sponsors, and regulating the tour. Most of the major tours are player-controlled organizations with the commercial objective to maximize the income of their members by maximizing prize money. Each tour has "members" who have earned their "tour cards". A tour card provides access to most of the tour's events. Each tour will have their qualification processes. A golfer acquire usually acquires their card by winning an entry tournament, often known as Qualifying School (or Q-School for short). They can also perform well enough in a qualification tour, or by achieving enough success in a tour's tournaments when competing as an invited non-member.

Most elite competitions are played over a four, day, 72-hole strokeplay format, with a cut after two rounds. A cut means only the players with the lowest scores, generally the best 70, progress to the final two rounds. Players who miss the cut usually do not receive any prize money.

Leading professional golf tours

Unlike tennis, golf does not have a genuine global tour like the ATP or WTA Tour. Instead, golf has a number of regional tours.

PGA Tour

The PGA Tour was originally the "Tournament Players Division " of the US PGA. In 1968 the division became a separate organization for tour players, as opposed to club professionals, the focal members of today's PGA of America. The PGA Tour organizes the week-to-week events, including The Players Championship and the FedEx Cup events, as well as the biennial Presidents Cup. The PGA Tour also runs the main tournaments on five other tours: PGA Tour Champions (for golfers age 50 and over), the Web.com Tour (the PGA Tour's qualifying tournament), PGA Tour Canada, PGA Tour China, and PGA Tour Latinoamérica.

European Tour

The European Tour is the primary golf tour in Europe. The British-based Professional Golfers' Association established the European Tour in 1972. An independent PGA European Tour organization was established in in 1984. Most European Tour events are held in Europe, but there is an increasing number being held outside Europe. The PGA European Tour is also responsible for the European Senior Tour and the developmental Challenge Tour.

Other golf tours

Official World Golf Ranking points can be earned at the PGA Tour, European Tour, Asian Tour, PGA Tour of Australasia, Japan Golf Tour, Sunshine Tour (Africa), Web.com Tour,
   Challenge Tour, PGA Tour Canada, OneAsia Tour, Korean Tour, PGA Tour Latinoamérica,
   Asian Development Tour, PGA Tour China, Alps Tour, Nordic Golf League, PGA EuroPro Tour,
   ProGolf Tour (Germany), Middle East and North Africa (MENA) Golf Tour.

The majors

In men's golf, there are four tournaments recognized as "majors". The Players Championship is often referred to as the unofficial "fifth major".

The Masters

The Augusta National Golf Club hosts The Masters. The Masters is the only men's major played at the same course every year. In 2017, The Masters had US$11 million in prize money with the winner receiving US$1.98 million. The Masters is synonymous with traditions - the green jacket awarded to the winner, the pre-event Par 3 tournament, referring to spectators as patrons, low ticket prices, absence of commercial signage, ceremonial opening tee shots, and the inclusion of former champions. Golf Digest reported that the 2015 event generated $115 million in revenue and a $29 million profit. The key revenue streams were merchandise ($47.5 million), tickets ($34.75 million), international TV rights ($25 million); concessions ($7.75 million). The ANGC receives no payment for its domestic broadcast rights. This arrangement allows ANGC to exert considerable influence on how the event is broadcast. For example, event sponsors are limited to four minutes of advertising time per hour. This is approximately one-third of the commercial interruptions of other sporting events

US Open

The United States Open is hosted by USGA and played at various locations in the United States. The US Open, was first played in 1895, but was not contested for two years (1917–1918) during the First World War and for four years (1942–1945) during the Second World War. US

Open venues are typically prepared with long, thick rough, narrow fairways and lightning-quick greens to prevent low scoring. Four US Opens since 2005 were won with a 72-hole total greater than par, including consecutive winning scores of five-over in 2006 and 2007. The US Open is on the official schedule of both the PGA Tour and the European Tour. The US Open is open to any professional (or amateur) with an up-to-date men's USGA Handicap Index not exceeding 1.4. Prize money at the 2017 US Open was US$12 million, with the winner receiving $2.16 million. Winners of the US Open are automatically invited to play in the other three majors (the Masters, The Open Championship (British Open), and the PGA Championship) for the next five years, as well as The Players Championship, and they are exempt from qualifying for the US Open itself for 10 years.

The Open

The Open Championship is hosted by The R&A. The event rotates through ten courses – The Old Course at St Andrews, Carnoustie, Royal St George's, Royal Lytham & St Annes, Royal Birkdale, Muirfield, Turnberry, Royal Liverpool and Royal Troon. St Andrew hosts the Open Championship every fifth year.

The PGA Championship

The PGA Championship is hosted by the Professional Golfers' Association of America and played at various locations in the United States. It is an official money event on the PGA Tour, European Tour, and Japan Golf Tour. Prize money at the 2017 PGA Championship was US$10.5 million, with the winner receiving $1.89 million. The event is the only major that does not explicitly invite leading amateurs to compete. Of the 156 places in the field, 20 are reserved for club professionals. This is one of the reasons why the PGA Championship is considered the weakest of the three majors.

World Golf Championships

At the 1996 Presidents Cup, the European Tour, Japan Golf Tour Organization, PGA TOUR, PGA Tour of Australasia and Sunshine Tour created the International Federation of PGA Tours. In addition to developing a generally accepted worldwide ranking system and a joint sanctioning process, the IFPGAT introduced the World Golf Championships (WGC). The four WGC events are the Mexico Championship, Dell Technologies Match Play, Bridgestone Invitational and the HSBC Champions. The World Golf Championships were developed to enhance the competitive structure of professional golf worldwide while preserving the traditions and strengths of the individual Tours and their events.

Elite competitions – women

Leading professional golf tours

LPGA Tour

The LPGA Tour is managed by the United States based LPGA. Unlike the PGA Tour and the US PGA, the LPGA is also an organization for female club and teaching professionals. Established in 1950, the LPGA also administers an annual qualifying school similar to that conducted by the PGA Tour. In addition to the main LPGA Tour, the LPGA also owns and operates the Symetra Tour, formerly the Futures Tour, the official developmental tour of the LPGA. Most of the LPGA Tour's events are held in the United States. But there is an increasing number played outside the US, some of which are co-sanctioned by other professional tours. Since the early 2000s, Korean golfers have enjoyed unprecedented success on the LPGA tour when compared to any other foreign group of players (Shin & Nam, 2004).

Ladies European Tour

In 1978 the Women's Professional Golf Association (WPGA) was formed as part of Professional Golfers' Association of Great Britain and Ireland and a women's tour was established in 1979. In 1988 the tour members formed an independent company, the Women Professional Golfers' European Tour Limited. In 1998 the Tour changed its name to European Ladies' Professional Golf Association and again in July 2000 to the Ladies European Tour. The LET Tour organizes The Solheim Cup when in Europe.

The Majors

Unlike elite tennis, there are no tournaments that integrate a men's and women's competition. Unlike men's golf, there are five tournaments that are considered majors. Unlike men's golf, the LPGA and LET do not share a common set of majors. Only the Women's British Open and The Evian Championship are currently recognized as majors by both organizations.

ANA Inspiration

Entertainer Dinah Shore established the tournament now known as the ANA Inspiration in 1972. The event is held annually at the Mission Hills Country Club in Rancho Mirage, California. The International Management Group (IMG) owns the event. The current title sponsor is All Nippon Airways (ANA). The tournament has been considered a major since 1983. As a major the tournament has been known previously as the Nabisco Dinah Shore, Nabisco Championship and the Kraft Nabisco Championship.

Women's PGA Championship

The Women's PGA Championship was established as the "LPGA Championship" in 1955. In 2015, the event's ownership was transferred to the PGA of America to become the Women's PGA Championship. Prize money at the 2017 Women's PGA Championship was US$3.5 million, with the winner receiving $525,000.

US Women's Open

Established in 1946, the US Women's Open is the only event recognized as a major by the LPGA since the group's founding in 1950. Prize money at the 2017 US Women's Open US$5 million, with the winner receiving $0.9 million. The championship is open to any female professional or amateur golfer with a USGA handicap index not exceeding 2.4. Players not qualified through previous performances, can qualify by competing in one of twenty 36-hole qualifying tournaments held at sites across the United States and at international sites in China, England, Japan, and South Korea. The event is played at various locations.

Women's British Open

The Ladies' Golf Union (LGU) managed the Women's British Open. The LGU was the governing body for women's and girls' amateur golf in Great Britain and Ireland, until its merger with The R&A in early 2017. The Women's British Open will continue to be managed by IMG in 2017 under the existing agreement with the LGU.

The Evian Championship

The Evian Championship is played annually at the Evian Resort Golf Club in Évian-les-Bains, France. Founded in 1994 it is one of two major championships on the LET, alongside the Women's British Open. The Evian became an LPGA co-sanctioned event in 2000, becoming the fifth major on the LPGA Tour schedule in 2013. Prize money at the 2017 Evian Championship was US$3.35 million, with the winner receiving $502,500.

Elite competitions – international golf

Golf is normally an individual game. There are only a handful of professional tournaments that involve national teams.

Ryder Cup

The Ryder Cup is a biennial men's golf competition between Europe and the United States. The venue alternates between courses in the United States and Europe. The PGA of America and Ryder Cup Europe jointly administer the Ryder Cup. Ryder Cup Europe is a joint venture of the PGA European Tour (60%), the PGA of Great Britain and Ireland (20%), and the PGA of Europe (20%). There are 12 players per team, eight of whom can play each day. Played over three days, the match-play format for the competition incorporates foursomes, four ball and singles competitions. Originally contested between Great Britain and the United States in 1927, the official title of the British Team was changed from "Great Britain" to "Great Britain and Ireland" in 1973. This reflected the fact that golfers from the Republic of Ireland and Northern Ireland were already playing on the team. American dominance promoted the decision to extend the representation of "Great Britain and Ireland" to include continental Europe from 1979. Since then, the United States team has won 8 matches, with Europe winning 10 matches, retaining the Ryder Cup once with a tie.

President's Cup

Similar in format to the Ryder Cup, the President's Cup is contested between United States and an International Team, representing the rest of the world minus Europe. It is hosted alternately in the United States and in countries represented by the International Team. The event was created and is organized by the PGA Tour. Of the 11 matches, the United States team has won 9, the International Team has won 1, with 1 match tied. There is no prize money awarded at the Presidents Cup, with net proceeds distributed to charities nominated by the players, captains, and captains' assistants.

Solheim Cup

The Solheim Cup is a biennial golf tournament for professional women golfers contested by teams representing Europe and the United States. The cup is played over three days. Since 2002, there have been 28 matches – eight foursomes, eight four-balls and 12 singles on the final day. This is the same format as the Ryder Cup. Of the 14 matches played since its inception in 1990, the United States have won 9 and Europe have won 5.

Olympics

Golf returned to the Olympics in 2016, for the first time since 1904. Men's and women's individual events were contested over 72 holes of strokeplay. The Olympic field was limited to only 60 players in both the men's and women's tournaments. Five of the men's top 10 players elected not to compete, citing concerns over the Zika virus epidemic and conflicts with the professional tournament schedule. The women's tournament was not affect to the same extent. The top 15 world-ranked players were automatically eligible for the Olympics, with a limit of four players from a given country. Beyond the top 15, there was a maximum of two eligible players from each country that does not already have two or more players among the top 15. The men's competition featured 34 nations. The US had four players in the men's competition. There were 23 teams with two competitors, while 10 countries have one Olympic participant. The women's tournament also has players from 34 nations. South Korea has the best representation, with four players, followed by the U.S. with three. Twenty-three countries have two female Olympians. The IOC will re-assess golf's return in 2017 and vote on whether to retain golf on in the Olympic program for 2024 and beyond.

Distinction between professional and amateur golf

Golf is one of the few sports that maintain a clear and strict delineation between amateurs and professionals. The purpose and spirit of the rules is to (1) Focus on the game's challenges and inherent rewards, rather than financial gain; (2) Maintain the distinction between amateur golf and professional golf; and (3) Keep the amateur game as free as possible from the pressures that may follow from uncontrolled sponsorship and financial incentive. While the actual rules are revised and amended by the R&A's Amateur Status Committee, the national golf union or association in each country is responsible for their enforcement and application.

Amateurs who breach their amateur status may lose their amateur status. Professionals may not play in amateur tournaments without committee approval. A professional player must apply to the relevant governing body to have amateur status reinstated. The R&A defines an amateur golfer, as "one who plays golf for the challenge it presents, not as a profession and not for financial gain". Amateur prize money is limited to £500 by the R&A and US$750 by the USGA.

Professional golfers are divided into two main groups. The vast majority of golf professionals are teaching professionals, golf instructors or golf coaches. Most will play few tournaments against their peers each year, occasionally qualifying to play in more important and lucrative tournaments. A smaller but much higher profile group of professional golfers play tournament golf. Their income is derived from prize money and in some instances appearance fees and endorsements.

Golf tourism

Golf tourism is a niche market within the broader sports tourism industry (Ermen & Frary, 2018). Golf tourism is premised upon travel from a place of origin to a destination for the purpose of either playing golf or observing golf. Mintel (2010) categorizes golf tourism into generic sports tourism (golf resorts), specialized sports tourism (famous golf courses), competitive sports tourism (world-class training), vacation sports tourism (golf activities), and high-end and residential tourism (residential golf courses).

Golf tourism can significantly contribute to growth of low season travel (Hudson & Hudson, 2004). There are significant golf tourism industries in the warmer southern states of the USA (e.g., Florida, Arizona) and in southern Europe (e.g. Portugal, Spain, Turkey). These types of destinations are attractive to golfers in the north that unwilling or unable to play locally during the winter months.

Not only do golfers extend the season for many destinations, they are also considered to be high yield tourists. In 2013, the Malaysian Tourism and Creative Economy Ministry added golf to its category of special interest tourism, citing that golfers spend between $2,500 to $5,000 during their golfing holiday in Indonesia, at least double that of a standard tourist (Osman, 2013).

Developing countries have not been left behind by the golf tourism bandwagon. "Export ready" golf courses now feature in non-traditional golfing nations such as Kenya, Vietnam, and Iceland. The expansion of golf tourism into these markets is not without its problems (Completo & Gustavo, 2014). These can include environmental concerns including water conservation and quality, energy efficiency, waste minimization and recycling, and respect for and rigorous compliance with current environmental regulations (Regules, Martinez & Moreda, 2015). While golf may provide local communities with employment leading to improved quality of life, playing golf remains inaccessible for the local residents. In this light, golf courses should be seen as a tool for economic development than sport development

Equity, discrimination and exclusion

There is little doubt that golf is male dominated, exclusionary and discriminatory (Kitching, Grix & Phillpotts, 2017). These are important issues for the golf industry and its long-term growth and survival, particularly at the recreational level.

Gender equity

Golf participation figures provide clear evidence of golf's gender divide. In Great Britain and Ireland, female golfers account for only 14% of golfers, approximately half of what is found in other European countries (England Golf, 2016). In New Zealand, females comprise about 30% of club members. Some golf clubs still exclude female members. Human Rights legislation in some jurisdictions uphold the right of golf clubs to pursue all male memberships, as long as it is written into the club's legal constitution. In 2017, Muirfield Golf Club members voted to allow women as members for the first time in its 273-year history. The decision came after the R&A, removed Muirfield as a host venue for The Open Championship because of men only policy. Ironically, the Royal and Ancient Golf Club of St Andrews had only introduced female members in 2014. Many clubs classify women as "associate members", effectively limiting their right to vote at club meetings. Beyond participation, golf's governance, administration and service provision is also male dominated. Female PGA golf professionals comprise less than 3% of all PGA professionals in Britain and Ireland, and less than 4% in America.

Racial and religious exclusion

In addition to gender, golf has also been characterized by a combination of implicit and explicit policies that has restricted access to golf and certain golf clubs by racial minorities. The United

States is rich with examples. At the professional level, PGA Tour had a "Caucasian only" clause until 1961. Althea Gibson becomes the first African-American to compete on the LPGA Tour in 1963. In 2011, Joseph Bramlett was one of two PGA Tour golfers of African-American descent on the 2011 PGA Tour, alongside Tiger Woods.

Some golf courses and country clubs retained Whites-only membership policies well after the removal of segregation. The argument from Shoal Creek Country Club founder that "we don't discriminate in every other area except the blacks" placed considerable pressure on the PGA Tour to not stage their events at clubs with whites only policies. In 1990, businessman Ron Townsend becomes the first African-American member of Augusta National Golf Club, site of the Masters. It would take until 2012 for AGNC to have a female member.

Elsewhere in the world, between the 1890s and the 1960s, Jews faced significant levels of racial discrimination within British golf (Dee, 2013). Some British golf clubs practiced a "Jewish apartheid", an unofficial racism, driven primarily by a middle-class desire for "exclusiveness" and "social demarcation". In response, Jewish golfers created their own clubs symbolically remaining open to all golfers, regardless of race or creed.

Participation decline

Golf participation declined markedly in golf's most developed markets – North America, Australia and western Europe – since the early 2000s. The National Golf Foundation (NGF) states that there were 30.6 million American golfers in 2003 and only 24.7 million in 2014. Golf club membership in Australia decreased every year between 2004 and 2015, a cumulative loss of 11% (Golf Management Australia, 2016). In Europe between 2009 and 2013, golf participation fell by 4%, whereas between 2014 and 2015 the trend stabilized to a very slight fall of –0.3% (KPMG, 2016).

There is no consensus on what caused this decline. Explanations include the global financial crisis, new courses being too difficult, a lack of star power – no golfer has emerged to repeat Tiger Wood's dominance, and . . . Many can be grouped under the heading of a growing incompatibility between golf and consumer demands. This includes golf's calm pace, four-hour (or thereabouts) duration, as well as its staid, elitist and sexist image.

Financial instability in the golf industry

This decline in participation numbers has negatively impacted the viability of many golf-related businesses. In the US since 2006, the number of permanent course closures per annum has always exceeded the number of new courses. As Deegan (2016) remarked, "Golf course closures aren't all that newsworthy anymore. Closures have become part of the current golf landscape." Other golf clubs are merging or selling their expensive inner-city land enabling them to retire debt and building a new facility on cheaper, peri-urban land. In 2016, America's largest specialty golf retailer filed for bankruptcy (Kosman, 2016), Nike stopped marketing golf clubs, golf balls and golf bags and Adidas announced its intention to sell its golf division consisting of the TaylorMade, Adams Golf and Ashworth Golf brands. The division was reportedly losing between $50 million and $100 million per annum (Kosman, 2017).

References

Breitbarth, T., Kaiser-Jovy, S. & Dickson, G. (2018). Global golf business and management: market issues and career prospects. In T. Breitbarth, S. Kaiser-Jovy & G. Dickson (Eds.), *Golf Business and Management: A Global Introduction* (pp. 3–19). Abingdon: Routledge.

Completo, F. & Gustavo, N. (2014). Golf tourism destination management: Looking for a sustainable demand: The case of Portugal. *Journal of Management and Sustainability*, 4(1), 142–153.

Dee, D. (2013). "There is no discrimination here, but the Committee never elects Jews": antisemitism in British golf, 1894–1970. *Patterns of Prejudice*, 47(2), 117–138.

Deegan, J. S. (2016). 12 golf courses that shuttered in 2016 we'll miss the most. *Golf Advisor*. Retrieved from www.golfadvisor.com/articles/closed-golf-courses-2016-16201.htm

Dickson, G., Zheng, J. & Chen, S. (2017). Golf in Asia and the Middle East. In T. Breitbarth, S. Kaiser & G. Dickson (Eds.), *Golf Business and Management: A Global Introduction*. London: Routlege.

England Golf. (2016). Positive signs for female golf participation in GB&I. Retrieved 5 June 2017, from www.englandgolf.org/news.aspx?sitesectionid=38&itemid=10190&search=

Ermen, D. & Frary, L. (2018). Golf tourism. In T. Breitbarth, S. Kaiser-Jovy & G. Dickson (Eds.), *Golf Business and Management: A Global Introduction*. Abingdon: Routledge.

Ferguson, N. (2012). *Civilization: The Six Killer Apps of Western Power*. London: Penguin.

Golf 20/20. (2013). KPMG: Golf in Scotland now a 1 billion industry, new study found. Retrieved 1 July 2017, from www.golf2020.com/reports/kpmg-golf-in-scotland-now-a-£1-billion-industry,-new-study-finds.aspx

Golf Europe. (n.d.). [Untitled]. Retrieved 1 July 2017, from www.golfeurope.com/almanac/history/history1.htm

Golf Management Australia. (2016). *Golf Club Participation Report 2015*. Melbourne: Golf Australia.

Hudson, S. & Hudson, L. (2004). *Golf Tourism*. Oxford: Goodfellow Publishers.

Kitching, N., Grix, J. & Phillpotts, L. (2017). Shifting hegemony in "a man"s world': incremental change for female golf professional employment. *Sport in Society*, 43 7(June), 1–18.

Kosman, J. (2016). World's largest golf retailer on the verge of bankruptcy. *New York Post*. Retrieved from http://nypost.com/2016/09/13/worlds-largest-golf-retailer-on-the-verge-of-bankruptcy

Kosman, J. (2017). Adidas struggling to sell TaylorMade brand. Retrieved from https://nypost.com/2017/02/27/adidas-struggling-to-sell-taylormade-equipment-brand

KPMG. (2016). *Golf Participation Report for Europe 2016*. Zug: KPMG.

Lane, J. M. (n.d.). History of golf management. Retrieved from http://golfmanagers.usgtf.com/the-history-of-golf-management

Mintel. (2010). Golf tourism: Travel & Tourism analyst. *Travel & Tourism*, 5, 13–16.

Moss, R. J. (2013). *The Kingdom of Golf in America*. Lincoln: University of Nebraska Press.

Osman, N. (2013, August 26). Indonesia wants to become major golf destination in Asia. *The Jakarta Post*. Retrieved from www.thejakartapost.com/news/2013/08/26/indonesia-wants-become-major-golf-destination-asia.html

R&A. (2015). *Golf around the World 2015*. St Andrews: R&A.

R&A. (2017). *Golf around the World 2017*. St Andrews: R&A.

Rankin, A., Bakir, A. & Bullock, E. (2018). Golf consumption. In T. Breitbarth, S. Kaiser-Jovy & G. Dickson (Eds.), *Golf Business and Management: A Global Introduction* (pp. 20–34). Oxon: Routledge.

Regules, A. F., Martinez, E. E. V. & Moreda, L. J. L. (2015). Developing golf tourism in Mexico: Environmental considerations. *The International Journal of Sustainability in Economic, Social, and Cultural Context*, 11(1), 1–17.

Shilbury, D. (2018). Governance. In T. Breitbarth, S. Kaiser-Jovy & G. Dickson (Eds.), *Golf Business and Management: A Global Introduction*. Abingdon: Routledge.

Shin, E. H. & Nam, E. A. (2004). Culture, gender roles, and sport: The case of Korean players on the LPGA tour. *Journal of Sport & Social Issues*, 28(3), 223–244.

Washburn, D. (2014). *The Forbidden Game: Golf and the Chinese Dream*. London: Oneworld Publications.

21

Snooker and billiards

Luke J. Harris

Snooker is Britain's most popular indoor sport, competed in within both social and recreational settings and boasts a professional circuit that gets significant media attention and enjoys a worldwide following. The sport, as long as its forefather; billiards are both played upon regular tables covered with cloth, which have pockets in the corners and along the longest sides, with the object being to pot balls into these pockets using long sticks of wood with leather tips on, known as cues.

These sports, although very much related are quite different. Billiards could be described as the father of table sports and has many variations, but is primarily played using three balls in total, with the object being to pot the balls, for which points are scored. Snooker originated from billiards at the end of the nineteenth century and is a game which consists of 22 coloured balls, of which 15 are red, along with a cue ball. Both players compete for the same balls, by potting the red balls, then the coloured balls in sequence, with the winner being the person who scores the most points. Pool, otherwise known as pocket billiards in the United States, has many different forms, with the majority revolving around potting one type of ball of which there will be several of and potting the black before your opponent has the opportunity. Although pool has popularity and a professional circuit in North America, the story and history of 'cue sports' is primarily a British one, and one dominated by snooker. Consequently this chapter will primarily focus upon the evolution of the professional game within Britain, along with its diffusion across the world.

All three sports are almost without academic writing. Within some general academic sports on sporting history there are mentions of primarily billiards and snooker, but these are often quite brief and focus upon the popularity of the sport in the 1980s. There are several fine non-academic works which contribute a great deal to uncovering these sports history, such as Clive Everton's *The History of Snooker and Billiards* and Mordecai Richler's *On Snooker*. These are works that are extensively utilised within this chapter.

Billiards

The origin of billiards is obscure; there are claims that it was initially played within several countries including France, Spain, Italy and Britain, although there is no definitive answer of where it originated from.[1]

In Britain, billiards was played with three balls and six pockets upon a rectangular table; its early origins and popularity came from purposes along with its social aspect. As Richard Holt describes: 'It offered older men the blend of skill, drinking, banter, and gambling they found so congenial.'[2] It particularly enjoyed popularity within the upper classes, as described by Mike Huggins:

> Billiard rooms began to appear in country houses in small numbers in the late eighteenth century. Of houses built between 1835 and 1870m about two-thirds were designed with a billiard room, sometimes paired with smoking rooms, and by the 1860s these were a common feature of more masculine suites in country houses. This might suggest that billiards was a male game, but a range of evidence suggests that in many houses mixed billiards was quite usual. By the late nineteenth century, when the Prince of Wales played, furnished billiards rooms were a standard feature, and the segregated male suite was unfashionable. In many houses, souvenirs of the eighteenth century Grand Tour found themselves joined by the new products of taxidermy, the big game and other sporting trophies.[3]

Although popular with the elite, billiards, like snooker in the twentieth century, was something which was enjoyed across the social classes. Holt describes it as being played 'from a royal table at Sandringham to the scruffy back room of a workman's bar.'[4] It was its popularity in Industrial Britain and emergence of its tables within social and working man's clubs that ensured that it became the domain of men, a legacy which has almost entirely excluded women from the game at both a recreational and elite level. One of the positives of industrialisation was a refinement in manufacturing techniques, with 'smoother tables, sprung cushions, and perfect balls',[5] changing the nature of the game forever.

The popularity of billiards within the working classes saw the sport, like so many others (such as athletics, association football and cricket) emerge as sports in Victorian Britain where elite athletes competed for money. The first recognised professional billiards championships were held in February 1870 for the 'considerable' sum of £100, with the holder of the title; John Roberts junior, facing challenger; William Cook. After a five-hour match Cook won by a score of 1,200 to 1,083[6] in front of a crowd that included the Prince of Wales. Just two months later, in April 1870, the championship was fought for again, after Cook was challenged by John Roberts Junior and the challenger was able to take back family honour by defeating Cook. This match saw the emergence as John Roberts Junior as the dominant figure within the sport until the end of the century. Although he was not always the Champion, it is generally accepted that he was the outstanding participant in the sport at this time.[7]

Roberts senior had entered the 1870 match as the 'Champion', although this was not a formalised championship and it had been determined by acclaim by the public, whose opinion ultimately determined the champion after a series of challenge matches for money.[8] The first player to be recognised as a champion was Jonathan Kentfield in 1820. Kentfield was to hold onto the title until 1849 when he refused to play the challenger; Roberts, owing to controversy over pocket size and the table. Roberts then assumed the title, for which he held until his match with Cook.

Following the 1870, match the old practice of a contender challenging the Champion continued into the 1910s, with the challenge needing to be accepted within two months of it being issued and if ignored the challenger would become 'The Champion'. The main problem in organising such matches was agreement upon the rules between players, something which changed in February 1885, when a meeting took place between the leading figures in the sport and they formed the Billiards Association, with rules being agreed shortly afterwards.

The agreement of rules encouraged Roberts, who had declined to the play in for the Championship over the issue of rules to do so once again. Subsequently he challenged Cook, in what turned out be a close match, with Roberts winning by a score of 3,000–2,908. From this point on Roberts was the dominant figure in the sport. His dominance did not mean that he was always 'The Champion' as W.J. Peall challenged and defeated Roberts in a controversial match that caused severe damage to the sport. This came because Roberts refused a re-match because of his refusal to play the 'all-in' format of the game, knowing that he was supreme at the other form 'spot barred'. Everton explains the damage that this match did:

> As happened before and was to happen many times again, internal strife was to interfere with the championship which, despite the promise which the formation of the Billiards Association had seemed to indicate, feel into abeyance between 1885 and 1899 for no other reason than that Roberts was supreme at sport barred but would not play all-in.[9]

The problem for the newly formed association was that Roberts had become the sport, giving him the authority to override the billiards association, ensuring clashes between the two for a number of years. Consequently Roberts turned his attention away from playing to manufacturing equipment for the sport, and he made billiards part of the period that Tony Collins describes as the 'Industrial revolution for sports equipment'[10] in the concluding years of the nineteenth century. Like his play, Roberts' equipment was of the finest quality and did much to make the sport playable amongst the masses, through affordable and reliable equipment. He was not to play in the Championships again until 1899.

In 1901, H.W. Stevenson, became Champion for the first time and he would become along with Melbourne Inman the dominant figure in the sport up to the outbreak of the First World War after defeating Charles Dawson. In the process, Stevenson is believed to be the first player to make a break of a thousand or more (1016).[11] Although later in 1901, Dawson, retook his title, between 1908 and 1914 it would be Stevenson and Inman who dominated the sport, with Tom Reece providing the main opposition for Inman in the later years, challenging him upon several occasions, although never to defeat him.

Reece would also provide the main opposition to Tom Newman, and would in-fact challenge for the title of Champion no less than six times without success. The 1920s would belong to Newman, from Lincolnshire, who would hold the Championship exclusively between 1921 and 1928, excluding 1923 when Willie Smith held the title. Newman was the first of the leading billiard players to play snooker seriously and although he regarded it the lesser of the two games he did play Joe Davis for the 1934 World Championship, losing 25–22.

The afore-mentioned Joe Davis, was born Derbyshire in 1901 and became a professional billiards player at the mere age of 18. In 1926, he lost the first of two consecutive world finals to Tom Newman, although he would have his revenge in 1928 when he finally defeated him to become Champion for the first time. Davis would remain Champion until 1933 when he was defeated by Australian Walter Lindrum. The two would compete for the Championship the following year, by this time Davis's attention was firmly focused upon snooker, where he was the outstanding player.

While Davis was concentrating upon snooker, billiards was dominated, by Australian Walter 'Wally' Lindrum, who held the World Championship between 1933 and 1950- when he retired as the uncontested champion of the world. John Bissett, Chairman of the Billiards Association & Control Club stated in 1933 that 'Lindrum to billiards is what a Shakespeare is to literature, one of those rare beings, gifted with supreme genius who only appear once in the history of a nation.'[12]

In the post-Second World War era billiards would play second fiddle to snooker, both in terms of competition and interest owing to the popularity of snooker. The first World Professional Billiards Championships took place in 1951, but the next did not take place until August 1968.'[13] The Championships itself was not restored to a tournament basis until 1980 and later in that decade only was there a growth in interest.

The 1980 Championships were won by the 67-year-old Fred Davis, and since this there have been regular championships, which were first run by the WPBSA (1980–2011) and since 2012 it has been the World Billiards Limited that has run the Championships. These championships have seen titles in both the timed and points formats. India has been the dominant nation in the modern history of the game, with Geet Sethi and more recently Pankaj Advani both having been multiple champions.

Snooker

John Roberts, along with having a big influence upon billiards, had perhaps even a bigger impact upon snooker, as he was responsible for bringing it to England after he had first witnessed it being played in India during a tour of the country in 1885. Up until this point snooker had been the preserve of British officers in the army who were looking for new ways to amuse themselves during the boredom of the Indian Monsoon season.

Credit for the game is widely given to Colonel Sir Neville Chamberlain and the Officers of the Devonshire regiment, who added balls to the game of Black Pool[14] which they widely played. This is where if a player potted their allocated coloured ball they could attempt a go at the black. Although early snooker had many forms, the one that became popular involved fifteen reds, along with a single yellow, green, pink and black ball. This was a game which provided great entertainment for both players and spectators who commonly bet on the match and elements within it. Rules along with the blue and brown balls were added and when Roberts toured India in 1885, he met Chamberlain and duly brought the game back with him to England. Although the cost of extra balls meant that not every billiard club played, the new game did take off across Britain.

During the following decade snooker became popular across Britain, and its rules were codified in 1919 following the amalgamation of the Billiard Association and Billiards Control Club. In the immediate years following the First World War it was seen as 'chiefly a gambling game or a respite from billiards',[15] although it was to become the dominant table sport in the late 1920s and 1930s owing to the success of one man: Joe Davis.

It was through the hard work and dedication of Davis that the first World Professional Snooker Championships were staged in 1927. These were Championships where he flourished, winning the first fifteen Championships held between 1927 and 1946.

His unbelievable and unparalleled success has seen him described by snooker historian and commentator, Clive Everton, as 'the greatest of them all'.[16] He remains the only undefeated player at the Professional Championships after his retirement in 1946. Such was Davis's popularity that he raised £125,000 for charity through playing exhibition matches and trick shot shows during the Second World War.[17] After his retirement in 1946, the sport went into decline for a decade, with snooker historians relating to the fact that the sport revolved so closely around him.

In the inter-war period Davis's popularity reached as high as any leading soccer or cricket star in Britain, while the accessibility and the social aspect of the sport helping to promote it as a whole. By the 1930s, social and working man's club up and down Britain had tables and it became a popular way for men to spend their spare time while enjoying a pint. For example, Holt explains its popularity in the Miners' Institute in Tredegar, Wales in the late 1930s: 'Unemployment had left many men from the Valleys with nothing to do but hang around the miner's welfare listening to the clinking of the balls, eking out their beer and tobacco between spells at the table.'[18] Such a description could have been made almost anywhere across the British Isles at this time, such was the popularity of snooker.

Despite its popularity as a favourite pastime, snooker struggled to attract attention as a popular spectator sport in the same way other sports did. Consequently, it enjoyed little success as a commercial activity, with little sponsorship and this saw Davis take it upon himself to attempt to encourage sponsors. This was something he enjoyed limited success in:

> I thought of every product, that might conceivably-and-sometimes inconceivably-have any bearing on billiards and snooker and then offered my services in endorsing them. I tried eye lotions and hair lotions, shirt makers and shoe makers, without eliciting the slightest flicker of interest. The only contract for endorsing a product that I obtained in those days was for Churchman's Top Score cigarettes, which I used to smoke.[19]

New sponsors did emerge, such as in 1936 when *The Daily Mail* newspaper's tournament was switched from billiards to snooker, reflecting the change in the nation's premier table sport. Snooker's new found popularity was also demonstrated by the periodical *The Billiard Player* changing its name to *Billiards and Snooker* in the same year, although after the Second World War it reversed to its original title.[20]

Following the retirement of Davis, the mantle of the leading player in the World went to his brother; Fred, who won every world championships between 1948 and 1956 excluding the 1950 event (where he was the runner up) and the 1952 championships. In 1952 a fall out over prize money between the Professional Billiards Players Association (PBPA) and the Billiards Association and Control Council (BACC) led to all of leading players boycotting the tournament. Consequently, the PBPA created their own event the World Professional Match play Championships, which Davis was victorious in. Despite the boycott, the BACC still held their event, but only Horace Lindrum and Clark McConachy entered, and Lindrum won the 145 match easily by a score of 73–37. From reading different histories of the sport, there are some disputes as to who is the correct 1952 champion. Davis was undoubtedly the sports premier player as Lindrum was some way past his best, having primarily been a force prior to the war, having been runner up in the Championships in 1936 and 1937, along with 1946, although he had not featured since.

After these issues were settled Davis once again became the undisputed champion in 1953. His quality being further demonstrated on 22 January 1955 when at the News of the World Tournament, he became the first person to make an official maximum break of 147.[21] His eight championships were then equalled by another Englishman; John Pullman, who after finishing runner up to Davis in 1955 and 1956, won a record eight times between 1957 and 1968.[22] The matches that took place between 1958 and 1964 were challenge matches, explaining why there was less than one contest in a calendar year.

The lack of formal sponsorship and the general organisation of the sport contributed to the lack of a championship and this threatened the sport as a professional entity, despite it prominence as a pastime. The formation of the World Professional Billiards and Snooker Association in 1968 helped to change the fortunes of the sport. It organised its first world championship in 1969, with John Spencer taking the title 37–24 in the final, having beaten Pullman in the first round.

The WPBSA did much to help organise championships, but the success which the sport was to enjoy over the following decades owed to the advent of colour television. Everton states that this transformed professional snooker from being 'a low-key, low-budget affair in obscure venues to a professionally staged sporting spectacle'.[23] It was the British Broadcasting Corporation (BBC) that brought about this revolution beginning in 1969 and occurred because they were looking for ways to use their new colour cameras. The idea was first suggested in a meeting of the corporations' executives, when head of sport Bryan Cowgill suggested using snooker, which director general David Attenborough was enthusiastic about:

> In terms of production of colour pictures it was an absolute godsend and absolutely invaluable in getting the service on the air. Then there was the sport itself, and the obvious drama with all the characters involved. I watched it all the time when it was on.[24]

The BBC's first venture into the sport came via a single-frame tournament, *Pot Black*, which was created by the corporation and initially featured eight players who played a single frame match that was filmed at the Pebble Mill studios. This was then broadcast as thirty-minute programmes beginning on 23 July 1969. Clive Everton remarks:

> it was a series which was to introduce snooker to sections of the community who had previously scarcely known of its existence. It was to make reputations for those players who appeared on it, which reached far beyond the traditional bounds of the snooker world. A player invited to appear on *Pot Black* usually found himself in much greater demand for the club exhibitions which still yielded the bulk of his income.[25]

The tournament continued until 1986 and did enormous amounts to popularise the game and its leading stars, many of whom became household names. The early success of *Pot Black* witnessed in the further expansion of the coverage by the BBC culminating in covering the entirety of the seventeen days of the World Championships. Its first live coverage of the event occurred in 1978; 'and by the end of the 1980s, snooker was the most popular televised sport in Britain, particularly amongst viewers from over the age of 50'.[26] In 1978, there were 35 hours of coverage, and the growth in interest was reflected in the size of the coverage, which had risen to 130 hours from the World Championship alone, with substantial coverage of other tournaments. By the early 1980s, snooker was already the most popular sport on television.[27]

Live television coverage of the World Championships had been made possible by the moving of the event to the Crucible Theatre, an in-the-round venue in Sheffield in 1976. The first event attracted more than 20,000 spectators and record prize money of £17,000. Despite complaints that the venue is no longer big enough in terms of spectator numbers, practice facilities or media space the venue has a deal in place to hold the tournament until at least 2018.

In the 1980s there began extensive television coverage of other top events, most prominently the Masters event from Wembley, but also the UK Championships. Everton describes the impact that this had upon the sport; 'Suddenly, snooker was full of managers, middlemen, entrepreneurs of varying degrees and probity and swarms of hangers-on, buzzing around this new overflowing money pot.'[28] This money pot came primarily from tobacco sponsorship, such as Benson and Hedges and Embassy, who sponsored the World Championships between 1976 and 2006, following the ban on tobacco advertising in Britain. In 1978, the total prize money was £24,000 by 1985 this had reached £300,000. For the sponsors, along with a couple of hundred thousand pounds for backup facilities it gave 'the sort of advertising exposure that, at average television commercial rates, would have cost something in the region of £75 million. And this was on the supposedly commercial-free BBC.'[29] Such sponsorship undoubtedly helped snooker 'boom'.

The potential for snooker was perhaps best recognised by a man who today is an integral part of its organisation: Barry Hearn, from Dagenham, Essex. Hearn began to invest in the game in the 1970s when he brought two snooker halls in nearby Romford. Soon after he began he had his own chain of halls, 'Lucania', promoting events and managing players; most prominently Steve Davis, a local boy who had been practising in his halls. In 1984, Hearn saw the end of the sponsorship of 'The International Tournament' by Jameson Whisky as an opportunity for another brand to step into the sport. Hearn saw the event, which happened in the Autumn, as an opportunity to promote the brand 'Goya' and its toiletries for men for Christmas. Launching the Goya 'Matchroom' range in October 1984, with the tournament happening shortly afterwards, it gave the new range a minimum of 30 hours peak-time viewing.[30]

Hearn, who by the late 1970s had established himself as Davis's manager did not stop there. The pair, along with professional Tony Meo, formed Matchroom Sports in the early 1980s. This was a management group for player and by the middle of the decade the group was managing a large number of leading players in the game, including Terry Griffiths, Willie Thorne, Dennis Taylor and Jimmy White. It was these players who under the title of 'The Matchroom Mob' that provided the back singing for the Chas and Dave's hit single 'Snooker Loopy' in May 1986. The single reached number six in the British charts, and included lyrics that humorously mocked the players involved and helped to raise their public profile, along with the sports.

The early years of television coverage during the 1970s was helped by the emergence of its first modern superstar: Northern Irishman Alex 'The Hurricane' Higgins, whose fast and attacking style of play was the like of which had never been seen before. At the age of just 23, he won the first of his two World Championships in 1971, after defeating John Spencer in a best of 73 frames final at the British Legion in Birmingham.

David Hatrick describes that the victory sent 'shockwaves through the tight-knit snooker community'.[31] Higgins's victory did not bring a string of successes, as in the years that followed he won minor tournaments, but none of the 'majors': 'His opponents had worked out a plan to nullify him as best they could by pulling him back to their level with long-drawn out frames and safety battles. His impatience and subsequent desire to please the crowd would always cost him.'[32] It was such displays that helped him earn the title of the 'People's Champion'.

A second world title was to follow ten years after his initial success, when he beat the five-time Champion, Ray Reardon, in 1982. Higgins's victory ended Reardon's period of dominance in the sport, where he had been world number one since 1976. Higgins, alongside his 'People's Champion' tab, had a less likeable side; he punched a referee and tournament director, along with once head-butting an official who required a random drugs test from him.

Fred Davis described him as 'the only true genius snooker ever had'.[33] There was little doubt that Higgins was a genius on the table and played shots which others could only dream, but he was undoubtedly a flawed genius. Like Belfast's other famous son of the period, George Best, he was an alcoholic, something which saw him in a nursing home in 1981.[34] After this came scandals involving cocaine and alcohol in 1986. Despite his off-the-table problems and moderate amount of success upon it, Higgins was not modest in his role in the game's growth in popularity. He said in 1999:

> I was a major force in bringing snooker out of the shadows. I was the one that made it a spectator sport, an entertainment. If I hadn't started the ball rolling like that, I doubt that you'd have the young boys in the game that there are now, because most of them were inspired by Alex Higgins. I have created an audience of millions who have never even played the game.[35]

Snooker had also made Higgins a wealthy man, with suggestions that in his career he had earned and spent £4 million.[36] Both his world titles brought about talk of Higgins becoming the dominant force in the game, this was not to happen upon either occasion, as first it was Reardon, then in the 1980s a young Englishman by the name of Steve Davis who became snookers leading figure.

In Clive Everton's *The History of Snooker and Billiards*, the twelfth chapter covering the period 1980–1986 is called 'The Steve Davis era'. This is an apt title, as during this seven year period he dominated the sport, winning six world titles, and twenty-eight ranking tournaments that he won during his career.

Despite his success, it is perhaps the 1985 World Championship final which he lost that Davis is best remembered for. The final is known as the 'black ball final' and Davis took on 11th seed Dennis Taylor, in a 35 frame final that came down to the final black. The climax of the match which was played out in the early hours of 29 April was watched by 18.5 million people in the UK, a record for any programme on BBC 2 and the highest post-midnight audience for any channel in Britain. 'The Times' declared the match as 'heart-stopping' and Holt claims that this was the culmination of the interest in snooker and 'what began as an attempt to diversify and cater for minority interests on BBC 2 turned into an extraordinary national obsession'.[37]

The popularity of the sport not only owed to the quality and drama of the play, but also the rivalries which existed between the top players. Certainly some of the rivalry and showmanship was part of a public relations exercise, but amongst this the competition between the men at the top certainly added to the drama. The visibility of snooker within the British sporting consciousness during the 1980s was demonstrated through the number of appearances of the sport's top players made within the prestigious BBC Sports Personality of the year award. The high point of this came in 1988, when Steve Davis took the title (Davis also finished as runner-up and third placed twice). The achievements of Alex Higgins and Stephen Hendry saw them finish in second position in 1982 and 1990 respectively.

In much the same way that *Pot Black* turned snooker players into recognisable public figures in the 1970s and 1980s, the prime time games show *Big Break* did the same in the 1990s for a new generation of players. Beginning in 1991 and aired on early Saturday evening prime-time slot on BBC1, *Big Break* was hosted by comedian Jim Davidson and former top ten player John Virgo, and mixed a light-hearted comic tone with snooker and trick shots. The show gave snooker players not only the chance to demonstrate their skills but also their personalities.

The man who replaced Davis as the dominant figure in the sport was Scotsman Stephen Hendry, someone considered to be by some commentators as the greatest player of all time. After coming to the sport relatively late at the age of twelve, he was Scottish Amateur Champion at the age of fifteen in 1984, before turning professional the following year. In 1986, he made his Crucible debut at the age of just seventeen and although eliminated in the first round, in 1987, he became the youngest ever winner of ranking title after winning the Grand Prix.

In 1990, he began a decade of dominance with a first of seven world Championships, when he became the youngest World Champion in snooker history. In 1992 Hendry began a run of five consecutive World Championships. Those who disagree with the suggestion that Hendry is snooker's greatest, certainly of the modern players, would most likely argue that Ronnie O'Sullivan is in fact the greatest. O'Sullivan announced himself on the world stage at the 1993 UK Championships, when he became the youngest winner of a ranking event at the tender age of 17 years and 358 days. Further success was to follow and explanation for his nickname 'The Rocket' was demonstrated when he made a maximum 147 break in just five minutes and twenty seconds.

Despite his acclaim and victory in both ranking and non-ranking, it wasn't until 2001 that O'Sullivan became World Champion. The inconsistencies and self-doubt that had plagued his career prior to this had certainly were certainly not expelled by this victory. In the following season he was defeated in the semi-final and the year after that witnessed him being eliminated in the first round. A second victory followed in 2004, with further titles in 2008, 2011 and 2012. Although very much the premier player at this time, he held the world number one ranking for just five years in the period between 2004 and 2013.

The twenty-first century has seen the game expand in popularity across the world, with ranking events taking place in both India and China. For the 2015/16 season, three of the eleven ranking events were hosted in China, demonstrating the prominence of the game within the country. The popularity of the game in China has seen the emergence of players from the country to inside the world's top 16. The most prominent of the Chinese players is Ding Junhui who has won two UK Championships (2005 and 2009), along with being runner-up at the 2016 World Championships.

The expansion of the game into China, along with other new places such as Germany has provided the sport with new and much needed momentum since interest and audiences for snooker in the United Kingdom have dwindled. This has been prescribed to a number of causes; the amount of sport and variety of sports on offer upon television in the modern era.

Snooker's demise has partially owed to the rise of satellite television and in particular Sky Sports in Britain. In the late 1980s Hearn's attention turned away from snooker, primarily firstly to boxing, but 'through his televisions promotions company, he identified, as he had identified in snooker, niche markets like darts, pool, angling and even ten pin bowling which had not been exploited to the potential which the new multiplicity of television channels now offered. With Sky as his bedrock client, thousands of hours of sports programming rolled off his production line'.[38] Snooker was no longer the primary sport on television and others with new innovations and exciting coverage have overtaken snooker in the popularity stakes.

Snooker still enjoys favourable television coverage and there is coverage of the UK Championships, Masters and World Championships upon the BBC. The audience of the sport is reflected in the times of the coverage, as now the main players play in the afternoon sessions, popular with the over 50s. The sports main sponsorship no longer comes from tobacco, but from betting organisations, which bring in significant amounts of money, such as a total prize pot of £1,500,000 awarded at the 2016 World Championships. There have been five separate betting companies which have sponsored the Championships since 2006.

Apart from O'Sullivan and Scotsman; John Higgins, who have won seven of the world titles between them in the twenty-first century the sport has been largely open, with eight different World Champions since the year 2000. These have all been from Great Britain excluding Australian Neil Robertson, the 2010 Champion. In 2016, Englishman Mark Selby won his second world title, having previously been the winner in 2014.

Women's snooker has had next to no visibility compared to the men's game. Women playing the sport continually face the obstacle of struggling to get access to facilities; particularly as many tables are in clubs and halls, which are often deemed to be the male preserve. Sponsorship for both players and events are a real issue, as Jenny Hargreaves states; 'It has been claimed that lack of sponsorship for women's professional snooker has nearly killed the game-even though there are sixty or more women snooker players who are as good as men players, they fail to secure adequate sponsorship.'[39] She continues to argue that sponsors argue that they don't want to take risks with sports that don't have a proven record of audience interest. She also argues that snooker is a sport of masculinity.[40]

The inequality between the men's and women's games can be seen in the two world championships. The women's event, organised by the World Ladies Billiards and Snooker, began in 1976. Although after the inaugural event it was not held again until 1980, (there have been four times since that there has been no championship). Comparable with the men's event it was sponsored by Embassy, but this ended in 2003 when tobacco sponsorship was banned. Consequently, in 2004, because of a lack of a new sponsor there was no event.

The 2016 final was contested over the best of ten frames and the total prize fund was £6,000, by contrast the men's event was for the best of 35 frames and there was just over £1.5 million given away as prize money.

Notes

1 Norman Clare, *Billiards and Snooker Bygones* (Shire, London, 1996), p. 5.
2 Richard Holt, *Sport and the British* (Bristol, Oxford University Press, 1996), p. 190.
3 Mike Huggins, 'Sport and the British upper classes, c1550–2000: A historiographic Overview', Sport in History, 28, 3 (2008), p. 376.
4 Holt, *Sport and the British*, p. 191.
5 Ibid, p. 190
6 In billiards two points are given for a shot if they strike the cue ball, their ball and their opponents ball in the same shot, while a point is given for potting their ball.
7 Clive Everton, *The History of Snooker and Billiards*, (Letchworth, Partridge Press, 1986), p. 23
8 Ibid., p. 12.
9 Ibid., p. 95.
10 Tony Collins, *Sport in Capitalist Society: A short history*, (Abington, Routledge, 2003), p. 49.
11 'H.W. Stevenson: Past Masters, No 7 – July 1984', www.snookerheritage.co.uk/normans-articles/past-masters/hw-stevenson/ accessed on 25/5/2016.
12 Peter Ainsworth, 'Walter Albert Lindrum: His life and times', www.eaba.co.uk/eaba/?p=5787
13 Everton, *The History of Snooker and Billiards*, p. 76.
14 Black pool is a game where if a player potted a coloured ball they could attempt the black, which yielded more points
15 Everton, *The History of Snooker and Billiards*, p. 50.
16 Ibid., p. 7.
17 Holt, *Sport and the British*, p. 191.
18 Ibid.
19 Mordecai Richler, *On Snooker* (London, Yellow Jersey Press, 2001), p. 47.
20 Everton, *The History of Snooker and Billiards*, p. 53.
21 Ibid., p. 61.
22 There was no world championship between 1957 and 1963, the two held in 1964 and the three in 1965 were all single challenge matches.
23 Everton, *The History of Snooker and Billiards*, p. 95.
24 Eloise McNaulty, 'BBC Snooker: Pot Black and beyond', www.bbc.co.uk/informationandarchives/archivenews/2015/snooker_pot_black_and_beyond
25 Everton, *The History of Snooker and Billiards*, p. 95.
26 John Nauright, 'Snooker', *Sports around the World* (USA, ABC-CLIO, 2012), p. 191.
27 Gordon Burn, *Pocket Money: Britain's Boom-Time Snooker* (Croydon, Heinemann, 2008), p. 36.
28 Ibid., p278
29 Ibid., p. 37.
30 Ibid., p. 39.
31 David Hatrick, 'How Alex Higgins rode the Hurricane to produce one of snooker's greatest breaks', *The Guardian*, 25 January 2016, www.theguardian.com/sport/in-bed-with-maradona/2016/jan/25/alex-higgins-hurricane-snooker-jimmy-white-crucible
32 Ibid.
33 Everton, *The History of Snooker and Billiards*, p
34 Richler, *On Snooker*, p. 119.
35 Ibid, p. 118.

36 'Alex "Hurricane" Higgins dies, aged 61', *The Telegraph*, 25 July 2010, www.telegraph.co.uk/sport/othersports/snooker/7908867/Alex-Hurricane-Higgins-dies-aged-61.html
37 Holt, *Sport and the British*, p. 319.
38 Burn, *Pocket Money*, p. 279.
39 Jennifer Hargreaves, *Sporting Females: Critical Issues in the History and Sociology of Women's Sport* (London, Routledge, 2001), p. 204.
40 Ibid., p. 273.

22

Table tennis

Tsz Lun (Alan) Chu

The history of table tennis, also known as ping pong in some countries such as the United States (US), could be traced back to the 1890s. Despite some evidence that British were trying to create some kind of indoor tennis games, the origin of table tennis could not be identified accurately. After lawn tennis gained popularity during that time, people spontaneously created a table game of tennis for fun using cigar box lids as bats, corks as balls, and a row of books as the net. In 1884, a famous British sporting goods company F.H. Ayres produced a more structured game of "Miniature Indoor Lawn Tennis." Seven years later, this game advanced to a more modern version when a British athlete carried some celluloid balls from the US in 1891. In this decade, a national craze for "ping pong" began, while bats with a hollow parchment or vellum face were used. Due to the increased popularity, the Ping Pong Association was formed and held a championship before Queen Victoria's death. After the game was played for 18 years in England, it was introduced to Japan and Central Europe in 1902. A critical developmental period of table tennis happened after the First World War when the Ping Pong Association was replaced by the Table Tennis Association in 1922. Americans, Australians, French, Spaniards, and Swedish took this game to their country after visiting England and seeing table tennis. The game became more competitive after the equipment production and advertisement from major game companies such as Jaques & Son in England and Parker Brothers in the US Soon after, the International Table Tennis Federation (ITTF) was formed in 1926 by Hon. Ivor Montagu (1904–1984), involving 29 countries in the organization and holding first World Championships in London.[1]

Ivor Montagu is a name that everyone who enjoy table tennis nowadays should know. Montagu was a British-born Jew in an upper-class society, a leisure class that gained power largely from state service and land ownership. Whereas most of the upper classes enjoyed "elite" sports such as hunting and fishing exclusively, he was enthusiastic in soccer and table tennis instead. Indeed, he was different than his peers in many other aspects as well. For instance, he believed in left-wing politics and joined the British Socialist Party at the age of 15, which was atypical for the upper class and shocked his parents. Montagu was a brilliant student who mastered several languages, including German, French, Spanish, Italian and Russian, as well as some Chinese and Japanese. He was later admitted to Cambridge University and graduated from King's College in zoology in 1924 at the age of 20. Furthermore, he was knowledgeable in technology and played a significant role as the director, writer, and producer in the film industry. Combining his interest in both film and sports, Montagu produced the movie *Table Tennis Today* in 1928.[2]

Montagu had been very actively involved in table tennis when he was in college. At the age of 19 and 22, respectively, he founded the English Table Tennis Association (ETTA) in 1923 and the ITTF in 1926. Additionally, Montagu set the record of holding a president position for any sport by being the ITTF President for 41 years. When table tennis was an upper-class parlor game, Montagu wrote the book *Table Tennis Today* in 1924 in order to set rules and promote table tennis as a competitive sport across social classes. Over the years as the ITTF president, he devoted himself to table tennis in ways that are consistent with his political views – creating opportunities for the middle and lower classes to experience the sport. Montagu wrote, "I saw table tennis a sport particularly suited to the lower paid, above all – since it was played indoors – in crowded towns. Its equipment was relatively cheap, it did not require extensive or expensive special premises."[3] There were followers who helped promote the sport across diverse ethnic groups in England, including Jews and Indians, so the popularity of table tennis continued to grow. The sport even broke through the political division between the socialist and the communist parties and was listed as one of the recreations by a socialist organization – the National Workers Sports Association.[4] Beyond England, Montagu developed good connections with Hungarian players, especially since Jews were their prominent national champions during the 1920s.[5] These early events demonstrated that table tennis is a sport not only for leisure and competition but also for political relations and diplomacy.

To further promote internationalization of table tennis, Montagu invited other countries to participate in the first World Championships in London after he established the ITTF in 1926. The World Championships was intended to be a European Championship in the first place, but was renamed due to the presence of Indian representatives who indeed lived in England. In the tournament, four players formed a team to compete in men's singles, women's singles, men's doubles, and mixed doubles. Eventually, 50 men and 14 women from nine countries participated: Austria, Czechoslovakia, Denmark, England, Germany, Hungary, India, Sweden, and Wales. Hungary won the first team title and the following eight (except 1932 in which Czechoslovakia won) due to their male players' dominance. Separate team events by gender started in 1934. Throughout his presidency and championship organizations, Montagu imposed two principles that might be attributed to his amateur upbringing. First, the ITTF members were not defined as national representatives but table tennis entities or organizations. Second, national flags and anthems were discouraged outside the world championships, because he emphasized friendships between players as human beings instead of their nationalities. His viewpoints fostered a harmonious environment that not a single entity (e.g., Rhodesia, Taiwan) has been excluded from the World Championships. The following ITTF President Evans as well as table tennis historians claimed that table tennis became a universal sport because of Montagu. Perfect though as he may seem, Montagu was criticized by some for his sense of superiority and dictatorship. Even Montagu referred to himself as "a crotchety old cross-patch" and stated his reasons for a long presidency as political.[6] Regardless, his commitment to both socialism and sports has greatly contributed to the East–West relations.

By now, you may have realized the terms of both "ping pong" and "table tennis" in this chapter. So, how should we call this game and/or sport? Well, both terms may work depending on the context. "Ping pong" was the most widely accepted name under the trademark of Jaques and Son and was later bought by Parker Brothers, which produced equipment for the game at that time. USATT historian Tim Boggan wrote:

> think "Ping-Pong" and think what you might of yesteryear "family" entertainment – of bygone board games stretched over an all-purpose dining-room table . . . Table Tennis,

in having its own World Championships since 1926 and in participating in the Olympic Games since 1988, is undeniably, a sport.[7]

The division between ping pong and table tennis in the US occurred in 1930, when the American Ping Pong Association (APPA) spokesman Schaad attributed the origin of the game to Parker Brothers, which began to promote tournaments with a commercial mind such that every participant could only play with Parker Brothers' equipment.

Parker Brothers worked with the New York Metro Ping Pong Association (MPPA) to organize the first national tournament in 1929 in order to build up the sport with the first National Champion. The rules of the ping pong tournament are very similar to those of modern table tennis, except that players would have to use an underhand one-bounce "tennis serve" with the ball struck from anyplace up to the server's waistline. Four hundred participants entered the tournament, and Marcus (Mark) Schussheim won the first national title. Since then, Schussheim had won all important leagues and tournaments organized by Parker Brothers. After playing these tournaments, some table tennis players wanted to use other equipment that is superior to the one manufactured by Parker Brothers. At a meeting in New York City in 1931, therefore, the MPPA members voted to form another organization – the New York Table Tennis Association (NYTTA). To adapt to this change, the ITTF immediately transferred its allegiance to the NYTTA. At the same time, Schussheim went along with the NYTTA instead of the APPA, because he did not like the upper-class, black-tie image of Parker Brothers. The NYTTA then organized their first National Championships in 1932, and Schussheim won the national title again. He also went on to play in the World Championships for the US team later.[8]

Table tennis is a relatively inclusive sport that has been played by diverse populations. The 1933 APPA National Championships was the first time that Black players entered a table tennis tournament in the US In the same year, both APPA and the NYTTA organized the Women's National Championships and attracted 40 local Illinois players to participate. Whereas most men used a penhold grip to gain an advantage on the one-bounce serve, women began to switch to a shakehand grip that requires less strength for an average woman to handle.[9] With a ball weighing less than three grams, table tennis is deigned in a way that muscle mass does not play as much of a role, so men are not necessarily favored over women in the sport.[10] There are three traditional competition formats divided by gender: men's and women's singles, doubles, and team events. In addition, there is mixed doubles, which will be held for the first time in the Olympics in Tokyo, Japan in 2020.[11]

After the hard rubber paddles were invented in the 1930s, the sport totally changed to a different level in that players were able to put spin to the ball and use various strategies with spin. This change led to more league and club establishment in Europe and the US. The Communist Party in China also instilled a "passion for the English game of table tennis." More international events were held and more table tennis books were published compared to the previous decade.[12] The United States Table Tennis Association (USTTA; now USATT) was founded in 1933 and helped promote the sport in the country. About 1,500 players signed the Articles of Agreement to form this non-profit, non-commercial association dedicated to amateur play in a "sportsmanlike" manner. Soon after, the US national team won a few World Championships titles, including the US's only world men's team title in 1937 and only women's singles title earned by Ruth Aarons in 1936.[13]

Despite the growth of table tennis participation in various countries, the development of the sport stopped and no World Championships were held between 1940 and 1946 due to the Second World War. In 1946, the ITTF was reactivated and held a conference meeting after the war to discuss a few important issues that pertains to harmony and fairness in table tennis participation. Some established rules included suspending ITTF membership of the associations that were opposed to the Allies during the war, restricting of World Championships participation to only ITTF members, and forbidding ITTF affiliates to discriminate against race, skin color, or religion. In the same meeting, the issue whether table tennis should be added to Olympics was raised and discussed. Alongside President Montagu, the majority of the ITTF committee members were against the idea due to a potential overlap between the Olympics and the already established World Championships.[14]

For people who play or watch table tennis, it seems clear that table tennis is an "Asian sport." Thus, many may be surprised to know that Asian countries started competing in the sport and experiencing successes later than Western countries. In the 1950s, the modern game of table tennis finally began after the invention of sponge or sandwich rubber, so an offensive style of play was made possible. With a thin covering of pimpled rubber, Japan was the first country that was able to dominate the sport with great speed and spin for a decade in the 1950s by training players with powerful strokes. In 1951 – two years after the People's Republic of China (PRC) was established – the ITTF recognized the Communist Chinese government and invited the country to enter the World Championships. This recognition led Mao Zedong, the Chairman of the PRC, to promote table tennis as the national sport. China then became a member of the ITTF in 1953. Because of this move, China was able to catch up in the international arena and defeated Japan to win their first World Champion title in table tennis and any sport, led by Rong Guotuan (1937–1968) who won the men's singles in 1959. In fact, Rong was born in Hong Kong and represented its team as a junior player. He only moved to China two years before he won the World Championships. This triumph resulted in the brand name of the famous table tennis manufacture today – Double Happiness – first happiness representing the first World Champion in China and the second happiness indicating the 10th anniversary of the PRC. Under the order of Zhou Enlai, the first premier of the PRC, Double Happiness started making equipment the next year that popularized table tennis across different social classes due to the low equipment cost. After winning the world singles title, Rong further helped the Chinese men's team win the first team title by defeating Japan and Hungary in 1961. Afterwards, he coached the women's team who won the first team title at the 1965 World Championships.[15]

The defeat of China over Japan in the 1961 World Championships team finals meant more than just a world team title, but a symbolic revenge of Imperial Japan's invasion of China in 1930. Once again, it showed that achievements in sports did not only represent athletic strength but also political power and relationships among different countries. Chairman Mao even claimed victories in table tennis as China's "spiritual nuclear weapon." Since then, table tennis tables could be found everywhere in China, such as in train stations, schools, parks, for the general public to hit a few balls when they need to take a break or kill some time. Even Mao Zedong and Zhou Enlai would play table tennis for fun. China took a dominating role in international competitions in the 1960s with its players' fast, offensive style. Zhuang Zedong (1940–2013) was one of the best table tennis player in the history who won three world singles titles (1961, 1963, and 1965). Chairman Mao also congratulated Zhuang and praised him for playing in a Chinese way – the penhold grip with a dual-sided style that emphasizes offensive backhand drives.[16] In 1966, the Cultural Revolution began such that China had to stop all professional sport competitions, including the 1967 World Championships. Rong Guotuan, along with two other national team players, Fu Qifang and Jiang Yongning, were arrested by the Red Guards as spy suspects. Sadly, these three players committed suicide soon after they were humiliated and jailed in 1968.[17]

On the other hand, Zhuang Zedong was not only famous for his three-time world singles title but also for his important role in ping-pong diplomacy. In the 1971 World Championships held in Japan, the US and Chinese teams met each other during a tour on April 2. Although a US player jokingly asked whether they could visit China for table tennis, the Foreign Affairs Ministry and the National Committee on Physical Education replied with a negative response. On April 4, a US player, Genn Cowan, missed the team bus to his hotel and got on the bus that carried Chinese players instead. Because of the conflicts in the Cold War, Chinese athletes were discouraged from interacting with American athletes during that period. Despite the regulation, Zhuang handed Cowan a silk portrait of Huangshan ("yellow mountain") as a gift. This act was noticed by the journalists who took a picture of the two players with the banner. Cowan returned the favor the next day by giving Zhuang a T-shirt with the image of a red, white, and blue flag and the words "Let It Be" as a gift, which attracted interviews from journalists. These brief contacts turned out to be historical breakthroughs when Zhou Enlai submitted the request of ping-pong diplomacy to Mao for approval.[18]

In the night of April 6, Mao changed his mind from denial to approval when he saw the news about Zhuang and Cowan in a government official newspaper and said, "This Zhuang Zedong not only plays table tennis well, but is good at foreign affairs." In the morning of April 7, the last day of the World Championships, the Chinese table tennis delegation received the message of approval and invited the US team. The US President Richard Nixon then received a telegraph about the invitation and immediately accepted it in that afternoon. This series of prompt actions led to one of the biggest events in the history of foreign affairs – ping-pong diplomacy. Finally, on April 10, the US table tennis delegation started a seven-day trip with table tennis plays in China. Under the principle of "Friendship First, Competition Second," instead of the likely straight-match wins, the Chinese men's and women's teams won 5–3 and 5–4, respectively, over the US teams. During the trip, Zhuang toured the US delegation to famous tourist spots such as the Great Wall and the Summer Palace while he was appointed the Minister of Physical Culture and Sports. Despite his contribution, Zhuang was investigated and sentenced to prison for four years from 1976 to 1980 after Mao's death and the arrest of related political affiliates. After he was released from the prison, Zhuang worked as a coach returned to Beijing. In 2013, Zhuang died at the age of 72 due to cancer.[19]

As most of us know, the ping-pong diplomacy long-lasting "butterfly effect" on the US–China relations after the visit. The 15 US table tennis delegation members, including the only African American player George Braithwaite, offered overwhelmingly positive feedback about the trip to the US media. The US government invited the Chinese table tennis team to visit the US, and President Nixon indicated his plan for visiting China the next year (1972). One year after the ping-pong democracy held in China, Chinese table tennis delegation had an 18-day trip visiting the US, Canada, Mexico, and Peru on April 12–30, 1972. In 2011, the White House in the US hosted a rematch of ping-pong diplomacy with participation of both current national players and the original 1971 and 1972 players to celebrate its 40th anniversary.[20]

Ping-pong diplomacy, in fact, was one of the several events that showed table tennis and politics were inseparable for China based on the principle of "Friendship First, Competition Second" from the 1950s to the 1980s. For instance, China paid for the expenses for players from more than 50 countries to participate in the Asian–African Table Tennis Friendship Invitational Tournament in Beijing in October 1971. During the tournament, the United Nations accepted China as a member in place of Taiwan. Afterwards, China further utilized table tennis as a means to develop relations with other countries, such as inviting Thailand Malaysia, and the Philippines teams for visits in 1972 and hosting the Asia–Africa–Latin America Table Tennis Friendship Tournament in 1973. To further demonstrate the concept of "Friendship First" in sport, in the 1975 World Championship, China dominated all of the events but let North Korea win the women's singles. Therefore, ping-pong diplomacy should not be viewed as a way to develop relations only with the US but around the world. China also used other sports in addition to table tennis as means to build friendships with 79 countries in 1972 alone. In the 1980s, however, the sport ideals of "Friendship First" stemmed from the Cold War was transformed to "patriotism first" by winning gold medals and showing national pride. In addition to the World Championships and Olympic Games, the World Cup is the most important competition in table tennis held annually since 1980. China continued to dominate in table tennis in the 1970s and 1980s, especially for the women's team who won 20 World Championships titles and only lost two from 1975 to 2016.[21]

Table tennis became an Olympic sport in 1988 in Seoul, Korea. Initially, there were singles and doubles events for both men and women; doubles events were replaced by team events since 2008. Becoming an Olympic sport, table tennis gained attention and financial investment from various countries, which led to more advanced equipment with continual improvement in technology.[22] During this time, the Chinese men's team experienced challenges when Sweden won three consecutive world team champion titles in 1989, 1991, and 1993. The Swedish team was led by table tennis legend Jan-Ove Waldner. Waldner has the nickname "Evergreen Tree" due to his extraordinary longevity and competitiveness in table tennis – playing international-level table tennis for 30 years since he was 16, including five Olympic Games. Moreover, he is first male player (1992) and the only non-Chinese who accomplishes a table tennis grand slam – World Champion, World Cup Winner, and Olympic Gold Medal – in the history. There are only four other male players who reach this pinnacle as of 2017: Liu Guoliang (1999), Kong Linghui (2000), Zhang Jike (2012), and Ma Long (2016).[23]

In addition to being the second male player who achieved a grand slam, Liu Guoliang is considered one of the greatest coach. He was appointed as the Chinese Men's National Team Head Coach when he retired at the age of 27 in 2001. Liu is particularly famous for using tactical and mental strategies in in and outside of the sport. For instance, he built a communication system with his players by clapping hands and shouting specific cues when actual coaching was not allowed during the game. Moreover, Liu taught his players the degree of aggressiveness they should play and when to take risks in competitions based on the game scores. Outside of the sport, he understands his players very well and uses effective strategies to motivate individual players by considering their personality. For example, Liu helped World Champions Ma Lin and Wang Hao gain motivation and confidence through goal setting and external motivators.[24]

Liu Guoliang's advanced tactical and psychological strategies, however, could seem unfair to his players. At the 2012 London Olympics, Wang Hao and Zhang Jike competed for the men's singles gold medal. Both players had relatively equal chance to win a gold medal and also earn a career grand slam as both of them had already won the World Championships and the World Cup. The night before the match, surprisingly, Liu privately told Wang to lose the finals match to Zhang. The reason was that the Chinese team had to play against South Korea the next day for the team's finals; Liu thought that Wang was more mature and would recover psychologically after a loss much better than Zhang in order to win the team match the next day. Wang proudly told *Telegraph* before the finals match, "I don't feel any pressure now because we are both playing for China." Liu's strategy was successful, because Zhang won his singles match and Zhang and Wang won their doubles match the team match against South Korea, winning another gold medal for China. Nevertheless, the strategy could seem a disservice to Wang, especially since he received his third silver medal in singles instead of a gold, and he could never achieve a career grand slam as a result.[25] Regardless, Wang was a player who made a big impact in the world of table tennis due to his unique playing style. He was the first penhold player who brought to the world unprecedented offensive penhold backhand using the reverse penhold backhand (RPB) technique rather than the traditional defensive backhand technique. Since then, the majority of the penhold player adopt his dual-sided offensive style using RPB. Another "first" about Wang was related to his personal life, in which he was the first Chinese table tennis player who was ever allowed to date a fellow player.[26]

As previously mentioned, Chinese female players have dominated the table tennis world to an even greater extent than the male players. While Yao Ming may be the tallest (2.26 m), famous male basketball player from China, Deng Yaping may be the shortest (1.50 m), famous female table tennis player from China. Deng was indeed rejected by the national team at a young age due to her height. After Deng managed to be selected to the team at the age of 15, she set several records in women's table tennis, such as winning 18 World Championship and World Cup titles and four Olympic gold medals including singles, doubles, and team events. Moreover, Deng maintained the number one ranking for eight years and was voted Chinese female athlete of the century. Deng is as successful off the table as she is on the table. After she retired at a relatively young age of 24, Deng went back to school and eventually earned her doctorate at Cambridge University with her thesis titled "The impact of the Olympic Games on Chinese development: A multi-disciplinary analysis." Deng also received a seat at the People's Political Consultative Conference of the Chinese Communist Party. Beyond Deng, Wang Nan and Zhang Yining are the other two female table tennis legends who won four Olympic gold medals.[27]

With such a great pool of table tennis players in China during the past two decades, making the Chinese team is often harder than defeating the top players from any other countries. Many of the second-tier players who are not selected represent China in big competitions, therefore, emigrate to other countries in order to reach their dream of competing at the World Championships and the Olympic Games. At the 2016 Rio Olympics, 44 table tennis players were Chinese-born but only six of them actually represented China; others represented countries such as the Singapore, Germany, Spain, Brazil, and so on. The six players representing China still dominated and won all four events, which extended the number of table tennis gold medals to 28 out of the 32 possible total.[28]

Because of China's dominance in table tennis, the ITTF has changed the rules multiple times in the past two decades in an effort to enhance the chance of other countries winning in competitions. In 2001, the ITTF increased the size of the ball from 38 mm to 40 mm diameter so as to reduce the speed and spin of the shots, changed the game from 21 to 11 points which increased the chance for an upset, and set a service rule that players cannot hide their serve. Since Chinese table tennis players are famous for their serve and spin, these changes might attenuate their strengths. These changes seemingly did not stop China from winning more titles. We used to see three Chinese table tennis players on the Olympic podium for the singles events, but it would have been impossible since the 2012 London Olympics. The rule change was that a maximum of only two players can represent one country to play a singles event, and only three players can play a team event in the Olympics. The ITTF President at that time, Adham Sharara, admitted the change was targeting China's dominance, "The [Olympic] tournament cannot be dominated as before by the Chinese."[29] Once again, the rule change did not stop Chinese players from winning gold medals in men's and women's team events and both gold and silver medals for men's and women's singles in 2012 and 2016 Olympics. In 2014, the table tennis ball material was changed from celluloid to non-celluloid (as called plastic or poly balls), and the size of the ball was enlarged to 40+ mm diameter. The rationale behind this change was to lower the cost and reduce the risks of fire hazard. More recent change was the implementation of a new World Ranking system in 2018. The aim of creating this ranking system was to "count on a larger variety of nationalities and higher presence of players proceeding from all continents"; therefore, some top-ranked Chinese players who do not participate in many tournaments would be affected. The accuracy and effectiveness of this system would debut soon around the time of this book publication.[30]

Today, table tennis is one of the largest sports in the world based on participation. The ITTF consists of 226 member associations, which include 58 in Europe, 51 in Africa, 45 in Asia, 40 in Latin America, 24 in Oceania, and four in Northern America. Table tennis an inclusive sport not only across gender and countries but also across social classes and levels of physical and mental ability. The ITTF has been developing a "Table Tennis for ALL" program to promote universality and inclusiveness of the sport. For instance, an annual World Table Tennis Day is held on April 6 to celebrate the universality of table tennis, with 453 events in 93 countries in 2017.[31] Table tennis was included as a para sport early in the first Paralympic Games in 1960. Currently, para table tennis participation is estimated to be over 40 million competitive players in more than 100 countries. Players are classified into one of the 11 categories based on physical disability ranging from sitting in a wheelchair (Class 1–5) to standing (Class 6–10) or intellectual impairment (Class 11). These events are more balanced in terms of competitiveness across different countries, because they are not dominated by Chinese players. Ibrahim Hamato, an armless Class 6 Champion from Egypt, is arguably the most famous Para table tennis players due to his unique playing style – holding the racket with his month and tossing the ball with his foot when serving. A YouTube video *Nothing is Impossible* of his plays with other world-class players such as Wang Hao and Ma Long has accumulated more than 3 million views as of 2017.[32]

You may now know much more about table tennis. But does ping pong still exist? Ping pong tournaments might have been long forgotten since ping pong has been perceived as a basement game instead of a real sport. Yet, ping pong tournaments were brought back to the world when the chairman of a British promotion company Matchroom Sport, Barry Hearn, started organizing the World Championships of Ping Pong in 2011. Tournament participants have to play with a sandpaper wood instead of sponged rubbers as a rule of ping pong. In 2013, the championships became an annual event held at the Alexandra Palace in London and attracted more than 8,000 spectators every year. The attraction might have come from a more balanced competition not dominated by China, since only one Chinese player had won the title (2017).[33]

Although the sport of table tennis, or ping pong if you prefer, has largely given way to competitiveness mostly in Asia and Europe, it still entertains many other regions of the world. Easy access to tables, cheap equipment, and inclusive atmosphere of the sport have reached a diverse group of players across the world – playing at a gym, a park, school, home, a bar, or anywhere you can imagine. It may be shocking to some that table tennis was once a black-tie sport, played only among the Victorians who had high social status in England. To end this chapter, let's appreciate what Ivor Montagu and the ITTF, as well as all table tennis enthusiasts, have done in the past century to popularize this sport for its global reach and inclusiveness.

Notes

1   C. Tennyson, "They Taught the World to Play," *Victorian Studies*, 2,3 (March 1959), 211–22.
2   J. Riordan, "The Hon. Ivor Montagu (1904–1984): Founding Father of Table Tennis," *Sport in History*, 28,3 (September 2008), 512–30.
3   Riordan, "The Hon. Ivor Montagu (1904–1984): Founding Father of Table Tennis'; I. Montagu, *The Youngest Son: Autobiographical Sketches* (London: Lawrence & Wishart, 1970), 220 (quote).
4   S. G. Jones, *Sport Politics and the Working Class: Organised Labour and Sport in Inter-war Britain* (Manchester: Manchester University Press, 1988), 108.
5   See G. Eisner, H. Kaufman, and M. Lammer, *Sport and Physical Education in Jewish History* (Netanya: Wingate Institute, 2003), 48–55, 157–69.
6   Montagu, *The Youngest Son*, 220 (quote).

7 T. Boggan, *History of US Table Tennis Vol. I: 1928–1939* (Geneva: Below the Line Productions, 2000), 9–11 (quote, 9).

8 Ibid., 12–40.

9 Ibid., 43–53.

10 See www.ittf.com/2017/05/10/a-question-of-gender (May 10, 2017).

11 See www.bbc.com/sport/olympics/40226990 (June 9, 2017).

12 E. Snow, *Red Star Over China* (New York: Grove Press, 1938), 281 (quote).

13 Boggan *History*, 67–72; R. McAfee, *Table Tennis: Steps to Success* (Champaign, IL: Human Kinetics, 2009), 9.

14 T. Boggan, *History of US Table Tennis Vol. II: 1940–1949* (Geneva: Below the Line Productions, 2003), 184–85.

15 McAfee, *Table Tennis*, 9; www.nytimes.com/2012/07/30/sports/olympics/china-brings-its-past-to-ping-pongs-birthplace.html (July 30, 2012); http://factsanddetails.com/china/cat12/sub77/item1015.html#chapter-0 (June 2015).

16 McAfee, *Table Tennis*, 9; http://factsanddetails.com/china/cat12/sub77/item1015.html#chapter-0 (quote, June 2015).

17 See http://home.covad.net/~chunglau/021002.htm (February 10, 2002).

18 Z. Hong and Y. Sun, "The Butterfly Effect and the Making of 'Ping-Pong Diplomacy'," *Journal of Contemporary China,* 9,25 (2000), 429–48.

19 Hong and Sun, "The Butterfly Effect and the Making of "Ping-Pong Diplomacy""; www.historyinanhour.com/2011/04/10/ping-pong-diplomacy (April 10, 2011); www.nytimes.com/2013/02/12/world/asia/zhuang-zedong-winner-in-china-foreign-relations-and-ping-pong-dies-at-72.html (February 11, 2013).

20 Hong and Sun, "The Butterfly Effect and the Making of "Ping-Pong Diplomacy""; http://china.usc.edu/calendar/40th-anniversary-ping-pong-diplomacy-rematch (April 10, 2011).

21 Hong and Sun, "The Butterfly Effect and the Making of "Ping-Pong Diplomacy""; P. Luo, "Political Influence on Physical Education and Sport in the People's Republic of China," *International Review for the Sociology of Sport,* 30,1 (March 2000), 47–58; G. Wang, ""Friendship First": China's Sports Diplomacy during the Cold War," *The Journal of American–East Asian Relations,* 12,3–4 (Fall-Winter 2003), 133–53.

22 McAfee, *Table Tennis*, 9.

23 See www.theguardian.com/sport/2012/aug/02/london-2012-table-tennis-zhang-jike?newsfeed=true (August 2, 2012); www.gametablesonline.com/blog/jan-ove-evergreen-waldner-table-tennis-legend (December 15, 2013).

24 See www.experttabletennis.com/liu-guoliang-on-psychology-tactics-and-player-development (April 29, 2013); https://pingsunday.com/liu-guoliang-genius-table-tennis-tactics (November 2, 2017).

25 See www.theatlantic.com/international/archive/2012/08/china-still-the-world-champ-is-falling-out-of-love-with-table-tennis/260845 (August 8, 2012); www.experttabletennis.com/liu-guoliang-on-psychology-tactics-and-player-development (April 29, 2013).

26 See www.theatlantic.com/international/archive/2012/08/china-still-the-world-champ-is-falling-out-of-love-with-table-tennis/260845 (August 8, 2012); http://factsanddetails.com/china/cat12/sub77/item1015.html#chapter-0 (June 2015).

27 Y. Zhao, *Deng Yaping's Arduous Study Years* (Beijing: China Youth Press, 2008), 223–28; http://factsanddetails.com/china/cat12/sub77/item1015.html#chapter-0 (June 2015).

28 See http://factsanddetails.com/china/cat12/sub77/item1015.html#chapter-0 (June 2015); www.businessinsider.com/why-china-is-so-good-at-table-tennis-2016-8 (August 18, 2016).

29 See http://factsanddetails.com/china/cat12/sub77/item1015.html#chapter-0 (June 2015, quote).

30 Y. Inaba et al., "Effect of Changing Table Tennis Ball Material from Celluloid to Plastic on the Post-Collision Ball Trajectory," *Journal of Human Kinetics,* 55 (January 2017), 29–38; www.ittf.com/2017/11/07/ittf-implement-new-world-ranking-system-2018 (November 7, 2017).

31 See www.ittf.com/det/tt4all (December 7, 2017).

32 See http://tabletennis.about.com/od/disabledplayers/fl/Ibrahim-Hamato-The-Armless-Table-Tennis-Player.htm (August 22, 2016); www.paralympic.org/table-tennis (December 7, 2017) www.youtube.com/watch?v=aDdh2439hnU (May 9, 2014).

33 See www.bbc.com/sport/35418169 (January 27, 2016).

23

Tennis

Chad Morgan and Samuel Nabors

Tennis began with a couple of "gents" named Fore and Marshall hitting rubber balls back and forth between each other on a strip of greensward. This was the beginning of the first and still the most prestigious tournament in tennis. Thus, Wimbledon was born, or so people think. Surely but mysteriously, from much deeper in history, a descendant of an old sport which evolved, was refined and continues to exist on its own as a separate pastime – played outdoors in curiously conformed, concrete-walled courts – known variously as real tennis, royal tennis or court tennis.[1] Its precise origins remain shrouded in conjecture, contrasting notions and theories, and lack of documentation despite the diligent delving of historians.[2] Many historians believe that the game came from northern France. It was here that tennis first developed into an upper-class game that was played by none other than the kings of France. The game moved from royal palace to royal palace. Rackets first appeared in the 16th century in France. Originally, they were used to play a game called *gioco di rachette*. It is believed that the scoring system sprang from the simple nature of a clock. But even this stirs confusion due to the score going from 30 to 40 and not 45. The roots of tennis are hazy through the history's unforgiving fact that if there is no record, then we have no concrete proof as to where to origins began. All we have are the clues. From those clues, we can try and piece together the puzzle of where this game began. Where the name of the game comes from isn't clearly known. One of the explanations was that the term "tennis" derived from the French *tendere* meaning "to hold." In 1918, C.E. Thomas offered a slightly more logical explanation of where "tennis" comes from. According to him, the derivation is from the French word *tenez*, meaning "take it." The reason that most historians thinks that this game began in France is that all of the common roots involve the French language. Another explanation points to two towns that are widely separated, one on the Nile River in Egypt, and the other in northern France, having "tennis" as their name.[3]

Everything becomes much clearer when the subject changes to modern lawn tennis. The history is clear and well documented. Its arrival was announced on March 7, 1874, in two papers, the Court Journal, read by almost all of the British upper class as well as those who aspired to join, and the Army & Navy Gazette, read by the military, which was stationed worldwide – for them the sun truly never set on the vast British Empire.[4] Major Walter Springfield received a patent (no. 685) for "A Portable Court of Playing Tennis." Those who read *The Field* on March 21, 1874 were informed in detail of the new game, for it reproduced much of the information about the Major's game of lawn tennis. The game grew rapidly. It was sold in a painted box, 36 × 12 × 6 inches and contained poles, pegs, and netting for forming the court, 4 tennis bats, a bag of balls, mallet, brush, and the instructive book titled *The Book of the Game*. It wasn't long before countries such as India, China, Russia were being sold the set. Wingfield was smart in that he marketed the game as a method to exercise for both male and females of all ages. It was a simple game that could be played without buying a set. Rackets from other sports could be used to try out the new phenomenon.

It is believed that Earnshill in Somerset was the first place that the game was played officially. Several other sites of early play have been put forth but again, lacking in documentation. The first documented exhibition occurred following The Field announcement of May 4, 1874, which read in part, "It [lawn tennis] may be seen and played next week, on and after the opening of the Princes Cricket Ground, and also at the Polo Club – Lillie-bridge."[5] Private homes with croquet lawns, public parks, and clubs became the playing grounds of tennis. The first London clubs to take up the sport were Marylebone Cricket Club, Hurlingham Club, and Princes Club.

In the spring of 1877, the All England Club, behind the leadership of Henry Jones, decided to hold a tennis tournament. And with Wingfield's failure to renew his patent on the game, there was nothing stopping them. This tournament would be known as the original Wimbledon. The inaugural Wimbledon embraced only one event, the men's singles.[6] Only 22 players made up the tournament in 1877. It cost about one shilling (then 25 cents) to see the final. Ultimately, Spencer Gore, a rackets player defeated William Marshall, a refugee from real tennis, in the final, 6–1, 6–2, 6–4.[7] A year later, the Scottish Championships in Edinburgh was inaugurated. The Irish Championships shortly followed with the introduction of women's singles as well as mixed events which was more an exclusive event, only allowing members of the Fitzwilliam Club to view. A few years later the first tennis association was formed. The Northern Lawn Tennis Association (of England) took over the reins of tennis until it joined forces with the All England Club in 1888. These two organizations would share funds raised by The Championships. However, the decline in the popularity of tennis brought small draws and reduced attendance.[8] The introduction of the women's singles and men's doubles events came about in 1884. Maud Watson emerged as the first Wimbledon women's singles champion out of a draw of 13 competitors. Although, officially, there was not a women's championship until 1913.

In 1922, the All England Club moved to its present-day site in a picturesque hollow at the foot of Church Road near Wimbledon Common, at a construction cost of 140,000 pounds. The new Centre Court had 9,989 seats, with room for 3,600 standees. The new arena was rung in with the attendance of King George V and Queen Mary.

Tennis followed *The Field* to North America through trade and naval passageways from continent to continent. The first recorded is October 8, 1874. It took place in the then-remote Camp Apache, Arizona Territory, and north of Tuscan. The East coast is where tennis really started to pick up some steam. Port cities such as Boston, Newport, New York, and Philadelphia became hubs of the sport. It also independently made its way to New Orleans and San Francisco. The first tennis club in the US was the New Orleans Lawn Tennis Club established in 1876. Clubs such as Boston's Longwood Cricket Club would add lawn tennis to their list of amenities two years later. A clear leader emerged within the tennis scene in the form of James Dwight. He was known as "the father of American lawn tennis" and organized the first tournament to take place on American soil in 1876. He was also the president of the United States Lawn Tennis Association, which formed in 1881. Dwight was president for 21 of the associations first 31 years. Not only was he successful on his home soil but he was the first American tennis player to win a title in the motherland in 1885. Through his ventures through competition on British soil and the connections that he was establishing within the LTA, he brought about the development of the Davis Cup. The Davis Cup began in 1990 and Dwight drew up the rules himself. The Davis Cup, at this point in time, was an international competition between the United States and Great Britain.

After a couple of tournaments with no standardization of the rules or equipment established, controversy about the correct way to play lawn tennis highlighted the need for fully accepted regulation became an issue. To resolve this, a meeting was arranged at the Fifth Avenue Hotel in New York on May 21, 1881, in the name of three prominent clubs: The Beacon Park Athletic Association of Boston, the Staten Island Cricket and Baseball Club of New York, and the All Philadelphia Lawn Tennis Committee.[9] Thirty-three clubs were represented at the meeting where the United States National Lawn Tennis Association was born. The rules that were already in place in Britain with the LTA were adopted and first implemented in the inaugural National Championships (hereinafter call the US Championships) that took place at Newport Casino in Newport, Rhode Island. It began on August 31st, 1881 and saw Richard "Dick" Sears win the final without losing a single set. Sears like the Renshaw's in Great Britain would dominate the early stages of American tennis.

The women's game in the US started mainly because the women came forward themselves with a desire to participate. In 1887, the first US Women's Championship was held at the Philadelphia Cricket Club. Ellen Hansell, a representative of the host club, was crowned the victor in a 6–1, 6–0 dismantling of Laura Knight.

In 1923, a new stadium was constructed at the West Side Tennis Club grounds in Forest Hills. Built at a cost of $250,000, the concrete horseshoe that would eventually seat 14,000 opened on August 10 with the inauguration of Wightman Cup matches. The Wightman Cup, much like the Davis Cup at the time, was a women's team competition that would see the US against Great Britain. It was an ideal way that Julian Myrick, a US Lawn Tennis Association official, had thought up that would be perfect for the opening of the new venue at Forest Hills. The competition itself consisted of five singles matches and two doubles.

The US Open moved for the third time in 1978 to a public park in Flushing Meadows, Queens, New York. The US National Tennis Center was dedicated on August 30, and its main arena Louis Armstrong, named for a local jazz legend, accommodated 20,000 spectators, with barely a bad seat in the house. In addition to the steeply banked, red, white and blue stadium, the complex included a 6,000 seat grand stand, 25 additional light courts and nine indoor courts, all with the same acrylic asphalt surface that approximates the hard courts most Americans play on.[10] This was a state of the art facility that was meant to become the center of the tennis universe.

The growth of lawn tennis around the rest of the world was fast. Clubs were founded in Scotland, Brazil, and India in 1875. It was played in Germany in 1876. In 1877, the Decimal Club was started in Paris, the first club in France. Australia, Sweden, Italy, Hungary, and Peru had lawn tennis courts in 1878, and the first Australian tournament was the Victorian Championship in 1879.[11] Denmark and Switzerland date their beginnings from 1880, Argentina from 1881, the Netherlands in 1882, Jamaica in 1883, and in 1885 both Greece and Turkey were all embracing the new game. Lawn tennis came to Lebanon in 1889, to Egypt in 1890 and to Finland in the same year. The Australian Championships, which would become known as the third major, was staged in 1905. South Africa's first championship was staged in 1891. The fourth major was the French Championships which didn't take place until 1925 due to war times. Davis Cup played a huge part in boosting tennis internationally. Prior to 1914, when war brought the competition to a temporary halt, there were nine entries: The US, British Isles, Belgium, France, Australasia, Austria, Germany, Canada, and South Africa were all involved. 6 years after South Africa staged its first tournament, tennis was featured as a part of the modern Olympic games in Athens,

Greece. With more and more countries getting involved with lawn tennis, and its popularity surging after its appearance in the games, it was necessary for the International Lawn Tennis Federation to be established to govern tennis throughout the world. In its inaugural meeting in Paris on March 1, 1913, 12 countries made up the foundation. This excluded the United States because they felt slighted by the various "World Championship" titles that were embraced by the French and Brits. The US would not join with the ITLF until 1978, after the war and the titles of the tournaments were abolished.

On October 11, 1940, international play ceased to continue due to four bombs being dropped on Centre Court in London in the midst of World War II. There was a huge hole in Centre Court as a result of the bombing and Wimbledon became a civil defense center. Stade Roland Garros had a shameful wartime chapter as a concentration camp, first run by a frantically French government to intern political dissidents, aliens and other suspect types.[12] Wimbledon and Roland Garros (the French Open) were out of commission until 1946. This halt in play in Europe was advantageous to the Americans because the state of tennis wasn't affected as significantly as other countries that had been seeing success prior to the war. Despite Pearl Harbor in 1942, the White House saw sports as a means to boost moral for the home front and troops overseas. Tennis in the US continued. Tennis players involved with the defense of the United States including Naval Seaman Bobby Riggs, Army Air Force Sergeant Frank Parker, and Army Air Corps Lieutenant Don Budge were all still able to play.

In 1947, four countries were re-instated to rejoin the International Tennis Federation. These countries included Italy, Hungary, Romania, and Finland. Germany and Japan were re-admitted in 1950. That same year, Althea Gibson broke the color barrier in tennis by becoming the first black tennis player to play at the US Championships. Gibson didn't stop there. She won the French Championships in 1956 as well as the US Championships and Wimbledon in 1957 to become the first woman of "color" to do so. Richard Nixon presented her with the US trophy. As the issue of equality progressed even further, the Davis Cup nations eventually voted South Africa and Rhodesia out of the competition in 1970 for its demonstrations against their racial policies. Players from various countries refused to play them which made the draw disruptive.[13]

Women's international tennis was taken to a new level when the Federation Cup was launched on the 50th anniversary of ILTF. The competition attracted 16 entries. During a time of pure dominance by US women, nothing changed. They won the first Federation Cup in 1963. Women's tennis in its entirety, made gigantic strides forward in the 1970's. Gladys Heldman splitting away from the ILTF to create a separate tour due to the difference in prize money collected between men and women was the first step forward. The "Battle of the Sexes" in 1973, was a match that involved 29-year-old Billie Jean King against Bobby Riggs, the outspoken hustler and former Wimbledon champion. It was a sociological phenomenon that drew a crowd of 30,472 as well as 50 million television viewers. King won the match 6–4, 6–3, 6–3. The whole ballyhooed extravaganza was just right for the times, and it became a national media event, front page in papers and magazines across the country, even the world. King exulted in her victory, not as a great competitive triumph but as the "culmination" of her years of striving to demonstrate that tennis could be big-league entertainment for the masses and that women could play.[14]

By 1900, all the strokes, tactics, and strategies had become a part of the game. Willie and Ernest Renshaw, who dominated the tennis courts in its elementary stages, contributed to the net game and tactics such as the "serve and volley." The serve and volley, throughout the history of tennis, especially at Wimbledon, was the chosen strategy utilized by many champions to claim glory until the technology related to the strings and rackets surpassed the strategy itself. Herbert Lawford won Wimbledon in 1887, and he is credited to be one of the first to impart topspin onto the clothed-rubber ball. The serve evolved in 1878 when a former Cambridge real tennis player, A. T. Meyers showed up to the court serving overhand instead of underhand. Holcombe Ward and Dwight Davis were also pioneers of a technique that was known then as the American twist serve and is known today as the "kicker." The two-handed backhand was introduced in 1933 by an Australian by the name of Vivian McGrath. This technique was revolutionary. That same year, Jiro Satoh was the first tennis player to wear shorts on Centre Court at Wimbledon. The Prince of Wales said, "I see no reason on earth why any woman should not wear shorts for lawn tennis. They are comfortable, and quite the most practical costume for the game; and I don't think the wearers lose anything in looks," about the shorts.[15]

More people than ever before were exposed to the game in 1937 when Wimbledon was covered on Television. With 4 × 3 inch screens, televisions were now a vehicle of growth for the sport even though American Lawn Tennis Magazine said, "When the entire court was shown the figures of the players were so small and far-away-looking that only general movements could be followed; the ball was seldom discernable."[16]

Racket technologies leaped forward in 1967 with the introduction of steel being integrated into the frames. Prince released the famous T-2000, made famous by Jimmy Connors, was a milestone for racket technology. The technology has continued to evolve since, offering easier access to more power, spin and speed of the ball coming off of the racket, thus making the game progressively quicker year after year. Oversized rackets were introduced in 1976, which increased the head size. This allowed for a much bigger "sweet spot" and an increase in power. With no limits to what companies could do to enhance equipment, there was loop hole that was ceased upon by a German former horticulturist named Werner Fischer. He invited the "spaghetti" racket which used a radical stringing technique that could be applied to any standard racket at the time. It involved two sets of vertical strings, supported by five or six cross strings threaded through them, and braced with fish line, adhesive tape, rope or other protuberances. These "spaghetti" could supply tremendous power because of the "trampoline-effect" where the ball would sink deep into the double layer of strings and being propelled out. This invention led to the development of the rules for the racket and enforcement of those rules.

From the late 1980s to the present day, tennis has seen many new innovations and technologies implemented, including changing the color of the balls from white to yellow, the utilization of sports sciences to enhance the performance of tennis athletes, strings, material to craft rackets and Hawk-Eye. Hawk-Eye is a complex computer system used to visually track the trajectory of ball and display a record of its statistically most likely path as a moving image. This would allow players to challenge the umpires initial call on whether or not a ball was "good" or not. The system was first on a professional level at the Hopman Cup in 2006 and at the Nasdaq-100 Open for a tour level event. On March 19, 2008, the organizing bodies announced a uniform system of rules: three unsuccessful challenges per set, with an additional challenge if the set reaches a tiebreak. In an advantage set (a set with no tiebreak) players are allowed three unsuccessful challenges every 12 games. The next scheduled event on the men and women's tour, the 2008 Sony Ericsson Open, was the first event to implement these new, standardized rules.[17]

In 1927, the first professional tournament played was in the United States in New York. Vinnie Richards won $1,000 dollars in a $2,000 pot over Howard Kinsey, 11–9, 6–4, 6–3 at the public courts of the long since disappeared Notlek Tennis Club in Manhattan. The idea of pro tennis at this time didn't have much appeal to it but it would soon become a hot topic of much debate and controversy in the tennis world. Three years later the most dynamic figure in the sport at the time, Bill Tilden, decided to turn pro. In the beginning, professional circuits usually involved a promoter and two well-known players that would tour around the United States playing exhibition matches against one another time after time for pay. For example, one of first circuits involved Tilden playing Karel Kozeluh 76 times on a cross-country tour that grossed $283,000.

The start of the real transition from amateurism to professionalism was in 1946. Professionals wandered almost anonymously, city to city, continent to continent, a gypsy band on a treadmill of one-nighters plus a few tournaments. They took their money in broad daylight, on the table, but in doing so, reaped minimal attention when compared to the "shamateurs," who were often paid generous "expenses" as gate primers by tournaments or by their national federations, thereby maintaining their eligibility for team events such as Davis and, later, Federation Cups.[18] There were harsh punishments enacted by the associations to anyone that entertained the idea of going pro. None made more of an example of then, Pauline Betz, who was indefinitely suspended in 1947 for simply discussing turning professional. The power that the associations had over the players was on full display again when Earl Cochell was banned for life after his outburst and unacceptable behavior at the US Championships in 1951. However, the growth in popularity of professional tennis was undeniable as a match between Jack Kramer and Bobby Riggs attracted 15,114 customers to Madison Square Garden on December 26, 1948. That night Kramer earned $89,000 while Riggs earned $50,000. The late 50's a trend developed that saw Kramer, a former player and promoter, pick off champion after champion to add them to the professional ranks. Amateur tournaments became a farm for professionals.

1967 was last year of the amateur era. Signs such as the Laver vs. Rosewall match that was televised on BBC dwarfing the Wimbledon final in sheer audience numbers shed light on the fact that tennis was about to change. The first step in bringing in the "Open" era was when the LTA voted overwhelmingly to make British tournaments Open in 1968. They chose to go it alone causing the rest of the tennis world to follow suit. Due commercial pressures and amateurs continuing to take money under the table, Hernan David felt comfortable with pushing this initiative forward. Hernan, along with the support of USLTA president Bob Kellenher, created enough momentum to cause emergency meeting was held by the ILTF in Paris where it was decided that there would be 12 open tournaments in 1968. In order to make this happen four compromises were made between the support parties. The first two were that amateurs could not accept money and teaching professionals could only compete with amateurs only in open events. Also, two terms were coined. A "contract professional" made their living playing tennis but did not accept the authority of their national associations affiliated to the ILTF. The signed on with independent contractors and promoters such as Jack Kramer. A "registered player" could accept prize money in open tournaments but still obeyed their national associations and retained eligibility for international competition although it only lasted until 1969.[19] The first Open tournament was launched a month after the contract was approved. The British Hard Court Championships had a total purse of $14,000. With the introduction of the open tournaments, it finally allowed for the question of, "Who is the best?" to be answered. Amateurs and professionals were now competing against one another for the first time in tennis history. This monumental change within the sport saw the beginning of the International Lawn Tennis Federation and revenues from television rights grow which, ultimately, helped grow the popularity of the game even more on an international level. The ITF's main competitor was the World Championships of Tennis which was founded in 1966 by Texas oilman Lamar Hunt and his nephew, All Hill, Jr. Both the ITF and WCT put together new systems where points where accumulated throughout the year to determine bonuses and top finishers in the standings. The players became the beneficiaries of this new model making more money than ever before.

Another significant development came along in 1972. The Association of Tennis Professionals was formed. Some 50 players paid $400 initial dues, and Washington attorney Donald Dell, the former US Davis Cup captain and personal manager for a number of top players, enlisted none other than Jack Kramer as executive director.[20] The ATP was carefully constituted and loomed as a major new force in the pro game's politics and administration.

The complete breakdown of amateurism occurred in 1988 when tennis returned to the Olympics as a medal sport. Tennis led the way with this movement of professionals competing in international competition with the "Dream Team" for the United States basketball following in 1992. The same year, John McEnroe announced that the ATP would be taking over the men's tour in 1990 after a long stint of the ITF and WCT running the show their own tours. Under complete control by the players, the ATP launched 75 tournaments on six continents and a season ending singles and doubles championship.

Billie Jean King is an American former tennis player who was formerly world number one and is known as a major trailblazer in women's tennis. Widely regarded as one of the greatest female tennis players of all time, she won a total of 12 Grand Slam titles and six Wimbledon singles crowns and was known for her clinical volleying and offensive minded play.[21] However, more famously, she is known as the "pioneer, godmother and midwife of women's tennis"[22] for her tireless work in promoting and legitimizing women's tennis in the early 1970s. She famously defeated male tennis player Bobby Riggs in the *Battle of the Sexes* in 1973 and was the founder of the Women's Tennis Association. She was inducted into the International Tennis Hall of Fame in 1987 and has won a host of other awards for her work including the Presidential Medal of Freedom for her work in advocating women's and LGBT rights.[23]

Chris Evert is an American former tennis player and former world tennis number one. Evert is a highly influential and emulated role model in the history of tennis. She reached 34 Grand Slam singles finals, a record that continues to stand to this day. She burst onto the world tennis scene as a 16-year-old semifinalist in the 1971 US Open and by age 19 she was world number one and Grand Slam champion. She still holds records for the most French Open women's titles and the highest winning percentage in the Open era, coming in just below 90%. Evert won at least one Grand Slam title for 13 straight years and her dominance was only kept in check by her intense rivalry with Marina Navratilova.[24] She also served as president of the Women's Tennis Association on two associations and was unanimously inducted into the International Tennis Hall of Fame in 1995. Her dominance at such a young age helped usher in the "age of prodigy" and had a profound impact on women's tennis that is still felt today.[25]

John McEnroe is an American former tennis player and former world tennis number one. McEnroe was known as the "high priest of serve-and-volley" for his quality attacking play and his record year of 1984 in which he won 13 titles and achieved a winning percentage of 96.5% has never been bettered.[26] However, McEnroe's major impact on the tennis world comes from his volatile on-court demeanor that earned him the "Superbrat" nickname. McEnroe's constant screaming at officials and nasty spats with umpires helped illuminate the fact that tennis was being played by professional players but officiated by amateurs.[27] McEnroe's temper would eventually bring about the use of professional officials and helped introduced technology to assist officials in line calling. In addition, McEnroe popularized Nike tennis shoes and his use of graphite frame racquets helped eliminate the use of wooden racquets.[28] His *"you cannot be serious!"* outburst at Wimbledon was named the "top Wimbledon moment of all time" by readers of the British newspaper *The Telegraph*.[29] McEnroe was inducted into the International Tennis Hall of Fame in 1999 and continues to work in the tennis world as a highly esteemed and influential commentator.

Steffi Graf is a former German tennis player and world number one. At age 19, she became the sport's first and only winner of the Golden Grand Slam, achieved by winning the Grand Slam and Olympic gold in the same calendar year.[30] Graf is the only tennis player to have won each Grand Slam event on four separate occasions and she holds the record for longest reigning number one in the history of computer rankings.[31] Her playstyle changed the sport for men and women as she was the first "aggressive baseliner" in women's tennis and set a template for women in the sport to come.[32] Her dominant forehand shot led to the forehand being taught as a primary focus of attack.[33] In addition to her numerous on court achievements, Graf personified the power shift in tennis from the United States to Europe, since Graf's era, many more Europeans have held the top ranking in the sport compared to Americans.

Andre Agassi is a retired American tennis player who was world number one and is known as one of the best players of the 1990s and early 2000s. Agassi won eight Grand Slam titles, was the first male player to win four Australian Open titles and is the only player to win what *Sports Illustrated* dubbed the "Career Super Slam," achieved by winning all four Grand Slam titles, the Olympic Gold Medal and the ATP World Tour Finals. Upon his retirement, the BBC called him "the biggest worldwide star in the sport's history."[34] His turbulent career captivated fans, rising and falling in rankings throughout his career and hitting peaks and valleys along the way. Agassi was the oldest man to rank number one in the world and set the standard for the "transformative career."[35] In addition to his on-court accomplishments, Agassi is renowned for his philanthropy work and has said his biggest career regret is not starting his philanthropic activities earlier.[36]

Venus and Serena Williams are American tennis players who, together, have shifted the culture of tennis with their athleticism, personalities and style. Between them they have 57 Grand Slam trophies and 8 Olympic gold medals in a dominant period stretching well over a decade. Both Venus and Serena have been ranked as world number one and despite questions early in their careers about their commitment to the game, both are still extremely competitive well into their 30s, outlasting the vast majority of their contemporaries. Serena holds the record for most Grand Slam singles titles in the Open era with 23 and as a doubles pair, the Williams sisters are undefeated in Grand Slam finals. Their dominance in the sport and presence in pop culture has normalized the sight of African-Americans in a sport traditionally dominated by white faces and they successfully pushed for achieving equal prize money in Wimbledon in 2007.[37] Their power and athleticism changed the women's game with their powerful serves and the dominance of their open-stance backhands helped make the shot a standard.[38] As they approach the age of 40, the ends of their careers are drawing closer but their legacies will be felt for generations to come.

Roger Federer is a Swiss professional tennis player who has won the most Grand Slam titles in the history of male tennis players. Federer's total of 302 weeks at the top of the ATP world rankings is another world record and he is considered by some to be the greatest tennis player of all time. Federer's massive on-court accomplishments have turned him into one of the most recognizable athletes in the world and his calm and composed demeanor and eloquent manner of speaking has helped restore tennis to a game of "sporting gentlemen" after a period when "bad boys" ruled the roost.[39] Federer's massive success and worldwide admiration has led to increased interest and investment into the sport with prize money soaring over the course of his career.[40] Federer has helped to establish the Laver Cup, which pits a team made up of European players against players from the rest of the world. The initial Laver Cup was contested in September 2017. Federer is one of the game's greatest ambassadors and his legacy will long be remembered both in and out of the game.

Maria Sharapova is a Russian professional tennis player who is one of the most famous female athletes in the world. Sharapova was born in Russia but moved to the USA with her father at a young age to further her career. She was Wimbledon champion at age 17 and by age 18 she was world number one, a title she has held on five separate occasions.[41] Her streak of winning one singles title per year from 2003 to 2015 is only bested by Steffi Graf, Marina Navratilova and Chris Evert and she has been called one of the best competitors in the sport by the likes of John McEnroe.[42] She was also the highest paid female athlete in the world at one point and has proven to be very smart with her money throughout her career, showing up in Forbes lists regularly.[43] Sharapova was the subject of controversy in 2016 after she tested positive for doping and was banned for two years by the International Tennis Federation. This suspension was later shortened to 15 months and Sharapova has recently resumed her career.

Li Na is a retired Chinese tennis player who was massively influential in popularizing tennis in China. She was the first Chinese player to win a pro title, the first to be ranked in the top 10 and the first to contest a Grand Slam final. She won the 2011 French Open and 2014 Australian Open and became the first player from East Asia to win a Grand Slam title. Her non-conformist attitude and style endeared her to fans and her success caused an influx of popularity and spending on tennis in China. Following her rise of success, prize money and events have exploded in China and she was recently named in *Time Magazine* as one of the 100 most influential people in the world.[44] Li Na's on court accomplishments made not match up with other tennis superstars but she represents the massive potential lying in the world's most populous nation.

Arthur Ashe was an American tennis player who won three Grand Slam titles and was the first black man to win Wimbledon. Ashe remains the only black man to win a singles title at Wimbledon, the US Open or the Australian Open and is one of the only two black men, the other being Yannick Noah, who Ashe discovered, to win a Grand Slam title at all.[45] Beyond his on-court accomplishments however, Ashe was a monumental figure off the court. He was an activist and role model who campaigned for civil rights in equality in America and campaigned against the apartheid regime in South Africa. As the second president of the ATP after his retirement, Ashe also helped establish the modern rules of the game. After retiring in 1980, Ashe was inducted into the International Tennis Hall of Fame in 1985 prior to his tragic death from AIDS in 1993 after contracting HIV from a blood transfusion.[46] Prior to his death he publicly announced that he had the disease and started work and philanthropic activities in HIV and AIDS education. Ashe was posthumously awarded the Presidential Medal of Freedom and his legacy lives on today.

Martina Navratilova is a retired tennis player who is considered one of the greatest, if not the greatest, women's tennis players of all time. Navratilova left her native Czechoslovakia as a teenager to come to the United States to advance her tennis career. Shortly after coming to the United States, she defected from communist Czechoslovakia and eventually became an American citizen. She developed a massive rivalry with Chris Evert, changing her diet and fitness regimen, and in turn forcing Evert to do the same to keep up, to compete at the highest possible level. Navratilova would go on to meet Evert in 61 different finals. By the end of her career, Navratilova had won 18 major singles titles, 31 major doubles titles and had won more singles tournaments, doubles events or matches than any player, male or female, in the history of the sport.[47] She was inducted into the International Tennis Hall of Fame in 2000. Along with Evert, Navratilova was instrumental in setting the standard for women's tennis and her legacy is still felt today.

Gladys Heldman was the founder of *World Tennis* magazine and most famously worked with Billie Jean King to establish the women's game. Heldman founded the magazine in 1953 and in the 1950s and 1960s, the magazine was run solely by Heldman as she served as editor-in-chief, layout editor, art director and advertising director.[48] The magazine became quite popular around the tennis scene and at the advent of the Open Era, Heldman used the magazine as a platform to advocate for equality in the sport. In 1970, she established the first all-woman's professional tour with the Virginia Slims of Houston event and by 1971, with the backing of Philip Morris, the women's pro game was under way.[49] By the mid-1970s, Heldman had sold World Tennis magazine and was out of the tennis politics world. As Billie Jean King said, "Without Gladys Heldman, there wouldn't be women's professional tennis."[50]

With massive stars such as Rafael Nadal, Novak Djokovic, Venus and Serena Williams and Maria Sharapova reaching the tail end of their careers, it is yet to be seen who the next major tennis stars will be in the coming decades. Further technological changes and advancements will surely come to the sport and bringing and popularizing the game is new areas of the world will define the future of tennis as one of the major world sports.

Notes

1 Bud Collins, *The Bud Collins History of Tennis: An Authoritative Encyclopedia and Record Book* (New York: New Chapter Press, 2016), 4.
2 Ibid.
3 Ibid.
4 Ibid., 5.
5 Ibid., 6.
6 Ibid., 8.
7 Ibid., 6.
8 Ibid., 7.
9 Ibid., 10.
10 Ibid., 192.
11 Ibid., 10.
12 Ibid., 67.
13 Ibid., 151.
14 Ibid., 167.
15 Ibid., 52.
16 Ibid., 65.
17 "Hawk Eye," retrieved from https://en.wikipedia.org/wiki/Hawk-Eye (accessed December 10, 2017).
18 Collins, *History of Tennis*, 79.
19 Ibid., 144.
20 Ibid., 165.
21 J. Le Miere, *International Business Times*, 28 August 2015, retrieved from www.ibtimes.com/top-10-womens-tennis-players-all-time-where-does-serena-williams-rank-list-greatest-2073830 (accessed December 10, 2017)
22 S. Petovski, *TennisMash*, September 15, 2016, retrieved from https://tennismash.com/2016/09/15/10-influential-players-history-tennis/ (accessed December 10, 2017)
23 S. Stolberg, *New York Times*, August 13, 2009, retrieved from www.nytimes.com/2009/08/13/us/politics/13obama.html (accessed December 10, 2017)
24 G. Vecsey, *New York Times*, August 30, 2010, retrieved from www.nytimes.com/2010/08/30/sports/tennis/30vecsey.html (accessed December 10, 2017)
25 S. Petovski, *TennisMash*, September 15, 2016, retrieved from https://tennismash.com/2016/09/15/10-influential-players-history-tennis (accessed December 10, 2017)
26 Ibid.
27 Ibid.
28 T. Newcomb, *Sports Illustrated*, November 18, 2015, retrieved from www.si.com/tennis/2015/11/18/tennis-shoes-stan-smith-john-mcenroe-pete-sampras (accessed December 10, 2017)
29 See www.tennisfame.com/hall-of-famers/inductees/john-mcenroe
30 R. Greenstreet, *The Guardian*, June 22, 2013, retrieved from www.theguardian.com/lifeandstyle/2013/jun/22/steffi-graf-interview (accessed December 10, 2017)
31 See www.tennisfame.com/hall-of-famers/inductees/stefanie-graf
32 S. Petovski, *TennisMash*, September 15, 2016, retrieved from https://tennismash.com/2016/09/15/10-influential-players-history-tennis (accessed December 10, 2017)
33 See http://news.bbc.co.uk/sport2/hi/tennis/wimbledon_history/3742103.stm
34 See http://news.bbc.co.uk/sport2/hi/tennis/5113548.stm
35 S. Petovski, *TennisMash*, 15 September 2016, retrieved from https://tennismash.com/2016/09/15/10-influential-players-history-tennis (accessed December 10, 2017)
36 Ibid.
37 A. Sreedhar, *New York Times*, July 10, 2015, retrieved from http://nytlive.nytimes.com/womenintheworld/2015/07/10/the-inspiring-story-of-how-venus-williams-helped-win-equal-pay-for-women-players-at-wimbledon (accessed December 10, 2017)

38 S. Petovski, *TennisMash*, September 15, 2016, retrieved from https://tennismash.com/2016/09/15/10-influential-players-history-tennis (accessed December 10, 2017)

39 Ibid.

40 See www.atpworldtour.com/en/players/roger-federer/f324/overview

41 A. Tullouch, *NewsHub*, June 8, 2012, retrieved from www.newshub.co.nz/sport/maria-sharapova-reclaims-world-number-one-ranking-2012060818 (accessed December 10, 2017)

42 K. Fleming, *New York Post*, March 29, 2016, retrieved from http://nypost.com/2016/03/29/why-eve ryone-in-tennis-hates-maria-sharapova (accessed December 10, 2017)

43 S. Petovski, *TennisMash*, September 15, 2016, retrieved from https://tennismash.com/2016/09/15/10-influential-players-history-tennis (accessed December 10, 2017)

44 C. Evert, *Time*, April 18, 2013, retrieved from http://time100.time.com/2013/04/18/time-100/slide/li-na (accessed December 10, 2017)

45 See www.tennisfame.com/hall-of-famers/inductees/arthur-ashe

46 J. Goldman, *Los Angeles Times*, February 13, 1993, retrieved from http://articles.latimes.com/1993-02-13/sports/sp-1301_1_arthur-ashe (accessed December 10, 2017)

47 See www.tennisfame.com/hall-of-famers/inductees/martina-navratilova

48 See www.tennisfame.com/hall-of-famers/inductees/gladys-heldman

49 Ibid.

50 Ibid.

Part IV
Racing sports

24

Athletics/track and field

Katja Sonkeng, Marques R. Dexter, Robert Matz, Jepkorir Rose Chepyator-Thomson and Kipchumba Chelimo Byron

Introduction

Throughout human history, fundamental physical movements are deeply interwoven within the cultural or social activities of many societies. Whether it's jumping over barriers, running to complete a task, or throwing objects like spears, for centuries these activities have been practiced and used for purposes of cultural cohesion as well as for individual development, and have formed an integral part of many cultures and ethnic groups worldwide. Gradually, these activities have been transformed into not only "basic exercises in athletics" (Costache, 2015, p. 9), but also into the competition characteristic of track and field events. Track and field derives its name from its typical competition venue: "a stadium with an oval running track enclosing a grass field where the throwing and jumping events take place" (CISM Europe, 2017, p. 1).

As previously alluded to, track and field origins can be traced to cultural and exercise activities practiced among many ethnic groups across the continental regions of Africa, Asia, Europe, and the Americas, including the areas of Oceania and the Caribbean. While in some nation-states' ethnic groups, track and field is incorporated into ways of life, such as training the youth for adulthood, to settle disputes in society or as a tool for preservation of physicality of ethnic groups across generations (Chepyator-Thomson, 1990). In other areas of the world, track and field underscores social identity formation, as can be seen in examples such as characteristic of Kalenjin ethnic groups in the eastern region of Africa or among aboriginal people of the Americas, Asia and Oceania, and among the historic people of Europe, particularly the Greeks, where "creation of individual and civic and identities were considered significant" (Newby, 2005, p. 7). No matter the location or region, track and field is part of people's culture and social history. These events have come to form part of major sporting competitions like the Olympics, World Championships and Commonwealth Games.

Across different areas of the world, individuals from varying ethnic groups engaged in inter-group competitions throughout history, but it was not until the 1896 Olympic Games that competitions of global magnitude were performed. The track and field running events being held included 110 meters hurdles, 100 meters dash, 400 meters dash, 800 meters dash, 1500 meters race and the marathon. In addition, the field events of shot put, high jump, long jump, triple jump and pole vault were contested. Initially, men were the only persons allowed to compete (Costache, 2015).

The Olympic Games were famous in Greek society and were held during the first full moon following summer solstice every four years, for which the Greek city-states set aside "their political disputes during the athletic competitions" (ibid., p. 1). Two competitive events during this time were foot racing and track events. According to Costache (2015), long jump was part of the competition in pentathlon in Ancient Greece, but long-distance events were not included at the ancient Games in Olympia, as the longest event was three miles, which is equivalent to 4.8 kilometers. In fact, the first recorded race was held at the very first Olympic games in 776 BC, a stadium footrace. The marathon as we know it today was first introduced at the inaugural modern Olympics in 1896. The event was specifically created as the link between ancient Greek traditions and modern Olympics held in Athens, Greece in 1896 (Cooper, 1996; Peiser & Rielly, 2004). The purpose of this chapter is therefore to discuss and extend current knowledge and discourse that highlights the paramount significance of track and field in terms of culture, society, and geography. Particular attention is paid to its use as an element of cultural preservation, identity formation, a tool for diplomacy, a weapon of justice and reconciliation in society, and as a vehicle for social change across many countries worldwide. For the remainder of this chapter, the authors discuss the beginnings of track and field in a global context in term of sociocultural and geographical aspects, and deliberate on its impact on social change in increasingly globalized societies.

Track and field across cultural, geographical and social terrains

Running as means of survival, recreation and religion in Native American traditions

In North America, the First Nations people had festive activities that were ceremonial, recreational and competitive. Running was a prominent sport among the Native Americans, with the Tarahumara people bringing a wave of change through foot racing. The Tarahumara came from the Sierra Madre of the north-western region of Mexico. Two Native American runners – Tomas Zafiro and Leconcio San Miguel – took part in what came to be known as the 100-kilometer Tarahumara foot race (Dyreson, 2017). Their participation symbolized "post-revolutionary Mexico's commitment to "*indigenismo*," which was a concerted effort to incorporate the nation's many indigenous peoples into the cultural and political mainstream of Mexican life" (ibid., p. 3). The two Tarahumara runners served as "icons of Mexican efforts to build a new post-revolutionary national culture" (ibid.). Dryeson posits:

> In running a modern version of their traditional tribal races in the center of Mexican urban life, the Tarahumara runners signified the hope that Mexico's proletariat could be rapidly assimilated into the modern mainstream Mexican society and yet still preserve their essential folkways.
>
> *(Dyreson, 2017, p. 3)*

People hoped Zafiro and San Miguel would represent Mexico at the 1928 Olympic games in Amsterdam, Netherlands. Tarahumara runners were a force to be reckoned with in Mexico and a force of change in global distance running. Meanwhile, the United States, feared Mexico's athletic world power would be a potent threat at the 1928 Olympics (ibid.). Foot runners in the United States were regarded as sports-entertainers, emerging in the sport industry in 1920s, with

Tarahumara runners inspiring an amazing race that started in Los Angeles and ended in New York City among other foot races (Dyreson, 2017). According to Williams (2013), 199 men took part in the coast-to-coast race, with C.C. Pyle the sponsor, "who made his fortune as a sport agent" (p. 11) in the 1920s, promising to award $48,500 as prize money.

The Native American James "Jim" Thorpe is the best all-around athlete of all times

One of the most celebrated Native Americans in modern times and one of the greatest athletes of all time is Jim Thorpe. Thanks to his spectacular performance at the 1912 Olympic Games in Stockholm, he inspired not just those in attendance but also sport followers across the globe. Thorpe won gold medals in pentathlon and decathlon, in addition to the 200 meters hurdling event where he set a world record that stood for 36 years (Cooper, 1996). Sweden's ruler, King Gustav, who declared him to be the greatest athlete in the world at the medal ceremony, publicly recognized Jim Thorpe's excellent performances at the Olympics (ibid.). Since then, the United States has produced dominant figures in the long jump events such as Jesse Owens (1936), Carl Lewis (1988, 1992 and 1996), and Jackie-Joyner Kersee (1988).

Track and field's place in African Asian and European societies

In African and Asian societies, running in all shapes and forms was common among the populace. The continent of Africa houses a diverse population, whose lives are punctuated by a variety of activities that utilized sports and games used to perform cultural and social functions. Due to the vast geographical terrains in these regions, along with a multitude of cultures, sport disciplines like track and field are supreme, among other sporting forms of physical activity. Participation in games in culture promoted physical development of children and youth, as well as interpersonal relationships or social interactions among children of different ages and age-groupings (Chepyator-Thomson, 1990).

In post-colonial Africa, track and field has been featured prominently in many countries across the continent. British speaking countries, notably Kenya, Nigeria and South Africa, as well as other countries such as Arab speaking northern African nations of Algeria and Morocco, and the eastern African country of Ethiopia, are well-known for their spectacular track and field performers. Particularly Kenya, where the country was introduced to global athletics at the British Empire and Commonwealth Games in Vancouver, Canada, in 1954, has distinguished itself as a powerful track and field nation with a long list of well-known world-class long-distance runners. In these games, Kenya was represented by a small group of track and field athletes, behind the notable performance by Nyandika Maiyoro, who finished 4th in the three-mile event. This international exposure prompted the formation of Kenya Olympic Association in 1954 and the International Olympic Committee (IOC) ratified its membership in 1955. Thanks to the financial support from the colonial government, the Kenya Olympic Association was able to send a team of 32 athletes, comprised of individuals of Africans, Asian and European descent to take part in the XVIth Olympiad at Melbourne in 1956. They participated in several events, which included track and field (Bale & Sang, 1996).

In Asian societies track and field played vital role in the sociocultural landscape. In China, for instance, track and field along with other sport disciplines has equally played a vital role in all aspects of the People's Republic of China since its establishment in 1949 (Hong & Zhouxiang, 2011). However, it's not until recently that scholars have turned their attention to sports in Asia as a lens to examine its societal processes (Mills, 2005; Morris, 2004). According to Morris

(2004), the groundbreaking year in the understanding of sports in China was 1912, which he reportedly depicts as a "time of frantic experimentation with and participation in an array of 'modern' sports" (p. 1144). Drawing from European countries' sport models, as well as Japanese and US style of sport competitions, national meetings quickly emerged to which teams and athletes from abroad were invited to challenge the cream de la crème of China, and in no time a fan culture and large spectatorship was developed (Mills, 2005). Meanwhile, a growing women's sports movement in Europe and North America swept the world and reached the Chinese culture in 1920s (Morris, 2004). Exclusive to women until then, the international driven campaign ultimately led to the establishment of the Women's World Games in 1921, followed immediately by inception of five women's track and field events in the 1928 Summer Olympics (Leigh & Bonin, 1977). Simultaneously, in China, track and field events for women were established, however, were met with resistance, criticism and disrespectful responses from audiences (Morris, 2004). It was Kinue Hitomi's gold medal in 1928 for Japan that set the stage for the growth and popularity of women's track and field in East Asia (Buchanan, 2000).

In Europe, track and field events began emerging in the Northern parts in medieval times, with the stone put and weight throw competitions most popular among Celtic societies such as Ireland and Scotland (CISM Europe, 2017). These were the predecessors of the modern shot put and hammer throw disciplines, as pointed out on the official web site of the International Association of Athletics Federations (IAAF) (IAAF, 2017). Pole-vaulting, on the other hand, is among the youngest track and field disciplines. Originally for distance, the sport can be traced back to at least the 16th century, although there is also evidence for its practice in Ancient Greece. Fast forward to the 19th century, the modern form of pole vaulting is first reported in Germany in the 1850s, when the sport was added to the gymnastic association. Approximately 20 years later, in 1870, physical education for girls was introduced in Germany, which laid the first foundation for women's track and field disciplines such as running, jumping and throwing (Bahro, 2010). Simultaneously, other forms of vaulting emerged in the Lake District region of England, where competitions took place that involved ash or hickory poles equipped with iron spikes (IAAF, 2017). According to the IAAF, the first recorded use of bamboo poles was in 1857, and yet it took almost another century before pole vaulting became widely popular in the late 1950s (ibid.). Headquartered in Monaco since 1993, the IAAF was founded in July 1912 as the world governing body for the sport of track and field athletics. At that time, there was an assertion "to fulfill the need for a world governing authority, for a competition program, for standardized technical equipment and for a list of official world records" (ibid., p. 1).

More than a century later, the goals and objectives remain the same, withstanding the tests and challenges of time and society thanks to the dynamic, life-enhancing sports' ability to continuously adapt to the ever-changing political and socio-economic changes and evolution of the world. For instance, in 2001, the adoption of the "International" as part of the IAAF's reflected the growth of a globalized professional sporting world, which did not exist yet in the pre-First World War era (ibid.).

Fifty years of social change in track and field: its impact on society

The historical founding of the Olympic Games had little diversity, as men, mainly those from Anglo-Saxon background, belonging to upper echelon of society were responsible for the development of modern games. Women participated in sporting activities across many cultures and nations, but the degree of participation was sanctioned by culture and social requirements commissioned by various entities throughout the 20th century. In early days, track and field was for men and elite women, which happened in the United States as "field day" (occurred for the first time at Vassar College in 1886, United States) and appropriateness of the track and field activities was grounded in white hegemonic femininity (Gilreath, Zupin & Judge, 2017, p. 359). De Coubertin, founder of the modern Olympics, wanted the games to educate people "and to inculcate ideals of life philosophically," as he viewed sport as a means to "conditions the moral fiber of a people" (Houghton, 2005, p. 160), focusing mainly white Europeans at the time. People of color – Africans, South Americans and Asians – took part in the 1904 Olympics not as participants but as a sideshow display, as they "were paraded before the public and were made to look like as barbaric and backward as possible" (ibid., p. 161). In the 21st century, "all persons take part in the Olympics and in many sport activities, with women participating as professionals and as amateurs in practically every sport" (Gilreath, Zupin & Judge, 2017, p. 360), and with men and women of color, reigning supreme in many track events.

Intertwined history of track and field and Olympic Games

Track and field events are widely considered the leading sport of the Olympic Games, and they play a central role in each summer celebration, while undergoing constant changes to withstand the political and social changes of the time. Consequently, both the IAAF and the IOC recognize their "social responsibility, the environment and all matters that help advance athletics as a force to change the world for good" (IAAF, 2017, p. 2). Athletes have been found to extend the Olympic creed to not only participation in the sporting events, but also as an agent for global change. Accordingly, the Olympic Games have been viewed as "promoting peace among peoples of different cultures" (Buller, 2016, p. 1). This credence became a game changer, as it triggered a period of revolutionary transformation at the 1968 Olympic Games, where Bob Beamon of the United States, and Kipchoge of Kenya, went into the annals of track and field as legends in Long Jump and 1500 meters race, respectively. The then 27-year-old touted underdog, Kip Keino, handed an upset to the heavily favorite US runner, Jim Ryan, who was expected to bring home to United States a gold medal. For 50 years, the world has seen phenomenal performers such as Carl Lewis of the United States, and most recently the great sprinter, Usain Bolt of Jamaica who has dominated the sprinting events – 100 meters dash and 200 meters dash – in the last decade, debuting on the world sports scene at the 2008 Olympic games, where he won squarely the 100- and 200 meters events.

Nation-states use track and field as soft power

Increasingly, nations seek to "affirm themselves on the world stage" (Houghton, 2005, p. 160) and this has led to individuals being used as soft power functioning as representatives of nation-states. The high performers in track and field events at international levels recognize notoriety accorded to individual athletes or players as well as prestige to the participating nation-states, while influencing foreign policies of nations. Eisenhower, for instance, recognized the value of international sport participation in sending Black athletes as cultural ambassadors to Europe and developing nations. By enlisting Black women as diplomats to represent US opportunity during the Cold War, Eisenhower hoped to establish a softening U.S. image that was marred with racial issues (Blaschke, 2016). President Ford of the United States also recognized the benefits of athletes' involvement in the 1976 Olympic Games in Canada. This is reflected in his foreign policy that shows how sport is entangled with aspects of US politics. President Ford learned that sport could function as a cultural diplomacy during his presidency, thus he sent athletes to the Montreal Olympics to drum up patriotism and promote diplomacy (ibid.). Blaschke thus noted that: "sport could function as effective cultural diplomacy … [and he] sent athletes to the games to build expressions of patriotism at home and diplomatic friendships abroad" (ibid., p. 826). As Blaschke expressed: "men and women athletes remained a key component of the foreign policy that actors on the cinders and in the White House calibrated to reflect changing gender roles in the United States from 1955–1975" (ibid., p. 844). As further suggested by Blaschke, President Ford saw "athletes" diversity as "bringing domestic and diplomatic pressures, with athletes remaining a policy constant from 1950s to the mid-1970s" (ibid., p. 840).

Kenya became part of the global sporting arena with the colonial encounter which changed indigenous sporting traditions. This brought a host of new sporting cultures that changed people's livelihood and involvement in recreational, celebratory, and communal activities. Utilization of track and field as soft power was increasingly used after the 1968 Olympic Games. For instance, Kenya cultivated competitive balance in track and field, which was used to enhance national unity and to project the country as a powerful political nation globally. Kenya began its involvement in global mega sport events such as the Olympics, World Championships, and Commonwealth games, where the athletes made history in many track and field events. At the summer Olympics in Mexico City in 1968, Kenya established itself as an athletic powerhouse (Onywera et al., 2006). The track and field team achieved success in middle and long-distance events, a feat that proclaimed the country's international prestige and recognition (Bale & Sang, 1996). The Kenyan athletes won many medals, making them national icons, and cultural and political ambassadors.

Globalization and commercialization of track and field

According to Stiglitz (2006), globalization broadly means "the international flow of ideas and knowledge, the sharing of cultures, global civil society, and the global environmental movement" (p. 4) and this includes movement of sport labor in track and field. Specifically, in reference to Byron (2014), globalization involves the movement of athletes who travel to participate in international competitions across the world. Nations allow their athletes to participate in global competitions to promote national goals and place them at the global stage through athlete performances (Horton & Saunders, 2012). The "commercialization of sport has become a major milestone in professionalization of athletics worldwide, [which] enable elite athletics to transition from amateur to highly paid professionals globally" (Byron, 2014, p. 50).

It was not until the early 1990s that the IAAF started to transform athletics from amateur to professional sport. The IAAF action opened up the athletics landscape through enhanced athletic development and provision of international competition opportunities. As Tanser (2008) explained, athletic competitions mushroomed globally, with the introduction of not only Olympics but also professional athletic competitions that included awards in the form of prize money. In Tanser's view, this commenced the international travel of athletes, allowing free market exchange of their labor, with permission from the International Amateur Athletic Federation. The professionalization of athletics led to visible economic returns of athletes' earnings with increasing sponsorships and television rights. This mediated athletic success enhanced the new scramble of athletics in corporate competitive sports markets. Thus, occurred the emergence of the search for stellar athletes in what is called training camps in many parts of Kenya for participation in global competitions. It may be said that globalization transformed may countries' track and field programs. In the United States, for instance, it has helped in the address of human rights in society, and in promoting social mobility through professional athletes' travel overseas to participate in Grand Prix track and field competitions.

In Kenya, globalization led to intense development of athletics, reaching places distant from the country's capital Nairobi. In Elgeyo Marakwet County, northwest of the capital, athletics took off like a wild fire, with many camps receiving many champions from all areas of the globe. In fact, Iten Athletics Community has become the epicenter of international athletics training for distance running, with a huge global corporate athletic presence escalating training activities and elevating performance requirements for the sports industry. The significance of Iten Athletics Community, in the field of athletics, has attracted international media and its branding in the international athletic performance. Iten has become a place most international athletes call their training home or destination while seeking international glory in the process. Most of Kenyan elite long distance runners attribute their global spectacular achievements in the sport of athletics to Iten Athletics Community. Over the last 20 years, this community has defined the scope and depth of athletic performances around the globe, particularly in distance running. Thus, Iten Athletics Community has seen an increased global sport labor migration to this community in search of ideal training conditions.

The impact of globalization in track and field

Globalization brought things good and bad, with record performances implicating athletes in doping issues, marring otherwise great track and field events worldwide. While globalization provided opportunities for women to demonstrate their high caliber performances at the Olympics level among other international sporting events like World Championships, emerging at the center of these great competitive events is the questions of who counts as female in track and field mega-events. One case is that of Caster Semenya, who first came to attention at the 2009 IAAF World Championships held in Berlin, Germany. Young notes that "Semenya's muscular appearance and extraordinary performance prompted many to ask whether she was 'really' a woman" (Young, 2015, p. 331). Young indicated that the concern was about whether Semenya was female biologically. This caused a lot of commotion, and in the end, she underwent sex verification testing, which was conducted to provide whether there was a "scientific evidence to prove if Semenya was a 'real' woman and thus eligible to compete at the international level" (ibid., p. 335). Whatever the evidence, Caster Semenya has continued to run as female in all track and field competitions. In 2017 she won a gold medal in 800 meters at the World Championships in London, United Kingdom.

Doping, physicality and performances in track and field

Doping issues have marred the sport of track and field. From the alleged systematic doping programs in the 1980s of the Soviet Union and East Germany, to Ben Johnson and Marion Jones (Aschwanden, 2017), to the most recent blanket ban of all Russian athletes from the Rio 2016 Summer Olympic Games (Shuster, 2016), doping has a long history in the sport of track and field. To combat the damaging stigma, the IAAF aims to push a reset button, figuratively speaking. Since May 2017, track and field's international governing body has been reviewing a proposal that essentially intends to erase any world record set before 2005. That is the year when the IAAF began to store athlete samples for enhanced testing (Payne, 2017). "We need decisive action to restore credibility and trust", explained Arne Hansen, the European Athletics Council President (ibid., p. 2).

While wiping the slate clean may help to improve the international reputation of the sport, the proposal seems to overlook the symbolic meaning associated with the athletes' accomplishments, transcending the individual's success and affecting cultural, political, racial and social relations across borders. Specifically, the total of 74 of the 145 records to date that would disappear from history books, including most famously Mike Powell's (1991) and Carl Lewis's (1984) long jump records or Kevin Young's record-breaking 400 meters hurdles time set in 1992. Not to mention the records set by legendary American sprinter Florence Griffith-Joyner in the women's 100 meters and 200 meters dashes in 1988, Jesse Owens's gold medals in 1936, Tommie Smith's and John Carlos' gold and bronze medalists in the 200 meters dash in 1968. The list goes on and on, and as Powell remarks," they would be destroying so many things with this decision without thinking about it" (Payne, 2017, p. 3). In addition to Powell, there are growingly more affected athletes speaking out against this proposal, even considering filing a lawsuit against the IAAF if the plan goes through (ibid.). By the end of 2017, the decision has yet to be made.

While the usage of performance-enhancing substances in contemporary track and field is undeniably prevalent among high-profile athletes, the negative side effect is the emergence of a toxic climate of suspicion, stereotypes and constant accusations (Plymire, 1999). As a direct outcome, when female long-distance runners from the People's Republic of China (PRC) stunned the track and field competition during the 1993 World Championship of Track and Field in Stuttgart, Germany, and the 1993 Chinese National Games in Beijing, their world-record setting performances (six for nine gold medals in the 1500, 3000 and 10,000 meters races) did not merit its well-deserved praise and standing ovations from the track and field world, their fellow athletes and sports journalists, but instead raised all kinds of eyebrows and concerns regarding its legitimacy and the potential abuse of steroids. As Plymire (ibid.) suggests, such reservations might have been primarily driven by stereotypical views and prejudices held by Americans and other westernized nations regarding communist countries. These beliefs are further nurtured by the disclosure of highly "centralized, state-controlled sport 'machines' that systematically distributed steroids to their athletes" (ibid., p. 159) as proven in East Germany and Soviet Union, hence so-called "Big Red Machine" (ibid., p. 160).

Although those systemic doping systems largely contributed to the increasingly prevalence of steroid use in track and field, Waddington and Murphy (1992) rather account doping in sport as a concomitant effect of "commercialization, de-amateurization, politicization and medicalization of sport" (Waddington & Murphy, 1992; Plymire, 1999, p. 159). Indeed, as Plymire suggests, the growing winning mentality among athletes, coaches, and administrators makes them more susceptible to abuse the knowledge and expertise of sport medicine experts to use steroids to improve performance (Plymire, 1999).

Track and field as a weapon of justice and reconciliation in society

African distance runners from across the continent played a critical role in the history of social change, as they were instrumental in ending the Apartheid system in South Africa by primarily using the Supreme Council of Sport. The Council used African runners' athletic prowess (Abibi Bikila and Mamo Wolde, Ethiopia; Kipchoge Keino and Naftali Temu, Kenya; and Mohammed Gammaoudi, Tunisia) to eradicate Apartheid policy (Nixon, 1977). Through the Council, 23 African countries were asked to pledge a boycott of the 1968 Mexico Olympic if South Africa was allowed to participate, and the strategy panned out (ibid.). 2018 marked the 50th anniversary of one of the most iconic and pivotal moments in the history of sport and the Olympic Games: When sprinters Tommie Smith and John Carlos, gold and bronze medalists in the 200 meters dash, raised their black-gloved fists in a black power salute on the medal podium during the 1968 Summer Olympics in Mexico City. With this act of resistance to the traditional hand over heart while the US national anthem is played, Carlos and Smith exploited their success and platform to draw notice to the injustices Blacks suffer within United States society. Even their Australian peer, silver medalist Peter Norman, understood the significance of the moment and wanted to join in, as he was in opposition to the Australian government's policies and treatment of the Indigenous and "non-white" populations in his home country (Osmond, 2010). Collectively, the athletes set in motion a movement of change and progress throughout both nations. There was a clear understanding of the implications their disruption would have in progressing notions of equity and equality to those who are often underrepresented and devalued by the dominant culture.

This wasn't the first time that we have seen track and field athletes of different nation-states and races came together in solidarity to utilize their talent to disrupt racist and ill-conceived perceptions of superiority. At the 1936 Berlin Olympics, sprinter and jumper Jesse Owens tallied four gold medals, not only setting a record that has yet to be broken, but also defying Nazi Germany in the process (Broughton, 2009). Equally significant was the relationship Owens and German competitor Carl Ludwig "Luz" Long developed through their competition against one another. Their talent was the only thing they cared about: racial differences didn't matter. As with Norman's relationship with Carlos and Smith, Owens and Long developed a brotherhood between each other that eradicated all political and racial barriers, disrupting the salient disparities throughout society.

Even prior to the legendary moment in 1968, the Olympics and other major sports have long been served as a wide-reaching platform to draw attention to social injustice and the abuse human rights. In fact, as Cotrell and Nelson (2010) argue, taking a symbolic stance for a variety of political protests are an integral part of both modern and ancient Olympics held in Athens. "The venue's attractiveness stems from of the high-profile nature of the global event, the events accessibility, the availability of transnational allies or supporters, and the 'symbolic meaning that facilitates collective claim-making and widens political opportunity'" (ibid., p. 5).

In terms of individual contributions of track and field athletes, Kenya's Kipchoge Keino made a profound statement, when he publicly praised "sport is one of the tools that can unite youth–sport is something different from fighting in war and it can make a difference–we can change this world by using sport as a tool" (Jarvie, 2008, p. 5). One of the premiere female distance runners is Tecla Loroupe, who used athletics to nurture peace in her West Pokot community in Kenya. By hosting the annual Tegla Loroupe Peace Race, she brought peace and stability to the Horn of Africa. With the Pokot warriors' participation in the annual race, they act as peace ambassadors upon return to their own communities, helping curb social conflicts in the region (Chepyator-Thomson, 2012). In addition to the race, the Tegla Peace Foundation holds conflict resolution activities to bring an end to warring relationships in the region, basically because young men armed with automatic weapons kill hundreds of people each year.

These are just two examples of a long list of defining moments in sporting and track and field events at Olympic games that underscore sports' ability to provide opportunities and a platform to create social change. Particularly in regard to women's struggle for equality and equal rights, Geer (2016) contends that: "athletic competition in the Olympics has invariably preceded social improvement in any country" (p. 1). Indeed, in 1900 women could participate in the Olympic Games for the first time – 20 years before the Congress ratified the 19th Amendment, which granted women the right to vote (ibid.). And yet, it took another 84 years for the first African Muslim woman to win a gold medal in a track and field event. With Nawal El Moutawakel's win in the 400 meters hurdles, she became a strong voice for women's equality, which led to social advancements in her home country.

Gender equity in track and field: making great strides, but still a long way to go

Despite all the strides made toward gender equity in track and field, there is still a long way to go, considering that certain views regarding women's participation in sport have lingered around for centuries. For instance, as highlighted by Plymire (1999), "track and field has typically been viewed as a masculine sport and one that has the potential to 'masculinize' women" (p. 157). Indeed, Plymire even contends that women who excelled in track and field were looked down on and considered as "failed women" (ibid., p. 157). Similarly, in Germany during the 1920s, Karl Ritter von Halt, a German decathlete published a textbook in 1922, claiming that competing in physical exercise and sport "disfigures the female face" and "is not in the female nature" (Bahro, 2010, p. 268). Building on his arguments, even physicians at that time then publicly warned of the perils of masculinization and "serious injuries, including the potential for dislocation of female reproductive organs" (ibid., p. 268). The direct outcome of those "protective provisions" (ibid., p. 268) was a delayed development of women's sport competitions due to enforced restrictions. Hence, as Bahro determined, the official birth of German women's track and field was not until 1919 upon the founding of a separate women's division within the Deutsche Sportbehörde füer Athletik, which was one of the major "bourgeois sports movements" in Germany at that time (ibid., p. 268).

Fast forward to the dawn of the new millennium, we saw further progress for women within the sport of track and field towards progressing equality throughout society. In 1996, Peris-Kneebone became first Australian Aboriginal to win an Olympic gold medal as a member of her country's winning field hockey team. Just a short four years later, fellow Australian, Cathy Freeman, captured the hearts of her country and the entire world, sprinting to a gold medal win at the 2000 Olympic games, carrying both the Aboriginal and Australian flags throughout her victory lap. With their performances, they not only represented progressive strides for women, but also personified the ability for sport – primarily track and field – to enable ethnic and cultural advancement.

Whether it's the Olympic Games or any other international track and field event, all of these global sporting events provide its spectators a glimpse into a leveled and equal playing field of athletes coming from all over the world, ultimately exposing the viewer to unknown cultures and countries (Geer, 2016). Figuratively, therefore, track and field events and the Olympic Games have the power to temporarily yet substantially tear down geographical, cultural and social borders. Through this lens, track and field events and Olympic Games provide a brief yet powerful peek into a unified world and its possibilities. As Geer indicated, "the people of the world are able to see what is possible when so-economic, political, gender and racial barriers don't exist. When you see what is possible, you can change the world" (ibid., p. 2). Thus, every four years at Olympic Games and at every track and field event, sports and its actors remind us on our communalities, a shared humanity. This is the living legend of track and field.

Conclusion

In closing, track and field has been a fundamental physical activity incorporated into various aspects of culture in worldwide communities. While it was used in some cultures to settle social issues, in others it served as a tool for cultural preservation and identity formation. As a central event in modern Olympic Games, the sport of track and field has become a soft power for small nations to increase their visibility and to garner international prestige. Nations like South Africa, individuals like Jim Thorpe of the United States and Kipchoge Keino of Kenya used their platform and popularity acquired through track and field as a weapon of justice and reconciliation by addressing issues of power and colonialism in society. Globalization and commercialization revolutionized the sport in terms of performance and economics. Many nations and individuals profit from mega events that include Olympic Games and World Championships, albeit marred by doping issues. The future of track and field is promising, given the increasing involvement of girls and boys in the sport across the globe.

References

Aschwanden, C. (2017). Track and field may scrap its records because of doping scandals. Is that a good idea? Retrieved from https://fivethirtyeight.com/features/track-and-field-may-scrap-its-records-because-of-doping-scandals-is-that-a-good-idea/

Bahro, B. (2010). Lilli Henoch and Martha Jacob: two Jewish athletes in Germany before and after 1933. *Sport in History, 30*(2), 267–287.

Bale, J. & Sang, J. (1996). *Kenyan running: Movement culture, geography and global sport.* New York: Frank Cass.

Blaschke, A. M. (2016). Running the cold war: Gender, race, and track in cultural diplomacy, 1955–1975. *Diplomatic History, 40*(5), 826–844.

Broughton, P. D. (2009). Forget Hitler – It was America that snubbed black Olympian Jesse Owens. Retrieved from www.dailymail.co.uk/news/article-1205901/Forget-Hitler--America-snubbed-black-Olympian-Jesse-Owens.html

Buchanan, I. (2000). Asia's first female Olympian. Retrieved from http://isoh.org/asias-first-female-olympian-kinue-hitomi/

Byron, K. C. (2014). Global-local examination of athletics in Kenya: A case study of Kaptuiyoot community. Doctoral Dissertation. University of Georgia.

Chepyator-Thomson, J. R. (1990). Traditional games of Keiyo children: A comparison of pre-and post-independent periods in Kenya. *Interchange, 21* (2), 15–25.

Chepyator-Thomson, J. R. (2012). Promoting human dignity through sport activism: The case of Africa. In F. G. Polite and B. Hawkins (Eds.), *Sport, race, activism and social change* (pp. 93–112). San Diego, CA: Cognella.

CISM Europe (2017, November 4). History track & field. Retrieved from www.cismeurope.org/history-trackfield/

Cooper, P. (1996). Marathon and distance running. In *Encyclopedia of world sports, volume I* (pp 599–605). Santa Barbara, CA: ABC-Clio.

Costache, R. M. (2015). The history and evolution of horizontal track and field events. *Labour, 2,* 140–156.

Cotrell, M. P. & Nelson, T. (2010). Not just the games? Power, protest, and politics at the Olympics. *European Journal of International Relations, 17*(4), 729–753.

Dyreson, M. (2017). The Super Bowl as a television spectacle: global designs, glocal niches, and parochial patterns. *The International Journal of the History of Sport, 34*(1–2), 139–156.

Geer, J. (2016). How the Olympics have changed the world. Retrieved from www.insidesources.com/how-the-olympics-have-changed-the-world/

Gilreath, E. L., Zupin, D. & Judge, L. W. (2017). How black women revitalized track and field in the United States. *The Physical Educator, 74,* 359–376.

Horton, P. & Saunders, J. (2012). The "East Asian" Olympic Games: what of sustainable legacies? *The International Journal of the History of Sport, 29*(6), 887–911.

Houghton, F. (2005). Latin America and the Olympic ideal of progress: an athlete's perspective. *The International Journal of the History of Sport, 22*(2), 158–176.

IAAF (2017). History. Retrieved on 8/November. Retrieved from www.iaaf.org/about-iaaf/history

Jarvie, G. (2008). Sport as a resource of hope. Retrieved from www.fpif.org/fpiftxt/5474

Leigh, M. H. & Bonin, T. M. (1977). The pioneering role of the role of Madame Alice Milliat and the FSFI in establishing international track and field competition for women. *Journal of Sport History. 4(1),* 72–83.

Mills, J. H. (2005). Asia. *The American Historical Review, 110*(4), 1144–1145.

Morris, A. (2004) *Marrow of the nation: A history of sport and physical culture in Republican China.* Berkeley and Los Angeles, CA: University of California Press, Ltd.

Newby, Z. (2005). *Greek Athletics in the Roman World: Victory and Virtue.* Oxford: Oxford University Press.

Nixon, R. (1977). Apartheid on the run: The South African sport boycott. *Transition, 58,* 68–88.

Onywera, V. O., Scott, R. A., Boit, M. K., & Pitsiladis, Y. P. (2006). Demographic characteristics of elite Kenyan endurance runners. *Journal of Sports Sciences, 24*(4), 415–422.

Osmond, G. (2010). Photographs, materiality and sport history: Peter Norman and the 1968 Mexico City black power salute. *Journal of Sport History*, *37*(1), 119–137.

Payne, M. (2017). To combat doping stigma, track and field officials propose erasing world records set before 2005. Retrieved from www.washingtonpost.com/news/early-lead/wp/2017/05/03/to-combat-doping-stigma-track-and-field-officials-propose-erasing-world-records-set-before-2005/

Peiser B, Reilly T (2004) Environmental factors in the summer Olympics in historical perspective. *Journal of Sports Sciences*, *22*, 981–1001.

Plymire, D. C. (1999). Too much, too fast, too soon: Chinese women runners, accusations of steroid use, and the politics of American track and field. *Sociology of Sport Journal*, *16*(2), 155–173.

Shuster, S. (2016). In sports and more, Moscow is bending the rules to get ahead. *Time*, *188*(1), 9.

Stiglitz, J. E. (2006). Global public goods and global finance: does global governance ensure that the global public interest is served? Retrieved from www.elgaronline.com/view/9781845427184.00016.xml

Tanser, T. (2008). Exceptional gathering at Shoe4Africa run. International Association of Athletics Federation (IAAF). Retrieved from www.iaaf.org/news/news/exceptional-gathering-at-shoe4africa-peace-ru

Waddington, I. & Murphy, P. (1992). Drugs, sport and ideologies. In E. Dunning & C. Rojek (Eds.), *Sport and leisure in the civilizing process: Critique and countercritique*, 36–64. London: Macmillan.

Williams, G. (2013). *C. C. Pyle's amazing foot race: The true story of the 1928 coast-to-coast run across America.* Old Saybrook, CT: Tantor Media.

Young, S. L. (2015). Running like a man, sitting like a girl: Visual Enthymeme and the case of Caster Semenya. *Women's Studies in Communication*, *38*(3), 331–350.

25

Cycling

Kieren McEwan and Joseph Muller

Introduction

The bicycle has always been viewed as an object of social interest. From the late 18th century when the Comte de Sivrac drew significant public attention as he rode the oddity that became known as the Celerifere around a Paris garden[1] all the way through to the present day, the bicycle has occupied a unique place within culture and society. This is empathised by the socially constructed nature of the bicycle itself as a piece of modern technology[2] and in this sense it must be viewed as being more than simply a functional object for recreation, pleasure and sport.[3] Failing to account for the bicycle's significant social impact would be to sell it short and research has emphasised its importance as a form of transport,[4] a means of improving health,[5] as an important component of individual identity[6] as well as having played a part in developing greater social mobility in society[7] and gender equality.[8] In this sense the bicycle, as well as the sport of cycling as a whole, should be viewed as a reflection of society through its 'modern' constructed nature as seen through the importance of technology within its development[9] and as a symbol of liquid modernity via its links to identity and subculture.[10]

Cycling is, therefore, worthy of note as a global sport for several reasons. Firstly, it is a sport which is both simultaneously modern and postmodern in its nature. Secondly, it has evolved pluralistically into a fascinating range of diverse activities, reflecting the kind of fragmented social space described by Jenks.[11] Finally, cycling also facilitates a number of participant outcomes (e.g. competition, challenge, travel, etc.). This allows cyclists to individualise their goals and outcomes within the sport, therefore meaning that this sport can simultaneously be many things to many people and this is its inherent beauty. For some cycling is a field of competitive pursuit while others view it as a means of recreation. Furthermore, it can also facilitate a feeling of thrill and exhilaration in the more daring and risk-based formats. Taken collectively, this serves to make cycling a sport which epitomises the ideals of liquid modern culture[12] and its links to individualised consumption.[13] This chapter seeks to explore this concept focusing on three forms of cycling; road cycling, mountain biking and bicycle moto-cross (BMX). During this chapter we attempt to demonstrate the fragmented and pluralised nature of the sport as well as exploring key issues and controversies. However, prior to this we must explore the global nature of the cycling market, its level of popular appeal, as well as evaluate why and how the sport became 'fragmented'.

The cycling market

Cycling represents a significant global sports market, which was worth €38.5 billion in 2013.[14] The following year alone over 20 million cycles were sold in Europe, 3.5 million of which were in the United Kingdom (UK).[15] Indeed, the UK market grew by 14% between 2008 and 2013, significantly contributing to the national economy.[16] This was also a global trend emphasised by the 14% increase in profits (up to $3.2 billion) for the global component manufacturer Shimano in 2015[17] and $1.8 billion revenue reported in 2012 by Giant, the world's largest cycle manufacturer.[18] In the UK the increasing sales has been evidenced by the threefold increase in turnover for the UK retailer Evans Cycles between 2008 and 2015[19] and based on this evidence both the national and global the market appears to be in great health prior to the end of 2015.

However, at the same time, in the UK in particular, fears had also begun to be raised about the continued growth of the cycling market and whether sustaining the increase in turnover experienced over the previous decade would be possible, given the state of the global economy. Indeed, the previously mentioned Evans Cycles have recently had to seek to financially restructure their business[20] and ultimately seek new ownership,[21] realising the fears that had been previously voiced within the industry and emphasising the increasingly challenging trading conditions within the cycling market.

Despite the perception of a possible downturn in sales within the industry, cycling as a whole remains a popular activity with increasing participation rates over recent years. In 2016, two million individuals in England over the age of sixteen participated in cycling for sport and pleasure (excluding active transport), making it the third most popular sport after swimming and athletics, and notably Association football.[22] However, information gathered the following year suggested that this might be much higher and that 8% of the adult population in the UK cycled for pleasure on a weekly basis.[23] Participation rates in particular formats of cycling in the UK are less clear. Information on mountain biking suggesting that 421,700 individuals regularly participated in 2014 in England, representing just short of 0.8% of the population.[24] The popularity of mountain biking has also grown considerably in the United States (US). Between 1987 and 2000, mountain biking participation increased by 419.4%[25] and by 2008 it was being reported that more than 50 million Americans regularly rode mountain bikes.[26] This provides evidence of a vibrantly growing sport, which presents the cycling industry, with an expanding consumer base into which to sell products. Part of cycling's broad appeal centres on the range of activity formats which make up the sport and diversity of opportunity that it offers its participants. In order to understand this fully we need to appreciate the fragmented nature of the sport cycling.

The development of cycling as a 'fragmented' sport

As already mentioned cycling is a diverse and arguably fragmented sport. Under its umbrella term, a vast range of other 'cycle sports' exist that exhibit differing characteristics and cultures. The process under which cycling has pluralised is only weakly understood and scarcely covered within the academic literature. However, recent research focused specifically on mountain biking has begun to uncover important characteristic differences between styles of off-road riding. This has manifested in the uncovering of distinct market segments for consumers to purchase products within,[27] varying patterns of identity[28] as well as subcultural values.[29] Although this research focuses solely on mountain biking, anecdotal evidence to suggest similar dynamics exist across other categories of cycling such as road cycling and BMX.[30]

The theoretical underpinning behind the pluralisation of cycling is important. In this respect the greatest insight can be found by linking the evolution of cycling to the increasingly fluid, self-regulated and individualised society arriving in the aftermath of modernity. By offering up numerous 'types' of activity to potential participants, cycling as a sport allows individuals to engage with the format that fits best them and their leisure goals. It also allows cycling to become a component part of an individual's negotiated identity[31] and a prominent part of 'acted out' persona during social interactions when viewed through the theoretical perspective of dramaturgy,[32] and often its associated conspicuous consumption,[33] thus, emphasising its socially constructed nature as a sport. A good starting point to observe this phenomenon is to begin by looking at the competitive formats of cycling which are sanctioned through the sport's international federation.

The Union Cycliste Internationale (UCI) was formed in 1900 when the national cycling federations of France, Belgium Switzerland, the United States and Italy met to create an overarching global administrative system to govern and control the expanding number of professional and amateur cycle races that were emerging at the time.[34] Currently the UCI are responsible for cycling and para-cycling events and competitions which fall in one of seven categories and these are: road, track, mountain biking, BMX, trials, cyclo-cross and indoor cycling, these themselves can be further subdivided into more niche formats as shown in Table 25.1. This

Table 25.1 Categories of competitive cycling controlled and sanctioned through the UCI.

Categories	Events	Description
Road	Road race	Road racing can take two distinct formats differing mainly the type of course upon which the athletes compete. These consist of road races, which are usually long courses where the race starts and finishes in differing places, or circuit races where riders compete of a number of laps of a smaller course.
	Time trial	As the name suggests, this form of road racing pits riders against the clock over a set course with the winner having the quickest time. This form of road racing can be further split into either individual or team time trials.
Mountain bike	Cross-country racing	This format of mountain biking involves riders competing solo over an off-road course. This can be separated into two differing racing formats based on the type of course involved. Cross-country is raced over short circuit courses of no more than 10 km where a number of laps are completed, while marathon cross-country is raced over longer distances usually between 60–100 km.
	Downhill racing	Downhill racing involves riders competing against the clock on a descending off-road track which often contain large obstacles, including drops, jumps and berms.
	Four-cross racing	Within four-cross racing athletes compete in groups of four on a short BMX-style track, making the racing time brief (commonly under 60 seconds). The tracks themselves contain features such as jumps and berms.

(Continued)

Table 25.1 (Continued)

Categories	Events	Description
BMX	Supercross racing	Similar to four-cross racing in mountain biking, this form of racing sees riders compete over short courses of up to 350 m, that contains berms, banks and jumps. However, in BMX supercross eight, rather than four, individuals compete with each other.
	Freestyle	Freestyle BMX is a pluralised category in its own right and contains five further sub-categories; Street riding (based on the use of cityscape and urban furniture), park (which occurs within dedicated skate parks), dirt (where riders perform tricks over a series of jumps constructed out of soil and dirt), vert (where riders preform tricks on large half-pipe ramps where the sides extend to a height where the extremities become sheer and vertical) and flatland (where riders use the bikes to perform on flat ground that involve the balance and coordination).
Track cycling	Sprint events	These shorter distance events pit opponents against each other as a test of power and strength and can be sub-categorised as being either individual or team sprint (raced over three laps of a velodrome), the kilometre (where athletes race over a 1km distance for men and 500 m for women against the clock with the two fastest riders then facing each other in a finals race) and the Keirin (which involves a group of athletes completing 750 m in the wake of a motorised bike, after which they complete three laps of the velodrome as a competitive sprint).
	Endurance events	These are longer distance events and include; Individual and team pursuit (where athletes attempt to chase down, and ideally pass their opponent(s) having started on each side of the velodrome track), the points race (individual) and the Madison (pairs of riders) where athletes compete for points awarded at intermediate stages during a number of laps of the velodrome circuit) and the scratch race (which is a long distance race in the velodrome with a large number of competing athletes and often ending in a sprint finish).
	Omnium	This is a combined velodrome-based competition containing a number of the events. Athletes score points based on their placement in individual races over two days with the most consistent rider winning the overall Omnium.
Trials riding	N/A	Trials riding is a highly skill and coordination orientated event, where riders hop and jump their bikes over a series of obstacles without any part of their body touching the floor. This is an offshoot of motorbike trials riding.
Cyclo- cross	N/A	Cyclo-cross is an off-road event where athletes' complete circuits of a short course on drop handled bikes. The courses often contain technical obstacles such as barriers or staircases that riders must cross.

Categories	Events	Description
Indoor	Artistic cycling	This is an aesthetic based form of competitive cycling which has links to dance and gymnastics. In this form of cycling athletes perform a routine to music and are scored on the quality of their movement and grace. This style of cycling requires high levels of skill, balance and coordination.
	Cycle ball	This is team sport played in teams that is similar to football.

serves to demonstrate the diversity and range of competitive activity formats which fall under the umbrella term on cycling and provides an insight into the pluralised nature of cycling.

It must also be recognised that a number of additional formats exist in parallel to those presented in Table 25.1, which possess a more recreational focus and therefore do not enter the orbit of control of the UCI. This is an emerging area within the academic literature and the work of McEwan and his co-authors[35] have done much to explore and chart the differing subcategories in mountain biking and its impact on the emergence of specialist markets catering for participants with varying identities.

Although, as yet uncharted to the same degree it is easy to view similar processes in play in other formats of cycling. For instance, the road bike market is made up of products with differing functional designs which on face value are all road bicycles but perform different duties such as racing, touring, endurance or sportive riding and time trials. Likewise, BMX products vary in accordance with their purpose and usage, so strong evidence exists to indicate an intensely pluralised market space across cycling as a whole.

It is also important to note that the organic evolution of cycling is continuous and the emergence of Gravel riding as the newest subcategory in cycling provides evidence of this.[36] However, it also indicates where the impetus for the sport's evolution comes from. In the case of gravel riding, which is a cross between road cycling, cycle touring and cyclo-cross, it emerged through the innovations of riders who sought to create new recreational opportunities for themselves and only then was it picked and marketed by the cycling industry. In essence this is a common process and as will be seen later in this chapter this mirrors the way in which mountain biking and its different formats were developed.[37]

Although it is acknowledged that there are numerous forms of cycle sport, three of the most popular are road cycling, mountain biking and BMX and these will form the remaining body of this chapter. By exploring these formats, it will become possible to provide a brief commentary of how they were developed and some of the main cultural and societal issues that they present when viewed analytically.

Road cycling: for fun and profit

Bicycles as we would recognise them began to emerge in the late 1830's with the development of the Velocipedes.[38] These differed from the earlier incarnations, commonly referred to as Hobbyhorse or Dandy-horses, in one respect- they were propelled using pedals rather than by scooting along using feet placed on the ground.[39] However, it was the emergence of the safety bicycle and the newly invented air-filled types in the late 1880s that allowed the sport of road cycling to develop. These along with other new technologies such as free-wheels, ratchet gearing and increasingly reliable braking systems[40] meant that bikes were increasingly able to deal with roads which were too treacherous on previous models. These newer bicycles therefore extended the boundaries of the sport and increased the scope for cyclists to ride longer distances and further afield. Unsurprisingly, the period around the turn of the 20th century saw cycling develop significantly and by the mid-1910s a number of the major events that we still see running today were born, such as the Tour de France and the Paris–Roubaix races. In this respect the impact of technology serves to highlight the thoroughly modern nature of cycling at that time as a newly emerging sport.

Social change and the popularity of road cycling

It is important to recognise the societal backdrop to road cycling's increasing popularity towards the end of the 19th century. Firstly, cyclists were beginning to organise and the emergence of a pan-global organisation in the form of the Cyclist Touring Club in 1878 with members in both Europe and continental America is evidence of this.[41] One reason for the increasing interest in cycling can possibly be drawn from the growing cultural importance of recreationalism as an escape from work and the urban setting.[42] Many upwardly mobile members of societies in Europe and America, recognising the benefits of exercise-based leisure, began to look towards the bicycle as a means of exploring beyond the towns and cities they lived and worked within.[43]

This change in attitude toward physical leisure during the late Victorian and early Edwardian era would become known as the Rational Recreation Movement[44] and it was the development of, initially, the ordinary bicycle[45] and later the safety bicycle[46] that made this possible. However, cycling at this point was far from acceptable to all. Bikes remained a relatively expensive and luxury item and this ensured that cycling continued to be viewed as a somewhat bourgeois pursuit well into the 20th century.[47] However, despite this, the situation did begin to change around the turn of the century. This was due to increasing intolerance towards what were perceived as unsavoury working-class urban leisure pursuits[48] and the paternalistic desire amongst the middle-class population to steer the working-class towards more palatable leisure pursuits.[49] This coupled to an increased influx of cheap mass-produced bicycles arriving in Europe from the United States[50] served to democratise cycling as a leisure activity.

Competitive cycling and resulting issues and controversies

Towards the latter stages of the 19th century a group of sports began to move away from a purely Corinthian sporting ideal and become early adopters of professionalism. Notable among these were football[51] and cycling,[52] as opposed to others sports such as rugby union, which did not professionalise until 1995,[53] and cricket, which retained at least a semblance of amateurism until into the 1960s through the bizarre fig-leaf of distinguishing between gentlemen and players.[54] However, this raises significant questions over why this was the case. Why was cycling so ready to professionalise as a sport?

In addressing this question, a fruitful perspective can be found in the work of Allison[55] and earlier works by Holt[56] and Dunning and Sheard.[57] In their view, observing the onset of professionalism in sport as an encroaching process which degraded the moral ethic in sport is misguided. Rather it was amateurism that was the reaction against the evolving sense of modernity. Therefore, it would be easy to suggest that cycling was more open to reflecting the specialised and rationalised society where professionalism was becoming increasingly prevalent[58]. Therefore, cycling as a sport can viewed as thoroughly 'modern' and a truer representation of society at the turn of 20th century.

In terms of this brief appraisal of road cycling, it is not possible to provide a detailed overview of the sport's professional history. However, an excellent account is provided by Mignot.[59] What is particularly worthy of note within his work is the environment that made professionalism possible within cycling. In his view professional cycling required four components in order to flourish. Firstly, the sport needed to be a spectacle in order to capture the imagination of the general public. Prior to the 1890's the main draw for spectators were races on the track and such events have been described as a 'crowd magnet'.[60] So when newer more capable bicycles made road racing possible it was fully understood that there was an opportunity to exploit the sport's popularity. This directly leads into both the second and third factors identified by Mignot,[61] the emergence of event organisers and team sponsors. As Mignot[62] points out, early cycling events were organised by newspapers in order to 'boost their sales and increase their advertising revenue' and team sponsors, for similar reasons, became aware of benefits to be gained via association to popular riders. To a degree this relationship was symbiotic in the early years of the Grand Tours, where riders relied upon sponsors to provide 'food and accommodation'[63] during the events. This relationship can be seen modelled below[64] and is deliberately presented as a cycle in order to emphasise the important association which also existed between professional riders and the spectators. In this respect it is the performance of the professionals that creates the interest that draws in the spectators and thus completes the linkage between the four elements that made the emergence of professional cycling possible.

What is also interesting to note from the relationships modelled in Figure 25.1 is that, while also explaining the emergence of professional cycling it also serves to explain and rationalise one of the darker elements of the sport, the issue of doping. Again, in order to fully understand this, the sociological backdrop must be appreciated. Firstly, professional cyclists were, in the main, drawn from the working class, and was reportedly the case right up until the late 1950.[65] As such the pressure to win, possibly at all costs, could arguably stem from a rider's need to protect their income. Secondly, Brewer[66] highlights how doping can be viewed as an unintended outcome of the commercialisation of cycling, where professionalism drives a win at all cost mentality. Arguably the relationship shown in Figure 25.1 remains true for today's professionals and as such provides an insight into why doping and cycling have continued to be connected.[67]

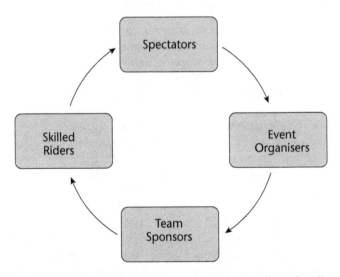

Figure 25.1 Model of the factors facilitating the early professionalism of cycling.

Source: adapted from Mignot (2015)

Undoubtedly, cycling has a long association with doping[68] and this perception has remained to the present.[69] However, it must be noted that at the outset of the 20th century pharmaceutical performance boosting was common across many of the professionalised sports.[70] Right up to the present, sporting achievement and financial rewards are an ever-present temptation, which could result in athletes engaging in doping or other methods which mean 'departing from the spirit in which games should be played'.[71] However, cycling has a notably bad reputation for doping and this is arguably due to organisational failure within the UCI and their perceived inability to grip and deal with the problem of drug cheats,[72] thus allowing the Lance Armstrong situation to become such a scandal. Equally the public's focus on the issue of doping has become increasingly focused through media attention. The eventual fall of Armstrong came about in no small part through the coverage provided by cycling journalists such as Paul Kimmage and David Walsh, with the latter publishing a best-selling account of his experiences with the seven-time Tour de France champion.[73]

However, if there is a temptation to consider the doping issue to be receding, then this would be naïve. The issue has ceased to be purely one focused on the taking of banned substances and has now migrated into the use of therapeutic use exemptions (TUEs).[74] Whether or not this is cheating or extreme gamesmanship is a debatable point but it does indicate the continuing imperfect systems of regulatory control within cycling. However, yet again singling out cycling as a main offender is easy due to the prominence of cases within the media, but it is clear that TUEs and doping more generally continue to be an existential threat throughout all sports.[75] Cycling just happens to find itself again at the forefront of an emerging issue in sport.

In conclusion with regard to road cycling, it was clear that the sport emerged as a result of social change and as the sport has evolved it has done so in parallel with society itself. In terms of sport, cycling was an early adopter of professionalism as a result of its attachment to commercialism, which arguably could be seen as the genesis point of some the problems the sport continues to face. To a certain degree road cycling is and continues to be a product of its time, born of modernism and beholden to its characteristics and also its issues.

Mountain biking: cycling into postmodernity

There is a conspicuous absence of literature pertaining to the development of the sport of mountain biking. However, a solid grounding can be found in Berto's book, *The Birth of Dirt*.[76] It was Berto's work as the engineering editor of *Bicycling Magazine* which brought him into contact with the individuals who would later become known as the 'Klunkerz',[77] and as a resident of the San Francisco Bay area he was located close to the birth place of mountain biking in Marin County.[78]

From the outset of the sport in the 1970s mountain bikers presented counter-cultural identities. The Klunkerz were 'tired of criticism and of being excluded from cycling competitions because of their long hair' and thus sought to establish an alternative pursuit where they would be welcomed regardless of how they looked.[79] Groups of riders began to emerge in the early stages of mountain biking's development with names like 'Lake Spur Canyon Gang', 'Cupertino Boys', 'East Bay Bicycle Coalition', 'San Francisco Bike Coalition' and 'The Derailleurs', indicating the birth of a new subculture as well as a new sport. By 1976 mountain biking was beginning to spread to other mountain-based locations, most notably Colorado[80] and the development of the first specifically engineered mountain bike, the Breezer in 1977/78[81] marked a turning point in the development of the sport, as the mountain bike itself became a consumer product.

Savre et al. describe the period between 1976 and 1981 as a 'golden age of the pioneers'[82] of mountain biking as the trips to the hills for the Klunkerz, gained a purposeful focus – to compete – with the emergence of the Repack Races. The track itself was a popular haunt for the Klunkerz[83] and was a natural choice for the first competition in the sport. More importantly, the event served to begin the process of 'sportisation' in mountain biking[84] that continued with the emergence of the National Off-Road Bicycle Association (NORBA) in 1983.[85] More importantly though, as Savre and co-authors[86] have rightly pointed out, this process also conforms to Guttmann's characteristics of modern sport.[87] However, this leaves questions over the continued evolution of mountain biking beyond the 1990s. Historical research covers some of the period between 1990 and 1996 when cross country racing entered the Olympic programme but collectively this only then accounts for two formats of mountain biking (downhill and cross country).[88]

Contemporary literature on mountain biking and its sub-formats has established a greater variety of styles within the sport[89] but the evolution of the sport from the 1990s to the present day remains to be fully explored and this represents a gap in the research on mountain biking's evolution. What is clear within recent research on mountain biking is that the sport in its current state has pluralised radically.[90] Taken collectively this body of evidence suggests that mountain biking has become a fragmented sport with differing formats demonstrating their own subcultural values and identities, as well as unique and distinct specialist product market. This evidence links to the kind of fragmented social-scape described by Jenks[91] and also Bauman's description of liquid modernism[92] where opportunity and plurality are a central part of culture in the aftermath of modernism.

The fact that mountain biking has developed into a highly pluralised sport is therefore unsurprising. It is widely agreed that sport mirrors society and both evolve in parallel.[93] Therefore, the social conditions into which mountain biking emerged must be explored. Its development in California is itself significant in that it ensured that it was a product of the social upheaval that had taken place within the state over the previous decade.[94] Dyreson's depiction of the effects of 'Californication'[95] therefore take on increased relevance in in respect to the neo-sports such as skate boarding, BMX, snowboarding and mountain biking that developed during the 1970s and 1980s. Such sports became imbued with a latent ethic of cultural resistance which McEwan argues has become a central concept in extreme or as they are often referred to as 'lifestyle sports'.[96]

The inescapable conclusion to these points is that mountain biking has been formed and shaped if not directly by postmodern attitudes, then at least under the influence of liquid modernity. Its plurality reflects the choices and opportunities that individuals have to shape their identity and portray themselves to the outside world. Like road cycling, mountain biking is a cultural product of its time. However, while road cycling became defined through a modernist nature, mountain biking has come to be defined by its postmodern and pluralistic character but importantly both reflect the eras in which they were launched.

BMX: artistry and excellence

Having demonstrated the pluralistic nature of road cycling and mountain biking it is unsurprising to discover that BMXing is also made up of subcategories. However, these fall under one of only two categories; BMX racing and BMX freestyle.[97] The former of these two categories was the first to be developed and, like mountain biking, originated in California only slightly earlier during the late 1960s and early 1970s.[98] As such it also came under the same cultural influences of freedom, individualism and deviance from the social norm of the time and significant parallels can be drawn between these two forms of cycling.

As with mountain biking, equipment was also central to the development of BMX. The introduction of the Schwinn Sting-Ray to the market within its rugged motorcycle inspired styling proved to be popular product, allowing its users to emulate their motocross heroes.[99] It wasn't long before groups of young riders began to arrange races on bikes like the Sting-Ray and thus the earliest form of BMX was born.[100] Eventually this kind of practice became increasingly controlled by on-looking parents and local entrepreneurs as the popularity of these races started to grow[101] and again this is remarkably similar to the way in which mountain biking developed.[102] By the late 1970s, participation in BMX racing had grown to the degree that more control of the sport was needed in the form of the American Bicycle Association, which would later become USA BMX, in 1977.[103] Similar bureaucratisation was also seen six years later in mountain biking with the creation of NORBA but more importantly both these examples present a process of sportisation[104] which fits, if only in the early stages of each sport's development, with the model of modern sport described by Guttman.[105] If further evidence of this were needed one only need look at the acceptance that BMX racing has gained from 'mainstream' sport, having been accepted into the Olympic programme for the 2008 Beijing games.

In contrast to the description of BMX Racing, is the other category of riding; BMX Freestyle. This format emerged as a more aesthetic pursuit with links to other urbanised sports such as skateboarding.[106] Developed as a means of expanding BMX practices, freestyle riders shared both the physical spaces – parking lots, skate parks and emptied swimming pools – and counterculture ideologies of their fellow action sport counterparts to create a practice based upon the performance of tricks and stunts. With a lack of organised control and particularly the absence of framework of rules and regulations, freestyle BMX could be described as deviating from the modern sporting ethos[107] and thus challenging the modern sporting construct created by Guttmann.[108] Therefore, this begins to play with the notion of the competitive and non-competitive dialectic in the same way as McEwan did with his appraisal of the sportsman and the neo-sportsman in mountain biking.[109] In essence this draws in an element of psychology into this point of analysis in the form of task and ego orientation related to the kind of motivation participants experience,[110] where the pull of the sport is not the chance to succeed over others.

Throughout the 1980s, freestyle BMX experienced varying levels of popularity as it was often seen as a by-product of the racing format.[111] This led innovators and entrepreneurs to develop new technologies and variations of the discipline to engage a wider market and provide outlets for freestyle enthusiasts.[112] Previously in this work we identified that the UCI sanction and recognise four formats of freestyle BMX and this is important on two levels. Firstly, it demonstrates the plurality within freestyle BMX, evidencing the influence of liquid modernity within the sports evolution. However, as a second point it also highlights an increasingly obvious attempt to sportify freestyle BMX.[113] The UCI are an organisation focused on competition, so what would prompt such interest? An answer rests in pure economics and in particular the increasing rates of participation in BMX. In the US this stood at 3,104,000 participants in 2016, which was 43.2% up from 2013 and amazingly 87.6% higher than in 2006.[114] Obviously, this represents BMXing as a whole but what it does indicate is that there is a rapidly growing consumer base for the UCI to tap into, echoing the way in which early road race organisers tapped into the increasing public interest to promote their events. Arguably this looks like history repeating itself yet again but it remains to be seen whether or not this will be viewed positively within the participant base or whether it may be viewed as the sport selling out its anti-competitive ideals.

In conclusion, BMX too shares the same fragmented and pluralised nature as other forms of cycling. However, there are significant common threads that exist between BMX and mountain biking in terms of how it has evolved. In this sense it is possible to hypothesise that the developments in both BMX and mountain biking centre around similar processes. Both began with a process of 'sportification' and developed formats which align to Guttmann's characteristics of modern sport.[115] However, subsequent newer formats developed often with a non-competitive focus, possibly under the influences that Dyreson describes as Californication.[116] However, in parallel to this, organisations like the UCI will always be drawn to the opportunities presented by increasing participation, possibly chipping away at any anti-competitive ethic present within BMX. It will be interesting to view over the coming year what if any effect this has on the sport.

Conclusion

Within this chapter we have tried to make coherent sense of the plurality that exists within cycling. It is clear that cycling is a complex sport and it is too naive to think of cycling as a sport that is easy to define. In this chapter we have discussed road cycling, mountain biking and BMX as three of the more popular categories of the sport and this only begins to scratch the surface of the nature of these forms of cycling. Arguably they deserve to be viewed, due to their differences as sports in its own right. It is also important to note that there are other formats of cycling that have escaped our focus here such as cycle touring, cyclo-cross trials riding. Also, niche activities such as cycle-ball, artistic cycling and cycle polo, which has been described as 'the most popular sport you've never heard of'[117] have managed to evade our evaluation, but we will leave this to others to pick up on run with.

In evaluating the three focus formats within this chapter attention must be drawn to the distinct natures of road cycling, mountain biking and BMX, each imbued with a powerful sense of the eras into which they emerged. Sport and particularly the ideas of modern sport are clearly visible across all the three formats. However, within road cycling, this led to professionalism with all its resultant issues and controversies. While mountain biking and BMX, as products of an emerging postmodern ethos were able to break free from the shackles of sportisation and go on to diversify into more non-competitive realms. This arguably makes cycling a sport which is fundamentally reflective of society and particularly the movement between modern and postmodern societies, making it one of the most interesting global sports to investigate.

Notes

1 F. Alderson, *Bicycling: A history* (Newton Abbot: David & Charles, 1972).
2 See P. Rosen, The social construction of mountain bikes: Technology and postmodernity in the cycling industry. *Social Studies of Science*, 23, 3 (1993), 479–513.
3 See O. A. Van Nierop, A. C. M. Blankendaal, and C. J. Overbeeke, The evolution of the bicycle: a dynamic systems approach. *Journal of Design History*, 10, 3, (1997), 253–267.
4 See E. Fishman, Cycling as transport. *Transport Review*, 36, 1, (2016), 1–8.
5 See S. D. Fraser and K. Lock, Cycling for transport and public health: a systematic review of the effect of the environment on cycling. *European Journal of Public Health*, 21, 6, (2011), 738–743.
6 See K. McEwan, N. Weston and Gorczynski, Differentiating identities within an extreme sport: A case study of mountain biking print advertisements. *Frontiers in Psychology*, 9, 1668, (2018).
7 See T. Pinkney, Cycling in Nowhere. *Journal of the William Morris Society*, 13, (1999), 28–33.
8 See J. Bonham and A. Wilson, Bicycling and the Life Course: The Start-Stop-Start Experiences of Women Cycling, *International Journal of Sustainable Transportation*, 6, 4, (2012), 195–213.
9 See J. Woodforde, *The story of the bicycle* (London: Routledge Kegan Paul, 1970).
10 See the following B. Downs, Small bikes, big men, In R. E. Rinehart, & S. Sydnor (eds.), *To the extreme: Alternative sports, inside and out.* (pp. 145–152). Albany: State University of New York Press, (2003); K. Kusz, BMX, extreme sports, and the white male backlash, In R. E. Rinehart, & S. Sydnor (Eds.), *To the extreme: Alternative sports, inside and out.* (pp. 153–175). Albany: State University of New York Press

(2003); P. Cox, *Cycling cultures* (Chester: (University of Chester Press, 2015); H. Oosterhuis, Cycling, modernity and national culture. *Social History*, 41,3, (2016), 233–248; K. McEwan, The future of sportsmanship: A narrative expression of in-group support and respect in the postmodern sport of mountain biking, in T. Delaney (ed.). *Sportsmanship: Multidisciplinary perspectives* (Jefferson, NC: McFarland, 2016), pp. 269–280; K. McEwan and Weston, N. (2017). Different spokes: A multidimensional scale analysis of market segmentation in mountain biking. *International Journal of Sports Management and Marketing*, 17,3, (2017), 162–181; McEwan, et al., Differentiating identities within an extreme sport.

11   C. Jenks, *Subculture: The fragmentation of the social* (London: Sage, 2005).

12   Bauman has produced numerous publications on liquid modernity. For a more complete overview of this theoretical perspective see the following: Z. Bauman, *Life in fragments: Essays in postmodern morality* (Chichester: Wiley, 1995); Z. Bauman, *Liquid Life* (Cambridge: Polity Press, 2005); Z. Bauman, *Liquid times: Living in an age of uncertainty* (Cambridge: Polity Press, 2007)

13   It is important to recognise the links between liquid modernity, identity and patterns of consumerist behaviour. For an detailed overview see: Z. Bauman, Consuming life. *Journal of Consumer Culture*, 1, 1, (2001), 9–29; Z. Bauman, *Consuming life*. (Chichester: Wiley, 2013).

14   J. Oortwijnjn, Global cycling market valued at €38.5 billion. *Bike Europe*, 27 August 2013. Retrieved from www.bike-eu.com/sales-trends/nieuws/2013/8/global-cycling-market-valued-at-e-38-5-billion-10110007 (accessed 26 November, 2018)

15   Confederation of the European Bicycle Industry. (2015). European bicycle market, 2015. Retrieved from https://issuu.com/conebi/docs/european_bicycle_industry___market__8e7511a5a2e3fe (accessed 26 November 2018).

16   The cycling market in the UK contributed £745m to the economy in 2014. See Mintel, Going up a gear – Britain's cycling enthusiasts trade up to better quality models, 25 April 2014. Retrieved from www.mintel.com/press-centre/social-and-lifestyle/going-up-a-gear-britains-cycling-enthusiasts-trade-up-to-better-quality-models (accessed 26 November 2018)

17   Bicycle Retailer, Shimano sales up 14%, 10 February 2016. Retrieved from www.bicycleretailer.com/international/2016/02/10/shimano-sales-14-last-year#.V1gzhVcwzkw (accessed 26 November 2018)

18   A. Ramzy, A maker of bikes now makes a point of riding them. *The New York Times*, 30 August 2013. Retrieved from www.nytimes.com/2013/08/31/world/asia/a-maker-of-bikes-now-makes-a-point-of-riding-them.html?_r=1 (accessed 26 November 2018)

19   M. Moore, UK cycling industry sees space for more growth. *The Financial Times*, 4 September 2015. Retrieved from www.ft.com/cms/s/0/67eafdf2-5319-11e5-b029-b9d50a74fd14.html#axzz4CIR2i0S0 (accessed 26 November 2018). Around the mid-point of 2015, reports in the cycling industry press began to emerge which voiced concerns over sales in the market beginning to show a slowdown in growth. For examples see: J. Harker, Sales rep's view: Showrooming is the least of your worries. *BikeBiz*, 23 June 2015. Retrieved from www.bikebiz.com/news/read/sales-rep-s-view-showrooming-is-the-least-of-your-worries/018023 (accessed 26 November 2018); J. Harker, Poll results: Has 2015 been a vintage year for bike sales? *BikeBiz*, 4 August 2015. Retrieved from www.bikebiz.com/news/read/straw-poll-has-2015-been-a-vintage-year-for-bike-sales-2/018211 (accessed 26 November 2018); J. Harker, UK bike sales rise 8%. *BikeBiz*, 22 October 2015. Retrieved from www.bikebiz.com/news/read/uk-bike-sales-rise-8/018554 (accessed 26 November 2018); M. Sutton, Sales reps view: There's no big thing, but lots of little things. *BikeBiz*, 20 October 2015. Retrieved from www.bikebiz.com/news/read/sales-rep-s-view-there-s-no-next-big-thing-but-lots-of-little-things/018543 (accessed 26 November 2018).

20   C. Reid, Evans Cycles in talks with lenders to raise £10 million. *BikeBiz*, 7 September, 2018. Retrieved from www.bikebiz.com/business/evans-in-cash-talks (accessed 26 November 2018).

21   R. Morley, Evans sold to Sports Direct. *BikeBiz*, 30 October 2018. Retrieved from www.bikebiz.com/business/evans-sold-to-sports-direct (accessed 26 November 2018).

22   Sport England, Once a week participation in funded sports among people aged 16 and over (April 2015–March 2016), n.d.. Retrieved from www.sportengland.org/media/10746/1x30_sport_16plus-factsheet_aps10q2.pdf (accessed 26 November 2018).

23   Details of the Department of Transport statistics can be down loaded in raw format from www.gov.uk/government/statistical-data-sets/walking-and-cycling-statistics-cw

24   Outdoor Industries Association & Sport England, Getting active outdoors: A study of demography, motivation, participation and provision in outdoor sport and recreation in England, 2015. Retrieved from www.sportengland.org/media/3275/outdoors-participation-report-v2-lr-spreads.pdf (accessed 26 November 2018)

25 G. Jarvie, *Sport, culture and Society: An introduction* (Abingdon: Routledge, 2006).

26 Shimano & International Mountain Bike Association (2008). The economics & benefits of mountain biking, 2008. Retrieved from www.singletracks.nl/Portals/5/documents/Economics%20and%20benefits%20of%20mountainbiking.pdf (accessed 26 November 2018).

27 McEwan & Weston, Different spokes.

28 McEwan et al., Differentiating identities within an extreme sport.

29 McEwan, The future of sportsmanship.

30 In both road cycling and BMX the different markets that have developed serve to provide individuals with differing recreation experience. This is important within the fragmentation process as it drives plurality and creates distinction between the various sub-formats that emerge. Further research of the type conducted on mountain biking would assist greatly in formally charting the impact of this process in BMX and road cycling.

31 See A. Giddens, *Modernity and self-identity: Self and society in the late modern age* (Stanford: Stanford University Press, 1991).

32 See E. Goffman, *The presentation of self in everyday life* (New York: Doubleday, 1959).

33 See T. Veblen, T. (2005). *Conspicuous consumption* (New York: Penguin Books, 2005); T. Veblen, *Theory of the leisure class* (Oxford: Oxford University Press, 2007).

34 L. Rebeggiani and D. Tondani, Organisational Forms in Professional Cycling: Efficiency Issues of the UCI Pro Tour, Diskussionspapiere des Fachbereichs Wirtschaftswissenschaften, Universität Hannover (2006).

35 See McEwan, The future of sportsmanship; McEwan and Weston, Different spokes; McEwan et al., Differentiating identities within an extreme sport.

36 J. Petri (2017). Everything you need to know about gravel bikes, the latest trend in cycling, *Bloomberg*, 11 May 2017. Retrieved from www.bloomberg.com/news/features/2017-05-11/everything-you-need-to-know-about-gravel-bikes-the-latest-trend-in-cycling (accessed 26 November 2018).

37 F. J. Berto, *The birth of dirt: The origins of mountain biking* (San Francisco: Van Der Plas, 1999).

38 Woodforde, *The story of the bicycle.*

39 Alderson, *Bicycling: A history.*

40 Van Nierop, et al., The evolution of the bicycle: A dynamic systems approach.

41 Woodforde, *The story of the bicycle.*

42 N. Wigglesworth, *The story of sport in England.* (Abingdon: Routledge, 2007).

43 Oosterhuis, Cycling, modernity and national culture.

44 See B. Beaven, *Leisure, citizenship and working-class men in Britain, 1850–1945.* (Manchester: Manchester University Press, 2013); P. Bailey, *Leisure and class in Victorian England: Rational recreation and the contest for control, 1830–1885* (Abingdon: Routledge, 2014).

45 See Alderson, *Bicycling: A history.*

46 See Woodforde, *The story of the bicycle.*

47 R. Holt, The bicycle, the bourgeoisie and the discovery of rural France, 1880–1914, *The International Journal of the History of Sport*, 2, 2 (1985), 127–139.

48 R. Vorspan, Rational recreation and the law: The transformation of popular urban leisure in Victorian England. *McGill LJ*, 45, (2000), 891–973.

49 G. Biddle-Perry, Fashioning suburban aspiration: Awheel with the Catford Cycling Club, 1886–1900. *The London Journal*, 39, 3 (2014), 187–204.

50 A. K. Ebert, Cycling towards the nation: The use of the bicycle in Germany and the Netherlands, 1880–1940, *European Review of History*, 11, 3 (2004), 347–364.

51 T. Webb, *Elite soccer referees: Officiating in the Premier League, La Liga and Serie A* (London: Routledge, 2017).

52 J. F. Mignot, The history of professional road cycling, in D. Van Reeth, & D. J. Larson (eds), *The economics of professional road cycling* (Cham: Springer, 2016), pp. 7–31.

53 M. Rayner, *Rugby union and professionalisation: Elite player perspectives* (London: Routledge, 2017).

54 C. Williams, *Gentlemen & Players: The death of amateurism in cricket* (London: Weidenfeld & Nicolson, 2012).

55 L. Allison, *Amateurism in sport: An analysis and defence* (London: Routledge, 2012).

56 See R. Holt, *Sport and the British: A modern history* (Cambridge: Cambridge University Press, 1989); R. Holt, Amateurism and its interpretation: The social origins of British sport, *Innovation: The European Journal of Social Science Research*, 5, 4 (1992), 19–31.

57 See E. Dunning and K. Sheard, *Barbarians, gentleman and players* (2nd ed.). (Abingdon: Routledge, 2005).

58 H. Perkin, *The rise of professional society: England since 1880* (Abingdon: Routledge, 2003).

59 See Mignot, The history of professional road cycling.

60 Alderson, *Bicycling: A history*, p. 163.

61 Mignot, The history of professional road cycling, p. 11.

62 Ibid.

63 Ibid., p. 10.

64 The model presented in this work is draw from the narrative presented by Mignot. See ibid.

65 C. Thompson, *The Tour de France: a cultural history* (Berkeley: University of California Press, 2006).

66 B. D. Brewer, Commercialization in professional cycling. *Sociology of Sport Journal*, 19, 3 (2002), 276–301.

67 See S. Morrow and C. Idle, Understanding change in professional road cycling. *European Sport Management Quarterly*, 8, 4 (2008), 315–335.

68 Ibid

69 V. Moller, *The doping devil* (Copenhagen: Books on Demand, 2008).

70 See I. Waddington, *Sport, health and drugs: A critical sociological perspective.* (London: Taylor Francis, 2000); I. Waddington and E. Dunning, Sport as a drug and drugs in sport: Some exploratory comments. *International Review for the Sociology of Sport*, 38, (2003), 351–368; I. Richie, Understanding doping as 'cheating' form a historical perspective, In T. Delaney (Ed.), *Sportsmanship: Multidisciplinary perspectives* (Jefferson, NC: McFarland, 2016), pp. 31–41.

71 B. Smart, Sportsmanship in question: The impact of professionalism and commercialization on the ethos of sport, In T. Delaney (Ed.), *Sportsmanship: Multidisciplinary perspectives* (Jefferson, NC: McFarland, 2016), pp. 222–233.

72 L. Freeburn, The Union Cycliste Internationale: a study in the failure of organisational governance of an International Federation. *The International Sports Law Journal*, 13, 1–2 (2013), 71–81.

73 D. Walsh, *Seven deadly sins: My pursuit of Lance Armstrong* (London: Simon & Schuster, 2012).

74 See P. Dimeo, Five questions for cycling chief Dave Brailsford. *The Conversation,* December 2016. Retrieved from https://theconversation.com/five-questions-for-cycling-chief-dave-brailsford-70365 (accessed 26 November 2018); P. Dimeo and V. Moller, Elite sport: time to scrap the therapeutic exemption system of banned medicines. *The Conversation*, December 2017. Retrieved from https://theconversation.com/elite-sport-time-to-scrap-the-therapeutic-exemption-system-of-banned-medicines-89252 (accessed 26 November 2018); P. Dimeo and V. Moller, *The anti-doping crisis in sport: Causes, consequences, solutions* (London: Routledge, 2018); L. Cox, A. Bloodworth and N. McNamee, Olympic Doping, Transparency, and the Therapeutic Exemption Process. *International Academic Journal on Olympic Studies*, 1, (2017), 55–74.

75 See Dimeo and Moller, *The anti-doping crisis in sport: Causes, consequences, solutions.*

76 Berto, *The birth of dirt.*

77 Klunkerz received their name due to the bike they rode, which were self-innovated using older style beach cruiser bikes, upgrade with the addition of road bike parts. See Berto, *The birth of dirt.*

78 See Berto, *The birth of dirt*; F. Savre, Mountain bike: Californians reinvent the bicycle, In D. S. Coombs & B. Batchelor (Eds.). *American history through American sport: From colonial lacrosse to extreme sports* (Santa Barbara: Praeger, 2013), pp. 281–296; F. Savre, J. Saint-Martin, and T. Terret, From Marin County's seventies clunker to the Durango World Championship 1990: A history of mountain biking in the USA. *The International Journal of the History of Sport*, 27, 11 (2010), 1942–1967.

79 Savre et al., From Marin County's seventies clunker.

80 ibid

81 Berto, *The birth of dirt.*

82 Savre et al., From Marin County's seventies clunker, p. 1949.

83 J. Breeze, Repack history, n.d.. Retrieved from http://mmbhof.org/mtn-bike-hall-of-fame/history/repack-history (accessed 26 November 2018).

84 For a full overview of the process of sportisation see: N. Elias, Introduction. In N. Elias, & E. Dunning, E. (Eds.) *Quest for excitement* (pp. 126–149). Oxford: Blackwells, (1986); N. Elias, The Genesis of sport as a sociological problem. In N. Elias, & E. Dunning, E. (Eds.) *Quest for excitement* (pp. 126–149). Oxford: Blackwells, (1986); R. Gruneau, *Class, Sport and Social Development* (Amherst: University of Massachusetts Press, 1983).

85 See Savre et al., An odyssey fulfilled: The entry of mountain biking into the Olympic Games, *Olympika: The International Journal of Olympic Studies*, 18, (2009), 121–136.

86 See Savre et al., An odyssey fulfilled; Savre et al., From Marin County's seventies clunker.

87 See A. Guttmann, *From Ritual to Record*. (New York: Columbia University Press, 1978); A. Guttmann, The Development of Modern Sports. In Coakley, J & Dunning, E (Eds.) *Handbook of Sports Studies* (London: Sage Publications, 2000), pp. 248–259.

88 See Savre et al., An odyssey fulfilled.

89 See McEwan and Weston, Different spokes; McEwan et al., Differentiating identities within an extreme sport.

90 See K. McEwan, An analysis of pluralised markets, identities and participant trait characteristics in mountain biking (Unpublished doctoral thesis, 2016). University of Portsmouth, Portsmouth; McEwan and Weston, Different spokes; McEwan et al., Differentiating identities within an extreme sport.

91 Jenks, *Subculture: The fragmentation of the social*.

92 See Bauman, *Life in fragments: Essays in postmodern morality*; Bauman, Consuming life. *Journal of consumer culture*; Bauman, *Liquid Life*; Bauman, *Liquid Times: Living in an Age of Uncertainty*; Bauman, *Consuming life*.

93 The argument that sport is reflective of society and that both evolve in tandem continuously is commonly held view in sports sociology, see E. G. Dunning, J. A. Maguire and R. E. Pearton, *The sports process: A comparative developmental approach*. (Leeds: Human Kinetics, 1993); J. Horne, A. Tomlinson and G. Whannel, *Understanding sport: An introduction to the sociological and cultural analysis of sport*. (London: Spon Press, 1999).

94 See T. M. Kerstetter, Rock music and the new west, 1980–2010. *Western Historical Quarterly*, 43,1 (2012), 53–71.

95 M. Dyreson, Crafting patriotism: Meditations on 'Californication' and other trends. *International Journal of the History of Sport*, 25, 2 (2008), 307–11.

96 McEwan, *An analysis of pluralised markets, identities and participant trait characteristics in mountain biking (p. 80)*.

97 J. C. Honea, Beyond the alternative vs. mainstream dichotomy: Olympic BMX and the future of action sports. *The Journal of Popular Culture*, 46, 4 (2014), 1253–1275.

98 Ibid; also see W. Nelson, The historical mediatisation of BMX-freestyle cycling. *Sport in Society: Cultures, Commerce, Media and Politics*, 13, 7–8 (2010), 1152–1169; H. Thorpe and B Wheaton, 'Generation X Games', action sports and the Olympic movement: Understanding the cultural politics of incorporation. *Sociology*, 45, 5 (2011), 830–847.

99 See W. Nelson, W. (2010). The historical mediatisation of BMX-freestyle cycling; C. Powell, C (2011). Premises liability in California: Chilling the diffusion of bicycle motocross. *California Western Law*, 47, (2011) 329–368.

100 See Honea, Beyond the alternative vs. mainstream dichotomy: Olympic BMX and the future of action sports.

101 See B. Edwards and U. Corte, Commercialization and lifestyle sport: Lessons from 20 years of freestyle BMX in 'Pro-Town, USA'. *Sport in Society: Cultures, Commerce, Media and Politics*, 13, 7–8 (2009), 1135–1151; S. Scott, A subcultural study of freestyle BMX: The effects of commodification and rationalization on edgework. (Unpublished Master's thesis, 2013). University of Louisville, Louisville.

102 As described by the likes of Berto and Savre, et al. See Berto, *The birth of dirt*; Savre et al., From Marin County's seventies clunker.

103 See USA BMX, History, 2018. Retrieved from www.usabmx.com/site/sections/7 (accessed on 26 November 2018)

104 See Elias, Introduction; Elias, The genesis of sport as a sociological problem; Gruneau, *Class, Sport and Social Development*.

105 Guttman, *From ritual to records: The nature of modern sports*.

106 See Scott. *A subcultural study of freestyle BMX: The effects of commodification and rationalization on edgework*; Nelson, The historical mediatisation of BMX-freestyle cycling.

107 Downs, Small bikes, big men.

108 Guttman, *From ritual to records: The nature of modern sports*. New York: Columbia Press.

109 In McEwan's analysis, he draws out two outcome focused narratives in mountain biking. In the first he identifies the 'sportsman' as a competitor who actively engages with others through rule-oriented contests. In the second, he identifies the 'neo-sportsman' who is focused more on personal outcomes without becoming oriented on benchmarking prowess and achievement against that of other participants. See McEwan, The future of sportsmanship.

110 For an overview of task and ego orientation see: J. L. Duda, Relationship between task and ego orientation and the perceived purpose of sport among high school athletes. *Journal of Sport and Exercise*

Psychology, 11,3 (1989), 318–335; L. L. Duda, Goal perspectives research in sport: Pushing boundaries and clarifying some misunderstandings. In G.C. Roberts (Ed.), *Advances in sport and exercise motivation* (pp. 129–182). Champaign, IL: Human Kinetics (2001); M. Newton and J. L. Duda, The relationship of task and ego orientation to performance: Cognitive content, affect, and attributions in bowling. *Journal of Sport Behavior*, 16, 4 (1993), 209–220.

111 Downs, Small bikes, big men.

112 Ibid

113 This point is emphasised through the inclusion of freestyle BMX (park) in the Olympic programme for the Tokyo games in 2020 and within the UCI Urban Cycling Championships in 2018. See R. Pearson, R. (2017). BMX in the Olympics: BMX freestyle park confirmed for Tokyo 2020, *Ride UK, 9 June 2017*. Retrieved from https://rideukbmx.com/news/bmx-olympics-bmx-freestyle-park-confirmed-tokyo-2020.html#IU0T8kgwZZDpelU0.97 (accessed 26 November 2018); UCI (n.d.). *2018 Urban cycling world championships*, n.d.. Retrieved from www.urbanworlds.cn/en/ (accessed 26 November 2018).

114 Outdoor Foundation, *Outdoor recreation participation: Topline report, 2017*. Retrieved from https://outdoorindustry.org/wp-content/uploads/2017/04/2017-Topline-Report_FINAL.pdf (accessed 26 November 2018).

115 See Guttmann, *From Ritual to Record*

116 Dyreson, Crafting patriotism: Meditations on 'Californication' and other trends.

117 D. Utton, Cycle-polo: 'The most popular sport you've never heard of'. *The Telegraph,* 28 May 2015. Retrieved from www.telegraph.co.uk/sponsored/why-not/11609512/try-cycle-polo.html (accessed 26 November 2018).

26

Equestrian

Susanna Hedenborg and Gertrud Pfister

Introduction

> The essential joy of being with horses is that it brings us in contact with the rare elements of grace, beauty, spirit, and fire.
>
> Sharon Ralls Lemon

> The wagon rests in winter, the sleigh in summer, the horse never.
>
> Yiddish Proverb

> To ride the horse is to ride the sky.
>
> Anonymous

Several aphorisms and proverbs from all over the world indicate the multiple roles of horses, and the various relations between horses and humans: horses have been working companions, subjects of love and admiration, and tools and partners in various sports competitions. Horses have also been valuable property and sources of prestige. Historically, kings, queens and members of the ruling classes were often portrayed on horseback, and early photographs of farming families in Europe often featured horses. Yet, horses were not only partners and friends of human beings; they were also (and continue to be) an important source of nutrition in many countries and cultures. All horse-riding peoples, from the Huns to the Native Americans, seem to have considered horsemeat a vital part of their diet. The numerous ways in which humans have used horses have made, and continue to make them one of the most important domesticated animals.[1]

During the 20th century, horses lost their role in transportation to motor vehicles in many areas in the Western world. Trains, cars, buses, and trucks increasingly replaced horse-drawn vehicles as means of transport, and the tractor proved to be a far more efficient tool in agriculture and forestry than the horse. The number of horses decreased as a consequence of motorization, and the role of horses changed; horses were, to an increasing extent, used for leisure pursuits, including competitive events.[2]

The purpose of this chapter is to map and analyse the use of horses in sport using Allen Guttmann's definition of modern sport.[3] Horse sports are in many ways unique, in that the relationship between a human athlete and animal is central. Yet, there are a wide variety of sports in which horses and humans are active. Individual humans and horses compete both as teams against other equipages (e.g. in horse racing), and in teams of several equipages (e.g. in polo). In some horse sports, other animals are also included (e.g. bull fighting, rodeo, working equitation). Humans ride or drive horses in competitions, and in the way in which the winner is decided depends on the specific event. The winner may be the equipage that is the fastest, jumps the highest, scores the highest number of goals, or exhibits the most precise movements. In this chapter, the analysis will be limited to horse racing; equestrian competitive activities organized by Fédération Equestre Internationale (FEI); and Olympic events. More specifically, we will focus on horse racing; dressage and para-equestrian dressage; jumping; eventing; driving and para-equestrian driving; vaulting; polo; driving; endurance; reining, and pentathlon. A more detailed description of what these activities entail will be provided below.

Although we have attempted to outline the uses of horses in as many settings as possible, and covering a breadth of time periods and regions, attempting to trace all contexts where horses have played a role would far have exceeded the scope of this contribution.[4] We were also dependent on available studies of our topic in English, French, German, or one of the Scandinavian languages. It is our hope that this chapter will encourage research that will shed light on further topics, contributing to a comprehensive body of knowledge about horses, and the ways in which humans have used and related to them.[5]

This chapter will focus especially on women's entrance into different events, in congruence with Guttmann's characteristic of "equality", which demands that nobody is excluded from participation in sports due to factors such as age, social class, ethnicity, gender and (dis)ability. It will be argued that equestrianism can only be defined as modern sport, in Guttmann's sense of the concept, if men and women, able-bodied/disabled persons, members of all social classes, and non-majority ethnicities can partake in competitions.

Concepts of sport and gender

In all ages and regions of the world, people have engaged in a multitude of physical activities with various aims and meanings, ranging from hunting for food, running to worship gods, or dancing for pleasure. People have also competed and attempted to outdo each other's strength, speed, or skills. Historically, however, competitions were restricted to selected groups of people – often young men – and the results were not registered and could not be challenged in future contests. Historians and sociologists trace the origin of modern sport to England, and claim that it emerged in the wake of Western industrialism.[6] Often used examples are football and rugby and their development in public schools, where young men from the aristocracy were moulded into the future leaders of society. Over time, different forms of sports spread from Britain to other countries and continents, when British students, merchants, or soldiers brought their leisure activities to the places they visited or resided. In addition, sport was used by Englishmen to "teach" and "civilize" people in the colonies.[7] Not all sports were diffused from England; some, like American football and baseball, developed as ways to distance America from England.[8]

In his book *From ritual to record*, Guttmann distinguishes modern sport from earlier movement cultures on the basis of seven characteristics: secularism/secularization, equality, specialization, bureaucratization, rationalization, quantification, and obsession with/the quest for records.[9] Several researchers have used Guttmann's characteristics in order to problematize what can and cannot be seen as modern sport. In this chapter, Guttmann's definition of modern sport will be used in order to discuss competitive activities involving humans and horses. Special attention will be given to the characteristic of equality. As historian and sociologist Gertrud Pfister and others have underlined, "sport was invented by men and for men; women were latecomers and – with regard to performance – the second sex".[10] As modern sport aims at the selection of the "best" athlete, equal access to competitions must be guaranteed so as not to exclude the potential winner. Yet, most sports are gender-segregated and men seem to have a biological advantage in metres, grams, and seconds. However, research has proven that a biological understanding of gender cannot explain participation patterns in sport, nor the feminization and masculinization of different movement activities. In this chapter, a starting point for the analysis is the recognition that the social construction of gender has a decisive effect on who is participating and not in a specific sport at a certain time. Furthermore, it needs to be stressed that what is perceived as masculine or feminine may vary between different social settings and time periods. Yet, masculinity and femininity are seen as separate, opposed, and attracted to each other, and masculine traits are considered the norm.[11]

Like other human practices, the use of horses has been gendered. Horses have had a more or less prominent position in the lives of men in many geographical areas and time periods. Men have traditionally used horses in agriculture, forestry, the transport sector, and in the army. The strong connection between horses and masculinity is indicated by the Swedish saying "a real man is a horseman".[12] Widespread practices and especially the symbolic correlation between masculinity and horsemanship may give the impression that women have, historically, had nothing to do with horses. However, while the use of horses has often been a male privilege, women's relationship with horses has varied considerably across different social and cultural contexts.[13] In the last century, a general trend in relation to the gendering of equestrian sports is that an increasing number of women partake in horse-related activities, and that several forms of femininity seem to develop in stable cultures.[14] However, this development progresses at different paces depending on location and competitive event. The equestrian sport activities studied in this chapter initially emerged as masculine activities, practised by men. This chapter will analyse the point at which they were opened to women, and the circumstances leading to gender inclusivity, also tentatively discussing gender constructions in the different sports.

Horses and competitions

Horse racing

Horse races emerged as important cultural and even political events in Greek antiquity, gaining increasing popularity in the Roman Empire. Numerous sources including pictures, statues, and written texts refer to races taking place as early as the 11th century BC.[15] An impressive narrative of the competitive use of horses is provided in Homer's *Iliad*, which describes the chariot race during the funeral games held in honour of Patroclus. In the Roman Empire, horse races were extremely popular albeit highly dangerous sports, mostly conducted in special arenas such as Circus Maximus outside of Rome, which seated around 250,000 people. The races kept the people entertained, and (perhaps) distracted them from political engagement.[16]

Over the centuries, racing remained an important form of equestrian competition. Guttmann indicates that horse racing is one of the oldest modern sports. Secularization was an early characteristic in horse racing (already under Antiquity), but specialization, bureaucratization, rationalization, quantification and obsession with the quest for records are more recent historical developments. Economic historians Joyce Kay and Wray Vamplew have argued that horse racing had developed the characteristics defined by Guttmann, thus becoming a modern sport, at the end of the 19th century.[17] Jockey clubs were first established in England and Ireland during the 18th century. Over time, these clubs established regulations, took charge of the registration of horses, and eventually licensed riders, trainers, and owners. In France, the revolution and the Napoleonic wars delayed the development of horse racing; although a jockey club was established in 1834, the first official races were not held until the mid-nineteenth century. In the United States and Sweden, jockey clubs were established somewhat later: in 1894 and 1890, respectively.[18] In other words, horse racing was in many respects one of the earliest modern sports, and jockey clubs now also exist in Africa and Asia. Horse racing has continued to advance its position in global sport, and today the horse racing industry is blossoming in the Arab countries.[19]

Equestrian sports

During the late 19th century, men and women alike flaunted their wealth by showing off their horses, but also through their audacity in hunting on horseback and their skills in carrousels.[20] 1921 witnessed the establishment of an international organization for equestrian sports: Fédération Equestre Internationale (FEI). The founding members were representatives of France, the United States, Sweden, Japan, Belgium, Denmark, Norway and Italy.[21] Today, FEI has 132 affiliated national federations, and is the governing body for equestrian programmes at Championships, Continental, and Regional Games, as well as for the Olympic and Paralympic Games. All international events in dressage and para-equestrian dressage, jumping, eventing, driving and para-equestrian driving, endurance, vaulting, and reining are governed by FEI.[22]

The performance of horses and riders vary between the different events, which are more or less difficult to understand for an inexperienced audience. Dressage, jumping, and eventing were the first three equestrian disciplines to be instated as Olympic events in 1912. They were also the first events recognized by FEI. Dressage has a long history, and is connected to prestigious riding academies in Europe in which members of the male nobility and their horses were trained for war.[23] In competitive dressage, an equipage performs movements of varying difficulties, which are judged by referees. The equipage with the highest scores wins the competition.

Jumping competitions in arenas did not appear until the late 19th century in France, Ireland, and the UK, although jumping over obstacles had been practised earlier. National organizations promoting show jumping were established, and the sport began to spread globally, at the beginning of the 20th century.[24] In show jumping, an equipage jumps a set of obstacles along a predetermined course, trying to avoid knockdowns of the obstacles and refusals. The equipage with the lowest number of faults (and sometimes also that which completes the course in the least amount of time) wins the competition.

In eventing (in French titled 'concours complet'), horse and rider compete in three different disciplines: a dressage programme, a jumping programme, and a cross-country ride including steeplechase obstacles (to be completed without falls and as quickly as possible). The winning equipage has to perform well in all of these. Dressage, jumping, and eventing have changed over time. Whereas the dressage movements and jumping obstacles and courses have become more difficult, the cross-country ride has become somewhat easier – not least to spare riders and horses' lives.[25]

Vaulting can be described as gymnastics or dance on horseback. It has its historical background in equestrian circus acts. Vaulting has, thus far, been part of the Olympic programme only once, at the 1920 Olympic Games in Antwerp. Army officers from Sweden, Belgium, and France competed jumping on and off horses from a standing position from the side and from the back. Some of the jumps entailed a board used to perform somersaults over one or more horses. Modern vaulting was developed in Germany after the Second World War as a way to introduce children to horse riding. It was included in FEI in 1983, and in the World Equestrian

Games in Stockholm in 1990. In modern vaulting, the horse moves around in a 15 metre circle, guided on a long rein by a lunger standing on the ground. Artistic mounts and dismounts, stands (on feet, knees shoulder or hands), and the carrying of another vaulter are included in the exercises.[26]

Polo, which is not under the auspices of FEI, was included in the Olympic programme in 1900, 1908, 1920, 1924, and 1936, after which it was removed.[27] Polo is a team sport with four equipages in each team (in arenas it is played with three equipages). It is played with a long-handled mallet, which is used to drive a ball forwards and to score goals. A modern game lasts about two hours. Presently, polo is a recognized sport in 77 countries, and world championships are held every three years, organized by the Federation of International Polo.[28]

Driving was recognized by FEI in 1970, and has never been an Olympic event. In driving, the driver sits on a vehicle drawn by one or more horses, and today there are competitions in dressage, marathon, and obstacle driving. In dressage, a number of compulsory movements have to be performed. These include speed and gait transitions as well as differently sized circles, and halts. In the marathon, horse and driver compete on a course with several hazards such as turns, water, hills, and labyrinths. In the final event, obstacle driving, the equipage must drive around cones with balls balancing on top. The winner is the driver who succeeds in completing the course in the shortest amount of time without knocking down the balls.[29]

In the early 20th century, the development of endurance riding was closely connected to the demands of the army. It was a military test for the cavalry where the horses were required to compete for five days for 483 kilometres carrying 90 kilograms. Endurance riding became a competitive sport in the USA in the 1950s, and was brought to Europe in the 1960s. At that time, there were only four international events. Endurance is not an Olympic event, but has been organized by FEI since 1978.[30] The number of events has increased over time; in 1998 there were 18 international events, and the first World Championships were held in the United Arab Emirates. In 2005, there were 353 international events.[31] Today, endurance riding is possibly the fastest-growing equestrian sport, and in 2014 there were more than 900 competitions within FEI.[32]

Organized endurance rides are usually 160 kilometres, and take approximately 10–12 hours. Veterinarians attend to the horses before and during the ride, and the horses must be found fit and in good condition in order for horse and rider to be allowed to continue. There are two types of endurance riding sports: endurance rides, and competitive trail riding. In endurance rides, the winner is the horse and rider first to cross the finish line. During the race, horse and rider stop periodically for a veterinary check, so as to assure that the horse is in good health. In competitive trail riding, horse and rider follow a marked trail, covering between 25 and 65 kilometres per day. The competitions can last between one and three days. In pace riding, the race has to be performed within a minimum and maximum time, whereas on a judged trail ride the horse is evaluated on performance and manners. In addition, the riders are assessed on the basis of how they handle the ride and manage their horse.[33]

As in running, the last decade has witnessed the increasing popularity of racing as an extreme sport. One example is an endurance race developed in Mongolia, spanning 1,000 kilometres, with riders changing horses every 40 kilometres during the race. Riders have ten days to finish the course, which is modelled on a 13th century long-distance postal route, so as to attract tourists to Mongolia. The first race was held in 2009, and 13 countries represented by 44 riders (21 men and 23 women) will partake in 2016.[34]

Reining was recognized by FEI in 2000, although it was accepted as a sport by the American Quarter Horse Association as early as 1949. Reining has thus far never been included in the Olympic programme. It originates from movements required by cattle horses while herding cattle. Competitions take place in arenas, and horses and riders are to perform small and large, slow and fast circles, as well as flying lead changes, 360-degree spins, and sliding stops.[35]

In 1996, para-equestrian dressage was included in the Olympic programme for the first time. Ten years later, in 2006, para-equestrian sports (dressage and driving) were incorporated into FEI. Para-equestrian dressage and driving use the same basic rules as conventional dressage and driving, but riders are divided into different competition grades based on their functional abilities.[36]

Pentathlon is a combination of five events, designed to discover the "perfect athlete" and the perfect soldier through running, swimming, shooting, riding, and fencing contests. Modern pentathlon was part of the Olympic programme for the first time in 1912.[37] It is not organized by FEI.

Today, all events described above are open to both men and women in international competitions and, for the ones that are part of the Olympic programme, in the Olympic Games. In contrast to many other sports, men and women compete with and against one another in the equestrian disciplines (in vaulting, however, men and women compete in separate events). In some of the events, mixed competitions have been the standard since the inclusion in FEI or the Olympic programme, such as in the case of para-equestrian events.[38] In the case of other events, exclusion and inclusion has a long history, and the chapter will now turn to an analysis of this process for dressage, jumping, eventing, polo, endurance, and pentathlon.

Modern sports

One of the lads?

Although horse racing fulfils many of Guttmann's criteria for modern sports, it is important to emphasize that women were barred from competing professionally in horse racing in many countries up until the 1970s. A majority of professional jockeys and trainers are still male in most countries. Nonetheless, male and female jockeys compete against each other. The development is complex. In amateur races, women started to compete in the first half of the 20th century.[39] At first, women competed in 'amazon races' (women's only races).[40] During the Second World War, women broke through the barriers and were allowed to compete with and against men. It seems that access was contingent on social class background and context. In other words, horse racing could be seen both as an old modern sport, and a sport whose modernization, in relation to Guttmann's criteria, happened late.

Although people from different social classes and ethnicities meet at the race course, it is evident that owners and trainers are more likely to be white and middle- or upper class, whereas grooms are generally drawn from a working-class background, as well as a range of ethnicities.[41] Previous research has shown that black jockeys were common in the late 19th and early 20th century, after which they disappeared.[42] In a study of race and social class in 19th century American horse racing, Mooney demonstrates how white men in power viewed the race track as a quintessential image of a harmonious society, representing white privilege and black slavery in harmony. Still, horse racing was not as harmonious as the actors in power would have preferred. On the contrary, struggles for patriarchal and social privileges and prestige were evident around the racetrack, which can be seen as a symbol for power relationships in the American South.

In addition, gender constructions in the groups meeting at the racecourse and in different locations warrant further research. An interesting conclusion in relation to the inclusion and acceptance of female stable hands in Britain is that they have to become "one of the lads".[43]

Graceful and dangerous

In Paris in 1900, five equestrian events were held: jumping, high jump, long jump, hacks and hunter combined (an event in which the rider showed the horse in walk, trot, and canter on the flat, and jumping over obstacles) and "four-in-hand mail coach".[44] It is difficult to talk about equal access during this period. Like most of the events in the Olympic Games at this time, the equestrian events were dominated by male athletes, and the sport was predominantly shaped by military influences.[45] Yet, in one of the equestrian events, "hack and hunter combined", two women competed. For one of them, a French woman named in the Olympic report as "Moulin", information is lacking, but the other one, Elvira Guerra, was a highly appreciated circus rider performing 'haute école' (dressage) at different circuses all over Europe.[46] In the second half of the 19th century and the beginning of the 20th century, the circus constituted a particular arena in which female horse riders were accepted. Despite performing imaginative and dangerous acts, which were not considered to be feminine activities at the time, the écuyères were nonetheless admired for their skills. On her horse Libertin, Guerra finished 9th out of 51 participants in the Olympic event, in which otherwise mostly cavalry officers competed.[47]

The equestrian disciplines currently included in the Olympics (dressage, show-jumping and eventing) were first part of the programme in the 1912 Stockholm Olympic Games. At the time, officers and gentlemen partook in the events, and an all-male committee for arranging these events had been organized.[48] Although women had competed in the Paris games in 1900, and competed in hunting, dressage and jumping on different levels, they were excluded from the Olympic Games from 1912 until the mid-20th century. Horse riding and a specific form of masculinity – a military masculinity – were closely connected.[49] Not until 1952 did women gain access again to Olympic competitions in dressage. At the same time as women were permitted to compete in the Olympic Games, regulations keeping low-ranking officers out of the Games were changed. From 1952, they were allowed to compete with the high-ranking officers and the so-called gentlemen, and were thus seen as amateurs. This marked the end of the military dominance over the Olympic equestrian events.[50] Four women out of 134 participants competed in the dressage event in 1952, and two of them became medallists: Lis Hartel of Denmark (silver); and Liselotte Linsenhoff of Germany (bronze). At the time, the prerequisites for riding dressage were debated in the media – was it (masculine) strength or (feminine) elegance that was required? There was also a discussion on opening separate events for women and men. However, a decision was never made.[51]

Before allowing women to compete in jumping and eventing, other discussions occurred. Some voices argued that the best athletes ought to compete in the Olympic Games, regardless of sex. Other voices emphasized that especially eventing at this level was too dangerous for women.[52] In the Equestrian Olympics in 1956, however, 13 women out of 158 participants competed in the equestrian events, a majority of them in dressage. Hartel and Linsenhoff once again won medals, and Pat Smythe, a well-known athlete and author at the time, competed in show jumping and won a bronze medal with the British team.[53] Smythe's book *Jump for joy* (1954) clearly reflects the changing use of horses during the 20th century, and Smythe's own story is significant in relation to women's access to the world of show jumping.

Women were not allowed to compete in eventing until 1964, when 13 women out of 103 competitors participated. A majority of the female competitors partook in the dressage event. Only one woman, Lana du Pont (USA), competed in eventing.[54] In relation to Guttmann's concept of "equality", equestrian sports have, in other words, been "modern" since the mid-20th century.

In contrast to most other sports, men and women compete with and against each other in equestrian sports, and from 1964 onwards the proportion of female competitive riders has increased. Yet, the majority are still men. In the most recent Olympic Games, Rio 2016, 224 athletes (38 percent women) from 43 countries competed in the equestrian events.[55] Gender distribution differs between the events: dressage has the largest proportion of female participants.[56] However, a high percentage of competitive eventing riders are also female. Prior to 1964, eventing was considered too dangerous for women. Eventing remains a dangerous sport, and the risks have not been eliminated: between 1993 and 2015, there were 59 fatal accidents in eventing, and three more riders died in the months preceding the Olympics in Rio.[57] The social construction of gender in relation to horse sports is complex,[58] and further research is needed to understand how femininity and masculinity are perceived and performed in the different events. Furthermore, although the equestrian events in the Olympic games are opened to men and women, the accessibility and equality of the competitions must be questioned in relation to social class and ethnicity. To compete in equestrian sports on this level requires bid sponsors or wealth. Furthermore, Western European countries and the USA have dominated the events during the 20th century.[59]

Played by men – watched by women?

The modern game of polo developed in India, in which the first polo club was established in 1833. In the 1860s, Polo was exported to England by British soldiers, after which it spread to other parts of the world. It arrived in Argentina in the 1870s, and today Argentina is the world-leading nation in polo. Players are ranked on the basis of their skills, and polo regulations allow both female and male players on the same team.[60] Historically, women appear to have participated in polo when it was introduced in Europe. The game was played by members of the aristocracy, and initially women played in their long skirts, riding sidesaddle. This practice was abandoned in the early 20th century.[61] Although women were allowed to play, their entrance in to polo appears to have met with resistance and gender stereotyping as well as recognition. In a study, Gilbert and Gillet report that women hold very few positions of authority in the world of polo, and gender stereotyping in relation to the dangerous nature of the sport is usually used to explain why women's participation on higher levels is resisted. Polo is described as played by men, and watched by women and families. Women can also participate as fundraisers. Similar to many other equestrian activities in Canada, however, Gilbert and Gillet demonstrate that grassroots polo is dominated by women.[62]

A good Muslim girl and a great rider

According to Guttmann, modern sport was more common in Protestant, capitalist, and industrialized countries.[63] It is thus perhaps surprising that horse sports play a seminal role in the Arab countries. However, it is important to recognize that Islamic sport scientists, both male and female, emphasize that health and fitness are important for men and women alike, and should be sustained by sporting activities.[64] In various sayings of the *hadith*, the Prophet Mohammed advocated living a healthy life and recommended running, swimming, archery, and horse riding. According to *hadiths*, the Prophet's wife Aysha raced with her husband. For this reason, it is less surprising that women from Muslim countries have, historically, ridden on donkeys, camels, and horses. Currently, several riding events, especially long-distance competitions, are organized for Arab women, one of them being the 100-kilometre "Sheikha Fatima bint Mubarak Cup". In 2011, this event attracted 60 participants who competed for a Dh800,000 prize at the Emirates

International Endurance Village in Al Wathba.[65] Since then, this event has served as the Sheikha Fatima Bint Mubarak Ladies' World Championship.[66] "It is restricted to the Arab women as to encourage and provide more winning opportunities for them", said the organizer Lara Sawaya, the director of the Sheikh Mansour bin Zayed Global Arabian Flat Racing Festival.[67] An exploration of the webpage on "Arabian Races", which covers races held since the 1980s, reveals that there are several women among the jockeys, trainers, and horse owners.[68] This explains why several of the best female riders are Muslims, such as HRH Princess Haya, who has competed for Jordan in international show jumping competitions. She is also the current president of the FEI. Another excellent horsewoman is Sheikha Latifa bint Ahmed, a multiple show jumping medallist competing for the UAE.[69]

The Hanan al Muhairi documentary *Arabyana* (2009) portrays the six members of the Emirati female riding team. The film demonstrates the struggles and hardships facing these women, practising what is still perceived as a man's sport. The documentary emphasizes women's right to ride. Some female horse riders are interviewed in the film, among them Sheikha Madeya Bint Hasher Al Maktoum, a young United Arab Emirates rider who specializes in endurance races, and champion rider Sheikha Latifa Al Maktoum. In addition to these women, the film features Sheikh Nahyan Al Mubarak and Sheikh Talib Al Qassimi. HRH Princess Haya supported the film. In the documentary, Hanan al Muhari wears a black scarf and loose clothing in order to demonstrate that "you can be a good Muslim girl and a great horse rider".[70]

The perfect athlete

Because of its military imagery, a majority of the pentathlon competitors in the 1912 Olympics were military officers. Many of the competitors came to the modern pentathlon from other sports, using their proficiency in those sports to aid their training for the combined event. In Stockholm, 12 of the 32 modern pentathletes also competed in another sport during the Olympics. The oldest participant in 1912 was Carl Pauen from Germany. Born on 7 April 1859, he was 53 years old in 1912. He retired, for unknown reasons, after the first event, which was shooting.[71] Surprisingly, there was also one female athlete in the 1912 Modern Pentathlon. Who, then, was the woman who wanted to compete against men in these disciplines? The applicant was fifteen-year-old Helen Preece, an excellent rider, who put her male competitors to shame in 1911 at the Olympia Horse Show in London, and who had also won a race with a prize of US$ 1,000.[72] On 7 July, 1911, the *Louisville Courier Journal* commented that: "English women are expecting Miss Helen Preece, a 15-year-old horsewoman, to accomplish great things at the Olympic Games". In an interview, Preece reported that she had trained hard, supported by her father and friends, to prepare herself for the contests in the five different disciplines. She was confident that she could win the pentathlon.[73] The *Evening Independent* of 9 July also mentions the participation in the Olympic Games "of the greatest girl rider in the world". However, the organizing committee in Sweden had already decided on 14 May 1912 by ten votes to two not to allow her to carry out her plan. It was not until the 2000 Olympic Games that the modern pentathlon was integrated into the women's programme.

Equestrian sports and 'equality'

This chapter has discussed several competitive activities wherein humans and horses take part: horse racing, dressage, jumping, eventing, para-equestrian dressage and driving, vaulting, polo, driving, endurance, reining, and pentathlon. All of these events are organized on national and international levels, and competitive conditions are standardized and regulated by organizations like FEI and IOC. Some of the records are more easily compared than others. It is simple to determine whether one racehorse runs faster than another on a particular distance, whereas the performances of dressage equipages demonstrating kür (the free programme) in different competitions are not as easily comparable. However, comparisons are made, and records are kept for the horses and riders with the highest scores. Thus, several of Guttmann's characteristics for modern sport are fulfilled in the activities presented here as early as the beginning of the 20th century. It is more questionable, however, whether the characteristic of "equality" was met at this point. This is especially interesting in regards to equestrian sports, as women and men compete in the same events. The commonly used argument of "women's weakness" does not hold for these sports, as physical strength is not decisive in horse riding. Women have proven that they can claim victories, and barring them would mean excluding potential winners. Still, many of the competitive activities described in this chapter were not initially open to women – and even if they were, gender stereotypes restricted women's performance. A hundred years ago, masculinity was symbolically connected to horses and horsemanship. Today, the stable is an arena for women and girls. Yet, a majority of the competitors on an international level are men.

Horse riding is one of the biggest sports for the disabled. Yet, there is segregation between able-bodied and disabled riders and, thus far, only para-equestrian dressage is part of the Olympic Games. In addition, horse riding on this level is an expensive sport, and is therefore not open to all. Sponsorship is a necessary prerequisite for (most?) competitors.[74] How this affects men's and women's participation, as well as members of different social classes and ethnicities, has yet to be studied. Additional research on the formal and informal gender regulations in equestrian sport is needed. In addition, social class seems to have a crucial influence on participation in equestrian sports, and it may be questioned if and how the marginalization of women and members of the lower classes contradicts the modern sport principles of inclusion und universal propagation.

Notes

1 Charles Chevenix Trench, *History of Horsemanship* (New York: Prentice Hall Press, 1970); Peter Mitchell, *Horse Nations: The Worldwide Impact of the Horse on Indigenous Societies,* Oxford: Oxford University Press, 2015).

2 Trench, *History of Horsemanship*; Susanna Hedenborg, "The horse in Sweden: workmate and leisure pursuit", in Hans Antonsson, & Ulf Jansson (eds), *Agriculture and Forestry in Sweden since 1900: Geographical and Historical Studies* (Stockholm: The Royal Swedish Academy of Agriculture and Forestry, 2011).

3 Allen Guttmann, *From Ritual to Record: The Nature of Modern Sports* (New York: Columbia University Press, 1978).

4 For instance, an interesting analysis of rodeo can be found in Miriam Adelman & Gabriela Becker, "Tradition and transgression: women who ride the rodeo in southern Brazil", in Miriam Adelman & Jorge Knijnik (eds), *Gender and Equestrian Sport: Riding Around the World* (London: Springer, 2013); Mary-Ellen Kelm, *A Wilder West: Rodeo in Western Canada* (Vancouver: University of British Columbia Press, 2011); Susan Nance, "A star is born to buck: animal celebrity and the marketing of professional rodeo", in Gillet, J., & Michelle, G. (eds), *Sport, Animals, and Society* (New York: Routledge, 2014).

5 Cf., Miriam Adelman & Jorge Knijnik (eds), *Gender and Equestrian Sport: Riding Around the World* (London: Springer, 2013); Dona Davis & Anita Maurstad (eds), *The Meaning of Horses: Biosocial Encounters* (London: Routledge, 2016); Miriam Adelman & Kirrilly Thompson (eds), *Equestrian Cultures in Global and Local Contexts* (London: Springer, 2017).

6 Guttmann, *From Ritual to Record...*; Norbert Elias & Eric Dunning, *Quest for Excitement: Sport and Leisure in the Civilizing Process* (Oxford: Blackwell, 1986); John Maguire, *Global Sport: Identities, Societies, Civilizations* (Oxford: Polity, 1999); J.A. Mangan (ed.), *Europe, Sport, World: Shaping global societies* (London: Frank Cass, 2001).

7 Mangan, *Europe, Sport, World...*

8 Mark Dyreson, Mark, J.A. Mangan & Roberta J. Park (eds), *Mapping an Empire of American Sport: Expansion, Assimilation, Adaptation and Resistance* (London: Routledge, 2013).

9 Guttmann, *From Ritual to Record…*

10 Gertrud Pfister, "Women in sport – gender relations and future perspectives", *Sport in Society* 13, no 2 (2010), 234–248.

11 Judith Lorber, *Breaking the Bowls: Degendering and Feminist Change* (New York: W.W. Norton & Company, 2005); Susanna Hedenborg & Gertrud Pfister, "Écuyères and 'doing gender': Presenting femininity in a male domain – female circus riders 1800–1920", *Scandinavian Sport Studies Forum*, vol 3, (2012), pp. 25–47.

12 Hedenborg, "The horse in Sweden: workmate and leisure pursuit"

13 Adelman & Knijnik, *Gender and Equestrian Sport*; Susanna Hedenborg, "Gender and sports within the equine sector – a comparative perspective", *International Journal of the History of Sport*, Vol 35, no 4 (2015), pp. 551–564; Davis & Maurstad, *The Meaning of Horses*; Miriam Adelman & Kirrilly Thompson (eds), *Equestrian Cultures in Global and Local Contexts* (London: Springer, 2017).

14 Gertrud Pfister, "Women in sport …"; Hedenborg, Susanna & Manon Hedenborg, "From glamour to drudgery – changing gender patterns in the equine sector. A comparative study of Sweden and Great Britain in the 20th century", in Miriam Adelman & Jorge Knijnik (eds), *Gender and Equestrian Sport: Riding Around the World* (London: Springer, 2013).

15 Sean Hemingway, *The Horse and Jockey from Artemision: A Bronze Equestrian Monument of the Hellenistic Period* (Los Angeles: University of California Press, 2004).

16 Hemingway, *The Horse and Jockey from Artemision* …

17 Kay, Joyce & Vamplew, Wray, "A modern sport? 'From ritual to record' in British *horseracing*". *Ludica*, 9 (2003), pp. 125–139; cf., Mike Huggins, *Flat Racing and British Society, 1790–1914: a Social and Economic History* (London: Frank Cass, 2000); Mike Huggins, *Horseracing and the British 1919–39* (Manchester: Manchester University Press, 2003).

18 Trench, *History of Horsemanship*; Wray Vamplew, *Pay Up and Play the Game: Professional Sport in Britain, 1875–1914*, (Cambridge: Cambridge University Press, 1988); Carole Case, *Down the Backstretch: Racing and the American Dream* (Philadelphia: Temple University Press, 1991); Fergus A. D'Arcy, *Horses, Lords, and Racing Men: The Turf Club, 1790–1990* (The Curragh, County Kildare: The Turf Club, 1991); Ghislaine Bouchet, *Le cheval à Paris de 1850 à 1914* (Genève: Droz, 1993); K. Arne Blom & Jan Lindroth, *Idrottens historia: Från antika arenor till modern massrörelse* (Farsta: SISU idrottsböcker, 1995).

19 Phil *McManus*, Glenn Albrecht, Raewyn Graham, *The Global Horseracing Industry: Social, Economic, Environmental and Ethical Perspectives* (Abingdon: Routledge, 2013).

20 Smith, Stephan J., "Human–horse partnerships: the discipline of dressage", in James Gillet & Michelle Gilbert (eds), *Sport, Animals, and Society* (New York: Routledge, 2014).

21 See www.fei.org.

22 See www.fei.org.

23 Lawe, Kari, "Några milstolpar i ridundervisningens utveckling vid Uppsala universitet", in Marianne Andersson & Johan Sjöberg (eds), *Till häst: Ridundervisning vid Uppsala universitet 350 år* (Uppsala: Uppsala universitet, 2013), pp. 81–97.

24 Kirrilly Thompson & Linda Birke, "'The horse has got to want to help': human–animal habituses and networks of relationality in amateur show jumping", in James Gillet & Michelle Gilbert (eds), *Sport, Animals, and Society* (New York: Routledge, 2014).

25 Hedenborg, "Gender and sports within the equine sector …"

26 See www.fei.org.

27 Horace A. Laffaye, *The Evolution of Polo* (Jefferson: McFarland & Co, 2009).

28 Michelle Gilbert & James Gillet, "Women in equestrian polo: cultural capital and sport trajectories", Miriam Adelman & Jorge Knijnik (eds), *Gender and Equestrian Sport: Riding Around the World* (London: Springer, 2013).

29 See www.fei.org.

30 Ibid.

31 See www.endurancegb.co.uk.

32 See www.fei.org.

33 Ibid.

34 "Adventure Tourism" (2016), retrieved from www.theadventurists.com/mongol-derby

35 See www.fei.org.

36 Ibid.

37 Ansgar Molzberger, *Die Olympischen Spiele 1912 in Stockholm–"Vaterländische" Spiele als Durchbruch für die Olympische Bewegung* (Köln: Dissertation 2010); Ansgar Molzberger, "Patriotic Games as a breakthrough for the Olympic movement", in Leif Yttergren & Hans Bolling (eds) *The 1912 Stockholm Olympics: Essays on the Competitions, the People, the City* (Jeffersen: McFarland, 2012); Sandra Heck, "Modern pentathlon and symbolic violence – a history of female exclusion from Stockholm 1912 to Paris 1924", *International Review on Sport and Violence*, 4, (2010), pp. 1–14; Heck, Sandra, *Von spielenden Soldaten und kämpfenden Athleten: Die Genese des Modernen Fünfkamps* (Göttingen:V & R unipress, *2013)*; Sandra Heck, 'Modern pentathlon at the London 2012 Olympics: between traditional heritage and modern changes for survival', *International Journal of the History of Sport* 30, no 7, (2013), 719–735.

38 For thorough analyses of gender constructions in relation to the (dis)abled body, see Kate Dashper, "'It's a form of freedom': the experiences of people with disabilities within equestrian sport", *Annals of Leisure Research* 13 (2011), no 1–2, pp. 86–101; Marie Larneby & Susanna Hedenborg, "(Dis)abled riders and Equestrian sports, in James Gillet & Michelle Gilbert (eds), *Sport, Animals, and Society* (New York: Routledge, 2014); Donna De Hann, Popi Sotiriadou & Ian Henry, "The lived experience of sex-integrated sport and the construction of athlete identity within the Olympic and Paralympic equestrian disciplines", *Sport in Society*, 19 (2016), no 8–9.

39 Wray Vamplew & Joyce Kay, *Encyclopedia of British Horse Racing* (London: Routledge, 2005); Susanna Hedenborg, "Female jockeys in Swedish horse racing 1890–2000: From minority to majority – complex causes", *The International Journal of the History of Sport*, 4, vol 24 (2007), pp. 501–519; Deborah Butler, *Women, Horseracing and Gender: Becoming 'One of the Lads'*(London: Routledge, 2017).

40 Hedenborg, "Female jockeys in Swedish horse racing 1890–2000 ..."

41 Huggins, *Flat Racing and British Society, 1790–1914;* Wray & Kay, *Encyclopedia of British Horse Racing*; Hedenborg, "Female jockeys in Swedish horse racing 1890–2000 ..."; Butler, *Women, Horseracing and Gender.*

42 James Robert Saunders & Monica Renae Saunders, *Black Winning Jockeys in the Kentucky Derby* (Jefferson: McFarland, 2003); Joe Drape, *Black Maestro: The Epic Life of an American Legend* (New York: William Morrow/HarperCollins, 2006); Katherine C. Mooney, *Race Horse Men: How Slavery and Freedom Were Made at the Racetrack* (Cambridge, MA: Harvard University Press, 2014).

43 Butler, *Women, Horseracing and Gender.*

44 Susanna Hedenborg, "Unknown soldiers and very pretty ladies: challenges to the social order of sports in post-war Sweden." *Sport in History*, 4, vol 29, (2009), 601–622; Donna De Haan, Donna & Lucy Claire Dumbell, "Equestrian sport at the Olympic games from 1900 to 1948", *The International Journal of the History of Sport*, vol 33 (6–7), (2016), pp. 648–665.

45 De Haan & Dumbell, "Equestrian sport at the Olympic games ..."

46 Hedenborg & Pfister, "Écuyères and 'doing gender'".

47 Ibid.

48 De Hann & Dumbell, "Equestrian sport at the Olympic games ..."

49 Hedenborg, "Unknown soldiers and very pretty ladies ..."

50 Ibid.; Susanna Hedenborg & Manon Hedenborg White, "Changes and variations in patterns of gender relations in equestrian sports during the second half of the twentieth century", *Sport in Society*, vol 15, no 3 (2012), 302–319. ; De Hann & Dumbell, "Equestrian sport at the Olympic games ..."

51 Hedenborg, "Unknown soldiers and very pretty ladies"; Hedenborg & Hedenborg White, "Changes and variations in patterns of gender relations".

52 Hedenborg & Hedenborg White, "Changes and variations in patterns of gender relations ..."

53 Hedenborg, "Unknown soldiers and very pretty ladies; Jean Williams, "The immediate legacy of Pat Smythe: the pony-mad teenager in 1950s and 1960s Britain", in: Dave Day (ed.) *Sporting Lives* (Manchester: MMU Institute for Performance Research, 2011), pp. 16–29; Hedenborg & Hedenborg White, "Changes and variations in patterns of gender relations".

54 Hedenborg & Hedenborg White, "Changes and variations in patterns of gender relations".

55 See www.sports-reference.com/olympics

56 Ibid.

57 Denzil O'Brien, "Look before you leap: what are the obstacles to risk calculation in the equestrian sport of eventing?" *Animals*, 6(2), (2016), 13.

58 Cf., Kate Dashper, Kate, "'Dressage is full of queens!' Masculinity, sexuality and equestrian sport", *Sociology* 46(6), (2012), 1109–1124.

59 Susanna Hedenborg, "Gender and sports within the equine sector".

60 Gilbert & Gillet, "Women in equestrian polo ..."; Laffaye, *The Evolution of Polo...*

61 Gilbert & Gillet, "Women in equestrian polo …"
62 Ibid.
63 Guttmann, *From ritual to record*…
64 Tamsin Benn, Tamsin, Gertrud Pfister & Haifaa Jawad, *Muslim Women and Sport* (London: Routledge, 2011).
65 See www.thenational.ae/sport/arab-women-get-sole-shot-at-endurance-horse-race-1.602406
66 See the website of International Federation of Arabian Horse Racing (IFAHR) at www.ifahr.net.
67 See www.thenational.ae/sport/arab-women-get-sole-shot-at-endurance-horse-race-1.602406
68 "Arabian Racing Cup" (2017), retrieved from www.arabianracingcup.com/champions.html
69 See www.thenational.ae/sport/arab-women-get-sole-shot-at-endurance-horse-race-1.602406
70 Ibid.
71 Molzberger, *Die Olympischen Spiele 1912 in Stockholm* …
72 *New York Times*, 5 November 2011.
73 Bill Mallon & Ture Widland, *The 1896 Olympic Games: Results for all competitors in all events, with commentary* (McFarland & Company, Inc., Publishers, 2009).
74 Hedenborg & Hedenborg White, "Changes and variations in patterns of gender relations"; Adelman & Knijnik (eds), *Gender and Equestrian Sport* …

27
Motor sports

Brandon Mastromartino

Introduction to motor sports

Motor sports is an overarching term to describe competitive sporting events that involve the use of motorized vehicles for racing or non-racing competition. Motor sports have been around since the late 1800s, originally as a way to test the functions of cars and improve their capabilities, but eventually became a spectator sport to marvel at the fast speeds and challenging tracks.[1] Primarily, most motor sports use cars or motorcycles as the main vehicle and the competition usually involves racing against other drivers in the same type of vehicle. The Federation Internationale de I'Autombile (FIA) globally governs most motor sport competitions, and the Federation Internationale de Motocyclisme (FIM) governs motorcycle competitions. There are various types of racing, the most prominent are open wheel racing or enclosed wheel racing. The most notable open wheel racing competitions are Formula One and IndyCar Series, and for enclosed wheel racing you'll find sports car, stock car, and touring car racing.

The rules and regulations of motor sports are vast and vary greatly depending on the type of vehicle and race taking place. Often it has been technology and safety that dictate the rules and regulations and they have evolved greatly since the beginnings of motor sport. Most motor sports are generally a race where the driver of a vehicle who goes from the start to finish line in the fastest time is declared the winner. However, there are other types of events such as time trials, endurance competitions, and showcases that don't necessarily follow the traditional race format.

Although specific details vary from competition to competition, FIA is the international body that governs most motor sport organizations and acts as the overarching regulator. One of their main objectives is to "encourage and implement the adoption of common regulations for all forms of motor sports and series across the world".[2] Their common regulations are divided up into circuits, rallies, off road, and hill climb sections, and they also have a safety guide and international sporting code that are applicable to all organizations that operate within FIA. The safety code covers many items including protective equipment mandates, vehicle component regulations, and track standards. FIA publishes their international sporting code on their website in English and French and it is updated every few years.[3] This is a comprehensive document that features regulations on competitions, officials, protests, and commercial inquiries amongst others. FIA provides general rules and regulations that must be abided by their member organizations, but since motor sport competitions can be vastly different from one another, specific rules and regulations can differ greatly depending on the event.

It is generally recognized that the birth of motor sport occurred in France in the 1890s based on the model of bicycle races.[4] City to city automobile races in France was used as tests for the technology of the car as well as an advertising platform where manufacturers could display their products. Due to the expensive nature of this venture, it was mostly France's upper class who were among the first to participate in these events. Typically, it was wealthy white men who had exclusive access to these events. Although the creation of the automobile internal combustion engine is credited to Gottlieb Daimler in Germany, the more developed road network in France provided a better testing ground for automobiles.[5] Around the same time, growing levels of literacy in society led to an increase in the popularity of newspapers. Needing content to fill their newspapers, a strong link began to form between journalism and the expansion of sport.[6] The coverage of a sporting event that lasted over a number of days, such as a car race, was used as a tool to promote the purchase of newspapers on a consistent basis.

In 1894, the owner of Le Petit Journal, a Parisian newspaper, sponsored the first recorded motor race. The race spanned 78 miles between Paris and Rouen and the winner was not the person who would cross the finish line first, but the one who completed the course "without danger, and was easy to handle and in addition was cheap to run".[7] Although not originally a spectator sport, word began to spread about these trials and people began to flock to watch these events. The following year, some vehicle makers arranged a 1200 km round trip race from Paris to Bordeaux where prize money went to the car that finished first for the first time. This event was heavily publicized and sponsored by newspapers and other notable corporations.[8] This was a turning point for motor sports and it began to spread elsewhere in Europe and North America.

The early days of motor sports were not without controversy and tribulations. The governments of Britain and Germany banned the use of their roads for racing out of fear for dangerous collisions. These fears were realized in 1903 when driver Marcel Renault died in the Paris to Madrid race, with an estimated 3 million spectators lined up to witness the horror.[9] This caused French authorities to ban regular roads for races, leading to the first "Grand Prix" in 1906 at Le Mans on closed roads. The concept of circuit races and other grand prix were still two decades away but this was a key development in motor sport as we know it today.

Although the first grandstands were built in Europe, America was where circuit racing was developed. On Europe's road races spectators would be able to watch for free, but enclosed in a circuit, spectators in America would have to pay for admission to the track. Race organizers and sponsors initiated this, but it was also beneficial to spectators because they could see more of the race from the vantage point in a grandstand.[10] As the Europeans led the way for the technical aspects of the sport, it was the Americans that led the way in commercializing it. This began in the 1930s during Prohibition in the United States. Modified cars were developed to quickly transport illegal alcohol and had to be illusive enough to escape authorities. Drivers would have competitions to see who could have the fastest car and sporadic organized races began to pop up.[11]

Stock car racing

In 1947, a group of drivers, mechanics, and promoters gathered in Daytona Beach, Florida, USA to discuss the future of auto racing in the United States. For decades there had been local races in various areas of the country, but there was no unifying body or championship that united all the races. This meeting is where the National Association of Stock Car Automobile

Racing (NASCAR) was born.[12] Entrepreneur and race promoter Bill France led the charge as he wanted to bring back a "golden age" in car racing where manufactures would sponsor racing teams to travel around the country and promote their brand.[13] From this, their notion that cars racing in NASCAR should resemble regular production cars but be modified to be able to race at high speeds became standard for their races. France believed that their first priority would be to serve the public by entertaining them instead of having the races as a test or exhibition of regular production cars.[14]

Entertainment came first for NASCAR, which set them apart from other organizations who attempted to rival them. The rise of NASCAR also occurred as mass automobile production in the United States rapidly grew in the 1950s and many smaller racing leagues already existed for them to unify. NASCAR initiated a points system for drivers, which allowed for closer competition. The system of flat distribution of points encouraged drivers to compete in the maximum number of races and made it feasible to make a career of racing for owners and drivers. This model helped keep more competitors of limited means financially viable and contributed to the growth of the sport.[15] NASCAR's popularity grew fast, and by 1955 they staged 45 races in the Grand National championship series with over $225,000 in prize money awarded.[16] This was a large step up from their inception in 1949 when they had just 19 races. However, due to growing violence in the sport, many states had banned car racing, forcing NASCAR to adapt. Through the 60s, NASCAR found a home in the southern United States where a large fan base was developed.[17] Quick population growth, rising income, and lack of major professional sports team in the south allowed for NASCAR to find their footing before eventually expanding nationwide once bans were lifted and race tracks became more safe. While NASCAR was on the rise in America, motor sport was also experiencing important growth in Europe.

Formula One (F1)

In 1950, Formula One (F1) was created when FIA unveiled plans for a Formula One world driver's championship. Drivers and promoters were frustrated by this unification though, because FIA banned commercial sponsors even though in America, motor racing was pulling in millions of advertising dollars each year.[18] Various races occurred over the next two decades, but it was in the 1970s where Formula One began to find their footing as one of the most powerful sport organizations in the world. Rapid growth in technology led to some of the fastest and most precise vehicles ever seen and driver rivalries such as the one between Jack Hunt and Niki Lauda took centre-stage as the sport grew in popularity.[19] With the explosion of popularity in the 1970s and 80s, Bernie Ecclestone became a key figure in moving away from the amateur model of motor sports and monetizing it, making himself and many others around him multimillionaires.[20] Under Ecclestone's leadership, F1 rights began to get sold on television and corporate sponsorship skyrocketed, leading to an increase for prize money for drivers and owners, and firm control for Ecclestone on all of F1's business matters; control he still holds to this day.

Like the globalization of many other industries, the growth of technology and communication are major factors in motor sports growing from a regional sport to an international one.[21] From a consumer perspective, the rise of television is at the forefront of motor sports going global. Motor races are one of the most exciting and unpredictable events to see on television and there is a high demand for it. High demand from consumers leads to advertisers paying large sponsorship fees, and as the importance of live sports on TV continues to grow, so does the amount TV networks will pay to get access to this content.[22] Having motor sports on television allows consumers from all over the world to watch races from every corner on the planet and makes that content all that more valuable for TV networks and advertisers. It can be argued that without the impact of television, NASCAR would not be as popular as it is in the United States today.[23] Although NASCAR is the largest motor sport industry in one country, the USA, Formula One racing is the apex of global motor racing.

Research from the Deloitte Sports Business group found that Formula One was the most valuable sport shown on TV globally. Each of their 17 races produced an average revenue of $229 million per event – the next closest competitor was the National Football League, who generated $24 million per game.[24] In 2007, Formula One earned $3.9 billion in worldwide revenues from three main sources. One was commercial rights revenues, which included race sponsorship, corporate hospitality, and broadcast fees. Second are team revenues that include sponsorship and contributions from partners and owners. Third are circuit revenues, which come from ticket sales and sponsorship.[25] Each event features a unique track in a different country that provides different challenges to the drivers and crew. The F1 circuit can be compared to a travelling circus that appears in different countries across the world each week to dazzle the crowds that come to watch.

This type of international attention has led to large corporate sponsorship deals and television partnerships that are among the most lucrative in all of sports.[26] Not only do these events take place in many countries around the world, the races feature competition between the top drivers and automakers representing their country. This national pride is highlighted through the intense rivalries through the years. Some examples include the rivalry between Brit James Hunt and Austrian Nikki Lauda, or between Frenchman Alain Prost and Brazilian Ayrton Senna.[27] Not only did these drivers represent their car manufacturer and corporate sponsors, their nations get behind them as a form of national pride.

Although there are events all around the world, there are certain nations where motor sports have more prominence. At the forefront of global motor sports are the USA, UK, Japan, Germany, Italy, and France who dominate international and global motor sport. Between them they account for 75 percent of the world market of spectators and 41 percent of the global racing series events.[28] Europe is consistently at the top when it comes to spectators but growth of the sport in other continents is contributing to a more globalized sport. Along with spectators, the production of motor sport vehicles and equipment is the most prominent in those aforementioned countries as well. However, there has been a shift in recent years that is allowing for some other nations behind those dominant countries to become major players in the motor sport industry. Countries such as Australia, South Africa, and Brazil have developed solid track records in terms of producing quality vehicles and hosting large scale motor sport events, but due to lower market opportunities, there is limited growth possible for these up and coming nations.[29] Behind them is a group of nations that are in the early stages of building an interest in the business of motor sport and have government funds and mandates to grow the sport. These countries are Malaysia, Gulf Region, Turkey, China and Czech Republic.[30]

Notable figures in motor sports

Over the years there have been thousands of drivers, mechanics, managers, promoters and other individuals that have contributed to the prominence of motor sports on the global stage.[31] The very nature of the transcendent personalities in motor sports explains why it is such a global sport. Going back to the early days of the sport, drivers were viewed as heroic individuals and even political figures would seek to align themselves with those heroes as the drivers exuded a personality that those leaders wanted to be associated with.[32] An example of this is Angel Nieto whose impact had greater meaning that just sport for the people of Spain.[33] In modern-day racing, not only do individuals represent the auto manufacturer they drive for, they also represent their country and discussions on which nation producers the best drivers is a constant among motor sports discourse. Among the thousands of transcendent personalities, some stand out amongst others. However, of notable importance, the history of motor sport is filled with white, wealthy men and the barrier of entry is strong for anyone in other social classes, gender and ethnicity. This is especially the case in F1, where no woman has started in a race since Italian Lella Lombardi in 1976. In recent years, Susie Wolff became the first woman to participate in a Grand Prix weekend in over 20 years, but just drove in a practice session before she retired because she felt breaking the gender barrier in FI "isn't going to happen".[34] In North America, it is more common to see women participating in the NASCAR series, but they are still significantly underrepresented when compared to the participation of male drivers.[35] This isn't just the case for drivers – male dominance in motor sport is also seen in the pit crews, course marshals, and team owners.[36] The FIA has made attempts in recent years to increase the role of women in motor sport through the creation of a women-focused commission, but there is still much work to be done to make motor sports more inclusive.[37]

Other notable exceptions include Lewis Hamilton, the British born mixed-race driver who rose to prominence in F1 racing. Hamilton become the first black driver on the F1 circuit in 2007 and become the youngest world-champion the following year at just 23 years old.[38] He now drives for team Mercedes and has claimed five world titles in his career.[39]

Richard Petty

Richard Petty is an American driver, known for his dominant NASCAR career that spanned over 35 years from the late 1950s to early 1990s. He won the NASCAR Championship seven times, only one of two drivers to ever accomplish that feat and won 200 races during his career, an all-time record. Petty grew up with the sport as he was a member of his father's pit crew at the age of 12 and moved up the ranks to become a driver himself. Petty's accolades are numerous and statistically he is the most successful driver in the history of NASCAR and among the top in all of motor sport.[40] The 1967 season was particularly noteworthy for Petty as he won 27 races, 10 of them consecutively. Off the track, Petty endeared himself to fans by spending countless hours signing autographs after races and attracted large crowds to any event he was participating in.[41] The dominant force that Petty was earned him the nickname "The King" and he was inducted into the inaugural class of the NASCAR Hall of Fame in 2010.

Mario Andretti

Mario Andretti was an Italian driver who immigrated to the United States and began participating in sprint and midget car racing at a young age. He entered the Indy 500 for the first time in 1965, driving to a third place finish and eventually captured a victory in Indianapolis in 1969. He spent a few years driving in the American Champ Car series before heading back to Europe to participate on the Formula One circuit. Andretti is known for his versatility as a driver, he is one of only three drivers in history to win races on road courses, paved ovals, and dirt track in one season, something he accomplished four times in his career.[42] Andretti drove up until his early 50s and finished second in the 1995 Le Mans 24 Hours. The Andretti name is famous throughout motor sports, which started with Mario, but his son's Michael and Jeff, nephew John, and grandson Marco have all had successful motor sport careers as drivers.[43] Mario Andretti drove in his last official race in 2000 and was inducted into the International Motor Sports Hall of Fame that same year.

Ayrton Senna

Ayrton Senna was a Brazilian Formula One driver who tragically passed away as the result of an accident on the track at the 1994 San Marino Grand Prix. Senna was known for his exceptional performances on wet tracks and impressive qualifying speeds, which earned him the pole position 65 times.[44] He won three Formula One world championships in 1988, 1990, and 1991 and is the fifth most successful driver in terms of wins in the history of Formula One. Although Senna's death is one of the most tragic incidents in motor sports history, it paved the way for dramatic changes to safety in motor sports. Improved crash barriers, redesigned tracks, higher crash safety standards, and changes to engine power were instituted to improve the safety of the sport's drivers.[45] Senna's legacy in Brazil still stands strong as the major freeways in Sao Paulo and Rio de Janeiro is named after him. Ayrton Senna was inducted into the International Motor sports Hall of Fame in 2000.

Alain Prost

Alain Prost was a French racing driver who won the Formula One championship four times. He was active from 1980–1993 and he held the record for most Grand Prix victories from 1987 until the record was broken in 2001. He joined the McLaren Formula One team at the age of 24 and went on to become one of the greatest drivers in the sport's history. He was nicknamed "The Professor" because he took an intellectual approach to the sport and would study every element of it.[46] His style behind the wheel was a relaxed and smooth presence and cited classic drivers such as Jackie Stewart and Jim Clark as his inspiration.[47] Post-retirement, Prost worked as a TV analysis for French F1 coverage and eventually went back to McLaren as a technical advisor. He was inducted to the International Motor Sports Hall of Fame in 1999.

Dale Earnhardt

Dale Earnhardt was an American NASCAR driver who recorded over 70 race wins during his career. He won seven NASCAR championships in the 1980s and 1990s and was known for his unrelenting and unwavering style of driving, earning himself the nickname of "The Intimidator".[48] He also became known for his business acumen and built up one of the most famous family driving dynasties in motor sport that has become a multimillion-dollar racing company. Like some other racing legends, Earnhardt faced a tragic end and passed away in a fatal crash at the 2001 Daytona 500. At the time of his death, Dale Earnhardt had accomplished more than most drivers ever have and his legacy lives on through his sons Dale Jr. and Kenny who have had successful driving careers as well. Along with Richard Petty, Dale Earnhardt was inducted into the inaugural class of the NASCAR Hall of Fame in 2010.

Michael Schumacher

Michael Schumacher was a German Formula One driver who holds the record for most F1 World Championships with seven. He is widely regarded as the best F1 driver in the history of motor sport as he has countless accolades and accomplishments.[49] Schumacher was at his best when he drove for Ferrari and was particularly dominant from 2001–2004 when he won five titles in a row. He was especially known for his technical abilities and how he strove for perfection in every little detail on the track.[50] His mental toughness and physical fitness set him apart from other drivers and he holds almost every major F1 record. Schumacher retired in 2012, but in 2014 he suffered a life threatening head injury in a skiing accident in Switzerland. To this date, Schumacher is paralyzed in a wheelchair and has severe memory and speaking issues. Progress has been slow for him but doctors remain optimistic that his quality of life will continue to increase over time. Although a tragic incident in the life of the great F1 driver, Schumacher's legacy as arguably the greatest driver is unrivalled by anyone.

Danica Patrick

Danica Patrick is an American professional race driver who achieved many "firsts" for women in motor sports. Patrick began racing go-karts at the age of 10 and at age 16 moved to England to pursue a career driving open-wheel cars.[51] There, her career blossomed and in 2005 earned the Indianapolis 500 Rookie of the Year and the IndyCar Series season Rookie of the Year awards. By 2008, Danica Patrick was ranked as high as 6th overall in the IndyCar Series driver standings, the highest ever for woman.[52] In 2010, Patrick began driving on the NASCAR circuit and continued to set the pace for female motor sport drivers, such as becoming the first woman to win a Cup Series pole position, and setting the record for most top ten finishes by a woman in the Spring Cup Series in 2015. In addition to her success on the track, Patrick has paved the way for women in motor sports in terms of endorsements, television commercials, and media attention, which has contributed to her large fan following that continues today.[53]

Tracks around the world

A unique aspect about motor sports is that not only are the individual drivers key personalities, the tracks and races themselves have a personality of their own and are important elements of the sport. In motor sports, the "Triple Crown" of motor racing refers to the three most significant races in the sport.[54] They are The Indianapolis 500, the Le Mans 24 Hours, and the Monaco Grand Prix. Each event in the world of motor sport has unique traditions and attraction, but these three races stand out from the rest because of their heritage and legendary status. Through the decades these races have existed, only one driver has achieved the illusive Triple Crown. This was English driver Graham Hill who won five Monaco Grand Prix championships (1963, 1964, 1965, 1968, 1969), and went on to capture the Indianapolis 500 in 1966 and the Le Mans 24 Hour Race in 1972.[55] He is the only individual to win all three, and only 11 other drivers in history have won two out of the three races to highlight how difficult it is. Despite the extreme challenge obtaining the Triple Crown poses, it "retains a revered and mythical status among motor sport enthusiasts" (p. 282).

The Indianapolis 500, also known as the Indy 500, is a 500-mile race in Indianapolis, United States. It first ran in 1911 and it has become an American tradition to run the race annually on Memorial Day weekend at the iconic Indianapolis Motor Speedway. The speedway is a two and a half mile banked oval with four 60-foot wide bends which drivers approach at the highest of speeds. Since it takes place on Memorial Day, a day in the United States to honor military members, it is often associated with the American spirit as many references to patriotism are made.[56] Over 400,000 people show up every year to witness the race, and perhaps the most unique aspect of the Indy 500 is that amateur drivers can attempt to qualify for the race. As long as the individual has paid the entry fee and attended a mandatory orientation session, anyone can attempt to qualify for the race, even if they are not part of any driving circuit or association.[57] Also unlike most American races, the Indy 500 attracts drivers from all over the world for the chance to compete in the famous and historic event. It is the challenge of the speed and danger mixed with the American spectacle and tradition that has made the Indy 500 so iconic in the motor sports world and part of the Triple Crown.

The Monaco Grand Prix is often viewed as the "jewel in the crown".[58] It is part of the Formula One world championship circuit and is one of the most prestigious motor races in the world. The race takes places through the streets of Monaco, along the French Riviera. At the centre of it all, Monaco, is infamous for its casinos, glamorous attractions, and the fact it is a tax haven, attracts attracting the world's wealthiest individuals – a perfect place for the high octane showcase of motor sport. The first running of the Monaco Grand Prix took place in 1929 and the challenge of this race lies in the fact the route takes places on a narrow street circuit through Monaco, where there is slim room for error. It is a very dangerous race as there are tight corners, frequent elevation changes, and the famous tunnel where drivers go from light to dark visibility. The track remains mostly the same since its inception in 1929 but car speeds have increased by 70% in that time, making it more dangerous and challenging than ever before.[59] The speed, glamour, excitement, and prestige of the Monaco Grand Prix is symbolic of the factors that attract drivers and spectators to the world of motor sport and has stood the test of time as one of the most important races on the planet.

The 24 Hours of Le Mans is a sports car endurance race that started in 1923. The race lasts for a 24-hour period and tests the reliability and durability of the vehicle more so than just speed. Designed to test the limits of new cars, this event focuses more on the car manufacturers over the driver. Le Mans is significant to motor sport because it as led to many technical innovations over the years as car manufactures needed to find ways to combine speed and durability in order to be victorious.[60] The race takes place on a combination of city streets and permanent racetrack, different from most races in the world, and has changed over the years as a result of safety concerns. In addition to there being one overall winner, there are other categories based on engine size that are awarded prizes, keeping the field very competitive. Since the crash in 1955, the race now mandates that each car entry have three drivers with no individual allowed to drive for more than 14 hours and only four consecutive hours at a time. Separating this race from most others as well is the freedom manufacturers have to make design adjustments to the vehicle. There are some regulations they must conform to, but most manufacturers use this race as an opportunity to show that their sports cars have both speed and reliability to make them stand out from their competitors.[61] Legendary sports car manufacturers such as Ferrari, Jaguar, Mercedes-Benz, and Porche made their debuts at Le Mans and have stood at the forefront for sports car design through many decades. Although a glamorous event, Le Mans is home to one of the most tragic accidents in motor sports history when a collision in the 1955 event caused the death of a driver and over 80 spectators.[62] Despite the dangers of Le Mans 24 Hours, the race has always attracted the best drivers and car specialists from all over the world. It gives the Triple Crown an extra element in that it rewards reliability and durability as opposed to outright speed like the other two Triple Crown events.

The Triple Crown of motor racing is a big piece of the long-standing tradition and history in motor sports. Combining multiple race victories adds to the legacy of the driver, similar to a Grand Slam in tennis, and gives added significance to each victory. As shown by the fact only one driver has won all three, winning all three takes a rare combination elite speed and car control with the ability to adapt and modify the vehicle to be the best of the best. Although extremely rare, winning the Triple Crown is the most sought after achievement in motor sports.

The world of motor sport has evolved greatly over 100 years of racing. Driving techniques, vehicle technology, and track design is continuality improving and the entertainment value of the sport is at an all-time high. One of the true global sports, motor sports has stood the test of time and continues to be one of the most popular sports in the world.

Notes

1 Éamon Ó. Cofaigh, "Motor Sport in France: Testing-Ground for the World", *The International Journal of the History of Sport* 28.2 (2011): 191–204.
2 See www.fia.com/regulations.
3 See www.Fia.com/regulations "International Sporting Code".
4 Cofaigh, "Motor Sport in France", 193.
5 Ibid., 193.
6 Ibid., 193.
7 Russell Hotten, *Formula 1: The Business of Winning*, Orion Business, 1998, 3.
8 Ibid., 4.
9 Ibid., 5.
10 Ibid., 5–6.
11 Clive Gifford, *Racing: The Ultimate Motorsports Encyclopedia*, Kingfisher Books, 2006.
12 Ben Shackleford, "NASCAR Stock Car Racing: Establishment and Southern Retrenchment", *The International Journal of the History of Sport* 28.2 (2011): 300–318.
13 Ibid., 301.
14 Ibid., 302.
15 Robert G. Hagstrom, *The NASCAR Way: The Business that Drives the Sport*, John Wiley & Sons, 2001.
16 Shackleford, "NASCAR Stock Car Racing", 307.
17 Ibid., 311.
18 Hotten, *Formula 1: The Business of Winning*, 7.
19 Ivan Rendall, *The Power Game: The History of Formula One and the World Championship*, Cassell & Company, 2000.
20 Hotten, *Formula 1: The Business of Winning*, 23–33.
21 Hagstrom, *The NASCAR Way*, 75–100.
22 Tom Evens, Petros Iosifidis, and Paul Smith, *The Political Economy of Television Sports Rights*, Palgrave Macmillan, 2013.
23 Michael Kackman et al., eds, *Flow TV: Television in the Age of Media Convergence*, Routledge, 2010.
24 Sport Business Group, "F1 Generates More Money Per Event than any Other Sport", www.motorsport.com/f1/news/f1-generates-more-revenue-per-event-than-any-sport.
25 Barbara Bell, *Sport Studies*, Sage, 2009, 113.
26 Hotten, *Formula 1: The Business of Winning*, 162–182.
27 Jose Rosinski, *The Formula 1 Saga Vol 7: Great Rivalries and the Alain Prost Story*, 1992.
28 Nick Henry, Tim Angus, Mark Jenkins, and Chris Aylett, *Motorsport Going Global: The Challenges Facing the World's Motorsport Industry*, Springer, 2007.
29 Ibid., 96–116.
30 Ibid., 117–131.
31 Anne B. Jones and Rex White, *All Around the Track: Oral Histories of Drivers, Mechanics, Officials, Owners, Journalists and Others in Motorsports Past and Present*, McFarland & Company, 2007.
32 David Hassan, "Prologue: The Cultural Significance and Global Importance of Motor Sport", *The International Journal of the History of Sport* 28.2 (2011): 187–190.
33 Teresa González Aja, "From Dictatorship to Democracy in Spain: The Iconography of Motorcyclist Angel Nieto", *The International Journal of the History of Sport* 28.2 (2011): 240–252.
34 Andrew Benson, "Susie Wolff: Female F1 test driver to retire after Race of Champions", www.bbc.co.uk/sport/formula1/34714704 (accessed 04 February 2018).
35 David A. Charters, "It's a Guy Thing: The Experience of Women in Canadian Sports Car Competition", *Sport History Review* 37 (2006).
36 Ben A. Shackleford, "Masculinity, Hierarchy, and the Auto Racing Fraternity: The Pit Stop as a Celebration of Social Roles", *Men and Masculinities* 2 (1999): 180–196.
37 Jordan J.K. Matthews and Elizabeth C.J. Pike, "'What on Earth are They Doing in a Racing Car?': Towards an Understanding of Women in Motorsport", *The International Journal of the History of Sport* 33.13 (2016): 1532–1550.
38 Coulthard, D. (2015). "Lewis Hamilton Has Proved Himself to be the Best F1 Driver of His Generation," *The Telegraph*, www.telegraph.co.uk/sport/motorsport/formulaone/lewishamilton/11954394/Lewis-Hamilton-has-proved-himself-to-be-the-best-F1-driver-of-his-generation.html

39 Duncan, P. (2019). "Lewis Hamilton Says Mercedes Will Be Underdogs for Russian GP and Rest of F1 Season," *The Telegraph*, www.telegraph.co.uk/formula-1/2019/09/26/lewis-hamilton-says-mercedes-will-underdogs-russian-gp-rest

40 Ed Hinton, *Daytona: From the Birth of Speed to the Death of the Man in Black*, Warner Books, 2002.

41 Richard Petty and William Neele, *King Richard I: The Autobiography of America's Greatest Auto Racer, Richard Petty*, Macmillan, 1986.

42 Larry Schwartz, "Super Mario Had Speed to Burn", http://espn.go.com/classic/biography/s/andretti_mario.html (accessed 1 June 2016).

43 Gifford, *Racing*, 114.

44 Clive Gifford, *Racing: The Ultimate Motorsports Encyclopedia*, Kingfisher Books, 2006.

45 Giuseppe Lippi, Gian Luca Salvagno, Massimo Franchini and Gian Cesare Guidi, "Changes in Technical Regulations and Drivers' Safety in Top-Class Motor Sports", *British Journal of Sports Medicine* 41.12 (2007): 922–925.

46 Gifford, *Racing*, 108.

47 Roebuck, Nigel. *Grand Prix Greats: A Personal Appreciation of 25 Famous Formula 1 Drivers*, Patrick Stephens, 1986.

48 Gifford, *Racing*, 100.

49 Ibid., 111.

50 Christopher Hilton, *Michael Schumacher: The Whole Story*, Haynes, 2006.

51 Connie Colwell Miller, *Danica Patrick*, Minneapolis, MN: Abdo Publishing, 2013.

52 Ibid., 21.

53 Shaughan A. Keaton, Nicholas M. Watanabe and Christopher C. Gearhart, "A Comparison of College Football and NASCAR Consumer Profiles: Identity Formation and Spectatorship Motivation", *Sport Marketing Quarterly* 24.1 (2015): 43.

54 Philip O'Kane, "A History of the 'Triple Crown' of Motor Racing: The Indianapolis 500, the Le Mans 24 Hours and the Monaco Grand Prix", *The International Journal of the History of Sport* 28.2 (2011): 281–299.

55 Bette Hill and Neil Ewart, *The Other Side of the Hill: Life with Graham Hill*, Hutchinson, 1978.

56 O'Kane, "A History of the Triple Crown", 283.

57 Ibid., 287.

58 Ibid., 287.

59 Ibid., 288.

60 Cofaigh, "Motor Sport in France", 198.

61 O'Kane, "A History of the Triple Crown", 294.

62 Gerald Donaldson, *Fangio: The Life Behind the Legend*, London: Virgin Books, 2009.

28

Sailing

David Black

Intrinsic diversity and 'apex' practices

A distinctive feature of sailing compared with most sporting practices is the exceptional diversity of forms it has taken. The array of craft that sailing takes place in, as well as the various locales where it occurs, are remarkable. Sailors pursue their sport, whether recreationally or as fierce competitors, in boats ranging from two to fifty metres and beyond; in popular designs spanning 'classic' classes with their origins in the early 20th century to the latest 'breakthrough' designs, which emerge annually; made of materials ranging from wood to fibreglass to plastic to an array of exotic high-tech products; with one, two, or three hulls and, increasingly, hydrofoils; from blindingly fast to 'dog slow'; and making athletic demands on their crew ranging from negligible to extreme. The range of locales where the sport is pursued, often in local clubs, runs from rivers, ponds and gravel pits to globe-spanning ocean races and everything in between.

The extraordinary range of sailboat classes and the diverse locales where they are utilized are, of course, intrinsically linked. For example, the enduring popularity of the inland scow classes pioneered in the American Midwest is directly linked to their suitability to the windy, flatwater lakes of this part of the world.[1] They are distinctly unsuited to large lakes or oceans with large waves. The upshot, however, is that sailing is a sport that can be actively and successfully pursued by an exceptional range of participants. Depending on boat design and crew role, sailors can remain successful competitors well into their 70s. While sailing, like most sports, was for many years dominated by men, there are many classes in which men and women can race with complete equality and mixed crews are increasingly common at the highest levels of competition.[2] Appropriately adapted designs are particularly well suited for physically disabled sailors, who can also race level with 'able-bodied' peers. Because of these features, the sport is in some respects exceptionally accessible.

Yet there is no denying the extraordinary expense that many forms of the sport involve, the privileged settings (and iconic yacht clubs[3]) where it often occurs, and the elitist and classist connotations it has come to bear as a result.[4] Moreover, notwithstanding Bourdieu's suggestion that these forms require 'little physical exertion', many of the sailors who crew these vessels must be exceptional (even extreme) athletes who are richly compensated for their roles.

One of many such apex practices is the new/latest generation of 'superyachts' – astounding vessels of well over 30 metres. A second instance, which truly warrants the 'extreme sport' appellation, is the Volvo (previously Whitbread) Ocean Race which in 2017–2018 pitted 7 vessels and their crews in a round-the-world race involving 11 legs between some of the world's most iconic venues, including Cape Town, Melbourne, Hong Kong, Newport, Itajai and the Hague. Like many contemporary forms of elite sailing, this event requires the latest high technology designs, and exceptionally skilled multinational crews prepared to confront the most extreme conditions, while 'representing' an odd blend of corporate, national, and cosmopolitan identities seeking to capitalize the exceptional branding opportunities these events offer.[5] One particularly interesting entrant in the 2017/2018 race is *Clean Seas*, representing 'the United Nations' and crewed by a gender-equal and multinational team of under-30-year-old sailors promoting a campaign to 'Turn the Tide on Plastic'. Tellingly, while the majority of vessels and sailors still 'represent' Western countries and corporations, they have been joined in recent years by entrants from China and Hong Kong, including the 2017/2018 champion – the Chinese-flagged Dongfeng Race Team.[6]

By far the most famous sailing competition, however, and the only one that might properly be thought of as a Sports Mega-Event (SME) – albeit a peculiar one (see below) – is the America's Cup. The 'Auld Mug' self-identifies as 'the oldest sporting trophy in the world', having first been contested at the Isle of Wight in 1851 (Smith 2002, 30). For more than a century, it was emblematic of American global ascendance, having been successfully won and defended by the New York Yacht Club from 1851 until 1983 against all comers. 'All comers', however, was exceptionally narrowly defined, however, with challengers hailing primarily from the United Kingdom and Australia, along with two 19th century outliers from Canada. During this time, it was 'sportingly' contested by some of the world's most iconic capitalists, including (from the US) J.P. Morgan, the Vanderbilts, Ted Turner, and Bill Koch, and (from the challengers) Sir Thomas Lipton, Sir Thomas Beckwith, Alan Bond, and Baron Marcel Bich of Bic pen fame (who was a repeat competitor for France, though he never succeeded in winning the challenger trials). The competition was staged in yachts designed and built according to several different 'rating' rules, allowing for innovation and competition in design and construction as well as sailing skill. The most famous such 'classes' were the mighty J-Class craft in the 1930s, and the 12-metre rule yachts from 1958 through 1987.

The character of the competition changed forever in 1983, however, when Australia wrested the cup from the American defenders with a breakthrough design, involving keel 'wings' on *Australia II* (see Chisnell 2013). This unleashed a surge in international and corporate interest, as well as a dramatically heightened 'science and technology' design race. The competition moved from Newport, RI in the US for the first time since 1851, to Fremantle in Western Australia, and there were more countries, clubs, and wealthy backers entering the competition than ever before, with 13 challengers from 6 countries. Since that time, the Cup has been contested in boats conforming to several different design rules – most recently the truly extreme (in terms of speed, technical difficulty, and expense) foiling catamarans used to contest the 2013 and 2017 competitions. Any pretence of 'nationality' rules among the crew has virtually disappeared, as a new generation of wealthy contestants (including Oracle's Larry Ellison, the Swiss biotechnology billionaire Ernesto Berterelli, and the Italian luxury brand Prada) aggressively recruited (and handsomely compensated) top sailing talent from all over the sailing world (see Woo and Kuriloff 2015). The most dramatic and controversial of such 'recruiting drives' occurred when Berterelli successfully lured away much of the Cup-winning NZL 60 crew from the New Zealand defender, including skipper Russell Coutts, from the 2000 New Zealand defender, setting up Alinghi's successful assault on the Cup and marking the first victory by a vessel 'representing' a landlocked country (Switzerland).[7]

The result has been a very distinctive type of SME. Because of the historic inaccessibility and unfamiliarity to the 'average' sport consumer (both participant and spectator), it has not enjoyed the same mass appeal as most other SMEs – although the Cup's inheritors have made great strides to improve the televisual appeal of the competition through the advent of 'arena' sailing in confined spaces like San Francisco Bay or Bermuda's Great Sound (Campbell 2017). Yet it enjoys a strong appeal and exceptional 'brand power' among a powerful cluster of companies, countries, and captains of industry. John and Jackson (2010) aptly note:

> the America's Cup is distinctive given its status as a competitive international sports event which is structured and operated by private yacht clubs, involving 'corporatized' global syndicates with few regulations about citizenship, yet represented and marketed under the banner of national flags.
>
> *(John and Jackson 2010, p. 402)*

This has made it a powerful vehicle for 'corporate nationalism', most strikingly in the 'David and Goliath' competitions between New Zealand's highly successful entrants (including the 2017 Cup winner) and their global competitors from the United States and Europe (John and Jackson 2010, 402). Moreover, the extraordinarily sophisticated technological demands and achievements of the Cup competitors make it a uniquely attractive platform for the branding efforts of high-tech and science-based corporations, as well as luxury brands. Smith (2002, 3), cites Hewlett-Packard as having asserted in a press release that, 'We would have a really hard time with (marketing via) the NFL, or even ice hockey, but the America's Cup is the one internationally recognized sporting event that even the farmer in Iowa traditionally associates with technology'. The distinctive, high-end and 'knowledge-intensive' marketing power of the Cup also helps explain why the New Zealand government has continued to invest public funds (via state-owned enterprises) in the privately managed Cup campaigns of its 'yachties' (see John and Jackson 2010).

If the America's Cup represents the pinnacle of 'apex' sailing, a close second is Olympic sailing. The sport has been present, with a shifting array of classes, since the second modern Games in 1900. Yet as the Summer Games have begun to transcend their Eurocentric roots, and as new sports agitate for a place on the Olympic stage, sailing's position as an Olympic sport has become relatively insecure. The number of countries who could, and do, compete has remained small beyond the sport's European and Inter-American 'core' due to their small sailing communities and limited resources, while some of the classic classes in which competition was held were either exceptionally expensive, not particularly athletic, or both. Examples include a number of the keelboat classes of past Games, including the Dragon, Soling and Tempest. Moreover, because events are typically contested far from shore and are hard to track for even the most expert spectator, they have been poorly suited to the media-sports complex (web-based media excepted) that has become such a pivotal and lucrative feature of the Games in the post-Los Angeles (1984) era.

World Sailing (the sport's international governing body) has attempted to respond by revising the classes and formats (within a ten event limit) in ways designed to ensure gender equity, athleticism, and (televisual) spectator appeal. The process of class selection is, predictably enough, intensely political. The upshot has been it has added classes (like the 49er and 49er FX skiff class sailboats and the foiling, mixed-gender Nacra 17 catamaran) that remain exceptionally expensive and difficult to sail. They therefore lack mass appeal among sailors and a market in relatively affordable second-hand boats – further exacerbating the challenge of extending the sport's appeal in the Global South. Gladwell (2018) summarizes that, 'with the various reviews and out of the box thinking Sailing is at real risk of positioning itself once again as a narrowly based, high technology, high-cost sport largely practised in "first world" countries'.

There are exceptions to the narrow base and limited appeal of Olympic sailing classes, however – the principal one being the Laser (men's) and Laser Radial (women's) single-handed classes. Indeed the Laser is emblematic of a very different trend to those described above, towards a more accessible, participatory, and 'democratic' sport.

Bringing sailing to the people? Post-war expansion and 'democratization'

Beginning in the 1930s and accelerating during the 'long boom' following the Second World War, a plethora of innovative new classes emerged with the expressed intent of expanding access to and participation in the modern variant of the sport. Concomitantly, many new sailing clubs sprang up to support the growth of the sport – often with a grassroots, self-help ethos that contrasted sharply with the more prestigious and elitist yacht clubs that predated them.[8] These processes were concentrated in the 'Anglosphere' (the United States, the United Kingdom, and the 'settler dominions' of the Commonwealth) and Western Europe, but were broadly diffused to Latin America and the 'new' (post-colonial) Commonwealth as well as other areas (like Japan) within the US sphere of influence.

These trends were enabled by innovations in design and materials, enabling relatively simple and affordable home construction in wood and, later, the beginnings of mass production in fibreglass. They were also enabled by the parallel development of purpose-designed youth classes to foster new (and greatly enlarged) generations of young sailors. More broadly, many new classes were relatively light, fun, and easy to sail – often by family combinations (husband-wife, father-son, etc.) – though still with few female 'skippers'.

While hundreds of new designs emerged in the 1930s, 1940s, 1950s and 1960s, most remained in or have faded into obscurity. However, a significant number have endured to become exemplars of the new face of the sport. In the United States, for example, the Snipe (1931) and the Lightning (1938) classes grew rapidly in popularity across North America, Latin America, and a few parts of Europe. They remain highly competitive international classes, with over 30,000 and 15,000 boats built, respectively (see Powlison 2012; Atkinson 1959). Even more successful was the pioneering 'beach boat' – the lateen-rigged Sunfish Class. Originally built of plywood when it was launched in 1951, it transitioned to fibreglass in 1959 and has become one of the most popular sailboat classes ever, with more than 300,000 built and sailing principally in North America, South America, and the Caribbean.[9] Another highly successful class, confined principally to the United States and explicitly targeted at a wide range of skill levels and family combinations, was the 19-foot Flying Scot, introduced in 1957. Now with over 6000 boats built and still very actively raced, it was distinguished by the fact that it was designed from the outset for fibreglass production, reducing costs and maintenance.

Nowhere was the trend towards growth of the sport through the spread of new small boat (dinghy) classes more pronounced than in the UK and, concomitantly, the 'old (settler) Commonwealth' countries of Australia, Canada, New Zealand and (apartheid-era) South Africa. In the UK, much of this growth was enabled by innovations in plywood construction, including 'do-it-yourself' (DIY) kits, which in effect directly challenged the class composition of the sport by enabling its popularization among the middle and working classes. At the forefront of this process were the designs of Jack Holt – one the country's and the world's most successful designers – whose path-breaking designs (all suitable for plywood construction) included the GP (General Purpose) 14 (1950), the single-handed Solo dinghy (1956), and the International

Enterprise (1956) – the latter commissioned for promotional purposes by the *News Chronicle* (see Moore 1995). By far his most successful design, with over 70,000 sailing, was the Mirror Dinghy (1963), on which he collaborated with the popular television DIYer Barry Bucknell to produce a small, light, easily car-topped and inexpensive design that could be easily built at home from a kit (see Jackson 2006). While each of these (and many more Holt designs) has subsequently been adapted for construction in fibreglass, new wood ones continue to be built and they remain very popular classes for racing and recreation, in the UK and other (mostly Commonwealth) countries.

Meanwhile, a similar movement was unfolding in continental Europe. An early breakthrough, paralleling the British pattern of cheap and easy wood construction, was the J.J. Herbulot-designed Vaurien, introduced at the 1952 Paris Boat Show and reportedly sold for the equivalent of the cost of two bicycles (Herbulot 2002). In Europe (notably but not exclusively France), however, many of the most successful classes were early adopters of fibreglass construction, enabling 'soft-chined' (rounded) hulls. Some of the most noteworthy and enduring examples include the 470 (introduced in 1963, and an Olympic class since 1976) and the 505 (introduced in 1954) – both of which remain exceptionally popular 'high performance' racing dinghies with spinnaker and trapeze (e.g. Powlison 2012). Unlike the Commonwealth-centric British designs, moreover, the pattern of diffusion of these and other classes was more geographically dispersed, with tens of thousands being built and sailed throughout Europe and in other parts of the world (including the UK and North America).

Reflecting and reinforcing this trend towards diffusion and popularization of the sport was the emergence of a number of purpose-built and increasingly internationalized youth classes. These included the Jack Holt-designed Cadet (1947) and, by far the most successful, the Optimist Pram (1947), conceived by Clark Mills in Florida as the sailing analogue to the Soapbox Derby and initially constructed from two 4 × 8 foot sheets of plywood. Today it is the most popular youth boat ever, with more than 150,000 registered boats in well over 100 countries.[10] Almost uniquely, it is widely sailed in Africa and Asia as well as the traditional sailing heartlands of North America, Europe, and South America. Also exceptionally successful was the International 420 class, designed by the French designer Christian Maury in 1959, which is used by both youth and adults and has 70 national associations with well over 50,000 boats built.

Beginning in the late 1960s and 1970s, a new turn in the diffusion of the sport gathered momentum which, on the one hand, significantly enhanced its visibility and reach and, on the other hand, introduced a new set of tensions, strains, and limitations. This was the advent of manufacturer based one-design classes that were uniform in design, equipment, construction and allowable modifications, and were mass-produced and marketed by a small set of licensed builders on a global scale. It was thus a reflection of the broader trend towards economic globalization. One of the most striking early examples was the adaptation of these techniques to the two-hulled catamaran, which made up in speed and stability what they gave away in manoeuvrability. Historically, catamarans had been heavy, awkward, and expensive, and therefore very limited in popularity. This changed when the California surfboard innovator and popularizer, Hobie Alter, turned his creative imagination to the sailing world. In 1968, he introduced a simplified, inexpensive, beachable catamaran – the Hobie Cat 14 – which quickly achieved widespread commercial success. This was soon followed by the even more successful, two-person and twin-trapeze Hobie Cat 16, launched in 1971, that spawned a class of more than 100,000 boats worldwide. Alter sold his catamaran company to Coleman Corp (see Anton 2014) in 1976, but the Hobie brand has persisted, with a succession of innovative, multi-hulled craft to follow.[11] Other catamaran designers and manufacturers quickly entered the scene, seeking to emulate the successful Hobie formula. None, however, achieved the success of the original 14 and 16, which along with the Sunfish have become the most ubiquitous 'beach boats' in the world and led to the popular slogan, 'have a Hobie day'.

Another pivotal development (two, in fact) was prompted by a unique event – the 'America's teacup' – held in 1970 at the Lake Geneva, Wisconsin Playboy Club as a 'one-of-a-kind' competition to showcase a range of innovative 'funboats', with the only restriction being that they had to be under US\$1,200 in price (Reed 2007; Reed 2016). Of the forty-nine entries, two changed the sport in fundamental and enduring ways. The first was the Bruce Kirby-designed Laser. This fast, light, inexpensive, accessible and rigidly one-design class became arguably the most successful sailboat in history, with well over 200,000 built since its introduction. Its global diffusion (with the exception of the tiny, youth-focused Optimist) has been more extensive than any previous design. More to the point, no other boat has more successfully straddled the twin imperatives of grassroots recreation and elite competition. Lasers are just as (in fact more) likely to be seen on cottage lakes and beaches as on World Championship race courses. As noted above, it is by far the most popular Olympic class and, by adopting three different rig sizes, appeals to virtually all weights, shapes, and sizes of sailors. It has become the single-handed class of choice for both youth and adult learners and competitors (though to be raced competitively, it requires a high degree of athleticism).

The second 'game-changing' entry was the 'Windsurfer' – the first ever commercially marketed sailboard. In fact, as Dant and Wheaton (2007) discuss, it pioneered a form of sailing that, though related to the sport as a whole, is properly thought of as a different sport altogether. Nevertheless, because of its ease of entry, exceptionally low cost, and portability, it drew hundreds of thousands of converts. Indeed, it can be argued that it was directly linked to the relative decline of popular interest in sailing, since many new sailboarders were potential sailors. Yet once mastered, its unique form of 'embodied' and lifestyle expression (Dant and Wheaton 2007, 12) only remained rewarding for expert sailboarders with highly specialized equipment under relatively extreme (windy and wavy) conditions, limiting its appeal and the range of locations where sailboarders were inclined to congregate. Thus, while it experienced an initial, unprecedented surge of interest, its numbers waned considerably in the mid-1990s and have never recovered, despite the growing popularity of the latest offshoot, kite sailing.

The final breakthrough design to be highlighted here is the Topper – primarily (though not exclusively) a youth-oriented single-handed design introduced in 1977, with more than 50,000 built.[12] The Topper's critical innovation was the use of injection-moulded polypropalene, enabling mass production of exceptionally inexpensive, durable, and uniform boats. It set the stage for the recent trend towards a growing range of roto-moulded (plastic) dinghies, resulting in lower production costs and greatly increased durability that make these designs especially popular with sailing schools and in other institutional settings.

These and many other manufacturer-produced one designs (from companies such as Laser-Performance, Topper International, RS Sailing, JBoats, or Melges Boatworks) have led to important developments and refinements in the sport. In part because of the size, scale, capitalization, and sophistication of the research and marketing that these companies are able to achieve, they have generated a succession of increasingly refined designs across a wide range of market 'segments'. Indeed, the array of more-or-less 'breakthrough' designs they have produced and marketed is quite head-spinning. Nevertheless, these advances have come at a cost: because the business model of these companies demands a steady diet of innovative new designs (similar to car makers), the impact has been to diffuse and 'splinter' the global community of sailors, diminishing support for and participation in the activities of established classes (new and old) in a seemingly endless, cyclical process. I will return to the implications of this cycle in the concluding section, below.

Future challenges

To be sure, this is a very partial account of an exceptionally diverse sport. Missing, for example, are some of the most prominent trends of the recent past, including the emergence of readily available (hydro)'foiling' dinghies, achieving spectacular speeds and equally spectacular 'wipe-outs', and the growth and proliferation of high-performance, planing keelboats, or 'sportsboats' (including among others the pathbreaking J24, the Melges 24, the Viper 640, the VX One, and the J70). Also missing are an array of iconic Offshore Races for ocean-capable race boats (Sydney-Hobart, Victoria-Maui, Bermuda, etc.); and a range of 'human-against-the-elements' single-handed races (including the 'extreme', technology-intensive Mini-Transat). The list goes on.

What this chapter has aimed to do, however, is outline the extremities of the sport, from its most elite and 'extreme' forms in terms of size, skill, prestige, and expense, to its most grassroots and participatory forms. In doing so, it has highlighted both the growth in accessibility and popularity of the sport, as well as some important, interrelated challenges – enduring and novel – that continue to constrain its visibility, appeal and growth. I will conclude by highlighting several of these.

The first is that the sport is both driven forward and fundamentally constrained by an unending cycle of advances in design, technology, and materials that produce a chronic succession of aggressively marketed new designs and a fetishization of the new and innovative. This means that successful, established classes with strong organizational structures and communities of committed participants are constantly struggling to hold their place, and often losing the struggle. The number of once-popular classes that have now disappeared is a long one. But, given advances in materials and construction (notably the advent of fibreglass), these 'good old boats'[13] rarely disappear, and can be purchased at very low cost from owners anxious to rid themselves of their space and running demands. This, of course, makes the challenge of commercial success for new entrants exceptionally high. In short, these inherent features of the sport make it hard to consolidate and stabilize accessible patterns of participation.

A second, related challenge is that in this process of innovation, there is an inherent bias towards greater speed and challenge. This is reflected in the growth of foiling and sportsboats, for example. These are exciting developments for both participants and the relatively limited community of spectators, but they make the challenge of mastering the sport for newcomers increasingly intimidating. They often serve as barriers to entry for the many more 'average' participants who found a place in the sport during its democratizing heyday in the 1950s through the 1970s.

A third related issue is that, notwithstanding advances in design and innovation, the sport remains an exceptionally expensive one, and also one that remains inaccessible to most sports consumers who can neither aspire to participate in nor view events held on race courses far from land, according to rules that remain elusive and arcane. This means that, despite the opening up of sailing in the post-war era, it remains out of reach to the majority of the world's people, and in some respects fundamentally elitist. This also means its place in the Olympic movement, among other markers of sport 'legitimation', is chronically fragile and uncertain. It remains to be seen how the sport will navigate these ongoing challenges, and the uncertain future they imply.

Notes

1 For more on the long history of the Inland Lake Yachting Association (ILYA), for example, see www.ilya.org.
2 The latest Olympic class is a mixed-gender foiling catamaran (two-hulled boat) – the Nacra 17. Separate women's sailing events were first introduced at the 1988 Olympics in Korea.
3 Exemplified in the 'Anglosphere' by such storied venues as the New York Yacht Club, the St. Francis Yacht Club, the Royal Yacht Squadron, or the Royal Canadian Yacht Club.

4 Dant and Wheaton (2007, 8) cite Pierre Bourdieu's argument that, 'yacht sailing is one of those sports in which 'gains in distinction' can be achieved and in which all the features that appeal of the dominant classes are involved – an exclusive setting, little physical exertion, ritualized competition'. Paul Henderson (2010, 263–279), the President of the International Sailing Federation (now World Sailing) from 1994 to 2004, devotes 16 pages of his autobiography to his sailing-based relationships with various European royals.

5 See www.volvooceanrace.com/en/teams/Turn-The-Tide-On-Plastic.html (accessed 28 July 2018).

6 See www.volvooceanrace.com/en/news/12024_FLASH-NEWS-Dongfeng-Race-Team-wins-the-Volvo-Ocean-Race.html, accessed 30 July 2018.

7 On the resulting 'Blackheart' campaign in New Zealand, see John and Jackson (2010).

8 Andrew Jackson (2006, 67) cites data from the British Royal Yachting Association indicating that the number of RYA-affiliated sailing clubs in the UK expanded from 8,403 in 1959 to 31,089 in 1970.

9 See www.sunfishclass.org/about/the-sunfish-class-history (accessed 1 August 2018).

10 See www.optiworld.org.

11 See http://hobieclass.com.

12 See www.itcaworld.org/about-topper.

13 The title of one popular sailing magazine.

References

Anton, M. (2014). 'Hobie Alter Dies at 80; Shaped Southern California Surf Culture'. *Los Angeles Times*, 30 March.

Atkinson, T. (1959). 'For Hustle and Plain Fun'. *Sports Illustrated*, 3 August 1959.

Campbell, A. (2017). 'Cats in a Dogfight'. *Sailing World*, May/June, 72–77.

Chisnell, M. (2013). 'The Cup Changes Hands'. In *Sailing on the Edge: America's Cup*. San Rafael, CA: Insight Editions.

Dant, T. and B. Wheaton. (2007). 'Windsurfing: An Extreme Form of Material and Embodied Interaction?'. *Anthropology Today*, 23 (1), 8–12.

Gladwell, R. (2018). 'World Sailing to Put Five Olympic Classes under the Scalpel for Paris'. *Sail-World*, 2 February. Retrieved from www.sail-world.com/news/201692/Five-Olympic-classes-recommended-for-Review (accessed 30 July 2018).

Henderson, P. (2010). *The 'Pope' of Sailing*. Toronto: Paul F. Henderson.

Herbulot, F. (2002). '1952–2002: Fifty Years of Vaurien'. Retrieved from www.vaurien.org/index.php/thevaurien/history (accessed 1 August 2018).

Jackson, A. (2006). 'Labour as Leisure – the Mirror Dinghy and DIY Sailors'. *Journal of Design History*, 19 (1), 57–67.

John, A. and S. Jackson. (2010). 'Call Me Loyal: Globalization, Corporate Nationalism and the America's Cup'. *International Review for the Sociology of Sport*, 46 (4), 399–417.

Moore, B. (1995). 'Obituary: Jack Holt'. *The Independent*, 16 November. Retrieved from www.sunfishclass.org/about/the-sunfish-class-history

Powlison, M. (2012). 'Then and Now: Enduring One-Designs'. *Sailing World*, October.

Reed, D. (2007). 'My One and Only'. *Sailing World*, March.

Reed, D. (2016). 'Bringing the Laser to Life'. *Sailing World*, May.

Smith, N. (2002). 'Passing the Cup: The Meaning of the America's Cup at the Global Table'. *Harvard International Review*, 24 (1), 30–33.

Woo, S. and A. Kuriloff. (2015). 'Low-Ranked Sailor Paid $300,000, Lawsuit Reveals'. *The Globe and Mail*, 11 March.

29

Skiing

Zachary Beldon, Hongxin Li and Sandy Nguyen

History

During the 1960s archaeologist Grigority Burov discovered the oldest ski-like artifacts in northern Russia, dating back to around 6000 BC.[1] When the Cro-Magnon man first attached sticks to his feet to traverse the snow, over 22,000 years ago, skiing was born.[2] During skiing's formative years, it was not viewed as a sport or competition, instead it was viewed as a mode of survival. More specifically, skis were used in central Asia's Altai region for traveling northeast and northwest behind glaciers in order to capture elk herds and reindeer.[3] Throughout the middle ages, skis were being regularly used by farmers, hunters and warriors in Scandinavian countries and by the 18th century, some units of the Swedish military were trained and competing on skis.

Within the last eight millennia, skis have improved the lives of many individuals through survival and transportation.[4] Skiing began to appear in cultural productions (i.e., art and mythology) in nations where skis played a dominant role in everyday life.[5] For example, in mythology the goddess Öndergud, the "ski god," carries bows and arrows and moves effortlessly throughout the winter landscape, thus demonstrating the importance of skiing to everyday living in the Eurasian landmass.[6] Throughout the Eurasian landmass, art found in rock carvings and cave paintings are continuously found depicting humans using skis throughout prehistoric times, three to five thousand years ago.[7] Skiing is a physical activity where a person uses skis to slide down a snow covered hill.[8]

Around the 1840s, woodcarvers in Telemark, Norway redesigned their ski gear so that it would curve away from the snow in the middle and have the most contact near the edge of the skis.[9] Prior to the redesign, skis had to be thick so that they could glide without bending and sinking into the snow, causing the skier to constantly have to ski uphill out of the snow that they have sunk into. This new ski design, called a "cambered ski" allows the skiers to be faster and more agile then the previous generation of skis.[10] The mid-nineteenth century also saw the slow development of recreational skiing by the Norwegians. Specifically, on March 19, 1843 the first organized ski race was held in the port of Tromsø, Norway, one thousand miles north of Oslo.[11]

Throughout the 1840s and 1850s Trondheim, the capital of the Vikings, became the hub for ski touring. While Trondheim became the hub for skiing, it was not nearly as developed as the other areas of Norway in the actual practice of skiing and did not host an organized ski tournament until 1860.[12] The 1860s saw skiing build a public profile in Norway through the tremendous growth in organized ski tours and races. The first official national competition in Norway took place in 1868 and took place in the capital of Christiania (now named Oslo).[13] The same year also saw steam trains beginning to move skiers and other passengers into the mountains of Europe and North America.[14] A few years later, in 1875, the first ski club in the world was founded in Christiania, the "Christiania Ski Club."[15]

Students and teachers played a key role in the diffusion of skiing throughout Europe.[16] When Germany emerged during the late nineteenth century as a leading industrial power, many Norwegian students and teachers relocated to Germany.[17] Therefore, around the mid-1880s Germany saw a notable increase in participation in skiing in the Harz Mountains, thanks to the Norwegian youth that had relocated to the center of Germany.[18] The two most common mountains in Germany, the Harz and Black Forest mountain ranges, both had numerous technical and traditional universities that were located within 100 miles of them and were reminiscent of the ranges the Norwegian mountains, with rolling hills instead of soaring peaks and steep inclines.[19] With Germans and Norwegians both preferring rolling hills over steep and soaring mountains, the Norwegian model of skiing was the preferred model throughout Europe.[20] A cultural dynamic occurred over a course of time and as the formative years of skiing in Central Europe was establishing itself, skiers had to overcome the initial disbelief of the local citizens, who viewed skiers in the 1880s and 1890s as a "blend of madman and clown," thus leading to many skiers resorting to practicing either at night or in obscure locations.[21]

While skiing saw great growth in the smaller mountain ranges throughout Europe, tourism to the steeper Alpine mountains brought on a new challenge to skiers. The Alpine mountains, commonly known as the Alps, helped symbolize recreation and leisure for healthy Europeans'.[22] Around the 1880s, some tourists discovered the Alps as a great location for skiing to take place year round.[23] Doctors believed that the hygienic quality of the mountain air could serve as a panacea for a range of diseases that affected urbanites.[24] The Alps became such a tourist destination that by 1888, four major tourist centers had opened their doors for visitors.[25] With the Alps developed as a year round tourist destination, many tourists were surprised with how isolated the tourist centers were during the winter months.[26] To cope with the isolation, tourists looked to winter sports to amuse themselves. Skiing was not the first activity to have arrived at the Alps, other activities that preceded skiing in the Alps were: ice skating, tobogganing, and bobsledding, all of which saw an increase in popularity once the tourist centers opened during the 1880s.[27] When skiing first began to take place in the Alps, skiers largely limited themselves to the forests and foothills that resembled the landscapes of Scandinavia.[28] Leading writer, Arnold Lunn to describe ice skating as "the Queen of Winter sports" and skiing as "an uncouth intruder," Lunn went on to recall that when he first tried to ski in 1898, "the few visitors who bothered to ski in Chamonix were regarded as reckless faddists."[29]

The development of skiing both inside and outside of Norway in the later quarter of the nineteenth century can be characterized as both informal and isolated.[30] Skiing's growth benefited from the speculative socioeconomic and cultural shifts in Europe such as industrialization, the growth of the middle class and the growth of leisure.[31] While the early skiers outside of Scandinavia followed the models from Norway, they left the nationalistic and ideological concepts behind and gradually altered the practice and meaning of the sport.[32] Skiers in Central Europe prior to the start of the First World War are typically characterized into two groups: those who ski for pleasure and those who skied for utility.[33] Ski observers described skis as a perfect tool for integrating the people that live in the mountains into modern society by increasing movement freedom, especially in the Alps where the mountain people suffered a "disease of mobility."[34]

Shortly after the 20th century started, skiing began to be seen as a sport over being a recreational activity.[35] For example, ski racing competition evolved from cross country and jumping which sometimes was combined into one competition and downhill sledding.[36] In 1905, the United States of America created their own foundation recognized as the US Ski and Snowboard Association which provides thousands of young skiers and snowboarders with leadership skills, direction, to support and encourage them to achieve excellence.[37]

Skiing spread throughout the globe predominantly through the middle and upper social classes.[38] While the working classes preferred the sports of soccer, bicycling and boxing, skiing excluded the lower classes due to the expensive costs of equipment and participation.[39] Skiing was not only divided among social classes, but also by gender. When females accompanied their husbands on winter vacations, they were expected to abide by the Victorian moral codes while the men were skiing.[40] Doctors were concerned with women skiing due to the ideology that their bodies were unsuited to physical exertion and the climate of the mountains.[41] Despite the arguments of women not being physically prepared to ski, some middle-class women did partake in short ski tours while their husbands were enjoying longer tours.[42] French skier Marie Marvingt argued that "skiing was well suited to women's participation because it was not violent or brutal like other contemporary sports, and its flowing, graceful movement made it socially acceptable for women to participate."[43]

Skiing made its first appearance in 1908 when an Australian ski club, Kiandra Snow Shoe Club, held one of the first international ski running competition that saw Charles Menger from the United States come in first place.[44] In 1922, the first Vasaloppet race occurred and quickly became one of the longest cross-country ski races across Europe. Margit Nordin was the first woman to ever participate in the Vasaloppet race, doing so in 1923, the following year women were banned from competing due to the objection from the male participants and officials. 1924 also saw the first Winter Olympic competition and the creation of the International Ski Federation.[45] The first Winter Olympic competition saw the implementation of the Nordic style of skiing, with Alpine skiing being implemented in the 1936 Winter Olympic competition.[46] Women were not allowed to participate in the Olympic skiing competitions until 1952 when women's Nordic skiing debuted, however it took until 2014 for the inclusion of a women's ski jumping competition.[47]

Skiing around the globe

Today, many people are participating in skiing around the world. By now, 100 countries offer skiing in Africa, Asia, Europe, North America, Oceania, South America, 67 countries offer equipped outdoor ski areas covered with snow, and 2000 ski resorts have been identified around the world.[48] In addition, more than 20 countries offer indoor snow or artificial surface skiing at indoor centers. Of those 20 countries: Malaysia, Netherlands, Saudi Arabia, Singapore, Thailand, United Arab Emirates, Bahrain, and Egypt solely have indoor skiing slopes. It is estimated that there are 350 million skier visits worldwide.[49] Although the skier visits average tends to decrease in some major mature countries (e.g., Japan), the skiing markets in other countries (e.g., China) are emerging.

Of all the continents, Europe provides the most skiing resorts and opportunities for many people. Not only are its landscapes known to be unique, it also offers at least two-thirds of all the ski areas within the world. Without any question, the Alps offer the broadest range of skiing opportunities in Europe. The Alps are the largest ski market all over the world, which captures 43% of the worldwide skiing attendance.[50]

The French Alps are the largest and most renowned skiing areas in the world. Although France is the number one destination of tourists around the world, most of the skiers in France are from the domestic market. In France, some of the major resorts were created from the 1960s and 1970s. However, those resorts were dismantled and the lift operations were distributed in the 1980s. From then on, Compagnie des Alpes, the world's largest ski resort operator started to manage and operate these resorts and as of today, they are managing nearly all the lift operations of major resorts in France.[51] There are also some smaller operators managing lifts for some ski areas. Many of the ski lifts and resorts are owned or partially owned by municipalities, since people in France see the ski lift as a public service.

Austria has a strong ski culture and some schools in Austria still have ski weeks regularly. As for the ski market, more than 51.3 million skiers went to Austria during the 2015–2016 winter.[52] Over the last few years, the number of foreign skiers has increased in the Austrian ski resorts.

Switzerland has been commonly seen as the most well-known ski destination in the world for centuries. Many customers that contribute most to Swiss skiing derive from various countries such as: Germany, Italy, France, Spanish, Netherland, Russia and Asian countries. However, in recent years, the number of foreign customers in Swiss skiing is declining. Except for the Alpine countries, the other western countries, of Great Britain, United States, Canada, are the home to more than 30 million skiers. Currently, there are more than 1000 ski areas in those countries, making them the largest outbound skiing market currently.[53]

Skiing has been in Scandinavia for thousands of years. In the birthplace of the modern skiing, Norway, most of the country is dominated by mountainous regions. Norway is a skiing destination for many families, because children under the age of seven can ski for free.[54] In the 2015–2016 winter, around 7.4 million skiers visited Norway. Sweden has more than 200 skiing resorts, and the ski tourism is very stable there. Sweden has made new investments to ski tourism in the past years, and the hotel and lodging capacity will expand in the next few years.[55] In Finland, Levi, Ruka and Yllas are the main resorts, which primarily attract families and recreational skiers.

In Eastern Europe and central Asian countries, the ski industry is still developing. Although skiing is hardly new to the people living in these countries, many countries just began to develop international skiing resorts in recent years. Currently, the number of skiers in this area is much lower than the number of skiers in Alps and Western Europe, which indicates a big potential growth of ski industry in the countries of Eastern Europe and central Asia. By now, there are more than 1100 ski areas in this region.[56]

In Russia, the main ski resorts in the country are located in the Ural and the Caucasus Mountains. Since 2012, the ski areas have started to increase rapidly. By now, there are more than 350 ski areas in Russia. Since the Sochi Olympics in 2014, the ski market in Russia has been expanding through an increasing number of domestic skiers. In 2015–2016 winter, there were about 6 million skier visits in Russia.[57] The Czech Republic is another country that has maa lot of ski resorts in Eastern Europe. Rokytnice Nad Jizerou, Spindleruv Mlyn, Pec pod Snezkou, and Malá Moravka-Karlov are the most famous resorts in Czech Republic. Poland also has more than 200 ski areas.[58] The climate in Poland is suitable for skiing, and the best season is from January to March. Although most of the skiers that visit are from the domestic market; with the big expansion in tourism, Poland is becoming more popular with tourists from other countries.[59]

In central Asia, countries like Kazakhstan and Kyrgyzstan have some well-known ski resorts. Although the ski industry there is not widely developed, most of the ski areas in those countries are located near the capital city. However, many new resort development projects are under constructed and those countries were recognized as emerging ski markets.[60]

Many skiing resorts are located in North America, including Canada and the United States. However, the overall attendance of skiing in North America is half of the attendance in the Alps. In Canada, with a long history of skiing, a mature market has already been established. The famous ski areas are located in Rocky Mountains of the West, and in the Quebec, Ontario and Atlantic provinces of the East. The ski resorts in Canada strongly depend on the domestic and US customers. In recent years, the number of skiers continues to decline in Canadian skiing market. The United States is one of the largest and mature ski markets around the world. About 460 ski resorts and many independent ski areas are located throughout the United States.[61] Since 2011, the trend of skier visits started to increase. From winter 2010–2011 to winter 2015–2016, the five-year average skier visits are 60.5 million, and most of the skier visits are from the domestic skiers.[62] Although the ski areas in the United States are as big as Europe, they only manage one-third of the ski visits of European countries'. Therefore, there is still potential for developing the ski industry in the United States.

In South America, Argentina and Chile are the main countries where people participate in skiing. The ski season in Argentina starts in June and ends in mid-October. In the last decade, ski resorts in Argentina experienced new growth and development. Although Argentineans do not have the mountain culture like Alps, citizen's general interest in skiing is increasing. During the ski season, around 1.5 million skiers from Brazil, Chile, Mexico, and domestic market gather into the ski resorts in Argentina to enjoy skiing.[63] In Chile, there are three major ski regions: Central Chilean Andes, Southern Andes, and Patagonia.

The Asia-Pacific region has the largest potential market for skiing. In China, skiing started in the northeastern part of the country, including the provinces of Heilongjiang, Jilin, and Liaoning, which contain most of the ski areas. After winning the bid of holding 2022 Winter Olympics, the ski industry in China experienced a tremendous boom. In 2016, 78 new ski areas opened in many provinces, including some southern provinces. Since 2003, the number of skiers has been growing rapidly, from 23 million to 120 million.[64]

Japan has the most ski resorts around the world. There are 547 ski resorts throughout the four main islands of Japan. Those resorts are different in size. Some of them are large resorts with dozens of runs, whereas some of them are small ones with small one-lift slopes. The best ski resorts and snow conditions locate on Hokkaido and Tohoku, as well as the mountains along the sea of Japan Coast.[65] From 1980s, the skier visits in Japan began to decrease mainly due to the economic downturn and the warm weather condition. Although the number of domain skiers is continuously declining in Japan, Japanese ski resorts attracted an increasing number of foreign visitors.[66]

In Australia, skiing has a long history, and people started skiing in the 19th century. During the 1950s, skiing became more popular and ski resorts were built due to the influence of people from the United States, Canada, and European countries. There are 10 major resorts in "Australian Alps," which locate in the states of New South Wales and Victoria. Even in Tasmania Island, there are two small ski resorts. Most of the skiers in Australian skiing market are domestic, whereas foreign skiers are mainly from Japan, and South Korea. New Zealand is a major destination for skiers in the southern Hemisphere. There are 13 commercial ski areas and 10 ski clubs. Since 2000, every year there are more than 1 million skier visits.[67] Although the resorts are fairly located in the two main islands, the South Island offers the best ski areas in New Zealand.

Although most of the skiing areas are not well developed, in the Middle East and African countries, there are ski resorts in both the Northern and Southern hemispheres. For example, Turkey has more than 40 ski areas and it attracted foreign skiers from Russia, the Ukraine, and Iran.[68] In South Africa, there is one commercial ski resort with several ski areas. The Snow Sports South Africa (SSSA) organizes the South African National Skinning Championships every year.

Important personalities

Skiing had its first recorded use of an organized exercise and race; charted back to military use of skis in Norwegian and Swedish infantries for mobility and for getting through rough terrain, exceeding downhill target practice, and completing a journey with a full military backpack. The personality that lies within a skier is not only infused in their character, it is rather demonstrated in their actions to have no fear and test the limits of those before them. Many skiers carry a passion for being outside in nature and in the cold winter mountains; either taking on new destinations, new boundaries, and as well discovering what all the winters have in store for them. The first recorded and known ski jumper by the name Olaf Rye dates back to 1809. His personality frameworks the efforts presented in today's modern sport characteristics. Born on November 16, 1791 he was a Norwegian-Danish military general officer. Being held in Norway in the 19th century, Olaf Rye reached 9.5 meters (31 feet).

Later on, Sondre Norheim was regarded as the "father" of the modern ski jumping, and was recognized as the first-ever ski jumping competitor to win a prize in the Hoydalsmo in 1866.[69] Born on June 10, 1825 in Morgedal, Telemark, a little cotter's farm nestled in the hillside, he resided in this Southern Norway village. He grew up in a poor family, that included a generation of poor cotters and at the age of two, he lost his mother Ingerid. Sondre loved the winter hills in Morgedal, as a child he was lively, had a playful nature to him, and was very active and found the surroundings in beautiful Morgedal perfect for different activities.[70] Learning to read and write never interested Sondre, however he was found to be out in the hills skiing and playing constantly. His personality was fearless and daring as he ran straight down the most dangerous and challenging hills.

Although he had responsibilities to share the farm's work, his parents made some exceptions to his restless and dreaming nature. When the hills shouted for him, his quick response would be "I'm coming!" The people surrounding Sondre in his upbringing believed he was born with skis on, and it seemed like skiing was his natural way of moving. Sondre couldn't live without spending time on the hills and ski slopes. Sondre's passion was skiing, this was his escape, and his way of surviving.[71] He could always be himself on the slope and he felt the most complete while being a part of skiing. He later grew to have a family, and being away from home he felt guilt for leaving his wife Rannei at home alone. Sondre was his own versatile craftsman where he was able to provide the equipment he needed to have bindings with straps around the heel and curved his own skis. At age 42, Sondre was invited to the 1868, very first national skiing competition in Christiania (now Olso). He had skied for three days to reach the capital 200 kilometers away. Sondre, defeated many other competitors that were 20 years younger, people were overwhelmed with his breathtaking performance. Still today Sondre will be remembered for being the pioneer and champion of modern skiing. He developed slalom and introduced the Telemark and Christiania turns.[72]

Another established Norwegian Nordic skier by the name Karl Frithjof Hovelsen was born on March 23, 1877. His location of birth was in Kristiania (Oslo). Hovelsen is remembered in history for his success in winning the Nordic combined at the Holmenkollen ski festival in 1903. He won the 50 km cross-country skiing events both in 1902 and 1903. He earned himself the Holmenkollen medal in 1903 for his event in the 50 km as well as the Nordic combined events for that year.[73] Aside, from being a celebrity and admired for this passion in the sport in 1905, Hovelsen emigrated to the United States and settled in Steamboat Springs, Colorado where he was renamed Karl Howelsen.[74] His career lead him into holding training in cross-country technique and ski jumping. He was selected by the Ringling Bros. and Barnum & Bailey Circus and made an appearance that was marketed as "Ski sailing" and the "The Sky Rocket." Hovelsen took it upon himself to build a ski jump in 1905, where he showed locals that ski jumping was an exciting new sport.

He took on the name as the Flying Norseman, and built a jump, ski jump more than 100 feet of the jump. Now known as the Howelsen Hill in downtown Steamboat Springs, this 30, 50-, 70- and 90-meter jumps are used by Steamboat's future Olympians as a training site. Another accomplishment Karl marked in history was organizing the first Winter Carnival in 1914 as a way to introduce the competitive skiing and celebration of winter.[75] Karl Hovelsen is rated as one of the pioneers of skiing in America. In 1922, Hovelsen returned home see his parents and found his wife where he chose to live in Norway until his death in 1955. In the 21st century, he is now remembered in Steamboat Springs by a life-size statue of Howelsen, which is located on the main street. To commemorate all his attributions to this sport of skiing, Carl Howelsen was entered into the Colorado Ski and Snowboard Hall of Fame in 1977.

Other areas of the world such as New Zealand were making its own mark on skiing history in the Alpine Skiing. Annelise Coberger, born on September 16, 1971 in Christchurch, Canterbury, New Zealand was raised in the Coberger family whom were the pioneers of skiing in New Zealand. Her German grandfather established one of the first ski equipment businesses in the country. As an individual, she was the first New Zealander to represent her country and win a medal in the World Junior Championship when she took a bronze medal in the slalom in 1990.[76] Annelise Coberger became the first person from the southern hemisphere to win a medal at the Winter Olympics and placed silver in the slalom at Albertville in France in 1992.[77] She later transitioned from the junior form to the senior circuit later on in life. Annelise dedicated herself to compete in the 1001 World Championships placing thirteenth in the combined event. One year later into her career, Coberger in January 14, 1992 made a breakthrough that month and made a run of results that culminated in an FIS World Cup slalom win at Hinderstoder that elevated her from being relatively unknown to being one of the Olympic slalom favorites.[78]

Currently, she hold New Zealand's only medal from any Winter Olympics. For this success, at the annual Halberg Awards she was announced as the title of New Zealand Sportsman of the Year. Annelise Coberger was also relentless as well to attempt the 1994 Winter Olympics in Lillehammer but unfortunately was unable to finish her fun of the slalom. She later joined the New Zealand Police to fulfill the rest of her career.[79]

Michael Edwards is a remarkable individual who has left his imprint on the sport of skiing through his passion, dedication, and determination. Better known as "Eddie the Eagle," he was born on December 5, 1963 in Cheltenham. He is known worldwide for being a British skier to many. Eddie was taught how to ski at his local dry ski slope and rapidly picked up the skills to become a talented and accomplished downhill skier, and was nearly almost looked past as being selected for the Great Britain ski team in the 1984 Olympic Games.[80] To better his opportunity to qualify for the Calgary Olympics in 1988, he moved to Lake Placid in the US to train and enter races of a higher standard to qualify. In order to achieve his own dreams of participating in the Olympics he decided to switch into ski jumping for financial reasons and easier qualification, due to there not being any other British ski jumpers whom he would need to compete for a place. His coaches were John Viscome and Chuck Berghorn in Lake Placid. Michael used Chuck's old equipment and head to wear six pair of socks to make the boots fit. Michael Edwards had to overcome many challenges in order compete.[81] He had no financial support for training, and worked as a plasterer and slept in a disused Finnish hospital to save enough money to keep his Olympic dreams alive. He was longsighted, and had to wear his high strength spectacles at all times, and during his jumps, his glasses often fogged which gave him a huge disadvantage. In the 1987 World Championships he was the first to represent Great Britain and was ranked 55th in the world. He was the sole British applicant for the 1988 Winter Olympics and he was the British ski jumping record holder despite finishing last in the 70 m and 90 m events.[82] Eddie the Eagle is still famous today for personifying the Olympic spirit and for this determination to represent his country without any form of funding. Soon after the event, the 1988 Olympics entry requirements were raised to higher standards in order to make it impossible for anyone to follow his example. This is now known as the "Eddie the Eagle Rule."

Globally, skiing has been a success and triumphant sport that dominates the winter games and internationally captures the interest of many individuals all across the world. The personality that exemplifies the resilience, persistence, and dedication in breaking world records makes this sport well participated and interests many millions of fans and participants throughout the world. An individual that really carries the passion of skiing and exemplifies working towards his dreams, every day is Kasai Noriaki, born on June 6, 1972 in Hokkaido, Japan. This is the northern Japanese island where Saporro hosted the 1972 Winter Olympic Games a few months before his birth. Countless time and time again, Kasai Noriaki demonstrates his desire to never give up on his dreams, and through his career he marks his determination to be the best and to be the top finisher in these Winter Olympics.[83] He is a ski jumper, and in the 1992 ski flying world champion and 1999 Nordic Tournament winner he has made many great contributions to the world of skiing. In his honor, in 2016 the Guinness World Records presented him with a certificate for the most World Cup individual starts no just in ski jumping but in all world cup disciplines run by the International Ski Federation.[84] Currently he holds the record of 528 individual starts and has competed in his 28th season in the World Cup in four different decades: the 1980s, 1990s, 2000s and 2010s.[85] The reason Kasai Noriaki still is competing is he believes he is still lacking a gold medal. Kasai Noriaki holds the record for the world record as the longest jump for athletes over 35 years old with 241.5 meters (792 ft) that was set in 2017.[86] At the moment, he has the record number of appearances in ski jumping at the Olympics, the Nordic world championships, and the ski fling world championships. He is known for the oldest ski jumping Olympic medalist at age 42 and 256 days.[87] He also carries the title as the oldest individual World Cup winner at age 42 and 176 days. As of age 44 and 293 days, he still holds record for the oldest World Cup performer ever.[88] Kasai has hinted that he aims for an eighth Olympics in Pyeongchang, partly because his family has never seen him compete and South Korea is so close to Japan in 2020, as he feels it would be a good opportunity for them to watch him.

Many pioneers have, not only sculpted skiing as a sport, as whole, it has also allowed the introduction of the sport to expand in their own country. Skiers personality are an important aspect of the individuals that part take in the dangerous appeal to the downhill, ski-jumping, and cross country events that range in various events. The impact these individuals have contributed to the sport since its existence still continues to lead into more opportunities for the future and further include more females, as well as expand more resorts and tourism opportunity. In the United States there are various mountain tops to ski as well as take jump off, however there will be more skier personalities to come by as this sport continues to flourish and bring about more competitors as well as world champions that will make a break in skiing.

Skiing is one of the oldest forms of physical activity ever documented. Since its inception, skiing has expanded to almost every mountain or hill that can be covered by snow. Globally, skiing is a major tourist destination for many countries, impacting the economy in several different ways. Overall, skiing has a rich history of diversity and expansion and as long as there are hills to go down, skiing will prosper.

Notes

1 S. Sood (2010). "Travel – Where Did Skiing Come From?" Retrieved from www.bbc.com/travel/story/20101221-travelwise-where-did-skiing-come-from
2 Ibid.
3 "A Short History of Skis." (n.d.). Retrieved from www.skiinghistory.org/history/shorthistoryskis-0
4 Denning, A. (2015). *Skiing into Modernity: A Cultural and Environmental History.* Berkeley, CA: University of California Press.
5 Ibid.
6 Ibid.
7 "A Short History of Skis"; Denning, *Skiing into Modernity.*
8 "Ski Running at Kiandra – an International Contest." (n.d.). Retrieved from http://trove.nla.gov.au/newspaper/article/10178153
9 "A Short History of Skis."
10 Ibid.
11 Denning, *Skiing into Modernity.*
12 Ibid.
13 "Alpine Skiing Equipment and History – Olympic Sport History." (2017). Retrieved from www.olympic.org/alpine-skiing-equipment-and-history
14 "Two Planks and a Passion: The Dramatic History of Skiing." (2009). *Choice Reviews Online,* 46(9). doi:10.5860/choice.46-5097
15 Denning, *Skiing into Modernity.*
16 Ibid.
17 Ibid.
18 Ibid.
19 Ibid.
20 Ibid.
21 Ibid.
22 Ibid.
23 "What is Skiing." (n.d.). Retrieved from www.skicanada.org/ready/what-is-skiing
24 Denning, *Skiing into Modernity.*
25 Ibid.
26 Ibid.
27 Ibid.
28 Ibid.
29 Ibid.
30 Ibid.
31 Ibid.
32 Ibid.
33 Ibid.
34 Ibid.
35 Ibid.
36 "What is Skiing."
37 "About US Ski & Snowboard." (n.d.). Retrieved from https://usskiandsnowboard.org/about
38 Denning, *Skiing into Modernity.*
39 Ibid.
40 Ibid.
41 Ibid.
42 Ibid.
43 Ibid.
44 "Ski Running at Kiandra – an International Contest."
45 "FIS-Ski." (n.d.). Retrieved from www.fis-ski.com; "Chamonix 1924." (2017). Retrieved from www.olympic.org/chamonix-1924
46 "Chamonix 1924."
47 International Olympic Committee. (2018). Ski jumping: Vogt vaults into Olympic history with maiden ski jump gold. Retrieved from www.olympic.org/news/vogt-vaults-into-olympic-history-with-maiden-ski-jump-gold

48 "What is Skiing."
49 Ibid.
50 Ibid.
51 Ibid.
52 Ibid.
53 Ibid.
54 Ibid.
55 Ibid.
56 Ibid.
57 Ibid.
58 Ibid.
59 Ibid.
60 Ibid.
61 Ibid.
62 Ibid.
63 Ibid.
64 Ibid.
65 Sood, "Travel."
66 "What is Skiing."
67 Sood, "Travel."
68 Ibid.
69 "Sondre Norheim." (n.d.). Retrieved from www.sondrenorheim.com/history.htm
70 Ibid.
71 Ibid.
72 Ibid.
73 "Karl Hovelsen" (n.d.). Retrieved from www.revolvy.com/main/index.php?s=Karl-Hovelsen
74 Ibid.
75 "Karl Hovelsen."
76 "Annelise Coberger Bio, Stats, and Results." (n.d.). Retrieved from www.sports-reference.com/olympics/athletes/co/annelise-coberger-1.html
77 Ibid.
78 Ibid.
79 Ibid.
80 "Eddie the Eagle Bio." (n.d.). Retrieved from http://eddie-the-eagle.co.uk/bio/
81 Ibid.
82 Ibid.
83 "Who is Noriaki Kasai?" (n.d.). Retrieved from www.nbcolympics.com/news/who-noriaki-kasai
84 "Annelise Coberger Bio, Stats, and Results."
85 "Noriaki Kasai" (n.d.). Retrieved from www.revolvy.com/main/index.php?s=Noriaki-Kasai&uid=1575
86 Ibid.
87 "Who is Noriaki Kasai?"
88 Ibid.

30

Sliding sports

Susan Barton

The first recorded recognised toboggan race took place in 1882 in Davos, Switzerland. It was a competition between guests staying at the Hotel Belvedere and the Hotel Buol and their friends; this race was won by Mr Chitty with Mr Garrard coming in second place, the Belvedere representatives beating those of the Buol.[1] The race was run down the main road from Wolfgang down to Klosters. At that time there were few runs in existence and none long enough to hold such a race, therefore the roads were used. The racing and other indoor and outdoor entertainments and events were organised by representatives of the guests themselves who formed Amusement Committees in the larger, luxury hotels. It was these committees that organised the race between the guests of the two hotels and their friends. Of course this was not the first time anyone had ridden on a toboggan: straight slides down slopes had long been in existence in Britain, Russia, Canada and the USA. Sledges of varying sizes had been used for transport and carrying heavy loads, such as hay, in snowy regions and elsewhere since ancient times, even before the development of the wheel. Visitors to the Alps had seen farmers transporting loads down mountains on wooden sledges while small ones, *Schlittli*, speeded up winter journeys or provided fun for children.

Visitors to Switzerland, often health seekers, had begun to stay over the winter for the first time during 1864 to 1865 in both St Moritz and Davos. There was as yet no winter season, mountain resorts were open only for the summer. The high-altitude, Alpine air and sunny, sheltered valley, meant Davos was recommended for tuberculosis sufferers who flocked there in ever greater numbers through the closing decades of the 19th century and 1900s.[2] Those who were well enough were advised to take regular moderate exercise as well as to eat nourishing food and get plenty of rest. For them and their healthy companions, tobogganing was an ideal pastime and an alternative to walking and ice skating.

The earliest reports of tobogganing for fun on a specially made track come from Davos Platz where a short run was made near the Kurhaus in the winter of 1872–1873.[3] This may have been the track known as the Buol Run mentioned above, which was said to have been in use in the 1870s.[4] Banks with ice to protect the corners were added to the Buol Run in the winter of 1881–1882. Another run was created down the road in Davos Dorf by a wealthy Englishman, Hugh Verner Dobson, born in 1860 in Bath.[5] In nearby St Moritz an English visitor, John Franklin-Adams,[6] is credited with having improvised a toboggan run beside the Engadiner

Kulm Hotel where he was a guest with the approval of the hotelier Johannes Badrutt. This was said to be based on Franklin-Adams's experiences of riding a straight slide in St Petersburg. The Lake Run, then later the Kurverein's Village Run, and of course the roads, were also used for tobogganing in St Moritz.[7]

Soon, people who were not ill but had heard of the opportunities for sport and pleasure in the Alps joined those who were unwell. Many of these visitors were British or from the British colonies and they remained in Switzerland for months at a time.[8] With few designated toboggan runs, sledging along the village streets and roads was popular although hazardous as riders had pedestrians, animals and large horse-drawn sleighs to contend with. The races between representatives of the two main hotels, the Buol and the Belvedere were held annually on the road for the next five years until weather and snow conditions made it impossible in 1887 and 1888.[9]

A year after that first recognised race, the Davos Toboggan Club was formed in 1883 with English author John Addington Symonds as its founding president.[10] The Club organised its first competitive race in February of that year on the Klosters road, with Symonds acting as referee. With the idea of encouraging visitors and local Swiss residents to mix more, local riders were invited to take part and the competition was given the title of the International Tobogganing Race in recognition of this. Each of the districts adjacent to Davos Platz was invited to send three representatives to compete against three English riders in a friendly test of skill in the art of tobogganing.[11] There were 21 entrants: twelve Swiss, three English, two Australian, two German, a Dutchman and a Canadian.[12] Competitors slid down the road, one person at a time and were timed. The result of the race was a dead-heat with a time of 9 minutes 15 seconds, between Peter Minsch, a postal worker from Klosters and George Pringle Robertson, a wealthy Australian, in Davos for the benefit of his health. Although born in Hobart, Robertson went to Rugby School and then to Oxford University where he gained fame as a cricketer before returning to Australia to work in his family's estate and livestock business.[13]

The following year, 1884, Robertson was staying at the Engadiner Kulm in St Moritz. His friends in Davos invited him to come over and bring with him some St Moritz riders to join in the second International Toboggan Race. Five British toboggan riders from Davos and six from the Engadine, a group that included both visitors and local inhabitants, took part in a race with 25 competitors.[14] Peter Minsch won again with most of the top places going to Davos-based riders. The International Toboggan Race became an annual event with a trophy, the Symonds Cup, being offered as a prize from 1885.[15] The riders from the Engadine enjoyed the competition so much that they decided to reciprocate by inviting Davos competitors over to race in St Moritz the following year. As there was no suitable road coarse to race down in St Moritz, Robertson, with Charles Digby Jones, identified the route of a run down from St Moritz to the smaller village of Cresta; it is sometimes claimed that local mathematician, Peter Bonorand, was commissioned by the Badrutt hotel owners to design the course.[16] The Outdoor Amusement Committee of the Engadiner Kulm Hotel, Robertson, Charles Digby Jones, Major William Bulpett, Charles Metcalfe and John Biddulph, with boots wrapped in bandages, linked arms and trudged a staked-out line until the snow was trampled down for the frost to harden.[17] The banks of the new run were built by workmen supplied by Peter Badrutt, son of Johannes.[18] The new run took nine weeks to complete. To protect the walls of the run from damage by sledge runners, at the suggestion of Bulpett, the walls of the banks of the curved track were watered and allowed to freeze overnight. The iced walls made the run faster to ride on than the Davos to Klosters road. This was to be the famous Cresta Run although it doesn't seem to have been referred to by that name in its early years. The St Moritz Toboggan Club was formed in 1885 and remains British run and managed to the present day. After the International Race, won that year by G. Dale of Davos, Robertson issued a challenge on behalf of the Engadine to the Davos tobogganers, to compete against them on their new course in a race, the Grand National, to be held on 16 February 1885.[19] For the Davosers this was to be their first time on an ice course. The Engadiners of St Moritz were confident they would at last beat the Davos riders but they over-rated their capabilities and all but Bulpett, who came 19th, had falls. No one was seriously hurt but Metcalfe, one of the best St Moritz riders, was carried off after hitting a post at the bottom of the gully. The first four places all went to Davos men, Charlie Austin the winner, with Peter Minsch coming in second place, G. Dale third and Tobias Branger fourth.[20] According to Symonds's wife, the Davos riders, unfamiliar with the course, "were cautious and ran for safety, while the Engadiners, confident in their knowledge of their own course, threw themselves out by the most terrific spills".[21] The artificial ice run at St Moritz inspired the Davos tobogganers. The next year, 1886, the Buol Run, which until that time had been purely a pleasure run, was transformed into a half-mile long ice run. To manage its use, the Buol Toboggan Club was formed.

Pegging was an innovation in tobogganing, as the sport was called by the British who organised the first clubs, competitions and determined the rules. Hand-held wooden pegs were used to propel the toboggan along in deep or heavy snow. Mr Garrard is credited with introducing this idea to racing in Davos in 1884.[22] Using wooden pegs for propulsion was not an entirely new idea as paintings from the Netherlands in the seventeenth century. For example the painting "Warmond Castle in a Winter Landscape" by Jan Abrahamsz Beerstraten, includes an image of a child seated on a small sledge, pushing themself along on ice using pegs.[23] Saddles, or cushions, on the toboggan were first seen in St Moritz in 1885 and the idea was copied in Davos the following year.[24]

Stop watches were first used in the Grand National in 1886, accurate to a fifth of a second, although each competitor had to be a clear second in front of their nearest rival.[25] The earlier method of timing was for two race officials to have synchronised watches with one of them noting the start time and the second the finish time. They then met to calculate the time the rider had taken on the course.[26] Nowadays, in the 21st century, electronic timing devices measure competitors' speeds with accuracy up to 1/1,000th of a second. Two independently functioning timing devices are always employed for verification purposes.[27] Races consist of two, three or four timed heats.

Peter Badrutt had financed the construction of the first three Cresta Runs but in 1887 he suggested the users form a club like the Buol Tobogganing Club to manage the course. Therefore on 17 November 1887 the St Mortiz Toboggan Club was formed with its first committee consisting of Captain Bulpett, Major Lambert Dwyer, Clarence Barker and Duke Grazioli.[28]

Tobogganing began to diffuse to other mountain resorts, for example, British guests staying at the Bear Hotel in Grindelwald, open in winter for the first time from 1888, formed the Bear Toboggan Club which organised races for gentlemen, ladies, children, singles, doubles and mixed doubles. Local people there and tourists of other nationalities joined in and rode with them.[29]

Thanks to the enthusiasm of public school educated British visitors for amateur sporting activities and their cultural propensity to form clubs, funds were raised to create and maintain runs, to provide prizes and rules were devised to ensure fair play. Women could take part, often on equal terms with men. Tobogganing in those early years was an inclusive sport in which anyone could participate, whether they had health problems or were fit and well, so long as they had the time and financial means for a lengthy stay in the Alps. As the pastime evolved into a sport things became more organised and competitive from the late 1880s. Specialisms evolved and elite sportsmen began to take part, who took training and winning seriously. It is from this time that the separate disciplines of skeleton, luge and bobsleigh began to emerge.

Skeleton

The modern sport of skeleton is characterised by competitors riding a lightweight sledge head-first on an ice run. Riding a sledge head first was first recorded in 1887 when an Australian, Mr Cornish, staying in St Moritz was reported as riding a long ordinary Swiss "on his waistcoat" in the Grand National.[30] He lay "his body on the toboggan, grasping its sides well to the front, his legs alternating between a flourish in mid-air and an occasional contact with mother earth or rather ice and snow, for the purpose of controlling his course".[31] Cornish had several falls and finished in thirteenth position so was no threat to established tobogganing conventions.

The following year, 1888, was described by Davos Toboggan Club member, Charlie Austin, as a time of great revolution in the sport. The International Race switched, for one year only, from the Klosters road to a new road from Davos to Clavadel which was more convenient for the growing numbers of spectators. The rules for toboggan racing had been passed on through word of mouth and there was an assumption that competitors would always ride sitting up on a wooden Swiss toboggan with no additional weighting with metal bars but there were as yet no written regulations. That year though, the race was won by an American, Lewis Peck Child of Rhode Island, mounted on the type of sledge known as a Boston Runner or coaster which had metal runners. He had already done a good deal of coasting on straight chutes in America and when he arrived at once set to work to have a "clipper sled" of the American type made in Davos.[32] Child rode his sledge, which could go much faster than the traditionally used Swiss toboggan, head first, lying on his side. Mr Child wasn't the only competitor to try out a different style in the race. Mr Scharp from Sweden experimented with the head first style on his Swiss toboggan and St Moritz-based Mr E. Cohen rode his coaster sitting upright into 22nd place. The newly introduced sledge soon became known as an "America" after Child's machine. Of the new America style of sledge Austin, who had been beaten by Child into joint second place with Harold Freeman, wrote "there is no doubt they are faster both on ice and in deep snow than the old Swiss though how they travel better on the latter I do not pretend to understand".[33] The controversy continued in the Davos visitors' press. A letter in the *Davos Courier* complained about the "unsportingness of healthy tobogganers using American machines they knew invalids could not use. Davos is made for invalids and tobogganing is made for invalids".[34] As the Grand National in St Moritz approached, the appearance of Child and his America sledge, where the Cresta could provide perfect conditions for a record speed, was awaited with eager anticipation. This raised the question of whether or not the new style machine should be allowed to compete. The idea of a sledge, that because of its design was faster than others, outraged the sense of fair play. It was unfair that this style of tobogganing was unsuited to the sick, many of them tuberculosis sufferers, who were supposedly so well-suited to the Swiss *Schlittli* that a number of them generally managed to beat those who were healthy. The event proved an anti-climax as although he was allowed to compete in the Grand National, Child himself decided to withdraw as he felt the conditions would be too dangerous. Another America-style sledge won the race, ridden by Cohen, but in an upright sitting position. In third place came Mr Watts of St Moritz who rode another innovation, a spring runner sledge, sitting up. Captain Wilbrahim of Davos came sixth riding an America head first but he fell off twice in the second heat.[35] The fastest time of the day was still achieved by a Swiss sledge, ridden by Harold Freeman, but the future divergence of the sport was beginning to emerge as it was realised that the America was most suited to racing. From then on lightweight sledges ruled the runs and the Swiss style became obsolete in competition. There are echoes of this controversy in the modern sliding sports, where rules govern materials used and the temperature of the runners, to ensure fairness in competition.

Innovation and design improvements led the way in the developing sport. In St Moritz, Bulpett, who is credited with the invention of the skeleton,[36] designed his own lightweight machine made to his own specification, by local blacksmith Christian Mathis. It had runners made of steel imported from England. The design was improved in 1892 by H. W. Topham whose sledge was made entirely of steel.[37] Another design was that of H.E. Forster who grooved the last few inches of his wooden sledge's steel runners to give a firmer grip. These new designs could all be ridden at greater speeds than those in which the rider sat upright, without the rider being thrown off at bumps and curves. This allowed courses to be built with more curves, leaps and twists and the surface made more slippery with ice to increase speed. More skill was now required to safely complete the course. Over a period of just eight years speeds attained on the Cresta increased rapidly. Calculations show that in 1887 Cornish travelled at 40.9 mph. In 1893 Forster travelled at 68.5 mph and in 1894 Topham reached 70.5 mph.[38] Modern skeletons can travel at speeds upwards of 80 mph (129 kph).

Within a very few years no Swiss toboggans were being used in racing. The last person to ride in a sitting position in the Grand National was Mr Butler in 1891.[39] All the competitors in this race rode Americas in the head first position apart from Butler who finished last. In recognition that some people, especially the local Swiss competitors, would still wish to continue using the traditional wooden sledges, a new trophy was introduced in Davos, the Symonds Shield, to be competed for by Swiss toboggans only.

The new sport spread and by 1905 there were skeleton events in Styria and Austrian Championships were organised from 1906. In 1923 the governing body, the International Bobsleigh and Tobogganing Federation (FIBT) was formed in Paris with delegates from Great Britain, France and Switzerland and with representatives from Canada and the USA, showing how interest in the sport had spread internationally in just a couple of decades. Since June 2015 this body has been known as the International Bobsleigh and Skeleton Federation (IBSF).[40] Its headquarters are in Lausanne.

In 1926 skeleton became an Olympic sport and the rules devised in St Moritz became officially recognised internationally. The sport was included in the Winter Olympic Games on the Cresta in St Moritz in 1928 and again in 1948, the only times that skeleton appeared in the Olympic programme before 2002.[41] However the disruption of the Second World War caused a post-war decline of skeleton as a sport. Only the St Moritz Toboggan Club with its Cresta Run survived throughout the period. Skeleton was reborn in Munich in 1967 and the Bavarian Skeleton Club was formed there in 1969 led by Hans Riedmayer and Max Probst, designer of the modern skeleton sledge.[42] Also in 1969, the first artificially refrigerated track was built in Konigsee in Germany, which is also used for luge events.

In 1970 a new design of sledge that could be used on bobsleigh runs was introduced. Back in Switzerland there was a skeleton club in Zurich from 1976. In St Moritz, skeleton competitions, now distinct from the St Moritz Toboggan Club and the Cresta, were held on the Olympia Bobsleigh Run from 1977.[43] A World Cup series for male skeleton riders began in the season 1986/1987, the first winner being Andi Schmid of Austria.[44]

In 2002, skeleton was reintroduced as a Winter Olympic Sport after a 54-year absence. Since 2004 the World Championships have been combined events with bobsleighing. The sport has continued to expand with an International Cup circuit introduced, a competition a level below the World Cup standard, which has widened opportunities for competition. There are athletes from about thirty countries involved in the sport, including, Nigeria, the first African country to join the Federation in 2018.

Modern skeleton sleds have no braking or steering mechanism and unlike on the Cresta, competitors do not have rakes in their footwear, control being entirely through shifting the weight of the body. Riders wear spike shoes, a skin-tight aerodynamic body suit and a helmet. After a running start they ride lying on their stomachs in a head first position. In 2010 new rules on materials for skeleton manufacture were introduced. Frames must now be made of steel only, with no steering or brake mechanism. Only the base plate may be made of plastics. The skeleton is thinner and heavier than a luge and gives the rider more control so it is judged to be safer. As the slider travels in a head first position, it is less aerodynamic and is the slowest of the three sliding sports.

Luge

Luge is also derived from upright tobogganing with the International Tobogganing Race in Davos in 1883 cited as the first luge competition.[45] A modern luge sledge is made of fibreglass and steel, custom built for the individual athlete based on weight, height and physical proportions of the body. Weighing between 21–25 kg for a singles machine or pod, the sledge runs from the rider's shoulders to their knees and is aerodynamic.[46] There is no head support and G-forces prevent the rider from lifting their head to see where they are going during a run. The runners have steel blades which bow upwards at the front. The temperature of these steel blades are checked in each competition and may not be more than 5°C above a control temperature. Riders push off sitting upright on their sledge and then lie back in a supine, face upwards, feet first position, holding on to side handles. A skin tight, rubberised suit, helmet with face shield and booties that fix the feet in a straight position are worn by the slider. Steering is done by adjusting the pressure of the calves and shoulders. Luge sliders wear spiked gloves to give traction as they push off at the start of a run. The rules of the sport say that adult male competitors must weigh over 90 kg and female over 75 kg. Sliders can add weights to their luge to meet the requirements.[47] There are no brakes. There are separate races for men and women and also gender neutral doubles riding in tandem, although these are usually all male teams. A team relay event was introduced as an Olympic discipline in 2014. In Olympic competition luge, with speeds up to 140 kph (87mph), is one of only two sports timed at 1/1,000th of a second, the other being speed skating, making it one of the most accurately timed. There are separate rules for luge on natural tracks and artificial ones.

The first governing body of the sport, the International Sled Sport Federation (Internationaler Schlittensportverband) (ISSF), was founded in Dresden in 1913.[48] The first European Championships were held in 1914 in Reichenberg, at that time in Bohemia, nowadays in the Czech Republic. After the First World War, the ISSF was refounded in 1927 with a membership of German and Austrian sledge and bobsleigh organisations. The ISSF was incorporated into the Fédération Internationale de Bobsleigh et de Tobogganning (FIBT) in 1935. In Oslo in 1955, the first world championships were held. Increased popularity of the sport of luge led to its separation from other disciplines and the foundation of the International Luge Federation (FIL) in Davos in 1957 with Bert Isatitsch as its first president. The FIL is based in Berchtesgaden in Germany and has a membership of 52 national governing bodies of the sport.[49] Luge was included in the Winter Olympics programme for the first time at Innsbruck in 1964 when twelve nations took part in the event. At the Lake Placid Winter Olympics in 1980, luge events were run on a refrigerated track for the first time. There are differences in the rules for competition on artificial and natural tracks. Luge is most popular in Germany, Austria and Italy with three-quarters of world and European champions coming from these countries. The most successful Olympic luger is Georg Hackl of Germany who has won five medals in four consecutive Winter Olympics, three of them Gold.[50] Luge has taken longer to become established in the United States and the United States Luge Association was not founded until 1979, despite there being American luge entrants in every Winter Olympics from the sport's introduction in 1964.[51] America's first artificial luge track was created for the 1980 Winter Olympics in Lake Placid and a second for the 2002 Games in Salt Lake City.

As a fast sport, 96 mph was recorded for Manuel Pfister in Whistler in 2010, luge has a reputation for being a particularly dangerous sport, an impression reinforced most recently by a fatal accident, involving a Georgian luger, Nodor Kumaritashvili, whose luge left the track while travelling at 89.2mph during a training run at the Winter Olympics of 2010 in Vancouver.[52] Serious concerns about the pursuit of speed at the expense of safety were raised. As a result of Kumaritashvili's death the start was moved lower down the track to slow the sleds down in the interest of safety. This was the first fatality since an Italian luger was killed in 1975 and the sport's Olympic debut in Innsbruck was marred by the death of Great Britain's Polish-born team member, Kazimierz Kay-Skrzypecki during practice.[53]

Since 2014, a new event, the luge team relay has been introduced. Team relay competitions consist of one male, one female and a doubles pair. At the bottom of the run, a competitor touches a touchpad signalling to a teammate at the top of the run to start.

Bobsleigh

Another sledge of a new kind appeared at Davos when Stephen Whitney from Albany, New York, introduced a new sliding machine to Davos in January 1889.[54] Whitney's machine, which he named Maud S, was made up of two American style toboggans joined together by a long board.[55] Bobsleighs were inspired by the large sleds used in America by lumberjacks to carry tree trunks. Whitney's machine, the forerunner of the bobsleigh, came first in trials for the Symonds Cup International Race but, together with similar sleds made for other Davos sporstsmen, was not allowed to compete that year as the race was restricted to Swiss toboggans since the controversy surrounding Child's America sledge the previous season. As the machine was declared illegal by the race committee, Whitney went down head first riding on just the front section of his dismantled machine but still won the race by a wide margin.[56] His bobsled was made of wood and had no steering mechanism, Whitney used his hands to steer. The *St Moritz Post* remarked that "it looked a very dangerous machine to ride".[57] It was only intended that one person should ride in a head first manner on Whitney's innovation, unlike later bobsleighs that carried two or more people.

This elongation of the toboggan was developed further by the designer of the skeleton, Bulpett, with the aid of the St Moritz blacksmith, Christian Mathis, although a report of 1909 says that the bobsleigh was created by someone called Townsend in 1888–89 and improved on the following year by Saunderson and Mathis. All of these people could have experimented with their own designs at around the same time. In Bulpett's design two steel-runnered skeletons were joined by a flat board above. It was steered by pulling on cords or pulleys, rather like reins, on either side. Because of their length, bobsleighs offered social opportunities to carry several people at once and initially became popular for amusement rather than sport. The first race exclusively for bobsleigh, as the new machine came to be known, was held on the Cresta in St Moritz in March 1892. It took place at the end of the season when any damage to the track by the brakes would not have ruined the course for other users. These bobsleighs now carried four or five people. The winning bobsleigh was steered by Townsend. In Davos a report in the visitors' press stated that "Races for bob-sleds only were never held, except privately and late in the season, till about 1898."[58]

Bobsleigh soon became recognised as a separate discipline to tobogganing and in 1897 the St Moritz Bobsleigh Club was formed.[59] By the turn of the twentieth century rules governing bobsleigh competition were emerging. The first international championship for bobsleigh was the Manchester Cup, named after the Duke of Manchester who donated the prize. The competition was run on the road from Davos Wolfgang down to Klosters in 1900. This first championship was won by Trilby, a bobsleigh steered by Lawrence Gale Linnell, an artist from Leicester in England. Trilby was said to be the last wooden bobsleigh made in Davos.[60] Bobsleigh races became a feature of toboggan race weeks from then on, including one in nearby Arosa in 1901.[61] The enthusiasm of bobsleighers for their new sport was reflected in the names they gave their machines, such as Bobs, Blitz, Royal Flush, Trilby, Boule de Neige, Joker.

The St Moritz Bobsleigh Club worked to raise 5,000 Swiss francs towards the 12,000 Swiss francs needed to build a dedicated run they could use all through the winter season. Most of the subscribers were English visitors. The rest of the money was loaned by the Badrutt hoteliers over whose land part of the track was to run with 500 Swiss francs donated by the St Moritz *Kurverein* (Tourism Office).[62] A course was laid out from St Moritz near the Engadiner Kulm Hotel down to Celerina, almost parallel with the Cresta Run. Work began in 1903 and the track opened on 1 January 1904. Soon there were two more runs in nearby Pontresina. Davos bobsleighers no longer had to ride on the Klosters road from 1907 when a run was installed from Schatzalp. Arosa too had its own track from 1908.[63] In Leysin, a health station in the west of Switzerland, bobsleighing was enthusiastically taken up and a steering wheel was added to the design by Adolphe Roessinger in around 1903.[64] In St Moritz, bobsleigh retained the pulley system of steering, the method employed in competition. Christian Mathis, the St Moritz blacksmith, became well-known as a builder of bobsleigh and other types of sledge but Bachmann Brothers of Travers, whose machines had a steering wheel, and Hartkopf of Davos rose to prominence as manufacturers after 1920.[65] The early development of the sport was facilitated by newly opened railways and funiculars in the mountain resorts, that enabled competitors to transport their heavy machines uphill to the start of the runs rather than drag or carry them.

By the 1910/1911 season there were 61 bobsleigh runs in the Alps and the sport had spread to other mountain regions in the USA, Canada and elsewhere. Since 1923 the sport has been represented by its international governing body the Fédération Internationale de Bobsleigh et de Tobogganing, the FIBT. Bobsleighing was one of the original Winter Olympic sports at Chamonix in 1924, where there was a four man bobsleigh event on the programme but in 1928, at St Moritz, there were crews of five. The St Moritz track was part of the infrastructure for the 1928 Winter Olympics when it was renamed the Olympia Bobsleigh Run. This was used again for the 1948 Winter Games.[66] The Olympia, formed by 5,000 cubic meters of snow, shaped into a 1,700 metre long track with 19 turns and corners, is now the world's last surviving natural track. Modern tracks are now made of concrete, coated with ice. Two-man bobsleighing, with just a pilot and a brakeman, was introduced to the Olympics at Lake Placid in 1932.

A rule limiting the total weight of the crew and sledge was introduced in 1952. The entire crew had to run and push the sledge to get up a good speed from the start. Previously the pilot had to be seated at the start and being heavy was an advantage. In the early days of the sport there was nothing to prevent a strong crew pushing the bobsleigh most of the way down the run. Modern bobsleigh crew members are skilled and well-trained athletes, often recruited from other sports. It is a professional sport which needs wealthy sponsors to pay for aerodynamic steel and fibreglass sleds which reach speeds of up to 150 kph (93 mph). During the 1970s, East Germany was an important centre for the design of sleds which allowed them success in the sport. The modern bobsleigh was developed and produced in Great Britain by a small group of young engineers in Leeds before the 1980 Winter Olympics.[67] Since 1984, bobsleigh frames have to be of a standardised construction and, from 2003, all runners have to be of a standard steel, delivered by the IBSF. This makes it easier to check for forbidden treatments to the runners to make the sledge faster.

A World Cup competition for bobsleigh was introduced in 1984/1985, athletes compete over a season on different tracks in an international circuit. This rewards consistency and versatility. The first world champion was Anton Fischer of West Germany.[68]

A new version of bobsleigh to be included in the 2022 Winter Olympics is monobob. These were first successfully tried out in elite competition at the Winter Youth Olympics in Lillehammer in 2016. By making all athletes share the same sledges, fastest athletes exchanging sledges with the slowest, reliance on technology and the performance of team mates are taken out of the competitive equation. Winning is not down to who has the best equipment but individual driving and athletic skill.[69]

Bob-sleigh now has participants around the world in countries without the natural resources for the sport of snow and ice; there are 69 national governing bodies of bobsleigh and skeleton in the IBSF.[70] The supposed incongruity of a Jamaican bobsleigh team was celebrated in the 1993 Disney film *Cool Runnings*. Although the film helped the sport enter into popular culture, it was mostly fictional and only very loosely based on the story of the Jamaican bobsleigh team that competed for the first time at the Calgary Winter Olympics in 1988.[71]

Women's sliding sports

Right from the start, women and girls had joined in tobogganing both as a fun recreation and for competition. Charlie Austin wrote in 1883 that, as usual, the ladies' race was won by Miss MacMorland, implying that female competition was a regular feature and suggests that racing by women, even in informal events, had been going on for longer than acknowledged elsewhere. There were three starters and the winner covered the course in 8 minutes 13 seconds.[72] Women's names appear in the inter-hotel competition between the Buol and the Belvedere in 1886, the highest placed female, Miss Tetley of the Buol, finishing in tenth place, the others making up the last four out of 17 entrants. In February 1886, before the International Race, a race for women was organised on the Klosters road between five women from Davos and five from St Moritz. Austin described this as the first important race for ladies. The Davos women took the first five places in the race which was won by Miss Kelvey in 7 minutes 18 seconds. Although this was a faster time than that of Minsch and Robertson in 1883, Charlie Austin commented in his *Toboggan Racing Calendar* for that year "In my opinion this course is far too long and trying for ladies to race on". Harold Freeman, who succeeded Symonds as secretary of the Davos Tobogganing Club presented a prize, the Freeman Trophy, named after his toboggan-racing daughter, Edith, to be competed for annually by female riders. Following the example of Davos, came the St Moritz Ladies' Race the following month, February 1886. The women started their race in the middle of the gully, below the Church Leap of the Cresta Run. The winner was St Moritz-based Miss Vickers.[73] When the head first riding position became almost universal, female participants solved the problem of billowing long skirts revealing legs and underwear by tying three bands around their legs to hold their garments in position. In the early days of the Cresta, women were allowed to participate but in 1925 they were banned, first from competition and then in 1929 from practice. One reason given was the belief that the vibration could cause breast cancer. Women are still barred from the Cresta although a special invitation ladies' event – the first since women were banned in 1929, has been held on one day at the end of the season since 1987. A prize for women, the Ladies' Garland, was introduced in 2016.[74]

A women's Skeleton World Cup was introduced in 1996/1997, won that year by Steffi Hanzlik of Germany. In Britain, women skeleton athletes have had remarkable success during the 21st century, for a country with no natural facilities for sliding sports and no track of its own on which to practice, thanks to a selection programme for young female athletes and a push-track facility at the University of Bath. Building on the success of three-time world champion Alex Coomber, who won a bronze medal in the Salt Lake City Winter Olympics in 2002, Shelley Rudman won silver in 2006 in Turin and in 2010 a team of three female skeleton athletes went to Vancouver where Amy Williams achieved gold. At the 2014 Games in Sochi Lizzy Yarnold won a medal and repeated her success in Pyeongchang, to become Britain's most successful Winter Olympic athlete in 2018. Fellow British athlete, Laura Deas, won the bronze medal.[75]

In luge competition, while men's singles events consist of four runs, women's singles and doubles only include two runs. Women are also entitled to carry extra weight, an additional 50 per cent of the difference between their body weight and a base weight of 70 kilograms or 150 lb. Men may add 75 per cent of the difference between their weight and a base weight of 90 kg or 200 lb.

Women joined in bobsleighing as enthusiastically as men in the early years of the sport, often competing in mixed sex teams of four or even five in Davos and St Moritz. Until the 1920s, competition rules said that out of a crew of five there should be two women. This was probably due to the social nature of the experience. Females though were progressively excluded from competition. They were barred from the Olympics and world championships from before 1924. In 1938 a female athlete, Katherine Dewey, won the American Athletic Union Championship, following which women were barred from that competition. Women's bobsleighing began again in the United States in 1983 when there was a demonstration event at Lake Placid.[76] It wasn't until 1993/1994 that the FIBT organised the first world bobsleigh championship for women which was won by Barbara Muriset of Switzerland, although this title is often credited to Claudia Bühlmann, who was official champion for the 1994/1995 season.[77] The International Olympic Committee added two-women's bobsleigh to the list of full-medal sports at the Winter Games. Female competitors made their Olympic two-woman bobsleigh debut in 2002 in Salt Lake City when the gold medalists were Americans Jill Bakken and Vonetta Flowers, the first African heritage athlete to win a gold medal in a Winter Olympics.[78] In September 2014 the IBSF declared the 4-man version of the sport to be gender neutral, allowing women to compete as part of a crew. Elana Myers Taylor (USA) and Kailie Humphries (Canada) were the first female athletes to compete against men in the World Cup series of 2014/2015.[79]

Women's bobsleigh caused controversy in Britain when just six months before the Winter Olympics in Pyeongchang, South Korea, in 2018, the British Bobsleigh and Skeleton Association (BBSF) announced it was cutting funding to the female team but would continue to finance and send three men's sledges to the Games. With public support, athlete Mica McNeil started a crowdfunding campaign to enable the women to compete which led to the BBSA reversing its decision.[80] The British women, Mica McNeill and Mica Moore raised more than £40,000 towards their costs and finished in eighth place, the best so far for a British female team. At the same Games, a Nigerian female pair's ambition to compete at the Winter Olympics was facilitated by crowdfunding.[81]

Although the men have four-man and two-man bobsleigh events at the Olympics there is still unequal treatment. For female athletes there is only the two-woman competition. Opponents of the inclusion of a four-woman bobsleigh event claim there are not enough females in the sport to justify a second event and they fear adding one to the Olympic programme could be at the expense of men's bobsleigh.[82] Although not meeting the demands for a four-women event a women's monobob event is to be included in the 2022 Winter Olympics.[83]

Para-sliding sports

For athletes with physical disabilities, there are para-bobsleigh and para-skeleton events. The IBSF Para-Sport Committee was formed in 2010 and became recognised as the International Federation for Para-Bobsleighing and Para-Skeleton in 2014.[84] The first para-skeleton World Cup, using conventional sleds, began in Park City, Utah in November 2014. World Championships were also held in Park City in 2016.

There is an International Para Sliding Club based in St Moritz and the first international competition for athletes with physical disabilities, the Prince Kropotkin Cup was held at Sigulda in Latvia in 2013.[85] The para-bobsleigh gold medal was won by Latvian Lavris Zutis and the para-skeleton by Matt Richardson of Britain.[86] The first World Championships at Park City included 19 athletes from 9 nations. The governing body, the International Federation for Para-Bobsleigh and Para-Skeleton, was recognised by the IPC in May 2014 and provisionally became a candidate for inclusion in Beijing in 2022.[87] A disappointing decision was made in September 2018, not to include para-bobsleigh in the 2022 Winter Paralympics in Beijing. The reason given was that the sport had fallen short of the minimum of 12 nations from at least three regions participating in the 2016/2017 and 2017/2018 seasons.[88] The sport is now working towards inclusion in the Paralympic Games of 2026. Unlike most other bobsleigh competitions, these are not team events. In these individual events athletes ride monobobs, steered and braked by one athlete only.

Notes

1 Austin, Charlie, *Toboggan Racing Calendar 1883–1888*, St Moritz: St Moritz Tobogganing Club, 2011, 1883
2 Barton, Susan, *Healthy Living in the Alps: the origins of winter tourism in Switzerland, 1860–1914*, Manchester University Press, 2008, pp. 20, 39
3 Ferdmann, Jules, *Der Aufstieg von Davos*, Davos, 1945, second edition, 1990, p. 160
4 Gibson, Hon. Harry, *Tobogganing on Crooked Runs*, Longman's, Green and Co., London, 1894, p. 82
5 Gibson, p. 86
6 Obituary Notice, *Monthly Notices to the Royal Astronomical Society*, 73, February 1913, p. 210
7 Gibson, p. 87
8 Barton, p. 138
9 Austin, 1888
10 Levinson, David and Christensen, Karen (eds), *Encyclopedia of World Sport: From Ancient Times to the Present*, Oxford University Press, 1999, p. 400
11 Austin, 1883
12 *Davoser Blätter*, 17 February 1883
13 *Melbourne Argus*, 25 June 1895
14 Austin, 1886
15 Gibson, p. 25
16 Seth-Smith, Michael, *The Cresta Run – a history of St Moritz Tobogganing Club*, Slough, 1976, pp. 18–19
17 Gibson, p. 28
18 Gibbs, Roger, *The Cresta Run 1885–1985*, London, 1985, p. 19
19 Austin, 1885
20 Ibid., 1885
21 Seth-Smith, p. 20
22 Austin, 1884
23 Beerstraten, Jan Abrahamsz, Warmong castle in a winter landscape, painted 1661 or 1665, Walker Gallery, Liverpool
24 Austin, 1885
25 Ibid., 1886
26 Gibson, p. 88

27 IBSF Rules, p. 24
28 Barton, p. 54
29 Rubi, Rudolph, *Im Tal von Grindelwald, der Sommer und Winter Kurort, Band III*, Grindelwald, 1986, p. 108
30 Austin, 1887
31 Gibson, p. 35
32 Ibid., p. 36
33 Austin, 1887
34 *Davos Courier*, 1 November 1888
35 Gibson, p. 39
36 Ibid., p. 58
37 *Alpine Post and Engadiner Express*, 2 November 1901
38 Gibson, p. 90
39 Ibid., p. 50
40 *IBSF History* on www.ibsf.org, accessed 15 July 2016
41 Winter Olympics Official Report 1928 and Winter Olympics Official Report 1948
42 www.britishskeleton.org, accessed 15 July 2016
43 Ibsf.org/history, accessed 16 July 2016
44 Ibid., accessed 15 July 2016
45 Highlights of Sledding and FIL history, www.fil-luge.org/history
46 International Luge Federation, IRO International Luge Regulations – artificial track, 2018 edition, pp. 22–27
47 Ibid., p. 39
48 Highlights of Sledding and FIL history, www.fil-luge.org/history
49 International Luge Federation, member countries, www.fil-luge.org, accessed 31 October 2018
50 Georg Hackl, Sports Reference, Olympic Sports, www.sports-reference.com, accessed 16 July 2016
51 www.teamusa.org/usa-luge/history-and-fast-facts accessed 31 October 2018
52 *The Telegraph*, 13 February 2010
53 *The Independent*, 13 February 2010
54 *The Courier*, Davos, 15 February 1901
55 Gibson, p. 42
56 Ibid., p. 43
57 *St Moritz Post*, 1888
58 The Courier, Davos, 15 February 1901
59 Barton, p. 55
60 *The Courier*, 15 February 1901
61 Danuser, Hans, *Arosa wie es damals war, Band 1, 1850–1907*, Arosa, 1997, p. 163
62 *Alpine Post and Engadiner Express*, 7 February 1903
63 Danuser, Hans, *Arosa wie es damals war, Band 2, 1907–1928*, Arosa, 1997, p. 24
64 Roessinger, P., La Luge, in *Les Sports d'hiver en Suisse, 2*, 1907, pp. 9–25
65 Triet, Max (ed.), *A centenary of bobsleighing*, Swiss Sport Museum, Basel, 1990, p. 64
66 Winter Olympics Official Report, Part II, 1928, pp. 12–13, Winter Olympics Official Report 1948, p. 6
67 Bobsleigh History, British Bobsleigh And Skeleton, www.thebbsa.co.k, accessed 16 July 2016
68 International Bobsleigh and Skeleton Federation, www.ibsf.org, accessed 15 July 2016
69 www.olympic.org/news/monobob-proves-an-instant-hit-at-lillehammer–2016 accessed 31 October 2018
70 www.ibsf.org/national-federations?start=60, accessed 30 October 2018
71 Engel, Pamela, *Here's the Real Story of the "Cool Runnings" Bobsled Team That the Movie Got Wrong*, Business Insider, 6 February 2014
72 Austin, 1883
73 Ibid., 1886
74 The Cresta Run, The Ladies' Event, www.cresta-run.com, accessed 20 July 2016
75 www.eurosport.co.uk/skeleton/pyeongchang/2018/why-are-britain-so-good-at-skeleton_sto6564066/story.shtml accessed 31 October 2018
76 Bobsleigh History, British Bobsleigh And Skeleton, www.thebbsa.co.k, accessed 16 July 2016
77 *Wiler Nachrichten*, 7 February 2013; *Bobsleigh History, British Bobsleigh And Skeleton*, www.thebbsa.co.k, accessed 16 July 2016

78 Historical Moments in the USBSF, p. 3
79 *The Guardian*, 18 December 2014
80 *The Guardian*, 21 February 2018
81 *The Guardian*, 20 February 2018
82 *The New York Times*, 20 February 2018
83 Palmer, Dan, *Women's monobob events announced as Olympic preparations continue*, Inside the Games, 18 September 2018, www.insidethegames.biz/articles/1070108/womens-monobob-events-announced-as-olympic-preparations-continue accessed 31 October 2018
84 Ibsf.org/history, accessed 16 July 2016
85 www.ibsf.org/en/our-sports/para-sport accessed 31 October 2018
86 IBSF Paralympic School Bobsleigh and Skeleton, Prince Kropotkin Cup, Para Bobsleigh and Skeleton, March 2013, Sigulda, Lavia, Official Results, pp. 3–4
87 www.ibsf.org/en/our-sports/para-sport accessed 31 October 2018
88 *TASS Russian News Agency*, 13 September 2018

31

Swimming and diving

Melly Karst and Sarah Zipp

Early history

Rock paintings of swimmers 10,000 years ago have been found in Egypt; a clay medallion from between 9000–4000 BC depicts four swimmers doing some sort of crawl. More wall drawings of a variant of the breaststroke have been found in Babylonia and Assyria. The most famous drawings of ancient swimmers are those found in the Kebir Desert dating back to 4000 BC. Pools and large baths were part of Indian palaces, Middle Eastern Civilizations and great houses in Ancient Greece and Rome.[1]

References to swimming can be found in literature from 2000-year-old writings such as *Gilgamesh*, *The Iliad*, *The Odyssey* and the Bible, with references included in the codices of the Vatican, Borgia and Bourbons. It was part of military exercises as early as 850 BC and, according to German folklore, used successfully in wars with the Romans.[2] Warriors in ancient Japan trained in swimming races, with historical reference to these events dating back to 36 BCE.[3]

Many techniques and crude technologies developed during the Renaissance. Da Vinci made sketches of life belts, Nikolas Wynmann, a German literature professor, wrote the first book on strokes and life-saving approaches in 1539.[4] In 1587, Everard Digby published a book with 40 illustrations of various methods including the breaststroke, backstroke and crawl.[5] Emperor Go-Yozei of Japan declared that all children of school age in the Empire should be taught to swim.[6]

Books from the Frenchman, Thevenot, in 1696 describing the breaststroke to the German, GutMuth who wrote about teaching techniques and safest apparatus were published through the end of the 1700s. A group of salt makers in Halle, Germany greatly advanced the cause by teaching young children to swim, setting an example for their community.[7]

Early competition history

Swimming emerged as a competitive sport during the early 1880s in England. The first pool, St George's Baths, were opened to the public in 1828. The National Swimming Society was holding regular swim competitions in six artificial pools, in various London districts, by 1837. The swimming of the English Channel, by Matthew Webb in 1857, sparked even more interest in the sport. By 1880 there were 300 regional clubs throughout the country with the Amateur Swimming Association acting as the sanctioning body.[8]

Two interesting, yet often overlooked, stories from this time were the contributions made by Native Americans from both North and South America. In 1844, two indigenous North Americans were brought to England to compete in a London competition. The British competitor used the then popular breaststroke while the Native American used a variant of the front crawl that had been used in the Americas for generations. "Flying Gull" swam the 130 foot length in 30 seconds, easily besting his British rival. The British witnesses to the event were "aghast" at the spectacle, according to the London Times. The Native American's style of rotating his arms "like a windmill" and the thrashing of his legs causing large splashes and actually keeping his head in the water were considered barbaric and "un-European". It seems the British swimmers of the era preferred, to keep their heads above water. The British swimmers continued to use the breaststroke until about 1873. Eventually they adapted the speedier sidestroke. J.H. Thayers of England set the 100 yard record, in 1895, by side-stroking the distance in just over a minute.[9]

Returning from Bueno Aires, in 1868, where he observed South American natives swimming, Sir John Arthur Trudgen debuted their powerful stroke and revolutionized British swimming. The "new" stoke was actually one that closely resembled the form depicted in Ancient Assyrian drawings. The "new" stroke involved bringing the arms forward, in an alternating fashion, while rolling the body side to side. While the native style was to use the flutter kick, Trudgen incorporated the scissors kick with the stroke. The new stroke took ten seconds off the existing 100 yard time and even though the splashing was still considered ungentlemanly, it became popular worldwide.[10]

In 1847, Nancy Edberg, popularized women's swimming in Stockholm. She made swimming lessons available to everyone, regardless of gender, in Denmark and Norway and her swimming exhibitions were likely the first public displays of women swimming in Europe.[11] Her cause was greatly helped by Louise of the Netherlands, then Queen of Sweden, and her daughter Louise, later queen of Denmark, when they both joined her classes in 1862. Swimming was not regarded as proper for women but when the Queen showed such enthusiasm for it, it not only became more accepted but also somewhat fashionable. Edberg is largely responsible for spreading women's swimming into: Norway, Denmark, Sweden and empirical Russia.[12]

Early Olympic era and milestones for inclusion

The first modern Olympics were held in Athens in 1896. This first Olympic Games were an all-male and all-white competition held in open waters. Swimmers were at the mercy of weather conditions and other factors. During that first Olympic swimming competition, six events were scheduled but only four were actually swam: 100m, 500m, 1200m freestyle and an event called "the 100m for sailors". In Paris during the 1900 Olympics, the competitions included: 200m, 1000m, 4000m freestyle, 200m backstroke and a 200m team race. Particular to the Paris games, there was also an obstacle swimming course in the Seine River and an underwater swimming race.

Various races, stroke styles and local oddity races continued until 1908 when the world swimming governance body, Federation Internationale de Natation Amateur (FINA), was born. While there were many more changes to come in competitive swimming, this was the first attempt to standardize and regulate international swimming competitions. That same year, the London Olympics was the first Games to host the swimming competition indoors. Although the venue changed, women and non-white athletes were still excluded.

Women were allowed to compete in Olympic swimming in 1912. They competed in the 100m freestyle and 4 × 100m free relay. The women's events were limited to these few events until 1924. Another factor concerning women swimmers was the concern of public nudity. In the early 1900s women, in much of the world were required to wear swim dresses that required them to be fully covered and had skirts that didn't reveal their lower bodies, however, in the 1912 Olympics, the woman swimmers competed in the scandalous attire of short sleeved tops over mid-thigh length shorts. This so scandalized American James E. Sullivan, head of the American Olympic Committee and the Amateur Athletic Union, that he forbade American women from participating. After his death in 1915, American women competed in the 1920 Olympics.[13] (There were no Olympics in 1916 due to the First World War.)

Non-white swimmers, such as the native Hawaiian Duke Kahanamoku, competed in the 1912 and 1920 Olympic Games. He paved the way for other dark-skinned Hawaiians in swimming and surfing.[14] However, it wasn't until the 1976 Montreal Olympics that a black swimmer won an Olympic medal. Enith Brigitha of Curacao won two bronze medals. She represented the Kingdom of the Netherlands, the colonial authority over Curacao.[15] The first black man to win an Olympic swimming medal was also from the Dutch Antilles, Anthony Nesty of Suriname. He won gold for the Netherlands in1988.

The exclusion and marginalization of black athletes is deeply rooted in colonial history and American racial segregation. British and European elites maintained strict amateurism regulations in Olympic sport for decades, which restricted participation to mostly white and wealthy persons. In the US, the restrictions were more clearly race based. From the early and mid-20th century, when public swimming pools became more common in the US, Jim Crow era segregation was at a peak. "Whites only" pools across the country meant that swimming became increasingly accessible for white children, while black children were excluded. As a result, competitive swimming remained a dominantly white sport in America, as opposed to other more accessible sports like basketball and athletics.[16] Barrier breakers such as Olympic medalists Maritza Correia (2004), Cullen Jones (2012) and Simone Manuels (2016) have helped generate a new movement in developing swimming amongst young black Americans.[17]

Swimming has been included in the Paralympic schedule since the first Paralympic Games in 1960 (Rome). Races and strokes are adapted for people with various disabilities, from sight impairment to amputees. Athletes compete within classifications for their disability type, regulated by World Para Swimming (formerly IPC Swimming) and in coordination with the FINA. In Paralympic swimming, athletes compete in backstroke, breaststroke, butterfly, freestyle, individual medley and relay races. Adaptations include how the race is started, standing in the water, diving in to the pool or entering from a sitting position. For the visually impaired or blind athletes, "tappers" are allowed to help them by touching them with a pole to indicate when they are near the wall for turns and when a race is over.[18]

Through innovation, diversity, inclusion and expansion the sport of swimming has become increasingly more accessible to participants and developing athletes. International swimming and Paralympic swimming now spans the globe and includes people from all walks of life, races, genders and social/geopolitical backgrounds. Despite these advances, cultural barriers and various limitations leave many poor, minority and disabled persons without access to competitive swimming.

Innovations in swimming techniques, training and technology

Development of techniques

In 1928, David Armbruster, a coach of the University of Iowa, began filming swimmers from underwater. He concentrated on the arm motion of the breaststroke. Finding that too much drag occurred during the extension of the arms underwater he developed what is now referred as the "butterfly" stroke. During this same time period the Japanese also began using underwater filming and further refined their strokes which led to their domination in the swimming event during the 1932 Olympics. The "butterfly" stroke was considered a variant of the breaststroke until 1952 when it changed to its own style with its own set of rules.[19] Australian swimmers changed the backstroke by bending their arms underwater instead of keeping them straight, increasing their vertical lift and increasing their speed. This is now the technique used worldwide.[20]

Further study of techniques lead to swimmers not breaking the surface for longer periods thus increasing their speed. While this lead to faster times it also meant more swimmers were suffering from oxygen deprivation and in some cases, passing out. Controversy erupted during the 1956 Olympics in Melbourne when six swimmers were disqualified for swimming great of distances underwater. The rule was changed, in the breaststroke, to require surfacing after the first surface and after each turn. Masaru Furkawa, of Japan, circumvented the rule by not surfacing at all after entering the pool. He swam but five metres underwater in the first three 50 metre laps, winning the gold medal. FINA again changed the rule, requiring the head to surface every stroke cycle. It was also at Melbourne that flip turn was introduced.[21]

The underwater swimming controversy didn't end there. At the 1988 Games in Seoul, Daichi Suzuki (Japan) and David Berkoff (USA) used the underwater technique in the 100m backstroke. Both men swam underwater over 30 metres during the first lap, using only the dolphin kick, far out distancing their competitors. Suziki went won the race in 55.05. Again, FINA changed the rules limiting the distance to 10 metres (increased to 15 in 1991) to ensure the health and safety of the swimmers.[22]

Today, the FINA events include four strokes: freestyle, backstroke, breaststroke and butterfly. Swimming competitions range in distance from 50 metres to 1500 metres and include medleys (mix of strokes), relays and mixed relays (mix of strokes and swimmers). The sport also includes various modes, such as open water swimming, artistic (synchronized) swimming and water polo. Each of these sports and disciplines is governed by the FINA and is included in the Olympic festival.[23]

Advances in swimwear

Due to fabric shortages during WWII, swimsuits went under dramatic changes. Men made their first topless debut in 1935. Two piece swimsuits made their debut and the bikini was invented in Paris by Louis Reard.[24] Innovations in swimwear in the late 1990s and early 2000s were dramatic and controversial. In 2000, "bodyskins" were introduced as advanced swimwear.

Swimmers reported the skins improved buoyancy. This is true for them as long as they stay dry and thus are recommended for distances of 200m and less.[25] The cost of the suits made them prohibitive for some competitors, a notable problem for the Olympic movement as it sought to develop sport in low and middle income countries. The bodyskins can only be used for a few races and become unusable after being taken off and put back repeatedly, further adding to the cost for the teams and individuals. They were banned by FINA from their sanctioned races, in 2010.[26]

Advancements in training

As cited earlier there have been numerous developments in stokes, kicks, techniques. Training includes arduous hours of pool time increasing lung capacity, muscle memory and endurance.

Robots are now used to replicate a swimmer's techniques and help them refine movements. The last half of 1900s and the first decades the 2000s have seen advancements in nutrition, the development of recovery techniques through sleep and dryland exercises and techniques. The use of biometrics, injury prevention and coaching techniques have helped the sport.[27]

Doping

Like other Olympic sports, swimming has a history of doping abuses.[28] Most recently, decorated American swimmer with an infamous past, Ryan Lochte, was banned from international competition for 14 months for posting a picture of receiving an intravenous drip on his Instagram account.[29] This is not Lochte's first time in the spotlight for his behaviour outside of the pool. During the Rio de Janeiro Olympics in 2016, he was caught vandalizing a store while on a drunken night out with three other USA swimmers. He claimed he was robbed, fabricating an elaborate cover story about a gunman assaulting them on their way home from partying.[30]

At those same Rio games, seven Russian swimmers were banned following a damming report by the World Anti-Doping Agency (WADA). WADA found evidence of systematic, widespread doping across multiple Russian sport federations. While the athletics team faced a complete ban, forcing clean athletes to compete under the Olympic banner, rather than the Russian flag, Russian synchronized swimmers, divers and the women's water polo team were permitted to compete for their country.[31]

Other notable doping scandals include the East German Women's Swim Team, which rose to prominence in the late 1970s and 1980s. After the collapse of East Germany in 1989, records detailing doping records were discovered. Much like the Russian federation prior to the Rio games, the East German system conducted widespread doping. Amongst the banned substances, East German swimmers were mainly using testosterone and steroids.[32]

In many cases the athletes didn't even know they were being doped. The banned substances were included in their meals, "inoculations" and supplements. It is believed 10,000 athletes were used by the East Germans, over many sports, as the government tried to enhance its international reputation. In 1964 no East German medalled in swimming, but by 1980 they were dominating, winning 26 medals in the Moscow games. In 1991, 20 former East German coaches admitted to the scandal. "We confirm that anabolic steroids were used in East German swimming, not all of us were involved in doping", the coaches stated in joint release.[33] Despite these revelations, the International Olympic Committee made no adjustments to the medals won in the Olympic Games during that period.[34]

The East Germans were not the only national swim team to cheat. The Chinese Women's Team went from no medals to four golds in 1992 World Championships to 12 golds in 1994. During the 1994 Asian Games, 11 Chinese women tested positive for testosterone and were disqualified.[35]

International swimming stars of the 20th and 21st centuries

Mark Spitz brashly predicted he would win 6 medals before the 1968, Mexico City Olympics, he won two. A wee bit burned by his disappointing performance, Spitz entered the 1972 Munich Olympics with something to prove, and he did. During the eight days of competition he not only won seven gold medals, he set the world record each of his races. This phenomenal achievement would stand until 2008.[36]

Spitz's achievements were unparalleled for decades, until Michael Phelps hit the water. As a child, Phelps suffered from attention deficit/hyperactivity disorder (ADHD) and began swimming as a way to burn off his excess energy. By the time he was fifteen he was an Olympian, finishing fifth in the 200m butterfly in Sydney's 2000 Olympics. During the 2004 Games in Athens he competed in eight events, winning five. He claims he never wanted to be Mark Spitz, he wanted to be, "the first Michael Phelps". And he was. At the Beijing Olympics in 2008 he won eight Olympic golds, setting world records in seven races and a new Olympic record in an eighth. Going into his fourth consecutive Olympics in London, with thoughts of retirement, he won four more golds and threw in a silver for good measure. His retirement didn't last long. He re-entered the pool to begin training for the 2016 Rio Olympics in 2014. He won the 200m butterfly for the third consecutive Olympics and the 4 × 200m freestyle for the fourth time. He left Rio with his 23rd Olympic gold and 28th overall Olympic medal.[37]

In the outstanding tradition of Australian swimming, Ian Thorpe holds the men's standard. Allergic to chlorine, Thorpe worked hard to overcome his illness and with the help of doctors and improved pool systems he quickly rose to the top of the swimming world. His first world title came in 1998 winning the 200 and 400m freestyle events. Competing at home in the 2000 Melbourne Games, he dominated his events by winning three golds and adding two silvers, becoming the most decorated swimmer at those games. The 2004 Olympics was to be the swimming world's "Race of the Century" between Thorpe, fellow Australian Grant Hackett, Peter van den Hoogenband of the Netherlands, and Michael Phelps. Trailing at the mid-point of the 200m freestyle by half a body length, Thorpe passed the Dutchman in the closing seconds bringing his medal count from those games to two golds, a sliver and a bronze. Illness, injury and missteps cut into his training for the 2008 Games and didn't qualify.[38]

At 6 feet and 7 inches, and with a matching arm span, Matt Biondi (The California Condor) was an eleven time Olympic medallist and competed for Team USA in the 1984, 1988 and 1992 Games. Winning a total of eleven medals (eight golds, two silvers and one bronze) he set the standard for American swimmers to try and attain. His five gold medals in 1988 at the Seoul Olympics was an impressive haul.[39]

American Dara Torres became the oldest swimmer to compete in the Olympics at the age of 41. She was the first swimmer to represent the United States in five Olympic Games. At the age of fourteen, she competed in the 1984 Los Angeles Games as a gold medal winning member of the 4 × 100m freestyle. She medalled at 1988 as part of the winning American 4 × 100 freestyle and repeated in the event in 1992.

Now this is when her story gets really interesting. She gave up competitive swimming for seven years but decided to try a comeback for the 2000 Sydney Games. She made the team and won five medals, including two golds, as a member of relay teams. At 33, she became the most decorated member of that team. She wasn't yet finished. After another seven year absence Torres, at the age of 41, and sixteen months after giving birth, competed in the 2008 Beijing Games winning silver while swimming the anchor of the 4 × 100m freestyle relay. With that medal, she became the oldest swimmer to win a medal in Olympic history. She went on to win the silver in the 50m freestyle and thirty-five minutes later another silver, swimming the anchor of 4 × 100m freestyle relay. Her split time in that race was the fastest split time in relay history.[40]

The first woman to win six gold medals in a single Games was East Germany's Kristin Otto. At the Seoul Games she dominated all the 100m and under races she entered. She was part of the East German team that took those games by storm. She dominated her events through most of the eighties but came under suspicion of doping when it was discovered that the East German teams had been systematically administered performance enhancing drugs through most of the 1980s.[41]

Dr Jenny Thompson of the USA is amongst the most decorated athletes in Olympic history, with twelve gold medals (eight gold) across four Olympic Games (1992, 1996, 2000, 2004).

During her twelve year Olympic career, she earned more medals than any other female swimmer in history. After retiring from competition, the swimming legend went on to earn her medical degree and is now a practicing anaesthesiologist and surgeon at the Maine Medical Center.[42]

Rising star Simone Manuel, also of the USA, broke swimming and cultural barriers at the 2016 Rio games when she became the first black female swimmer to win Olympic gold. In the process, she shattered stereotypes and the world record in the 100-metre freestyle.[43]

Paralympic swimming

Paralympic swimming is competition for athletes with disabilities. The sport is governed by the International Paralympic Committee with competitors using adapted rules set forth by FINA. These athletes compete in backstroke, breaststroke, butterfly, freestyle, individual medley and relay races.[44]

Adaptations include how the race is started, standing in the water, diving in to the pool or entering from a sitting position. For the visually impaired or blind athletes, "tappers" are allowed to help them by touching them with a pole to indicate when they are near the wall for turns and when a race is over.[45]

The most successful Paralympic swimmer in history is American Trischa Zorn, winner of 55 medals over the course of her 24 year Paralympic career (1980–2004). She garnered 41 golds, nine silvers and five bronze medals, making her the most decorated Paralympic athlete in history.[46]

Natalie du Toit from South Africa took up Zorn's mantle as the rising star at the 2004 Athens games, winning five gold medals and one silver. Du Toit brought home five more golds from the Beijing Paralympics in 2008, but the Paralympics were just one part of her Beijing journey. Weeks prior, she competed in the 10km open water swimming competition for the Olympic Games, becoming the first female amputee to compete in an Olympic event. She finished in 16th place. Du Toit was selected as the South Africa flag bearer for both the Olympic and Paralympic teams, becoming the first athlete to carry her nation's flag in both games.[47] In 2012, du Toit again dominated the pool, winning three gold medals and one silver. She is now retired from swimming.[48]

Brazilian Daniel Dias who won 5 five medals in his first international competition in 2006 after being inspired by watching his countryman, Clodoaldo Silva compete in the 2004 Athens Paralympics. At the 2008 Beijing Games, he brought home nine medals, including four golds. His haul was more than any other athlete at the games. In 2012, he was the flag bearer for the Brazilian Paralympic team and garnered five gold medals. In the 2016 Paralympics, at home in Brazil, he added nine more medals to his count, including four more golds. He is currently holds the Paralympic record for most medals won, at a total of 24. He hopes to add to his count in the Tokyo 2020 Paralympics.[49]

Diving

Early history

Water is a natural source of recreation and fun. Jumping in to it, in various forms, is part of that enjoyment. Diving was born from this joy.[50]

Evidence of some form of diving has been found in a 5th century burial vault paintings in Naples, Italy. On a roof slab of a vast burial vault south of Naples is a painting of a young man diving from a narrow platform. The discovery of the "Tomba Del Tuffatore" (The Tomb of the

Diver) shows us that the excitement and grace of diving from high places into water has lured people from at least 480 BC - the date established for the construction of the tomb.[51] Early references to diving can be found in Ancient Greek and Roman texts. Early diving was not so much about the ascetics but about commerce. Divers entered the water to search for sponges, salvage from sunken ships and for food. Diving in its more modern form which emphasizes grace, athleticism and technique, evolved in the early 19th century as a diversion for gymnasts and became a competition later that century.[52]

Early competitions, "plunging", began in Britain in 1883. At first the events were about how deep and far a diver could go. They evolved to also include "fancy" dives.[53]

In the beginning there was just "plain" dives. It was a simple front dive from platform referred to as a "swan" or "'swallow" dive. "Fancy" diving included twists and somersaults. Gymnasts used diving as an exercise to hone their skills. Swedish and German gymnasts used it to train by jumping off equipment into water. The origins of modern diving can be traced to two European venues - Halle in Germany and Sweden.[54]

It was a traditional specialty of the guild of salt boilers, called Halloren to practice certain swimming and diving skills. The Halloren used to perform a series of diving feats from a bridge into the River Saale. In 1840 in contact with the German gymnastics movement the world's first diving association was formed. Most of its members were gymnasts starting their tumbling routines as a kind of water gymnastic. Thus diving became very popular in Germany.[55]

In Sweden, wooden scaffolding was erected around many lakes, inviting courageous fellows to perform diving feats. Somersaulting from great heights and swallow-like flights of a whole team were common.[56]

Early Olympic history

"Fancy" dive competition began in 1903 and was added to the 1904 Olympics. Only two competitors competed in those games, one from Germany and one from the United States. Diving off a 33 foot platform, George Sheldon of the US, won the gold. Controversy, even then, surrounded this performance. Sheldon won because his dive was deemed "cleaner" (if simpler) than the German's who used a much more complicated plunge but didn't enter the water as crisply.

Springboards were added to the Games in 1908, using a part fashioned from an airplane wing. Wrapping a towel around the end for traction, the "board" gave but a few inches of "spring".[57]

Women were allowed to compete in diving at the 1912 Olympics but only from the platform. They weren't allowed to use any "fancy" dives, only straight forward dives. By 1920, the springboard was added for women and in 1928 games in Amsterdam they were formally allowed to add "fancy" moves to their repertoires. "Fancy' and "plain" diving were combined for the women's competition in the Amsterdam Olympics.[58]

At first the double somersault was thought to be too dangerous but as diver's pushed their abilities, they also pushed to expand the types of dives they could attempt. Originally there were only 14 platform and 20 springboard dives allowed, today there are, approximately, 60 one metre, 70 three metre and 85 platform contortions that can be performed.[59]

Diving competitions, with the additions of new moves, stayed larger the same from 1924 to 2000 when synchronized diving made its entrance. Synchronized diving is when two divers form a team and perform dives simultaneously. The dives are identical. It used to be possible to dive opposites, also known as a pinwheel, but this is no longer part of competitive synchronized diving. For example, one diver would perform a forward dive and the other an inward dive in the same position, or one would do a reverse and the other a back movement. In these events, the diving would be judged both on the quality of execution and the synchronicity – in timing of take-off and entry, height and forward travel.[60]

Criteria for diving

The FINA governs diving and has outlined extensive criteria for each diving discipline and scoring elements. Unlike swimming, diving is a judged sport and requires clear rubrics for evaluation. Dives are usually scored on three fundamental elements; the approach, the flight and the entry. For example, approaches may include hand-stands, which are judged for quality. The divers' flight is assessed for body position, rotation and distance from the diving apparatus, among other things. Body angle and amount of splash, the less splash the better, are aspects of the entry that judges review.

In international competitions, the FINA requires panels of between five and eleven judges. This method helps reduce subjectivity and maintain consistency across scores. Dives scores are also determined by the degree of difficulty they require. Scores are multiplied by degree of difficulty measures to enhance the scores of divers conducting more complex dives.[61]

While there are some diving competitions for disabled divers they are sparse and not well documented. Diving is not included in the Paralympic schedule.

Modern history

Americans had largely dominated international diving until the 1984 Olympics. The Chinese Team returned to Olympic competition and made a big splash (though not at the end of their dives.). Absent from the games since 1952, the women executed extremely difficult dives and entered the water with mere ripples. Chinese athletes, especially women, have dominated Olympic diving since the 1980s, winning 89 medals, more than half of them gold.[62]

The Chinese training methods are different than most other countries. Young children spend three years developing and honing techniques on dry-land, perfecting each movement before entering the water. This instils discipline, muscle memory and confidence. On Chinese training methods U.S. diving coach Ron O'Brien told Time, "the first three years the Chinese work on nothing but fundamentals of movement, with lots of dry-land repetition, and only then do the kids start to dive. In the US our athletes attempt difficult moves before they are ready . . . The Chinese live poor and train rich".[63]

Equipment developments

During the 1904 Olympics there were three methods for divers to enter the water, a platform, a low board constructed on the side of the pool or from the side of the pool itself. The springboard was not actually springy since it was merely a piece of wood that had little give and was, at times, wobbly. As noted earlier, the first actual springboard was fashioned from parts of an aluminium airplane wing. Over the next few decades, countries developed their own form of aluminium boards that were some form of an aluminium plank with varying degrees of spring and traction. This resulted in divers having to learn each new "board" they competed on resulting in a wide variety of success for each diver.[64]

The diving event was standardized in the 1928 Olympics with competitors using a 10 metre platform and a 3 metre springboard. Not until the 1960 Olympics in Rome did a well-designed and standardized springboard come into competition. Finally, a carefully engineered and scientifically design debuted, the Duraflex board. This board was designed by a self-taught engineer,

Ray Rude, and became the Olympic standard. Rude's form of board is still used in all major competitions.[65]

Famous Olympic divers

Wu Manxia is considered by many to be the greatest diver in history. She represented China in every Asian Games, Olympic Games and FINA World championships from 2001 until 2016. She is an eight time world champion, and a five time Olympic and Asian champion. There is no more decorated diver in the sport. She began as synchronized swimmer, with her partner Guo Jingjing in 2001, winning the World Aquatics Championships. She also specialized in the 3 metre springboard, winning the gold medal in 2012. She is the first woman in history to win gold medals in three consecutive Olympics.[66]

Guo Jingjing, Manxia's synchronized diving partner is also a giant in Chinese diving lore. Along with synchronized swimming gold, she also won the 2004 gold medal in the 3 metre springboard. After those games she became a Chinese national sports figure when her commercial endorsements ads worldwide. She was later banned by China team for "excessive commercial activities" and was not allowed to compete for the team until she gave up the nearly 44 million she had earned through her endorsements.

She went on to win two more golds in Beijing hosted Olympics in 2008, retiring as one of the most decorated divers in history.[67]

Greg Louganis, is the most decorated American diver in history. He is the only male and second in Olympic history to sweep the diving events in two consecutive Olympics.

His first Olympic competition in the 1976 Montreal Olympic Games. He placed second in the platform diving as a sixteen year old. He set records scorers in both events at 1984 Olympics. (The United States did not compete in 1980 Moscow Olympics due to a boycott. He was favoured to win two golds.) During the 1988 preliminary rounds at Seoul, he hit his head on the springboard resulting in a concussion. He went on to win the event by a margin of 25 points. After retiring he went on to work as an actor, an activist for LGBTQ rights and champion for HIV research.[68] Pat McCormick (USA), Klause Dibiasi (Italy) and Ingrid Kramer (Germany) are also considered to among the best divers in world history.[69]

Notes

1 McVicar, J.W. "A Brief History of the Development of Swimming". *Research Quarterly. American Physical Education Association* 7, no. 1: 56–67. 1936.
2 Ibid.
3 Kehm, Greg. *Olympic Swimming and Diving*. The Rosen Publishing Group, 2007.
4 Lixey, Kevin. *Sport and Christianity: A Sign of the Times in the Light of Faith*. Washington, DC: Catholic University of America Press, 2012.
5 Digby, Everard. *De Arte Natandi Libri Duo: Quorum Prior Regulas Ipsius Artis, Posterior Vero Praxin Demonstrationemque Continet*. London: T. Dawson, 1587.
6 McVicar, "A Brief History of the Development of Swimming".
7 Ibid.; Kehm, *Olympic Swimming and Diving*.
8 Love, Christopher, ed. *A Social History of Swimming in England, 1800–1918: Splashing in the Serpentine*. Routledge, 2013.
9 Ibid.
10 Ibid.
11 Porter, Lisa. "The History of Competitive Swimming". *Livestrong*. www.livestrong.com/article/342427-the-history-of-competitive-swimming
12 Love, *A Social History of Swimming in England, 1800–1918*.

13 Welch, Paula, and D. Margaret Costa. "A Century of Olympic Competition". *Women and Sport: Interdisciplinary Perspectives*. Champaign, Human Kinetics. 1994. 123–138.

14 Pitts, Lee. "Back splash: The History of African-American Swimmers". *The International Swimming Hall of Fame*. 2007. Accessed March 15, 1019 www.kintera.org/atf/cf/%7B09E41378-901D-47D3-91DE-C700B1371B1F%7D/history AA swimming.pdf

15 Pitts, "Back splash".

16 Scott, Jaqueline L. "Swimming while Black". *The Conversation*. August 19, 2018. Accessed on March 13, 2019 https://theconversation.com/swimming-while-black-101354

17 "Why Simone Manuel's Olympic Gold Medal in Swimming Matters". BBC News. August 12, 2016. Accessed March 13, 2019 www.bbc.co.uk/news/world-us-canada-37057236

18 Kehm, Greg. *Olympic Swimming and Diving*. The Rosen Publishing Group, 2007.

19 "Coach Dave Armbruster". *American Swimming Coaches Association*. Accessed March 01, 2019 https://swimmingcoach.org/about/hof/armbruster-dave/

20 Porter, "The History of Competitive Swimming."

21 "Did You Know: Swimmers Must Not Remain Submerged for More than 15m". Nabaiji. June 8, 2017. Accessed March 1, 2019. www.nabaiji.co.uk/blog/did-you-know-swimmers-must-not-remain-submerged-more-15m-b_25967.

22 "David Berkoff and Daichi Suzuki's Underwater Duel in '88". SwimSwam. June 11, 2015. Accessed March 1, 2019. https://swimswam.com/david-berkoff-daichi-suzukis-underwater-duel-88/

23 Swimming. Federation Internationale de Natation (FINA). Retrieved from FINA Diving Rules 2017–2021. www.fina.org/sites/default/files/2017-2021_diving_12092017_ok.pdf

24 Roberts, Jacob. "Winning Skin". Science History Institute. April 20, 2017. Accessed March 1, 2019. www.sciencehistory.org/distillations/magazine/winning-skin

25 Rushall, Brent. "What are the Reasons for Wanting/Allowing More Material in Competitive Swimsuits?" *Swimming Science Journal*. San Diego State University. 2010. Accessed March 1, 2019 https://coachsci.sdsu.edu/swim/bodysuit/July2010.pdf

26 "Hi-tech Suits Banned from January". BBC Sport. 31 July 2009. Accessed March 13, 2019. http://news.bbc.co.uk/sport1/hi/other_sports/swimming/8161867.stm.

27 Longman, Jeré, and Gina Kolata. "As Swimming Records Fall, Technology Muddies the Water". *The New York Times*. August 11, 2008. Accessed March 1, 2019. www.nytimes.com/2008/08/12/sports/olympics/12records.html

28 Kumar, R. "Competing against Doping". *British Journal of Sports Medicine*. 2010. 44: i8.

29 "Ryan Lochte Banned 14 Months for Doping Violation Revealed on Instagram". www.theguardian.com/sport/2018/jul/23/ryan-lochte-doping-rule-ban-14-months-swimming

30 Graham, Bryan Armen. "Ryan Lochte Banned 14 Months for Doping Violation Revealed on Instagram". *The Guardian*. July 23, 2018. Accessed March 18, 2019. www.theguardian.com/sport/2018/jul/23/ryan-lochte-doping-rule-ban-14-months-swimming

31 Macguire, Eoghan, and Steve Visser. "7 Russian Swimmers Banned from Rio amid Doping Scandal". CNN. July 26, 2016. Accessed March 13, 2019. https://edition.cnn.com/2016/07/25/sport/russia-olympics-doping/index.html

32 Dimeo, Paul, and Thomas M. Hunt. "The Doping of Athletes in the Former East Germany: A Critical Assessment of Comparisons with Nazi Medical Experiments". *International Review for the Sociology of Sport* 47, no. 5 (2012): 581–593.

33 Janopsy, M. "Olympics; Coaches Concede that Steroids Fuelled East Germany's Success in Swimming". *New York Times*. 1991. Accessed March 13, 2019 www.nytimes.com/1991/12/03/sports/olympics-coaches-concede-that-steroids-fueled-east-germany-s-success-in-swimming.html

34 Rutemiller, B. (2013). "Doping's Darkest Hour; The East Germans And The 1976 Montreal Games". *Swimming World News*. April 28, 2016. Accessed March 1, 2019. www.swimmingworldmagazine.com/news/dopings-darkest-hour-the-east-germans-and-the-1976-montreal-games/

35 Ibid.

36 "Mark Spitz". Biography.com. November 11, 2014. Accessed March 1, 2019. www.biography.com/people/mark-spitz-9490898

37 "Michael Phelps". International Olympic Committee. January 8, 2019. Accessed March 1, 2019. www.olympic.org/michael-phelps

38 "Ian Thorpe". Biography.com. April 2, 2014. Accessed March 1, 2019. www.biography.com/people/ian-thorpe-20930179

39 "Biography of Matt Biondi". https://thebiography.us/en/biondi-matt. Accessed March 01, 2019.

40 "Dara Torres". International Olympic Committee. May 11, 2017. Accessed March 1, 2019. www.olympic.org/dara-torres

41 "Kristin Otto". *Encyclopedia Britannica*. February 03, 2019. Accessed March 1, 2019. www.britannica.com/biography/Kristin-Otto

42 "Jenny Thompson". International Olympic Committee. May 11, 2017. Accessed March 13, 2019. www.olympic.org/jenny-thompson

43 "Why Simone Manuel's Olympic Gold Medal in Swimming Matters". BBC News. August 12, 2016. Accessed March 13, 2019 www.bbc.co.uk/news/world-us-canada-37057236

44 www.paralympic.org/swimming/about

45 "A-Z of Paralympic Classification". BBC News. August 28, 2008. Accessed March 1, 2019. http://news.bbc.co.uk/sport1/hi/other_sports/disability_sport/7586684.stm

46 "Stoke Mandeville 70: Trischa Zorn's Legendary Triumphs". International Paralympic Committee. Accessed March 1, 2019. www.paralympic.org/news/stoke-mandeville-70-trischa-zorn-s-legendary-triumphs

47 Turnbull, S. (2009). "Natalie du Toit: 'If I Can Achieve a Dream, then Anyone Can'". *The Independent*. Retrieved from www.independent.co.uk/sport/olympics/natalie-du-toit-if-i-can-achieve-a-dream-then-anyone-can-1688566.html

48 "Paralympian Natalie Du Toit Aims to Make Impact New Role". Retrieved from www.bbc.co.uk/sport/disability-sport/21394927

49 www.paralympic.org/Athletes/Biographies?athlete=Daniel%20Dias

50 Kehm, *Olympic Swimming and Diving*.

51 "The Tomb of the Diver". www.ajaonline.org/article/151. Accessed March 1, 2019.

52 Edmonds, Carl, Christopher Lowry, and John Pennefather. "History of Diving". (1975).

53 Sinclair, Archibald, and William Henry. *Swimming*. Vol. 11635. Longmans, Green & Company, 1901.

54 Marx, Robert F. *A History of Diving*. London: Pelham, 1968; "History of Diving". Diving Australia. Accessed March 2, 2019. www.diving.org.au/about/history

55 Ibid.

56 "History of Diving". Diving Australia. Accessed March 2, 2019. www.diving.org.au/about/history/

57 "Swimming". Epicsports.com. Accessed March 2, 2019. https://swimming.epicsports.com/diving-history.html

58 Edmonds et al., "History of diving".

59 "History of Diving". British Swimming. Accessed March 2, 2019. www.britishswimming.org/browse-sport/diving/learn-more-about-diving/history-diving/.

60 "Who We Are". International Olympic Committee. February 18, 2019. Accessed March 2, 2019. www.olympic.org/about-ioc-olympic-movement

61 "FINA Diving Rules 2017–2021". FINA. 2017. Accessed March 2, 2019 www.fina.org/sites/default/files/2017-2021_diving_12092017_ok.pdf

62 "Diving Equipment and History – Olympic Sport History". International Olympic Committee. December 13, 2018. Accessed March 2, 2019. www.olympic.org/diving-equipment-and-history

63 Beech, Hannah. "Rio 2016 Olympics: Inside China's Diving Dominance". *Time*. August 09, 2016. Accessed March 2, 2019. http://time.com/4442329/china-diving-rio-2016-olympics/

64 "Diving Equipment and History – Olympic Sport History". International Olympic Committee. December 13, 2018. Accessed March 2, 2019. www.olympic.org/diving-equipment-and-history

65 Ibid.; "Swimming". Epicsports.com. Accessed March 2, 2019. https://swimming.epicsports.com/diving-history.html.

66 "China's Five-time Olympic Champion Diver Wu Minxia Retires". *South China Morning Post*. July 20, 2018. Accessed March 02, 2019. www.scmp.com/sport/china/article/2054903/chinas-five-time-olympic-games-champion-diver-wu-minxia-retires

67 Whitten, Phillip. "Guo Jingjing". *Encyclopedia Britannica*. October 11, 2018. Accessed March 02, 2019. www.britannica.com/biography/Guo-Jingjing

68 "Greg Louganis". Biography.com. April 19, 2016. Accessed March 2, 2019. www.biography.com/people/greg-louganis-9386797

69 Kehm, *Olympic Swimming and Diving*.

Part V
Judged sports

32

Figure skating

Ellyn Kestnbaum and Cheryl Litman

Introduction

Figure skating takes its English name from the concept of skating "figures" on the ice (i.e., specific moves or patterns). The term came to refer specifically to a series of exercises performed on two tangent circles (drawing a figure 8 shape on the ice) or three circles laid end to end making a pattern like OOO, often elaborated by specified turns, which formed a significant portion of competitions and scoring for approximately the first century of figure skating as an internationally organized sport. In this context, these basic specified patterns were referred to as school figures or, competitively, compulsory figures.

In other languages, the sport is known as artistic skating (e.g., *patinage artistique* in French, Eiskunstlauf in German).

At its most fundamental level, figure skating can be defined as the practice of using the body to control blades attached to the soles of the feet moving across the ice in curves produced by leaning over one side (edge) or the other of a blade and the various methods of transitioning from one edge to another: forward and backward, right and left feet, inside and outside edges.

Throughout skating's history, the visual appearance of the body has also been a point of focus, with the shapes and movement qualities most valued varying across eras, national and other cultural subcommunities within skating culture, and the gender of the skater.[1] Spectacular athletic feats such as jumps and spins that take advantage of speed and rotational forces have become staples of the sport, often driving results in modern era singles and pair skating.

In addition to organized sport and casual pastime, figure skating has also maintained a history as a performing art, with cross-fertilization of technical and presentational developments between the worlds of competition and show skating.

Early ice skating and the beginnings of figure skating

Gliding on ice in the cold climates of Europe by means of bone blades attached to the soles of their feet as early as 3000 years ago.[2] Written accounts, drawings, and other artifacts from medieval and early modern times attest to skating as a winter pastime and means of transportation, especially in the Netherlands with its numerous canals.[3] The 14th-century Dutchwoman

Lydwina, who suffered aftereffects of a teenage fall while ice skating with friends, was later canonized and recognized as the patron saint of ice skaters.[4]

Use of sharpened iron blades allowed for skating on one foot at a time, on either the inside or outside edge of the blade, beginning with a technique known as "the Dutch roll." In Britain, where skating took place more often on frozen ponds and fens than on canals, techniques for skating in circles and other patterns suitable to smaller surfaces took precedence over the Dutch preference for speed and distance.[5]

Tsar Peter I is said to have pioneered the permanent attachment of blades to boots.[6]

During the 18th and 19th centuries, additional developments in blade technology from skating enthusiasts in Britain, the European continent, and North America advanced skaters' ability to control the blades and what could be done with them. By 1784, the Edinburgh Skating Club was formed, with a proficiency test required for admission. Other skating clubs soon sprang up across Europe and in Canada and the United States.[7]

Skating experts of the late 18th and 19th centuries published how-to books to encourage would-be skaters to master figure skating techniques.[8] Some male experts encouraged female readers to take up the activity, but it was not until 1894 that a female skater contributed a chapter to one of these treatises.[9]

British and North American emphasis tended toward technical, edge-based skills, whereas French skaters showed more interest in body positions and dancelike movements.

Because of the need for leisure time to perfect increasingly difficult skills and the advantages of belonging to a club of like-minded practitioners, advanced figure skaters tended to come from more moneyed social strata and to advocate what they considered graceful, aristocratic-looking body postures.

Canadians pioneered erecting covered sheds over ice surfaces and North Americans experimented with creating artificial ice; however, the first successful indoor rink opened in London in 1876. "Ice Palaces" enjoyed a wave of popularity with the general public, followed by continued use of artificial indoor ice by hockey and figure skating clubs.[10]

British skaters developed a practice of "combined skating" in which groups of adept skaters created symmetrical patterns on the ice by skating the same edges and turns in different directions at the same time[11] – a forerunner of both pair skating and synchronized skating.

American Jackson Haines, a ballet dancer as well as an accomplished skater, introduced innovations to the skate blade that allowed greater control and attention to body carriage. His use of music and emphasis on body lines (including the sitspin, which he invented), theatrical costuming, and posing as well as technical skating drew scorn from American skating experts, but his style found greater acceptance in continental Europe.[12]

Haines's legacy was especially strong in Vienna, where performing to music and couples dancing on ice to waltzes and march tunes became popular.

The freer, more artistic "Viennese" or "International" style of skating vied with the more rigid precision and scientific approach of the "English style" through the late 19th century and eventually came to predominate.[13]

Competitions using figure skating skills began to appear in the second half of the 19th century.[14] A competition held in Vienna in 1882 established trends for competition structures to come. A panel of judges evaluated contestants on 23 prescribed moves or "compulsory figures," a four-minute freeskating performance, and "special figures" that allowed each contestant to present moves or combinations of moves highlighting his best skills. The winner, Austrian Leopold Frey, "linked an outside spread eagle to a back outside eight and terminated on a Jackson Haines sitting pirouette." Norwegian speedskater Axel Paulsen demonstrated the one-and-a-half-revolution jumps from forward to backward that bears his name. Another entrant, Theodor Langer, drew a symmetrical four-point star on the ice.[15]

Skating as organized international sport

The International Skating Union (ISU) formed in 1892 to govern international competition in speed skating and figure skating[16] and within a decade had twelve European members.[17] European Championships in figure skating were first held in 1892 and World Championships in 1896. As part of the nascent modern Olympic movement in the organization of sports in this era, the ISU held to a strict policy of amateurism, such that anyone who received remuneration for skating performances or teaching – or initially for other sport-related businesses – would be disqualified from competition.[18] This principle, combined with the need for leisure and access to uncrowded and where possible clean-surfaced ice for practice, meant that competitive figure skating at the highest levels remained in reach only for those who could control their own hours and often purchase ice time at indoor rinks or travel to suitable training locations. Although the advent of artificially produced ice allowed for practice outside of winter months or in locations with less reliably frozen natural surfaces, for the most part figure skating remained physically and culturally accessible only in cold-weather climates with a culture of winter sports. Ski resorts such as St. Moritz and Davos, Switzerland, and later Lake Placid, NY and Sun Valley, Idaho in the United States offered skating opportunities for the general public and for competitors' training at times of year when ice might not be available at home.

Early entrants in ISU competitions were all male, until 1902 when Madge Syers of Great Britain entered the world championship and placed second to defending champion Ulrich Salchow of Sweden. The following year, the ISU prohibited women from entering the championships and instituted a separate Ladies' Championship beginning in 1906, which Syers won. Pair skating competitions, for teams of one lady and one man, were initiated in 1908. The 1908 (Summer) Olympics, held in October in London, offered all three disciplines and the first opportunity for women to participate in any Olympic competition. A Special Figures competition, in which (male) skaters drew elaborate designs of their own devising on the ice with their blades was also part of the 1908 Olympics (won by Russian Nikolai Panin) and various lesser competitions in the late 19th and early 20th century, but the event was never part of the world championships.

Early ISU singles competitions consisted of up to 12 compulsory figures (6 types, in most cases begun on both the left and right foot) based on a now-standardized syllabus of two- and three-circle patterns.[19] Judges stood on the ice nearby each skater performing the compulsories and afterward knelt to examine in detail the tracings of the circles and turns carved on the ice by the skaters' blades and award marks for ease of execution and precision of the tracings left behind. Skaters also performed a freeskating program linking established and novel moves together into an aesthetically pleasing performance, and the results of compulsories plus freeskating were combined to determine final placements.

Pair skating competitions consisted of freeskating only, including side-by-side and reciprocal moves demonstrating equality between the partners as well as lifts and other pair moves.

In 1911, Hungarian world champion Lily Kronberger introduced rinkside musical accompaniment to her freeskating performance, a practice that was soon adopted by all competitors.[20] At first a rinkside band would provide background music for all skaters, who might time their skating to the musical rhythms. During the 1930s, it became common for skaters to bring specially cut phonograph records and perform programs personally choreographed to their musical arrangements.[21]

German skater Charlotte Oelschlagel never tested herself in the amateur competition but made a sensation as a professional show skater under the single name Charlotte. As a teenager during the First World War she left Germany to perform in ice shows in New York and across the US and to star in a film called *The Frozen Warning* before returning to Europe in the late 30s. She became known for her signature move, the Charlotte spiral or Charlotte stop, and with partner Curt Neumann in the 1920s introduced the (backward outside edge) death spiral that has become a standard element in competitive pair skating.[22]

Early in the century male skaters experimented with various means of jumping from one edge to another, with and without assistance from the toe of the other skate. In addition to Axel Paulsen as mentioned above, Ulrich Salchow, Austrian Alois Lutz, and German Werner Rittberger each invented a jump that bears his name and has become a standard part of the freeskating repertoire (the Rittberger jump is generally referred to as a loop jump in English), with the backward outside edge being established as the most secure landing. In the 1920s, Gillis Grafström of Sweden perfected the axel jump and introduced several spin innovations includ-ing the flying sitspin, change-foot spin, and an arabesque spin variation known as the Grafström spin and was also known for his interpretation of music. Grafström along with Karl Schäfer of Austria pioneered double jumps (two revolutions in the air) during the 1920s, while jumps with lower revolutions could land facing forward or emphasize spectacular air positions.[23] Canadian Montgomery Wilson was reportedly the first to attempt double jumps in competition.[24]

American Theresa Weld is one of the first women known to have performed a salchow jump in 1920, meeting with disapproval because her long skirt would fly up to her knees.[25] By 1924, 11-year-old Sonja Henie of Norway was executing the same single jumps and flying spins as the men in age-appropriate shorter skirts. Austrian Herma Szabo also shortened her skirts and was known for her daring jumps.[26] As hemlines rose off the ice so too women's skating apparel adapted to allow for greater freedom of movement and athleticism.[27]

Henie dominated competition from 1927 through 1936 with her athletic power and perfor-mance quality, winning 10 world titles and 3 Olympic gold medals. She parlayed competitive success into a professional career as a star of Hollywood films and touring ice shows, which boosted awareness and popularity of figure skating in the US.

Cecilia Colledge and Megan Taylor of Great Britain brought further athleticism into wom-en's skating of the 1930s. Colledge is credited with landing the first double salchow by a woman in competition; she also popularized the camel spin and introduced the layback spin position.[28]

Early 20th century skating competitions were held outdoors, often in frigid weather – although unseasonably warm weather could also pose a challenge by melting ice. Wind and ice conditions often presented challenges to the execution of the figures and freeskating moves.

For most of the first century or so of ISU competition, judges awarded one score for each compulsory figure on a scale of 0 ("not skated") to 6 ("perfect and faultless") with one deci-mal place allowed. Freeskating programs were given two scores on the 6.0 scale, the first mark reflecting the technical difficulty of the performance as a whole and the second the quality of its execution. These separate scores were factored and combined to produce rankings, or "ordinals" of the skaters by each judge, with those rankings then combined with those of the rest of the judging panel. Specific details of the scoring calculations changed over the years.

Since the Viennese waltz craze of the 1870s, skaters had experimented with translating waltzes and other ballroom dances onto ice for social and performance purposes. These efforts showed fruit in danced portions of pair skating programs with partners briefly joining together in ballroom dance holds. Informal competitions of dancing on ice began to spring up; for exam-ple, the first US championships in 1914, along with men's, ladies', and pairs' events, also included a "waltz" competition, to which the Fourteenstep (a march) was added in 1921. During the

1930s, with ballroom dance popular in Great Britain, English rinks encouraged development of ice dances suitable for use during "dance intervals" of adult skating sessions and ice dance competitions for professional or amateur skaters. Several dance patterns created there have remained standard fare in competitive and social ice dancing ever since[29].

Additional countries joined the ISU including Canada in 1911, Czechoslovakia and the United States in 1923, Poland in 1925, Latvia and Japan in 1926, followed by Italy, Estonia, Yugoslavia, and then Australia in 1932, Romania in 1933, and South Africa in 1938.[30] In the period between wars, skaters from twenty-one countries competed in international championships.

Post-Second World War era

The Second World War required a suspension of international competition but after a seven-year gap from 1940 to 1946 figure skating was revived with vigor. While many European rinks were destroyed and remained closed across war-torn Europe, North Americans competitors continued to train and compete through the war years. The first postwar ISU congress was held in 1947 and the number of compulsory figures was cut in half from twelve to six. The World Championships resumed in 1947 and singles skating underwent an athletic transformation. The 1948 Olympic Games in St. Moritz were the first games to be held (either winter or summer) since 1936; although neither Germany nor Japan were participants,[31] it was a meaningful opportunity for countries to unite in a peaceful event.

Dick Button won his first of two Olympic gold medals at the 1948 games and included a double axel jump; his second Olympic program at Oslo in 1952 included the first triple jump – a loop. Button's style typified the more athletic "American School" combining speed and big jumps with artistry and musicality. The era 1947–1960 in singles skating was dominated by North American skaters such as Button, Hayes and David Jenkins, Carol Heiss, Tenley Albright, and Barbara Ann Scott.[32]

The ISU continued to expand. Austria, Hungary, and Italy rejoined the ISU in 1947. The Soviet Union and South Korea (Republic of Korea) joined in 1948. Germany and Japan were readmitted in 1951. During the 1950s China, Spain, the Democratic People's Republic of Korea (North Korea), Mongolia, Romania, and the newly created nation of the German Democratic Republic (East Germany) were admitted to the ISU.

Ice dancing continued to evolve following the wartime stoppage. Ice dancing was competed at the 1950 World Championships as a special event. It became an official discipline at the World Championships in 1952. Jean Westwood and Lawrence Demmy of Great Britain dominated through 1955 – winning every European and World title. In 1955 British ice dancers swept the medals and repeated their sweep for the next two years as well.

In 1967 the value of compulsory figures, unchanged since the beginning of ISU competitions, was reduced from 60 to 50% of the overall score. 1967 also marked the last World Championship where events were skated outdoors. Pair skating had long been a freeskate-only competition, with nothing comparable to singles' compulsory figures or the compulsory dances used in ice dance. In the 1960s a pairs technical "short program" was implemented, eventually settling at one-third of the total score. Ice Dance expanded by adding new compulsory dances as options but for competition purposes replaced one of the four compulsory dances with an "original dance" with a set pattern and tempo. Three compulsory dances were combined for 30% of the score, the free dance was set at 50% of the score.

During the period of the 1950s to 1980s, the U.S. and the Soviet Union did not actively war since mutually assured destruction was a likely outcome. However, figure skating and other sports were a common arena for "proxy wars" allowing the two rivals to prove their superiority in other ways. One common feature of this era was the rise of "bloc judging." Judges from Warsaw Pact countries awarded higher marks to skaters from those countries while judges from NATO countries did the same for their competitors. While not an "accepted" practice sanctioned by the ISU, a tendency toward "bloc voting" was assumed to exist and discussed by commentators and journalists.[33]

Is it possible that the appearance of "bloc voting" is due to preferences for specific styles of skating, music, and artistry that vary by location? Unlike other sports that are suitable for objective measurement of time or distance, objective measurement of figure skating competitors has always proved elusive. Judging controversies abound. Sonja Henie triumphed over Herma Szabo at the 1927 World Championships in Oslo where the three judges from Norway all marked Henie first in both compulsory figures and freeskate while the other two judges from Austria and Germany placed Szabo first.[34] In the 1950s the ISU recognized the need for judge training and certification. A system for the evaluation of judges was adopted in the 1950s. In 1961 the first Judges Handbook was published covering compulsory figures with additional handbooks for the other disciplines following over the next few years.[35]

Like the competitors, figure skating officials are required to maintain amateur, now "eligible," status and are forbidden to earn income related to skating by serving as a coach, choreographer, or consultant to skaters. Because officials are assigned to international competitions by their national federations, there is incentive to overmark their own countries' skaters or otherwise to follow the federations' bidding.[36]

Skaters of the period 1960–1990

Pairs skating in the 1960s was dominated by Ludmilla and Oleg Protopopov, who created a new style based on the Russian style of classical ballet. Their programs integrated the athletic technical elements in a more continuous vision of a program showcasing an on- and off-ice romantic relationship that shone through in their skating.[37] In 1964, at ages 31 and 29, they won their first Olympic Gold medal. From 1965 through 1968 they won every competition they entered including four World and two Olympic Championships. This began a stretch of Russian domination of pairs skating.

On the way to the 1961 World Championships in Prague, the plane carrying the entire U.S. World team crashed with no survivors. The United States tragically lost its best skaters and a group of strong coaches. The World Championships were cancelled by the ISU out of respect for the loss to the sport. Several European coaches subsequently relocated to the US to fill the void, notably Carlo Fassi and John Nicks.[38]

Peggy Fleming revived the post-plane crash fortunes of US skating by winning 1966–1968 Worlds and 1968 Olympic gold. Fleming furthered the artistry of women's singles discipline with varied positions in spins and double jumps and an emphasis on refined body line and music interpretation. After turning professional Fleming headlined large ice shows and TV specials and performed shows in communist China (the first introduction to figure skating for many Chinese) and in the USSR.

In the 1970s Canadian Toller Cranston flouted the staid athletic tradition of men's skating, using his entire body in a wide variety of traditional and nontraditional movements exhibiting extreme flexibility to create original shapes on the ice. His creative choreography and flamboyant costuming along with technical prowess in jumps and spins made him a leading artistic skater of his time. His style was copied by others and he had great success both as a professional skater and choreographer.

Briton John Curry, a balletic skater considered one of the greatest artistic classicists, lacked strong jumps and compulsory figures. Improved technically after relocating to the United States to train under Gustave Lussi of Lake Placid and Carlo Fassi of Colorado Springs, Curry won every major competition in 1976. After retiring from amateur skating Curry developed a training regime for skaters with a ballet-style school and attitude.[39] For the next decade Curry formed small professional skating companies focusing on classical music and performance.

Although international skating was televised on ABC's Wide World of Sports in the US and on international broadcast networks since the early 1960s, the 1971 World Championships in Lyon, France demonstrated the impact of television on the sport. At that time compulsory figures and freeskating both counted for 50% of the total score in singles. Trixi Schuba of Austria excelled in compulsory figures, which were performed first, and entered the freeskating portion of most events with a commanding lead. Her leading competitors were Canadian Karen Magnussen and American Janet Lynn who were outstanding freeskaters. However, compulsory figures were not televised while the freeskating events were. Viewers around the world saw Janet Lynn skate an extraordinary first place freeskate but because she was in fifth place after the compulsory figures she did not receive a medal. Thus, viewers around the world were mystified as to the outcome based upon that broadcast, leaving figure skating with a credibility problem among fans.[40] By 1973, a short or technical program was adopted worth 20%, figures were reduced to 40%, and freeskating was reduced to 40%. This was the beginning of the devaluation and eventual elimination of figures in 1990.

In 1978, the ISU World Junior Figure Skating Championships were established for skaters under the age of 18 who did not compete in a senior-level championship competition nor medaled in a senior-level international competition.

Irina Rodnina of the Soviet Union was unquestionably the champion of pairs skating in the 1970s. She skated with two partners from 1969 to 1980 and won every title – European, World, and Olympic. Continuing in the tradition of the Protopopovs, but with a more athletically focused style of skating, Rodnina and her partners received at least one perfect score each year. Soviet domination of pair skating resulted with the Soviets/Russians winning thirty of the thirty-eight world championships from 1965 to 2002.

The USSR also wrested control of ice dancing from the British beginning in the 1970s, led by Lyudmila Pakhamova and Alexandr Gorshkov, who won the first ice dance Olympic gold medal when ice dance became an Olympic sport at the 1976 games. Soviet or Russian dance teams have medaled at every Olympic Games from 1976 to 2014.

English ice dancers Jayne Torvill and Christopher Dean won their first world championship in 1981. They were unbeatable for the next four years, winning every international competition. Up until that time ice dance programs were ballroom dance brought onto the ice with movements to the music. Torvill and Dean created routines with storyline and characters. In the Olympic year 1984 they created an original paso doble with Dean as a matador and Torvill as a cape. The brilliant choreography, costuming, and skating received straight 6.0 marks at the Sarajevo games for artistic impression. Their iconic Bolero free dance received twelve perfect scores.

Soviet ice dancers Natalia Bestemianova and Andrei Bukin competed in the shadow of Torvill and Dean. Bestemianova and Bukin had a four-year unbeatable streak of their own following the retirement of Torvill and Dean after their Olympic gold. The Soviet partners of Marina Klimova and Sergei Ponomarenko won almost every competition from 1989 to 1992. Klimova and Ponomarenko, along with fellow Soviets Maia Usova and Alexander Zhulin and the Canadian-French siblings Isabelle and Paul Duchesnay, led an era of artistic experimentation in early 1990s ice dancing. Upon International Olympic Committee objections that ice dance judging had become too subjective, mid-90s ice dance rules reinforced an emphasis on ballroom rhythms.[41]

East Germany became a dominant force, second only to the USSR in pair skating in the 1970s and early 80s and often chief rival to Western skaters in the singles disciplines. Katarina Witt, Olympic champion in 1984 and 1988, became the seductive face of Communism for Western audiences. Witt's 1988 *Carmen* freeskate in which she portrayed the title character furthered the trend toward thematically unified programs; her showgirl short program performed at Europeans that year in only a leotard with a few feathers around the hips prompted enactment of a requirement, known as the "Katarina rule," for ladies' costumes to include a skirt that covered the hips and posterior.

Triple jumps, first introduced in men's competition by Dick Button in the 1950s, gradually gained importance over the subsequent decades. The triple axel (3½ revolutions in the air) was first landed in competition in 1978 by Canadian Vern Taylor; as the 1980s progressed a full repertoire of all six triple jumps became expected for top male freeskaters.

Denise Biellmann of Switzerland was the first woman to land a triple Lutz but is better known for the spin that bears her name in which she reached back over her shoulder, grabbed the blade of her free leg skate and raised her foot above and towards her head, requiring great strength and flexibility.

American Elaine Zayak won the World Championship in 1982 with a program containing six triple jumps – four toe loops and two salchows – while most women attempted no more than two. This resulted in a 1983 rule change referred to as the "Zayak rule" that prohibited the repetition of triple jumps except once and only when repeated in combination or in sequence.

Japan joined the ISU in 1926 and sent skaters to competitions only twice before the Second World War. Japanese skaters competed regularly beginning in the 1950s but won no medals until the 1970s. In 1989 Midori Ito became the first World Champion from Japan. Ito included all the triple jumps including the triple axel. This signaled a new era for the ladies freeskating program in which six or seven triple jumps, including salchow, loop, toe loop, flip, and lutz, were expected in a winning performance.[42]

Professional skating

Large vaudeville-style ice shows such as Ice Capades, Ice Follies, and Holiday on Ice featuring elaborate sets and costumes continued to tour. Not finding a place for himself in the big tours, 1984 Olympic champion Scott Hamilton of the US was a key impetus for the foundation of Stars on Ice,[43] a more intimate show focusing on technically advanced skating and individual personalities as means for star competitors to capitalize and extend their name recognition after turning professional. Curry, Cranston, and Torvill and Dean headlined tours that pushed artistic limits of the form. Russian coach Tatiana Tarasova formed an ice ballet company called Russian All-Stars that traveled the world in the late Soviet and early post-Soviet era performing full ballets on ice in addition to the variety show format.

The Dick Button production company produced professional skating competitions including the World Challenge of Champions, World Professional Figure Skating Championships,[44] and many one-time special events featuring invited stars of the sport and others Button believed would appeal to American audiences.

Meanwhile, inspired by the British professional competitions of the 1930s,[45] between 1974 and 1998 Jaca, Spain hosted an event also called World Professional Figure Skating Championships (Campeonatos del Mundo de Patinaje Artístico Professional Sobre Hielo) organized by professional skaters. The Professional Skaters Association has similarly hosted a U.S. Open championships for professional skaters beginning in the 1980s.

1990s BOOM

In 1992 the International Olympic Committee shifted the cycles of the Summer and Winter Olympic games so that instead of being competed in the same year they would alternate in biennial years. Instead of the next Winter games being held in 1996 they were moved to 1994. This allowed Olympians to remain eligible amateurs for only two additional years in order to compete at the next Olympics. Along with this change was a decision by the ISU to allow a controversial[46] one-time reinstatement of ineligible skaters to allow them to return to competition in 1994.

At the same time, amateur rules had relaxed to allow the introduction of Pro-Am competitions featuring well-known eligible and ineligible skaters. Competitors were also now allowed, with ISU or national federation approval, to accept sponsorships and remuneration for coaching and for performing in shows such as the Tour of World Figure Skating Champions (later Champions on Ice), first organized as a postseason amateur exhibition tour in 1969.[47] The line between amateur and professional increasingly blurred, and terminology changed to a distinction between "Olympic eligible" and "ineligible."

Entering the 1994 season American Skaters Tonya Harding and Nancy Kerrigan were rivals competing at the National Championships in Detroit. Following a practice session a man approached Kerrigan and struck her knee with a metal bar. She was physically unable to compete in the championships but was chosen by the US Figure Skating Association to represent the US at the Lillehammer Olympics. Harding won the competition and was also named to the Olympic team. An investigation of the attack pointed to Harding's husband and his friends. Harding competed at the Games with a shadow hanging over her. The scandal was intoxicating to casual skating fans and American interest in figure skating spiked.[48] Harding was eventually implicated in the attack and was banned for life from US Figure Skating and stripped of her title.[49]

The explosion of professional (lucrative) skating opportunities boomed following the 1994 Olympics as did the pressure for amateur competitive skaters to turn professional once achieving success in a championship. American networks and production companies created a plethora of made-for-TV competitions offering employment to numerous elite skaters from around the world. Often skaters performed the same programs week after week that lacked the cutting edge technical difficulty of amateur competitive skating, eventually leading to audience fatigue.[50]

ISU competitors were not able to accept money for professional skating. The professional skating boom threatened the potential competitor pool for ISU events; as a result the ISU instituted prize money for ISU Championships starting in 1995. They also formalized a number of existing and new fall competitions into a Champions Series, later retitled Grand Prix, held over six weeks in the fall in which skaters could earn points to qualify for the Grand Prix Finals, with prize money available at each competition. In 1999 the Four Continents Championships was established for skaters from the Americas, Africa, Asia, and Australia/Oceania to have an ISU championship comparable to the European Championships, with new and increased participation from Asian countries and the southern hemisphere.

Over the next decade the ISU signed agreements for TV broadcasting and brought in more money from the televising of the Grand Prix Series and European and World Championships. The ISU allowed and later sponsored open competitions between professionals and amateurs with ISU judging; these proved unsuccessful with professionals performing entertaining performances and the amateurs more technical programs. The big names of the Olympics did not need to turn pro in order to make money and with the lack of recognizable stars professional skating declined.

Michelle Kwan served as the face of American skating for a decade from the mid-1990s to a retirement in 2006. She became the most decorated figure skater in U.S. history, widely considered one of the greatest of all time.[51] She was one of the most popular female athletes in the US[52] known to those who follow skating and millions of others who did not.

In the early 1990s Germany reunified and the Soviet Union dissolved. With former Soviet republics now each sending entries to the World and European championships (along with the splitting of Czechoslovakia and Yugoslavia), the fields grew larger and deeper. Qualifying rounds became needed in singles disciplines. Russia remained strong in pairs and dance, while in the singles events Ukrainian skaters won the 1992 men's and 1994 ladies' Olympic titles and Russia took home four straight Olympic golds in the men's discipline 1994–2006, with the turn-of-the-century rivalry between Alexei Yagudin and Evgeny Plushenko proving especially captivating to audiences worldwide. Russian women also took their first steps to the top of the world podium with Maria Butyrskaya's title in 1999 and Irina Slutskaya's in 2002 and 2005. Russian girls born during that era have taken up the mantle to lead the ladies' field in the 2010s, winning Olympic gold in 2014 and 2018 and demonstrating even more dominance at the junior level.[53]

Building on Midori Ito's pathbreaking, Japanese ladies of the next generation found success with Shizuka Arakawa's 2006 Olympic gold and Mao Asada's command of the triple axel, three world titles, and 2010 Olympic silver. Japanese men have also earned numerous medals in the 21st century, most notably Yuzuru Hanyu's repeat 2014 and 2018 Olympic titles. Figure skating became a national obsession in Japan, with extensive TV coverage both of skating events and of star skaters as celebrities, Japanese fans traveling the world to enjoy their favorites' live performances, and a popular skating-based anime series.[54]

Yuna Kim's multiple titles including 2010 Olympic gold and her touring shows have inspired similar enthusiasm in South Korean fans and young skaters.[55]

Chinese pairs, led by Xue Shen and Hongbo Zhao, first challenged for world medals in the late 1990s and went on to win multiple world and Olympic medals in the 21st century. Though less successful competitively, Chinese men proved instrumental in driving the quad revolution of the 1990s and 2000s, with Boyang Jin leading the way onto the world podium in the late 2010s.

Meanwhile, Russian dominance in ice dance declined as former-Soviet coaches have led Canadian and American teams to the tops of podiums, and France has fielded several champion teams.

Far from its northern European origins or the anglophone West vs. Soviet and East German rivalries of the Cold War era, skating in the 21st century has become a global sport, with medalists hailing from less traditional skating countries such as Italy, Spain, and Kazakhstan.

Competition judging

At 1998 the Olympic games in Nagano, judges were booed for seemingly biased judging[56] and a Ukrainian judge was caught on tape explaining the predetermined results of the ice dance event. In Salt Lake City in 2002, a decision was made to award two gold medals in the pair event following evidence of collusion by a French judge and others.[57] Following the scandal of the Salt Lake City games, the ordinal placement system using 6.0 was replaced with a points-earning system in order to reduce subjectivity in judging. After testing in 2003 the International

Judging System (IJS) was officially implemented in 2004. The panel of officials was split into a technical panel and a judging panel. The points score was divided between a technical score and program components score, replacing the old two marks. Members of the technical panel call which element the skater performed. Elements have a base value relying on difficulty, measured in points. Each judge then assigns a Grade of Execution (GOE), ranging from –3 to +3, to each of these elements. These GOEs are averaged, scaled, and added to the each element's base value. In 2018, the GOE scale was enlarged to –5 to +5. The sum of all the adjusted base values and GOEs comprises the technical elements score. For the program component score, each judge assigns a mark to each of the five individual components: skating skills, transitions, performance, composition, and interpretation. Judges mark each component on a scale from 0.25 to 10.0, in increments of 0.25.

During the entire event, judges are not permitted to discuss their evaluations among themselves. For the evaluation of the technical elements, judges have very specific guidelines for reductions and deductions marking the GOE scores. All marks are posted publicly shortly following the conclusion of each skating event. The system as originally implemented still lacked transparency as the marks were reported anonymously so there was a lack of accountability for the judges, but in 2016 the ISU acceded to public clamor for accountability by allowing judges' marks on the published protocols to remain in the same order that their names are published.[58]

While skaters, coaches, and technically minded fans can find copious details in the protocols about how each competitor gained and lost points, for fans in the arena or watching on television or online streaming video at home, the immediate experience of summary scores being announced may prove less satisfying than the 6.0-era association of two Technical Merit and Presentation scores with each individual judge.

Synchronized skating

Synchronized skating began as "precision skating" in Ann Arbor Michigan in 1954. Dr. Richard Porter created a skating program for girls and called it the Hockettes. The Hockettes performed programs similar to drill teams with marching and clear shapes on the ice. It took two decades for the first precision team skating competitions to be held. By the late 1970s teams from Canada and the United States were in regular competition with each other. Multiple skill and age levels of teams were organized and codified over time. During the 1980s precision skating became international with teams formed in Japan, Finland, and Sweden. In 1993 competition were first held under ISU regulations which required a short technical program and a freeskating program. In 1998 the ISU adopted the name "synchronized skating" for the discipline. The first world championship was held in 2000 with twenty-one teams from sixteen countries competing. Of the 19 World Championships held, fifteen gold medals were won by teams from Sweden or Finland. Team Surprise of Sweden has won six while Marigold Ice Unity has won five. Nexxice of Canada is the only North American team to win, in 2009 and 2015. Team Paradise of Russia were champions in 2016 and 2017. Teams may change members but retain the same name, colors, and allegiance of their fans and alumni. Synchronized skating competitions are very well attended and can be financially lucrative for their organizers. As of 2018 it is not an Olympic sport despite the lobbying efforts of the ISU with the support of the synchronized skating community.

Synchronized skating is primarily but not exclusively a women's discipline with some teams now including men. Synchronized skating includes formations such as blocks, circles, lines, wheels, and intersections with requirements for rotating, travelling, and pivoting. Elements and transitions include jumps, spins, and freeskating moves such as spirals and ina bauers. Handholds, unison, shapes, speed, and quality of movements are all evaluated. Synchronized skating is judged using the IJS.

The state of figure skating 2018 and beyond

1988 was the beginning of a revolution in men's skating – the quad jump with four or more revolutions. Kurt Browning of Canada landed the first quad jump, a toe loop, at the World Championships. Quads remained rare for a decade; the 1997 Champions Series final was the first time three skaters landed quads in the same event (Russians Alexei Urmanov and Ilia Kulik, and the first quad-triple combination by Canadian Elvis Stojko). In 1998 while still a junior skater, American Timothy Goebel landed the first ratified quad salchow. That year a quad became an option for the solo jump in the men's short program. In 2010, American Evan Lysacek won the Olympic gold medal without attempting a quad jump but by executing excellent triple jumps, high level spins and footwork, prompting runner-up Evgeny Plushenko to object that quads were undervalued and the ISU to revise the Scale of Values in response.[59] It took until 2011 for Brandon Mroz of the US to land the first successful quad lutz. Points earned for a poor but rotated quadruple jump often beat a very good triple jump and so the quad became an essential for the most competitive skaters to earn a medal. By 2015 Boyang Jin of China landed six quads in two programs at the Grand Prix Final. In 2018 skaters such as Nathan Chen of the US and Yuzuru Hanyu of Japan regularly attempt four or more quadruple jumps in freeskating programs. At the Rostelecom Cup in November 2018, Artur Dmitriev Jr. of Russia included a quad axel attempt which was downgraded[60] but raised the bar for the future of men's figure skating.

The technical level for other disciplines continues to increase as well. Ladies require a triple-triple jump combination to be competitive. Before 2018 only seven women had ever landed a triple axel but in 2018 there have been many including American Mirai Nagasu at the Winter Olympics and a Junior level skater – American Alysa Liu. Alexandra Trusova of Russia won the world junior title in 2018 with two quadruple jumps,[61] raising the bar further.

Popularity of the sport

The popularity of figure skating peaks each quadrennial with the world-wide televised events of Olympic games. The ISU receives approximately $15 million each year for television rights.[62]

Skating's popularity with American audiences has seen a decline since the 1990s, from a combination of fatigue with the oversaturation of the boom years, disenchantment with perceived corruption and a less fan-friendly new scoring system, and the retirement of superstar Michelle Kwan in 2006.[63]

Live skating shows have been flourishing in Asia with star Yuzuru Hanyu packing arenas with fans anxious to reward his quad jumps with a shower of Winnie the Pooh stuffed animals. Japanese sponsorships are commonly seen on skating shows with companies' logos on the rink boards at televised competitions around the world.[64]

Both live and televised skating is quite popular in Russia, not only competition with Russia's recent domination of the ladies' event but also a long-running *Ice Age* television series and numerous live tours.[65]

Challenges to figure skating

Many skaters in colder climates around the world begin skating on outdoor ice on ponds, rivers and backyard rinks. Climate change has begun to affect that way of life.[66] The scoring of skating is still difficult to understand for fans. The sport is considered to be for the elite with the cost of training escalating.

As the technical content of skating programs increases – not only jumps, but also difficult spin and lift variations requiring extreme flexibility, and more complex connecting moves between elements – so too does the incidence of injury. The gap between what a recreational figure skater and an elite competitor can accomplish becomes ever wider, and young skaters seeking to bridge that gap may burn out physically before reaching senior competition level.

Regardless, figure skating continues to engage recreational skaters around the world, nurture devoted athletes, and entertain millions of fans.

Notes

1 For analysis of the presentation of gender in figure skating, see Cynthia Bauman, editor, *Women on Ice: Feminist Essays on the Tonya Harding/Nancy Kerrigan Spectacle* (New York: Routledge, 1995); Mary Louise Adams, *Artistic Impressions: Figure Skating, Masculinity, and the Limits of Sport* (Toronto: University of Toronto Press, 2011); Ellyn Kestnbaum, *Culture on Ice: Figure Skating and Cultural Meaning* (Middletown, CT: Wesleyan University Press, 2003); Erica Rand, *Red Nails, Black Skates: Gender, Cash, and Pleasure On and Off the Ice* (Durham, NC: Duke University Press, 2012).

2 See Federico Formenti and Alberto E. Minetti, "Human locomotion on ice: the evolution of ice-skating energetics through history," *Journal of Experimental Biology* 210 (2007), 1825–1833; Hans Christian Küchelmann and Petar Zidarov, "Let's skate together! Skating on bones in the past and today," in *From Hooves to Horns, From Mollusc to Mammoth: Manufacture and Use of Bone Artefacts from Prehistoric Times to the Present. Proceedings of the 4th meeting of the ICAZ Worked Bone Research Group at Tallinn, 26th–31st of August 2003*, ed. Heidi Luik, Alice M. Choyke, Colleen E. Batey, and Lembi Lõugas (Tallinn, Estonia: The Authors, 2005), 425–445.

3 Sandra Alvarez, "Did People Ice Skate in the Middle Ages," Medievalists.net, www.medievalists.net/2015/12/did-people-ice-skate-in-the-middle-ages/, accessed December 1, 2018.

4 Johannes Brugmann, *Vita alme virginis Liidwine* (Schiedam, Netherlands: Otgier Nachtegaal), 1498, https://commons.wikimedia.org/wiki/Category:Johannes_Brugman#/media/File:Heilige_Liduina_van_Schiedam.jpg; Thomas a Kempis, *St. Lydwine of Schiedam Virgin* (London: Burns & Oates, 1912), 58.

5 Nigel Brown, *Ice-Skating: A History* (New York: A. S. Barnes, 1959).

6 Russian figure skating history, All Russia, Russian culture, http://allrus.me/russian-figure-skating-history/, accessed November 26, 2018.

7 Brown, *Ice-Skating: A History*.

8 E.g., Robert Jones, *A Treatise on Skating* (London: J. Ridley, 1772); Jean Garcin, *Le vrai patineur, ou Principes sur l'art de patiner avec grâce* (Paris: Delespinasse, 1813); Christian Siegmund Zindel and Johann Adam Klein, *Der Eislauf, oder: das Schrittschufahren: ein Tasschenbuch fü Jung und Alt* (Nürnberg: Campe, 1825); George Anderson ("Cyclos"), *The Art of Skating* (London, Horace Cox, 1868); H. E. Vandervell and T. Maxwell Witham, *A System of Figure-Skating: Being the Theory and Practice of the Art as Developed in England, with a Glance at its Origin and History* (London: Macmillan, 1869).

9 Miss L. Cheetham, in Douglas Adams, *Skating* (London: George Bell, 1894).

10 Brown, *Ice-Skating: A History*.

11 Montagu S. F. Monier-Williams, *Combined Figure Skating* (London: Horace Cox, 1883); Cheryl Richardson, "Combined Skating," Skating Ahead of the Curve, www.skatingaheadofthecurve.com/CombinedSkating.html.

12 James R. Hines, *Figure Skating: A History*, 1st edition (Urbana, IL: University of Illinois Press, 2006).

13 *George H. Browne,* "Artistic Skating in the International Style," *New York Times, November 28, 1909;* Irving Brokaw, *The Art of Skating* (Carlisle, MA: Applewood Books, 1910); Brown, *Ice-Skating: A History*; Gregory R. Smith, "Skating: Pictures, prints, & histories," *Skating*, June/July 1978.

14 See, e.g., Hines, *Figure Skating: A History*; Ryan Stevens, "The 1889 Championships of America," Skate Guard (blog), October 4, 2018, https://skateguard1.blogspot.com/2018/10/the-1889-championships-of-america.html.

15 Brown, *Ice-Skating: A History*.

16 "History," accessed December 1, 2018, www.isu.org/isu-history.

17 "Member federations – ISU," accessed December 1, 2018, www.isu.org/member-federations.

18 Eugene A. Glader, *Amateurism and Athletics* (West Point, NY: Leisure Press, 1978).

19 Susan A. Johnson, "And then there were none: A fond remembrance of compulsory figures at the World Championships, Part I," *Skating*, Mar. 1991.

20 Brown, *Ice-Skating: A History*; Frank Loeser, "Loeser on Music," *Skating*, Oct 1979, 7.

21 Ryan Stevens, "Marches and mazurkas: Music's role in figure skating history," Skate Guard (blog), May 7, 2016, http://skateguard1.blogspot.com/2016/05/marches-and-mazurkas-musics-role-in.html.

22 Smith, *Figure Skating: A Celebration*, 23; "Charlotte – Broadway's skating superstar" Roy Blakey's IceStage Archive (blog), accessed December 1, 2018, www.icestagearchive.com/charlotte.html.

23 Beverley Smith, *Figure Skating: A Celebration* (Toronto: McClelland & Steward, 1994); John Misha Petkevich, *Figure Skating: Championship Techniques* (New York: Sports Illustrated/Winners Circle Books,1989); Josef Dedic, *Single Figure Skating for Beginners and Champions* (Prague: Olympia, 1982).

24 International Skating Union, "III Olympic Winter Games – men's figure skating – Lake Placid 1932." Filmed February 1932. YouTube video, 11:00. Posted October 5, 2017, www.youtube.com/watch?v=9h0RK6h7h5A, accessed December 1, 2018.

25 Smith, *Figure Skating: A Celebration*, 22.

26 James R. Hines, *Figure Skating in the Formative Years: Singles, Pairs, and the Expanding Role of Women* (Urbana: University of Illinois Press, 2015).

27 Amanda Schweinbenz, "Not just early Olympic fashion statements: Bathing suits, uniforms, and sportswear," in *Bridging Three Centuries: Intellectual Crossroads and the Modern Olympic Movement. Fifth International Symposium for Olympic Research* (London, Ontario: The University of Western Ontario, 2000), 135–142.

28 *Heir to Henie*, Time Magazine, March 15, 1937; Cecilia Colledge, "The birth of a camel," *Skating*, July 1987, 11; Cecilia Colledge, "Breaking the back of the layback," *Skating*, Nov. 1987, 7.

29 Brown, *Ice-Skating: A History*, 169–172; Lynn Copley-Graves, *Figure Skating History: The Evolution of Dance on Ice* (Columbus, OH: Platoro Press, 1992).

30 "Member federations – ISU," accessed December 1, 2018, www.isu.org/member-federations.

31 John E. Findling and Kimberly D. Pelle, *Encyclopedia of the Modern Olympic Movement* (Greenwood Publishing Group, 2004).

32 Hines, *Figure Skating: A History*.

33 Ryan Stevens, "Unravelling the Russian Judge Stereotype," SkateGuard (blog), April 6, 2018, http://skateguard1.blogspot.com/2018/04/unravelling-russian-judge-stereotype.html; Eric Zitzewitz, "Nationalism in Winter Sports Judging and its Lessons for Organizational Decision Making," *Journal of Economics and Management Strategy*, 15, no. 1 (2006), 67–99.

34 Smith, *Figure Skating: A Celebration*, 83.

35 Hines, *Figure Skating: A History*, 196–197.

36 Eric Zitzewitz, "Does transparency reduce favoritism and corruption? Evidence from the reform of figure skating judging," *Journal of Sports Economics*, 15, no. 1 (2014), 3–30.

37 Hines, *Figure Skating: A History*, 192.

38 Nikki Nichols, *Frozen in Time: The Enduring Legacy of the 1961 US Figure Skating Team* (Cincinnati, OH: Clerisy Press, 2006); Patricia Shelley Bushman, *Indelible Tracings: The Story of the 1961 US World Figure Skating Team* (Stewart & Gray, 2010).

39 "John Curry's magic skates," *Washington Post*, August 5, 1984, www.washingtonpost.com/archive/lifestyle/style/1984/08/05/john-currys-magic-skates/6af849c6-c9ef-4910-acfd-be06514d00e4/.

40 Kelly Lawrence, *Skating on Air: The Broadcast History of an Olympic Marquee Sport* (Jefferson, NC: McFarland & Company., 2011), 41.

41 Ellyn Kestnbaum, *Culture on Ice: Figure Skating & Cultural Meaning* (Wesleyan University Press, 2003), 231–234.

42 Kestnbaum, 139.

43 Scott Hamilton with Lorenzo Benet, *Landing It: My Life On and Off the Ice* (New York: Pinnacle Books, 1999), 291.

44 Lawrence, *Skating on Air*.

45 Hines, *Figure Skating in the Formative Years*.

46 Lisa Luciano, "Backtalk; Pandora's box of problems for figure skating," *The New York Times*, December 5, 1993, sec. Sports, www.nytimes.com/1993/12/05/sports/backtalk-pandoras-box-of-problems-for-figure-skating.html.

47 "Champions on ice – Tommy's tour," Roy Blakey's IceStage Archive (blog), accessed December 2, 2018, www.icestagearchive.com/champions.html.

48 Lawrence, *Skating on Air: The Broadcast History of an Olympic Marquee Sport*.

49 "'Olympic Ice' Relishes Fun of Games," accessed November 24, 2018, https://usatoday30.usatoday.com/sports/columnist/hiestand-tv/2006-02-15-hiestand-oly_x.htm.

50 Lawrence, *Skating on Air: The Broadcast History of an Olympic Marquee Sport*.

51 Christine Brennan, *Inside Edge: A Revealing Journey into the Secret World of Figure Skating*, Reprint edition (New York: Anchor, 1997).

52 Jose Antonio Vargas, "The Michelle Kwan myth, worth its weight in gold," February 14, 2006, www.washingtonpost.com/wp-dyn/content/article/2006/02/13/AR2006021302412.html.

53 Patrick Reevell, "In Russia, skating booms again," *The New York Times*, January 31, 2014.

54 Bunny Bissoux, "From Yuzuru Hanyu to 'Yuri on ice': Japan's fascination with figure skating," *Tokyo Weekender*, March 5, 2018, www.tokyoweekender.com/2018/03/from-yuzuru-hanyu-to-yuri-on-ice-japans-fascination-with-figure-skating/.

55 Kibum Kim, *Korea's Golden Girl*, Foreign Policy, February 23, 2010, https://foreignpolicy.com/2010/02/23/koreas-golden-girl/; Flora Carr, "5 things to know about Yuna Kim, lighter of the Olympic cauldron," *Time*, February 9, 2018, http://time.com/5141402/yuna-kim-olympics-2018/.

56 E. M. Swift, "Blind justice figure skating judges are booed and viewed as mean-spirited and incompetent. And it didn't take long for controversy to break out in Nagano," Vault, accessed November 24, 2018, www.si.com/vault/1998/02/16/238916/blind-justice-figure-skating-judges-are-booed-and-viewed-as-mean-spirited-and-incompetent-and-it-didnt-take-long-for-controversy-to-break-out-in-nagano.

57 Joy Goodwin, *The Second Mark: Courage, Corruption, and the Battle for Olympic Gold* (New York: Simon & Schuster, 2004); Christopher Clarey, "Figure skating: 2 French officials suspended 3 years in skating scandal," *The New York Times*, May 1, 2002, sec. Sports, www.nytimes.com/2002/05/01/sports/figure-skating-2-french-officials-suspended-3-years-in-skating-scandal.html.

58 "ISU vote to abolish anonymous judging system in figure skating to 'increase transparency'," www.insidethegames.biz/articles/1038244/isu-vote-to-abolish-anonymous-judging-system-in-figure-skating-to-increase-transparency

59 E. M. Swift, "Last Word Judgment on the Judging in Figure Skating: More Rotten than Ever," Vault, accessed November 24, 2018, www.si.com/vault/2002/02/13/322403/last-word-judgment-on-the-judging-in-figure-skating-more-rotten-than-ever.

60 "ISU GP Rostelecom Cup 2018," accessed November 21, 2018, www.isuresults.com/results/season1819/gprus2018/.

61 Nick Zaccardi, "13-year-old is first female figure skater to land two quads (video)," *Olympic Talk* (blog), March 10, 2018, https://olympics.nbcsports.com/2018/03/10/alexandra-trusova-quads-video-figure-skating-world-junior-championships/.

62 "Financial and other reports – ISU," accessed November 25, 2018, www.isu.org/financial-and-other-reports.

63 Sidney Randolf, "What happened to America's love of figure skating?" Odyssey, Nov. 3, 2015, www.theodysseyonline.com/what-happened-americas-love-figure-skating; Ahiza Garcia, "U.S. figure skating used to be wildly popular. What happened?" CNN Money, February 13, 2018, https://money.cnn.com/2018/02/13/news/figure-skating-popularity-us-olympics-pyeongchang/index.html.

64 "Claira Triniti, on thin ice: Figure skating in Japan and some popular Japanese skaters," Japan Info, August 23, 2016, http://jpninfo.com/58891.

65 Anna Kozina, "The show must go on: Russian skaters turn to TV to keep career alive," Russia Beyond (blog), December 6, 2014, www.rbth.com/arts/2014/12/06/the_show_must_go_on_russian_figure_skaters_turn_to_tv_to_keep_career_ali_42019.html.

66 John Schwartz, "Canada's outdoor rinks are melting. So is a way of life.," *The New York Times*, June 8, 2018, sec. Climate, www.nytimes.com/2018/03/20/climate/canada-outdoor-rinks.html.

33

Gymnastics

Anne L. DeMartini

Introduction

Definition

Though early practitioners attempted to define it, gymnastics is not a uniform concept or practice.[1] The word gymnastics derives from the Greek *gymnos* (naked), referring to the practice of men engaging in physical training unclothed, and a gymnasium originally meant a public place where Greek youth exercised.[2] From characterizing gymnastics as 'movements chosen . . . with the object of giving the body . . . harmonious development',[3] to an 'application of postures in harmony with the conditions and needs of the organism, and predetermined with regards to space and time, for the purpose of pacing the body under control of the will',[4] the activity is difficult to describe. Authors, historians, scientists, doctors and others approach gymnastics differently and gymnastics communities' interests vary widely.[5] Contemporary gymnastics encompasses a myriad of disciplines including artistic gymnastics, rhythmic gymnastics, trampoline, aerobics, acrobatics, gymnastics for all, and parkour.[6]

Early history

All over the world, ancient cultures participated in physical exercises very early in human history. Sumerians, Egyptians, Chinese, and Persian peoples participated in some version of acrobatics.[7] Arguably, the origins of gymnastics are rooted in Ancient Greece, arising from the bull-leaping of Crete in the Minoan era (2800–1100 BC).[8] Ancient Greeks considered gymnastics an indispensable part of young men's education and in Sparta gymnastics was also a part of women's education.[9] Bibliographic research reveals gymnastics through the Mycenaean (1600 BC) eras, Homeric years, classical years, and the Byzantine era in Greece.[10]

Following the Roman era, societies across the world continued developing military arts and valued physical fitness and prowess; therefore, the training of soldiers continued to employ gymnastics-type skills.[11] During the Renaissance (13th–16th cent.) and Enlightenment periods (17th–18th cent.), great thinkers across Europe saw a connection between a healthy body and healthy mind, endorsing physical exercises.[12] Many military physical training instructors subsequently became the physical education teachers and sport masters in the schools of Europe, thus establishing a prominent place for gymnastics in school physical education.[13]

In the early 1800s, the German Philanthropists, aligned with progressive ideals, believed in physical education as a pre-condition for mental development and intellectual learning.[14] They introduced exercises referred to as 'gymnastics' into the education system including high bar, balance, floor exercises, rings, dangles, and pommel horse, though they focused solely on boys.[15] The Philanthropists' instructive and written work created a general gymnastic movement, from which all the subsequent main gymnastic systems (German, Swedish, English, and Slavic) emerged.[16] During the 19th century, 'gymnastics' did not mean a separate and specialized sport, with precise regulations, common dimensions and functional specifications of equipment as it is known now. Gymnastics constituted various apparatus included in a general, mixed system.[17]

The German system

Johann Christoph Friedrich GutsMuths (1759–1839), a philanthropist, served as the linchpin between the ancients' athletic exercises and what is commonly recognized as the base of modern artistic gymnastics, the German system.[18] He published *Gymnastik Fur Die Jugend* in 1793 and maintained an outdoor gymnasium with devices for physically developing his students, inspiring many later educators including Prussian Friedrich Ludwig Jahn (1778–1852).[19] Jahn created the first gymnastic equipment and gymnastic exercises in 1811 as part of the Turner movement in the region now known as Germany.[20] This 'Turnen' German gymnastic system was characterized by the acrobatics, the steady gymnastic apparatuses (horizontal bar and parallel bars), and the founding of gymnastic associations.[21] Jahn's practice was refined, and Turnen became a social force in clubs called Turnvereins and then as a fixed part of the national physical education curriculum.[22]

Nationalism suffuses the origins of gymnastics, as the Turner movement reacted to the Napoleonic occupation of the German states.[23] Turnen's exercise repertoire was used to instil national ethics and indoctrinate boys and young men so that they would accept their duty to fight and sacrifice themselves for the German fatherland.[24] Women and girls were initially excluded from gymnastics, female physical education was introduced later against Jahn's will.[25] Kant argues the Turnen system 'should be recognized as one of the earliest modern examples of a nation as a community becoming, forming, and defining itself through physical movement'.[26] With an authoritarian leader leading and the group voluntarily submitting to orders, Turnen established hierarchies based on physical abilities.[27]

Jahn's Turnen movement method became the most widely taught and most influential gymnastics practice in Prussia and later in united Germany.[28] The origins of the 'rhythmic', 'aesthetic' and 'expressionist' gymnastics of the later nineteenth century as well as modern German dance of the twentieth century can be found in Turnen.[29] Up to the end of the 19th century, this German gymnastic system reigned supreme and provided the foundation of European and world artistic gymnastics, especially for men.[30] The early 1800s saw the spread of this Germanic system to England, Italy and the Netherlands.[31]

Other gymnastics systems

During this time, across the continent other pioneers created their own gymnastic regimens. Building on the early institution of a daily training program for school children in Denmark, Franz Nachtegal (1777–1845) began the legacy of Danish gymnastics.[32] The forward thinking Dane educated others and his student, Pier Ling, founded the Swedish gymnastic system.[33] The

Swedish system omitted the horizontal bar and the parallel bars and focused less on physical strength.[34] The Swedish gymnastic system rivalled the German system through the 1850s, not because of a significant difference between or supremacy of one over the other, but due to political, national, and racist motives. [35] Generally, Swedish gymnastics was thought to be suited for educational and medical purposes, while Jahn's apparatus gymnastics more suited for military training and sport.[36]

Francisco Odeano Amoros (1770–1848), a colonel in the Napeolonic army, founded French and Spanish gymnastics and invented the swinging horizontal bar.[37] Though rational and scientific, Amoros's method was not as defined and methodical as Ling's or Jahn's and later incorporated characteristics of Swedish gymnastics.[38] Gymnastics were used in France as a model of bodily excellence. Similar to its use in Germany, through the military and physical education, gymnastics in France disseminated values recognized by the Republic, such as discipline, morality, respect for hierarchy and laws, and solidarity.[39] Also in France, but in contrast to Amoros's militaristic use of gymnastics, Fancois Delsarte (1811–1871) developed exercises meant to assist actors develop natural poses and expressive gestures for use in acting.[40] This system brought new qualities of aesthetics and expressiveness into gymnastics and became a popular form of women's gymnastics due to its emphasis on grace and poise.[41]

Gymnastics began in Slavic countries in 1862, founded by Miroslav Tyrs (1832–1884) in Bohemia.[42] Tyrs, a professor of history and art and an expert in ancient Greek gymnastics, created a new gymnastic movement with elements from various other gymnastic systems mixed with national, cultural, and folklore elements of the Czech nations.[43] Similar to Jahn's, this movement was also based in patriotism. Tyrs believed that the nation was progressing linguistically, artistically, scientifically, economically, and socially, but that it lacked physical excellence.[44] Tyrs understood physical exercise not only affected one´s physical wellbeing, but could also affect the development of one´ s character and social attitudes.[45] Therefore, he chose gymnastics as the means for training the nation in the qualities he saw as necessary for its preservation and complete fulfilment.[46] The organization held a democratic spirit, attracting participants from a broad swath of society. Tyrs and his associates named the movement 'Sokol' (Falcon) and utilized a falcon in flight as a symbol of its lofty aims and courage.[47] The movement quickly spread in Bohemia and Moravia, and Sokol units were established among the Slovenes and in America followed by Poland, Croatia and Serbia.[48] By 1871, there were 120 units with 11,000 members. Tyrs recognized a nation was not just its men, and initiated the 'Gymnastic Society of Women and Girls of Prague', conveying the Sokol idea to women.[49]

Spread of gymnastics

During the mid-nineteenth century, the German system spread in both directions – to the Americas in the west and to Russia and Ukraine in the east – through immigration. European tradespeople, teachers, politicians, and economic refugees settled in Latin America, primarily Chile, Argentina, and Brazil, and brought Jahn's gymnastic methods with them, setting up gymnastic associations.[50] Though in Brazil the German system faced competition, as France attempted to use physical instruction as a part of the new French cultural imperialism.[51] These German gymnastics associations also popped up across the world through the late 1800s – as far away as Australia, Istanbul and the Congo.[52]

The first wave of gymnastics in the United States began in Northeastern cities when Jahn's adherents immigrated and instituted physical training at schools including Harvard and Yale Universities.[53] Turnen in the United States linked with educational institutions, promoting gymnastics as compensation for long hours of sitting and learning.[54] After the failed revolution of

1848, thousands of political refugees for whom Turnen was not only a recreational activity but also an identity and a political platform, came to the United States.[55] This second wave of immigrants founded Turnvereins, the first in Cincinnati, Ohio in 1848.[56] Turnvereins developed into social and cultural centres, preserving German culture and language.[57] Since women played an important role in maintaining that social cohesion, women took part in Turnen and Turner festivals much earlier in the United States than women in Germany.[58] The number of clubs grew quickly. By 1860, 157 clubs appeared in 26 states with approximately 10,000 members and by 1894, there were 317 Turner clubs with 40,000 members.[59] The Slavic gymnastic movement also appeared in the United States. The first Sokol in America was established in Saint Louis in 1865, soon after Tyrs founded the organization in Bohemia and rapidly Bohemian, Slovakian, Slovenian and Polish Sokols spread across the US.[60] After its introduction, gymnastics in the United State grew extensively and intensely.

The growth of gymnastics in Britain was less pronounced than overseas.[61] When gymnastics first came to the British Isles is uncertain, but Phokion Henrich Clias (1782–1854) travelled to London in 1822. Clias, born in the United States to Swiss parents, instructed gymnastics to the Swiss Army.[62] He impressed English observers, published influential books, and is credited with being chiefly responsible for spreading military gymnastics in England.[63] Gymnastic clubs using Jahn's German system opened in London and found initial success, but had limited influence.[64] Interest waned and peasants, labourers, and the new artisan classes remained satisfied to seek a traditional way of life, unable to find time or money to indulge in regular sessions at the gym park, and the novelty wore off.[65]

However, the British Army recognized the importance of fitness and created an army gymnastic training staff, appointing Archibald McLaren to organize military physical education.[66] McLaren, born in Scotland, studied gymnastics and fencing on the continent. He built a gymnasium at Oxford and was likely the first British national to teach gymnastics in England.[67] Clias and McLaren both wished to see some form of gymnastics suitable for masses of British schoolchildren, but did not agree on the form it should take.[68] Swedish gymnastics arrived in Britain in 1840, producing a rivalry between the Swedish and German systems.[69] Thought more suitable for girls, Ling's system was instituted in London girls' schools before a program of physical education was made compulsory across English elementary schools.[70]

Meanwhile, as the German, Swedish and Slavic systems spread across the world, forming the foundation of what would become artistic gymnastics, a Swiss educator created exercises that would evolve into rhythmic gymnastics.[71] Jacques Dalcroze (1865–1950) devised eurhythmics, a system of muscular and musical instruction, to develop the musical sensitivity of his Geneva Conservatory of Music students through natural body movement.[72] Dalcroze opened training institutes for eurhythmics teachers in Germany and Switzerland. Students of Dalcroze conceived movement programs that incorporated contraction and relaxation, hand apparatus (balls, hoops and clubs), and partner work.[73] Together, these teachers pioneered rhythmic gymnastics sharing a belief in natural, total body movement, using a rhythmic flow of motion and disapproving of artificial movement.[74]

Governance and organization

Gymnastics' governance and organization evolved over time. The first gymnastics festivals (Turnfests) were established in German speaking Europe in 1860.[75] The Czech Sokol movement also initiated a large gymnastics festival, called a Slet, in 1882 and by the end of the century hosted thousands of participants.[76] Similar large gymnastics festivals occurred in Scandinavia as well as multisport, multinational athletic exhibitions and competitions in conjunction with national and international trade and commerce fairs.[77] For many years, gymnastics lacked a commonly accepted competitive system and rules.[78] The end of the 19th century to the second decade of the 20th century (1896–1913) revealed the most important period in the history of gymnastics, when the sport became more formalized, specialized, popular, and international.[79] The roots of gymnastics governance grew in two major branches.

Governing bodies and competitions

The first governing body, the Federatious Europeennes de Gymnastque (European Federation of Gymnastics), later changed its name to Fédération Internationale de Gymnastique (FIG).[80] FIG, founded in 1881, is the world's oldest international sport governing body.[81] However, FIG was not the only international sport institution governing gymnastics. The International Olympics Committee (IOC) controlled gymnastics at the Olympic Games.[82] Both agencies organized competitions, but the lack of permanent and commonly accepted rules and specifications of gymnastic apparatus created tension between the two which impacted the progress and development of the sport.[83] Gymnastics organizers debated the virtues of the German versus the Swedish styles of gymnastics, and both of those systems versus the English sporting approach in education.[84] Countries participating in the competitions accepted, more or less, the different rules and competitive systems applied each time.[85]

FIG's original members included two Belgium federations, France, and the Netherlands.[86] FIG organized a 'world – international' competition from 1903 to 1913, which would later be deemed the World Championships.[87] By that first championship, Great Britain, Czechoslovakia, Canada, Italy, Spain, Luxemburg and Hungary had also joined FIG.[88] Rotating European cities hosted these early championships every two years, where exclusively men participated in gymnastics apparatus events (pommel horse, rings, parallel bars, and horizontal bar) in addition to track and field, swimming events, weight lifting, and/or rope climbing.[89]

Concurrently, athletes were competing in 'gymnastics' in the Olympics run by the IOC. At the first modern Olympics in Athens (1896), the host country itself formed the rules for the competition, with little guidance from the IOC and founder Pierre de Coubertin.[90] Though the German gymnastics federation submitted a request to the IOC for formation of unified and commonly accepted rules as early as 1901, the IOC refused, and from 1896 to 1912 there were no commonly accepted rules.[91] Therefore, the number of events, nature of the events, rules and scoring varied depending on the host country, allowing for forming a competitive system that gave a competitive advantage to the organizing country.[92] At the suggestion of the well-organized Czechoslovakian gymnastics federation, FIG formed a technical committee in 1906.[93] This committee, consisting mostly of active athletes, discussed and offered solutions to problems arising from the primitive existing rules, but still did not form a commonly accepted system.[94]

During this era there was no cooperation at all between FIG and the IOC.[95] The German and Swiss gymnastics federations held the most power and possessed the most athletes.[96] These Federations did not like the international agency nor the competitions organized by them, refusing to participate.[97] The German Federation believed that the competitive system and the judging were not proper or objective, and also ignored the institution of the Olympic Games, advocating for use of their own federation's standards in international competition.[98] The IOC and FIG began collaborating for the first time at the Stockholm Olympic Games (1912), where in order to maintain balance and please multiple constituencies, they organized the Games in competitive rounds that that rotated Swedish and German gymnastics systems.[99]

All the way until 1950, the World Championship competitive format often differed from the Olympic Games format because FIG governed the World Championships and the IOC governed the Olympic Games.[100] Competitive format – the frequency and length of competitions, the participants, the venues, the specific apparatuses, the division between group and individual routines, the equipment, the scoring, and requirements of compulsory versus free exercises continued to change.

Female participation in gymnastics appeared at the Olympic Games in Amsterdam, in 1928, with a team event.[101] In 1932, the Olympic Games did not stage women's artistic gymnastics, but it reappeared in 1936. In 1933, the IOC formed a female technical committee, which summarized its rules in the Code of Points and has governed the development of female artistic gymnastics ever since.[102] Women began participating in the World Championships for the first time in 1934.[103] Women's gymnastics in the 1940s and 1950s reflected societies' belief about the appropriate place of females.[104] Since those values were in flux, so was the nature of women's gymnastics and the apparatuses on which they competed.[105] A men's code of points wasn't established until 1949.[106] Changes to both men's and women's Codes of Points occur from one Olympic cycle to another, strongly influencing gymnastics development.[107]

Only European nations took part in World Championships up until 1950 when Egypt participated with a full team of eight gymnasts, the first from the African continent.[108] The Soviet Union and Japan made World Championships debuts in 1954. Their men's teams placed first and second respectively, beginning a tradition of long-running dominance of men's artistic gymnastics by the two countries.[109] China and the United States entered teams in 1958.[110]

FIG held all World Championship competitions up through 1954 outdoors.[111] Since 1958 World Championship have been held indoors and the gymnasts compete on a raised podium, where judges are seated well below the top of the podium to minimize obstruction of spectators' view and better highlight gymnasts' performances.[112] Gymnasts in international competition perform routines on multiple apparatus and receive scores on each. Those scores may be combined for an 'all-around' and team competition. Before 1956, competitions determined all-around medallists based on common competition that contained all apparatuses and also served as a qualification for apparatus finals.[113] All-around winners were those who had scored highest in team competition with the highest total scores from compulsory and optional exercises.[114] Apparatus finals was organized for the first time at the Olympic Games in Melbourne, 1956 and all-around finals started to be organized as a separate competition in Munich, 1972.[115]

Rhythmic gymnastics organization

Modern rhythmic gymnastics started as a separate, competitive sport in Russia in the early 1950s.[116] International competitions had previously included group rhythmic routines with hand apparatus in the Olympic Games and World Championships, but in 1956 FIG excluded these routines.[117] FIG resurrected modern rhythmic gymnastics as an internationally recognized independent sport in 1962.[118] The first World Championships were held in Prague in 1963, though no distinct rules were developed until 1968.[119] A Commission for Modern Gymnastics approved three hand apparatus exercises – ball, hoop and rope – and clarified techniques and penalties for international competition which were codified in a Code of Points in 1970.[120] In the early 1970s, FIG introduced a new hand apparatus with the addition of a compulsory ribbon routine, and changed the name of this new sport to Modern Rhythmic Gymnastics.[121] FIG submitted a request to the International Olympic Committee for admission of the sport to the Olympic Games, but it was not added to the Olympic program until 1984, when only individual gymnasts were allowed to participate.[122] All Eastern European countries except Romania boycotted the Los Angeles Olympic Games in 1984, therefore commencing Olympic rhythmic gymnastics without the nations that dominated at the time – Bulgaria and the Soviet Union.[123] In 1996, the Atlanta Olympic Games welcomed the first group competition, where Spain triumphed over Bulgaria and Russia.[124]

Significant rule changes

Even after the initial cooperation between the IOC and its Olympic Games and FIG and its World Championships, gymnastics rules continue to evolve. Significant changes occurred in scoring, the structure of competitions and athlete ages. Until the 1987 World Championship, athletes' scores were carried over from the qualifying rounds to the succeeding rounds of competition or finals.[125] Starting with the 1989 World Championships, gymnasts were given 'a clean slate' or 'new life' for each round of competition as scores were no longer carried over to the team, all-around and individual events finals.[126]

Individual event apparatus finals were introduced in the 1958 World Championship with the top six qualifiers advancing to event finals, who could be from any country.[127] After previously having huge numbers of gymnasts competing in all-around, starting in the 1972 Olympic Games and followed up in the 1974 World Championship, only the top 36 all-around gymnasts from the qualifying round advanced to the all-around finals. The top 36 did not have a limit in number from any one country.[128] In 1972, few countries' gymnasts qualified into and then dominated the event finals.[129] Only three countries were represented in the event finals: the Soviet Union, East Germany, and Hungary.[130] Those countries' gymnasts also monopolized the all-around competition, winning the top 7 spots.[131] Therefore, starting with the 1976 Olympic Games and the subsequent World Championship, no more than three all-around and two individual event qualifiers per country could advance to the finals.[132]

Before 1966, top-level international female gymnasts were usually fit, grown women in their early twenties.[133] In the early twentieth century, women's gymnastics was burdened with gender expectations that limited the activity's daring and explosiveness, the movements graceful and slow.[134] The athletic prowess of the female gymnasts escalated through the late 1960s and 1970s, the sport attracting younger girls with a different mind-set and more dynamic acrobatics.[135] Successful gymnasts got younger, starting in the 1966 World Championship, where 17-year-old girls competed on the gold medal team.[136] In 1970, the first age minimum was introduced to the sport. The new rule, ostensibly about protecting very young gymnasts from harsh training methods, also provided protectionism, maintaining the image of the sport as a feminine pursuit suitable for adult women as younger gymnasts adopted more and more complex skills.[137] Then, in the 1976 Olympic Games, the women's all-around gold medallist, Nadia Comaneci, was just 14 and her Romanian team averaged 15.8 years old.[138] The minimum age limit was changed from 14 to 15 before the 1980 Olympic Games, and raised to 16 years in 1997, with justifications similar to the earlier rule: equal parts protection and protectionism.[139] Men's gymnastics have not had the same problem of young teenagers in elite competition, likely due to the need of post-pubertal strength for the male gymnasts' apparatus and the minimum age is 18 for senior men.[140]

Gymnasts traditionally engaged in compulsory exercises, where each gymnastics competitor performed an identical routine comprised of basic movements meant to show the gymnasts' virtuosity.[141] FIG eliminated the compulsory exercises in the 1997 World Championships.[142] This substantial change shortened the competition, making it less taxing for gymnasts.[143] It also simplified competition results and increased spectator interest, making gymnastics more attractive to the public.[144]

Contemporary governance and disciplines

The International Gymnastics Federation (FIG) currently governs gymnastics worldwide.[145] FIG, headquartered in the Olympic Capital of Lausanne, Switzerland counts 146 national member federations.[146] FIG's Congress, the biennial general assembly of the delegates of the affiliated member federations, takes place in even years and deals with financial matters, considers admissions and expulsions of federations and carries out elections.[147] At the Tokyo Congress in October 2016, the Congress elected Morinari Watanabe, the first non-European to hold the post, to a four year term as the ninth President of the FIG.[148]

Gymnastics disciplines have broadened considerably. The FIG now governs eight sports: gymnastics for all, men's and women's artistic gymnastics, rhythmic gymnastics, trampoline – including double mini-trampoline and tumbling, aerobics, acrobatics and parkour.[149]

Artistic gymnastics, the oldest discipline, combines speed, strength, power and flexibility with tumbling and acrobatic skills, all performed with an emphasis on style.[150] Male artistic gymnasts compete in six separate events: floor exercise, pommel horse, still rings, vault, parallel bars and horizontal bar.[151] While female artistic gymnastics has undergone many transformations, gymnasts currently perform elements on four apparatus: vault, uneven bars, balance beam and floor exercise.[152] Floor exercise is the only event set to music and features tumbling, leaps, turns and choreography on a spring-loaded mat.[153]

Currently, rhythmic gymnastics characterizes itself as the juncture of sport and art.[154] Rhythmic gymnasts perform routines with music, either as individuals or in groups, executing difficult manoeuvres requiring enormous flexibility with hand-held apparatuses of hoop, ball, clubs, ribbon and rope.[155]

The first FIG Sports Acrobatics World Championships occurred in 1995 and FIG adopted it as a new discipline in 1998.[156] Acrobatic gymnastics is equal parts performance and partnership, as groups of gymnasts work together in pairs, trios or groups, where each of the individual gymnasts' size and skill are used to complement each other.[157] Set to music and interspersed with choreography, the gymnasts perform static elements such balances and holds, dynamic elements such as lifts, throws with complex somersaults and twists, and tumbling skills.[158] Pairs and group exercises must include human pyramids and each pair or group performs three routines in competition: balance, dynamic, and combined.[159]

FIG welcomed trampoline as a new discipline in 1998 and it debuted at the Olympic Games in 2000.[160] Trampoline gymnasts compete in one of four categories: individual trampoline, synchronised trampoline, double mini-trampoline and tumbling.[161] Athletes use the trampoline to catapult themselves to heights that can surpass 10 meters without technological devices or safety harnesses.[162] Unlike in other forms of Gymnastics, a fall from the trampoline ends a routine.[163]

In 2004 FIG formalized the discipline of aerobic gymnastics.[164] Arising from the fitness explosion of the 1970s and 1980s, aerobic gymnastics fuses mainstream aerobic exercise sequences with gymnastics elements, creative transitions, interactions between members and lifts.[165] Gymnasts perform routines inspired by and synchronized with music.[166] Competitive aerobic gymnastics offers several platforms.[167] Gymnasts may compete singly, or in mixed pairs, trios, groups of five or in the case of aerobic dance and aerobic step, teams of eight.[168] In all categories, continuous movement covers all the competition space, including floor and aerial movements to the music.[169]

In 2017 FIG agreed to develop Parkour as a new sport and launched the first FIG Parkour World Cup in 2018.[170] Originating on the streets, Parkour exhibits the art of getting from one point to another efficiently.[171] In FIG events, athletes use of a range of techniques, such as the cat leap, arm jump, drop jump and wall run to overcome obstacles.[172] In the Speed-run event, athletes strive to reach the finish line in the quickest time.[173] In the Freestyle event, athletes use the obstacles to demonstrate their style and creativity and receive a score on their technical performance.[174]

Both a discipline and concept, Gymnastics for All presents an all-inclusive philosophy of 'Fun, Fitness, Fundamentals and Friendship'.[175] Gymnastics for All offers movement opportunities suitable for all genders, age groups, abilities, and cultural backgrounds and its activities – gymnastics with or without apparatus and gymnastics and dance gymnastics for all – can be showcased through either demonstration, performance, or competitive team events.[176] The World Gymnaestrada, the premiere Gymnastics for All event, occurs every four years.[177] Since 1953, myriad gymnastics groups unite for a festival week of city and gala performances to illustrate the richness and variety of the activity.[178]

Judging

Subjectivity

Other than in Parkour's Speed-run event, judges determine the success of performances in the gymnastics disciplines. Performance results do not arise from an objective measure like many other sports, but from an intricate judging process.[179] Though the details of scoring change over time, generally, judges subjectively evaluate the performance in competition by applying a tool, the Code of Points, and giving a score that determines the value of the routine and the position of the gymnast in the final ranking.[180]

Judged sports always create controversy. Much of this controversy stems from the claim that judges are biased, that their judgments might be influenced by the intention to favour athletes or to put them at a disadvantage.[181] Controversy in gymnastics decisions may stem from bias or may arise from the great difficulty of assigning an objective value to a gymnastics performance.[182] Evaluating gymnastic routines accurately on the basis of the Code of Points is an extremely complex task.[183]

Problems with gymnastics judging are not a new phenomenon. The formation of the competitive system and judging in favour of the organizing country was a fact for almost all Olympic Games, especially in the early era when there were no technical specifications for the various gymnastic exercises.[184] Just before the end of the 19th century, European gymnastics federations used a detailed scoring system with the highest score being the 10 or 20, but it was not always used in competitions.[185] At the first modern Olympics in Athens (1896), the all Greek committee altered those European gymnastics regulations to fit the abilities of local athletes, aiming to increase participation and the chance for distinction.[186] The trend of changing rules and selecting judges with favourable attitudes to suit the host country continued in Paris (1900) with an unprecedented triumph of French athletes and the Americans adjusted the competitive systems and the rules based on their own preference at the Olympic Games in St Louis (1904).[187]

Contemporary researchers found gymnastics judging to be affected by judges' prior exposures to the same move presented in a worse performance, the order in which the gymnast performs, and influenced by the scores of other judges.[188] Former gymnasts alleged plausible claims of intentional cheating in gymnastics judging, asserting scores and pre-determined placings ensued from behind the scenes deal making.[189] Retired judges confirmed declarations of rampant judging corruption, often linked with politics.[190]

The perfect 10

In the mid twentieth century, the Code of Points was quite short and scores were out of possible 10.0 points.[191] This scoring system did not reflect the true distance between excellent, if elementary, routines and those athletes who innovated new skills.[192] Judges awarded a 10 to gymnasts who were not perfect, but were demonstrably better than other high scoring athletes in order to rank them correctly.[193] From 1976 to 1992, the perfect 10 went from rare occurrence to commonplace. Judges awarded more than 100 perfect scores in international competition.[194] The proliferation of perfect scores indicated gymnasts had mastered and surpassed the rules. Scoring at or near perfection illustrated the rules had become obsolete for the top tier of athletes.[195] The desire to establish a grading curve led to a cycle of rule revisions every four years, meant to make it more difficult to achieve the perfect 10.[196]

In 2006, international elite level gymnastics rid itself of the perfect 10 in favour of open ended scoring.[197] This scoring system allows for more difficult skills to add to the total value of the routine, so each athlete begins with a unique start value not capped at 10. Proponents believe it advances gymnastics, promoting progress and increasing the objectiveness of judging.[198] Critics contend the new system is less marketable, arguing that spectators will not understand the new scoring, will mourn the loss of one of the hallmarks of gymnastics, and will lose interest in the sport.[199] Opponents disapprove of differing start values, since it limits the number of athletes who are truly competing for podium spots, as those with lower starting values cannot win even with perfect execution. Open ended scoring escalates the difficulty levels, requiring gymnasts to crowd as many hard moves into a ninety second exercise to accrue the highest staring score, which also elevates the injury risk.[200]

Many criticisms of the new scoring system belie political and racial undercurrents of the sport. Critics argue the new Code of Points does not emphasize artistry strongly enough, turning women's gymnastics into simply tricking.[201] When Russia and Romania dominated women's gymnastics, traditional Eastern European style gymnastics focused on elegance.[202] Under the new open-ended scoring system which emphasizes strength and speed, American gymnasts dominate women's international competition.[203] The new Code of Points is seen as punishing the sport's traditional powers.[204]

'Artistic' and 'artistry' not only describe types and qualities of movement, but are coded language for body type and race.[205] Commentators describe long and lean female gymnasts as 'artistic' regardless of their performance and call stocky, often non-white, gymnasts 'powerful'.[206] This new Code of Points not only changed the way the scores looked, but how the female gymnasts looked.[207] The rules that reward difficulty favour a different breed of gymnast who is more powerfully built and athletic.[208]

Scoring

Currently, in artistic and rhythmic gymnastics, two panels of judges with different processes evaluate the athletes and calculate two separate scores, 'D' and 'E'.[209] The final score of an exercise is established by adding together the D and final E scores.[210] The difficulty jury (D jury) judges the routines' content, what skills the gymnast performs, giving a D score.[211] The execution jury (E jury) evaluates the quality of the routines, how the gymnast performs, providing an E score.[212] The E Jury evaluates the aesthetic, execution and technical performance aspects of an exercise as well as its compliance with the exercise construction expectations for that apparatus.[213] For women, the E jury also evaluates artistry.[214] Each apparatus prescribes special requirements unique to the event and judges take deductions for technical errors – large and small – which are subtracted from the E score.[215] Judges keep record of the ongoing presentation of a routine with a judging shorthand system.[216]

Icons

Gymnastics generates athletic icons. The former Soviet Union and Eastern Europeans nations produced many of gymnastics' greatest stars and the political climate of these regions impact gymnasts' careers. Historical and current gymnastics legends also hail from Japan and the United States.

Larissa Latynina (Ukraine SSR) dominated women's artistic gymnastics in the 1950s and 1960s when the sport focused on artistry and was largely inspired by ballet.[217] Latynina (born 1934) set the standard by which later gymnasts were measured.[218] She was the first female athlete to win nine Olympic golds.[219] For 48 years, Latynina held the record for winning more Olympic medals than anyone in history, male or female, in any sport. Her record of eighteen Olympic medals stood from 1964 until the London 2012 Games.[220] She coached the Soviet national gymnastics team from 1966 until 1977 and organized the gymnastics competition at the 1980 Olympic Games in Moscow.[221] The International Olympic Committee awarded her the Olympic Order and in 1998 she was inducted into the International Gymnastics Hall of Fame.[222]

In the same time period on the men's side, Soviet gymnast Boris Chakhlin shone. Born in Siberia in 1932, Shakhlin earned the nickname 'Man of Iron' for his steely determination and calm consistency.[223] Shakhlin earned individual gold medals at three straight Olympic Games (Melbourne in 1956, Rome in 1960, Tokyo in 1964), as well as five gold medals at the 1958 World Championships.[224] Since his retirement in 1966, he has served as an international judge and a member of the International Gymnastics Federation's Men's Technical Committee.[225] Both Shanklin and Latynina were products of the stark war and immediate post-war years, participating in Ukrainian civic life as Kiev city councillors.[226]

Vera Čáslavska, a Prague native, achieved worldwide admiration for not only her dominating performances, but her dignified defiance of political and social strife in her homeland.[227] Čáslavska, the most successful female gymnast of the 1960s, won seven gold medals at Olympic games and every event at the 1965 and 1967 European Championships.[228] She may be best remembered for her protest against the Soviet-led invasion of Czechoslovakia in 1968 when on the medal podium she turned her head down and to the right when the Soviet national anthem was played.[229] Vivacious and talented, Čáslavska became one of the most popular competitors in the history of the sport.[230] However, her public anti-Soviet display of Czechoslovakian patriotism made her an outcast upon her return to her country, which was still under Soviet influence.[231]

On the men's side, Sawao Kato's (born 1946 in Japan) technique and style defined men's gymnastics for three Olympiads.[232] Judges admired his originality and his level of refinement, form and execution.[233] At the 1968 Olympic Games, as team captain, Kato won the all-around title and led Japan to their third successive victory in the event, with Japanese gymnasts filling four of the top five individual places.[234] His medal count over three Olympic Games totalled 12 Olympic medals, eight of them gold.[235]

Perhaps no other gymnast ever did more to promote participation in the sport of gymnastics than Olga Korbut (born in Belarus), who won the hearts of millions of viewers.[236] Her performances at the 1972 Games brought unprecedented interest in the sport, displaying a cheeky style different than the traditional flowing grace of classic Russian gymnasts.[237] At the height of the Cold War, Korbut's daring innovation and display of emotion broke the mould of the stoic Soviet gymnast, which endeared her to fans worldwide.[238] Though criticized that her skill level lagged behind her competitors, crowds adored her precisely because she erred at crucial moments.[239] Korbut drove advancement in gymnastics elements including a dramatic back flip on the uneven bars and originating the back salto on balance beam.[240] Korbut won six Olympic medals and in 1988, became the first inductee into the International Gymnastics Hall of Fame.[241]

Nadia Comaneci (born 1962 in Romania), the most celebrated gymnast in the history of gymnastics, starred in the 1976 Montreal Olympics when she earned the very first perfect 10 score.[242] Comaneci demonstrated a technical perfection that had not been seen in the sport before, likely due to the intense conditioning required by coach Bela Karolyi.[243] She revolutionized the uneven bars, originating release moves and the back salto dismount.[244] Comaneci won nine total Olympic medals and earned three European Championships titles.[245] Comaneci modelled a new, more child-like look for an Olympic champion, free from associations with womanhood or politics.[246] Receiving global recognition, she appeared on the covers of Time, Newsweek and Sports Illustrated, United States' popular magazines, all in the same week.[247]

Comaneci inspired a new generation of powerful, acrobatic gymnasts. Mary Lou Retton (born 1968) catapulted to international fame at the 1984 Olympic Games in Los Angeles, becoming the first American woman ever to win the gold medal in the all-around in women's gymnastics.[248] Her five medals were the most won by any athlete at the 1984 Olympics.[249] Karolyi, who defected to the United States, also coached Retton.[250] Retton is credited with popularizing a more athletic style of tumbling and represented a departure from 1970s stereotype of a female gymnast.[251] Sports Illustrated magazine named her Sportswoman of the Year and General Mills placed her likeness on boxes of Wheaties, a ubiquitous American breakfast cereal, the first time the company bestowed that honour on a female athlete.[252]

Epically battling the Japanese since the 1950s, the Soviet Union's men's gymnastics squads finished first or second at the Olympics for 40 years, with the exception of the boycott year of 1984.[253] For the 1992 Olympics Games most of the individual republics of the former Soviet Union banded together to form the Unified team, the last demonstration of Soviet dominance with star Vitaly Scherbo.[254] Scherbo (born in 1972 in Belarus), considered by many as the best male gymnast of all time, won world titles in all eight events: the individual all-around, the team and the six disciplines.[255] Scherbo, nearly untouchable at the Barcelona Olympics, won six gold medals at the 1992 Games, the most by any gymnast in the history of the Games.[256] By the time his career ended in 1996, he had won 10 Olympic medals (six gold) and an incredible 23 world championship medals (12 gold) and would be remembered as much for his propensity to openly react unfavourably to scores and to speak his mind as for his dynamic gymnastics.[257]

Now rivalling Scherbo for the honour of greatest male gymnast of all time, Japan's Kohei Uchimura (born 1989) has dominated men's gymnastics for the last decade.[258] Nicknamed 'Superman' and 'the King', Uchimura displayed near-technically-perfect and wildly difficult men's gymnastics for years.[259] A legend in his native Japan, Uchimura won six world championships in a row, every major all-around title since 2009.[260] His streak included the Olympic all-around titles in 2012 and 2016 and Uchimura ranks second on the list of male gymnasts with the most medals at the Worlds with 19, 10 of them gold.[261]

Though there is controversy regarding the men, most observers agree on the greatest female gymnast of her, or any, generation: Simone Biles (born 1997, United States).[262] Biles won a record fourth world all-around title in 2018 and the 14th medal of her career, the most ever by any gymnast at Worlds.[263] Biles has won every meet she's entered since the US championships in 2013 and usually the scores are not close.[264] Described as a 'phenomenon who is born once in 100 years', and so 'preternaturally talented ... she can do heretofore-unthinkable skills cleanly'.[265] She competed in the 2018 World Championships despite being hospitalized during the competition with a kidney stone and returning from a year-long break following the Rio Olympics.[266]

Conclusion

Gymnastics progressed through a long and fascinating journey with foundations in the performing arts, military training, the medical professions, and the education professions.[267] Gymnastics skills, rules, and equipment continue to advance, resulting in an incredible increase in the activity's difficulty and popularity.[268] In its current form, gymnastics fans demand televised international coverage of gymnastics competitions.[269] Since 1972, gymnastics has become one of the most widely viewed sports on television during the Olympic Games.[270] Expanded television coverage and nascent online platforms for user-generated content raise the public's awareness of and knowledge of gymnastics.[271] This attention created a tremendous increase in participation and treats gymnastics athletes as global superstars.[272] The International Olympic Committee declared gymnastics in the top three most popular and highest revenue producing Olympic sports.[273]

As gymnastics remains popular and continues to evolve, significant developments in the sport require increased financial, material, and human resources support.[274] While celebrating its positive aspects and growing the sport, fans and critics, coaches and governing bodies must not ignore gymnastics' challenges. The sport must monitor the serious, documented consequences for athletes participating in the sport and create and maintain ethical, responsive structures to address the problems.[275]

Notes

1 Pfister, *Gymnastics, a Transatlantic Movement*, 3.
2 J. Goodbody, *The Illustrated History of Gymnastics* (London: Stanley Paul & Co. Ltd., 1982), 11.
3 K. Knudsen, *A Textbook of Gymnastics, Volume I* (London: J&A Churchill, Ltd., 1947), 3.
4 J. Bolin, *What is Gymnastics? Volume I historical reprint* (New York: Nabu Press, 2012), 28.
5 I. Cuk, 'Foreword', *Science of Gymnastics Journal* 1,1 (2009), 3.
6 'About the FIG', International Gymnastics Federation, accessed 23 November 2018, www.fig-gymnas tics.com/site/about.php
7 A. Frantzopoulou, S. Douka, V. Kaimakamis, A. Matsaridis, and M. Terzoglou, 'Acrobatics in Greece from Ancient Times to the Present Day', *Studies in Physical Culture and Tourism* 18, 4 (2011), 337–342.
8 Ibid.
9 Ibid.
10 Ibid.
11 Russell, 'The Evolution of Gymnastics', 3–11.
12 Frantzopoulou, et al., 'Acrobatics in Greece', 337–342.
13 Russell, 'The Evolution of Gymnastics', 3–11.
14 K. Hardman and R. Naul (Eds.), *Sport and Physical Education in Germany* (London: Taylor and Francis, 2005); Also, Frenchman Jean-Jacques Rousseau wrote, 'Exercise his body continually; make him strong and healthy that you may make him wise and reasonable.' J. Goodbody, *The Illustrated History of Gymnastics* (London: Stanley Paul & Co. Ltd., 1982), 12.
15 Frantzopoulou et al., 'Acrobatics in Greece', 337–342; Hardman and Naul, *Sport and Physical Education*, 15–16.
16 V. Kaimakamis, G. Dallas, P. Stefanidis, and G. Papadopoulos G., 'The Spread of Gymnastics in Europe and America by Pedagogue-Gymnasts During the First Half of the 19th Century', *Science of Gymnastics Journal* 3, 1 (2011), 49–55.
17 Ibid.
18 Frantzopoulou et al., 'Acrobatics in Greece', 337–342.
19 Russell, 'The Evolution of Gymnastics', 3–11.
20 Frantzopoulou et al., 'Acrobatics in Greece', 337–342; Pfister, *Gymnastics, a Transatlantic Movement*, 3.
21 Kaimakamis et al., 'The Spread of Gymnastics', 49–55.
22 M. Kant, 'German Gymnastics, Modern German Dance, and Nazi Aesthetics', *Dance Research Journal* 48, 2 (2016), 4–25.

23 G. Gems, 'The German Turners and the Taming of Radicalism in Chicago', in *Gymnastics, a Transatlantic Movement: From Europe to America*, ed. G. Pfister (Abingdon: Routledge, 2011), 38–57.

24 Kant, 'German Gymnastics', 4–25.

25 Ibid.

26 Ibid.

27 Ibid.

28 Ibid.

29 Ibid.

30 Kaimakamis et al., 'The Spread of Gymnastics', 49–55.

31 Ibid.

32 Ibid.

33 Ibid.

34 Ibid.; A student of Ling criticized the German system as overly straining the upper body, overworking the heart and lungs, and producing heavy shoulders and a stopping gait. Goodbody, *The Illustrated History*, 15.

35 Kaimakamis et al., 'The Spread of Gymnastics', 49–55.

36 J. Prestidge, *The History of British Gymnastics* (Shropshire: British Amateur Gymnastics Association, 1988), 7.

37 Kaimakamis et al., 'The Spread of Gymnastics', 49–55.

38 T. Terret and L. Tesche, 'French Gymnastics in Brazil: Dissemination, Diffusion and Relocalization' in *Gymnastics, a Transatlantic Movement: From Europe to America* ed. G. Pfister (Abingdon: Routledge, 2011), 95–110.

39 Terret and Tesche, 'French Gymnastics in Brazil', 95–110.

40 A. Schmid, *Modern Rhythmic Gymnastics* (Palo Alto: Mayfield Publishing Company, 1976).

41 Ibid.

42 Kaimakamis et al., 'The Spread of Gymnastics', 49–55; A. Gajdoš, M. Provaznikova, and S. Banjak, '150 Years of the Sokol Gymnastics Czechoslovakia, Czech and Slovak Republic', *Science of Gymnastics Journal* 4, 2 (2012), 5–26.

43 Kaimakamis et al., 'The Spread of Gymnastics', 49–55.

44 Gajdoš, Provaznikova, and Banjak, '150 Years', 5–26.

45 Ibid.

46 Ibid.

47 Ibid.

48 Ibid.

49 Ibid.

50 Kaimakamis et al., 'The Spread of Gymnastics', 49–55.

51 Terret and Tesche, 'French Gymnastics in Brazil', 95–110.

52 Kaimakamis et al., 'The Spread of Gymnastics', 49–55.

53 A. Grossfeld, 'A History of Artistic Gymnastics in the United States', *Science of Gymnastics Journal* 2, 2 (2010), 5–28.

54 G. Pfister, 'The Role of German Turners in American Physical Education', in *Gymnastics, a Transatlantic Movement: From Europe to America*, ed. G. Pfister (Abingdon: Routledge, 2011), 5–37.

55 Ibid.

56 Ibid.

57 Ibid.

58 Ibid.

59 Gems, 'The German Turners', 38–57; Grossfeld, 'A History of Artistic Gymnastics in the United States', 5–28.

60 Grossfeld, 'A History of Artistic Gymnastics in the United States', 5–28.

61 Goodbody, *The Illustrated History*, 17.

62 Ibid., 16.

63 Ibid.

64 Prestidge, *The History of British Gymnastics*, 8–9.

65 Ibid., 9.

66 Goodbody, *The Illustrated History*, 16.

67 Also spelled MacLaren. Prestidge, *The History of British Gymnastics*, 7.

68 Prestidge, *The History of British Gymnastics*, 7–8

69 Goodbody, *The Illustrated History*, 16; Prestidge, *The History of British Gymnastics*, 7.

70 Goodbody, *The Illustrated History*, 16; Prestidge, *The History of British Gymnastics*, 8.

71 A. Schmid, *Modern Rhythmic Gymnastics* (Palo Alto: Mayfield Publishing Company, 1976), 1–6.

72 Ibid., 2.

73 Ibid., 2–3.

74 Ibid., 3–4.

75 Russell, 'The Evolution of Gymnastics', 3–11.

76 Ibid.

77 Ibid.

78 G. Papadopoulos, V. Kaimakamis, D. Kaimakamis and M. Proios, 'Main Characteristics of Rules and Competition Systems in Gymnastics from 1896 to 1912', *Science of Gymnastics Journal* 6, 2 (2014), 29–40.

79 Papadopoulos et al., 'Main Characteristics of Rules', 29–40.

80 Ibid., 29–40; A. Grossfeld, 'Changes During 110 Years of the World Artistic Gymnastics,' *Science of Gymnastics Journal* 6, 2 (2014), 5–27.

81 Russell, 'The Evolution of Gymnastics', 3–11.

82 Grossfeld, 'Changes During 110 Years', 5–27.

83 Papadopoulos et al., 'Main Characteristics of Rules', 29–40.

84 Russell, 'The Evolution of Gymnastics', 3–11.

85 Papadopoulos et al., 'Main Characteristics of Rules', 29–40.

86 Grossfeld, 'Changes During 110 Years', 5–27.

87 Ibid.

88 Ibid.

89 Ibid.

90 Papadopoulos et al., 'Main Characteristics of Rules', 29–40.

91 Ibid.

92 Ibid.

93 Ibid.

94 Ibid.

95 Ibid.

96 Ibid.

97 Ibid.

98 Ibid.

99 Ibid.

100 Grossfeld, 'Changes During 110 Years', 5–27.

101 M. Pajek, 'Individual Apparatus Results of Female All Around Olympic Champions', *Science of Gymnastics Journal* 10, 3 (2018), 357–368.

102 Ibid.

103 Grossfeld, 'Changes During 110 Years', 5–27.

104 D. Meyers, *The End of the Perfect 10: The Making and Breaking of Gymnastics' Top Score–from Nadia to Now* (New York: Touchstone, 2016).

105 Meyers, *The End*, 33–37.

106 Grossfeld, 'Changes During 110 Years', 5–27.

107 Pajek, 'Individual Apparatus Results', 357–368.

108 Grossfeld, 'Changes During 110 Years', 5–27.

109 The USSR maintained its dominance in 1958 with Japan, again, placing second. Then for the next five World Championships (WC) – 1962, 1966, 1970, 1974 and 1978 – dominance switched, with Japan's team winning and the Soviet team placing second. The Soviets regained the top spot in the next two WC – 1979 and 1981–with Japan being second. In 1983, China was the top team with the USSR second. The USSR was most dominant in the 1985, 1987, 1989 and 1991 WC. See Grossfeld, 'Changes During 110 Years', 5–27.

110 Grossfeld, 'Changes During 110 Years', 5–27.

111 Ibid.

112 Ibid.

113 Pajek, 'Individual Apparatus Results', 357–368.

114 M. Simons II, *Women's Gymnastics: A History. Volume I: 1966 to 1974* (Carmel: Welwyn Publishing Company, 1995).

115 Pajek, 'Individual Apparatus Results', 357–368.

116 Schmid, *Modern Rhythmic Gymnastics*, 5.

117 Ibid., 5.

118 Ibid., 6.

119 Ibid., 6–7.

120 Ibid., 7.

121 Ibid., 7–8.

122 R.A. Pelin, 'Studies Regarding the Rhythmic Gymnastics from the Olympic Games', *Sport & Society*, 13 (2013), 61–65.

123 Pelin, 'Studies Regarding the Rhythmic Gymnastics', 61–65.

124 Ibid.

125 Grossfeld, 'Changes During 110 Years', 5–27.

126 Ibid.

127 Ibid.

128 Ibid.

129 In 1972, the all-around and all podium spots in the event finals were claimed by only 5 gymnasts: Lyudmila Turischeva, Karin Janz, Tamara Lazakovich, Erika Zuchold, Olga Korbut, from only two countries, the Soviet Union and East Germany. Pajek, 'Individual Apparatus Results', 357–368.

130 M. Simons II, *Women's Gymnastics: A History. Volume 1: 1966 to 1974* (Carmel: Welwyn Publishing Company, 1995).

131 All-around competition results: 1. Turischeva (USSR) 2. Janz (GDR) 3. Lazakovich (USSR) 4. Zuchold (GDR) 5. Burda (USSR) 6. Hellman (GDR) 7. Korbut (USSR). Qualifiers for event finals: Lyudmila Turischeva (USSR), Karin Janz (GDR), Tamara Lazakovich (USSR), Erika Zuchold (GDR), Olga Korbut (USSR), Ilona Bekesi (HUN), Monica Csaszar (HUN), Angelika Hellman (GDR) See Simons, *Women's Gymnastics*, 247.

132 Grossfeld, 'Changes During 110 Years', 5–27.

133 Ibid.; Meyers, *The End*, 33.

134 See Meyers, *The End*, 33 describing women's gymnastics as not demanding above average strength or coordination and athletes' physiques possessing evident breasts and wide hips.

135 Meyers, *The End*, 33–52.

136 Grossfeld, 'Changes During 110 Years', 5–27.

137 Ludmilla Tourischeva, though known for her balletic, graceful movements pushed the envelope on difficulty, performing a back flip on beam and a full twisting somersault off. Her European Championships routine contained so much difficulty she was deducted points for it. Meyers, *The End*, 39–40.

138 Grossfeld, 'Changes During 110 Years', 5–27; The Soviet team, the overall winner in the 1976 Olympic Games, averaged 19.8 years of age. See A. Gajdoš, *Aristic Gymnastics: A History of Development and Olympic Competition* (Loughborough: British Amateur Gymnastics Association Limited, 1997).

139 Grossfeld, 'Changes During 110 Years', 5–27; Bela Karolyi, famous gymnastics coach, said that a female gymnasts' best training years were from eight to twenty. Meyers, *The End*, 38–39.

140 Grossfeld, 'Changes During 110 Years', 5–27.

141 Meyers, *The End*, xiii.

142 Grossfeld, 'Changes During 110 Years', 5–27.

143 Ibid.

144 Ibid.

145 'About the FIG', International Gymnastics Federation, accessed 23 November 2018, www.fig-gymnastics.com/site/about.php

146 Ibid.

147 'Congress', International Gymnastics Federation, accessed 23 November 2018, www.fig-gymnastics.com/site/pages/about-congress.php

148 'The President', International Gymnastics Federation, accessed 23 November 2018, www.fig-gymnastics.com/site/pages/about-president.php

149 'About the FIG', International Gymnastics Federation, accessed 23 November 2018, www.fig-gymnastics.com/site/about.php

150 'Men's Artistic Gymnastics', International Gymnastics Federation, accessed 23 November 2018, www.fig-gymnastics.com/site/pages/disciplines/pres-mag.php

151 Ibid.

152 'Women's Artistic Gymnastics', International Gymnastics Federation, accessed 23 November 2018, www.fig-gymnastics.com/site/discipline.php?disc=3

153 Ibid.

154 'Rhythmic Gymnastics', International Gymnastics Federation, accessed 23 November 2018, www.fig-gymnastics.com/site/pages/disciplines/pres-rg.php

155 Ibid.

156 'History – Milestones', International Gymnastics Federation, accessed 23 November 2018, www.fig-gymnastics.com/site/figbrief/history.php

157 'Acrobatic Gymnastics', International Gymnastics Federation, accessed 23 November 2018, www.fig-gymnastics.com/site/pages/disciplines/pres-acro.php

158 Ibid.

159 Ibid.

160 'History – Milestones', International Gymnastics Federation, accessed 23 November 2018, www.fig-gymnastics.com/site/figbrief/history.php

161 'Trampoline Gymnastics', International Gymnastics Federation, accessed 23 November 2018, www.fig-gymnastics.com/site/pages/disciplines/pres-tra.php

162 Ibid.

163 Ibid.

164 'History – Milestones', International Gymnastics Federation, accessed 23 November 2018, www.fig-gymnastics.com/site/figbrief/history.php

165 'Aerobic Gymnastics', International Gymnastics Federation, accessed 23 November 2018, www.fig-gymnastics.com/site/pages/disciplines/pres-aer.php

166 Ibid.

167 Ibid.

168 Ibid.

169 Ibid.

170 'History–Milestones', International Gymnastics Federation, accessed 23 November 2018, www.fig-gymnastics.com/site/figbrief/history.php

171 'Parkour', International Gymnastics Federation, accessed 23 November 2018, www.fig-gymnastics.com/site/pages/disciplines/pres-pk.php

172 Ibid.

173 Ibid.

174 Ibid.

175 'Gymnastics for All', International Gymnastics Federation, accessed 23 November 2018, www.fig-gymnastics.com/site/pages/disciplines/pres-gfa.php

176 Ibid.

177 Ibid.

178 Ibid.

179 C. Leandro, L. Ávila-Carvalho, and E. Sierra-Palmeiro. 'Judging in Rhythmic Gymnastics at Different Levels of Performance,' *Journal of Human Kinetics*, 60 (2017), 159–165.

180 Ibid.

181 H. Plessner, 'Expectation Biases in Gymnastic Judging', *Journal of Sport & Exercise Psychology* 21, 2 (1999), 131–144

182 Plessner, 'Expectation Biases', 131–144.

183 Ibid.

184 Papadopoulos et al., 'Main characteristics of Rules', 29–40.

185 Ibid.

186 Ibid.

187 Ibid.

188 Plessner, 'Expectation Biases', 131–144.

189 Meyers, *The End*, 61.

190 Ibid., 59–62.

191 Ibid., 11.

192 Meyers, *The End*, 25–28.

193 Ibid., 16.

194 Ibid., 29.

195 Ibid., 66.

196 Ibid., 64.

197 Ibid., 74, 103.

198 'A Decade of Change', FloGymnastics, last modified December 2, 2011, www.flogymnastics.com/articles/5047179-a-decade-of-change

199 Meyers, *The End*, 71, 91; Chloe Angyal, 'Why Gymnastics Abandoned The Perfect 10 And Embraced Jaw-Dropping Athleticism', *HuffPost*, 3 August 2016. Retrieved from www.huffingtonpost.com/entry/gymnastics-olympics-perfect-10-scoring_us_57a0fdc7e4b08a8e8b5fe129 (accessed 24 November 2018).

200 Meyers, *The End*, xvi.

201 Ibid., 259.

202 Ibid., xiv, 119, 232, 241, 252–256.

203 Angyal, 'Why Gymnastics Abandoned'

204 David Ciaralli, the spokesman for the Italian Gymnastics Federation, 'The Code of Points is opening chances for colored people (known to be more powerful) and penalizing typical Eastern European elegance, which, when gymnastics was more artistic and less acrobatic, allowed Russia and Romania to dominate the field.' See Meyers, *The End*, xiv, 119, 232, 241, 252–256.

205 Ibid., 119.

206 Ibid., 119.

207 Ibid., xiv.

208 Ibid., xiv–xvi.

209 Leandro, Ávila-Carvalho, and Sierra-Palmeiro. Judging in Rhythmic Gymnastics', 159–165; '2017 Code of Points – Men's Artistic Gymnastics', International Gymnastics Federation, last updated January 2018, www.fig-gymnastics.com/publicdir/rules/files/en_MAG%20CoP%202017%20-%202020.pdf

210 '2017 Code of Points.'

211 Leandro, Ávila-Carvalho, and Sierra-Palmeiro. Judging in Rhythmic Gymnastics', 159–165; For men, 'D' score content will include by addition: 1. The additional difficulty value of 10 elements (8 for juniors), the best 9 (7 for juniors), but maximum 5 elements for the same Element Group, inside the best counting plus the value of the dismount, 2. The connections value, based on special rules on different apparatus, 3. The Element Group Requirements Value, performed among the 10 counting elements (8 for juniors). See ''2017 Code of Points'; For women, a) The D-Score on Vault is the Difficulty Value in the Table of Vaults. b) The D-Score on Uneven Bars, Balance Beam and Floor Exercise includes the highest 8 difficulties, compositional requirements and connection value. See '2017–2020 Code of Points'–Women's Artistic Gymnastics', International Gymnastics Federation, last updated December 2016, www.fig-gymnastics.com/publicdir/rules/files/en_WAG%20CoP%202017-2020.pdf

212 Leandro, Ávila-Carvalho, and Sierra-Palmeiro. Judging in Rhythmic Gymnastics', 159–165.

213 'E' score, will start from 10 points and will evaluate by deductions applied in tenths of a point: – The total deductions for aesthetic and execution errors. – The total deductions for technical and compositional errors. – The highest and the lowest sums of total deductions applied in tenths of a point for execution, aesthetic, technical and compositional errors are eliminated. The average remaining sums is subtracted from the 10 points in order to determine the Final 'E' Score. See '2017 Code of Points'

214 For perfection of execution, combination and artistry of presentation, the gymnast may earn a score of 10.00 P. The E- Score includes deductions for faults in execution and artistry of presentation. The E- judges will judge an exercise and determine the deductions independently. Each performance is evaluated with reference to expectations of perfect performance. All deviations from this expectation are deducted. Deductions for errors in execution and artistry are added together and then deducted from 10.00 points to determine the E- Score. See '2017–2020 Code of Points.'

215 '2017 Code of Points'; '2017–2020 Code of Points.'

216 Plessner, 'Expectation Biases', 131–144.

217 Pajek, 'Individual Apparatus Results', 357–368.

218 Goodbody, *The Illustrated History*, 30–31.

219 'Larissa Latynina, the 18 Times Record Olympic Medal Athlete, Congratulates Michael Phelps on Becoming the Record Gold Medal Athlete', *PR Newswire Europe* 15 August 2008. Retrieved from https://infoweb.newsbank.com/apps/news/document-view?p=AWNB&docref=news/12296E3AD4DBB8C0 (accessed 17 November 2018)

220 'Larissa Latynina', 1998, *International Gymnastics Hall of Fame*. Retrieved from www.ighof.com/inductees/1998_Larissa_Latynina.php (accessed 17 November 2018).

221 'Larissa Latynina, the 18.'
222 Ibid.
223 'Boris Chanklin', 2002, *International Gymnastics Hall of Fame*. Retrieved from www.ighof.com/induct ees/2002_Boris_Shakhlin.php (accessed 17 November 2018).
224 Ibid.
225 Ibid.
226 Goodbody, *The Illustrated History*, 32.
227 'Vera Caslavska' 1998. *International Gymnastics Hall of Fame*. Retrieved from www.ighof.com/induct ees/1998_Vera_Caslavska.php (accessed 17 November 2018).
228 Ibid.
229 K. Janicek, 2016. 'Czechs Mourn Gymnastics Great Vera Caslavska.' *Associated Press: Worldstream*, September 12. Retrieved from https://infoweb.newsbank.com/apps/news/document-view?p=AWNB& docref=news%2F15F5AC39CEE22A58 (accessed 17 November 2018)
230 Goodbody, *The Illustrated History*, 42.
231 'Vera Caslavska.'
232 'Sawao Kato' 2001. *International Gymnastics Hall of Fame*. Retrieved from www.ighof.com/inductees/ 2001_Sawao_Kato.php (accessed 17 November 2018)
233 Ibid.
234 Ibid.
235 Ibid.
236 'Olga Korbut' 1988. *International Gymnastics Hall of Fame*. Retrieved from www.ighof.com/inductees/ 1988_Olga_Korbut.php (accessed 17 November 2018)
237 Goodbody, *The Illustrated History*, 57–62.
238 'Olga Korbut Auctions Medals & Memorabilia', *International Gymnast* 59, 3 (2017) 12.
239 Goodbody, *The Illustrated History*, 57.
240 Simons, *Women's Gymnastics*, 363.
241 'Olga Korbut.'
242 'Nadia Comaneci' 1993. *International Gymnastics Hall of Fame*. Retrieved from www.ighof.com/ inductees/1993_Nadia_Comaneci.php (accessed 17 November 2018)
243 Meyers, *The End*, 18.
244 Gajdoš, *Aristic Gymnastics*, 261.
245 'Nadia Comaneci.'
246 Meyers, *The End*, 14.
247 'Nadia Comaneci.'
248 'Mary Lou Retton' 1997. *International Gymnastics Hall of Fame*. Retrieved from www.ighof.com/ inductees/1997_Mary_Lou_Retton.php (accessed 17 November 2018)
249 Ibid.
250 Meyers, *The End*, 48
251 Meyers, *The End*, 48; E. Almond. 'Catching Up With Mary Lou Retton, Olympic Darling of 1984.' *The Daily Review*, 30 March 2016. Retrieved from https://infoweb.newsbank.com/apps/news/docu ment-view?p=AWNB&docref=news%2F15BF719CB94B34B0 (accessed 17 November 2018)
252 Almond, 'Catching Up.'
253 J. Goodbody, 'Gymnast Proves His Mettle.' *The Sunday Times*, 15 January 2012. Retrieved from https:// infoweb.newsbank.com/apps/news/document-view?p=AWNB&docref=news%2F13C4C2BAF6A E1BA0 (accessed 17 November 2018). Goodbody, *The Illustrated History*, 111–141.
254 Goodbody, 'Gymnast Proves His Mettle.'
255 Ibid.; 'Vitaly Scherbo', 2009. *International Gymnastics Hall of Fame*. Retrieved from www.ighof.com/ inductees/2009_Vitaly_Scherbo.php (accessed 17 November 2018)
256 Goodbody, 'Gymnast Proves His Mettle'; 'Vitaly Scherbo.'
257 'Vitaly Scherbo.'
258 R. Schuman', The Greatest Gymnast of All Time–When Simone Biles Grows Up, She Wants to Be Like Kohei Uchimura.' *Slate*, 11 August 2016. Retrieved from https://infoweb.newsbank.com/apps/news/ document-view?p=AWNB&docref=news%2F15EB2838F0D22758 (accessed 17 November 2018)
259 Ibid.
260 Schuman, 'The Greatest Gymnast'; 'Injury Halts Japanese Gymnast's Run at Title.' *The Orange County Register*, 4 October 2017. Retrieved from https://infoweb.newsbank.com/apps/news/document-vie w?p=AWNB&docref=news%2F16752B18827E4288 (accessed 17 November 2018).

261 'Injury Halts Japanese.'

262 N. Armour. 'Just a Year into Return, Biles Better than Ever.' *USA Today*, 1 November 2018. https:// research.flagler.edu:2048/login?url=https://search.proquest.com/docview/2127539899?accoun tid=10900. (accessed 17 November 2018)

263 'With 13th World Title, Biles Sets Another Mark'. 3 November 2018. *New York Times* Retrieved from https://research.flagler.edu:2048/login?url=https://search.proquest.com/docview/2128416417?acc ountid=10900 (accessed 17 November 2018)

264 Armour, 'Just a Year.'

265 According to Dvora Meyers in Angyal, 'Why Gymnastics Abandoned'.

266 According to Uzbekistan's Oksana Chusovitina, a gymnast still competing at age 43. Armour, 'Just a Year.'

267 Russell, 'The Evolution of Gymnastics', 3–11.

268 Grossfeld, 'Changes During', 5–27.

269 B. McCarthy, 'From Shanfan to Gymnastike: How Online Fan Texts Are Affecting Access to Gymnastics Media Coverage', *International Journal of Sport Communication* 4, 3, (2011), 265–283. Grossfeld, 'Changes During', 5–27.

270 McCarthy, 'From Shanfan to Gymnastike', 265–283.

271 Grossfeld, 'Changes During 110 Years', 5–27. Gymnastics fans created and maintained spaces like the International Gymnast message board, Gymnastike (now FloGymnastics), and the gymnastics blogosphere, tailoring them to perform specific information functions. See McCarthy, 'From Shanfan to Gymnastike', 265–283.

272 Grossfeld, 'Changes During 110 Years', 5–27. FIG estimates 50 million people worldwide regularly participate in amateur gymnastics every year. Google search accessed 28 November 2018 for Simone Biles returned more than 10 million results and she maintains 3.4 million Instagram followers: www. instagram.com/simonebiles/?hl=en

273 Grossfeld, 'Changes During 110 Years', 5–27.

274 J. Zurc, 'It was Worth It: I Would Do it Again: Phenomenological Perspectives on Life in Elite Women's Artistic Gymnastics', *Science of Gymnastics Journal* 9, 1 (2017): 41–59.

275 Research has found injuries, negative weight control methods, eating disorders, severe physical injuries, corporal punishment, training and competing with injuries, psychological abuse, lack of time for resting and leisure activities, adverse effects on health and development, decreased school performance, absence from home, lack of social contact with non-athletes, sexual abuse, and substance abuse. See Zurc, 'It was Worth It', 41–59.

The United State Olympic Committee moved to remove USA Gymnastics' (USAG) National Governing Body recognition as USAG has been at the center of controversy for more than two years in the wake of revelations that disgraced sports doctor Larry Nassar was allowed to abuse gymnasts under the guise of medical care at national and international events, including the Olympics, and at the Karolyi Ranch, the former national training center for the women's team. See David Barron, 'USA Gymnastics refuses to step aside; USOC to continue with efforts to strip federation of ability to govern the sport', *Houston Chronicle*, 22 November 2018. Retrieved https://infoweb.newsbank.com/apps/news/document-view?p=AWNB&docref=news%2F16FE409B88BF78B0 (accessed 26 November 2018).

34

Weightlifting

Gherardo Bonini

Ancient populations idolized men with superhuman strength capable of leading them to victory in war or who saved people in emergencies or for carrying out feats otherwise impossible for ordinary people, such as lifting extremely heavy weights, removing obstacles, demolishing or even pulverizing objects, for carrying enormous weights over long periods of time and distances. In the Western world, Hercules had been the Greek mythological figure who had all powers, furthermore prehistoric inscriptions dating from 3600 BC bore witness on how in other cultures, stone lifters received attention and won fame. The Bible's Book of Judges recounts in detail the dramatic figure of Samson whose incredible strength came directly from God. However, the strongmen did not acquire celebrity status only because they were connected with mythological or sacred traditions, but because they were recognized "sportsmen" such as Milo of Croton, the legendary winner of wrestling games in the ancient Greek Olympics, famous for having lifted animals and objects in duration of space and time. The ancient athletes cultivated their strength with repetition lifts of *halteres* and this practice persisted through the centuries as a type of training for warriors.[1]

The Roman Empire and Middle Ages did not however neglect the use of physical power, however it was confined to war or in the field of circuses and sporadic popular festivals. Christianity preached another kind of strength, moral and religious vigour. Quoting Ulmann, Toschi wrote that Christianity made "any doctrine granting the body a value not deriving from soul unacceptable".[2] The champion has to prevail physically not just in respect to his faith in God but also for his physical training. The "chevalier" emerged as the strongest athlete, but his muscular skills could only be used to defend the faith.[3] Kings, generals and warriors acquired legendary attributes for their leadership; courage and dexterity but their strength was remembered as of secondary importance. They were physically powerful too, like the King of England, Richard Lionheart in the 11th century or King Scanderberg of Albania in the 14th century, but their strength remained biographically as a secondary attribute. Another exception was Empress Elizabeth of Pomerania, who reigned during the 14th century, she too was remembered for her feats of strength. The late Renaissance opened a new era and rediscovered the physique and its qualities. The gymnastic manual of Hieronymus Mercurialis (1582) exalted strong men and their muscular tone. Under the soldiers' armours, well-built masculine bodies served to express leadership, bravery and mastery. In the 17th century, the scientific revolution changed definitively the mentality. Measurements and sizes determined the rankings among men. On 24 May 1741 the Herculean Thomas Topham had lifted by means of special apparatus, casks of water weighing 833 kg. The physicist Theodore Desagulières studied him, detecting with precision the physiological base of Topham's energy.[4]

Embryo of a modern sport

The crucial passage towards the determination of strength as an autonomous sector of human activities emerged in the 19th century, in parallel with the industrial revolution and its innovative mentality. A new physical culture gradually put forward the idea of the body as a tool and target of its effort. Pushing up a wooden bar, lifting and managing the weights figured as fundamental steps in the gymnastic drills. Initially in his home town of Brussels, then after 1849 in Paris the grand hall of gymnasiarch Hyppolite Triat teemed of globular bells, the extended type of dumbbells and, as historian Jan Todd stressed "many of Paris distinguished citizens signed up for classes".[5] In 1834, Donald Walker diffused in America workouts with Indian clubs which flanked repetition lifts with dumbbells as the basis for building strong bodies. Strength became a tool for health. Men and, infrequently, women could build strong, healthy and beautiful bodies. Dudley Sargent observed that weakness in women was mostly a product of a peculiar dress mode and the pressure exerted on them (mainly by men) to please. He noted "girls need more muscle-making exercise" so as to narrow the gap, not to acquire greater physical strength but to be able to achieve more in their daily lives, even if their role in society remained separated and differentiated.[6]

Ancient mythological figures such as Hercules, Samson, Milo but also Goliath, Cyclops, Achilles were revived. Those were the preferred names assumed by strongmen who used their power as career resources in the new labour market. True strongmen and rarely strongwomen occupied the scenario beside normally-built men who used charlatanism to dupe spectators. Parodic figures of corpulent men who were breaking the chains in the touring circuses or caravans became a serious obstacle for the affirmation of a reliable sport.[7]

In the industrial era, the quantification of the raised weights required a certified authenticity. In 1859, William Curtis recorded a performance in curl and put-up for both hands of dumbbells of 100 pounds. Publications began to hand on for future generations the weights recorded. Strength played a fundamental role for the athlete who claimed victory in the multi-athletic games of the Highlands.[8] In Japan *chikaraishi* consisted in a competition in which the lifting of big stones were duly recorded and with the aim of being surpassed.[9] Did the weight carrying, harness lifting, burden lifting, tossing the caber or whatever weight game give rational fundaments to determine the true test of athleticism? How was it possible to define a possible modern sport of weightlifting from other circus acts and vaudeville? Defying gravity revealed the most fitting concept and this challenge had to be done using proven gymnastic tools; dumbbells or barbells. Weightlifting had to be the object of scientific elaboration, done by well-educated theoreticians. In the last two decades of the 19th century, four masters in Europe marked the emergence of a pre-history of weightlifting. Thanks to the increasing diffusion and specialization of the sport press, they knew each other and they debated on the definition of the sport.[10]

Towards standardization: conflict of styles

In France, Edmond Desbonnet, professor of physical education connected weightlifting with a new physical culture in which to work with weights acted as the driving force. His gym halls opened for improving health of French bourgeoisie (men and women). His schools offered tools but also refreshments and entertainment rooms. In the 1880s, Desbonnet founded or inspired the constitution of athletic circles in Roubaix, Lille and Paris. He strove for emancipating weightlifting from gymnastics, becoming the father of the so called French style. In Germany, Theodor Siebert opened a school in Halle and recorded the procedures of the lifting tests, used by the earlier clubs in Vienna in 1880 and in Cologne in 1882, but which were often too closely connected with the gymnastic tradition. Desbonnet called this way of lifting weights the German style. Siebert knew the French style. In the same period, in Russia, the Polish-born Dr Wladyslaw Krajewski and in Italy Marquis Luigi Monticelli Obizzi founded devoted circles. They advocated the necessity of standardizing the new sport and they knew both French and German styles. Both the styles were also known in the United States. However, private schools for physical culture taught predominantly Continental style that was also practiced by numerous clubs attached to German associations.[11]

The conflict between the two styles hampered a world-wide accepted codification and foundation of an authoritative international governing body until the Olympics of Antwerp in 1920. The two styles individualized the basic tests for the sport, one-handed and two-handed snatch, jerk and press, but, apart from the snatch (seldom practiced in Central Europe) undisputedly one move from ground to stretched arms, they differed in the effective practice of exercises with the same name. In Austria, Viennese taverns and inns had become popular centres for convivial meetings where corpulent and powerful men exhibited with weights. Most controversies surrounded jerk. German and Austrian practitioners strictly adopted from the gymnastic steps ground, waist, chest, stretched arms for raising the iron bar. Moreover, the one-handed jerk and press used only by the Germans and Austrians implied a two-handed move from ground to chest, and then the athlete could jerk or press with one hand. The French style imposed steady and parallel legs plus erect trunk for the slow raising called press, in which Germans divaricated their legs and indulged in back-bending. German-style lifts allowed more poundage.[12]

In Britain, since the beginning of the 19th century, strongmen toyed with multi-shaped weights and exhibited at circuses and theatres. At amateur level, the German Gymnastic Society based in London and founded in 1865 comprised weightlifting in its athletic meetings. Ravenstein's *Handbook of Gymnastics* (1867) acted as a peculiar reference for outlining terms of reference for weightlifting tests. This fundamental manual contained the terms of separation of the two styles. A demanding test for drills recommended the upraising of a wooden bar with ground, waist, chest steps and, more pages ahead, the text illustrated an athletic test which was identified in the lifting through ground-chest an iron bar, so complying with French rules, while Germans and Austrians had applied to iron contests the wooden bar procedures. Since 1886, Hungarian-born master Joseph Szalay taught in London the French style.[13] The German, Eugen Sandow, alias Friedrich Müller, was a disciple of Louis Attila who in his turn referred to Triat method of teaching. Sandow had built a statuesque body and exhibited in 1889 in London, showing bent press, a German-styled test with a two-handed elevation at chest level and one-handed screwing with stretched arm. Britons labelled the German style as Continental.[14]

Parameters for the resounding title of Strength Monarch implied the sovereign managing of barbells and dumbbells, but also impressive tests of burden and harness lifting. Weight carrying remained rather a domain for bet-involving open air dual matches engaging workers, peasants, and adventurers. The most credited strongmen for assuming the role of the Strongest were three super-sized men: the hero of Quebec, French Canadian Louis Cyr, the giant French Louis Uni, better known as Apollon, and the Austrian Wilhelm Türk. Cyr created a sensation during his tours in Britan in 1891 and 1892 and ended his career undefeated. Apollon excelled in a peculiar interpretation of the snatch, and lifted a van's wheeled axle of 366 pounds that demanded a problematic grip. The Apollon Axle's lift became since then a proof certifying absolute excellence. After performing initially in circuses stages, Türk dedicated to classic tests of Continental-styled weightlifting, winning in the summer of 1898 a famous World championship in Vienna.[15]

Anglo-Saxon circles gave their preference to Cyr, and Desbonnet put Cyr ex aequo with Apollon. Central European circles as well as Monticelli Obizzi praised Türk. The cultural atmosphere pervading Europe of Darwinistic concepts and the cult of human progress, inspired a common point for eligibility of the three super-champions. They were indicated as semigods and superhumans of archetypes for future generations, because they were oversized in comparison to their contemporaries. But Monticelli Obizzi stressed another difference separating Cyr and Apollon from Türk. The first two were Super strongmen, Türk was a super-lifter, exhibiting in front of certified juries.[16]

However, Britain became the cradle of modern weightlifting. After the Sandow tours, the aristocratic and middle class spectators became eager to watch a veritable competition for electing the strongest man. In early 1891, London hosted various events. On the 28 March at Café Monica, the first World event took place and muscular and the English Jew Edward Lawrence Levy won in front of representatives of Italy, Belgium, Austria, Germany. The programme was made up of repetition lifts of dumbbells. On 30 March, another World championship took place including a test of dead-lift, but this event had a very minor impact. The Italian Zafarana won.[17]

Weightlifting entered the first Olympics of Athens in 1896 with two competitions, single-handed and double-handed jerk with the French style with intermediation by Britons. The Danish gymnast Viggo Jensen won the single-handed laurel, and the globetrotter Briton Launceston Elliot won the double-handed contest and was admired for his statuesque body. The Olympics of Saint Louis in 1904 scheduled two weightlifting competitions, namely the double-handed jerk won by a Greek resident of the United States, Perikles Kakousis, plus a contest composed of ten various exercises won by the American Oscar Osthoff.[18] In the Intercalated Games of Athens in 1906, the Austrian Josef Steinbach won the single-handed competition while in the double-handed the noisy public and some wrong decisions by the Jury favoured the victory of local hero Dimitris Tophalos. This was the first controversial case of weightlifting in a scenario of large international attendance.[19]

Although the dominant Darwinistic assumptions stressed selective process where the most gifted athletes had the greatest advantage, the democratic principles allowed the widest access for entering. Also lighter lifters had demonstrated power and skills. The standing was mostly decided by summing the aggregated kilograms lifted in the single tests and the unique class penalized the light-weight performers. In 1899, the English Amateur Gymnastics Association established official championships for three classes, later copied by Austria, Germany, Italy and France. In Austria, using the Continental jerk, Emil Kliment lifted double his weight and in England, William Pullum equalled this feat but using the French style.[20]

In Europe, where most weightlifting was practiced, the two schools marched in autonomous directions. Both the schools set up international championships and rules varied. In 1910s the Central Europeans tried to settle French-styled world records, but in vain because France's circles accepted records only on French soil and abroad French-styled performances were ideologically reputed to be uncontrolled and erratic. However, in January 1912, Desbonnet was obliged to record that the 151 kg were correctly jerked in Paris by the German Hermann Gässler.[21]

Monticelli Obizzi acted as the driving force for the setting up a World Athletes Union (also included wrestling) in 1905. Italy, Germany, Denmark and The Netherlands joined the project, followed after a year by Switzerland and Sweden. The body collapsed in 1907 but produced a scheme for competition using a hybrid style that Monticelli Obizzi had already proposed in the Milan World Championships. 1899. In the press, the cleaning had to be done in French style, and then the elevation could indulge in slight back-bending. In the jerk, the lifter could choose Continental or French style, this latter awarded with extra points. After the Union collapse, some international championships and German festivals adopted the scheme. Launched in the Olympics of Stockholm of 1912, where weightlifting did not schedule as in London 1908, another body (again incorporating wrestling) was formalized in 1913, but the maintenance of the Continental style as a possible option meant that the French style was cast aside. Some powerful women came on the scene and they were allowed to exhibit mainly due to the fact that they were related in some way to well renowned figures in the theatrical or sporting fields. The Vienna and Berlin clubs officially measured the records of Käthe Brumbach, but the national and international bodies did not accept women's participation in the established sport. Käthe and her emulators remained in the vaudeville arena. The sport remained a male dominated reserve.[22]

French style becomes international style

France, as one of the victorious countries of the First World War succeeded in the definitive internationalization of weightlifting. During the Olympics of Antwerp 1920, where the contests included five bodyweight classes, a new federation (FIH) which didn't encompass wrestling was formed and the French style became the international mandatory style. Following Gässler, Germans had adopted French procedures, but political punishment left them outside the Olympics until 1928. Austrians stuck to the Continental style until 1927. They idolized their champions, from Türk to Steinbach and then to Karl Swoboda, whose image had been reproduced in a postage stamp, and who in 1912 raised 185.6 kg. His compatriot Josef Grafl acted as Ursus in the *Quo Vadis?* film of 1913.[23]

The heavier athletic events of Vienna in September 1920, one week after Antwerp, represented the most successful contra-Olympics. Again Vienna in 1923 hosted a pirate World championship attended by some athletes of the FIH. In June 1924, French troops still occupying Saar denied visas to athletes entering the "pirate" European championships in Neunkirchen. Austria joined the official French-driven international federation in the summer of 1924, and then Germany followed in 1925. All the eligible World records settled by German and Austrian lifters before these dates were ignored.[24] A separate story arose in the years between the two world wars. Austrian and German Workers lifters set 10 absolute performances. The management of elite lifters led Austro-Marxism to modify its sport policy; later the USSR considered these choices in regard to its athletes. Since 1934 Soviet lifters established a long list of veritable World records.[25]

An ideological conflict was caused by the evolution of styles. The techniques of deep knee bend revolutionized the performing of jerk and snatch specialties. The lifter lowered his body under the ideal line of his height until he was in the squat position, and then resumed an erect posture. As a moderate alternative, without bending completely the legs, but splitting them (grazing often with the ground by unpermitted knee touch), carried out the exercise. The first option, called "dive and squat", was risky and often costed honours and records to its interpreters. The second one, "get set", opportunely perfected became progressively more successful. Initially, conservative France did not accept the change, because the rules were dogmatically defended and because its old enemy, Germany, was the pioneer of the process. To lower oneself under the height level involved an acrobatic procedure, so that implied the intolerable transformation of athletes into circus performers. However, after the Olympics of 1928, French lifters increasingly used the new techniques for contrasting main opponents who were profiting from these.[26]

On the athletic side, women organized an international body, but strength sports remained a masculine reserve officially. However, Briton Ivy Russell strove to receive the official seal of approval. The British national body allowed for two national meets, but the resistance to holding regular events for women prevailed. After the Second World War, US Pudgy Stockton battled against similar obstacles. Male practitioners opposed women's participation in the sport and the Amateur Athletic Union, after having allowed some regional contests, decided to discontinue the short-lived practice.[27]

France defended its castling also showing a high resounding example. Charles Rigoulot, Olympic champion in 1924, turned professional and surpassed his contemporaries in the jerk and snatch. He exceeded 141 kg in snatch and 182.5 kg in jerk, when official amateur records remained at 135 kg by the Briton Walker (1936) and 167.5 kg by the Estonian Luhääar (1937) respectively. He had lifted also Apollon Axle. France was proud of its hero Rigoulot, *l'homme le plus fort du monde* as it corroborated their perception of a leading role in the World, and in his prime he was counted as an icon like the protagonists of the Tour de France and the Four Mosquetaires in tennis.[28] New techniques definitely adapted up to the present time.

From the Olympics of Amsterdam 1928, the programme became definitely composed of double-handed press, snatch and jerk. In these years, a solid international figure was another French Louis Hostin, who, after winning silver in Amsterdam 1928, became the first lifter in doubling an Olympic victory, triumphing in Los Angeles 1932 and in Berlin 1936, when he kept his nerve against the noisy and unfriendly attitude of German spectators instigated by anti-French Nazi propaganda. Noteworthy lifters were able to settle World records in more than one bodyweight class. Before Hostin, the Italian Carlo Galimberti became first lifter to get three Olympic medals, capturing the title in 1924 and silver medals in 1928 and 1932.[29]

The Olympics of Berlin 1936 marked several features. In the lightweight, the golden medal went *ex aequo* to Egyptian Ahmed Mesbah and the Austrian-Jew Robert Fein. Spectators and organizational staff damaged Fein, who in 1938 was disappeared from the scene with the Nazi annexation of Austria. In the middleweight, the Egyptian Touni proved the best lifter after explicating refusing the request of affiliation offered by Adolf Hitler. In the featherweight, Italian-born Anthony Terlazzo took first gold for United States. He was a product of the "York" school, where several sons of emigrants practiced, and led by Bob Hoffmann, who advocated the US national regeneration and the conquest of international strength field. Strength workouts were linked to severe diet and satisfying sexual activity.[30]

At the outbreak of the Second World War, Germans occupied the FIH's Secretariat in Paris and recognized records of Axis-aligned countries. Former Workers' World record holder Austrian Franz Huhsar was segregated in the concentration camps.[31] But the victors of the Second World War upset this trend. In 1946, the newly re-organized international governing body re-wrote, like in the 1920s, the history, re-instating three records of 1939 settled under the Japanese flag, as South Korean.[32] The Cold War exploded also through weightlifting, where the United States and the USSR acted as super-powers. The first black winner of World championships in 1938, John Davis became a hero, dominating the heavyweight field until 1953. Gradually, the USSR prevailed, but US lifters carried out great achievements with Japanese origins Tommy Kono or with Norbert Schemansky, first lifter to win four Olympic medals. In 1969, during the World championships of Warsaw, US-Pole Bob Bednarski was subject to unfair decisions, but finally won the title and the public supported him as a form of underground dissent to Communist regime.[33]

Post-war and the rising of powerlifting

The American, Paul Anderson, Olympic champion in Melbourne 1956, led the way for affirmation of powerlifting, setting World records in repetition squats. His compatriot Peary Rader popularized the ancient practice of lying press that developed soon into the bench press. Since its sporadic appearance in March 1891, dead-lift had developed underground and in 1920 the German Hermann Görner won sensational but still controversial records. The three competitions joined in a coded sport. Since 1963 in the milieu of bodybuilders and fans of muscular development, the term powerlifter had begun to circulate. Success was significant and rapid and in 1965 the AAU organized its first national meet, later in 1971 York organized the first World Championships.[34] Simultaneously, women's powerlifting was being organized and in 1980 the first World championships took place in Nashua, New Hampshire.[35]

In 1972, the press was excluded from official international championships because the lifters indulged excessively in the Continental-shaped backbending. According to John Fair this played a crucial role in the affirmation of powerlifting. Bench press allowed records over 500 kg, a significant and impressive note for the records. Young Anglo-Saxon talents chose massively powerlifting over Olympic weightlifting. First World championships took place in 1978 and later Ed Coan became a star. His fame as Strongest Man on Earth contrasted with that of Soviet Vassili Alexejev, ten-time world champion, winner of 80 world records and two Olympics. In the words of John Fair, in the 1980s steroid abuses led to a trivialization of the sport. He riterated that they ruined health and corrupted results and he denounced it as a dangerous social issue. As Todd emphasized, young people were attracted by the prospective of having a stronger and more successful physique through medical enhancement. The steroids could bring about the sports downfall.[36] However, in the same period, when the USSR defended its leading role from challenges of Eastern European and Asian countries, the re-named International Weightlifting Federation (IWF) confronted the plague of doping. IWF introduced random tests in 1985, and subsequently disqualified several athletes and even national teams.[37]

Strongmanism obscuring classic strength sports

From the second half of the 1970s, a form of strongmanism recuperated the older tradition composed of weight carrying, burden and harness lifting, and connected it with new televisual requirements of sporting spectacle. Covered by private network Trans World International (TWI) new industrially refurbished strength sports were affirmed. The reformulated Highland Games resumed and since 1977 the contest for World's Strongest Man challenged directly the results of Olympic weightlifting. Race carrying of sacks, pushing of stones, vehicle (trucks) pulls were introduced. Weight and power lifters, shot putters, wrestlers joined other strength-gifted people in these contests, characterized by ethnic distinctiveness particularly from Scandinavian and Baltic countries. Exuberant Jón Páll Sigmarsson became the hero of Iceland and an international star. As in the words of David Webster "these strongmen from different lands are the true modern gladiators". In 1995, the test of farmer's walk (weights in hand) added exciting appeal to the contests.[38] The contemporary sporting strength concept re-discovered the potentiality of the entire body that older pioneers set aside. To the contemporary eyes, tests of Olympic weightlifting appeared insufficient to be credible proof for measuring strength and power.

In 1981 the IWF mandated a Commission composed of historians and experts for retouching the official history. The results issued in 1986 and almost all the unofficial international events before the First World War and from 1920 to 1924 were a posteriori recuperated and a new numbered lineage of World and European championships released and archived. The championships of 28 March 1891 assumed the role of first of the list, while that of 30 March was discarded. Medals won by Austrian athletes for greater Germany in the World Championships of 1938 were attributed to Austria, so responding and accepting what had been done previously for South Korea.[39]

Since the 1960s, women fought for equal rights and social opportunities, obtaining some results. In the United States, Title IX of 1972 opened the possibility for women to access sport on an equal level to men; progress was also made in Europe on this front. Italy's Family Law in 1975 parified the legal status of women. These acquisitions radiated slowly into the sporting world, where the amount of female athletes increased. In weightlifting, women were able to officially enter regular competitions and in 1987 the first official World championships took place and the Olympics of Sydney 2000 was open to female competitors. Seven bodyweight classes had official schemes for women, being the heaviest reserved to lifters over 75 kg. Men's classes had increased to ten in 1980, from the year 2000 they were reduced to eight, with new weight limits and the heaviest class reserved to athletes over 105 kg. In women's weightlifting, China but also Columbia and Thailandia were successful and in these latter countries the achievements increased the social consideration of women. In male competitions, China reigns in lighter classes, while Kazakhstan, Russia, Ukraine and Iran are the other leading countries.[40]

The lightweight Turkish triple Olympic champion Halil Mutlu jerked the triple of his bodyweight, while superheavies elevated about two and a half times. The era of open professionalism allowed the prolongation of the careers. Ethnic appeals persuaded the triple Olympic champions Naim Suleymanoglu to leave Bulgaria for Turkey, Pyrros Dimas from Albania to Greece and Akiad Kakhasvili from Georgia to Greece.[41]

The Paralympics broke another barrier allowing access to strength sports for disabled people. Since Tokyo 1964 the bench press is the only competition in the Paraolympic programmes of powerlifting featuring a contest for four bodyweight classes for men with spinal cord injuries. In the successive years, the number of classes had increased and in 2000 women debuted for the first time. In the Paralympics of Rio de Janeiro 2016, ten contests for men and ten for women were scheduled. The most successful countries were China, Nigeria, Iran and Egypt.

Currently, the World's Strongest Man contests are given encouragement and meet with wide acceptance. For the public, the duel between the Pole Mariusz Pudzianowski and the Lithuanian Zydrunas Savickas represents the most reliable parameter for the proclamation of the Strongest Man on Earth.[42]

In 2017, Olympic weightlifting faced another crisis of credibility due to doping. The IWF banned for one year the teams from Russia, Kazakhstan, Armenia, Azerbaijan, Belarus, Moldova, Ukraine, Turkey and China. On the other side, strongmanism is enjoying increased popularity, television profits and growing consent. However, only oversized people tend to enter this sport while Olympic weightlifting can be practised by lighter men and women, so Olympic weightlifting keeps intact the values of a standardized and healthy sport.[43]

Notes

1 L. Toschi, *The Myth of Strength. Story of Weightlifting from the Antiquity to the nineteenth century* (Rome: IWF-EWF, 2001), pp. 30, 32, 24; D. Webster, *The Iron Game* (Irvine: IWF, 1976), pp. 5–6; Mark Holowchak, "Early Greek Influence on Sport. (Part III). Legendary Figures of Greek Sports" in *MILO. The Journal of Serious Strength Athletes*, 4(1996)3, pp. 44–46.
2 L. Toschi, *The Myth of Strength.*, cit. p. 60.
3 J. McLelland, *Body and Mind: Sport in Europe from the Roman Empire to the Renaissance* (London/New York: Routledge, 2006), pp. 88–89.
4 L. Toschi, *The Myth of Strength*, p. 66; E. Desbonnet, *Traité de l'athletisme* (Paris: Levrault & Berger, 1906), p. 115; D. Webster, *The Iron Game*, p. 9.
5 Jan Todd, "From Milo to Milo: A History of Barbells, Dumbells and Indian Clubs" in *Iron Game History*, 3(1995)6, p. 10.
6 E. Desbonnet, "Hyppolite Triat" (translated from French by D. Chapman), in *Iron Game History*, 4(1995)1, pp. 3–10; J. Todd, "The Strength Builders: A History of Barbells, Dumbbells and Indian Clubs"

in *International Journal of the History of sport*, 20(2003)1, pp. 73–75; D. Sargent "The Physical Development of Woman" in *Scribner Magazine*, 5(1899)1, pp. 172–188 (quote 184).

7 L. Toschi, *The Myth of Strength*, p. 78.

8 D. Webster, *The World History of Highland Games* (Edinburgh: Luath Press, 2011), pp. 69–78.

9 A. Krüger, A. Ito, "On the Limitations of Eichberg's and Mandell Theory for Sports and their Quantification in View of Chikaraishi", in (eds.) J.M. Carter and A. Krüger, *Ritual and Record. Sports Records and Quantification in Pre-modern Societies* (Westport: Greenwood Press, 1990), pp. 103–114.

10 *New York Clipper Annual 1900*, p. 115; G. Schödl, *The Lost Past. Concealed or Forgotten?* (Budapest: IWF, 1992), pp. 26–30.

11 G. Bonini, "The Father of Modern Weightlifting: Edmond Desbonnet" in *MILO. The Journal of Serious Strength Athletes*, 15(2008)4, pp. 108–110; Bernd Wedemeyer-Kolwe, *Der Athletenvater Theodor Siebert (1866–1961)* (Göttingen: Verlag Klatt, 1999); about masters and styles, *The First Italian Dictionary of Weightlifting* (Florence: Author, 2006), pp. 2–5, 50.

12 G. Schödl, *The Lost Past*, pp. 58–59; T. Siebert, *Katechismus der Athletik* (Weissenfels: Lehmstedt, 1898), pp. 98–104.

13 E. Ravenstein and J. Hulley, *Handbook of Gymnastics and Athletics* (London: Trübner & Co., 1867) pp. 258–260 and 268; D. Webster, *Iron Game*, pp. 13–14.

14 D. Chapman, *Sandow the Magnificent* (Urbana, IL: University of Illinois Press, 2003), pp. 23–32.

15 B. Weider, *The Strongest Man in History. Louis Cyr. Amazing Canadian* (Nevada City: Ironmind Enterprises, 2000); E. Desbonnet, "Apollon. The Emperor of the Athletes" (English version by D. Chapman), in *Iron Game History*, 4(1997)5–6, pp. 23–47; G: Bonini, "The Nietzschean Superlifter: Wilhelm Türk", in *MILO. The Journal of Serious Strength Athletes*, pp. 32–34.

16 E. Desbonnet, *Les Rois de la Force* (Paris: Librairie Berger & Levrault, 1911), p. 401; G. Bonini, *The first Italian dictionary*, cit. pp. 70–71.

17 G. Bonini, "London the Cradle of Modern Weightlifting" in *The Sport Historian* 21(2001)1, pp. 56–70; G. Fahey, *E. Lawrence Levy and Muscular Judaism, 1851–1932* (Miami: Eudun Mellen Press, 2014).

18 B. Mallon, *The 1896 Olympic Games. Results for all Competitors in all Events with Commentary* (Jefferson: McFarland Press, 1998), pp. 111–114; B. Mallon, *The 1904 Olympic Games. Results for all Competitors in all Events with Commentary* (Jefferson: McFarland Press, 1999), pp. 194–196.

19 B. Mallon, *The 1906 Olympic Games. Results for all Competitors in all Events with Commentary* (Jefferson: McFarland Press, 1999), pp. 144–147.

20 Amateur Gymnastics Association, *Handbook 1902–1903* (Birmingham: Hammond, 1903), p. 36; G. Bonini "Emil Kliment: The first Continental double raiser" in *MILO. The Journal of Serious Strength Athletes*, 19(2012)4, pp. 69–70.

21 G. Schödl, *The Lost Past*, pp. 20–21; D. Webster, *The Iron Game*, pp. 31–32, 80; G. Bonini, "The German Meteor: Hermann Gässler" in *MILO. The Journal of Serious Strength Athletes*, 13(2006)4, pp. 54–55.

22 B. Kidd, "Sports and masculinity", in *Sport in Society*, 16(2013)4, pp. 553–554.

23 B. Mallon, *The 1920 Olympic Games. Results for all Competitors in all Events with Commentary* (Jefferson: McFarland Press, 2003), pp. 303–308; D. Webster, *The Iron Game*, pp. 24–26.

24 W. Vierath, *Moderner Sport* (Berlin: Oestergaard Verlag, 1930), pp. 129–130.

25 G. Bonini "Politics and ideological representation in Weightlifting history with focus for years 1919–1947" in (eds.) C. Faniopoulos, E. Albanidis, *Sports in Education from Antiquity to Modern Times. Proceedings of the 18th International Congress of the European Committee for Sports History (CESH)* (Edessa: Municipal Enterprise, 2015), pp. 95–100; G. Schödl, *The Lost Past*, cit. p. 201 on Soviet records; G. Bonini, "Workers Weightlifting Movement" in *MILO. The Journal of Serious Strength Athletes*, 22(2014)3, pp. 56–58.

26 André Bourdonnay-Schwech, "Poids et haltères" in AA.VV. *Encyclopédie des Sports* (Paris: Librairie de France, 1924–1926), vol. 2, pp. 76–78; B. Hoffman, *Weightlifting* (York: S&H, 1939), pp. 170 and 172.

27 J. Todd "Weightlifting " in K. Christensen, D. Levinson, G. Pfister, *The International Encyclopedia of Women Sport* (Great Barrington: MacMillan Reference Group, 2001), volume 3, pp. 1261.

28 G. Bonini, "The Era of Rigoulot" in *MILO. The Journal of Serious Strength Athletes*, cit. 22(2014)1, pp. 70–71.

29 G. Bonini "The First Double Olympic Champion: Louis Hostin" in *MILO. The Journal of Serious Strength Athletes*, 22(2014)2, pp. 46–47; hints to Galimberti, see G. Bonini "Paris 1924: The Unforgettable Italian Triumph" in *MILO. The Journal of Serious Strength Athletes*, pp. 23–25.

30 Fein, Robert www.sports-reference.com (May 20, 2016); about Terlazzo, J. Fair "A Century of American Weightlifting in the Olympics, 1896–1996" in *The International Journal of the History of Sport*, 15(1998)3,

p. 22; J. Fair, *Muscletown USA. Bob Hoffman and the Manly culture of York Barbell* (Park: Pennsylvania University Press, 2000), pp. 2–4.

31 Walter Farthofer, *Tramway Geschichte(n). Strassenbahner im Kampf gegen der grünen und braunen Faschismus* (Vienna: OGB Verlag, 2012), p. 324.

32 G. Schödl, *The Lost Past*, pp. 210–212, 213; on South Korea *Strength and Health*, 16(1947)11, pp. 22, 37; criticisms G. Bonini "Politics and Ideological Representation in Weightlifting History with Focus for Years 1919–1947", p. 98.

33 Bednarski, Robert, https://en.wikipedia.org/wiki/Bob_Bednarski (Accessed 24 June 2016).

34 J. Fair "Powerlifting" in (eds) D. Levinson, K. Christensen *Berkshire Encyclopedia of World Sport* (Great Barrington: Berkshire Publishing Group, 2005), volume 3, pp.1212–1213; G. Bonini, M. Kodya, J. Roark, "Was Hermann Goerner really Mighty?" in *Iron Game History*, 9(2007)2, pp. 21–33.

35 J. Todd "Powerlifting " in K. Christensen, D. Levinson, G. Pfister, *The International Encyclopedia of Women Sport* (Great Barrington: MacMillan Reference Group, 2001), volume 2, pp. 899–902.

36 John Fair in www.post-gazette.com/news/health/2005/10/02/Never-Enough-Steroids-in-Sports-Experiment-turns-epidemic/stories/200510020264 (September 25, 2017); Terry Todd "Anabolic Steroids. The Gremlins of Sport" in Journal of Sport History, 14(1987)1, pp. 87–107.

37 G. Schödl, *The Lost Past*, cit. pp. 152–155; Bulgaria's case see www.nytimes.com/1988/09/24/sports/the-seoul-olympics-weight-lifting-team-lifted-after-2d-drug-test-is-failed.html (Accessed 24 June 2016).

38 D. Webster, *The Sons of Samson. Volume 2. Profiles* (Nevada City: Ironmind Enterprises, 1998) p. 63.

39 G. Schödl, *The Lost Past*, pp. 151–152.

40 J. Todd "Weightlifting" in K. Christensen, D. Levinson, G. Pfister, *The International Encyclopedia of Women Sport*, vol. 3, pp. 1260–1264.

41 P. Coffa, "Naim Suleimanoglu: Defection" in *MILO. The Journal of Serious Strength Athletes*, 15(2007)3, pp. 82–88; Dimas, Pyrros www.sport-references.com/olympics/athletes/di/pyrros-dimas-1.html; Kakhasvili, Akiad in www.sport-references.com/olympics/athletes/ka/akakios-kakiasvili-1.html (Accessed 24 June 2016).

42 A. Holowchak, "Pudzianowski vs. Savickas: Who is the Greatest All-Time Strongman?" in *MILO. The Journal of Serious Strength Athletes*, 18(2010)2, pp. 114–118.

43 Greg Everett, *Olympic Weightlifting for Sport: The Yes, When and How*, in *MILO. The Journal of Serious Strength Athletes*, 20(2012)3, pp. 48–49.

Part VI
Leisure and lifestyle sports

35

E-sports

Jacob Hindin, Matthew Hawzen, Hanhan Xue,
Haozhou Pu and Joshua Newman

In recent years, the world has witnessed a phenomenal growth of professional organized video game competitions, known more commonly as 'e-sports.'[1] The letter 'e' in e-sports represents 'electronic,' which denotes that e-sports is largely dependent on digital and computer-mediated content; 'sports' within such nomenclature refers to the gaming form's organized, immediate, and competitive features. Hollist describes e-sports simply as: 'professional video game matches where players compete against other players before an audience' (Hollist, 2015, p. 825). Taylor (2012) goes further to suggest that e-sports 'represents the configuration of competitive video gaming as spectatorial and professionalized sport' (p. 1).

E-sports is not limited to the digital gaming practices of 'traditional' sports such as soccer, basketball, or football – even though such simulations of 'traditional' sports could also be included as part of e-sports (such as EA Sports' FIFA and Madden NFL franchises) (Hamari & Sjöblom, 2017). It is also practiced through highly competitive, tournament-style, mass-mediated events that bring together top gamers from around the world to compete in avatar-based fantasy battle games. Hence, we might refer to e-sports as any organized multiplayer video game competition – such as *League of Legends, Dota 2* (Defense of the Ancients), and *Starcraft* – where individuals and teams assemble in stadia and arenas to compete in sanctioned, real-time, broadly-streamed, financially-incentivized, and widely-attended tournament events. The domain of e-sports now includes a vast variety of genres including fighting games, first person shooters (FPS), real time strategy (RTS), massively multiplayer online role-playing game (MMORPG), and multiplayer online battle arena games (MOBA). Each e-sports event consists of event organizers, officials, sponsors, broadcast teams, news reporters, and tens of thousands of spectators congregating in professional sports venues – while millions of 'gamers' watch live online streams and television broadcasts from other locales around the world.

When defined so broadly, today e-sports is an incredibly popular, deeply professionalized, and highly commercialized feature of the global sport-media landscape (Taylor, 2012, 1–33). By some estimates, global revenues from the e-sports market related to video gaming commerce are expected to reach $1 billion[2] by 2019 (Riddell, 2016). According to a *Sport Business Journal* report, 205 million people watched or played e-sports games in 2014. In 2015, corporate sponsorship of e-sports was estimated at $111 million in North America, and the total global prize pool for major e-sports events reached $165.4 million (Lefton, 2015).

Most recently, e-sports events have drawn considerable interest from traditional sports and media corporations. In January 2016, ESPN launched a vertical site dedicated to covering global e-sports tournaments, events, players, and gaming trends. In late 2015, Turner Broadcasting System (TBS) and IMG partnered to create a 20-event broadcast schedule of *Counter-Strike* e-sports events for the 2016 calendar year. Further, it has been reported that Disney/ESPN is in negotiations with Riot Games to broadcast League of Legends events across ESPN online and television platforms for $500 million.

Besides media corporations, universities and institutions are also making their incursions into the field of electronic gaming. In the United States, a number of university athletic programs have in the past three years developed university-sponsored competitive video gaming teams. Operating under the same budget as their competitive NCAA football, basketball, and baseball teams, e-sports teams at Robert Morris University, University of California, Irvine, Columbia College, Maryville University, and Southwestern University now compete in online and in-person tournaments around the United States. In Australia, Australian University Games (AUS) – the governing body for intercollegiate sport competitions – sanctioned League of Legends as an 'official sport' in May 2016, for which AUS will maintain governance oversight (Walker, 2016).

Are e-sports 'sports'?

Where e-sports sit relative to traditional sports is a matter of definition. Allen Guttmann developed a list of distinguishing features for modern sport in *From Ritual to Record* (1978), defined as activities that involve 'physical, competitive, and organized play in contrast to spontaneous play, non-competitive games and intellectual contests' (Jonasson & Thiborg, 2010, p. 289). In Guttmann's construct, unorganized, spontaneous play become games when rules and structure are added; some games can then be classified as contests dependent on adding the element of competition, and these contests can be divided into intellectual contests and physical contests, which he calls sports (Jonasson & Thiborg, 2010). E-sports can be seen as fulfilling the requirements of being organized, competitive, and physical. As Witkowski (2012) argues, e-sports differ from intellectual contests in that the kinesthetic ability of the player determines the outcome of the match. Compared to the intellectual contest of chess, where the movement of the piece is unrelated to the player's actions (e.g. a grandmaster could dictate orders to a stand-in with no difference in performance), the ability of an e-sport competitor to manipulate their avatar, select actions, or aim within a game will directly impact the result (Witkowski, 2012). Jenny, Manning, Keiper, and Olrich (2016), however, draw a distinction between fine motor skills and gross motor skills (moving large parts of the body), arguing that some definitions of sport require gross motor action, a requirement e-sports will not meet unless motion-based video games (those that track gross motor movements) are implemented.

Guttmann also argued that modern sports differ from ancient sports in certain aspects, namely a movement towards bureaucratization, rationalization, quantification, record-keeping, secularization, and equality (Jonasson & Thiborg, 2010). E-sports fulfill many of these qualifications, as they have no outward religious aspect (secularization), force players to abide by the same rules (equality), lend themselves more easily to quantification of performance than traditional sports, and have a long history of record-tracking (Jonasson & Thiborg, 2010). However, e-sports lack the overarching bureaucratization of global sports such as football (FIFA) or the Olympics (IOC), instead having several competing organizations competing for supremacy on the nascent international scene (Jonasson & Thiborg, 2010; Jenny et al., 2016). As discussed below, global governance is one of the current challenges facing the emerging e-sport market.

E-sports and the experience economy

E-sports fans tend to skew younger-roughly 28% may be over 35, although 84% are over 21 (Casselman, 2015). Seo (2013) has argued that e-sports represent a provision of the emerging experience economy driven by younger consumers. The experience economy represents a shift from the service sector to an economic sector where consumers pay to experience memorable events. There are four areas of perceived consumer experience collectively known as the '4Es': educational, escapist, esthetic, and entertainment, which many e-sports events fulfill, such as learning through education experiences or enjoying a performance through an entertainment experience, which may represent a shift towards the desires of younger adults (Seo, 2013).

The early development of e-sports

E-sports roots lie within the dawn of computerized gaming and the development of competitive game environments. Much of the current competitive videogame market may be traced back to the 1962 debut of *Spacewar,* one of the first multiplayer games distributed among multiple machines (Lowood, 2009). *Spacewar* was developed at MIT to demonstrate the power of a new microcomputer and included two players, each controlling a spaceship and attempting to eliminate the other. The program spread from MIT to other research institutions, adding in unique code at each spot. The game reached its zenith during the 1972 '*Spacewar* Olympics' at Stanford University (Lowood, 2009). The small competition of approximately two dozen players represented one of the first physical gatherings of competitive gaming and was covered by *Rolling Stone,* primarily for the novelty of the occasion (Lowood, 2009).

By the 1908s the arcade scene in the United States had fully exploded. A series of popular and inventive games such as *Centipede, Pac-Man,* and *Galaga* drew many players to the arcades (Borowy & Jin, 2013). Numerous live tournaments were also organized during this time period, primarily sponsored by game companies. The mid-1970s All Japan TV Game Championships in Tokyo were sponsored by Sega (a Japanese multinational video game company), while the 1980 First National *Space Invaders* Competition was sponsored by Atari, manufacturer of the arcade case (Borowy & Jin, 2013). The national *Space Invaders* tournament was the first large-scale videogame competition in the United States, attracting over 10,000 participants from the regional rounds through the final in New York (Borowy & Jin, 2013).

The new media attention birthed the first wave of e-sports (proto) celebrities and professionals. These included Ben Gold, a contestant on the reality game show *That's Incredible,* whom Walter Day considered the first video game champion; Leo Daniels, who earned five national records and used his celebrity to attract business to the arcade he managed; and Roy Schildt, whose expertise at *Missile Command* among others, earned him sponsorships from Taco Bell and Nike (Borowy & Jin, 2013). Similar to golf, contestants played against 'the course' and then compared performances. This, however, quickly changed with the widespread emergence of home consoles and the advent of the Internet age.

The widespread adoption of home video game consoles from the mid-1980s to 1990s brought gaming to living rooms across the world. Unlike personal computer gaming, consoles are stand-alone devices that are usually connected to televisions and played with specifically designed game controllers as opposed to mice and keyboards. Including consoles such as the Nintendo Entertainment System, Sega Genesis, Sony PlayStation, and Microsoft Xbox, the consoles of the late 20th century eased access to competitive gaming. Gaming magazines such as *Nintendo Power* and *Sega Visions* kept and published records to encourage competitions (Taylor, 2012, 6), and in 1990 Nintendo held the Nintendo World Championships, a touring competition within the United States. Consoles allowed multiple players to directly compete against each other without purchasing multiple play chances such as in an arcade, allowing for longer game sessions. By projecting the display of the game on televisions rather than personal monitors, consoles also acted as a catalyst for passive consumption of games by other members of the family or friends of players, prefiguring the rise of e-sport spectatorship (Taylor, 2012, 184).

The development of e-sports has also come about in conjunction with the digital interconnectivities brought about by the launching of the worldwide web in 1989. From the early 1990s onward, advances in software and hardware (network) technologies allowed video game players to connect in real-time multiplayer gaming scenarios. In the early days, competitions were carried out over the Internet or through Local Area Networks (LAN), where both smaller and larger numbers of computers were linked together in one network. The most popular genres within multiplayer online gaming environs were FPS, RTS, and sports games (see Jonasson & Thiborg, 2010). In FPS games, the player controls an avatar, the virtual representation of a human or creature in the game. The only thing visible of the avatars on the screen are the hands and the weapons they handle, with the goal being to 'shoot' enemy players, akin to an immersive, complex shooting gallery. FPS games may be structured for individual battles (such as in the *Doom* or *Quake* series) or as team-based matches with objectives such as in the *Team Fortress* series or *Counter-Strike* (a series which has sold more than 10 million copies since 2000). *Counter-Strike* in particular has remained popular, especially in Europe; the game pits teams of five against each other, one attempting to plant a bomb and the other attempting to stop it (Witkowski, 2012).

Emerging e-sports leagues

The late 1990s to early 2000s saw the development of the first organized e-sport leagues with regular scheduling and structured seasons. Over time the number of different games in which organized, prize-based competitions are held has increased. E-sports organizations defunct and ongoing such as the World Cyber Games (WCG), Electronic Sports World Cup (ESWC), Major League Gaming (MLG), Professional Gamers League (PGL), Championship Gaming Series (CGS), and Cyberathlete Professional League (CPL) – in cooperation with corporations within the computer game industry – arranged LAN competitions at both national and international levels. The earliest leagues consisted of both the PGL – an ephemeral production founded in 1997 that included competitions in *Quake* and *Starcraft* with Nolan Bushnell as its first commissioner – and the CPL that was founded by Angel Munoz in the same year (Taylor, 2012, 1–34).

The CPL attracted media attention (such as MTV specials) and offered an example for other leagues to follow (Kane, 2008, 117). However, after years of declining events, the league was sold in 2008, reorganized to host several events in China, and eventually stopped production. CPL management was later accused of shady business dealings, deception, and issues with delayed or never-paid prize money from tournaments, clouding its final years (Taylor, 2012, 9). The fickle nature of emerging markets meant that many of the first e-sports leagues were short lived, including the WCG.

The WCG began in 2000 as a product of the South Korean competitive e-sports scene, and was created by a collaboration of the South Korean government and private investors (Hutchins, 2008). The games patterned themselves after the Olympic Games, complete with medal count, opening and closing ceremonies, and nationalized competitors (Hutchins, 2008). Entrants would go through numerous rounds of regional qualifying before the winners were invited to the annual grand finals, held in South Korea for the first four years before being rotated among the US, Europe, and Asia. Total prize money for the competition rose from an initial $200,000 to approximately $500,000 at its peak, with over 70 nations and 700 competitors represented at the 2007 finals. The WCG claimed that approximately one million players globally entered the events, when all of the numerous national preliminary rounds were included (Hutchins, 2008). The 2009 finals in Chengdu, China attracted over 82,000 live spectators, while the 2010 finals in Los Angeles attracted over 32, 000 (Taylor, 2012, 206). The WCG also exhibited the push towards rationalization and bureaucratization that may increasingly be seen as e-sports undergoing 'sportification' (Jonasson & Thiborg, 2010, p. 292). As with many of the nascent e-sports organizations, the WCG did not prove to be as stable as some of the more well-established e-sports leagues – the competition was shut down in 2014.

That the WCG originated in South Korea is no surprise. Since the 1990s South Korea has taken a leading place in global e-sports structuring, acting not only as '…what a professional scene that has entered the cultural mainstream can actually look like, but for the imaginative (even mythical) power it holds for those trying to foster pro gaming in North America and Europe' (Taylor, 2012, p. 18). The emergence of e-sports in South Korea may be traced back to the 1997 Asian Financial Crisis. Following the crisis, the South Korean government decided to invest in information technology as a developmental goal. Between 1998 and 2002 $11 billion was invested into the country's Internet network (Li, 2016, 35). This investment has led to South Korean consumers having access to very fast Internet connections, with over 95% of the population having access to broadband Internet (Jin, 2010, 20). Access fees are also cheap – monthly fees for Internet usage fell from roughly $40 in 1999 to under $20 by 2006, at which time US consumers still spent on average more than $50 per month (Li, 2016, 35). PC bangs (24/7 Internet cafes that provide relatively cheap hourly access to gaming computers) became popular after the financial crisis as laid off workers searched for something to do. The PC Bangs then acted as primary setting for the development of competitive gaming (Jin, 2010, 22–25). As of 2012 the South Korean gaming economy surpassed $5 billion with over 50% of the population playing online games (Taylor, 2012, 17).

This level of activity has led to government involvement in the South Korean e-sports scene. In 2004 its Game Industry Promotion 5-Year Plan was instituted to foster online gaming and e-sports – included in the plan was support for e-sports festivals, academic research and game development (Jin, 2010, 67). The largest step South Korea has taken is the formation of the Korean e-Sports Association (KeSPA) in 2000, a nongovernmental body that was nonetheless created with the approval of the Ministry of Culture and Tourism (Taylor, 2012, 25). KeSPA catalyzed the bureaucratization of e-Sports within South Korea. KeSPA has managed numerous tournaments, overseen construction of dedicated e-sports stadiums, aided in securing sponsorships, handled broadcast rights, and registered and tracked professional gamers in South Korea as well as structuring their path to professionalization (Taylor, 2012, 161–162).

The rise of major e-sports events

While various e-sports leagues and organizations have experienced both pronounced successes and failures, game publishers and developers, such as Blizzard, Valve Corporation, and Riot Games, have become robust players in steering new development of e-sports. In particular, those game developers have specifically designed and modified games to attract more participants and spectators of different age and gender groups, leading up to the rise of large-scale professionalized e-sports events.

The most popular genre became known as multiplayer online battle arenas (MOBAs), which generally consist of two teams of five players and each player attempts to destroy their opponents' base. Each team consists of five 'heroes' who must strategically navigate pathways to their opponents' base that is occupied by enemy minions and powerful defensive turrets, while defending their own. The most popular MOBA titles include Riot Game's *League of Legends* (LoL) and the Valve Corporation's *Dota 2*. Both games operate on a free-to-play basis, with charges for extras such as unlocking additional characters. The low initial expense for participants has led up to massive player activity in both games – as of 2013 *Dota 2* had four million unique players each month, while LoL averaged 32 million per month (Funk, 2013).

LoL was launched by the Riot Games in 2009 and has been at the forefront of the e-sports revolution. In elite competition, LoL teams – similar to traditional sports teams – feature athletes, coaches, analysts, sponsors, fans, as well as media contracts and merchandise. To date, the game has been featured in more than 1,260 tournaments and over 2,700 professional players around the world (Aaron, 2015). In organizing their events, Riot Games has collectively offered over $19 million in prize pools, and viewership has skyrocketed as well. For comparison, in 2014, more than 27 million viewers watched the LoL World Championship and the average viewership number of the NFL was 17.6 million (Aaron, 2015). The 2014 competition as a whole saw 288 million cumulative daily unique impressions, according to the organizer Riot Games.

As large-scale international events, the production of major e-sports tournaments might be considered what Roche (2000) describes as mega-events. In 2015, for instance, several e-sports events – produced in joint effort by multinational corporations and governing bodies – substantially grew the e-sports market by facilitating competition and captivating audiences. In January 2015, the *Dota 2* Asia Championships in Shanghai, China, featured 20 teams made up of five players competing for a share of the $3 million prize pool. Later in August of that year, Valve sold out the KeyArena in Seattle, Washington for The International 2015, which featured 16 teams from around the world competing for a share of the $18.4 million prize pool.[3]

This trend has further expanded to another game genre: sports video games. Sports games have become increasingly popular. In sports games, game players control digital representations of popular athletes from traditional (or modern) sports in a simulated game, match, season, or race. Popular titles in this genre are the FIFA football series (nearly $10 billion in total sales) and the Madden NFL game (which has totaled more than $4 billion in sales in the US alone). Borrowing from the FPS and RTS platforms, the major sports game manufacturers EA Sports has in recent years enacted a number of initiatives to grow their live event market. 'It is evident to us that this represents a large and important growth opportunity for the company,' noted Peter Moore, chief operating officer at Electronic Arts, 'This has the feeling of a great startup, but a startup within a $4.5 billion company with three decades of experience in gaming' (quoted in Fisher & Thomas, 2016, 1).

Apart from MOBA, RTS, FPS, and sports genres, fighting games, as practiced by the fighting game community (FGC), have emerged as a major part of the e-sports biome. Most fighting games consist of two players controlling characters in a two-dimensional plane attempting to defeat the opposing player. Mimicking boxing or traditional combat sports, each player has commands that correspond to punches, kicks, throws, and special moves. Fast-paced execution and timing is paramount to victory. Popular titles within the FGC include the *Street Fighter* series, the *Mortal Kombat* series, and the *Super Smash Bros.* series. Fighting game competitions often revolve around locally organized match nights at arcades or gaming halls which function as both social occasions and opportunities for high-level competition and local bragging rights. Major e-sports events on fighting games are either organized wherein the players qualify through smaller regional events or are invited directly, or as 'open' competitions, where every player who attends is afforded a spot in the bracket. The most notable fighting tournament is the Evolution Championship Series, or simply Evo. Evo started as Battle by the Bay in 1996 within the San Francisco area, and was rebranded as Evolution in 2002, with the championship eventually moving to Las Vegas (Cravens, 2014, 18). The tournament now bills itself as the world's largest fighting game event, and has gotten significant number of spectators. The final of Evo 2016's *Street Fighter V* segment was broadcast live on ESPN2.

Media consumption of e-sports

While television coverage of e-sports, such as the EVO2016 final, is becoming more common, the primary ways for media consumption of e-sports continues to be online or in-person. Streaming sites, such as Twitch.tv, broadcast matches as well as provide a chatting service for viewers to communicate with each other in real-time. Streaming sites also provide a platform for individual professionals to host their own stream, broadcasting their recreational play or practice, allowing them to talk to fans directly (by reading the chat that accompanies their stream), as well as earning income from advertisers or sponsors. Online platforms may also host video on demand (VOD) or replays of concluded matches, mimicking a trend in traditional sports where VODs and replays are recycled and consumed at the viewer's leisure time (Taylor, 2012, 199–200). Games have also been adapted to make it easier to spectate. Popular titles such as *Starcraft* and *Counter-Strike* now have built-in functions to record and review matches (Taylor, 2012, 199). Originally, commentators would have to bundle audio with zip-files after the match or clumsily join as a neutral third-party and hide in order to observe the match from a non-playing computer. Developers eventually installed modes specifically for observation where commentators could view and move around a map naturally within the game (Li, 2016, 49).

Match commentators, often called 'shoutcasters' or simply 'casters,' have become an essential part of the e-sports consumption experience, and are often drawn from pools of ex- or current players (Taylor, 2012, 224–228). These announcers are used for all game types, although their roles may differ for certain genres that are difficult to understand by novices (fighting games, for instance, may be more 'viewer-friendly' than MOBAs that have complex tactical action across the broadcast). Matches may be wildly different in length (an RTS battle can be over in 10 minutes or an hour) and this uncertainty makes showing individual games difficult to fit with traditional advertisers (Taylor, 2012, 211–212). These difficulties present problems for television broadcasting for many games. However, successful television ventures have been undertaken, especially in South Korea, which has multiple channels devoted specifically to e-sports competition. For example, OGN (originally ongamenet), a South Korean e-sports-dedicated cable channel, was one of the first and has been in operation since 1999 (Jin, 2010, 68).

Emerging international e-sports governing bodies

The administration, governance, and management of various e-sports games/franchises has progressively been bureaucratized, taking a similar path to international sports such as football/soccer, volleyball, basketball, and athletics. Increasingly, governmental or pseudo-governmental institutions have been formed to administer e-sports. For instance, in early 2016 the Electronic Sports League – the world's largest competitive video gaming organization – announced the formation of the World eSports Association (WESA). The formation of the WESA represents the most significant effort (to date) to create an international governing body for competitive gaming. This international governing body will provide oversight of tournament scheduling and player contract mediation, look to curb the growing trend of match fixing, and seek to develop a comprehensive set of policies and procedures for dealing with the growing problem of doping in e-sports (see Waldron, 2016). WESA will also be responsible for promoting electronic gaming and tournament marketing in established and emerging markets across the global North.

Contemporary issues in e-sports

Violence in e-sports

One concern with the rise of E-Sports is the effect of violent games on behavior; many e-sports titles include actions that represent player avatars doing violence to other players (shooting, punching killing, etc. ...) and psychology researchers have warned that watching or playing violent media may make it more likely that individuals perform real-world violence (Anderson & Bushman, 2001). The results of studies have been mixed and the effect of violent media is an area of active research. Anderson and Bushman's (2001) meta-analysis found links between violent video games and aggressive behavior, cognition and affect. Anderson et al. (2008) found correlations between habitual violent video game play and later aggression within a longitudinal study of US and Japanese youth. Saleem, Anderson, and Gentile (2012) found that violent video games increased states of hostility, aggression, and mean feelings compared to neutral or 'prosocial games.'

However, the field is still unsettled on whether consuming violent video games leads to violence. Ferguson (2018) notes that 'false positive' results for studies linking violence to violent game consumption are prevalent and may be the result of publication biases favoring studies that show significant relationships. An open letter to the APA signed by over 200 scholars criticized making conclusions that violent games caused violence behavior as many studies in the field suffered from methodological issues and the meta-analyses of these papers may be flawed (Consortium of Scholars, 2013). The ultimate links between violence and gameplay remain at this time an open question.

Gender in e-sports

E-sports is played and watched primarily by men; there are no women players among the top 100 pro earners, and market research indicates 85% of the audience is male (Featherstone, 2017). Currently, most women's' teams and tournaments exist segregated from men's' tournaments in the fashion of traditional sports. Contemporary debate focuses on whether professional women competitors should participate within or parallel to existing tournaments. Arguments for separate women's teams note that women face institutional barriers to entry, including an 'initiation' culture that can be acutely sexist and the reticence of male organizers to include and 'skill-up' burgeoning female players in the same way they would male players. Separately organized and supported women's' teams allow for female gamers to benefit from networking opportunities as well as exposure. Conversely, arguments against separating women and men focus on how there may be no biological reason they cannot compete at the same level at e-sports and that separating players and tournaments reinforces divisions that may be more difficult to break down in the future (Taylor, 2012, 125–128).

These debates rest within a broader debate within gaming about traditional views of femininity and masculinity. Gaming, as a tech-heavy leisure pursuit, has often been associated with 'geek' culture, which provides opportunities for men to perform alternative masculinities or translate mainstream hegemonic masculinities. As a (once) marginalized subculture, this may display as either an embrace of alternative lifestyles or repudiation of traditional athletic norms, or as a reproduction and reclamation of masculine norms through the display of technological mastery as well as misogynistic behavior towards unproven female gamers. Many women choose to either hide their gender online, or to adopt hyper-masculinized or hyper-feminized identities within casual competitive play, a phenomenon reinforced by sponsors looking for particular identity displays for all-women teams. The complicated relationship between masculine and feminine performances are exacerbated as 'geek' culture and e-sports become increasingly mainstream, and the level of subculture differentiation dissolves. (Taylor, 2012, 110–125).

Disability e-sports

E-sports present uncertain opportunities for disabled gamers to compete. The nature of electronic interaction allows many gamers with impaired gross motor abilities chances to find workarounds, such as Mike 'Brolylegs' Begum, a fighting game competitor born with arthrogryposis and scoliosis who plays using his tongue for fine dexterity on a controller stick. Rumblevests have also been developed to assist hard of hearing or deaf gamers, while other competitions may alter their monitor/input setups to accommodate wheelchairs or other assist devices. However, there are currently no accessibility standards for tournaments and acceptance of certain modifications or adaptations will depend on the tournament organizer. Travelling to tournaments may impose financial costs on some competitors with disabilities, and whether modified controllers are allowed or other accommodations are made may depend on ad hoc decisions of tournament legality (Giampapa, 2016; Winkie, 2017).

Conclusion

While nascent compared to other sporting pursuits, the sustained growth of e-sports suggests that the activity will continue to play an important role within the sports ecosphere. The stakeholders and structure of the e-sports industry are still in flux. The connections between the tournament organizers, game developers, professional teams, sponsors, media organizations, and fans will continue to evolve to uncertain ends. Jonasson and Thiborg (2010) offer three scenarios: that e-sports develops into an alternative counterculture to mainstream hegemonic sports, that e-sports becomes accepted as part of mainstream hegemonic sports, or that e-sports itself becomes the new hegemonic sports, acting in concert within changing social conditions and the increasing importance of networked technologies. However e-sports ultimately ends up, its exploration of sporting spheres, both new and old, will continue to warrant further attention.

Notes

1 Exiting literature on e-sports has primarily focused on e-sports consumption, marketing, and experience economy (e.g. Borowy & Jin, 2013; Kirschner, 2015; Seo, 2013, 2016; Seo & Jung, 2014), legal aspects, ethical and moral issues, and regulation in e-sports industry (e.g. Blackburn, Kourtellis, Skvoretz, Ripeanu, & Iamnitchi, 2013; Comerford, 2012; Golub &Lingley, 2007; Hollist, 2015), e-sports and cultural life, social relations, and politics (e.g. Dyer-Witheford & de Peuter, 2009; Fisher & Jenson, 2016; Grimes & Feenberg, 2009; Hutchins, 2008; Millington, 2014; Simon, 2007), and the relationship between e-sports and the development of other industries and fields in particular sports and media (e.g. Burroughs & Rama, 2015; Crawford & Gosling, 2009; Jonasson & Thiborg, 2010; Rai & Yan, 2009).
2 Driven by the growth in e-sports market, the global digital gaming sales hit $61 billion in 2015 (DiChristopher, 2016).
3 Valve generates its record-size prize pools through crowdfunding and compendium sales—in game purchases that participants can make (during non-tournament play) (Tassi, 2015).

References

Aaron, J. (2015, February 18). The controversial dichotomy between sports and eSports. *The Huffington Post*, Retrieved from www.huffingtonpost.com/jesse-aaron/the-controversial-dichoto_b_6692052.html

Anderson, C.A., & Bushman, B.J. (2001). Effects of violent video games on aggressive behavior, aggressive cognition, aggressive affect, physiological arousal, and prosocial behavior: a meta-analytic review of the scientific literature. *Psychological Science*, 12(5), 353–359.

Anderson, C., Gentile, D., Anderson, C.A., Gentile, D.A., Sakamoto, A., Ihori, N., & . . . Naito, M. (2008). Longitudinal Effects of Violent Video Games on Aggression in Japan and the United States. *Pediatrics*, 122(5), E1067–E1072.

Blackburn, J., Kourtellis, N., Skvoretz, J., Ripeanu, M., & Iamnitchi, A. (2014). Cheating in online games: A social network perspective. *ACM Transactions on Internet Technology (TOIT)*, 13(3), 1–24.

Borowy, M., & Jin, D.Y. (2013). Pioneering e-sport: The experience economy and the marketing of early 1980s arcade gaming contests. *International Journal of Communication*, 7, 2254–2274.

Burroughs, B., & Rama, P. (2015). The eSports Trojan Horse: Twitch and streaming futures. *Journal For Virtual Worlds Research*, 8(2), 1–5.

Casselman, B. (2015, May 22). Resistance is futile: eSports is massive . . . and growing. *ESPN*. Retrieved from www.espn.com/espn/story/_/id/13059210/esports-massive-industry-growing

Comerford, S. (2012). International intellectual property rights and the future of global 'e-sports.' *Brooklyn Journal of International Law*, 37, 623.

Consortium of Scholars (2013). Scholar's open statement to the APA task force on violent media. Retrieved from www.scribd.com/doc/223284732/Scholar-s-Open-Letter-to-the-APA-Task-Force-On-Violent-Media-Opposing-APA-Policy-Statementson-Violent-Media.

Cravens, G. (2014) *Evo moment 37: One of the most famous moments in competitive gaming history.* Lexington, KY: Glenn Cravens.

Crawford, G., & Gosling, V.K. (2009). More than a game: Sports-themed video games and player narratives. *Sociology of Sport Journal*, 26, 50–66.

DiChristopher, T. (2016, January 26). Digital gaming sales hit record $61 billion in 2015: Report. *CNBC*, Retrieved from www.cnbc.com/2016/01/26/digital-gaming-sales-hit-record-61-billion-in-2015-report.html

Dyer-Witheford, N., & de Peuter, G. (2009). *Games of empire: Global capitalism and video games.* Minneapolis, MN: University of Minnesota Press.

Featherstone, E. (2017, June 8). Women in eSports: 'Ignore the stereotypes and do what you want'; Cyberbullying and the pay gap are just two of the hurdles facing female gamers, but that isn't holding them back. *The Guardian*.

Ferguson, C.J. (2018). The problem of false positives and false negatives in violent video game experiments. *International Journal Of Law And Psychiatry*, 56, 35–43.

Fisher, S., & Jenson, J. (2016). Producing alternative gender orders: A critical look at girls and gaming. *Learning, Media and Technology*, 1–13.

Fisher, E., & Thomas, I. (2016, January 4). E-sports ready for the big leagues? *Sports Business Journal*, p. 1.

Funk, J. (2013, September 2) MOBA, DOTA, ARTS: A brief introduction to gaming's biggest, most impenetrable genre [Web log post]. Retrieved from www.polygon.com/2013/9/2/4672920/moba-dota-arts-a-brief-introduction-to-gamings-biggest-most

Giampapa, J. (2016, July 26). S-S-S-S-Stigma breaker: gamers with disabilities are taking the fighting game scene by storm. Retrieved from www.ablegamers.org/stigmabreaker/

Golub, A., & Lingley, K. (2007). 'Just like the Qing Empire:' Internet addiction, MMOGS, and moral crisis in contemporary China. *Games and Culture*, 3(1), 59–75.

Grimes, S.M., & Feenberg, A. (2009). Rationalizing play: A critical theory of digital gaming. *The Information Society*, 25(2), 105–118.

Guttmann, A. (1978). *From ritual to record: The nature of modern sports.* New York: Columbia University Press.

Hamari, J., & Sjöblom, M. (2017). What is eSports and why do people watch it? *Internet Research*, 27(2).

Hollist, K.E. (2015). Time to be grown-ups about video gaming: The rising esports industry and the need for regulation. *Arizona Law Review*, 57, 823–847.

Hutchins, B. (2008). Signs of meta-change in second modernity: The growth of e-sport and the world cyber games. *New Media & Society*, 10(6), 851–869.

Jenny, S. E., Manning, R. D., Keiper, M. C., & Olrich, T. W. (2016). Virtual(ly) Athletes: Where eSports Fit Within the Definition of 'Sport.' *Quest* (00336297), 69(1), 1–18.

Jin, D.Y. (2010). *Korea's online gaming empire*. Cambridge, Mass: MIT Press.

Jonasson, K., & Thiborg, J. (2010). Electronic sport and its impact on future sport. *Sport in Society,* 13(2), 287–299.

Kane, M. (2008). *Game boys: Triumph, heartbreak, and the quest for cash in the battleground of competitive videogaming.* London: Plume.

Kirschner, H. (2015). Online livestreams, community practices, and assemblages: Towards a site ontology of consumer community. *Advances in Consumer Research*, 43, 438–442.

Lefton, T. (2015, November 2). It's game on for e-sports. *Sports Business Journal*, p. 1.

Li, R. (2016) *Good luck have fun*. New Yok: Skyhorse Publishing.

Lowood, H. (2009). Videogames in computer space: The complex history of Pong. *IEEE Annals of the History of Computing*, 31(3), 5–19.

Millington, B. (2014). Amusing ourselves to life: Fitness consumerism and the birth of bio-games. *Journal of Sport and Social Issue*, 38(6), 491–508.

Rai, L., & Yan, G. (2009). Future perspectives on next generation e-Sports infrastructure and exploring their benefits. *International Journal of Sports Science and Engineering*, 3(1), 27–33.

Riddell, D. (2016, May 29). ESports: Global revenue expected to smash $1 billion by 2019. *CNN*, Retrieved from http://edition.cnn.com/2016/05/29/sport/esports-revolution-revenue-audience-growth/

Roche, M. (2000) *Mega-events and modernity*. London: Routledge

Saleem, M., Anderson, C.A., & Gentile, D.A. (2012). Effects of prosocial, neutral, and violent video games on college students' affect. *Aggressive Behavior*, 38(4), 263–271. doi:10.1002/ab.21427

Seo, Y. (2013). Electronic sports: A new marketing landscape of the experience economy. *Journal of Marketing Management*, 29(13–14), 1542.

Seo, Y. (2016). Professionalized consumption and identity transformations in the field of eSports. *Journal of Business Research*, 69(1), 264–272.

Seo, Y., & Jung, S-U. (2014). Beyond solitary play in computer games: The social practices of eSports. *Journal of Consumer Culture*, 16(3), 635–655

Simon, B. (2007). Geek Chic: Machine aesthetics, digital gaming, and the cultural politics of the case mod. *Games and Culture*, 2(3), 175–193.

Tassi, P. (2015, February 25). New report details how eSports is an effective engagement and marketing tool. Forbes, Retrieved from www.forbes.com/sites/insertcoin/2015/02/25/new-report-details-how-esports-is-an-effective-engagement-and-marketing-tool/#5a5e866d62cc

Taylor, T. L. (2012). *Raising the stakes: E-sports and the professionalization of computer gaming*. Cambridge, MA: MIT Press.

Waldron, T. (2016, May 24). EA Sports is betting millions you'll watch this guy play 'FIFA.' *The Huffington Post*. Retrieved from www.huffingtonpost.com/entry/ea-sports-fifa_us_573f4c6be4b0613b512a2f43

Walker, A. (2016, May 27). League Of Legends was just sanctioned as a sport in Australia [Web log post]. Retrieved from www.kotaku.com.au/2016/05/league-of-legends-was-just-sanctioned-as-a-sport-in-australia

Winkie, L. (2017, July 14). For disabled gamers like brolylegs, esports is an equalizer. *Vice Sports*. Retrieved from https://sports.vice.com/en_ca/article/ywgqxv/for-disabled-gamers-like-brolylegs-esports-is-an-equalizer

Witkowski, E. (2012). On the digital playing field: How we 'do sport' with networked computer games. *Games and Culture*, 7(5), 349–374.

36

Fishing and Angling

Mike Huggins

Angling (from the word 'angle', referring to an early form of hook[1]) is the act of fishing with a rod, line, hook and bait or lure, celebrated as a pleasurable recreational activity rather than fishing for survival, subsistence or commercial capture. Though angling has always been an important participant activity, it has been regarded as a 'field sport' and has yet to receive the historical, social and cultural scholarly study it deserves. Some have viewed it somewhat sceptically as a 'sport', judgements usually based on ill-defined assumptions about physical activity levels, and because the various types of angling (such as sea fishing, coarse fishing and game fishing) are very different.[2] Indeed the 1975 *Oxford Companion to Sports and Games* omitted angling altogether.[3] But although *angling is not an Olympic event, it is recognized as a sport by policymakers and funding bodies in many countries, and is a large participant sport in many parts of the world. Whilst many participants are lone anglers,* an infrastructure of angling clubs, projects and governing bodies can be found across the globe. It has competition that can be formal or informal, elite or community, organized at local club, regional, national and international levels. Its activities can attract support and resources from public agencies.

Angling rarely attracts popular public attention. Whilst it is both a sport and an activity closely linked to leisure and recreation, it is often 'hidden', taking place well away from urban areas and the public and media gaze. So it has largely been ignored by sociologists and historians of sport and by students of cultural and leisure studies. Writers on sport in Britain and America have more generally concentrated on mass-audience and urban sports. Rural recreations have consequently been largely neglected. Likewise in France, even in 2015 it could be claimed that 'recreational fishing remains largely unstudied by the human sciences . . . physical and sports activities and their specialist journals'.[4]

Such omission has been blinkered and wrong. Angling has unique properties, qualities, histories and practices. It has had historically relatively high levels of active participation across the life stages for millions of people. Anglers have generally spent more daily time on the activity than on other sports, though its physical intensity is generally viewed as moderate by anglers. Angling provides opportunities for different levels of physical activity for people of all abilities and ages, including the retired and those with some form of illness or disability. The vast majority of anglers in recent decades began fishing well before their late teens, showing the importance of youth development. Family and friendship groupings were key factors in participation and most anglers were introduced by a parent, another family member or a friend.[5]

It has broad appeal. Thomas Barker, in his *The Art of Angling*, first published in 1651, argued that angling surpassed all other recreations in promoting health and pleasure.[6] Angling is a sensory pursuit embedded in nature. It has a range of personal and social attractions: personal health and an enjoyment of mental relaxation, calm and contemplative repose, wellbeing and peace of mind, with periods of anticipation, concentration, excitement and physical effort as well as the escape from the pressures of work and domesticity. Angling is a physical activity in a natural environment, sometimes the most meaningful contact many urban dwellers have had with wildlife. It is a problem-solving activity. Finding fish, approaching them, actually sensing the fish take and the choice of bait and equipment are all important, as are environmental influences such as the type of water fished, the time of day and the weather, since calm conditions, rain or wind speed and direction all affect results. For the experienced angler, catching a fish in the way that was wanted, with fullest respect for the fish and a real testing of one's skills was always the real challenge. Yet because chance and luck were also involved, and environment and fish are not always predictable, the non-expert and less expert could sometimes be highly successful. Catching fish was an instantly gratifying demonstration of success. This made it particularly appealing to young people, especially those with low confidence in their own abilities.

Angling's histories

Angling for pleasure amongst those with wealth and free time has a long prehistory based on archaeological evidence, but according to a variety of manuscript and printed sources it became a wider cultural phenomenon amongst the better off in the late middle ages, originating independently in the Balkans, England, France, Germany, Spain and other European countries.[7] In Britain recreational angling for 'game fish' more valuable as quarry and food, such as salmon and trout was quickly distinguished from 'coarse fishing' for other species, though this division hides the historically-rooted elite prejudice for more costly 'game' fishing as well as changing angling practices and boundary blurring. By the sixteenth century techniques such as float fishing, ledgering, live baiting and fly fishing were also already well understood.

British angling grew in popularity as a social diversion in the seventeenth and eighteenth century. Many rivers were still well stocked with salmon and trout, and some fishing beats quickly became valuable commodities which could be exclusively let by the season.[8] There are numerous references too for colonial fishing in America.[9] By the mid-nineteenth century many countries were finding declining numbers of river fish in their more industrialized and urbanized areas due to overfishing, man-made pollution and other environmental changes. However railway expansion allowed the wealthy to reach more remote rural areas and urban artisan anglers to enjoy fishing expeditions distant from their local waterways and ponds. Many artisan clubs increasingly organized matches and shared catches afterwards with friends, but this led to further overfishing. English anglers in Sheffield, a centre of coarse fishing activity, successfully lobbied their local MP to introduce an 1878 Act to protect freshwater fish and establish a close season, despite some debate about its timing with the leading London clubs.

Increased salmon stock decline was blamed on multiple factors: the increase in locks and weirs which kept fish from reaching spawning grounds; discharge of pollution from mills, mines, tanneries and factories; higher mill dams; extraction of gravel; unguarded turbines; lime washed from farmers' fields; better and more indiscriminate catching technologies; greater poaching; and overfishing. In Britain, in 1861 a Royal Commission into the Salmon Fisheries of England and

Wales investigated the problems.[10] It offered a range of fish conservation solutions: fish passes and ladders, the suppression of effluent and earlier popular forms of fish capture such as estuarine stake-nets, earlier closing of fishing seasons, the prohibition of poaching, the introduction of licenses for angling and commercial fishing, and the introduction of local river conservancy management boards to provide administration and enforcement. License revenue would pay for the employment of river bailiffs. Such recommendations were passed into law in later Salmon Acts, with conservancy boards often dominated by rich, landed riparian owners and enforced by a Salmon Fisheries Inspectorate. Salmon and trout fishing became commodified, and dominated by the upper and upper middle classes, privileging an elite ethics of fly fishing. To protect and preserve fish numbers some older and more popular working-class customary methods of fish capture such as estuary netting and spearing for subsistence or income augmentation became outlawed or restricted.[11]

Britain was not alone in such responses. Wherever rivers and lakes were still fishable the perception that traditional fishing methods and poaching had a serious impact on angling encouraged local power brokers to establish organizations and take individual initiative to protect their fishing. As angling waters became scarcer, collective purchase or rent of fishing rights to gain exclusive use by the better off allowed them to continue their hobby. Many purchased angling beats elsewhere. In America, the Blooming Grove Park Association established a summer fishing resort about four and half hours travel from New York. Shares were priced at $450 each.[12] To preserve fish stocks in Westmeath, in Ireland, members of the gentry, men with private income, army officers, administrative officers, substantial landowners and members of the higher status professions formed the Westmeath Fish Preservation society to preserve their fishing and prevent poaching on local loughs in the 1990s.[13] Such actions were not always successful. In Hamilton, Canada, in the early 1920s, the newly-formed Hamilton Angling and Casting Club set up a sport fishery in the Bay. Composed of better-off sport fishermen, its motto was 'protect, propagate and preserve'. It wanted to restock the Bay, and increase fish numbers, and it attacked or placed limits on traditional activities but succeeded only in placing limits on the season in the face of strong community resistance in a period of depression.[14]

Fishing clubs, syndicates and competition predated widespread industrialization, and even today angling is still an activity with a comparatively high proportion of club members compared to other sports.[15] Angling clubs have helped develop participation, skills and competitions, manage and sometimes regularly restock fishing waters, and generate social value to individuals and communities. Angling clubs have a long history. In America for example, The Schuylkill Fishing Company of Pennsylvania, also known as the State in Schuylkill, the first angling club in the American colonies, was established as early as 1732. Socially elite, it survives to the present day.[16] By the 1830s, there were upper and middle-class clubs in Boston, Cincinnati and New York too, and angling was soon booming on the east coast.[17] By the later nineteenth century American anglers were breaking away from English traditions, and the Catskill Mountains increasingly attracted leading fly-fishers.

In Britain numbers of clubs grew rapidly in the nineteenth century, aiding the structure and organization of angling. Clubs could gain permission from owners to fish specific waters, often for a relatively low rent, since in return they often protected the waters from poaching and encouraged conservation, and club membership encouraged competitions and was often attractive for social reasons too. In England the Angling Association was formed in 1869 and claimed that there were over 80 anglers' clubs. After The Scottish National Angling Clubs Association was formed in 1880 it began what was to become a highly prestigious Scottish national fly fishing championship.[18] A rival association, the Scottish Anglers Association, also held a national competition. The two organizations eventually merged as the Scottish Anglers National Association Limited in 2006.

British coarse fishing also developed some clubs and organizations more attuned to working-class culture. Headquarters were often local pubs, and timed sweepstake competitions were run on canals and river banks for members.[19] These clubs emerged first in large urban areas, and only reached the coalfields of northern England in the 1880s.[20] Sea fishing increased in popularity as seaside resort holidays became more popular with the middle classes, and members included professionals and businessmen who lived at the seaside and commuted to towns inland. Sea angling clubs organized beach-fishing competitions, and a British Sea Anglers Society was formed in 1893. For the wealthier offshore boat fishing for larger, more challenging fish became a popular sport, offering commercial opportunities for boatmen.

Angling was so popular that writers regularly referred to it in wider literature and writings. An analysis of the frequency of the word 'angling' in Google Books which plots its normalized frequency against the date of publication shows similar patterns in America and Britain. The word's use peaked in American texts in the 1840s, reached a major peak between c. 1860 and 1880, fell slightly, peaked again in the 1920s and suffered some decline from the 1960s until gaining slight recent renewed popularity. In British texts there were peaks in the 1830s, 1850s and a highest peak in the 1880s with lower peaks in the early 1920s and around 1950 before declining for some decades and then rising slowly.[21] This suggests that in wider discourse, at least, interest in angling peaked in America and Britain amongst the more literate in the late nineteenth century.

In Britain by the First World War local authorities were sometimes leasing fishing on their reservoirs. Following the hiatus of the war years, angling experienced renewed growth, and in 1923 the Salmon and Freshwater Fisheries Act encompassed earlier piecemeal legislation and established Fishery Boards. Membership of working men's fishing clubs expanded rapidly once again, and some midland clubs rented miles of rivers in the Fens and elsewhere, often filling excursion trains on Saturdays. By the late 1920s there were more than 600,000 members of the Working Men's Anglers Association.[22] Game fishing maintained its position, while for a brief period in the 1930s big-game tuna fishing off Scarborough was enjoyed by wealthy aristocrats and officers.[23] In America fly fishing peaked in the early 1920s, and the period saw a supposedly golden age of angling.

Following the Second World War, the increased availability of motor cars allowed anglers to travel to more distant venues, and opened angling up to a wider public, while air travel extended angling tourism. In America angling grew in popularity along the west coast. In Britain a boom in carp fishing from the 1950s saw widespread commercial exploitation of specially built artificial lakes well stocked with large fish. Coarse fishing rapidly developed new tackle, new baits, and new methods. Pike fishing also grew in popularity. Angling matches became increasingly competitive, with a complex structure of national and international tournaments, and some professional and semi-professional competitors. In Scotland, for example, the Glasgow and West of Scotland Coarse Fishing Association was formed in October 1966 and organized a competition the following month. With growing membership it held its first Scottish Open Championships in 1969, attracting up to 400 competitors in the early 1970s. In 1975 the Scottish Federation for Coarse Angling was formally created. Sea angling in Britain has become more common since the 1990s, with just over half fishing mainly from the shore, about a quarter from private boats, and around 22 per cent from charter boats.[24] In America and Britain, catching and then releasing fish became widely practiced to aid conservation.

Angling's actual popularity in different countries is hard to establish. Angling literature has often claimed it to be the most popular participant sport, especially in Britain, but such claims have proved hard to substantiate without quantitative data. In recent years however, the increased emphasis on evidence-based policy and practice has helped create a large body of survey data. This has allowed scholars to see angling's popularity in broader context.

In the USA angling is still a popular outdoor recreational activity, though American participation in angling overall has been declining since the 1960s due to a variety of factors including an aging populace, immigration, and busy lifestyles. According to the 1994 *Statistical Abstract of the United States* recreational fishing had been carried out annually by nearly 20 per cent of the population at least once. More than 55 million Americans took at least one fishing trip in 2013, though running and biking activities had even more participants. In recent decades bass fishing has gained in appeal, with specialist boats and elite bass anglers. In the Caribbean, and off Florida and Texas, charter boats offered expensive deep water big game angling for marlin, sailfish and swordfish. Angling was more popular with older men, and since 2000 paid fishing license holders in the USA have fluctuated between 29 and 28 million per annum.[25]

In England and Wales studies have not provided a consistent picture, though it would seem that though angling remained popular up to the 1970s the Sports Council believed there was some decline by the later 1980s partly due to the growing attractions of other leisure forms like golf and swimming, with the sport then attracting mainly manual working males. More recently the increased spending power of the better-off has driven some renewed growth in inland and sea angling. In 2004 it was estimated that in England and Wales there were four million anglers spending around £3 billion a year.[26] France, in comparison, had perhaps 1.4 million anglers at this time. Nevertheless, despite anglers' claims about its widespread popularity, recent surveys have made it clear that angling is not a leading British sport. In 2001 an estimated 9 per cent of the population of England and Wales had been angling in the previous two years, and similar results were obtained from a 2010 survey.[27] Sales of licenses have been over a million each year since the mid-1990s, lower than survey results because of a combination of evasion, changes in turnover, countryside access issues, falls in catch in some areas and because licenses are not necessary for sea angling. In 2002 fishing was estimated to be fourteenth in the list of active sports, with 5.6 per cent of over-sixteens taking part at least once, well behind sports like running, cycling, golf, football and tennis.[28] But a 2011 survey sponsored by Sport England suggested that angling was only the 16th highest participation sport in England, as did a further survey in 2012.[29]

In Australia sea fishing was the second most popular sport in the 1890s, when weekend fishing trips proliferated and most major cities had fishing clubs. It remains popular there and in New Zealand.[30] The Australian Recreational Fishing Foundation recently claimed that 'recreational fishing ranks as our largest participation sport and lifestyle activity', with $10 billion spent annually.[31] In 1991 the *Australian Sports Directory* made angling the seventh most popular male sport and the fourth most popular female sport. However the 2011 Australian Bureau of Statistics analysis of sport and physical recreation saw angling as relatively minor compared with more popular activities like walking, jogging, aerobics, swimming, cycling, golf, tennis and football.[32]

While transport change and fish availability have affected angling's history, it has been changes in fishing tackle (equipment) and the type of bait to attract fish to the hook which have been key to its development. Single or two piece rods of usually around 96 cm in length sometimes of hickory, with a fixed short thick length of line, often knotted horsehair, were in use by the late medieval period. Lines could not be cast or controlled, but landing nets helped get heavier fish to land. By the mid-seventeenth century running a line through a ring at the end of the rod allowed better casting and running of a hooked fish. To deal with stronger fish primitive narrow winches or reels, often made of brass, began to appear in Britain. They broke easily, had no check or drag mechanism and often jammed. Shops were selling tackle by the mid-seventeenth century. Simple multiplier reels with gearing (a reel design in which one turn of the handle produces more than one revolution in the spool) next began to appear, and from the first decades of the nineteenth century Kentucky watchmakers like George Snyder were producing even more effective American reels, and these were soon being mass-produced.[33]

Rods were now being made more often in three sections. Around mid-century leading anglers in Britain began to purchase 550–600 cm rods made of more pliant greenheart, a water-resistant and more elastic wood from Guiana and the West Indies. More often only the top section was greenheart, the rest from lancewood, hickory or whole cane. In the United States rods from mid-century began being made out of lighter, more flexible and durable first four then six-strip split bamboo cane, an industry initially centred on Vermont. These were copied in Britain by leading fishing tackle manufacturers, such as Allcock of Redditch (founded in 1803) who from the mid-1880s also increasingly dominated the mass production of angling goods for the less well off, with branches in London, Paris and Toronto and a factory for silk gut line production in Spain.[34]

Simpler winches with adjustable drag check mechanism began to be manufactured in the 1860s. These were initially made of brass but aluminium, Ebonite and Vulcanite were soon introduced and reels became lighter, more easily dismantled and more reliable. Fixed spool reels were being produced in Bradford by 1905. Through the twentieth century new developments included free spool reels, new rod tapers, electronic bite alarms, nylon monofilament lines and graphite rods. Much modern tackle development has been influenced in part by salt water angling techniques.

With better rods lines could be longer. Casting competitions based on distance and accuracy achievements emerged in America and Britain in the nineteenth century, often promoted by tackle manufacturers and angling writers. The finest and most expensive British rod production was dominated by the leading English tackle company, the North British Works (built in 1890) based in Alnwick, with retail branches in Edinburgh, Manchester, and London, as well as extensive overseas outlets. John James Hardy (1854–1932) had extended his family tackle business to become its managing director. He was a skilled publicist who used his angling prowess to win many competitions and publicize his Hardy production rods. One model first produced in 1911 was still selling in 1961. It was neatly named the Casting Club de France, one of many early twentieth century casting organizations and federations like the British Casting Association, Casting Club of Belgium and American Casting Club which began to organize tournaments. Hardy won the 1910 competition with a 25 yard cast, and since then across various weight classes distances have become far greater. A 300 metres world record cast (using a multiplier reel) is now getting ever closer.[35]

Fishermen have long recognized that flies attract some fish. Artificial flies were already in use in the fourteenth century if not before, but from the seventeenth century onwards there was more rapid development of artificial flies with a range of tying styles and materials, some imitators of fly surface movement, and some more brightly coloured attractors. 'Dry flies' were buoyant, landing softly on the surface. 'Wet flies' were meant to sink. Regional and national patterns emerged quite quickly. Fly tying became a specialized cottage industry, and an increasingly wide range of sophisticated, highly complex, ornate and expensive fly patterns, materials and construction became available for purchase. *The Salmon Fly: How to Dress it and How to Use It*, written by angling journalist George Kelson (1835–1920), provided 200 detailed fly patterns and explained how and when each might best be used.[36] From the 1890s Frederic Halford (1844–1914) dogmatically asserted and encouraged dry fly fishing upstream on the expensive, southern English clear chalk streams. He pulled together, systematized and further developed existing practices, but his inflexible principles of ethical purity encouraged a cultish, dominant ideology of angling amongst his supporters.[37] Halford's views circulated widely in the American press, and in book form, and his flies were copied by American tackle companies, though as American writers like George LaBranche pointed out the faster and rougher American trout streams of the Appalachians needed a modified approach.[38] Fishermen on the rougher, darker northern English rivers often used 'wet flies', and there was resistance to Halford's views. In the early twentieth century Halford's former protégé G.E.M. Skues (1858–1949) argued that using nymph flies, designed to resemble the immature form of aquatic insects and crustaceans, was often more effective and could be used on southern streams.[39] This ethical and part-regional debate continued in Britain into the 1930s.

Angling's cultural productions

Angling's popularity can be gauged through its cultural products. As early as the eighteenth century, its multiple representations ranged from art images of the fisherman as 'natural' gentleman to a tombstone in Ripon cathedral churchyard, North Yorkshire, devoted to 'poor but honest Bryan Tunstall' who 'was a most expert angler, until Death, envious of his Merit, threw out his line, hook'd him, and landed him here'.[40] Cultural material soon proliferated. Angling's popularity can be seen, for example, in railway companies' advertising posters, such as the English sea-fishing poster used as one of the 'East Coast Joys' in LNER railway company advertising, or 'Come Fishing', issued by Canadian Pacific. In Britain public house names such as 'The Angler's Arms', 'Jolly Anglers', 'Anglers' Rest' or even just 'The Anglers' signify its attraction. There is a market for television programmes such as 'Extreme Fishing', 'Passion for Angling', 'Fishing Adventure' or 'Hook, Line and Sinker', a Canadian digital TV station, 'World Fishing Network', launched in 2005, and occasional films such as the British comedy/romantic film *Salmon Fishing in the Yemen* (2011), as well as much commercial instructional material. Compared to some other sports, there are surprising few museums devoted to angling. The United States is fairly exceptional in having the American Museum of Fly Fishing in Vermont that preserves and exhibits artefacts relating to American angling, and the Fly Fishing Museum of the southern Appalachians, and there are scattered smaller angling museums elsewhere in the world. One British equivalent, The Fishing Museum, has only an online presence currently.

Despite a current lack of serious academic studies, there is a voluminous print literature on angling. It provides a useful historical perspective on angling, and the ways it has been interpreted, practiced and communicated. There have been weekly, monthly and annual publications over the past century and a half. In Britain the *Fishing Gazette* first catered for anglers in 1877. The first American magazine devoted to angling, *The American Angler*, began in 1881.

In the many magazines and books, enthusiastic anglers have discussed the effective practice, traditions, locations and successes of their sport, shared biographies of keen anglers and distilled their experiences for a wider angling audience. Fishermen's tales are a well-known genre, conveying a combination of adventure, combat with an exaggeratedly strong and large fish and sporting 'feeling'. A key British text was *The Compleat Angler*, first published in 1653 by Izaak Walton (1593–1683), one of the most famous and influential works in the history of sport. It celebrated innocent, carefree, contemplatively pastoral angling on rural river banks, and combined expert tuition about how to lure fish onto angles with verse, songs, quotations, enjoyable anecdotes and aphorisms. Its various revisions during his lifetime included contributions by Thomas Barker and Charles Cotton, who also wrote angling books. It is the second most-printed book in English after the King James Bible. Walton presented angling as in part a gregarious social enterprise with kindred spirits, and his work encompassed a deep understanding of natural history and angling ecosystems. Another early key text, James Chetham's *The Angler's Vade-mecum* (1681), was informative and influential but was published anonymously.[41]

Books on angling proliferated in the nineteenth century. In 1876 the editor of *The Field*, Francis Francis (1822–1886), author of *A Book on Angling*,[42] argued that in Britain 'the literature of angling is one of the richest branches of literature we have'.[43] Writers increasingly distinguished between 'true anglers' who *naturally* were gentlemen, and simply enjoyed catching fish, and those whose main aim was to get big catches, sell fish or win competitions. Angling writings by Frederic Halford, G.E.M. Skues and John James Hardy's standard work *Salmon Fishing*[44] were widely read. After 1945, books by E. Marshall Hardy became classic works. Richard Stuart Walker (1918–1985) was the leading carp fisherman of his generation. He wrote regular columns for the *Angling Times* which became a *tour de force* of angling journalism and contained considered, clearly written and entertaining angling stories and advice. His enthusiasm, clarity of expression, powers of angling observation and provocative writing made him widely known. His first major book, *Still Water Angling* (1953) remains a seminal work. Barrie Rickards (1938–2009) was even more prolific in terms of articles and books. His two most influential works were *Fishing for Big Pike* and *Angling: Fundamental Principles* , which sold 25,000 copies in its first year.[45] In 1997 there was a useful discussion of the authors and literature of Scottish angling up to the late twentieth century.[46] More recently British academic authors like John Lowerson, Harvey Osborne and Richard Hoffmann have produced articles exploring angling's history in more depth.

In America the first significant book was John J. Brown's, *The American Anglers' Guide* (1841), and publications grew in number thereafter. Prominent writers on angling have included Thaddeus Norris, John Harrington Keene, Theodore Gordon, Preston Jennings, and Vincent C. Marinaro, all covered in what is still the standard book-length history of American game angling by Paul Schullery.[47] Arnold Gimrich, an avid fly fisherman, has produced a useful survey of angling literature,[48] and Glen Law a succinct history of American fly fishing,[49] while Mark Browning's *Fly Fishing in North American Literature* also covers Canadian writers like Roderick Haig-Brown.[50] However academic writing on angling's American history is still rare.

Future research

In the last decade scholars and government agencies have begun to recognize the need for deeper research into angling. In Australia, for example, the Australian Recreational and Sport Fishing Industry Confederation have said that the social and economic importance of recreational fishing is a priority research area, and there have been expenditure surveys of angling there for some time.[51] In the USA there have been five-yearly series of national recreational fishing expenditure surveys since the 1970s. In Britain, the economic benefits of angling, participation levels and demographics, and public attitudes to angling are likewise increasingly being explored.

The history of angling tourism is under-researched, even though angling tourism has been extremely important in terms of the economic contribution that visiting anglers make to rural areas, lengthening the tourist season or helping to sustain employment in often economically fragile communities. In America, railroads were exploiting angling's potential by hotel building in places like St Pauls or Minneapolis from the mid-nineteenth century. Between the two world wars some of the best fishing reaches of the leading rivers and loughs in Scotland and Ireland were taken over by hotels. Studies of recent angling in Britain, USA, Canada and Australia have been largely at the regional rather than national level.[52] The many inland recreational fisheries often substantial capital value. In England and Wales this amounted to an estimated £3 billion in 2003/2004, while in 2009 over 37,000 jobs were generated by the industry. Estimations of annual gross expenditure by anglers in England and Wales on fishing licenses, tackle, travel and accommodation have varied in the last two decades but have always been over a billion pounds, much of it on coarse fishing, while a 2004 assessment of sea angling's economic contribution both nationally and more locally suggested that £538 million was spent annually by sea anglers fishing largely by boat or off beach, creating nearly 19,000 jobs.

Other under-researched areas concern ethical issues and questions about protection of fish stocks, river and environmental resource management; anglers' relationship with the natural world and new technologies; and conditions measurement. These have divided angling groups and scientists. For example there have been battles over access to facilities between anglers, farmers, and other recreational sports wanting river use such as boaters and canoeists. There has been an increasing trend towards fish capture and then release back, but not all anglers accept this, and some wish to retain and eat the fish they capture. As yet there has been little exploration of this particular theme, though a fascinating study of angling on the river Lot in France has carried out a ethnographic analysis of the standards and practices of two distinct groups of fishermen with different procedures and identities: shad fishermen using traditional approaches and eating their catch; and anglers catching carp who conceptualize the fish differently, use sophisticated, expensive equipment and more codified fishing tactics, and release after catching.[53] An American study has explored a historical conflict between traditional recreational spearing of pike through the ice and modern angling methods in terms of its impact on fish management issues.[54]

Little is also known about angling's impact in particular rural settings, the different ways in which it involved local people and visitors, how people benefited from it and the ways in which communities were helped by its development in terms of employment opportunities. Changes in the number of people earning a living from angling remain to be explored. The politics of fishing has also been neglected, especially the connections between angling, changes in biological knowledge and debates about the use and abuse of the landscape and natural environment. Up to and beyond the mid-nineteenth century, for example, little was known about the breeding cycle of salmon.[55] More detailed study of the historical relationship between angling and nature, between anglers and the environment and between anglers and their landscape is at an early stage.[56]

Britain's imperial connections ensured British trout were deliberately introduced into rivers in the Empire from Kashmir to New Zealand, though the brown trout was introduced to North America in 1883 from Germany, and American Pacific coast rainbow trout were introduced into British ponds and reservoirs between the wars. But how imported fish impacted on indigenous fish, the environment and angling practices remains unclear.

Anglophone research has largely concentrated on western angling, and neglected the histories of angling in other cultures so this too needs to be explored. In Japan for example, 'tenkara' fishing for trout on the high mountain streams, which has at least a 200 year history, uses a very long, light bamboo rod, with short tapered furled line attached to the end, to place and manipulate the fly more precisely on small pools. It does not use a reel. This is becoming popular on west coast America.

Angling as a gendered activity is another topic that needs far more explanation. Dominated by men, there is a strong male bias in its history and culture. Many fishing accounts and academic studies focus on masculine traits such as strength, resilience and competitive duelling with nature with trophies and captures, though additional subordinate masculinities can be exhibited.[57] Attention is now slowly shifting to women anglers, and the historical narrative of women and angling can currently be traced back to at least the seventeenth century.[58] In Britain in 2002, 10 per cent of men and 1 per cent of women had fished in the previous 12 months. Other studies on British angling participation have variously suggested that between 12 and 3 per cent of anglers are female. Of the 29,000 anglers who replied to the 2012 national angling survey, 97 per cent were male.[59] In countries such as the USA the proportion of women appears to be higher, but currently there is little research into the reasons for such disparity and how it has affected attitudes to angling. It may well be that its gendered character lies partly in its context, its offering of escape from wider public scrutiny and the domestic environment, but this needs further exploration.

Another debate has been over the reasons for women's disproportionate success in some fishing forms such as salmon fishing in Britain and musky fishing in America. One suggestion is that pheromones given off by male fishermen signal danger, and so women's scent more positively affected taking patterns. Others have suggested that women were more prone to take the advice of their professional guides and gillies.[60] Certainly women hold many of the leading salmon weight records. For example, in 1922 the largest salmon and heaviest freshwater fish ever caught by rod in the British Isles (64 lb) was landed by Georgina Ballantyne on the River Tay in Scotland.

The racial bias of fishing participation in In Western Europe and America towards white communities is another under-explored area. Little is known for example of the history of resistance to angling regulations by Native Americans, whose fishing practices were different. In Britain today most surveys suggest that anglers are about 97 per cent white. In America Anglo males were more likely than African-American or Mexican-American males to have started fishing at an earlier age, have more years of fishing experience, fish more days from a boat, belong to a fishing club or organization, fish in tournaments, and have less varied species preferences.[61] Selective law enforcement and discriminatory behaviour were constraints on participation.[62]

Changing attitudes to nature have ensured occasional attacks on fishing on humanitarian grounds for at least two centuries. In 1814 T.F. Salter felt the need to provide an 'apology' and defence of angling, admitting that 'many people speak of Angling as a cruel and reprehensible amusement, and feelingly describe the sufferings and torture endured by the harmless and unoffending fish, when on the angler's hook'.[63] In Britain, America and Europe, recreational fishing has recently come under moral pressure, especially from animal liberation and animal rights philosophies, though it remains largely free from widespread controversy. Opinion surveys covering a range of countries show that about 25 per cent of people already morally question recreational fishing for sport.[64] In Britain better-organized anti-angling groups appeared in the early 1980s. A campaign for the Abolition of Angling (CAA) began in 1985, promoting public awareness of its mission, campaigning for fish rights and drawing supporters together. It then turned to activities such as leafleting, demonstrations, picketing of tackle shops, sabotage activities to disrupt fishing, demonstrating the damage caused by discarded tackle and lobbying local authorities to restrict angling on their sites. In the 1990s there were similar small-scale movements in the USA, Australia, Belgium and several other European counties.

In the early twenty-first century the CAA became the Fish Protection League, stressing fish rights, welfare and conservation issues, and linked with a sister European organization. Membership levels remained low. It picked up on the intensifying scientific debate on the extent to which fish felt pain like humans.[65] Recent empirical studies have argued that fish probably have the capacity for suffering, though this may be different in degree and kind from the human experience of this state.[66]

Conclusion

Angling's history shows how over time anglers from different social backgrounds have emphasized and given status to particular angling methods and codes of sportsmanship, formed clubs for association, competition and access to waters, fought over access, and encouraged laws to restrict or protect particular fishing practices. Changes in transport, shifts in the availability of fish, and developments in tackle and bait all played a key role, while environments were reshaped and ecosystems rebalanced to facilitate fishing. Class, gender, race, and generation have all affected participation. Angling has made positive environmental contributions to the management of waterways and pools, action against pollution and over-fishing. But for most anglers the pleasure and enjoyment of being out of doors, pitting their wits against the fish, still lie at the heart of the sport.

Notes

1 See its use in the first-known written work on fly fishing, *Treatise on Fishing with an Angle* (1496), often erroneously attributed to Dame Juliana Berners. On the issue of attribution see Rachael Hands, 'Juliana Berners and the Boke of St Albans', *Review of English Studies* 18 1967, pp. 373–386.
2 Adam Bron, Natalie Djohari and Paul Stolk, *Fishing for Answers: Final Report of the Social and Community Benefits of Angling Project* (Manchester: Substance, 2012), p. 12.
3 John Arlott (ed), *The Oxford Companion to Sports and Games* (London: Oxford University Press, 1975).
4 Marie Cheree Bellenger, Review of Carole Barthélémy, *La Pêche Amateur au Fil du Rhône et de l'Histoire. Usages, Savoirs et Gestions de la Nature* (2013), in *European Studies in Sports History* 8 2015 pp. 201–202.
5 See www.resources.anglingresearch.org.uk/sites/resources.anglingresearch.org.uk/files/National_Angling_Survey_Report_2012.pdf.
6 Thomas Barker, *The Art of Angling* (London, J.H Burn, 1820 reprint of edition of 1651)
7 The work of Richard Hoffmann is important here e.g. Richard C. Hoffmann, 'Fishing for Sport in Medieval Europe: New Evidence', *Speculum*, 60,4, 1985 pp. 877–902; Richard C. Hoffmann, 'Carps, Cods, Connections: New Fisheries in the Medieval European Economy and Environment', in Mary J. Henniger-Voss (ed) *Animals in Human Histories: The Mirror of Nature and Culture* (Rochester NY: University of Rochester Press, 2002), pp. 3–55.
8 See, for example, 'To be let. A fine trout stream, well adapted for angling', *Times* 28 May 1789; p. 4.
9 See Charles Goodspeed, *Angling in America: Its Early History and Literature* (Boston: Houghton Mifflin, 1939).
10 Report of the Royal commission appointed to Enquire into the Salmon Fisheries (England and Wales) Parliamentary Papers 1861 [2678] XXIII.
11 Harvey Osborne, 'The Development of Salmon Angling in the Nineteenth Century', in R. W. Hoyle ed, *Our Hunting Fathers: Field Sports in England after 1850* (Lancaster: Carnegie 2007) pp. 187–211.
12 Colleen J. Sheehy, 'American Angling: The Rise of Urbanism and the Romance of the Rod and Reel', in Kathryn Grover ed. *Hard at Play: Leisure in America, 1840–1940* (New York: The Strong Museum, 1992), p. 79.
13 Tom Hunt, 'Angling in the Mullingar district in Victorian times: a class act?' In Seamus O'Brien (ed) *A Town in Transition: Post Famine Mullingar* (Mullingar; Rathlainne Publications, 2007), pp. 102–133.
14 Nancy B. Bouchier, Ken Cruikshank, *People and the Bay: A Social and Environmental History of Hamilton Harbour* (Vancouver: UBC press, 2016), pp. 103–106.
15 Kate Fox and Leicha Rickard, *Sport and Leisure, National HouseHold Survey* (London: Office for National Statistics, 2002), p. 11.
16 Schuylkill Fishing Company, *A History of the Schuylkill Fishing Company of the State in Schuylkill 1732–1888* Philadelphia, Privately printed for the Club, 1889; Gerald R. Gems, Linda J Borish and Gertrud Pfister, *Sport in American History* (Champaign Il: Human Kinetics, 2008), pp. 57–59.
17 Sheehy, 'American Angling', p. 79.
18 David A. Biggart, *SNACA: The First hundred Years* (Edinburgh: SNACA, 1979).
19 John Lowerson, 'Brothers of the Angle: Coarse Fishing and Working Class Culture 1850–1914' in J. A. Mangan ed., *Pleasure, Profit, Proselytism: British Culture and Sport at home and Abroad 1700–1914* (London: Frank Cass, 1988) pp. 105–127.
20 Alan Metcalfe, *Leisure and Recreation in a Victorian Mining Community: The Social Economy of Leisure in North-East England, 1820–1914* (Abingdon: Routledge, 2005), p. 116.
21 This figure was derived from Google's Ngram Viewer analysis, known as 'culturomics'.

22 Nicholas Goddard and John Martin, 'Angling', in Tony Collins, John Martin and Wray Vamplew (eds) *Encyclopaedia of Traditional Rural Sports* (Abingdon: Routledge, 2005), p. 24.

23 Mark Ross, *The Glory Days of the Giant Scarborough Tunny: The British Tunny Club, Hardy Bros. Tackle and Big Game Fishing in the 1930s* (Yeovil: Mark Ross, 2010).

24 Drew Associates, *Research into the Economic Contribution of Sea Angling* (London: DEFRA, 2004).

25 See www.statista.com/statistics/247669/fishing-license-holders-in-the-us.

26 Environment Agency, *Our Nation's Fisheries* (Bristol: Environment Agency, 2004), p. 1.

27 D. Simpson, D. and G. Mawle, *Public Attitudes to Angling. Environment Agency R&D Project W2–060/TR* (London: EA, 2001); D. Simpson and G.W. Mawle, *Public Attitudes to Angling 2010* (Bristol: Environment Agency, 2010).

28 Fox and Rickard, *Sport and Leisure*, p. 20.

29 Sport England, *Active People Survey 5* (April 2010–April 2011) and *Survey 7* (April 2012–April 2013) provide similar figures; Adam Brown, Natalie Djohari and Paul Stolk, *Fishing for Answers: Final Report of the Social and Community Benefits of Angling Project* (London, 2012), p. 12.

30 Bob Dunn, *Angling in Australia: Its History and Writings* (Balmain: David Ell Press, 1991).

31 See www.igfa.org/News/ARFF-Call-for-Charter-for-Recreational-Fishing-in-Australia.aspx.

32 See www.abs.gov.au/AUSSTATS/abs@.nsf/Lookup/4102.0Main+Features30Jun+2011.

33 James A. Henshall, 'The Evolution of the Kentucky Reel', *Outing Magazine*, December 1900, pp. 288–293.

34 For Alcock see John Lowerson, *Sport and the English Middle Classes* (Manchester: Manchester University Press, 1993), p. 231.

35 Cliff Netherton, *History of the Sport of Casting: People, Events, Records, Tackle and Literature, Early Times* (Lakeland, Florida: American Casting Education Foundation, 1981).

36 George Kelson, *The Salmon Fly: How to Dress it and How to Use It* (London: Wyman and Sons, 1895).

37 Tony Hayter, *F.M. Halford and the Dry Fly Revolution* (London: Robert Hale, 2002)

38 George LaBranche, *The Dry Fly and Fast Water* New York: Charles Scribner's Sons,1914

39 Tom Hayter, *G.E.M. Skues: The Man of the Nymph* (London: Robert Hale, 2013).

40 For art see Walter Shaw Sparrow, *Angling in British Art Through Five Centuries: Prints, Pictures, Books* (London: J. Lane Bodley Head 1923.)

41 James Chetham, The Angler's Vade-mecum (London: Thomas Bassett, 1681).

42 Francis Francis, *A Book on Angling* (London: Longmans, 1867).

43 Francis Francis, *On Angling* (London: Longmans Green, 1876), p. 2.

44 John James Hardy, Salmon Fishing (London: Hudson and Kearns, 1907).

45 Barrie Rickards, Fishing for Big Pike (London: A&C Black, 1971); Barrie Rickards, Angling: Fundamental Principles (London: The Boydale Press, 1986).

46 N.W. Simmonds *Early Scottish Angling Literature* (Shrewsbury: Swan Hill Press 1987).

47 Paul Schullery, *American Fly Fishing A history* (Nick Lyons Books, 1999).

48 E.g. Arnold Gimrich, *The Fishing in Print: A Guided Tour Through Five Centuries of Angling Literature* (New York Winchester Press, 1974).

49 Glen Law, *A Concise History of Fly Fishing* (New York: Lyons Press, 2003).

50 Mark Browning, *Fly Fishing in North American Literature* (Athens, OH: University of Ohio Press, 1998).

51 See www.recfish.com.au/research/RecfishingResearch.pdf'; Expenditure surveys in different states of Australia prior to the year 2000 were reviewed in A. McIlgorm and J. Pepperell, *A National Review of the Recreational Fishing Sector, A report by Dominion Consulting to Agriculture, Forestry and Fisheries*, (Canberra: AFF, 1999).

52 Environment Agency, *Our Nations Fisheries: The Migratory and Freshwater Fisheries of England and Wales – a Snapshot* (Bristol: EA, 2004), p. 15; A. Radford, G. Riddington, and H. Gibson, *The Economic Evaluation of Inland Fisheries: The Economic Impact of Freshwater Angling in England & Wales Science Report – SC050026/SR2* (2009). For Scotland see A. Radford, G. Riddington and J. Anderson, *The Economic Impact of Game and Coarse Angling in Scotland* (Edinburgh: Scottish Executive Environment and Rural Affairs Department, 2004); A. Radford, G. Riddington and H. Gibson, *Economic Impact of Recreational Sea Angling in Scotland* (Edinburgh: Scottish Government, 2009); a Queensland study is reported in J. Rolfe, and P. Prayaga 'Estimating Values for Recreational Fishing at Freshwater Dams in Queensland', *The Australian Journal of Agricultural and Resource Economics*, 51, 2007, pp. 157–174.

53 Carole Barthélémy, *La Pêche Amateur au Fil du Rhône et de l'Histoire. Usages, Savoirs et Gestions de la Nature* (Collection Eaux des villes, Eaux des Champs, Paris, L'Harmattan, 2013).

54 R.B. Pierce and M.F. Cook, 'Recreational Darkhouse Spearing for Northern Pike in Minnesota: Historical Changes in Effort and Harvest and Comparisons with Angling', *North American Journal of Fisheries Management* 20, 1, 2000, pp 239–244.

55 Osborne, 'The Development of Salmon Angling'.

56 Richard Coopey and Tim Shakesheff, 'Angling and Nature: Environment, Leisure, Class and Culture
in Britain 1750–1975', and Jean-Francois Malange, ' Les Pratiques de Pêche à la Ligne en France
(c. 1870–c. 1930): Aux Origines d'une Conscience Environnementale' in Genevieve Massard-Guilbaud
and Stephen Mosley (eds), *Common Ground: Integrating Social and Environmental History* (Newcastle:
Cambridge Scholars Publishing, 2011) pp. 16–41, 42–65.

57 Jacob Bull, 'Watery masculinities: fly-fishing and the angling male in the South West of England' *Gender,
Place & Culture: A Journal of Feminist Geogra*phy, 16, 4, 2009 pp. 445–465

58 Nicholas D. Smith, 'Reel Women: Women and Angling in Eighteenth-Century England', *International
Journal of the History of Sport*, 20, 1, 2003, pp. 28–49.

59 Judith Milner, *The Woman's Guide to Angling* Stoke Abbott: Harmondsworth, 1993) p. 129 estimated 10
per cent. See also Fox and Rickard, *Sport and Leisure*, p. 23. See also the Environment Agency report,
Our Nation's Fisheries; Adam Brown, *The National Angling Survey 2012 : Survey Report* (London: Substance 2012).

60 Wilma Paterson and Peter Behan, *Salmon and Women* London: H.F. and G. Witherby, 1990); Fred Buller,
'A list of Large Atlantic Salmon Landed by the Ladies', *The American Fly Fisher*, 39, 4, 2013 pp. 2–21.

61 K.M. Hunt and R. B. Ditton, 'Freshwater Fishing Participation Patterns of Racial and Ethnic Groups
in Texas', *North American Journal of Fisheries Management*, 22, 2002, pp. 52–65.

62 S.A. Schroeder, M.L. Nemeth, R.E. Sigurdson and R. J. Walsh, 'Untangling the Line: Constraints to
Fishing Participation in Communities of Color', *American Fisheries Society Symposium* 67, 2008, pp. 1–15.

63 T.F. Salter, *The Angler's Guide* (London: T. Tegg, 1814), p. xi.

64 Robert Arlinghaus, Alexander Schwab, Carsten Riepe and Tara Teel, 'A Primer on Anti-Angling Philosophy and Its Relevance for Recreational Fisheries in Urbanized Societies', *Fisheries*, 37, 4, 2012
pp. 153–164.

65 Tom G. Pottinger, *Fish Welfare Literature Review* (Institute of Freshwater Ecology, 1995).

66 See for example F. Huntingford, C. Adams, V. A. Braithwaite, S. Kadri, T. G. Pottinger, P. Sandøe & J.F.
Turnbull, 'Current Issues in Fish Welfare', *Journal of fish Biology*, 68, 2 2006 pp. 332–372.

Recommended reading

Bob Dunn, *Angling in Australia: Its History and Writings* (Balmain: David Ell Press, 1991).

John Lowerson, 'Angling' in Tony Mason ed. *Sport in Britain: A Social History* (Cambridge: Cambridge University Press, 1989), pp. 12–43.

Genevieve Massard-Guilbaud and Stephen Mosley (eds), *Common Ground: Integrating Social and Environmental History* (Newcastle: Cambridge Scholars Publishing, 2011), pp. 16–65.

Glen Law, *A Concise History of Fly Fishing* (New York: Lyons Press, 2003).

T. Miles, M. Ford, and P. Gathercoal, *The Practical Fishing Encyclopaedia: A Comprehensive Guide to Coarse
Fishing, Sea Angling and Game Fishing* (London: Lorenze Books, 1999).

Paul Schullery, *American Fly Fishing: A History* (Nick Lyons Books, 1999).

Colleen J. Sheehy, 'American Angling: The Rise of Urbanism and the Romance of the Rod and Reel',
in Kathryn Grover (ed.), *Hard at Play: Leisure in America, 1840–1940* (New York: The Strong Museum,
1992), pp. 76–92.

37

Climbing and mountaineering

Christopher Atwater

Early mountaineering history

If mountaineering is defined as the act of climbing a mountain, the official "beginning" of mountaineering history could be no more than a vague concept, as the scope of early human beings' ascension up mountains for reasons of survival, exploration or spirituality is immensely broad. However, it is valuable to consider how those in the past managed their way up a mountainside when examining the history of mountaineering. Early documentation of mountaineering ventures includes the writings of 16th- and 17th-century European scholars and scientists, who climbed mountains for the purpose of observation and discovery in fields including botany, geology and meteorology.[1] During this time, equipment used for traversing snow and ice-covered mountains included crampons, alpenstocks, ropes and snowshoes.[2] Such excursions revealed evidence of others having been there before them, particularly on the summits. For example, names, dates and family crests could be found carved into rock.[3] Sometimes an item was found on the summit, such as a cross.[4] Though it is clear from the writings of these early scientific mountain surveyors that the impressiveness of their surroundings was duly appreciated,[5] it wasn't until the 19th century that people in significant numbers began to climb mountains for the sole purpose of the experience itself. A mountain-top voyage directed by scientific pursuit was lengthy and permeated with regular stops. The mid-1800s brought forth an era of mountain climbing where climbers followed inspiration to reach the summit swiftly and directly. They tested their own limits against the challenge of climbing mountains which were fraught with threatening difficulty. These early mountaineers sought the fulfillment and oftentimes public fame that followed conquering the natural world's most breathtaking and dangerous mountains. This new enthusiasm for mountain climbing during the 1800s is best illustrated by the 11 years between 1854 and 1865, deemed the "Golden Age" of mountaineering.[6] As the Golden Age occurred in the European Alps, terms like "alpine scrambler" or "alpine traveler" were used to describe the sport. It is from this kind of language that the term "alpinist" was coined in 1874,[7] now widely used almost synonymously with the term "mountaineering."[8] Perhaps the Golden Age of Mountaineering then, could be identified as the beginning.

The Golden Age of mountaineering

The Golden Age of mountaineering is considered to have begun in 1854 with Alfred Wills's ascent of the Wetterhorn, 3,701 meters high and located in the Swiss Alps. In the true spirit of the Golden Age, Wills's motivation to climb the Wetterhorn came from a self-directed drive to overcome obstacles. Wills climbed as a way to advance in his field of profession, which was law. Unable to attend elite schools, he found a way to set himself apart. Accompanied by four guides and two local citizens, Wills successfully made the venture to the summit of the Wetterhorn and wrote a book about it. The undertaking earned him the notoriety he desired and he gained admiration from society's upper ranks including the Prince of Wales. Wills eventually went on to become a judge.[9]

As excitement for mountain climbing grew throughout the European Alps, alpine clubs were formed, beginning in London and spreading quickly through Europe. Clubs such as the Austrian Alpine Association, the Club Alpino Italiano, the Schweizer Alpen Club and the French: Society des Touristes Savoyards arose, exhibiting heightened enthusiasm for mountain climbing combined with a spirit of nationalism. The Italian club, created by scientist and politician Quintino Sella, was devised in 1863 after Sella had climbed Monte Viso and challenged his fellow countrymen, "What Italian not entirely insensible to the beauties of nature would not want to conquer this beautiful mountain, whose summit is entirely ours?" Sella portrayed the Alpine Club in London as made "for people who spend a few weeks of the year climbing the Alps, our Alps!"[10]

Competitiveness to conquer the Alps abounded throughout mountaineering's Golden Age and in 1865, the Matternhorn, a 4,478-meter mountain located in the Swiss Alps on the border of Switzerland and Italy, was the only remaining 4,000-meter peak that had not been summited.[11] Edward Whymper, a climber from England altered and improved traditional climbing tools,[12] determined to be the first to summit the Matterhorn. His first attempts began in 1861 on the Italian side of the mountain with his partner, Italian climber Jean-Antoine Carrell and continued over the course of several years. Eventually, Carrell left the partnership to continue his efforts with the Italian Alpine Club. Whymper then decided to change his approach to the Swiss side of the mountain and went to Zermatt, Switzerland.[13] In Zermatt, Whymper found guides to be scarce and it was rumored that Carrell's Italian sponsors were responsible for paying off many guides in Zermat in order to delay Whymper. Other climbers in Zermat at the time, also hoping to be the first to summit the Matterhorn were encountering similar problems. With almost no guides to be found, they decided to join together and form one group. Whymper, along with English climbers Lord Francis Douglas, the Reverend Charles Hudson and his protégé Douglas Hadow managed to hire two local Swiss guides, a father and son both named Peter Taugwalder as well as a French guide, Michel Croz.[14]

Whymper's party succeeded in reaching the top before Carrell's, but the race was so close that Whymper and Croz (who summited first from their team) could see the ascending Italian team from the peak.[15] However, disaster followed the group's triumph on their descent. Roped together, Hadow slipped and dragged French guide Croz over the edge of the mountain, followed by Douglas and Hudson. Whymper and the father–son Swiss guides, the Taugwalders, managed to stabilize themselves but the rope snapped and the unfortunate four others were able to be seen sliding on their backs for a few seconds before vanishing over the cliff.[16] Ropes used during the Golden Age of mountaineering were not strong enough to sustain tension caused by falls, especially of multiple people. Ropes were made of vegetable material that rotted when wet and even attracted animals to chew it. Ropes were used mostly for communication and steadying.[17] Whymper and the Taugwalders were the only survivors. In an interview with BBC news.com in 2015, Taugwalder descendant and Matterhorn climber Matthias Taugwalder, described the mountain as, "like walking on an ironing board, with a 2,000-metre drop on each side. . . . If you slip, your only choice is which side to fall: Switzerland or Italy."[18]

The Matterhorn incident brought forth an outcry of concern about the dangers of such extreme ventures. Queen Victoria stated, "England's best blood has been wasted" and called for a ban on mountain climbing.[19] The London Times published, "Well, this is magnificent. But is it life? Is it duty? Is it common sense? Is it allowable? Is it not wrong? There certainly are limits to audacity." Charles Dickens stated that justification of Alpine ascents, "becomes ghastly when it implies contempt for and waste of human life – a gift too holy to be played with like a toy, under false pretenses, by bragging vanity." Nonetheless, even after tragedy, the alternate viewpoint was not silenced. The *Illustrated London News* printed– "There would be small philosophy—nay, small knowledge of the world shown in discouraging adventure. It has given us the empire." In fact, adventuring mountaineers continued to be admired and acclaimed. William Matthews, a Bristol woolen merchant and Francis Fox Tuckett, an archeologist, were made knights in 1865 for summiting various peaks including first ascents of Monte Viso. Edward Whymper was knighted in 1872 by the king of Italy.[20]

Edward Whymper's ascent to the summit of the Matterhorn in 1865 is considered to be the conclusion of the Golden Age of mountaineering;[21] however interest in mountaineering continued to grow and by 1874, the Alpine clubs of Europe included approximately eleven thousand climbers.[22] After the Alps were summited, climbers took on the rest of the globe's highest peaks, scaling the mountains of North and South America, Africa and ultimately Asia,[23] where the Himalayas are home to nine of the ten highest mountains in the world including Mount Everest, the highest peak on earth at 8,850 meters.[24]

Women climbers during and following the Golden Age

Just six years after Edward Whymper's first ascent of the Matterhorn, the first female achieved the climb. Dressed in long skirts, Englishwoman Lucy Walker reached the summit in July of 1871. Similar to the circumstances of Whymper's quest, she also found herself to be in a race to be first to the top with another notable female climber of the time, Meta Brevoort, an American who had attempted to summit the Matterhorn two years earlier and almost reached 4,000 meters before harsh weather forced her to descend.[25] Walker was a founding member of the "Ladies Alpine Club," formed in 1907.[26] Following the Golden Age, mountaineering enthusiasm and rivalry among women mountaineers continued. Renowned American climber Fanny Bullock Workman, who climbed the mountains of northern India and the Himalayas with her climbing partner and husband William, accomplished three women's altitude records. In 1906 at age 47, when she set the bar once again by summiting Pinnacle Peak,[27] located in the Nun Kun Range of India, she was challenged by a rival American climber Annie Smith Peck, who set the women's altitude record in 1897 by climbing Mt. Orizaba in Mexico.[28] Peck disputed that her own venture to the summit of the Huascarán in the Andes in 1904 was higher than Pinnacle Peak. Workman answered by employing surveyors to determine Peck's 1904 destination, which proved to be lower than Pinnacle Peak by 1,000 feet, thereby defending her title.[29] Workman's persistent determination was applied in her unending efforts for women's rights and she used her athletic adventures to advance her agenda, publishing books and speaking for the progression of the rights of women globally. An iconic photo was taken of Workman on top of a 6,400-meter glacier in the Himalayas, where she reads a newspaper on which the headline states, "Votes For Women."[30]

Sherpas and the Nepalese community

In the 20th century, climbers around the world were determined to conquer the world's fourteen 8,000-meter peaks. Expeditions which usually lasted months included large numbers of people, substantial equipment and sizeable base camps. In the Himalayan region, Sherpas, local people known for their excellent mountaineering skills, made up a significant part of these teams and still do today.

The Sherpas as an ethnic group live primarily in the mountainous regions of Nepal, Tibet, India and the Sikkim state with the greatest number residing in Nepal. The Sherpa population is approximately 150,000. The word Sherpa in the mountaineering field refers to several ethnic groups, including ethnic Sherpas,[31] who have long been recognized for their aptitude at mountain climbing as well as unusual endurance in high altitudes.[32] Since the early 1900s,[33] Sherpas have been assisting mountain climbers in the role of guide and porter as well as providing other support such as securing ropes and setting up camps.[34] Over time, an entire industry of the Sherpa profession has unfolded. Sherpas in the Khumbu region of Nepal today are among the wealthiest of the local population and they have expanded their business offerings to other undertakings like hotels and trekking companies.[35] While Nepal's annual per capita household income is $430, Sherpas who lead or assist expeditions to Mt. Everest earn about $5,000 in the two-month climbing season.[36]

Among the local population of Nepal, the inclusion of women as mountaineers has become a recent occurrence. Pasang Lhamu Sherpa was the first Nepalese woman to climb Mt. Everest in 1993. Sadly, she did not survive the descent.[37] In 1994, Nepalese siblings Lucky, Dicky and Nicky Chhetri created the trekking agency 3 Sisters Adventure Trekking, a company of all women guides and porters which serves female clientele.[38] This was the first company to employ female guides in Nepal. In addition, the Chhetri sisters also founded the non-profit association Empowering Women of Nepal, which provides training to women to become employable as mountain guides, allowing them opportunity for income and independence in an environment which normally affords few prospects.[39] Empowering Women of Nepal has been the recipient of numerous accolades including awards in tourism, entrepreneurism and women's leadership.[40]

The subject of the Nepalese people and the impact of the mountaineering industry which brings 370 million dollars per year into their nation is complicated and controversial. Though acting as a guide and porter has historically provided a distinctive opportunity to earn a substantial income in an otherwise impoverished region, the occupation entails great risk for injury or death. Whereas the recreational climber may employ a Sherpa for a singular adventure, Sherpas who depend on mountain climbing for a livelihood make repeated journeys up the perilous routes to the summits. This is an especially serious concern for Sherpas who work on the very highest peaks, like Mt. Everest. In 2013, Outside Online published, "A Sherpa working above Base Camp on Everest is nearly ten times more likely to die than a commercial fisherman – the profession the Centers for Disease Control and Prevention rates as the most dangerous nonmilitary job in the US – and more than three and a half times as likely to perish than an infantryman during the first four years of the Iraq war."[41] Further, despite the work of a Sherpa being quite lucrative relative to other local people, the pay does not compare to that of a western guide, who on Mt. Everest, can make as much as $50,000 during a season.[42]

The pursuit of the summit of Mount Everest

Among the historical accounts of early climbers and their quest to be first to the top of the highest mountains, especially famous is the story of George Mallory and his partner Andrew

Irvine who disappeared during an attempt to summit Mount Everest in 1924. As a member of Britain's Alpine Club, and having excelled as a climber in the Alps and in Wales, Mallory was thought to have an exceptional chance of being the first to reach Everest's peak. After exploring and mapping the entire base of the mountain in order to find the best route, his first attempts failed due to weather and difficulties from the lack of oxygen in the high-altitude atmosphere.[43] Bottled oxygen was a new innovation at the time and still problematic,[44] and Mallory and his team experimented with the oxygen cylinders, trying some ascents with them and some without. His multiple attempts to reach the top of Everest presented the utmost physical and mental trials. During one of his attempts in 1922, seven Tibetan Sherpa porters on his team died in an avalanche.[45] When asked by the New York Times in 1923 why he wanted to climb Mount Everest, Mallory replied with a phrase that would become one of the most famous quotes in history, "Because it's there." Though the answer and famous quote may have seemed over-simplistic, its true implication was profound. In fact, Mallory did follow the quote with this explanation, "Everest is the highest mountain in the world, and no man has reached its summit. Its existence is a challenge. The answer is instinctive, a part, I suppose, of man's desire to conquer the universe."[46]

Mallory chose 22-year-old Andrew "Sandy" Irvine for his ultimate attempt to Everest's summit. Though he was not the most experienced climber, Irvine was exceptionally fit and especially skilled with the new oxygen cylinders. The last time Mallory and Irvine were seen was by a member of their expedition on the afternoon of June 8, 1924. They were ascending the Northeast Ridge.[47] Mallory's body was not discovered until 1999 when an expedition was arranged following the discovery of equipment that had dated back to the 1920s. Irvine's ax was found at 8,440 meters.[48] Mallory's body was found at 8,160 meters on the North Face.[49] It was determined that Mallory had died after a substantial fall.[50] Irvine's body is still missing. The discovery of Mallory's body raised new questions about whether Mallory did, in fact, reach the summit. It was known that he carried a photograph of his wife because he planned to leave it at the summit. When his body was discovered, there was no photograph, indicating that he could have made it to the summit and left it there as he intended. It was theorized by some that Mallory had actually been descending when he died, based on the amount of oxygen that was remaining in the oxygen cylinders and the fact that his snow goggles were found in his pocket, which could suggest that he descended after sunset when goggles would not have been necessary. Since the discovery in 1999, there have been searches for a camera known to have been carried by Mallory but it has not been found.[51]

Mount Everest was officially first summited in 1953 by Edmund Hillary from New Zealand and Sherpa Tenzing Norgay. Norgay had participated in six previous attempts to summit Everest, including a near successful effort with a Swiss team the previous year. He and Raymond Lambert made it as far as 8,598 meters before having to turn back. Norgay was then hired by a British team under leader Sir John Hunt as their lead Sherpa. The expedition included 350 porters, 20 Sherpas and 10 climbers. George Band, who was one of the party, told National Geographic in 2013, "Our climbers were all chosen as potential summiters. The basic plan was for two summit attempts, each by a pair of climbers, with a possible third assault if necessary." Tom Bourdillon, a former president of the Oxford Mountaineering Club, and Charles Evans, a brain surgeon, made the first attempt to the summit. Bourdillon and Evans made it to 101 meters short of the top, but they turned back, knowing that they would deplete their oxygen if they went on. Three days later Hillary and Norgay started from a higher camp than Bourdillon and Evans, therefore making it as far as their teammates had much earlier in the day. Their biggest hurdle was a 12-meter high rocky outcrop just before the summit. By repeatedly bracing his feet and back against opposite walls between the rock pillar and an adjacent ridge of ice (a technique referred to as "chimneying"), Hillary negotiated the formidable obstacle, later to be known as the Hillary Step. Upon reaching the summit, Hillary wrote later that he thought of Mallory and Irvine, and that he "looked around for some sign that they had reached the summit but could see nothing." Hillary, Norgay and John Hunt agreed not to reveal whether Hillary or Norgay actually stepped on the summit first. It was not until Norgay released his autobiography that it was announced Hillary was truly first.[52]

In 1975 Junko Tabei was the first woman to climb to the peak of Mt. Everest. An avid lifelong mountaineer, Japanese-born Tabei was five feet tall and weighed less than 100 pounds. Having a fierce commitment to climbing, she funded her mountain excursions by teaching English and piano. On her Everest climb, she was the co-leader of a team of 15 women who were assisted by six Sherpas. During the ascent, the team's camp was buried in an avalanche and Tabei was knocked temporarily unconscious. Her team's success was recognized as a victory for women in a society where females encountered continual difficulty breaking social barriers. After graduating from college with a degree in English Literature, Tabei organized a climbing club for women and was told they "should be raising children instead." As stated by Tabei, "Even women who had jobs, they were asked just to serve tea." Though she was the first woman to climb Mt. Everest, she described herself as the 36th climber to accomplish the feat.[53]

Progression of climbing equipment

The achievements of 20th-century mountaineering were intertwined with ever improving mountain climbing equipment. The turn of the century brought about the piton, an iron spike or hook which is hammered into the ice or a crack in the rock face to be used with rope as an anchor. Later, a ring was included through a small hole in the end of the spike.[54] Hans Feitchl further improved the piton by designing an eye directly into the spike.[55] Fiechtl, along with Ottos Herzog and Hans Dulfer also developed the first carabiner around 1910. The carabiner or "carbine hook" provided a safer and easier way to link ropes with anchors. Early carabiners were often not strong enough to support the weight of a person.[56] Synthetic ropes appeared after the invention of nylon in 1938. Ropes became smoother, stronger and even more durable when the kernmantle rope, made of an external sheath woven around a core of twisted nylon cordlets, came about in the 1960s. For securing footing on ice, early climbers drove nails or metal spikes into the soles of their boots. Early crampons were metal cleats which were tied on to the climber's boots. By the 1980s, crampons were available with step-in bindings. Advancements in climbing equipment provided opportunities to climb more safely and attempt more challenging climbs, but simultaneously brought about concern for the preservation of the mountain's natural state. Distressing to many was the unnerving site of great numbers of abandoned pitons as they began to build up on mountain walls. Reusable pitons were developed in 1947, designed to be placed by the leader of the climb and removed by the last climber. However, since a piton is hammered in, the process of removing the piton can oftentimes lead to damage and scaring of the rock face. Soon the phrase "clean climbing" was coined, meaning that one climbs a mountain without changing it. In this spirit, the chockstone (also called a chock or nut,) was developed, which is wedged into an existing crack and removed following the ascent. While improvements in climbing gear advanced the progression of clean climbing, they also inspired debates about the legitimacy of the climber who uses too many assistive devices. In the late 1970s a spring loaded caming unit was invented to be used in the same way as a chock. This invention was believed by many purists at the time to make climbing too easy and inauthentic.[57] Controversy regarding both the protection of the mountain face and the validity of the climber was significantly heightened when the practice of "bolting" or embedding pitons into drilled openings in the rock face came into play.[58] One of the most influential climbers to address this issue was Reinhold Messner (see Box 37.1). Along with often being identified as the greatest mountaineer in history,[59] he is also credited with advancing what is called "alpine style" climbing,[60] where minimal equipment is used.[61]

Box 37.1   Reinhold Messner

Reinhold Messner is often referred to as the greatest mountaineer of all time. In 1997, he was described in Outside magazine as the Michael Jordan of climbing, when it was written that, "He has taken the sport to a level not previously imagined."[62] He amazed the world by accomplishing a massive number of first time achievements in mountaineering, including being the first to summit all fourteen of the world's 8,000-meter peaks. He was the first to summit Mt. Everest without bottled oxygen, an undertaking which was thought to be impossible at the time. Later, he was the first to climb Mt. Everest solo.[63] His first ascents number over 100, as he pioneered the most difficult routes to the world's highest peaks. In his lifetime, he completed over 3,000 climbs.[64]

Messner is considered fundamental to the institution of "alpine style" mountaineering where the climber uses minimal equipment and climbs with very few people, only one partner or even alone. Before Messner's time, attempts to reach the world's highest summits utilized sizeable amounts of equipment, people and money. Messner rejected oxygen tanks, fixed ropes, porters and established camps, freeing himself to experience the mountain in an individual way while preserving the mountain from human alteration.[65] Messner's minimalist style of climbing contributed to his remarkable speed. His extraordinary abilities in the most life-threatening surroundings made him legendary in his own time. In 1979, he and Oswald Oelz performed a rescue on Nepal's Ama Dablam, saving the lives of three climbers including Peter Hillary, son of the famous climber Edmund Hillary, reaching them in a fraction of the time other climbers normally required to cover the same distance.[66]

Reinhold Messner was born in 1944[67] in northern Italy's South Tirol, among the Dolomite mountains, where most of the residents are Italian citizens who speak German.[68] As early as the age of five, he climbed the mountains of his homeland with his family.[69] By his early twenties he began to make his mark with many first ascents, climbing to mountain summits by the most challenging cliff side routes, known as Big Wall climbing, oftentimes solo or with his brother and childhood climbing partner, Gunther. In 1967, at age 23, he made the first winter ascent of the North Ridge of Monte Agner and the first winter ascent of the North Face of the Furchetta. The following year, he made the first winter ascent of the North Face of Monte Agner and together with his brother Gunther, he made the first ascent of the Eiger's North Pillar and the first ascent of the Central Pillar on the Heiligkreuzkofel. In 1970, he and Gunther climbed the Rupal Face Nanga Parbat: at 8,125 meters, one of the highest vertical rock and ice walls in the world. Reinhold ended up accomplishing the first ever traverse of the mountain, but tragically, Gunther was lost in an avalanche on the descent.[70] Messner searched for his brother for two days, developing severe frostbite on his hands and feet which required amputations of seven toes and three of his fingertips.[71] In 1971 he made another attempt to search for Gunther's body but was unsuccessful in finding it. Gunther's remains were finally found in 2005.[72]

Incredibly, despite any hardship or trial he faced, Messner's ambition never waned. He regularly established new routes, made first ascents and broke records on mountains ranging from

6,000–8,000 meters. In 1978, Messner and partner Peter Habeler made the first ascent of Mount Everest without bottled oxygen, despite the accepted belief of the time that it would be fatal.[73] Altitudes above 8,000 meters was identified as "the death zone."[74] Later the same year, he made the first solo ascent of an 8,000-meter peak: the Diamir face of Nanga Parbat, the same mountain where he had lost his brother eight years earlier. In 1980, he made the first solo ascent of Mount Everest,[75] a journey during which he fell into a crevasse at nighttime and managed to climb out.[76] Eight of the world's best climbers died at high-altitude between 1980 and 1982,[77] but Messner continued to realize repeated success. In 1982, he became the first to climb three 8,000-meter peaks in one season. Together with partner Hans Kammerlander, he was the first to traverse two 8,000-meter mountains together in one undertaking: the Gasherbrum Traverse. In 1986, when he and Kammerlander summited Lhotse, he became the first person to climb all fourteen 8,000-meter peaks. In the same year, he completed the "Seven Summits" (the highest mountains on all seven continents) when he climbed Mount Vinson in Antarctica,[78] and was the first to climb all seven without supplemental oxygen.[79]

Once his mountaineering goals were met, Messner's remarkable achievements continued. His next ventures included crossing the Antarctic, the Takla Makan Desert, Greenland, Tibet and the Gobi Desert all on foot.[80] His other accomplishments include being a member of European Parliament from 1999 to 2004,[81] authoring 50 books and creating the Messner Mountain Museum, which is actually a circuit of six separate museums located in his home of South Tyrol and Belluno, all dedicated to the mountains of the world.[82] Messner has been active in the film industry and a champion for the environment.[83] In 2010 Messner won Piolets d'Or Lifetime Achievement Award.[84]

The modern-day sport of mountaineering

Historically, mountain climbing required considerable funds for transportation, equipment and supplies, as well as substantial amounts of time for travel and the climb itself. Because of this, the activity was limited to specific men and women who had means and opportunity or who were accomplished enough at mountaineering that they could acquire sponsorship. Even for those whose resided in geographically mountainous regions, mountaineering was not necessarily considered appealing as a sport often due to social, cultural or religious reasons. At the time Edward Whymper climbed the Matterhorn, it was the shared belief of many local people that the mountain could not be climbed and should not be attempted because it was haunted by evil spirits. Zermatt was economically depressed and isolated in the winter months and those locals who participated in mountaineering were often acting in roles of guides and porters, climbing out of necessity rather than for recreation.[85] Sherpas did not climb to the peaks of mountains until the 20th century because they viewed the summit as home to the gods.[86] As late as the 1920s, Tibetan Sherpas had no word for "summit," and it was often believed that foreign mountaineers were climbing to the peaks in search of statues made of gold to take as treasure.[87] As late as 1981, it was commonly believed by local people that Mount Nanda Devi, the highest peak in India, could not be summited by a woman because the sacred peak would reject her. The belief was disproved that same year when the first female mountaineers did reach the summit.[88]

Along with changing attitudes about mountain climbing, in the later part of the 20th century separate elements of mountaineering developed into individual sports, changing the entire concept of the sport of climbing. Narrowing the experience to the singular element of climbing, it became possible to engage in the sport on a small boulder or a manufactured climbing wall. Equipment could be rented for a few hours or in some cases, it was not needed at all. With the growth of climbing gyms and outdoor adventure parks, adults and children alike began to attempt climbing activities in rising numbers. Along with developments in climbing equipment and the evolution of media and communication technology worldwide, the sport has expanded tremendously since the 1980s. According to the President of the International Federation of Sport Climbing, nearly 3,000 people try climbing for the first time every day worldwide, including in numerous developing countries.[89] As the sport of climbing has evolved, organized climbing competitions have emerged. The challenge of ascending a mountain initially involves a spirit of competition essentially against one's own limits. However, competition with other climbers has always been a significant part of the mountaineering tradition, demonstrated by a widespread race to be the "first" throughout mountaineering history. Today, climbing has a wide array of participants and the experience of the sport can vary greatly, ranging from climbing an indoor artificial climbing wall to climbing to the summit Mt. Everest.

High altitude mountaineering

"High altitude mountaineering," as it has been known historically, has grown substantially in magnitude. Reaching the highest mountain peak on each of the seven continents, referred to as climbing "the Seven Summits" is a goal of many and considered a mountaineering feat. The first to summit all seven was Richard Bass in 1985.[90] In 1992, the first woman accomplished the challenge, Junko Tabei, who was also the first woman to climb Mt. Everest.[91] Today's leading mountaineers embark on extremely high altitude alpine style climbs, with minimal equipment and support, seeking the most difficult routes requiring innovative techniques on the world's highest terrain. This elite community of mountaineers is recognized by the Piolets d'Or awards, which are awarded each year to esteemed climbers that exhibit exceptional creativity and independence.[92]

In non-alpine style high-altitude mountaineering, mountain peaks worldwide can be reached in organized expeditions. Climbers can utilize a variety of professional companies to guide and support them to the summits of the world's most breathtaking mountains. Costs to join an expedition vary depending on the excursion, the company used and what kinds of amenities are included in the purchased package. The cost can vary from several thousand dollars to well over $100,000. Climbing permits are a formidable portion of the cost; for example, in 2017 a permit to climb Mt. Everest was $11,000 from Nepal or $14,500 from Tibet.[93] Climbing companies arrange guides, porters, meals, tents and a variety of technical assistance including oxygen tanks, fixed ropes and ladders. Even with organized support and substantial dollars, climbing to high altitude peaks holds significant danger of injury or fatality from avalanches, storms, exhaustion, exposure, frostbite, falls and altitude sickness. Despite these risks, the number of people who participate in these types of climbs has increased dramatically since 1990[94] and the high number of climbers actually contributes to the danger, as waiting behind other groups increases susceptibility to frostbite.[95] The increased number of people has also had an environmental impact. 8.1 tons of garbage were removed from Mt. Everest in a clean-up effort in 2011.[96] By 2017, the total amount of waste removed had reached 16 tons.[97]

Mountaineering divided into individual sports

Eventually, mountaineering necessitates skill in multiple domains: hiking, rock climbing and ice climbing. Hiking is familiar to many people as a moderately achievable activity. Hiking trails are readily available to most people via public parks and forests. The hiker's destination is a scenic natural spectacle such as a high overlook or a waterfall. Hikers have the opportunity to challenge themselves at their discretion, choosing from trails that are usually well mapped and categorized for length and difficulty. Hiking can entail an easy walk through the woods or can involve heavy aerobic exercise and muscle building climbs which necessitate stamina and endurance.

Rock climbing skills become necessary once the climber encounters high boulders or cliffs. Rock climbing is where teamwork and equipment come into play. Two climbers work together, the first one climbing the full length of a rope before anchoring and then bringing up the partner, known as a *belay*. This process is repeated for each section.[98] Harnesses are normally used to attach oneself to the rope. The anchor, referred to as "protection" can be natural, like a tree or a boulder.[99] Otherwise artificial anchors are used such as a piton, chock or camming device, which are inserted into a crack or crevasse in the rock face, or a bolt which is hammered into a hole drilled into the rock. Rock climbing requires focus in order to enable the hands and feet to achieve a constant combination of grip, support and balance with each movement. Various scenarios necessitate different skills.[100] For instance, a climber must "chimney" to ascend or descend a vertical shaft by repeatedly bracing the feet and back against opposite walls.[101] On smooth rock, the palm of the hand[102] or even the foot[103] can be pressed against the rock with enough force to provide the friction necessary to hold the climber.

As a mountaineer climbs to higher altitudes, rock climbing inevitably becomes ice climbing. Ice climbing involves the same rope work used in rock climbing, but ice climbers must also know how to use other equipment. Ice pitons are driven into the ice walls and freeze in place. The ice ax can be used to cut steps in ice, provide a hand hold, arrest a slide and secure rope. Ice cleats, called crampons, are sets of spikes that are attached onto boot soles.[104] The two most common techniques used when climbing with crampons are called "flat footing" or "front pointing." With flat footing, the crampons are placed directly onto the ice whereas with front pointing the front crampons are pierced into the ice.[105] As with hiking, the other two phases of mountaineering are often enjoyed as individual sports. Ice climbing no longer takes place only while on route to the summit. Ice climbers can climb any vertical ice formation, such as frozen waterfalls or ice-covered cliffs.[106] In this vein, rock climbing of its own accord has gained significant popularity and has given rise to multiple different disciplines.

Sport climbing (a.k.a. lead climbing)

Sport climbers use expansion bolts in the rock for protection along a predefined route. Indoors, bolts are already part of the climbing wall. With the rope tied to his or her harness, the lead climber clips into each bolt to protect against a fall.[107]

Trad climbing (traditional climbing)

Trad climbers place their own removable anchors and remove them while they climb to maintain the purity of the route. The anchor is placed by the lead climber along the route and it is removed by the team's final climber. As there is no predefined route, exploration is a significant characteristic of trad climbing.[108]

Bouldering

Bouldering occurs mostly on boulders 2–5 meters in height or on artificial climbing walls. Bouldering is done without protection. When climbers fail to hold on, they simply jump to the ground,[109] or in some cases thick padded mats are used.[110] Bouldering is distinguished by short routes and high strength moves[111] in which the principles of gymnastics are utilized. The routes are often outlined exactly, and sometimes the ascent begins from a sitting or lying down position.[112] In bouldering, the routes are referred to as "problems."[113]

Rappelling

Rappelling capitalizes on the fast and fun way down from an ascent. Rope is wrapped around the climber's body and secured on one end. The rope is then fed out by one hand to lower the person gradually down the face of the rock.[114] The descent is controlled by the climber. Rappelling can become necessary in outdoor climbing when a climb becomes unsafe or impossible. In this case the anchor, either a permanent bolt or a strap around a rock or tree, will be left behind.[115]

Top roping

Top roping can be done indoors or outdoors, but it is one of the most popular types of indoor climbing.[116] Climbers are protected by a rope anchored from above while tension is applied to the rope from the ground by a partner, called a belayer. The rope runs from the belayer up to the anchor and down to the climber. With this system, potential falls are of a minimal distance, thereby allowing more difficult routes to be attempted. Outdoors, climbers participate in top roping in situations where other methods, like lead climbing, would be unsafe. Because most top-rope anchors can be retrieved by hiking or scrambling, top roping outdoors is also chosen in order to avoid environmental damage.[117] In this case, a tree or rock would be used for the anchor. However, some climbers use bolting to secure their anchors outdoors.[118]

Speed climbing

Speed climbers attempt to ascend to summits in the fastest time, beating the current record holder. In 1974, the record for climbing the North Face of the Eiger was accomplished in 10 hours. By 2007, the record was set at three hours and 54 minutes, only to be broken the next year by the same person, Ueli Steck, when he climbed it in 2 hours, 47 minutes and 33 seconds.[119] In indoor speed climbing, climbers race each other side by side along the same standardized route, determined by the International Federation of Sport Climbing (IFSC). Indoor climbing facilities set up practice courses according to IFSC standards. Though competitions include both 10-meter and 15-meter walls, international competitions are only held on 15-meter walls.[120]

Aid climbing

In *aid climbing*, the climber stands on a device attached to an anchor to ascend. This device is often a stirrup made of strong nylon webbing, called an aider. The lead climber will use the aider to place a higher anchor from which to hang the next aider. This method is normally used for extremely steep and long climbs, known as Big Wall ascents. Big Wall climbers use a multitude of hardware and equipment to move up the face of the cliff. The climbs take several days, so climbers carry substantial amounts of food and water with them and sleep on portaledges, which are semi-rigid cots that hang from anchors along the cliff side.[121]

Free solo climbing

Free solo climbing, or "free soloing" is done alone and without the use of any protective equipment including ropes or a harness. By definition, this could also describe bouldering except that free solo climbers usually ascend to heights that would be unsafe to fall from. The term "free soloing" is often confused with the term "free climbing." The term free climbing actually applies to most rock climbing in which equipment is used for safety and not to assist the climb. Aid climbing would be free climbing's opposite.[122] Despite the great risk, some free solo climbers push the ultimate boundaries of fear and danger, taking on the world's greatest Big Wall climbs without any protective equipment, often at great cost of injury or death. Alex Honnold, indisputably the world's most renowned free solo climber, amazed the world by climbing some of the world's steepest cliff faces without safety gear. On June 3, 2017, he accomplished his most impressive achievement to date when he free solo climbed Yosemite's El Capitan, a granite wall more than a half a mile high. The climb took him just under four hours. As described in National Geographic June 6, 2017, "Honnold squeezed his body into narrow chimneys, tiptoed across ledges the width of matchboxes, and in some places, dangled in the open air by his fingertips."[123]

Climbing in organized competitions

Climbing competitions originated with speed competitions held in the former USSR in the 1940s. Until the 1980s, these competitions primarily included Soviet Union participants. In 1985 the first international climbing competition, called "SportRoccia," was held in Bardonecchia, Italy and began what is known as Sport Climbing today. By the 1990s, competitive climbing escalated in popularity internationally. During this time, in order to standardize climbing routes and eliminate any differentiation caused by environmental elements, international events began to be held on artificial walls only. Today, male and female champions from over 75 countries compete against each other in the world competition events. In 2006, the inclusion of climbers with visual impairments and physical disabilities was celebrated with the first International Paraclimbing Competition.[124]

Sport climbing began to make its way into the Olympic domain when climbing demonstrations were presented at the 2006 Torino Winter Olympics.[125] In 2016, climbing was approved by the International Olympic Committee (IOC) to be an official part of the 2020 Olympic Games in Tokyo. Along with baseball/softball, karate, skateboarding and surfing, climbing was included with the goal of appealing to young people. IOC President Thomas Bach stated, "We want to take sport to the youth. With the many options that young people have, we cannot expect any more that they will come automatically to us."[126] The format chosen for the competition was a combination of three disciplines: lead climbing, bouldering and speed climbing. Sport climbing was also included in the schedule for the Youth Olympic Games Buenos Aires 2018, using the same combined three disciplines.[127]

As in the Olympic format, most climbing competitions feature the three disciplines of lead climbing, speed climbing and bouldering. In lead climbing, the winner is determined by who climbs the farthest within an established timeframe. In speed climbing, contestants climb alongside each other on identical routes and the winner is the climber who reaches the top first.[128] In a bouldering competition, climbers are judged on the number of problems they complete and how many attempts it takes to complete a problem.[129] Males and females compete separately.[130] Competitions utilize several formats. In a "Red Point" format, there are numerous climbing routes that vary in difficulty and potential points that can be earned. Within a predetermined time period, climbers must earn as many points as possible.[131] Because the climber cannot earn points if the route is not completed, the climber must strategize when choosing routes. In an

"On Sight" format, climbers are allowed to see the route one time and then make one attempt at the route. Points are determined by the height the climber reaches. In a "Flash" format, climbers are also only allowed one attempt at the route, but there is no limitation on visualization of the route; they can even watch their competitors climb.[132]

Governing bodies

The Union Internationale Des Associations D'Alpinisme (UIAA)

Translated as the International Union of Alpinist Associations, the UIAA is the International Olympic Committee(IOC) recognized international sanctioning body for international climbing competitions. It is only through sanctioned climbing competitions that climbers can earn points toward their national or world ranking. The UIAA has representatives from over 60 member countries[133] and represents the interests of over three million climbers and mountaineers from member federations worldwide.[134]

The International Federation for Sport Climbing (IFSC)

Formerly the International Council for Competition Climbing (ICC),[135] the IFSC is an international non-profit organization which provides direction and regulation as well as promotion and development for climbing competitions globally.[136]

History of competitive climbing timeline

1932 – *Union Internationale des Associations d'Alpinisme* (UIAA) is founded as the international federation for climbing and mountaineering.[137]

1985 – First "SportRoccia," a competition in lead climbing, marks the beginning of Sport Climbing.[138]

1988 – First World Series.[139]

1989 – First Speed and Lead Climbing World Cup.[140]

1991 – First IFSC World Championship, Lead Climbing and Speed Climbing.[141]

1992 – First Youth World Championship.[142]

1995 – The UIAA is recognized by the International Olympic Committee (IOC).[143]

1997 – International Council for Competition Climbing (ICC) is formed as part of the UIAA, for the purposes of autonomy and development.[144]

1998 – "Top Rock Challenge" – Bouldering is introduced as a new climbing discipline.[145]

2001 – IFSC World Championship includes Bouldering.[146]

2006 – The first International Paraclimbing Competition is held in Ekaterinburg, Russia.[147]

2006 – UIAA ends its governance of competition climbing, which leads to the formation of the International Federation of Sport Climbing (IFSC).[148]

2007–57 federations join together to create the IFSC.[149]

2008 – First IFSC Paraclimbing Cup is organized in Moscow, Russia [150]

2011 – The first IFSC Paraclimbing World Championships are organized parallel to the World Championships.[151]

2016 – Climbing is approved by the IOC to be an official part of the 2020 Olympic Games in Tokyo. Sport climbing is also included for the first time in the Youth Olympic Games Buenos Aires 2018.[152]

Notes

1 Peter H. Hansen, *The Summits of Modern Man: Mountaineering After the Enlightenment* (Cambridge, MA: Harvard University Press, 2013), 43, 54, 69–72.

2 Ibid., 40.
3 Ibid., 39.
4 Ibid., 69.
5 Ibid., 54.
6 "Wetterhorn during the Golden and the Post Golden Age" (January 31, 2010), www.summitpost.org/wetterhorn-during-the-golden-and-the-post-golden-age/593265 (accessed November 30, 2017).
7 Gilles Modica, *1865: The Golden Age of Mountaineering: An Illustrated History of Alpine Climbing's Greatest Era* (Sheffield: Vertebrate Publishing, 2016), 10.
8 Thomas Kublak, *Mountaineering Methodology – Part 1 – Basics* (MMPublishing, March 17, 2013), www.mountaineeringmethodology.com/history-of-techniques/.
9 Hansen, *The Summits*, 180–181.
10 Ibid., 186–188.
11 "Matterhorn," www.zermatt.ch/en/Media/Attractions/Matterhorn (accessed November 30, 2017).
12 David Pagel, "Great Innovations, the Evolution of Climbing Gear," *Climbing* (March 15, 2000): 122.
13 "First Ascent of the Matterhorn," www.alpenwild.com/staticpage/first-ascent-of-the-matterhorn (accessed November 30, 2017).
14 Imogen Foulkes, "Matterhorn: The Race to Conquer Swiss 'Z Hore' Mountain," (July 14, 2015), www.bbc.com/news/world-europe-33512241 (accessed November 30, 2017).
15 "First Ascent," www.alpenwild.com.
16 Hansen, *The Summits*, 190.
17 Pagel, "Great Innovations," 123.
18 Foulkes, "Matterhorn."
19 Ibid.
20 Hansen, *The Summits*, 190–192.
21 Ibid., 180.
22 Ibid., 192–193.
23 George Alan Smith and Carol D. Kiesinger, "Mountaineering" (February 25, 2016), www.britannica.com/topic/mountaineering (accessed November 30, 2017).
24 "Highest Mountain Peaks of the World," www.infoplease.com/world/world-geography/highest-mountain-peaks-world (accessed November 30, 2017).
25 Caroline Fink, "First Ladies: The first women to climb the Matterhorn" (2013), www.zermatt.ch/en/Media/Zermatt-inside-stories/focus-women-alpinists (accessed November 30, 2017).
26 Claire Jane Carter, "Lady-like Victorian Psyche: The Story of Lucy Walker and the Eiger" (December 9, 2014), www.thebmc.co.uk/ladylike-victorian-psyche-the-story-of-lucy-walker-and-the-eiger (accessed November 30, 2017).
27 "Fanny Bullock Workman Shows Rich Brits What an American Woman Can Do," www.newenglandhistoricalsociety.com/fanny-bullock-workman (accessed November 30, 2017).
28 "Annie Smith Peck," www.biography.com/people/annie-smith-peck-215064 (accessed November 30, 2017).
29 Evangeline Holland, "Fascinating Women: Fanny Bullock Workman" (May 22, 2011), www.edwardianpromenade.com/women/fascinating-women-fanny-bullock-workman (accessed November 30, 2017).
30 "Fanny Bullock Workman Shows," www.New England Historical Society.com.
31 "Sherpa" (June 28, 2017), www.britannica.com/topic/Sherpa-people (accessed November 30, 2017).
32 Krishnadev Calamur, "Who Are Nepal's Sherpas?" (April 22, 2014), www.npr.org/sections/parallels/2014/04/22/305954983/who-are-nepals-sherpas (accessed November 30, 2017).
33 "Sherpas: The Invisible Men of Everest," *National Geographic* https://news.nationalgeographic.com/news/special-features/2014/04/140426-sherpa-culture-everest-disaster (accessed November 30, 2017).
34 Calamur, "Who Are," www.NPR.org.
35 "Sherpas: The Invisible Men," *National Geographic*.
36 Calamur, "Who Are."
37 Bibek Bhandari, "Women Climb Indian, Himalayan Peaks to Defy Stereotypes," *South China Morning Post* (March 24, 2014): www.scmp.com/news/asia/article/1455696/women-climb-indian-himalayan-peaks-defy-stereotypes (accessed November 30, 2017).
38 "About 3 Sisters," www.3sistersadventuretrek.com/sisters/tourism_for_women (accessed November 30, 2017).
39 Harley Rustad, "Himalaya Girl Power: Treks 'by Women, for Women'" (November 8, 2013), http://travel.cnn.com/three-sisters-adventure-trekking-nepal-971486 (accessed November 30, 2017).

40 "Awards," www.3sistersadventuretrek.com/sisters/awards (accessed November 30, 2017).
41 Grayson Schaffer, "The Disposable Man: A Western History of Sherpas on Everest," *Outside Online* (July 10, 2013): www.outsideonline.com/1928326/disposable-man-western-history-sherpas-everest (accessed November 30, 2017).
42 Calamur, "Who Are," www.NPR.org
43 "George Mallory" (October 14, 2014), www.britannica.com/biography/George-Mallory (accessed November 30, 2017).
44 "George Mallory – from Life to Legend" (October 26, 2015), https://rsgsexplorers.com/2015/10/26/george-mallory-from-life-to-legend (accessed November 30, 2017).
45 "George Mallory," www.britannica.com.
46 "The origin of George Mallory's Famous Mountain Climbing Quote: 'Because it's There.'" (March 18, 2015), www.thisdayinquotes.com/2010/03/george-mallory-coins-because-its-there.html (accessed November 30, 2017).
47 "George Mallory," rsgsexplorers.com.
48 "George Mallory," www.britannica.com.
49 Nick Squires, "Mallory and Irvine's Everest Death Explained," *The Telegraph* (August 4, 2010): www.telegraph.co.uk/news/worldnews/asia/nepal/7925594/Mallory-and-Irvines-Everest-death-explained.html (accessed November 30, 2017).
50 "George Mallory," www.britannica.com.
51 Dan Mallory, "Mallory Expedition, George Mallory" (2007–2015), www.malloryexpedition.com/george.htm (accessed November 30, 2017).
52 David Roberts, "Everest 1953: First Footsteps – Sir Edmund Hillary and Tenzing Norgay," *National Geographic Adventure (April 2003): excerpted in "50 Years on Everest,"* National Geographic.com *(*March 3, 2013): www.nationalgeographic.com/adventure/features/everest/sir-edmund-hillary-tenzing-norgay-1953 (accessed November 30, 2017).
53 Sam Roberts, "Junko Tabei, First Woman to Conquer Everest, Dies at 77," *New York Times* (October 26, 2016): www.nytimes.com/2016/10/27/world/asia/junko-tabei-dead.html (accessed November 30, 2017).
54 Pagel, "Great Innovations," 124.
55 Maurice Isserman, *Continental Divide: A History of American Mountaineering* (New York, W.W. Norton & Company, Inc., 2016), 177–178.
56 George Chesterton, "Sportsactive: No turning back: The karabiner," *The Independent on Sunday* (November 3, 2002).
57 Pagel, "Great Innovations," 123–131.
58 Kublak, *Mountaineering Methodology,* www.mountaineeringmethodology.com.
59 Caroline Alexander, "Murdering the Impossible: How Reinhold Messner, the World's Greatest Mountaineer, Willed Himself to Shatter the Limits," *National Geographic* (Nov. 2006): 1.
60 Kublak, *Mountaineering Methodology,* www.mountaineeringmethodology.com.
61 Oliver Smith, "20 Reasons Why Reinhold Messner is the World's Greatest Living Man," *Telegraph.co.uk,* London (December 11, 2016): 1.
62 Alan R. Elliott "Top Climber Reinhold Messner; Goal Oriented: His Determination Helped Him Scale the World's Highest Peaks," *Investor's Business Daily (*November 27, 2006), 2.
63 Smith, "20 Reasons," 1–2.
64 "Reinhold Messner's Biography," www.messner-mountain-museum.it/en/mmm/the-messner-mountain-museum (accessed November 30, 2017).
65 Alexander, "Murdering the Impossible," 1–2.
66 Ibid., 4.
67 "Reinhold Messner" (April 1, 2016), www.britannica.com/biography/Reinhold-Messner (accessed November 30, 2017).
68 Alexander, "Murdering the Impossible," 2–3.
69 "Reinhold Messner / When You're Alone, Fear is All on You," *Columnists India/Pak* (March 1, 2014): 3.
70 Reinhold Messner, *My Life at the Limit* (Seattle, Mountaineers Books, 2014).
71 Alexander, "Murdering the Impossible," 6–7.
72 Messner, *My Life.*
73 Ibid.
74 Xan Rice, "Observer Sport Monthly: Home on the Range," *The Observer* (October 3, 2004), 2.
75 Messner, *My Life.*

76   "Reinhold Messner / When You're Alone," 2.

77   Rice, "Observer" 3.

78   Messner, *My Life.*

79   Smith, "20 Reasons," 1.

80   "Reinhold Messner's Biography," www.messner-mountain-museum.it.

81   Elliott, "Top Climber," 3.

82   "Messner Mountain Museum," www.messner-mountain-museum.it/en (accessed November 30, 2017).

83   Messner, *My Life.*

84   "2010 – Reinhold Messner," www.pioletsdor.net/index.php/en/the-lifetime-achievement-award/21-po-carriere/liste-po-carriere/22-2010-reinhold-messner (accessed November 30, 2017).

85   Foulkes, "Matterhorn," www.bbc.com.

86   "Sherpa," www.britannica.com.

87   "Sherpas: The Invisible Men," National Geographic.com.

88   Bhandari, "Women Climb Indian," www.South China Morning Post.com.

89   Marco Maria Scolaris, "President's Message," www.ifsc-climbing.org/index.php/about-ifsc/what-is-the-ifsc/president-s-message (accessed November 30, 2017).

90   "Seven Summits Expeditions," www.alpineinstitute.com/programs/expeditions/the-seven-summits (accessed November 30, 2017).

91   Roberts, "Junko Tabei," www.nytimes.com.

92   "The 2017 Piolets d'Or," www.pioletsdor.net/index.php/en (accessed November 30, 2017).

93   Devon O'Neil, "Everest 2017: New Routes, New Records and Lots of Climbers," *Outside Online* (April 3, 2017): www.outsideonline.com/2168681/everest-2017-new-routes-new-records-and-lots-climbers (accessed November 30, 2017).

94   Merrit Kennedy, "Dispute Reports of More Everest Deaths" (May 24, 2017), www.npr.org/sections/thetwo-way/2017/05/24/529855463/everest-death-toll-rises-to-10-this-season-after-4-more-climbers-found-dead (accessed November 30, 2017).

95   Pradeep Bashyal, Annie Gowen, "Mount Everest Is so Crowded This Year, There is a Risk of 'Traffic Jams'," *Washington Post* (May 3, 2017): www.washingtonpost.com/world/mount-everest-is-so-crowded-this-year-there-are-traffic-jams/2017/05/03/7b4f4fe6-2f3c-11e7-a335-fa0ae1940305_story.html?utm_term=.470d13667a14 (accessed November 30, 2017).

96   Neelima Shrestha, "Saving Mount Everest Clean-Up Expedition Team Successfully Brings Over 8 Tons of Garbage from Mount Everest and its Trekking Trails" (May 29, 2011), www.savingmountever est.org/index.php?id=70 (accessed November 30, 2017).

97   Michael Safi, "Mount Everest Climbers Enlisted for Canvas Bag Clean-up Mission," *The Guardian* (March 29, 2017): www.theguardian.com/world/2017/mar/29/climbers-prepare-clean-up-mission-mount-everest-nepal-waste (accessed November 30, 2017).

98   Mark Horrell, "What's the Definition of a Mountaineer?" (August 9, 2011), www.markhorrell.com/blog/2011/whats-the-definition-of-a-mountaineer (accessed November 30, 2017).

99   "Four Basic Types of Rock Climbing Protection," www.seekingexposure.com/4-basic-types-of-rock-climbing-protection (accessed November 30, 2017).

100 Carol D. Kiesinger, George Alan Smith, "Mountaineering" (February 25, 2016), www.britannica.com/topic/mountaineering (accessed November 30, 2017).

101 "Chimney," www.dictionary.com/browse/chimney (accessed November 30, 2017).

102 Kiesinger, Smith, "Mountaineering," www.britannica.com.

103 Mark Synnott, "Exclusive: Climber Completes the Most Dangerous Rope-Free Ascent Ever," *National Geographic* (June 3, 2017): www.nationalgeographic.com/adventure/features/athletes/alex-honnold/most-dangerous-free-solo-climb-yosemite-national-park-el-capitan (accessed November 30, 2017).

104 Kiesinger, Smith, "Mountaineering," www.britannica.com.

105 "Ice Climbing," www.topendsports.com/sport/more/climbing-ice.htm (accessed November 30, 2017).

106 "Ice Climbing," www.topendsports.com.

107 Chris Brinlee Jr., "The Beginner's Guide to Rock Climbing," *Outside Online* (March 16, 2016): www.outsideonline.com/2062326/beginners-guide-rock-climbing (accessed November 30, 2017).

108 Brinlee, "The Beginner's Guide," www.outsideonline.com.

109 Kublak, *Mountaineering Methodology*, www.mountaineeringmethodology.com.

110 Brinlee, "The Beginner's Guide," www.outsideonline.com.

111 "Climbing Competition Types and Formats," www.indoorclimbing.com/comp_types.html (accessed November 30, 2017).

112 Kublak, *Mountaineering Methodology*, www.mountaineeringmethodology.com

113 Brinlee, "The Beginner's Guide," www.outsideonline.com.

114 Kiesinger, Smith, "Mountaineering," www.britannica.com.

115 Brinlee, "The Beginner's Guide," www.outsideonline.com.

116 Ibid.

117 Aleksey, "Types of Climbing" (September 5, 2014), http://climbingschool.org/types-of-climbing (accessed November 30, 2017).

118 Brinlee, "The Beginner's Guide," www.outsideonline.com.

119 Lola Jones, "The North Face of the Eiger" (April 4, 2011), http://xtremesport4u.com/extreme-air-sports/base-jumping/the-north-face-of-the-eiger-switzerland (accessed November 30, 2017).

120 Brendan Blanchard, "What the Hell is Speed Climbing?" *Climbing* (September 26, 2016): www.climbing.com/news/what-the-hell-is-speed-climbing (accessed November 30, 2017).

121 Patrick Joseph, "For 'Big-wall' Climbers, Hanging Around Is A Way Of Life," *Chicago Tribune* (February 18, 2001): http://articles.chicagotribune.com/2001-02-8/travel/0102180076_1_portaledges-big-walls-durable-tape (accessed November 30, 2017).

122 Brinlee, "The Beginner's Guide," www.outsideonline.com.

123 Mark Synnott, "Exclusive: Climber Completes," www.nationalgeographic.com.

124 "History of International Climbing Competitions," www.ifsc-climbing.org/index.php/about-ifsc/what-is-the-ifsc/history (accessed November 30, 2017).

125 Dougald MacDonald, "Climbing at Olympics— [*sic*] Sort Of," *Climbing* (January 17, 2006): www.climbing.com/news/climbing-at-olympicsmdashsort-of (accessed November 30, 2017).

126 Kevin Corrigan, "Climbing Officially Approved for 2020 Olympics," *Climbing* (August 3, 2016): www.climbing.com/news/climbing-officially-approved-for-2020-olympics (accessed November 30, 2017).

127 "Five Things You Need to Know about Sport Climbing" (April 11, 2017), www.olympic.org/news/five-things-you-need-to-know-about-sport-climbing (accessed November 30, 2017).

128 "Sport Climbing," www.topendsports.com/sport/more/climbing-ice.htm (accessed November 30, 2017).

129 Charles Arthur, "How to Succeed in Bouldering Comps" (February 2001), www.ukclimbing.com/articles/page.php?id=19 (accessed November 30, 2017).

130 "Climbing Competition," www.indoorclimbing.com.

131 David Harmanos, "Guide to Rock Climbing Competitions" (November 10, 2012), www.teamprg.org/2012/10/guide-to-rock-climbing-competitions.html (accessed November 30, 2017).

132 "Climbing Competition," www.indoorclimbing.com.

133 Ibid.

134 "For the Climbers. For the World," http://theuiaa.org (accessed November 30, 2017).

135 "About Us," https://usa-climbing.myshopify.com/pages/about-us (accessed November 30, 2017).

136 "What is the IFSC?" www.ifsc-climbing.org/index.php/about-ifsc/what-is-the-ifsc (accessed November 30, 2017.)

137 "For the Climbers," www.theuiaa.org.

138 "History of," www.ifsc-climbing.org.

139 Ibid.

140 Ibid.

141 "Five Things," www.olympic.org.

142 "History of," www.ifsc-climbing.org.

143 "For the Climbers," www.theuiaa.org.

144 "History of," www.ifsc-climbing.org.

145 Ibid.

146 "Five Things," www.olympic.org.

147 "History of," www.ifsc-climbing.org.

148 Ibid.

149 Ibid.

150 Ibid.

151 Ibid.

152 "Five Things," www.olympic.org.

38

Snowboarding and skateboarding

Mikhail Batuev, Sarah Zipp and Leigh Robinson

Introduction

In the last 30–40 years, participation in and media coverage of "extreme" sports, which can be also labelled as "action", "young", "free", "lifestyle", "whiz", "new" or "adventure" sports have increased remarkably (Gillis, 2001; Bennett, Henson and Zhang, 2002; Puchan, 2004; Breivik, 2010; Vivirito, 2011). Examples of such sports include aggressive inline-skating, snowboarding, mountain-biking, motocross freestyle, and free climbing. Whereas the definition of "extreme" or "action" sports highlights the excessive levels of danger that athletes expose themselves to, the term "free" or "alternative" sports refers to the same range of sports but points out the distinctive nature of those sports, which is to symbolize an alternative to the mainstream sport culture with its rule-bound and competitive spirit (Midol and Broyer, 1995; Wheaton, 2000).

In this chapter we will discuss two core major action sports: snowboarding and skateboarding, which along with surfing and wake-boarding, constitute the groups of "board" sports. These activities (which later became sports) have evolved around the idea of using the boards to slide on various surfaces: snow, water, concret, metal rails etcetera. Board sports are characterized by a certain artistic sensibility and "express a particular and exclusive social identity" (Wheaton, 2000, p. 258).

Snowboarding

Snowboarding has grown from a participatory activity to an established Olympic sport over the last three decades. It must be noted that a strong distinction exist between "racing" (or "alpine") and "freestyle" snowboarding disciplines. Freestyle snowboarding includes the disciplines of Halfpipe, Slopestyle, and Big Air, where participants perform on their own and essentially free to perform any flips, rotations, slides and other tricks. On the other hand, in racing disciplines of snowboarding, Slalom and Snowboard Cross, participants compete directly against each other on the racing course as the ultimate goal is to cross the finish line first. While time and finishing ahead of opponents are the objective winning criteria in racing snowboarding, the judging in freestyle snowboarding is subjective as it is based on points for successful execution of tricks, creativity and style. Snowboarding equipment differs for racing and freestyle snowboarding, but most importantly they represent completely different communities and cultures, so they are often seen as different sports. To relate this to more established "mainstream" sports, these perceptions are, in some way, similar to those that exist between two Olympic sports on ice: figure skating and speed skating. One is about a subjective judgement of elements, while the other is about speed and finishing first. For the purposes of this chapter, we will be focusing on freestyle side of snowboarding, as it is meant to be the core of the activity and the very idea of snowboarding has always revolved around "freedom of expression" and creativity.

The culture of snowboarding activity was anti-competitive at the beginning as it was built on and characterized by the major features of all "board cultures", which emphasized individuality, play, and a strong sense of expressionism (Heino, 2000; Steen-Johnsen, 2008). The early snowboarders "embodied freedom, hedonism and irresponsibility" (Humphreys, 1996, p. 9) in contrast to the expensive and bourgeois sport of skiing, which was framed by a strong set of rules of conduct (Thorpe and Wheaton, 2011). A majority of ski resorts originally banned snowboarders because they behaved and dressed differently and often broke resorts regulations. The rise of snowboarding was described as "an opposition and protest against certain aspects of modern societies" (Breivik, 2010, p. 262) that was reflected in the way snowboarders dressed, behaved, and performed. Competitions were not common in first years of any alternative sports as these activities emerged not as a sports but "as a way of life and a form of resistance to the mainstream sport culture of particular groups of young people who were searching for alternative ways of expressing their identities and interacting with the world" (Girginov, 2010, p. 407).

So snowboarding was an underground activity in the backwoods with some competitions but in a form of social gatherings rather than organized contests (Rails, 2011). Individualism and non-competitiveness have historically been distinctive features of snowboarding more closely aligned with the precepts of "play" rather than with the routine of training and performance emphasized in the standardized environment of mainstream sports. A vivid example of this is the 2014 Olympic snowboarding champion Sage Kotsenburg from the USA, posting the following statement on Twitter shortly before the Olympics in an attempt to demonstrate how snowboarding culture is different from the mainstream sports: "'Training' and 'snowboarding' should never be used in the same sentence" (Kotsenburg, 2013).

Competitive snowboarding has always been a part of a bigger phenomenon of snowboarding activity. As professional snowboarding athlete Christian Haller suggests, competitive snowboarding is very different from most other sports, as

> it is not only sports, but also is a lifestyle and big community behind that . . . there are so many different approaches. People can never ride a contest, but they can live from snowboarding. And there is a competitive side of snowboarding, which is kind of another world. You know it is up to you – there are a lot of opportunities [to do snowboarding].

> *(Christian Haller in Batuev, 2016)*

The most popular of snowboarding non-competitive activities over the last two decades was filming the videos that represented "an alternative source of employment for snowboarders that are anti-competitions because they provide snowboarders the opportunity to receive sponsorship and recognition among their contemporaries" (Coates, Clayton and Humberstone, 2010, p. 1087). Therefore, while we summarize the main organizational developments of competitive snowboarding over the last three decades in Figure 38.1 and further discussion, it is important to acknowledge that the competitive aspect can be seen as only one of the opportunities for snowboarding participants.

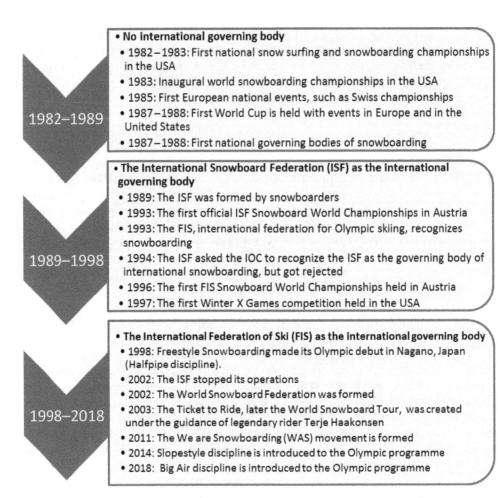

Figure 38.1 Timeline of the history of international competitive snowboarding.

Sources: Transworld Sport (1996), RAILS (2011), Natives (2002)

The grassroots and youthful appeal of snowboarding does not, however, make these sports easily accessible or inclusive. Snowboarding has long been perceived as a sport for whilte, middle class/upper class males, celebrating traditional masculinities and marginalizing women. Participation and media representation in this sport is dominated by young white men, with women and minorities only recently having increased presence in the sport (Thorpe, 2012). A National Ski Areas Association (NSAA) study showed that 86% of snowsport participants in the United States were white (Hunt and Secor, 2013). Although this study includes skiers, other studies confirm that minorities are under-represented in snowboarding, with only 11% of snowboarders identifying as ethnic or racial minorities (Thorpe, 2011). Women make up approximately 27% of snowboarders (Hunt and Secor, 2013). However, among the action sports that emerged in the 1960s and 1970s, snowboarding has been a more somewhat more welcoming to women compeitors. Women have been a part of the X-Games snowboarding programme since its beginning in 1997, while sports like skateboarding excluded women from competition well into the 2000s (Wheaton and Thorpe, 2016).

Snowboarding is also class-restrictive, as access to lessons, facilities (e.g. ski resorts) and equipment are expensive (Thorpe, 2011). Another NSAA study revealed that 58% of visitors to ski and snowboarding resorts were from households earning more than $100,000 annualy, an income level only 23% of US housholds achieve (Hamway, 2015). Although snowboarding can, and is often, practiced in "backcountry" locations, the majority of the world's 70 million snowboarders participate through resorts and rely on expensive equipment (Thorpe, 2011). It is hard to estimate the value of global snowboarding market, as most sources treat ski and snowboarding industry as one. For example, it was estimated that skiing/snowboarding industry contributes about 5 billion US dollars to the economy of Colorado state alone (Chapagain et al., 2018). While in terms of participation snowboarding was the second most popular winter sports behind downhill skiing in the United States in 2015–2016 season (Burakowski and Hill, 2018), it has recently become one of the most viewed Olympic sport. It had 28% of all worldwide TV exposure among the snow diciplines at 2014 Olympic Games beating traditional alpine skiing, cross-country skiing and ski jumping (Bridges, 2014). Four years later, Shaun White and Chloe Kim winning male and female Olympic golds in half-pipe achieved the highest median viewerships on the American national TV, overtaking the Opening ceremony (Samba, 2019). In the following sections, we will go through the history of organization of international snowboarding and major features that influenced its evolution over the last two decades.

Early history of international governance of snowboarding

The first national and international snowboarding competitions were held in the early eighties. The first national governing bodies were formed soon after in the USA: North American Snowboard Association in 1987 and United States Amateur Snowboarding Association in 1988. To facilitate the rapid growth of snowboarding as a professional sport, the International Snowboard Federation (ISF) was established by snowboarders in 1989. It was, however, very different from conventional sport federations. An earlier board member of the ISF, interviewed by Steen-Johnsen (2008, p. 344), emphasized that:

> snowboarding was a sport that from the outset was not particularly organized. But still we were running an internationally comprehensive work organizing competitions. And from the time when the first snowboard was seen on the slopes, we were innovators and created the culture and image around snowboard activities. But this was the snowboarders' own work; they determined the rules. They were behind the development and very few adults interfered.

The word "adults" here highlights not only that snowboarding has its roots in the youth culture, but also the idea that the ISF organized snowboarding differently from the mainstream federations. While mainstream sport organizations acted in a formal "adult" way, the ISF advocated an informal way of organization for snowboarding. This lack of formal organization meant that regulations emerged progressively, were developed by the snowboarding community and managed by the ISF, which described itself as not just a sport governing body but a "lifestyle/peace movement and philosophy" (Natives, 2002). The ISF played a leading role in the governance of the sport in the early 1990s representing "a common cause and a collective counter-culture identity to traditional sport" (Steen-Johnsen, 2008, p. 344) and developing snowboarding in a way to preserve the lifestyle (Popovic, 2006).

Due to this approach, the ISF evolution was very different from the development of a conventional sport governing body that usually involves formalization, bureaucratization, and "the new forms of integration and differentiation inside the organization" (Gomez et al., 2008, p.8). This was highlighted by Reto Lamm, a former elite professional snowboarder and the President of the TTR World Snowboarding Tour, who said that snowboarding "has been a progressive sport since the beginning . . . In the very beginning the idea of snowboarding was a new sport that has a different approach to everything" (Batuev, 2016).

The ISF had never been much concerned about formalization of competitions but, for example, rather had to push the progress of snowboard technology via contests:

> It [the ISF] was a bunch of riders who organized events and who organized the things to make it more fun for themselves . . . They were always willing to try something new. It was through competition in the ISF that modern race boards were designed. . . Unlike the more stuffy, bureaucratic International Ski Federation . . . [that] have a 300-page book to tell you how to do (an event).
>
> *(Christian Hrab, snowboard coach and former snowboarder, in Natives, 2002)*

Essentially, The ISF acted as a network. It served as a facilitating organization for professional snowboarders, event organizers, media, photographers, and producers but did not organize them in any formal sense (Steen-Johnsen, 2008). At the national level, snowboarding federations were created in countries such as the USA, Norway, Canada, Switzerland, and Japan. However, these federations were not directly governed by, but were aligned with, the ISF in an informal way. At the local level, these "soft" governance arrangements reflected quite a distinctive feature of the organization of snowboarding: grassroots participants were not institutionalized by governing bodies (Rinehart and Sydnor, 2003), or, in other words, the organization of snowboarding had been formalized only to a certain extent with regards to competition of elite athletes.

Snowboarding and the X-Games

Since the 1990s snowboarding has been an attractive platform for marketing of various brands to a young audience. Its popularity increased and made the ESPN to start organizing action sport event the X-Games, which included snowboarding. Athletes benefit from the X-Games, in particular, in terms of individual commercial opportunities due to the role of TV coverage and sponsorship in modern sport. However, their love for this event is not only due to commercial reasons. Winning the Olympic Games presents even greater opportunity in terms of commercial potential, but most athletes also indicate that, even though they put an extra effort in order to qualify for the Olympics because of the commercial benefits, they still consider winning the X-Games as the most credible competitive achievement within the snowboarding community.

> [The Olympic Games] . . . is not necessarily the biggest contest in snowboarding. But outside of the snowboarding it gives the viewers a perspective what is that sport like . . . But in the actual snowboard world I don't think it really matters. The X-Games feels just bigger, for example. The Olympics are just more credible to the outside world.
>
> *(Luke Mitrani, professional snowboarder, in Batuev, 2016)*

The reasons why the X-Games are more respected than the Olympic Games can be summarized in two arguments. Firstly, the X-Games are organized by the people from the snowboarding community and in consultation with the athletes in terms of contest setup, safety, judging system, and athlete facilities. So the X-Games are very much respected as a commercial organization with great understanding of snowboarding. There has been a difference in perception of commercial actors from snowboarding community and others who are not:

> A sharp line was drawn in the interviews between commercial actors that were not part of the snowboard culture and who seek to profit from it, such as banks or other commercial businesses. . . and commercial actors that belong to the snowboard network, such as board producers and magazines.
>
> *(Steen-Johnsen, 2008, p. 343)*

Many athletes express their honour at representing Burton, the manufacturer of snowboarding equipment and apparel, that is solely created and owned by snowboarders, rather than mainstream sport brands. For example, Cristian Haller, professional snowboarder from Switzerland, says that he is

> . . . really proud to ride for Burton cause it is snowboarder-owned, privately-owned company . . . It is hard these days for companies like this. They struggle and they don't do things like beachwear, skiing shirts etc. I like that. Snowboarding has its own thing, and it will always be like this I think.
>
> *(Batuev, 2016)*

In other words, the companies seeking only profits from snowboarding have not been welcomed by the snowboarding community, whereas commercial and media businesses integral to the activity have been respected. Therefore, even though the X-Games represented commercial interests, they have been always perceived as part of the snowboarding network.

Secondly, the organization and environment at the X-Games encourages creativity and self-expression and are more relaxed and closer to the snowboarding culture, rather than the very formalized, technical, and competitive Olympic culture.

> I would love to win the X Games more than have a gold medal [of the Olympic Games], for sure . . . [At the Olympics] it's not so much about who did the best run . . . It's about who did the most flips and the most spins. I hate that about it. I don't agree with it.
>
> *(Danny Davis, professional snowboarder, in New York Times, 2014)*

The example of the X-Games demonstrates that commercial actors have a deep credibility in snowboarding, and some of them have more cultural legitimacy than governing bodies.

Snowboarding and the Olympic Games

It was argued (Heino, 2000; Rinehart and Sydnor, 2003; Steen-Johnsen, 2008) that snowboarding gradually became more mainstream and lost a big part of its rebelliousness throughout the 1990s with the heavy spread of competitive snowboarding in mainstream media and its usage in marketing. As suggested by Rinehart and Sydnor (2003), this happened due to the move from expressive sport (driven by participants) to spectacle sport (driven by rewards), which led to the adoption of "must win" logic among at least some snowboarders. As competitions got extremely popular and became a source of income for athletes, by the middle of 1990s competitive snowboarding was accepted by most athletes, so it was not in a complete opposition to mainstream sports and skiing, in particular, anymore.

Commercialization and worldwide growth of popularity of snowboarding triggered its inclusion into the Olympic programme. Snowboarding became arguably the first and the best example of a action sport, which was selected by the IOC and included into the medal programme of the Winter Olympic Games since 1998. In order for a sport to become an Olympic sport, there must be an international governing body, which is recognized by the IOC as the one and the only legitimate (in terms of the Olympic movement) organization responsible for the sport globally (IOC, 2019). The introduction of snowboarding was different from the introductions of other new Olympic sports in the 1990s, for example, badminton in 1992 or triathlon in 2000, which followed the application of their respective international federations for IOC recognition and subsequent inclusion in the programme. However, it is argued by Steen-Johnsen (2008) and Rails (2011) that the ISF was never intending snowboarding to become a part of the Olympic movement. In other words, before 1994, the ISF, the leading international governing body of snowboarding run by the snowboarders themselves, never was pro-active in terms of the Olympic application and had no intention of fulfilling the IOC criteria in order to be recognized by the Olympic movement. As the snowboarding community were wary of a kind of organization such as the FIS, characterized by Transworld Snowboarding Magazine as a "bureaucratic giant", in 1994 the ISF asked the IOC to recognize the ISF as the governing body for international snowboarding but received "a three sentence reply" from the IOC that the FIS already governed that discipline (Transworld Sport, 1996).

There is an opinion that it is likely that the IOC decision to empower the FIS with the right to run Olympic snowboarding was driven by established commercial relationships between the IOC, the FIS, and the Olympic sponsors. This position has been mainly advocated by Terje Haakonsen, one of the best international competitive snowboarders of the 1990s, who has been an influential figure in snowboarding over the last two decades and is known as the only snowboarding athlete boycotting the Olympic Game in 1998. When explaining how iconic Terje Haakonsen was, Henning Anderson noted:

> Throughout the 1990s, Terje Haakonsen was more triumphant in halfpipe snowboarding than Christiano Ronaldo is in soccer today. He said no to the Olympics because the IOC gave his sport to the International Ski Federation (FIS). Terje was only twenty-four. According to his peers at the time he could easily have won the gold medal, but his consciousness said no. To this day, he is the only individual athlete having said no to the IOC and the Olympics based on sports political reasons. In all these years after his decision, he has been warning his fellow snowboarders about the Olympic pitfall …

> *(Henning Andersen, the organizer of the Arctic Challenge snowboarding event, in Bridges, 2014)*

Terje Haakonsen claimed that "they [the IOC] gave FIS, a ski federation, control of snowboarding, totally for commercial reasons" (Haakonsen, 2014). The Olympics are highly commercialized event, so the governing bodies in charge of Olympic sports are provided with significant funding from the IOC and also have indirect benefits, such as sponsorship and media rights valued at much more for Olympic sports than for non-Olympic sports. Terje's argument was that the IOC was clearly in a position to influence the FIS to bring the competitive snowboarding under its governance and into the Olympic programme. Similar opinions have been also raised by Heino (2000) who highlighted that the FIS accepted snowboarding as effectively one of the ski disciplines, having no prior interest in it and no understanding of its culture.

In opposition to the IOC and the FIS governance of international snowboarding, in 2002 a number of riders, event organizers, and sponsors established the TTR (Ticket to Ride) World

Snowboarding Tour, which has been managed by TTR Pro Snowboarding. In contrast with the FIS, the TTR Pro Snowboarding is a dedicated snowboarding organization, addressing the issues of competition safety and athletes' voice within its structures. This is highlighted by a Norwegian snowboarder Roger Kleivdal:

> . . . we can have no say there [in the FIS]. But in the TTR it has been better. We can actually tell them to change the course if that is scary or we don't want that or we need [half] pipe a little bit better. And they change it. That is pretty cool. So the TTR is better than the FIS for sure.
>
> *(Batuev, 2016)*

On a level of strategic decision-making, TTR Snowboarding has a substantial representation of the athletes and the event organizers. The President of the TTR Snowboarding, Reto Lamm, provides an example of the athletes' role in the decision-making process at 2014 General Assembly of the organization:

> it's actually the riders that are asking for this [the change of format of World Snowboarding Tour] from us. [The athletes] Stale (Sandbech), Torstein (Horgmo) and Kjersti (Buaas) came to us and were the representatives at the GA [General Assembly] and stood up in the open session and addressed the entire hall . . . and said "we want the World Snowboard Tour to run this. This is what we want, and exactly what the guys are presenting here is exactly what we need for our future". And so everyone could see that it was a necessity that everyone wanted. So . . . we were given the mandate both from riders and from the event organisations to roll this out.
>
> *(Boardsportsource, 2014)*

Therefore, apart from the Olympic snowboarding and the FIS World Cup tour that has been governed by the FIS since 1998, the TTR Snowboarding has been an alternative international snowboarding organization, which substituted the ISF in 2002 and organizes snowboarding competitions in a more flexible and athletes-driven way than the FIS does.

Essentially, the Olympic movement manifests the competitive aspect of sport and reflects the cultural ideals of western capitalist sport that snowboarders were opposed to. Therefore, the FIS and the IOC encountered a lot of cultural resistance since snowboarding was introduced to the Olympic Games. Brad Steward, one of the first influential snowboarders and entrepreneurs, provides several examples of how neglectful the FIS was to the culture of snowboarding:

> It's hard to imagine now, but some of the original FIS ideas for snowboarding included the following: Snowboarders will wear the same uniform as the ski team. Snowboarders will each be asked to do the same group of tricks, whoever completes that group of tricks the best will win. No music in the Pipe. Alpine will be the predominant discipline. All athletes will train solely with the team and all equipment used in the Olympics must pay a FIS Pool fee to belong (big money). Coaches will select all riders, none of the existing US events will qualify Olympic team athletes . . . I could go on.
>
> *(Brad Steward, former professional snowboarder, in Batuev, 2016)*

The ideas listed above are simply unthinkable for freestyle snowboarders because athletes in this sport have always embraced the culture of creativity, individuality, and fun. That is why it was unthinkable for them to wear uniforms, do the same tricks, train only within teams, and ban music. The mentioned ideas were not realized, but, inevitably, since the inclusion of snowboarding into the Olympic Games, snowboarders have been very concerned that "snowboarding values such as creativity and individuality would lose ground to nationalism and professionalism with FIS in the large Olympic machinery" (Rails, 2011, no page number). They resisted not the particular competition but rather the organizational hegemony and bureaucratic style of the IOC and the FIS that promoted snowboarding as part of the dominant culture under the discipline of skiing (Heino, 2000; Coates et al., 2010). Overall, cultural change was resisted among the elite international snowboarding in the early years of its Olympic journey, and traditional snowboarding values have remained relatively strong.

However, over the last two decades, the current international athletes have accepted what can be called "the positive aspects of mainstreaming and legitimation" of their sport (Heino, 2000, p.188). They now believe that snowboarding being an established part of the Olympic Games is beneficial for their careers and for the development of the sport in general. Although the acceptance of the Olympic Games by snowboarders does not necessarily suggest an acceptance of Olympic values, it still indicates a significant change from the view of Terje Haakonsen, the snowboarder of the earlier generation, who did not compromise on the values of snowboarding when he boycotted the Olympic Games. It did not happen immediately in 1998, but as suggested by snowboarding athlete Christian Haller, after three Winter Olympic Games, snowboarders accepted the Olympic Games as the most important contest, which the athletes and the sport benefit from:

> I think it is very logical that competitive snowboarding will go mainstream, or is mainstream [already]. That might sounds hard, but I think it is kind of the only way the sports get bigger . . . I feel that since Torino [2006] the Olympics are the most important snowboarding event. I feel like the media, snowboarding community itself . . . approved it.
>
> (Christian Haller, in Batuev, 2016)

This acceptance of the Olympic Games is largely due to commercial opportunities but is also due to the fact that competitive snowboarders have got younger over last two decades. Terje Haakonsen admits that the biggest difference in contemporary snowboarding from snowboarding of the 1990s is the age of the athletes: "there are 14-year-old guys now at the top level" (Batuev, 2016). Thus, the current generation of athletes has witnessed snowboarding only in Olympic era and are likely to perceive Olympic snowboarding as an integral part of the activity.

Overall, inevitably, due to the integration into the Olympic movement, international competitive snowboarding has become more homogenized into the mainstream sporting culture since 1998. As noted by Breivik (2010, p.270) "gradually parts of the snowboard milieu have been swallowed by the formalized sport culture and has become part of the Olympic sport culture with its competitive events and ideology". Traditional snowboarding values are still very much relevant for non-competitive snowboarding activities, such as freerising, but not that dominant in the competitive sport of snowboarding anymore. Nevertheless, even though the competitive dimension has changed, the sport still carries some major values of snowboarding, such as individualism, self-expression, and opposition for tight control.

Competitive skateboarding

Skateboarding is also a "board" activity, which emerged in America after the World War Two. Borden (2019) argues that skateboards evolved from the children's kick scooters shorn of the crate and handlebar components, which allowed the turning capacity to be similar to surfing, the activity that were enthusiastically practised in California and Florida at the time. The idea of "surfing" the streets quickly caught on among surfing participants and eventuall among the youth in the United States (Burke, 1999). Surf manufacturers and shops started to produce skateboards and their components in the sixties, and there has been a strong cultural bond between surfing and skateboarding ever since. Skateboarding industry has evolved on its own and experienced a few ups and downs over the years, but arguably it "has had little of the complex technological advances seen in other board sports like windsurfing and snowboarding" (Borden, 2019, p. 6).

While, technically speaking, skateboarding is a broad term for riding on a 4-wheel board, it has always entailed much more than that, for example, music, fashion, the way of life. The activity of skateboarding has been very diverse and has not fit to any conventional sport frameworks: "Skaters have a completely different culture from the norms of the world's society. We dress differently, we have our own language, use our own slang, and live by our own rules" (Maeda, 1991, p. 17).

The culture of the skateboarding community has always been based on opposition towards mainstream sport competitive values and towards corporate bureaucracy. The following quote illustrates values of skateboarding activity and the way a skateboarder is expected to perceive the world:

> Skateboarding, traditionally speaking . . . has always been "anti" all of this bullsh*t. Anti money. Anti corporation. Anti organization. Anti representation. Anti judgment. Anti hero. Anti team mentality. Anti segregation . . . Skateboarding, when viewed through a skater's eyes, is anti everything that sucks in the doldrums of the everyday world of "reality".
>
> *(Stratford, no date)*

It is difficult to define what sport of skateboarding is, as it has barely had any clear boundaries. In this section we will focus on competitive freestyle skateboarding that includes disciplines of Vert, Park, Street, Big Air, and Pool. Similar to snowboarding, in these disciplines participants have a freedom to perform slides, flips, jump, rotations and various other tricks on skateboard, which are judged subjectively on the basis of difficulty of the trick, landing, creativity and style. There are also "racing" disciplines of skateboarding, which in contrast to snowboarding, are considered relatively marginal in comparison to freestyle skateboarding.

The role of competition has been of very limited significance in skateboarding, especially in the early years of the sport. For instance, this is how Beal (1995) reported skateboarders' attitude to competition during the series of contests run by the Colorado Skateboard Association (CSA) in 1991:

> As Doug [a 25-year old skater from Welton] stated, "Skaters, even in contests, it's more an attitude of having your best run, making all your tricks as opposed to beating somebody. It's not 'I got to beat this guy, this is the guy I'm going to beat'". This negotiation between a corporate form of skateboarding and the interests of the skaters is reflected in the registration process. Contestants placed themselves into an appropriate category based on age and experience. Each contestant then had a corresponding registration number and color to denote the category pinned on his shirt . . . Many of the skaters pinned their numbers so they were difficult to read (e.g., upside down, or at the very bottom of the shirt). This intentional rejection of conformity demonstrates that these skaters were not fully dedicated to the values of the mainstream sport.
>
> *(Beal, 1995, pp. 259–260)*

While traditionally winning competitions was less important in skateboarding than enjoying the activity and having fun, there is now a much stronger emphasis on winning contests among the younger generation of skateboarding athletes. This focus on improving their contest performance in training, previously not a priority for skateboarders, indicates that the values of competitive skateboarding are changing and diverging from the traditional non-competitive values of this activity. The major reason for this was the growth of the X-Games and subsequent development of other competition platforms, e.g. the Street League Series (SLS), which have boosted the commercial potential of the sport and consequently increased the chances for athletes to make living from it.

A shift to the competitive side of skateboarding and suggested further institutionalization of sport have become a matter of concern to many athletes and members of the skateboarding community. For example, that is how Stratford (no date, p. 2) explains this stance:

> There has never been any serious movement that I know of, to legitimize skateboarding in the eyes of the powers-that-be that control which sports are recognized by the International Olympic Committee (IOC), and which aren't. . . Skateboarding already has a fairly effective infrastructure of industry, demos, contests, appearances, and media that works to promote, support, and grow skateboarding both locally, and worldwide, completely from within. So, there has traditionally been little to no need for any sort of outside entity to legitimize skateboarding in the eyes of the world (Although the "outside entities" usually feel like we do, anyway, regardless of what we might think about it) . . . It doesn't need to be hawked like an energy drink, or an extreme snack. It sells itself just fine on its own.

Nevertheless, with the upcoming first Olympic skateboarding competition in 2020, there has been an increasing acceptance of competitive skateboarding as an integral part of skateboarding culture. Acceptance into mainstream sport systems and competitions, such as the Olympics, reflects the global growth of skateboarding. Exposure of the sport through the X-Games and various online platforms has helped create skateboarding sub-cultures in places beyond North America, Europe and Ocenia, with emerging skateboarding cultures in the Middle East and Asia (Wheaton and Thorpe, 2016).

Inclusion in these structures has also compelled the sport to make room for women athletes. At skateboarding's debut in Tokyo 2020, women will participate alongside the men. It has been a long road to this milestone for women skateboarders. Skateboarding is typical of other action sports, built on a culture that is a "celebration of youthful, hedonistic fratriarchal masculinities" (Wheaton and Thorpe, 2016, p. 10). This environment, and an ethos that prizes close social ties among "competitors", tends to marginalize women and men who do not fit heterosexual norms.

> A lot of times at events where the guys are running the events and a lot of them really don't know who the girls are or what their needs are. A lot of times it just gets swept under the rug and the girls end up getting stuck with whatever they get. It's almost like the women's side is an afterthought.
>
> *(Professional female skateboarder, in Wheaton and Thorpe, 2018, p. 328)*

Skateboarding was slower to include women in competitions than snowboarding. While female snowboarders were competing in the X-Games since its beginning in 1997, skateboarding continued to exclude them until 2002 (Wheaton and Thorpe, 2016).

Overall, skateboarding today is a global industry worth around 5 billion US dollars (Wynn, 2018) with around fifty million skateboarders and thousands of skateparks worldwide (Borden,

2019). The X-Games have remained the main driver of international competition skateboarding with the following key indicators reported following the 2018 event in Minneanapolis (X-Games, 2019):

- 119,000 on-site attendance.
- Viewership across all telecasts increased by +21% year-over-year among fans aged 12–34.
- YouTube channel had more than 26 million minutes streamed, up +646% year-over-year.
- The Facebook page reached more than 9 million fans, up +120% year-over-year.
- The Instagram page reached more than 1.6 million people, up +225% year-over-year.

We discuss the main trends and issues of this rising sport in the following sections.

The early history of organization of competitive skateboarding

The history of organization of competitive skateboarding is much connected to the periods of its popularity in the USA and subsequent commercialization and professionalization of the activity. It is clear that the USA has always been the dominant country in terms of skateboarding development and the organization of skateboarding in the USA has mainly driven the global organization of the sport.

> Skateboarding is an extraordinary pastime in itself; that's almost totally obvious to anyone that's exposed to it. It's truly an American icon that has effectively spread itself all over the world, strictly based on its own merits, and its infectious appeal to kids and adults, young and old, everywhere.
>
> *(Stratford, no date, p. 2)*

The early 1980s marked the arrival of the first professional skateboarding athletes who were able to make a living thanks to commercial interest of the sponsors and competitive skateboarding. The arrival of Tony Hawk, as the role model athlete, who focused on the competitive side of skateboarding and benefited from his commitment to succeed in it, also facilitated a shift to a competitive side of skateboarding.

As Frank Hawk, the father of Tony Hawk, was "unimpressed by the level of organization of skateboarding competitions and wanted to create a more professional setting for his son and other young people who skateboarded" (Beal, 2013, p. 22), he created the National Skateboard Association (NSA), the first governing body for the sport in the USA, in 1981. In 1986, the NSA received non-profit corporation status from the State of California. It was quite different from what conventional sport governing bodies were as the NSA board of directors included the chief executive officers of the major commercial entities, which were involved in skateboarding, namely Vision, Powell/ Peralta, Santa Cruz, Transworld Skateboard, and Thrasher magazines (NSA, 1990). Such a heavy involvement of commercial actors underlined the NSA commitment to organize a corporate and commercialized form of sport through sponsoring amateur and professional events throughout the USA (Beal, 1995).

Throughout the 1980s, the NSA played the leading role in commercialization and legitimization of competitive skateboarding in the USA. The popularity of the sport started to spread outside the USA, and Beal (2013) highlights the contest in Vancouver, Canada, which was held during the World Expo Fair 1986, as the first international skateboarding competition. In the same year, the city of Munster, Germany hosted the first European Cup, which obtained the status of skateboarding's World Cup in 1989. However, in the beginning of 1990s skateboarding popularity began to

• First organisational steps
- 1981: National Skateboard Association (NSA) created
- 1986: The first international skateboarding competition in Vancouver, Canada
- 1987–1988: First World Cup in Muenster, Germany
- 1993: The NSA folded its operations

1981–1993

• The World Cup Skateboarding and the X-Games as the main competitive platforms
- 1993: World Cup Skateboarding (WCS) is established to replace the NSA
- 1995: The ESPN starts holding the X-Games with skateboarding as an integral part of the program
- 1995: World Cup Skateboarding Tour and ranking system started by the WCS
- 2002: United Professional Skateboarders Association (UPSA) created in the USA

1993–2002

• Olympic influence and various governing bodies
- 2002: The International Skateboarding Federation (ISF) is formed
- 2005: New USA Skateboarding Association becomes governing body for the USA
- 2007: Skateboarding is considered for 2012 Olympic Games inclusion under the International Cyling Federation (UCI)
- 2009: The first ISF World Championships is held in Boston
- 2010: Street League Skateboarding (SLS) starts
- 2011–2013: Various reports that the UCI proposes skateboarding for 2016 Olympic Games
- 2014: SLS and ISF announce partnership and SLS endorses ISF as official skateboarding federation
- 2014: Skateboarding debut at Youth Olympic Games as an exhibition event
- 2016: The IOC confirms skateboarding will make the Olympic debut in 2020
- 2018: The ISF merge with the FIRS to create the new governing body World Skate

2002–2018

Figure 38.2 Timeline of organization of international competitive skateboarding.
Sources: Batuev and Robinson (2017), WCS (2019), SLS (2019), Beal (2013)

decline, because of the US economy recession (Beal, 2013), so the sport faced difficult times both commercially and organizationally. The NSA President at that time, Don Bostick, was one of the organizers of the World Cup competitions in Munster from 1989 to 1993, and that is when it became clear to him that skateboarding needed "an Organization that encompassed more than just North America and one that worked for the skater's best interests" (WCS, 2019). As Don Bostick recalled in an interview, "after going to Europe, it opened my eyes to what skateboarding was internationally. When the NSA ... went under, I knew there was interest and a place for skateboard body in organizing and sanctioning events around the world" (interviewed by Young, 2013, p. 40).

Similarly to snowbording, the popularity of skateboarding started to build again with the launch of the ESPN X-Games. The impact on the X-Games of this sport has been huge and likely much bigger than any influence of any governing bodies that have ever been in charge of skateboarding. For example, Beal (2013, p. 40) notes that in 2000s the leading professional skateboarders demanded a pay raise and better working conditions from the X-Games organizers, not from any existing skateboarding governing bodies.

From the early years of alternative sports, their image and organization has been shaped by commercialism and brought forward by companies like Nike, Pepsi, MTV, and ESPN (Breivik, 2010). Likewise in case of snowboarding, competitive skateboarding has quickly become a corporate and commercialized form of sport. A number of skateboarders and representatives of skateboarding companies were behind the establishment of the International Skateboarding Federation (ISF) in 2002, including:

- Gary Ream, the ISF President, owner of the Camp Woodward, the biggest commercial operator of action sports and gymnastics facilities in the United States.
- Don Bostick, the President of the World Cup Skateboarding (WCS), former professional skateboarder, international skateboarding event organizer and entrepreneur.
- Dave Carnie, former Executive Director of the USA Skateboarding, editor of skateboarding magazine, owner of skateboarding decks brand.
- Tony Hawk, the most successful skateboarder in history, entrepreneur, millionaire.

The founders and the current officials of the ISF are coming from skateboarding industry and had held other positions in skateboarding commercial enterprises. Athletes have also been given substantial power within the ISF. The indicative example of the athletes' representation in international skateboarding is Tony Hawk, who is perceived as the voice of skateboarding globally. Overall, the ISF has existed to represent skateboarding on a bigger political stage, and specifically concerning the Olympic Games, and can be considered as the first international governing body of skateboarding.

Another issue, related to the history of organization of international competitive skateboarding, is whether this sport can be organized as a part of so called roller sports, which include inline-skating, inline hockey, roller derby, inline freestyle, and rink hockey. Since the 1960s, the leading international organization for roller sports has been the International Federation of Roller Sports (FIRS), which suggested roller sports included skateboarding in the following disciplines: slalom, downhill, street, and vert. However, the FIRS actions have always lacked any support from skateboarding athletes and community, while there has been a significant degree of support towards the ISF. Until recently, the FIRS had not been well connected with best athletes and event organizers in international skateboarding, so the FIRS statements and actions were not underpinned by any support from the actual sport and had no real consequences for organization of sport. However, the FIRS has recently become a major player in the Olympic perspective, which will be covered in the next section.

Skateboarding and the Olympic movement

As international skateboarding has grown and established itself as a competitive sport since the advent of the X-Games (Beal, 2013), reports and rumours about Olympic perspectives of this sport started to circulate (Koraeus, 2005; Buesing and Glader, 2011; O'Neil, 2012). Batuev and Robinson (2018) suggest that commercialism has been one of the major drivers of the Olympic "push" for skateboarding, as broadcasters, media, sponsors and event organizers have recognized business opportunities that introduction of skateboarding into the Olympic Games might bring. According to one of the most influential leaders of the skateboarding community, Don Bostick:

> NBC [broadcaster] . . . has a long term contract with the IOC, so they are trying to get Action Sports into the Olympics. The feeling is that the Olympics need to stay in tune with the times. Action Sports meaning; skateboarding, BMX Freestyle and Aggressive Inline. Vert is what excites NBC. It's really that simple.
>
> *(Don Bostick, cited in Koraeus, 2005)*

Therefore, it can be assumed that NBC, the American television broadcaster, has played the most active part in making the IOC consider skateboarding as a potential Olympic sport as it was interested in bringing it into the Olympic Games since the early 1990s.

There has always been a strong belief among professional athletes and key skateboarding influencers, such as Tony Hawk and Don Bostick, that skateboarding should enter only on "skateboarding's terms". As skateboarding has always been quite fragmented in organizational terms, there has never been a leading international federation responsible for the whole competitive skateboarding, which is a mandatory requirement for any potential Olympic sport. The establishment of the ISF in 2002 can be connected with a need to preserve skateboarding culture and protect competitive skateboarding from governmental control of non-skateboarding organizations, which was felt by key skateboarding organizers, companies, and athletes to be necessary as a result of the tensions following the the Olympic inclusion of snowboarding and a perceived interest of the IOC in skateboarding. Close cultural ties between two board sports meant that skateboarding athletes and influencers were very aware of issues that affected competitive snowboarding since it entered the Olympics. As skateboarding leaders did not want skateboarding values to be affected in the same way by global sport organizations, they have taken preventive actions in order to make sure skateboarding will enter the Olympic Games only "on skateboarding terms". According to Brixey, as the inclusion of skateboarding in the Olympic Games was inevitable, it should be done under control of people from skateboarding:

> as long as there's money to be made there are going to be people out there looking to take skateboarding, package it and sell the sh*t out of it. And there's no doubt that the Olympics will get hold of skateboarding at some point, whether that's 2016, 2024 or later ... But I feel a little better about it, knowing we've got people, like Dave Carnie or Tony Hawk [both the ISF founders] looking after it who are trying to ensure that the damage done is minimal.
>
> *(Brixey, 2012)*

However, the ISF itself has never been recognized by the IOC.

In the past, there was another international federation recognized by the IOC that indicated the willingness to take skateboarding into the Olympic programme under their patronage. This organization is the International Cycling Union (UCI), the global governing body of all cycling sports, from traditional road and track cycling to some modern disciplines such as BMX and mountain bike. Cycling has been present at all modern Olympic Games since 1896, and the UCI has been the international governing body for Olympic cycling since its creation in 1900 (UCI, 2019). An attempt to "fast-track" skateboarding to 2012 Summer Olympics via the UCI was well documented in media (Bane, 2011) and discussed in forums (Letsrun, 2014), as the UCI kept pushing and lobbying the idea of skateboarding entering the Olympics under its authority. For example, Pat McQuaid, the UCI president at time, declared again in 2011 that the "UCI could, without much difficulty but through a lot of work, bring skateboarding into the UCI structure and onwards into the Olympic program" (Bane, 2011). According to Sportcal (cited in Andersen, 2013), in 2013 during the IOC Executive Board meetings it was revealed that the UCI was ready to make a proposal to include skateboarding in the 2016 Olympic programme. However, despite the fact that UCI was thought to have some flexibility with regards to skateboarding, the sport did not make it to the list of the UCI disciplines.

As the IOC announced that Park and Street would be the two skateboarding disciplines that will make its Olympic debut at Tokyo 2020, it was also decided that the the FIRS would be rebranded into "World Skate", the international governing body for roller sports and skateboarding recognized by the IOC, The ISF has just joined this new international governing body in the form of its Skateboarding commission. At the time of publication, very little is known about the World Skate, which seems to be an organizational compromise between the FIRS and ISF. FIRS has not ever organized or sanctioned any significant international skateboarding competitions, but has been in the unique position as the only IOC-recognized international sport organization that claims skateboarding as one the disciplines under its jurisdiction. By contrast, the ISF has not been recognized by the IOC, but supported by international skateboarding athletes, community and key commercial ventures.

Even though many Olympic sports, such synchronized swimming, rhythmic gymnastics, and figure skating, include a subjective "artistic impression" as one of the judging criteria, one of the biggest concerns of the Olympic inclusion of skateboarding among the professional skateboarders has been about how skateboarding's flexible competition arrangements would fit into quite rigid Olympic frameworks. Skateboarding competitions encourage creativity and style,

> judging in skateboarding is so difficult . . . when it comes down to skateboarding, the style counts. You have to make it look good and smooth. And it comes down to a personal taste for the judge. So to put skateboarding in the Olympics, they [the IOC] have to really figure out the judging system that will be accepted by everybody. Otherwise you are going to have controversy for every single contest.
>
> *(Brad McClain, professional skateboarder, in Batuev, 2016)*

Arguably this concern can be addressed by existence of the SLS, the the major recent competition series in the Park discipline of skateboarding that has the Instant Scoring Experience judging system that

> provides instant, real-time results for every skateboarding trick . . . [and] creates fast paced real-time understanding of exactly what place every skater is in at every moment of the event. There are five Street League judges. Each judge has an ISX [Instant Scoring Experience] dial. They judge each trick that is done in each section. This will allow the viewers and skaters to know exactly what place everyone is at every moment of the event, allowing the winner to be known at the very instant the last trick the event is scored.
>
> *(SLS, 2019)*

This competition format and judging system became a completely new experience for international competitive skateboarding and again can be seen as a compromise between the traditional values of skateboarding creativity and certain standardization of competition judging required in the Olympics. As Batuev and Robinson (2017) suggested, the SLS format would, favour the technical side of skateboarding over the style as the instant scoring is focused on the difficulty of tricks. Overall, along with the merge of the FIRS and the ISF, this compromise is necessary to facilitate successful integration of international skateboarding into the Olympic Games.

References

Andersen, Henning. (2013) Post on personal Facebook page. Retrieved from www.facebook.com/henning.andersen.902?fref=ts (accessed 6 February 2019).

Bane, Colin. (2011) ISF, UCI, and the IOC. Retrieved from http://sports.espn.go.com/action/skateboarding/news/story?id=6361581 (accessed 6 February 2019).

Batuev, Mikhail. (2016) "Free sports": organizational evolution from participatory activities to Olympic sports. Doctoral thesis, University of Stirling.

Batuev, Mikhail and Robinson, Leigh. (2017) How skateboarding made it to the Olympics: an institutional perspective, *International Journal of Sport Management and Marketing*, 17, nos 4–6: 381–402.

Batuev, Mikhail, and Robinson, Leigh. (2018) What influences organisational evolution of modern sport: the case of skateboarding. *Sport, Business and Management: An International Journal*, 8, no. 5: 492–510.

Beal, Becky. (1995) Disqualifying the official: an exploration of social resistance through the subculture of skateboarding. *Sociology of Sport Journal*, 12, no. 3, 252–267.

Beal, Becky. (2013) *Skateboarding: the ultimate guide.* Santa Barbara, CA: ABC-CLIO.

Bennett, Gregg, Henson, Robin and Zhang, James. (2002) Action Sports Sponsorship Recognition. *Sport Marketing Quarterly*, 11, no.3: 174–185.

Boardsportsource. (2014) TTR Tour 2.0: Centralising riders & TV rights. Friday interview. Retrieved from www.boardsportsource.com/#!/article/the-friday-interview-ttr-tour-2-0-centralizing-riders-tv-rights (accessed 6 February 2019).

Borden, Iain. (2019) *Skateboarding and the city: A complete history.* Bloomsbury Publishing,

Breivik, Gunnar. (2010) Trends in adventure sports in a post-modern society. *Sport in Society*, 13, no. 2, 260–273.

Bridges, Pat. (2014) Boycott the Olympics: The IOC needs snowboarding more than we need them. 5 November. Retrieved from www.snowboarder.com/featured/boycott-the-olympics-the-ioc-needs-snowboarding-more-than-we-need-them/#RVq7OmeSCOCAKDqe.99 (accessed 6 February 2019).

Brixey, Webb. (2012) Skateboarding vs. The Olympics: a brief history. Retrieved from www.jenkemmag.com/home/2012/09/04/skateboarding-vs-the-olympics-a-brief-history (accessed 6 February 2019).

Buesing, Brock and Glader, Paul. (2011) Skateboarding in the Olympics? Retrieved from http://sports.espn.go.com/action/skateboarding/news/story?id=6274791 (accessed 6 February 2019).

Burakowski, Elizabeth, and Hill, Rebecca. (2018) *Economic Contributions of Winter Sports in a Changing Climate.* Boulder, CO: Protect Our Winters.

Burke, L.M. (1999) *Skateboarding!: Surf the Pavement.* The Rosen Publishing Group.

Chapagain, Binod P., Neelam C. Poudyal, J.M. Bowker, Ashley E. Askew, Donald B.K. English, and Donald G. Hodges. (2018) Potential effects of climate on downhill skiing and snowboarding demand and value at US national forests. *Journal of Park & Recreation Administration*, 36, no. 2.

Coates, Emily, Clayton, Ben and Humberstone, Barbara. (2010) A battle for control: Exchanges of power in the subculture of snowboarding. *Sport in Society*, 13, no. 7: 1082–1101.

Gillis, Richard. (2001) Ready to board? Richard Gillis on the rapid growth in extreme sports. *Sports Business*, 60, 14–17.

Gómez, Sandalio, Opazo Magdalena and Martí, Carlos. (2008) Structural characteristics of sport organizations: main trends in the academic discussion. Working paper, IESE Business School.

Girginov, Vassil. (2010) Culture and the Study of Sport Management. *European Sport Management Quarterly*, 10, no. 4: 397–417.

Haakonsen, Terje. (2014) Why I still hate the Olympics. Retrieved from http://whitelines.com/features/comment/terje-haakonsen-why-i-still-hate-the-olympics.html (accessed 6 February 2019).

Hamway, Stephen. (2015) Study identifies skiing trends. Survey shows average age of skiers, boarders has plateaued. *The Bulletin*, 27 December.

Heino, Rebecca. (2000) New Sports: What is So Punk about Snowboarding? *Journal of Sport & Social Issues*, 24 no. 2: 176–191.

Humphreys, Duncan. (1996) Snowboarders: Bodies out of control and in conflict. *Sporting Traditions*, 13 no. 1: 3–23.

Hunt, Katherine and Secor, Will. (2013) *A business case analysis of the snowboarding industry. Journal of Business Case Studies*, 9, no. 2: 111–120.

IOC. (2019) Olympic Charter. Retrieved from www.olympic.org/Documents/olympic_charter_en.pdf (accessed 6 February 2019).

Koraeus, Hans. (2005) Skateboarding (in general): getting organized. Retrieved from www.slalomskateboarder.com/phpBB/viewtopic.php?t=2336 (accessed 6 February 2019).

Kotsenburg, Sage. (2013) Twitter post. 2 October. Retrieved from https://twitter.com/sagekotsenburg/status/385580500737220609 (accessed 6 February 2019).

Letsrun. (2014) IOC may add skateboarding for London 2012. Forum thread. Retrieved from www.letsrun.com/forum/flat_read.php?thread=1957546 (accessed 6 February 2019).

Maeda, K. (1991) Rights for skateboarders [Letter to the editor]. *Windsor Beacon*, October, p. 17.

Midol, Nancy and Broyer, Gerard. (1995) Toward an anthropological analysis of new sport cultures: the case of whiz sports in France./Vers une analyse anthropologique des nouvelles cultures sportives: le cas des sports de glisse en France. *Sociology of Sport Journal*, 12, no. 2: 204–212.

Natives. (2002) ISF folds operations. Retrieved from www.natives.co.uk/news/international-snowboard-federation-folds/4625 (accessed 6 February 2019).

New York Times. (2014) Snowboarder Danny Davis's ambivalent comeback. 15 January. Retrieved from www.nytimes.com/2014/01/16/sports/snowboarder-danny-davis-sochi-olympics.html?_r=0 (accessed 6 February 2019).

NSA. (1990) *Packet for new members.* National Skateboard Association.

O'Neil, Devon. (2012) No rush for gold. Retrieved from http://xgames.espn.go.com/skateboarding/article/8253956/skateboarding-unlikely-become-olympic-sport (accessed 6 February 2019).

Popovic, Megan. (2006) From Terje to the Flying Red Tomato: snowboarding's incorporation into the Olympic Games. *Proceedings: International Symposium for Olympic Research*, 1 October: 157–168

Puchan, Heike. (2004) Living "extreme": Adventure sports, media and commercialisation. *Journal of Communication Management*, 9 no. 2: 171–178.

Rails. (2011) Project Rails: reviewing and analyzing the international level of snowboarding. Master's dissertation, University Of Oslo.

Rinehart, Robert and Sydnor, Synthia. (2003) *To the Extreme: Alternative Sports, Inside and Out.* Albany, NY: State University of New York Press.

Samba. (2019) Winter Olympics Viewership Analysis. Retrieved from https://platform.samba.tv/resources/insights/2018-winter-olympics-viewership-analysis (accessed 6 February 2019).

SLS. (2019) About the SLS. Retrieved from http://streetleague.com/about (accessed 6 February 2019).

Steen-Johnsen, Kari. (2008) Networks and the organization of identity: the case of Norwegian snowboarding. *European Sport Management Quarterly*, 8, no. 4: 337–358.

Stratford, B. (no date) Gary Ream Doesn't Speak For Me: Why I cannot and will never support skateboarding in the Olympics. Retrieved from http://realskate.com/MrReam.pdf.

Thorpe, Holly. (2011) *Snowboarding Bodies in Theory and Practice.* Berlin: Springer.

Thorpe, Holly. (2012) Transnational mobilties in snowboarding culture: Travel, tourism and lifestyle migration. *Mobilities*, 7, no. 2: 317–345.

Thorpe, Holly and Wheaton, Belinda (2011) "Generation X Games", Action Sports and the Olympic Movement: Understanding the Cultural Politics of Incorporation. *Sociology*, 45, no. 5: 830–847.

Transworld Sport. (1996) *Snowboard History Timeline Part 3(1990s).* Retrieved from http://snowboarding.transworld.net/uncategorized/snowboard-history-timeline-part-31990s (accessed 6 February 2019).

UCI (2019) About the UCI. Retrieved from www.uci.org/inside-uci (accessed 6 February 2019).

Vivirito, J. (2011) Action Sports Reach New Heights. *Sportstravel*, 15, no. 6: 21–26.

WCS (2019) World Cup skateboarding history. Retrieved from www.wcsk8.com/history-of-wcs (accessed 6 February 2019).

Wheaton, Belinda. (2000) "Just do it": consumption, commitment, and identity in the windsurfing subculture. *Sociology of Sport Journal*, 17, no.3: 254–274.

Wheaton, Belinda and Thorpe, Holly. (2016) Youth perceptions of the Olylmpic Games: Attitudes towards action sports at the YOG and Olympic Games. *The IOC Olympic Studies Centre.* June.

Wheaton, Belinda, and Thorpe, Holly. (2018) Action Sports, the Olympic Games, and the Opportunities and Challenges for Gender Equity: The Cases of Surfing and Skateboarding. *Journal of Sport and Social Issues*, 0193723518781230.

Wynn, Jonathan. (2018) "Skateboarding LA: Inside Professional Street Skateboarding by Gregory J. Snyder". *Social Forces* 97, no. 1.

X-Games. (2019) History of X-Games. Retrieved from www.xgamesmediakit.com/read-me (accessed 6 February 2019).

Young, Nicky. (2013) ICON: Don Bostick. *Topgrom,* Summer, 8 August, 38–41. Retrieved from http://issuu.com/sbittle/docs/topgrom-mag-22-issuu-190dpi?e=8384272/4355435 (accessed 6 February 2019).

39

Surfing

Dexter Zavalza Hough-Snee

Ancient and early modern surfing through 1800

Well before surfing's twentieth-century emergence as an international competitive sport and twenty-first-century crowning as a $13 billion industry,[1] surfing was a global cultural practice. With the sea central to many indigenous societies, waveriding demonstrated social, religious, and political importance prior to becoming a modern sport.[2] In fact, waveriding's global character long precedes notions of surfing as a regimented, judged set of athletic performances: while surfing as modern sport is a by-product of the twentieth-century institutionalization of surfing via surf and surf lifesaving clubs, competitive governance, and the surf industry, waveriding has long connected coastal cultures across the globe.

As early as 3000 BCE, the seagoing peoples of north-central Peru took to the waves atop the *caballito de totora* (*tup* in the now-extinct Mochica language), a single-manned vessel crafted of totora,[3] with a profile resembling an early hybrid of modern kayaks and standup paddle surfboards. The *caballito*'s pilots, predominantly adult male fishermen, would ride waves seated or kneeling when returning from nearshore fishing excursions or transporting goods along the coast.[4] Sixteenth-century Spanish explorers noticed that such indigenous navigational practices took on elements of a thrill ride and commented on wavecraft in their writings.[5] Similar wave-riding observed throughout South America and the Pacific have led to modern attempts to substantiate hypotheses of shared ancient Andean and Polynesian cultural and genetic ancestry.[6]

African peoples surfed with boards, as well. Representing the Dutch West Indies Corporation in West Africa, Nuremberg goldsmith Michael Hemmersam first observed Atlantic Africans surfing in the 1640s, although he mistook their adept waveriding as a means of learning to swim.[7] Jean Barbot observed children, perhaps boys and girls, "on bits of boards, or small bundles of rushes, fasten'd under their stomachs" near Elmina, Gold Coast (Ghana).[8] Though European observers conflated young Africans' proficient waveriding as a means of learning to swim, during the next two centuries these seventeenth-century accounts of African surfing would be replaced by unequivocal accounts of West African youths riding waves on boards.[9] James Edward Alexander's 1834 observations of bellyboarding at Accra, Ghana precede Thomas Hutchinson's accounts of fishermen surfing in now-southern Cameroon, where the former detailed emotive descriptions of recreational waveriding and racing atop dugout canoes.[10] Although materially different than modern surfboards, these crafts were roughly the size of modern-day surfboards and significantly smaller than the Hawaiian surfboards of the day.[11] As in South America, Europeans versed in oceanic navigation were not equally adroit in the surf zone and their observations reflect a marvel and respect for indigenous aquatic skills far exceeding those of Europeans.[12]

Likewise, diverse forms of waveriding were present throughout Oceania, including among Aboriginal peoples of Australia and New Zealand, where "surfing, or various forms of wave riding, have long been practiced."[13] Commented upon by British Captain James Cook, the aquatic cultures of Polynesia proved particularly adept at engaging the surf for food and recreation. In Tahiti, Cook's onboard surgeon, William Anderson, recorded a detailed account of canoe surfing in Matavai Bay.[14] In New Zealand, nineteenth-century observers documented the Maori practicing traditional Polynesian forms of surfing (*whakahekeheke*) on a range of surfcraft, including surfboards known as *kopapa*.[15] Similar displays were documented throughout Polynesia.

The most important indigenous surfing culture for modern surfing is that of Hawai'i, known as *he'e nalu*. With waveriding on wooden boards dating back several millennia, "the more developed form of *he'e nalu*, standing while riding," dates back to the sixth century CE.[16] Standup surfing for twelve centuries before Cook's crew documented surfing, Hawaiians of all ages and both sexes rode waves atop a variety of surfcraft that would impress Cook's crew in 1778.[17] Although the British expedition had seen surfing in Tahiti the year prior, the means by which surfing participated in Hawaiian cultural, social, religious, and economic life was unique to the island chain.[18] In fact, surfing was so central to Hawaiian culture that it garnered wonder and scorn from Europeans: wonder, at Native Hawaiians' athleticism and intuitive relationship with the ocean, and scorn, for the pervasiveness of surfing – instead of work – among all ages and sexes, at all times of day.[19]

The age of discovery revealed the global character of waveriding to explorers circling the world under the charge of their respective imperial and corporate flags. The spectacular nature of waveriding in its many forms – bodysurfing, swimming, diving, small-vessel navigation, and board surfing – was on display practically everywhere that European maritime explorers arrived. Manifest in aquatic cultures throughout the early modern world, surfing was truly a global pastime well before the emergence of modern sport. There was, however, one glaring exception: Europe.[20] Although Europeans circumnavigated the globe time and time again, mapping and colonizing the world's coasts, Europeans demonstrated an aversion to swimming, and thus surfing, until the nineteenth century.[21] In order for surfing to enter the matrix of institutionalized sport in the twentieth century, Europe had to overcome its uncomfortable physical and ideological relationship with ocean bathing, an uncomfortable process that would take centuries. The West would finally embrace the beach with the advent of surf lifesaving in the United States, Oceania, Europe, and South Africa, a trend seen as "making the beach safe for surfing."[22] And when they did, Hawai'i would be the locus for surfing's conversion into a modern sport through indigenous surfers, American profiteers, and ever-evolving surfcraft.

Surfing and European colonization: 1800–1910

As Europeans settled the globe through the nineteenth century, rising Western comfort with the sea and aquatics more generally led to rising Western beach culture centered around sea-bathing, which primed the water-going public for surfing's twentieth-century rise.[23] And nowhere was a more prominent site of nascent Western water culture than annexation-era Hawai'i. While Europeans first stigmatized Hawaiian surfing for its intermingling of sexes and a perceived licentiousness of the tropical beach space where Native Hawaiians generally went nude, countless Europeans tested surfboards in colonial Hawai'i,[24] beginning with the odd sailor and culminating in early-twentieth-century tourism promoters such as Alexander Hume Ford, who founded Waikiki's "de facto whites-only" Outrigger Canoe Club in 1908.[25] Ford "encourage[ed] all comers to pick up a board and give the new sport a try" and promoted the sport to white visitors in magazines and newspapers, even alleging that "those most expert in Hawaiian water sports were ... white boys and girls."[26]

Meanwhile, Hawaiians had continued to surf in spite of a century of population decline, missionary restrictions, and workforce pressures in the new colonial economy.[27] Native Hawaiians – like coastal populations worldwide, with their respective forms of waveriding – continued to surf throughout American colonization and annexation. Still, if the promotional wagers of Hume Ford and his collaborators with the Hawaiian Promotion Committee did not "revive" surfing, they did ardently package and promote the sport for tourists, introducing board surfing to visitors on a scale never seen before.

But Ford's efforts came decades after the first documentation of surfing in the mainland USA. In 1885, on the eve of Hawaiian annexation, surfing arrived to California through three Hawaiian princes attending military school in San Mateo.[28] The young royalty built boards from local redwood (instead of the traditional Hawaiian koa tree) and surfed in Santa Cruz, although surf culture never took off and "these earlier episodes left no roots."[29]

Surfboards circle the world, surfing gains ground: 1910–1960

Standup surfing on surfcraft fashioned after Hawaiian surfboards gained global reach in the twentieth century, in part due to tourism to Hawai'i and surf lifesaving's use of paddleboards worldwide. Through the 1950s, waveriding boomed in California, Australia, South Africa, and post-annexation Hawai'i, accompanied by small, isolated coastal enclaves riding waves around resort towns.[30] Through the circulation of surfboard technology, surfing spread across the globe as an outdoor pastime and took on a new identity as an avatar of modern leisure, competitive surfing – surfing as modern sport – appearing in local contexts through surf and lifesaving clubs.

As more and more tourists traveled through Hawai'i between American annexation and the Islands' Second World War militarization, Hawai'i became a global center for the dissemination of surfing during the early twentieth-century. International visitors regularly hired surf lessons from Waikiki's famed Beach Boys,[31] gaining varied levels of proficiency before returning home to try their hand at local beaches. Hawai'i and Native Hawaiian surfers – as instructors and practitioners – were central to modern surfing's arrival overseas. Part-Hawaiian George Freeth (1883–1919) and Native Hawaiian Duke Kahanamoku (1890–1968) are surfing's greatest Hawaiian exporters, the former surfing in Venice, California in 1907 and the latter giving surfing exhibitions in New Jersey (1912) and California (1915–1930s), before surfing in Australia (1914–1915) and New Zealand (1915). Freeth, who gave surfing demonstrations organized by industrialists promoting beach recreation to sell coastal real estate, surfed throughout Southern California for over a decade, pioneering the modern, proactive lifesaving techniques that primed American beaches for surfing's popularization.[32] Australian and New Zealand beaches followed suit, and surf lifesaving clubs exploded in the first decades of the twentieth century, responsible for organizing Kahanamoku's travels to Australia.[33]

But two men and a handful of promoters couldn't single-handedly birth surfing-as-sport. Interestingly, books and magazines supported surfing's growth on three continents, even if only in embryonic form. For example, First World War pilot Tony Bowman returned to South Africa from England in 1919, settling in Cape Town in 1921. There, he is said to have read Jack London's *The Cruise of the Snark*, an account of Freeth surfing in Waikiki. Aware of the potential to ride waves on nearby Muizenberg Beach, in 1922 Bowman set out to build a surfboard, requesting pictures of contemporary surfcraft from the Honolulu Tourist Association, which he used as boardbuilding plans. With friends Lex Miller and Bobby Van Der Riet, Bowman fabricated several timber-framed hollow surfboards, taking to the waves at Muizenberg Corner in the 1930s.[34]

In England, Londoner Lewis Rosenberg made a surfboard from balsa after seeing images of Australian surfing that inspired him to attempt surfing in Newquay circa 1929.[35] Nearly a decade later in 1941, Pip Staffieri was photographed surfing on a self-shaped hollow surfboard purportedly derived from the 1929 *Encyclopedia Britannica* entry on Hawai'i, which depicted surfers and their equipment.[36]

In Santos, São Paulo, Brazil, Osmar Gonçalves built a 3.9-meter, 80kg board after obtaining a 1937 *Popular Mechanics* magazine article depicting how to build the chambered surfboard pioneered by American surfer-inventor Tom Blake.[37] The sixteen-year-old Gonçalves enlisted friends João Roberto and Júlio Putz to build the craft, which they christened at Santos' Canal 3 beach in 1938. Portugal's first surfer, Nuno Fernandes, was similarly driven to build and surf a self-fashioned surfboard modeled after Blake's article, taking to the waves in Figueira da Foz. Another Portuguese, Pedro Martins de Lima, discovered surfing via American magazines[38] on a US Naval base in the Azores Islands, first improvising belly boards in the 1940s and later importing surfboards from Biarritz to Estoril, Portugal circa 1959.

More commonly though, through the mid-twentieth century, surfing arrived to distant shores via affluent tourists who visited Hawai'i and picked up the sport before returning home with surfboards. Before Kahanamoku's Australian tour, Charles Paterson, a Manly alderman and future president of the Surf Life Saving Association of Australia (1912–1933), imported a board from Hawai'i. According to Percy Hunter, head of the New South Wales tourism bureau, several surfboards dotted manly circa 1910.[39] Between 1911 and 1913, newspaper and oral accounts place youths Tommy Walker, Basil Kirke, and Jack Reynolds at the fore of Manly's surfing scene.[40] At Point Lonsdale, Victoria in 1915, Grace Smith Wootton took up surfing after riding a board brought from Hawai'i by a Mr. Jackson and Mr. Goldie.[41] Virginian Walter F. Irvin brought a redwood *olo* to Virginia Beach – the first of its kind on the American East Coast – as a gift for his nephew in 1912.[42] Before Bowman built South Africa's first surfboards, Cape Town resident Heather Price (a Zimbabwean national) learned to surf at Muizenberg in 1919 alongside two United States Marines who, mysteriously, had Hawaiian-styled surfboards with them while returning home from the First World War.[43] In the UK, Nigel Oxenden returned to Jersey after taking surf lessons with Kahanamoku at Waikiki in 1919, prompting the 1923 foundation of Jersey's Island Surf Club.[44] Prince of Wales, Edward VIII, also took lessons with Kahanamoku in 1920, raving about the experience in official correspondence.[45] Spanish consul in Hawai'i, Ignacio de Arana (1880–1918) introduced the first surfboards to Europe in Vitoria (Basque Country), Spain, circa 1914. Arana also brought with him a copy of *The Surf Riders of Hawaii*,[46] the world's first surf-specific book.[47] Another who introduced surf equipment was Kahanamoku, who left his boards with locals, such as Manly Beach surfer Claude West, a future Australian national champion (1919–1924).

1936 marked the year that Californian hoteliers Bob and Louise Koke first surfed in Indonesia, then the Dutch East Indies.[48] Having brought a surfboard with him to Bali after passing through Hawai'i, he rode waves adjacent to his Kuta Beach Hotel, where he gave lessons to Western guests. He amassed a fleet of surfboards via Hawai'i and surfing seemed poised to take off, had the hotel not closed in 1941 prior to Japanese invasion.

While Koke surfed in Bali, Carlos Dogny Larco, the Ivy-educated son of a powerful Franco-Peruvian agricultural family, imported surfing to Peru in 1937 after learning to surf in Hawai'i in the mid-1930s. There, he surfed with famed Waikiki Beach Boys, including Kahanamoku, who is rumored to have given Dogny his first surfboard. Upon intensification of the Second World War, Dogny returned to Lima with surfboards and introduced the sport to Peruvian shores. Surfing promptly took off around Lima, where the city's elite had taken to sea-bathing and coastal sporting leisure at private waterfront clubs. Modeled on the exclusive Club Regatas (1875) and Club Terrazas (1918), Dogny founded Club Waikiki in 1942, an upscale social club catering to surfers, further embedding surfing in the Peruvian elite.[49]

In Brazil, surfing was a regular pastime in coastal Rio de Janeiro and São Paulo by the 1950s.[50] During the 1940s American servicemen were stationed in Rio, some of whom brought surfboards with them, perhaps from Hawai'i.[51] By the 1950s, young *cariocas* were regularly surfing on solid wooden boards known as "*portas de igreja*" ("church doors," for their long, thin profile). As surfing grew from novelty pastime to sport in Rio, lighter wooden boards known as "*madeirite*" emerged, in part due to the local wood board's commercialization by an Ipanema carpenter circa 1962.[52] By 1964, Rio magazines and newspapers had announced surfing's arrival alongside American exportation of beach blanket films and surf music. Brazilian journalists quickly adapted an English-inspired lexicon that rendered all surfboards "*pranchas*" ("boards") and "*pranchistas*" became "surfers."[53] Surfing became tied to California (which enjoyed the largest global surfing population through the 1970s), post-annexation/statehood Hawai'i, and United States beach culture more generally as a symbol of international luxury and modernity.[54] 1965 saw the creation of the Federação Carioca de Surfe, which organized surfing competitions in Rio, followed closely by contests at Gonçalves' beach of Santos (São Paulo) in 1967.[55]

Across the Atlantic, the Muizenberg surfers of the 1910s and 1920s were followed by South African surfing's arrival to the temperate waters of Durban. Here, surfing arrived via members of the Durban Surf Life Saving Club (1927) and Pirates Surf Life Saving Club (1928), who, like their Californian and Australian contemporaries, had set out to improve public ocean safety, picking up surfboard riding along the way.[56] Fred Crocker, a member of the latter club, built a few modestly functional surfboards in the mid-1930s. When Durban SLSC member and South African national swim coach Alec Bulley returned from the 1938 Empire Games in Sydney with sketches of modern surfboards and surf skis, Crocker used the plans to build more advanced equipment with local materials, his boards garnering the name "Crocker Skis."[57] A Durban-based lifeguard crew attended the 1956 International Surf Carnival in Australia, where they were introduced to American Malibu boards, which they quickly began to improvise. Back in Cape Town, John Whitmore built the boards for local surfers from a magazine article. Whitman later acquired South African licenses for Clark Foam – the primary surfboard foam manufacturer for decades – and *Surfer* magazine after encountering Hobie Surfboards denizen Dick Metz during the Californian's visit to Cape Town in 1959. A local surf mogul, Whitmore hosted Bruce Brown and the *Endless Summer* crew around the country in 1963.

Mid-century New Zealand surf culture got a technological boost from magazines, which published blueprints for longboards, enabling local craftsmen to innovate equipment beyond the solid wooden boards found in Lyall Bay (Wellington), Muriwai (Auckland), and New Brighton (Christchurch) in the 1920s and 1930s. Californian lifeguards Rick Stoner and Bing Copeland visited in the summer of 1958–1959, surfing their imported Malibu boards for four months and further popularizing the sport and its modern technologies – fiberglass over balsa cores – at the Piha Surf Lifesaving Club.[58] Australian surfing evolved similarly, as Frank Adler built a hollow board known as "The Racing 16" in 1934, replacing solid timber boards before the introduction of Malibu boards to Australia by a team of American lifeguards participating in the Melbourne Olympics in 1956–1957.[59] On beaches across the world, it only took the arrival of a single surfboard – or even a picture of one – for local craftsmen to begin to make their own. Conspiring with the growth of surf lifesaving and the dawn of consumer air travel, surfing began to flourish in beach communities worldwide.[60]

In 1956, American film industry personalities and Southern California surfers Peter Vietrel and Richard Zanuck surfed in Biarritz, France, while filming on location for *The Sun Also Rises*, prompting well-heeled locals to pick up the sport in the ritzy coastal destination.[61] Two years later, in 1958, Dogny co-founded Biarritz's own Waikiki Surf Club in with French surfer Michel Barland on the model of the homonymous clubs in Honolulu and Lima. In 1959, Europe's first surfboard label, the French Barland-Rott brand, was founded. On the wind-ravaged German island of Sylt, lifeguard Uwe Drath was documented surfing a rescue board in the 1950s.[62]

Much of coastal Europe staffed growingly popular beaches with summer lifesavers in the 1950s and 1960s, enlisting Australians, South Africans, and Americans to train, staff, and oversee beach safety. These lifesavers brought surfboards from their respective corners of the world, establishing surf lifesaving and beach clubs as surfing hubs. The first surfing clubs appeared in Newquay and on Jersey Island in the mid-1950s. Surfing had arrived to most of Atlantic Europe by the time 1960s beach blanket films[63] had sent American and then global audiences into a surfing frenzy. With Bruce Brown's *The Endless Summer* (1966), which documented surfing in West Africa, South Africa, Australia, New Zealand, Tahiti, and Hawai'i, surfing's global character became unquestioned, grossing $20 million worldwide.[64]

But while surfing went global at mid-century, it retained an identity as a free-spirited outdoor pastime, not a competitive sport, even though local competitions pitted local and visiting surfers against each other, competition tying surfing to lifesaving, especially in Australia.[65] It would only be in the 1960s that surfing competition turned global and professional, its international character bolstered by emerging surf industry and an ever-growing surf tourism circuit.

Global surf travel, surf industry and professional surfing: 1950–1986

During the Second World War, American surfers were dispersed across the globe and countless American soldiers found themselves in Hawai'i and California, where they were first exposed to surfing. Some would anonymously take up surfing where they were deployed, mostly in the Pacific, but also in Brazil and North Africa, especially US Marines stationed at Kenitra (formerly Port Lyautey) after the Allies landed in 1942.[66] This pattern would be repeated through the 1960s during the Vietnam War, as well, with soldiers surfing in Morocco, Vietnam, Guam, and the Philippines during the 1960s.[67] Settling on both coasts of North America, veterans returned home with surfing on the brain, contributing to surfing enclaves and nascent surf industry in most coastal states. Notable among these surfing centers were southern California and Florida, where the climate and conditions were ideal for mid-century surfing styles and technologies. There, postwar surfing culture exploded, rendering the coastal stretch between San Diego and Santa Barbara a surfing epicenter, while Florida military towns Cocoa Beach and Pensacola anchored American east coast surf culture.[68] In Southern California, cottage surfing industry developed as figures such as Tom Blake (1902–1992), Bob Simmons (1919–1954), and Dale Velzy (1927–2005) began to craft more technologically advanced surfboards. Similar industries developed simultaneously in Hawai'i and throughout Australia, bolstered by contemporaries in Cape Town and Durban, Rio and São Paulo, and elsewhere where surfers provisioned themselves for the sport. By the late 1950s, surfers were not only crafting their own boards, surf shorts, and primitive cold-water wetsuits for local publics: they were beginning to convert their pastime-supporting crafts into consumer industries.

As local surfing communities expanded through the mid-1950s, more reliable and compact surfboards emerged, and consumer air travel became more accessible to well-heeled surfers. These conveniences enabled international competitions to become annual events with standardized, quantified judging criteria that often varied based on the venue and the nationalities of the judging panel. The Makaha International Surfing Championships (1954–1971), the Peru International Surfing Championships (1956–1974), and the World Surfing Championships (1964–1972) were mainstays in early global surf competition, and the early years of these contests saw a diverse cast of international actors formulate and implement judging criteria, revolutionizing competition. While the first Makaha contest was attended by Hawaiians and Southern Californians, surfers from Australia and Peru competed in subsequent years, garnering the contest the reputation of the unofficial world championships.[69] Broadcast by ABC for American publics from 1962 to 1965, the event had a unique format, with open registration for any surfer and heats allowing up to 24 surfers into the water during a single heat (American contests used heats of six), resulting in over 500 competitors, mostly Hawaiian, in 1965. This format, loathed by competitors from outside of Hawai'i, combined with competition from the Peru International and the World Surfing Championships to see the contest relegated to obscurity by the late 1960s.

The Peru contest was organized by Carlos Rey y Lama through Dogny's Club Waikiki. In spite of the club membership's travel bona fides and longstanding relationships with top Hawaiian surfers, early installments of the Peru International were just as insular as the inaugural Makaha. In 1956, only attendees from Club Waikiki and California's San Onofre Surf Club participated. A field of Peruvians and Hawaiians participated in 1957. After a three-year hiatus, the 1961 event saw a small California contingent attend (Southern Californian John Severson, *Surfer* magazine founder, won the event). Yet by 1962, surfers from California, Hawai'i, Australia, France, and Peru competed in the event, heralding in the first truly international field in competitive surfing, leading Severson to consider it "the first successful event where teams from most of the leading surfing areas of the world were represented."[70] 1964 saw the addition of a women's hotdogging category, among other events.[71] The 1965 event doubled as the World Surfing Championships, reflecting modifications to previous judging criteria that only took "speed, wave height, and length of ride" into consideration "instead of maneuvers and form."[72] Like Makaha, the judging criteria evolved as a result of conversations among the worldwide field and when surfing went professional in the late-1960s, responsive organizers ordained the 1969 Peru International the first professional event outside of the United States.

The inauguration of the World Surfing Championships in May 1964 saw over 100 Australian men and women and invited surfers from California, Hawai'i, Peru, England, South Africa, France, and New Zealand congregate at Manly Beach, Australia. In terms of global representation, the 1964 WSC surpassed the 1962 mark set in Lima, and conversations among the '64 participants led to the inauguration of the International Surfing Federation in Lima, Peru, which *limeño* Eduardo Arena chaired. In 1965, when the Peru International served as the WSC, twenty-two of fifty-four competitors were from California, with large groups of Hawaiians, Peruvians, and Australians alongside one-man selections from South Africa, Ecuador, and France. Future installments featured North American destinations and more contestants – competitors from Brazil, Mexico, Ireland, Panama, Japan, and India contested the 1968 final in excellent surf at Rincon, Puerto Rico – further heralding in surfing as a global competitive sport.[73] Yet by the final ISF-organized WSC in 1972, the event had gone the way of the Makaha International, plagued by competitor complaints, poor waves, and judging controversy. The next World Championships wouldn't be organized until 1978.

Parallel to these first decades of international surfing competition, surfers began to design and manufacture surfing goods and apparel. Half a desire to finance a surfing lifestyle and half a desire to proffer new products to improve the surfing experience, the surf industry emerged from surfing's two largest populations, Australia and California. As Hawai'i and Lima were 1960s competitive surfing hubs, Indonesia and Fiji became meccas for traveling surfers of the next decade. It was in Bali in 1974 that business student Bob McKnight would meet American-born Hawaiian professional surfer Jeff Hakman, a dominant presence in competitive surfing.[74] The two would be granted the American license for Quiksilver board shorts, a company founded in Torquay, Victoria, Australia, by Alan Green, Carol McDonald, and Tim Davis in 1969.[75] Basing Quiksilver USA in Orange County, "the OC" quickly became a surf industry hub around dozens of international surfing brands (including Rip Curl, Billabong, Stüssy, etc.). Quiksilver exploded, as did Brian Armstrong and Charlie Bartlett's Rip Curl (also founded in 1969 in Torquay) and Gordon and Rena Merchant's Billabong (founded on Australia's Gold Coast in 1973), each brand granting dozens of licenses worldwide to become surf apparel behemoths. Known as the "Big Three" by the 1990s, these companies introduced big-business approaches to the surf industry foreign to earlier companies. They also sponsored countless professional surf contests, a legacy established by predecessors Hang Loose and Ocean Pacific. As each respective company peaked, they put their name on unprecedented prize purses, making surfing a lucrative sport in the twenty-first century. They also exercised unparalleled influence on surfing's competitive governance – events were named for sponsors – and financed the world's best surfers.

No wave unridden: surf competition and exploration in the twenty-first century

In 1976, the ISF changed its name to the International Surfing Association (ISA), a move that accompanied the launch of International Professional Surfers (IPS), surfing's first professional world tour.[76] And while IPS founders supported the ISA, each organization championed their respective professional and amateur competitive missions. Under the leadership of Hawaiian-Americans Fred Hemmings and Randy Rarick, the 1971-founded Pipeline Masters event, the Duke Kahanamoku Classic (1965–1984), and the Smirnoff Pro contests (1969–1977), each organized by Hemmings on O'ahu's North Shore, became the nucleus of the new IPS world tour, inaugurated in 1976. While the ISA focused its energies on its annual, Olympic-styled amateur championships,[77] the IPS implemented an international ranking (based on points-per-placing), filtering previously unaffiliated events in Hawai'i, North America, Australia, and South Africa into a single tour of nine men's events in 1976.[78] With the IPS tour featuring anywhere from nine to fourteen events, prize money grew from $77,650 in 1976 to $338,100 in 1982.[79] Still, even top competitors, required to circle the globe to compete,[80] could barely afford travel costs on prize money alone. Notable IPS world champions including South African Shaun Tomson (1977), and Australians Wayne Bartholomew (1978) and Mark Richards (1979–1982) depended on corporate sponsorship, promoting brands in competition and advertisements to eke out a living, compensated well below contemporaries in traditional sports.

Although women were some of the first surfers from Cape Town to Victoria and competitive standouts Linda Benson, Joyce Hoffman, and Margo Oberg impressed the world with revolutionary performances on their way to national and world championships, female surfers confronted marginalization in nascent professional surfing.[81] In response, Jericho Poppler and Mary Setterholm founded the Women's International Surfing Association (WISA) in 1975 to "help address the sport's gender inequities."[82] The Huntington Beach-based WISA featured amateur and professional events, culminating in the Hang Ten Women's International Professional Surfing

Championships at Malibu with a $3000 purse. The 1975 Malibu finals were infamously interrupted by male recreational surfers who refused to clear the lineup for the women's event.[83] This event was symbolic of the extent of women's marginalization in surfing more generally: serious and highly respected female professional surfers had to battle with recreational male surfers for waves, even in organized and sanctioned competitive settings.

Select IPS women's events debuted in 1976, the women's tour officially launching with five events in 1977.[84] Oberg, the 1968 WSC and 1975 WISA winner, won the inaugural title, the women's tour featuring $19,000 in total prize money, a sum that would reach $42,000 by 1982.[85] The IPS Women's tour was a death knell for the WISA, which failed to attract major sponsors against the IPS, holding inauspicious events until its final 1991 contest.[86]

The IPS era introduced changes to judging criteria, previously based largely on length of ride and size of wave. The shortboard revolution – "from roughly 1967 to 1970, when average board specs dropped from 9'6" by 22" and 26 pounds [11.8 kg] to 6'6" by 20" and 10 pounds [4.5 kg]"[87] – and the acrobatic surfing that it facilitated had rendered previous equipment obsolete as surfers drew different lines and surfed closer to the curl of the wave. The advent of twin-fin surfboards in the late 1970s – pioneered by Mark Richards who surpassed single-fin adherent Shaun Tomson during his title years – also enabled looser turning and new techniques. These new technologies prompted IPS judging to reward radical maneuvers, and techniques of decades past became anachronistic on the judging scale of zero to ten (a perfect ride). In 1977, the IPS reduced heat sizes, previously of up to eight surfers, to two-competitors in "man-on-man" affairs, allowing individual riders to catch more waves and reducing the free-for-all wavecatching heats of earlier generations.[88] Existing rules against dropping-in on competitors – effectively stealing waves from competitors who were already up and riding – were systematically enforced to penalize offenders, allowing surfers to focus on technique instead of competitor interactions.

Parallel to the IPS, the ISA held their own world championships bi-annually from 1978 to 2002, adding a Junior (under-20) division in 1980 and other categories, held annually at distinct locations.[89] Rebranding its competition as the World Surfing Games, the ISA garnered IOC recognition in 1995, granting national and individual champions in a variety of disciplines (shortboard, longboard, bodyboard, standup paddling, etc.) and promoting its championships "as the true "Olympics" of surfing."[90] Santa Barbara-raised Tom Curren won ISA Junior (1980) and Men's titles (1982), foreshadowing later professional success.

As the IPS failed to prove lucrative for athletes and organizers alike, the IPS dissolved after 1982, replaced by the Association of Surfing Professionals (ASP; 1983–2014). Headed by vocal IPS-critic and world tour runner-up Ian Cairns, the ASP garnered sponsorship from surfwear brand Ocean Pacific and relocated from Hemmings and Rarick's home offices in Hawai'i to Huntington Beach, California, adjacent to the then-thriving California surfing industry. The ASP immediately added events and boosted prize money, featuring twenty events (sixteen tour stops and four Australian specialty events) for a first-year purse of $487,900.

The ASP introduced priority rules, giving one surfer "priority" to ride the next wave and alternating priority between competitors. This eliminated the aggressive lineup positioning and rough wavecatching tactics of pre-ASP competition, where surfers could bully or deceive opponents out of catching the best waves. Priority enabled surfers to focus on technical waveriding instead of holding inside position, and judging eventually came to reward the top two wave scores, for a heat total out of twenty points.

The ASP ushered in a new era of professional surfing with back-to-back titles by diminutive Australian power-surfer Tom Carroll in 1983 and 1984. Über-stylish ISA standout Tom Curren would reign supreme in 1985 and 1986. Carroll and Curren innovated new, techniques atop the responsive three-finned (thruster) shortboard introduced by Australian surfer-shaper Simon

Anderson in 1981, still prevalent in elite surfing today. But the ASP held up to twenty-five events in a single season and failed to forge lasting season-long sponsorship deals – Ocean Pacific and Coca Cola each briefly partnered with the ASP – relying on surf brands for individual event sponsorship. During the 1980s, the ASP also controversially built contests "into huge, added-attraction, beach-carnival surf extravaganzas" and continued to hold events in apartheid-era South Africa.[91] Many surfers, including Curren, quit in exhaustion or frustration. The global surf industry, housed largely in Australia and the US, crashed with the early 1990s recession, further limiting scarce sponsor dollars for ASP events and surfers alike. These factors caused the ASP to cut the number of events beginning in 1992 and move away from spectator-friendly contests in major cities to entice surfers, media, and industry to partake in fewer, better events at tropical world-class waves, such as Fiji and Tahiti.[92]

It would be on the new ASP "Dream Tour" that 20-year-old Floridian Kelly Slater would win his first world title, a feat that he would repeat eleven times (1992, 1994–1998, 2005–2006, 2008, 2010–2011). Raised in small surf, Slater dominated in waves of all sizes, amassing the career-event wins record (60) while battling several generations of competitors. His greatest rivals would prove to be a pair of three-time ASP champions: Kauai-born Andy Irons (2002–2004) and Australian Mick Fanning (2007, 2009, 2013). This was, in many ways, reflective of the national spread of surfing's most powerful nations: surfers from Australia, Hawai'i, and the US won the majority ASP titles, with Tomson and Martin Potter triumphing for South Africa (although Potter competed on a UK passport due to apartheid restrictions). The 1990s also saw Brazil, where surfing culture had thrived, take the world stage with Fabio Gouveia and brothers Flavio and Neco Padaratz achieving top-ten finishes and international recognition, preparing the way for subsequent waves of Brazilian tour surfers.

The women's tour, founded in 1984 and consisting of fewer events, often held at different locations for lower prize purses, also played host to dominant surfers. Floridians Frieda Zamba (1984–1986, 1988), and Lisa Andersen (1994–1997) and South African Wendy Botha (1987, 1989, 1991, 1992) each won four ASP titles. Australian Layne Beachley (1998–2003, 2006) dominated for nearly a decade, winning seven titles after wresting the crown from Andersen, her title run stopped by Peru's Sofia Mulanovich (2004), the first South American world champion in the professional era. Australian Stephanie Gilmore amassed six world titles (2007–2010, 2012, 2014), ceding the title to Hawaiian Carissa Moore three times (2011, 2013, 2015).

The same year as Slater's maiden title and Botha's last, the ASP implemented a two-tiered system, establishing the World Qualifying Series (WQS) to qualify surfers to the World Championship Tour (WCT) circuit. The WQS figured as "a sort of minor league for the WCT" where surfers accrued points towards qualification onto the WCT, the best competitors ascending to the dream tour while the lowest-ranked WCT competitors were cut, forced to re-qualify on the WQS. While the WCT held the moniker of the dream tour, the WQS was alternately known as a "slog" or "grind," in part due to its many events (up to fifty events, as in 2016) in small or lackluster surf. The WQS was also notoriously expensive to participate in, calculated to cost approximately $50,000 to compete in only the top dozen events,[93] most competitors relying on corporate sponsorship, which dwindled with each global economic hiccup.

The internet shifted media coverage of professional surfing. Through the 1990s, contest results were only available in major surfing publications (often released weeks after an event) or through an ASP hotline in Southern California. Select television broadcasts were tape-delayed for weeks or months, showing only event highlights and failing to yield mainstream viewing numbers. Yet after transmitting events sporadically through the mid-1990s, by 2000 the live webcast was a standard ASP media product, enabling surf fans to follow ASP events in real time. This was great for surfers but bad for the surf industry that competitive surfing depended upon, as the sport, even today, rarely garners mainstream viewership: with big wave, specialty, WQS, and WCT events, the ASP was projected to have operating costs around $100 million largely financed by major surf brands – Quiksilver, Billabong, Rip Curl – who sponsored most events for around $3 million per licensed event.[94]

In 2012, the ASP was acquired by Zosea Media, a company led by Kelly Slater's longtime manager, Terry Hardy, and Paul Speaker, former Quiksilver executive and CEO of America's National Football League. In 2015, the ASP relaunched as the World Surf League (WSL), largely retaining ASP governance and competition structures. At first, longstanding WCT competitions remained on the renamed CT tour (Snapper Rocks and Bells Beach, Australia; Rio de Janeiro, Brazil; J-Bay, South Africa; Cloudbreak, Fiji; Teahupo'o, Tahiti; Trestles, California; Hossegor, France; and Pipeline, Hawai'i), and the WQS – then the QS – offered new events in traditional and emerging surfing markets, often with better waves. The judging criteria, further refined to accommodate for aerial surfing under the ASP, made "speed, power, and flow" its mantra, rewarding innovative aerial maneuvers alongside classic power surfing and tuberiding. The advent of wavepool technologies revolutionized the business potential of competitive surfing events, and the 2018 WSL schedule will include an event at the Kelly Slater Wave Ranch in Lemoore, California.[95]

Brazilians, long active in international surfing, dominated the first years of the WSL, earning the media nickname "the Brazilian Storm." Twenty-one-year old Gabriel Medina handily won the WSL crown in 2014, followed by countryman Adriano De Souza in 2015. Filipe Toledo has dominated small-wave contests, winning multiple CT and QS events in recent years. Hawaiian John John Florence and Australian Tyler Wright won back-to-back titles (2016, 2017) in the men's and women's divisions, respectively.

During the ASP era, the ISA became a much-marginalized organization, as top talent chose to compete for ASP prize money instead of training for the one-off World Surfing Games (WSG). The United States failed to attend the games in 2008, and Brazil and Hawai'i also declined to participate alongside the US in 2014.[96] Peru has had tremendous success (especially considering that no Peruvian has qualified for the men's WCT/CT), winning the 2010, 2014, and 2016 WSG and regularly medaling in several categories. However, with IOC-recognition for all waveriding sports, the ISA began to add member nations in the 2010s, including more than a half-dozen landlocked countries, totaling 103 member nations in 2018. After decades of ISA petitioning, the IOC approved surfing as an Olympic sport in August 2016, to be first contested at the Tokyo 2020 games and later in the Paris 2024 games. The ISA also inaugurated the World Adaptive Surfing Championships in 2015, a discipline previously supported only by charity and non-governmental organizations. The annual event held in La Jolla, California was won by Brazil in 2016 and 2017 after no team score was kept in 2015. The 2017 event featured 109 athletes from 26 teams competing in stand/kneel, upright, prone, assist, and visually impaired categories.

Notes

1 The surf industry is estimated to reach US$13 billion in 2017, excluding the travel industry. See P. Kvinta, "Surfonomics 101," *Fortune.com*, 5 June 2013. Retrieved from http://fortune.com/2013/06/05/surfonomics-101/ (Accessed 1 May 2016). Quality surf breaks are estimated to generate US$50 billion in economic activity: T. McGregor and S. Wills, "Surfing a Wave of Economic Growth," CAMA Working Paper No. 31 (March 2017).

2 On modern sport, A. Gutmann, *From Ritual to Record*, (New York: Columbia UP, 1978).

3 *Schoenoplectus californicus*, subspecies *tatora*; colloquially, California bulrush.

4   F. Pomar. "Surfing in 1000 BC," *Surfer* April 1988. The ceramic record shows depictions of *caballito* navigators seated atop the craft, not standing.

5   For sixteenth-century Spanish references to pre-Hispanic waveriding: P. Cieza de León, *Crónica del Perú* (Caracas: Biblioteca Ayacucho, 2005 [1553]); J. de Acosta *Historia natural y moral de las Indias* (México DF: FCE, 2006 [1590]), 133; M. De la Rosa, *Huellas en el mar* (Lima: Elephant Press, 2010), 80–89.

6   See D. Zavalza Hough-Snee, "You Have the Right to Surf: Riding Waves of Decolonization, Modernity and Nationalism in Peru," in *Sports and Nationalism in Latin/o America*, eds. R. McKee Irwin, J. Poblete, and H. Fernández L'Hoeste (New York: Palgrave MacMillan, 2015), 201–223. Also, T. Heyerdahl, *Kon Tiki: Across the Pacific by Raft* (New York: Pocket Books, 1973). On modern excursions taking up ancient maritime navigation from the Hawaiian Islands to show ancient Hawaiian cultural ties to the Pacific World, see I.H. Walker, "*Kai Ea*: Rising Waves of National and Ethnic Hawaiian Identities," in *The Critical Surf Studies Reader*, eds. D. Zavalza Hough-Snee and A. Eastman (Durham: Duke University Press, 2017), 62–83; and I.H. Walker, *Waves of Resistance* (Honolulu: University of Hawai'i Press, 2011).

7   K. Dawson, "Swimming, Surfing and Underwater Diving in Early Modern Atlantic Africa and the African Diaspora," in *Navigating African Maritime History*, eds. C. Ray and J. Rich (St. John's Newfoundland: Memorial University of Newfoundland Press, 2009), 100. Also see, "Michael Hemmersan's Description of the Gold Coast, 1639–1645," in *German Sources for West African History*, ed. A. Jones (Wiesbaden: Franz Steiner Verlag, 1983).

8   J. Barbot in Dawson, "Swimming, Surfing, and Underwater Diving," 100.

9   Dawson, "Swimming, Surfing, and Underwater Diving," 100–102. See also K. Dawson, *Undercurrents of Power: Aquatic Culture in the African Diaspora* (Philadelphia: University of Pennsylvania Press, 2018).

10   Ibid.

11   Ibid.

12   For many such observations, see P. Moser, ed., *Pacific Passages* (Honolulu: University of Hawaii, 2008).

13   C. McGloin, *Surfing Nation(s) – Surfing Country(s)* (Wollongong: University of Wollongong Thesis Collections, 2005), 6. For comprehensive catalogue of sources citing Aboriginal surfcraft: "The Traditional Watercraft of the Australian Aboriginals," *SurfResearch.com.au* Retrieved from www.surfresearch.com. au/0000h_Australia_48,000bc.html (accessed 1 August 2016).

14   W. Anderson, "A Voyage to the Pacific Ocean," in *Pacific Passages*, 65–66.

15   B. Finney and J. Houston, *Surfing: A History of the Ancient Hawaiian Sport* (Pomegranate: San Francisco, 1996). Also, see "Story: Lifesaving and Surfing – The rise of Surfing," in *The Encyclopedia of New Zealand*. Retrieved from www.teara.govt.nz/en/lifesaving-and-surfing/page-4 (accessed 1 August 2016).

16   Walker, *Waves of Resistance*, 16.

17   The four primary types of ancient Hawaiian surf craft were the *paipo* or *kioe*, a 60–120cm bodyboard often used by children; the *alaia* or *omo*, measuring approximately eight feet (I use American measurements consistent with contemporary surfboard dimensions); the 12–18 foot *kiki'o*; and the *olo*, the longest surfboard measuring up to 24 feet in length and reserved for royalty.

18   P. Moser, ed., *Pacific Passages: An Anthology of Surf Writing* (Honolulu: University of Hawai'i Press, 2008).

19   See M. Warshaw, *Zero Break: An Illustrated Collection of Surf Writing, 1777–2004* (Orlando: Harcourt, 2004); S. Laderman, *Empire in Waves* (Berkeley: University of California Press, 2014); Moser, *Pacific Passages*; P. Westwick and P. Neushul, *The World in the Curl: An Unconventional History of Surfing* (New York: Crown, 2013).

20   Dawson, "Swimming, Surfing, and Underwater Diving" explores this hypothesis in Africa and Oceania.

21   Ibid; S. Meacham, "Myths of Aborigines and Saltwater Culture," *Sydney Morning Herald* 26 November 2011. Retrieved from www.smh.com.au/national/writer-challenges-myths-of-aborigines-and-saltwater-culture-20111125-1nz6q.html (accessed 1 August 2016).

22   Westwick and Neushul, *World in the Curl*, 64.

23   D. Booth, *Australian Beach Cultures* (London: F. Cass, 2001); Booth, "Surf and Surf Lifesavers as Safety Hazards: The Myth of Bondi's Black Sunday," *New Zealand Physical Educator* 49, no. 1 (2016): 20–22; M. Warshaw, *The History of Surfing* (San Francisco: Chronicle, 2010), 57.

24   Laderman, *Empire in Waves*, 8–40.

25   Warshaw, *History*, 44–45.

26   Ibid.

27   See Walker, *Waves of Resistance*, 19–25.

28   Ibid.

29   Westwick and Neushul, *World in the Curl*, 65.

30 Warshaw, *History*, 133.

31 See Walker, *Waves of Resistance*, 70–82.

32 Westwick and Neushul, *World in the Curl*, 65–68.

33 Ibid., 147.

34 "Surfboards Made in Muizenberg in 1920's," *Surfing Heritage South Africa*. Retrieved from http://surf ingheritage.co.za/site/1922_tony_bowman (accessed 1 August 2016).

35 D. Esparza, "Towards a Theory of Surfing Expansion: The Beginnings of Surfing in Spain as a Case Study," *RICYDE* 44, no. 12 (2016): 199–215.

36 R. Mansfield, *Surfing Tribe: A History of Surfing in Britain* (Newquay: Orca Publications, 2009), 24. Staffieri was inspired by boards fabricated by non-surfing dentist Jimmy Dix, after his own encyclopedia-inspired attempts. See M.S. Moore, *Sweetness and Blood* (New York: Rodale, 2010), 145.

37 "Historia do Surf no Brasil: Cidade Natal do Surf no Brasil," *SurfinSantos.com.br* Retrieved from http:// surfinsantos.com.br/historia-do-surf/ (accessed 1 August 2016). For the plans used by Gonçalves: T. Blake, "Riding the Breakers on this Hollow Hawaiian Surfboard," *Popular Mechanics* 68, no. 1 (1937), 114–117.

38 American monthlies *Popular Mechanics* and *Popular Science* published plans of prone solid timber boards in July 1934 (reprinted 1937) and August 1935 (reprinted 1939), respectively. An additional *Popular Mechanics* article, "Hitch-Hiking on the Big Waves," ran in 1942.

39 G. Osmond, "Myth-making in Australian Sport History: Re-evaluating Duke Kahanamoku's Contribution to Surfing," *Australian Historical Studies* 42 no. 2 (2011): 260–276.

40 Ibid.

41 L. Wells, *Sunny Memories: Australians at the Seaside* (Richmond, Victoria: Greenhouse, 1982), 157.

42 S. Ferebee, "A History of Surfing in Virginia Beach," *The Surfer's Journal* 23, no. 6 (Dec.-Jan. 2015).

43 "Surfing at Muizenberg, Cape Town, 1919," *Surfing Heritage South Africa*. Retrieved from http:// surfingheritage.co.za/site/1919_heather_price (accessed 1 August 2016).

44 Moore, *Sweetness and Blood*, 146–147.

45 Ibid.

46 There are only eight known copies of the handmade book. See A.R. Gurrey Jr., *The Surf Riders of Hawaii* (Honolulu: Gurrey, 1914).

47 P.M. de Lima, "Surfing Pioneers in Europe," *olosurfhistory.com* Retrieved from https://olosurfhistory. com/tag/pedro-martins-de-lima/ (accessed 1 August 2016).

48 Moore, *Sweetness and Blood*, 37–39.

49 On the elite standing of Club Waikiki: Warshaw, *History*, 133.

50 C.G. Dias, "Especial Surfe: Na crista da onda," *Revista de Historia* 13 (2009). Retrieved from www. revistadehistoria.com.br/secao/artigos/especial-surfe-na-crista-da-onda (accessed 1 August 2016).

51 "História do Surf," *Surf Ingleses* Retrieved from www.surfingleses.net/historia.html (accessed 1 August 2016).

52 Dias, "Especial Surfe."

53 Ibid. Also: C.G. Dias, R. Fortes and V. Andrade de Melo, "Sobre as ondas," *Estudos históricos* 25, no. 49 (2012): 112–128.

54 Ibid.

55 Ibid.

56 S. Pike, *Surfing South Africa* (Cape Town: Double Storey, 2007). Retrieved from: www.wavescape.co.za/ culture/history/part-1-as-early-as-ww1.html (accessed 1 August 2016); "Durban's Surfing Birth," *Surfing Heritage South Africa*. Retrieved from http://surfingheritage.co.za/site/1938_fred_crocker (accessed 1 August 2016).

57 Ibid.

58 "Lifesaving and Surfing," *Te Ara: The Encyclopedia of New Zealand*. Retrieved from www.teara.govt.nz/ en/lifesaving-and-surfing/page-4 (accessed 1 August 2016).

59 D. Booth, "Beach Sports," in *Youth Sport in Australia*, eds. S. Georgakis and K.M. Russell (Sydney: Sydney University Press, 2011), 149–164.

60 Warshaw, *History*, 133.

61 Ibid.

62 Moore, *Sweetness and Blood*, 74.

63 The precursor *Gidget* films (1959 and 1961) introduced surfing to mainstream America, making way for *Beach Party* (1963) and a dozen other surf-inspired titles in the beach party genre between 1964 and 1967.

64 Brown's earlier films *Slippery When Wet* (1958), *Surf Crazy* (1959), *Surfing Shorts* (1960), *Barefoot Adventure* (1960), *Surfing Hollow Days* (1961), and *Water-Logged* (1962) exported surfing in Mexico, California, and Hawai'i to a worldwide viewership.

65 Evolving from the Australian Rescue and Resuscitation and Surf Race Championships (1915) was the Australian Board Riding Championships (inaugurated 1924). California's Pacific Coast Surf Riding Championship, organized by Tom Blake, was held at Corona del Mar (1928–1935) and San Onofre (1935–1941). See Warshaw, "Pacific Coast Surf Riding Championships," *encyclopediaofsurfing.com*.

66 Moore, *Sweetness and Blood*, 100.

67 Warshaw, *History*, 202.

68 Surfing was also popular further north in California, although more isolated from the surfing culture of Southern California, which focused around Malibu, San Onofre, and San Diego.

69 Warshaw, "Makaha International Surfing Championships," *encyclopediaofsurfing.com*. Retrieved from: http://encyclopediaofsurfing.com/entries/makaha-international-surfing-championships (accessed 1 August 2016).

70 Warshaw, "Peru International Surfing Championships," *encyclopediaofsurfing.com*. Retrieved from: http://encyclopediaofsurfing.com/entries/peru-international-surfing-championships (accessed 1 August 2016).

71 Ibid.

72 Ibid.

73 The 1966 and 1972 WSC were held in San Diego, California, 1968 in Rincón, Puerto Rico, and 1970 at Bells Beach, Australia.

74 On McKnight, see Zavalza Hough-Snee, "Bob McKnight and Quiksilver," in *Sporting Entrepreneurs*, eds. J. Nauright and D. Wiggins (Fayetteville: University of Arkansas Press, 2018); P. Jarratt, *The Mountain and the Wave* (Huntington Beach: Quiksilver Entertainment, 2010).

75 See Laderman, *Empire in Waves*, 139–140; Westwick and Neushul, *World in the Curl*, 287–289.

76 Fred Van Dyke had attempted to organize such a professional tour under the moniker the "International Professional Surfers Association" in 1968, giving up on the idea in 1969 due to logistical difficulties.

77 The ISF did not organize world championships from 1973 to 1975 due to a lack of sponsors.

78 Warshaw, "International Professional Surfers," *encyclopediaofsurfing.com*. Retrieved from http://encyclopediaofsurfing.com/entries/international-professional-surfers (accessed 1 August 2016). Also: "History," *WorldSurfLeague.com* Retrieved from: www.worldsurfleague.com/pages/history (accessed 1 August 2016).

79 Ibid.

80 The IPS tour held most events in Hawai'i, Australia, and South Africa, with tour stops in Brazil, New Zealand, Florida, and California.

81 Westwick and Neushul, *World in the Curl*, 270–280.

82 Warshaw, "Women's International Surfing Association," *encyclopediaofsurfing.com*.

83 Ibid.

84 Warshaw, "International Professional Surfers," *encyclopediaofsurfing.com*.

85 Ibid.

86 Warshaw, "Women's International Surfing Association," *encyclopediaofsurfing.com*.

87 Warshaw, "shortboard revolution," *encyclopediaofsurfing.com*.

88 Warshaw, "International Professional Surfers," *encyclopediaofsurfing.com*.

89 "50th Anniversary ISA History," *ISAsurf.org* Retrieved from: www.isasurf.org/isa-info/history-of-the-isa/ (accessed 1 August 2016).

90 Ibid.

91 Warshaw, "Association of Surfing Professionals," *encyclopediaofsurfing.com*.

92 Ibid.

93 J. Howard "The Price of Qualifying," *Stab*. Retrieved from: http://stabmag.com/news/the-price-of-qualifying/ (accessed 1 August 2016).

94 S. Nettle, "The ASP: It's on but Who's Watching?," *Swellnet.com* 8 May 2014. Retrieved from: www.swellnet.com/news/surfpolitik/2014/05/08/asp-its-whos-watching (accessed 1 August 2016). Also: Sean Doherty, "The New ASP," *Surfermag.com* 01 July 2013. Retrieved from: www.surfermag.com/features/the-new-asp/#KGk6ETEFjwaxmqB0.97 (accessed 1 August 2016).

95 "Surf Ranch Announced as 2018 Championship Tour Venue," *WorldSurfLeague.com* 17 November 2017. Retrieved from: www.worldsurfleague.com/posts/283223/surf-ranch-announced-as-2018-championship-tour-venue

96 Jake Howard, "US, Hawaii and Brazil Don't Send Teams to Peru," *Surfline.com* 25 October 2014. Retrieved from: www.surfline.com/surf-news/but-the-u.s.,-hawaii-and-brazil-don't-send-teams-to-peru-1_119602 (accessed 1 August 2016).

Part VII
Heritage sports

40

Gaelic games

Joe Bradley

Origins and evolution

In varying forms and styles the Irish sport of hurling has a history going back at least two thousand years. The tribes and heroes of ancient Ireland's sagas, the Firbolgs, Tuatha de Danaan, the Red Branch Knights and Cuchulainn, have all made their mark in the story of hurling and this has contributed to the games' contemporary national mystique and narrative.

This narrative has been enhanced further with authentic historical events and processes. For example, there was an attempt to ban the game in the 14th century under the English colonial administration's 'Statutes of Kilkenny'. Again in 1527 the 'Statute of Galway' ordered that no hurling should take place, while the 1695 Sunday Observance Act enacted, 'that no person or persons whatsoever, shall play or exercise any hurling'.[1] Although acts like the Statutes of Kilkenny and of Galway were meant to dissuade early colonists from adopting Irish ways and becoming 'more Irish than the Irish', in creating these laws the forces of conquest in Ireland also made clear their intention to subvert Irish pastimes. Thus, for many centuries, even before the birth of the Gaelic Athletic Association, sport in Ireland exhibited resonances that were linked to ethnic and national identity, resistance, culture and politics.

In terms of the development of Gaelic sport, by the 18th century it is clear there were two principal, and regionally distinct, versions of hurling in Ireland. The northern half of the country played the version called caman, anglicised as 'commons'. The southern half of the country played the game known as ioman or baire. The main difference in each version was that the latter was played during the summer with a soft ball or sliothar which could be handled. The version played in the northern part of the country was mainly a winter game in which the ball could not be handled.[2] Although the game today is unrecognisable from its unstructured and often violent antecedents, of all Gaelic sports it is hurling which owes its origins to the Gaelic world of the past.

Gaelic football and other Gaelic sports of camogie, handball and rounders, have a more recent history. In football, there are few references before the 1600s, but these are more frequent by the late 1700s.[3] Tipperary, Clare, Wexford, Wicklow, Monaghan, Armagh and Donegal are some of the counties from where there are reports of both hurling and football matches from the early modern period. In addition, by the time of the organisation of Irish sports in the late

19th century, it was probably football as opposed to hurling that was more in need of preservation and cultivation. Even though the Great Hunger of the mid-19th century killed over one million people and provoked the mass emigration of at least one million more in the space of only a handful of years, proved demoralising for those who survived and almost destroyed the rural social system, in one form or another, Gaelic sport survived.

From the 12th century, few comments regarding social or political developments in Ireland can be made without reference to the context of Ireland's relationship with its militaristically powerful and ambitious neighbouring island: Gaelic sports are no different. Ireland's link with Britain was of a complex colonial nature. Subject to rule from London, this relationship invariably had a vast number of economic, social, cultural and political consequences for the indigenous people of the island – including the great Irish starvation. One result of this domination was that by the late 19th century, as organised sport began to develop in much of Europe due to the extension of the recreational aspects of contemporary lifestyles, in Ireland regulated sport was largely the preserve of the upper and middle classes. These were invariably recognised by the rest of the population as British, Colonist and Unionist. Controlled by those who retained privilege and power, this meant that organised sport in Ireland also served as a vehicle for the promotion of British and Unionist identities. The rest of the population demoralised and lacking resources, were largely excluded from regulated sport.

Features of life in Ireland considered worthwhile and held in esteem were inevitably British influenced. Colonial Ireland was multi-faceted in its Anglicisation. Sugden and Bairner emphasise this:

> While British domination had always been challenged by the indigenous population, only gradually did this resistance take an overtly nationalist form. Sensitive to the threat of emergent Irish nationalism, the British endeavoured to suppress expressions of Gaelic culture. Part of this programme included the discouragement or prohibition of Gaelic games. At the same time distinctively Anglophile sports, introduced into Ireland by settlers and the agents of the Crown, and encouraged by British landlords, grew in popularity. In addition to these factors the devastating effects of famine pushed Gaelic games nearer to extinction.[4]

As a cultural, sporting and political reaction to this state of affairs, Cumann Lúthchleas Gael (Gaelic Athletic Association or GAA) was founded in 1884:

> On All Saints' Day, 1 November 1884, a small group of men met in the billiard room of Miss Hayes Commercial Hotel, Thurles; they formally founded 'The Gaelic Athletic Association for the Preservation and Cultivation of National Pastimes', ever since known as the Gaelic Athletic Association or, more familiarly, the GAA.[5]

Michael Cusack, Pat Nally and Maurice Davin among others, became synonymous with the Association's beginnings. Its patrons, Michael Davitt (founder of the Land League), Charles Stewart Parnell (leader of the Irish Parliamentary Party) and Archbishop Croke (Catholic Archbishop of Cashel) became equally associated with the origins of the new organisation. A letter received at the founding of the Association from Archbishop Croke remains an important statement with regard to the GAA:

> if we continue travelling for the next score years in the same direction that we have been going in for some time past, condemning the sports that were practised by our forefathers, effacing our national features as though we were ashamed of them ... we had better at once,

and publicly, abjure our nationality, clap hands for joy at sight of the Union Jack and place 'England's bloody red' exultantly above the green …[6]

Croke made it known that although he supported Irish sports, especially at the expense of the growing British domination of the country, he felt sure that there was room for all recreation: he had no wish to deny other sports and pastimes simply because they were not national. Michael Davitt stressed that as far as he could interpret, the GAA did not begin with any great political ideal though its aims were national.

> When the Gaelic Association movement was first projected … the idea was national and not political. It was intended to counteract to some extent the denationalising work and tendencies of systems specifically framed to destroy every remnant of our Celtic institutions.[7]

The idea of political assertion aligning itself with any national project during these years in Ireland seems inevitable. Mullan writes that conflict between native and coloniser over scarce economic resources and occupational life chances 'established a set of conditions that, by the 1880s, undermined any possibility for the peaceful integration of modern sports'.[8]

For Tierney:

> the founding and consolidation of the GAA was part of the social revolution, perhaps its most vital expression. Popular sports, it was said, should be open to all and should be organised by the people not by the ruling class. Here was democracy working its way into rural Ireland, asserting the rights of the Irish people to control their own pastimes … Working class people might watch while the gentry hunted, shot or played tennis, but they must not be allowed to compete. The same applied in athletics, where gentlemen could not imagine themselves having to compete against artisans or agricultural labourers … The GAA hoped to provide a counterblast to the existing class distinction in sport.[9]

Former Fenian Michael Cusack believed that though every social movement in Ireland was to some extent political, the Gaelic Athletic Association was not a political organisation.[10] In relation to the history and contemporary constitution of the Association the thinking of Cusack is important to understanding the political as well as non-political nature of the GAA. For Holmes, 'Irish nationalism in the nineteenth century revived Gaelic football', while the founding of the GAA is seen as an important step in the assertion of an Irish national identity.[11] Cultural and political activists in Ireland demonstrated that they wished to reclaim cultural influence and authority, to begin the process of reviving confidence and pride in being Irish and end the ascendancy and hegemony of British Protestants over Irish Catholics. Likewise, the Association's founding allowed for the inclusion of the impoverished majority in Ireland in sporting activities. Therefore, as well as the greater political situation, the GAA also had significance in challenging both the class and the religious domination of sport.

Apart from its objectives of celebrating and promoting Irishness through sport, its political consequences, and its aim of achieving the democratisation of sport in Ireland, the greatest immediate impact of the GAA was the organisation, standardisation and modernisation of games throughout the island. As a result of the nationalisation of Irish sport, Gaelic games were both saved and rejuvenated. The 'movement' took root rapidly throughout the country. Indeed, using the southern version of hurling as his measure, Michael Cusack codified hurling along the lines of which he had known himself as a child in County Clare. For one historian, 'the founding of the GAA caused something of a social revolution'.[12]

Cusack and his GAA backers used Gaelic games as a nationalising idiom, a symbolic language of identity filling the void created by the speed of the British influence in the country. Cusack and others recognised that colonialism in Ireland meant that Ireland's was a significantly politicised culture and any attempt to promote and defend Irishness in the context of a country ruled from London within the British Empire was bound to have political resonances, to a greater or lesser degree. To resist British colonialism in Ireland, or to labour to sever relevant political, economic, social, cultural or sporting domination, was invariably a political act or aspiration.

Only a few years after its' founding, the GAA was already aligning itself with various groups of evicted tenants as well as the building of nationalist monuments. Its principal backers were those already active in the nationalist political culture of the time, classically the IRB (Irish Republican Brotherhood). Its spread depended on the active support of an increasingly nationalist Catholic middle class and its social constituency especially included journalists, publicans, schoolteachers, clerks, artisans and clerics.[13]

The revival of Gaelic sports in Ireland also paralleled the success of the codification of games such as soccer and rugby in Britain. With the shortened working week, its' associated concept of 'the weekend', rising spending power and a general organisation of society, conditions suited the development and expansion of sporting activity. It can be argued that precedents created and set in place for the development of sport in Britain also helped shape sporting developments and progress in Ireland. The sporting revival in Ireland also mirrored events in Australia and the USA. Indeed, Australian Football and American Football (more recent inventions) can also be viewed partly as avenues for the construction of national identities.

> The growth experienced by the GAA was essentially imitative of the world-wide phenomena whereby various types of ball-games were becoming an integral part of the social fabric. In effect, the growth of Gaelic games as popular sports paralleled the growth of like organisations in North and South America, in Australia, New Zealand, South Africa, India and much of Europe.[14]

Development of the GAA

Despite the GAA's initial successes, many practical problems faced the organisation. Years of internal struggles (financial and personal) and the effects of the national question (including Fenian against constitutionalist and Parnellites versus anti-Parnellites) had their negative effects, although the latter also had a positive influence. A patriotic consciousness provided the Association with more members than might otherwise have been the case, while many activists were certainly motivated by the organisation's political nature. Although patriotic and nationalist, the Association also declared its intention of acting independently of political parties, following its own principles and concentrating on its own success and prosperity.[15] The Association experienced years of slumps and difficulties before it became firmly established. By the early 1900s, it came under the guidance of a set of officials who brought a slow, intermittent, but undoubted revival. This revival also coincided with a general upsurge and participation in cultural activities.

By 1909, with every county represented on Central Council, the GAA finally became a genuine, though with varying strengths and weaknesses throughout the counties, national body. In addition, the fortunes of the Association became increasingly tied with those of the growing Irish Ireland bodies of the Gaelic League and Sinn Fein, aligning with the political and cultural mood of the time.

In relation to the sporting activities that forthwith slowly began to prosper in Ireland, De Búrca states:

> These pastimes now passed for ever out of the hands of people like landlords, military and police, who belonged to a class that was opposed both to nationalist political aspirations and to nationalist cultural ideals.[16]

Mullan refers to:

> The pre-GAA Victorian sporting elite – the high professions, the higher echelons of urban commerce, the officer corps of the military and even the upper echelons of the state civil service, by virtue of a centuries-old system of entrenched Protestant control dating from the Penal Laws – were automatically assigned and isolated to the Anglo-Irish camp of modern sport.[17]

Not for the last time this century, and not in any way restricted to Ireland or the Irish, sport became a repository of a national identity: in this instance, one that contested the dominance of an alien colonising 'national' identity. The alliance of the GAA in Ireland with nationalism was a regional variation on an almost universal theme. Two decades before the GAA was born, the Czechoslovakian Sokal Gymnastic Association was formed. The threat of Germanisation and the loss of Czech cultural identity motivated leading patriots to revive Czech cultural activities, 'to combine physical education and fitness with specific political objectives – primarily the Czech struggle for national independence . . . in the face of Austro-Hungarian political and cultural oppression'.[18] For Mandle, 'the use of sport to proclaim national distinctiveness was a British invention: imitations might be made in Melbourne or Tokyo, even in Thurles, Co Tipperary, but imitations they were, not originals'.[19]

Combining with the contemporary cultural revival in Ireland, the Irish language movement of the late 19th and early 20th centuries attracted women activists. In turn, this also encouraged them to perform an important role in the playing and promotion of Gaelic sports. In Ireland, as elsewhere, sport has frequently been a male preserve.[20] However, camogie, a women's version of hurling, developed, thus establishing women's contribution to the revival of Gaelic sports. The first recorded camogie game was played in Navan, County Meath in 1904, between Keatings and Cuchulains of Dublin. *Cumann Camogaiochta na Gael* was founded at a meeting in Dublin's Gresham Hotel in 1932. Ladies Gaelic Football was to explode on to the scene some decades later.

The years following the 1916 Easter Rising saw the GAA's support for the revolutionary nationalist movement further establish it as an important body in Irish society, although the years of the War of Independence (1919–1921) and the Civil War (1922–1923) had a detrimental effect on the Association in many areas. Indeed, much of the 1930s had passed before Ulster began to function in a similar way to other provinces: the hostility experienced by the Association in Unionist dominated Northern Ireland proving a severe handicap to the expression of native Irish culture and identity. In fact, it might be argued that it was only after the foundation of the Irish Free State that the GAA was firmly able to establish itself and henceforth flourish, liberated from any substantial political or military pre-occupations or obstacles.

In 1906 there were 750 GAA clubs throughout the country, one thousand three hundred and seventeen by the 1927 Congress and almost two thousand, including those in Britain and the U.S.A., by the mid-1930s. The 1920s witnessed a rising wave of popularity for the Gaelic sport of handball. During the same period minor (under-age) Gaelic sports competitions were started. At the Easter Congress of 1925, National League Games in hurling and football were inaugurated. The same Congress also decided that 'no club be called after a living person or after any political or semi-political organisation'. New peaks in the standard of play, growing attendances and the building of Croke Park in Dublin, also marked important developments. With the welcome entry of Queen's University in Belfast to the GAA in the 1930s and the expansion of third level education in Ireland, university Gaelic sports began to develop.

Since the 1950s, and the 1960s in particular, the parish GAA club in Ireland has become an important focus for community leisure and social activities in the locality. The revival of traditional music and other forms of native culture contributed to a growing strength and significance for the GAA. An effective administrative machine and adequate financial resources and commercial advertising and support have also contributed to its importance in Irish life.

Ironically, notwithstanding sporting competition from soccer as the pre-eminent world team game, the widely acclaimed Irish soccer successes of the 1980s and 1990s also coincided with an era of great progress, classic games and vibrant attendances in Gaelic sports. This has continued throughout the years of the new millennium.

The 21st century

In terms of culture, identity and the mass numbers of participants playing and spectating, Gaelic games of hurling and football are considered the island's national sports. Though today it has many hundreds of paid employees acting as administrators, directors, coaches, etc., throughout Ireland and beyond, the GAA has remained an amateur body since its birth. This, despite the wealth that the Association has accumulated over the fourteen decades of its life, particularly in the modern era of live television, radio and internet broadcast games and the involvement of sponsors bearing national and international brand names.

Although there are numerous social, cultural and economic privileges associated with being a top GAA player, it also remains that such players do not receive payment for their involvement on the field of play. No transfers exist in Gaelic Football and the vast majority of players demonstrate their heritage with respect to, and fondness and loyalty towards, their locality, by traditionally playing for their community club (geographically designated and usually by means of the Catholic Church parish system) and, if good enough, for the county they were born or live in. One of the greatest distinguishing features of the GAA is the millions of hours historically and contemporaneously spent on its survival, welfare, growth and vibrancy, on the part of known and less well known volunteers across the country and beyond the island: this has continued to be the Association's greatest resource since its' founding in 1884.

Camogie has long been popular among many women in Ireland, but it is ladies Gaelic football that has enjoyed noteworthy successes since the 1990s in particular. Many (if not most) GAA clubs in and beyond Ireland have under-age and adult women's football teams. As females continue to break out of the real and imagined chains that have suppressed their sporting expressions on the field of play for many years, a new found respect for these efforts is widespread and further growth in this area remains significant for numerous clubs, counties and communities throughout Ireland and its diaspora. Ladies Gaelic Football remains one of the fastest growing sports in the world. The sport is governed by the Ladies Gaelic Football Association (LGFA).

The GAA has hundreds of stadiums scattered throughout Ireland and beyond. Every county, and nearly all clubs, has grounds, sometimes numerous, often acquired, maintained and developed over several decades, on which to play, with varying capacities and utilities. Befitting the efforts of thousands of volunteers, benefactors and fund raisers, as well as its community roots and identities, the GAA, its member clubs and counties, own various stadiums around

Ireland with spectating capacities of 15,000–50,000. Croke Park Stadium in Dublin, including its administrative offices and museum, is the Association's flagship venue and headquarters. With a capacity of 82,300, it ranks among the top five stadiums in Europe by this measure. On St Patrick's Day every year, after several months of contestation, including winning their respective County and Provincial Finals, the country's top hurling and football clubs meet to contest the All-Ireland club finals in front of tens of thousands of spectators. Every September, considered the highpoint of every season, a sold-out Croke Park hosts the All-Ireland Inter-county Hurling and Football Finals as the conclusion to the national championships. The GAA also hosts international fixtures with respect to often annual or bye-annual hurling/shinty compromise games with Scotland's *Camanachd* Association and with respect to Gaelic football/Australian rules football competitions.

The skills and athleticism of the greatest and most well-known Gaelic players of over one hundred years have found their way into the annals of national sporting and cultural achievements. Despite the Association's amateur status, such players and many others like them have long been professional like as well as frequently exceptional in aptitude, dedication, fitness and ability. In Football, Martin O'Connell (Meath), Mick O'Connell (Kerry) Matt Connor (Offaly), and in Hurling, Lory Meaghar (Kilkenny), Jimmy Barry-Murphy (Cork) and Tommy Walsh (Kilkenny), represent but a small number of hundreds of outstanding and honoured Gaelic Sportspersons in the life of the GAA and Ireland's sporting history.

The island of Ireland contains four provinces and thirty-two counties. All-Ireland Football Championships have been won mostly by Munster's Kerry and Leinster's Dublin. Around a quarter of All-Ireland county champions since 1884 have come from the provinces of Ulster and Connacht. Most Hurling Championships have been won by Counties Cork, Kilkenny and Tipperary.

Ireland's diaspora

Gaelic games have either been played or continue to be played in countries that have traditionally hosted small as well as larger Irish ex-patriot communities. GAA teams and clubs recently, or currently exist, and games frequently or occasionally played in; South Africa, Myanmar, China, Indonesia, Japan, South Korea, Thailand, Malaysia, Gaza, Singapore, and Vietnam. In Bahrain, Kuwait, Oman, Qatar, Saudi Arabia and particularly in the United Arab Emirates. In Europe, Gaelic games are played in various cities in Austria, Belgium, Czech Republic, Denmark, Estonia, Finland, France, Germany and Holland (and Jersey).

Gaelic Games are also of significance among Irish ex-patriot communities all over New Zealand and especially Australia where several dozen clubs exist: in South Australia alone over thirty clubs can often compete. Well known clubs in Australia are; Cormac McAnallens, Sydney Shamrocks, Na Fianna Hurling Club and Wolfe Tones: in New Zealand, Connemara Gaels and Celtic.

Records show that Gaelic Sports have been played in North America since the late 18th and early 19th centuries. Today, the North American and New York Boards are the continent's main organisers and administrators for Gaelic games. In numerous US states, Hurling and Football Championships are held annually. As of 2018/19, Gaelic games, hurling, Gaelic football, camogie and ladies Gaelic football were being organised and played in over sixty cities across the US, including Baltimore, Los Angeles, Philadelphia, Chicago, San Antonio, New York and Dallas. With a variety of economic and political changes taking place in North America and Ireland, numerous areas and clubs have responded with varying levels of youth development, among second- and third-generation Irish born in the USA and also involving numerous youngsters with little or no Irish ethnicity. Some of the longest established and most well-known GAA clubs in North America are; Denver Gaels, Kevin Barrys (Philadelphia), Padraig Pearse (Chicago) and Aidan McAnespie (Boston). All over the USA various clubs are called after counties in Ireland as they contain many and sometimes mostly players from those areas. In the Boston area alone there are clubs called after counties Cork, Limerick, Galway, Mayo, Roscommon, Tipperary, Wexford, Armagh and Kerry.

Historically, the nearest destination for Irish emigrants has of course been Great Britain. In 1885 the first GAA club in Britain was founded in Wallsend near Newcastle-on-Tyne, an area of high Irish migration. Again in England in 1900 the first provincial council for the administration and organisation of Gaelic games was established. In a more formal sense, the Gaelic Athletic Association was founded in London in 1895 though it would be around 1903 before Central Council in Dublin began reporting on Gaelic activities in Britain.

Reflecting the sense of patriotism often felt by Gaelic minded people, one of the first clubs' affiliated to the growing GAA in London was the Robert Emmet's club of Marylebone. The idea of calling a club after a perceived patriot has been a hallmark of GAA club's since the founding of the Association. Indeed, when the Tuam Krugers Club was founded in County Galway around 1900, that club's name amounted to a clear statement with regards hostility towards British colonialism and the Boer War then underway in South Africa.

London has played a significant role in GAA history and Michael Collins, Liam McCarthy and Sam Maguire, figures involved in the struggle for Irish independence in the early part of the 20th century, all played Gaelic Sports in London. McCarthy and Maguire of course give their names to the All-Ireland Hurling and Football trophies respectively.[21]

Beyond London, in 1960 the Herefordshire County Board was formed by a small group under the leadership of its first founder chairman, Cork's Father Jerome O'Hanlon. Gloucestershire formed its first Gaelic hurling club The Emmetts, in 1928. Yorkshire formed the first County Board spearheaded by Father Donal Stritch in 1949. In the same year famous Yorkshire Gaelic clubs' like Hugh O Neills and St Brendans of Leeds were also founded. The Warwickshire County Board was formed in 1944.

In west-central Scotland, linking with the development of the Irish language organisation the Gaelic League, as well as plethora of other political and cultural activities among the diaspora there, the first GAA club was founded in the east end of Glasgow in 1897.[22] 1903 marked the formation of Glasgow's first county board, which included Rapparees, Wishaw Shamrocks, Fagan-bealachs Carfin, Patrick Sarsfields Coatbridge, Finn MacCumhails Anderston and Partick, Hibernians Pollockshaws and Cuchulains Polmadie: all clubs in and around the city of Glasgow.[23]

The GAA in Scotland experienced numerous successes and downturns, much of its fortunes like elsewhere in the diaspora, related to the presence or otherwise of first-generation Irish immigrants in providing various skills with regards playing, planning and organising, but mostly, in terms of knowledge, expertise and enthusiasm brought from home clubs in Ireland. By the new millennium, Scotland contained five football clubs, Glaschu Gaels, Tir Conail Harps, Dundee Dalriada, Sands MacSwineys and Dunedin Connollys: this in addition to a number of minor successes in the promotion of youth football among second- to fifth-generation Irish boys and girls and among others with little or no Irish connections. This includes participating under the 'Scotland' banner in the annual boys and girls aged under fourteen Feile competitions held annually in Ireland, for scores of clubs in Ireland as well as for a number from England and the USA (usually representing counties such as London, Lancashire, New York, etc.).

The GAA: history, politics, diaspora and sport

Today, the Association and its members retain unique identities amid a growing emphasis on globalisation, commercialism and 'world sports'. Gaelic sports remain a forum through which cultural, national and local identities are projected, maintained and celebrated. It size and signifi-cance to people in and beyond Ireland disrupts its amateur status, also raising questions about where much sport in the world has travelled – often to their detriment – in terms of media control and athletes salaries.

The beauty, skills, artistry, athleticism, passions and emotions linked to playing and watching Gaelic Sports, means that the Gaelic Athletic Association has become part of the fabric of life in Ireland since 1884. Amid the diaspora, as well as the qualities involved in playing fast and excit-ing field based team games, Gaelic sports are also a vehicle for ethnic Irishness. The GAA pro-vides a concrete link with the country of birth or origin. The history of the GAA has become one of the outstanding stories of modern sport.

Notes

1 From the Irish Parliament of William 111, National Library of Ireland.
2 Kevin Whelan, 'The Geography of Hurling', *History Ireland*, 1, 1 (1993), pp. 27–31.
3 M. De Burca, *The Story of the GAA*, Wolfhound Press, Dublin, 1990, p. 5.
4 J. Sugden and A. Bairner, 'Northern Ireland; Sport in a Divided Society', in L. Allison, *The Politics Of Sport*, Manchester University Press, 1986, pp. 90–117.
5 P. Puirseal, *The GAA in its Time*, The Purcell Family, Carrigeen, Dublin, 1982, p. 10.
6 *GAA Official Guide*, 1994.
7 From P. Healy, 'Irish Nationalism and the Origins of the Gaelic Athletic Association', unpublished dis-sertation, history BA degree, University of North London, 1994.
8 Michael Mullan, 'Opposition, Social Closure, and Sport: The Gaelic Athletic Association in the Nine-teenth Century', *Sociology of Sport Journal*, 12 (1995), pp. 268–289.
9 Mark Tierney, 'Croke of Cashel', All-Ireland Final match programme, 17 September 1995, p. 78.
10 The Fenians was the name of the mid-19th century Irish organisation who engaged in military struggle against Britain for an independent Ireland.
11 M. Holmes, 'Symbols of National Identity: The Case of the Irish National Football Team', *Irish Political Studies*, 9 (1994), pp. 81–98.
12 De Burca, *The Story of the GAA*.
13 Whelan, 'The Geography of Hurling'; also Mullan, 'Opposition, Social Closure, and Sport'.
14 P. Rouse, 'The Politics of Culture and Sport in Ireland: A History of the GAA Ban on Foreign Games 1884–1971. Part One: 1884–1921', *The International Journal of the History of Sport*, 10, 3 (1993), pp. 333–360.
15 Puirseal, *The GAA in its Time*, p. 103.
16 De Burca, *The Story of the GAA*, p. 100.
17 Mullan, 'Opposition, Social Closure, and Sport', p. 283.
18 Flanagan, cited in G.A. Carr, 'The Spartakiad: Its Approach and Modification from the Mass Displays of the Sokol', *Canadian Journal of History of Sport*, 18 (May 1987), p. 87.
19 W.F. Mandle, 'The Irish Republican Brotherhood and the Beginnings of the Gaelic Athletic Associa-tion', *Irish Historical Studies*, 20, 80 (1977), pp. 418–438; also W.F. Mandle, *The GAA and Irish Nationalist Politics*, Helm, Gill and MacMillan, Dublin, 1987.
20 R. Holt, 'Sport and History: The State of the Subject in Britain', *Twentieth Century British History*, 7, 2 (1996), pp. 231–252.
21 J.M. Bradley, *The Gaelic Athletic Association and Irishness in Scotland: History, Ethnicity, Politics, Culture and Identity*, Argyll Publishing, Scotland, 2007.
22 *Glasgow Examiner*, 11 September 1897.
23 Bradley, *The Gaelic Athletic Association and Irishness in Scotland*.

41

Highland games

James Bowness and Aaron Zipp

Introduction

The Highland games take place around the world, but nevertheless remain strongly related to the Highland regions of Scotland. The games involve a series of sporting events that include running, jumping, dancing, cycling, tug-o-war, wrestling and heavy athletics. Surrounding the sporting events are musical performances with bagpipes, parading clans, food and drink stalls and a variety of vendors. Of all aspects of the games, the heavy athletics is the best known. In being the focal point of the games, this chapter will focus upon the heavy events and will explore the variation in how the games are played across the world.

Heavy athletics consists of a variety of strength, power and co-ordination challenges. Many of the events originate and were developed from the requirements of agricultural labour.[1] The 'open stone' is an event that led to the introduction of the shot put found in track and field athletics.[2] Confined to a box, the athlete must throw the weight as far as possible. Athletes often utilise a series of full body rotations to build momentum before release. The 'Braemar stone' is similar to the open stone but with a heavier weight. This is another event with the aim of throwing the object as far as possible, yet rotational movement is not allowed and the throw consists of a standing putt. The 'heavy weight throw' and the 'light weight throw' both involve an object that descends from a short metal chain. The athlete must throw the object as far as possible. There is no stipulation on technique but the thrower must not cross a demarcated line. The light weight throw follows the same rules as the heavy weight throw, but weighs just over half as much. The 'heavy hammer' and 'light hammer' are similar to track and field's hammer throw, with the only difference relating to the implement itself. Whereas track and field's hammer involves a weighted ball sat at the end of a wire, the Highland version has a more rigid shaft. Typically the heavy hammer weighs 22 lb for men and 16 lb for women, while the light hammer weighs 16 lb for men and 12 lb for women.[3] The 'weight over bar' event involves athletes throwing a weighted ball over a framework that raises a bar to ever increasing heights. A range of techniques are used, from a rotational throw to a static overhead throw. Three attempts are permitted.[4]

The centrepiece of any Highland games is the 'caber toss', an event that developed from the traditional methods of roofing in the agrarian Highlands.[5] Today's cabers are wooden poles that must fulfil certain girth and length requirements. In Scotland, cabers can vary between 4 and

5 meters; have a diameter of 25–35cm at the thick end and 10–15cm at the thin end.[6] However, the weight and not length is not standardised between all games across the globe. The thrower must attempt to flip the log and is marked upon its landing position. The best possible outcome is a successful flip where the log lands at a 12 o'clock position in relation to the thrower. This means that the flipped caber will lie on the ground along a straight line directly ahead of the athlete. The caber toss normally takes place individually, but in the last 5 years there have been multiple successful attempts at breaking the world record for the number of cabers successfully tossed simultaneously. In 2014, at the Masters World Championships in Inverness, 160 throwers concurrently tossed 66 cabers.[7] Less than a year later, the Fergus Scottish Festival and Highland games, Canada, regained its world record with 80 throwers flipping 69 cabers in unison.[8] The transatlantic exchanging of caber toss world records is only one signifier of the global spread within the games. This chapter will now map the movement of the Highland games from its Scottish origins to its global location in the 21st century.

History of the games

The Highland games make up a key aspect of Scotland's cultural history and a number of scholars have examined the socio-historical context of its transformations. One of the most complete accounts of this history comes from the sociologist Grant Jarvie.[9] This section will recount much of his work on the history of the Scottish Highland games.

Verifying the origins of the Highland games has been troubled by paucity of authentic sources. Credible historical sources on the history of the games stretch back only to the late 18th century.[10] Nevertheless, various accounts suggest its origins lie in the 11th century and a single event that took place in Braemar.[11] Plagued by a lack of textual evidence, these previous historical accounts have relied upon folklore and often embellished into the form of a myth. [12] The original tale suggests that King Malcolm (Malcolm Canmore 1058–1093) had organised a footrace to the summit of Craig Choinnich, a hill in the area known locally as the Braes of Mar. The winner of the race would gain the honour of becoming the king's messenger. Allegedly, two brothers were engaged in a dramatic finish that was celebrated in proceeding years by a gathering of locals. These gatherings developed into a tradition, one that would eventually flower into the creation of the Braemar Highland games some seven centuries later. [13] The terms 'Gathering' and 'games' are often used interchangeably. The early use of the term gathering refers to the congregation of clans which over time, developed into the festival style gatherings that now surround the games. [14]

The 700 years between the 11th and 18th centuries saw the initial formation of the cultural forms that we understand as being typical of 'Highlandesque' today.[15] This period provided the antecedents that led to the creation of a romantic Scottish cultural identity in the early 19th century. Images of the kilt, clan tartan and of Scotland's rurality produced what has been termed 'tartanry' and 'kailyardism'.[16] These stereotypical cultural icons have come to represent Scotland and are often assumed to have a longer history than they really have. Various accounts highlight how the historical origin of the kilt, and various clan tartans, is much more recent than popularly believed.[17] Beliefs around the longevity of such items were often propagated by romanticist literary men of the early 19th century.[18] Popular culture of the 20th century has also propagated these myths, with the film *Braveheart* (1995) portraying Scots wearing kilts some 400 years before their actual origin.

The period between 1740 and 1850 marked the cultural marginalisation of Highlanders by the English crown. In quelling the Jacobite uprising of 1745, the British state pursued an 'anglicisation' of the Highland region.[19] The act of proscription (1746) banned the communal gatherings of Highlanders and prohibited the wearing of Scottish dress.[20] The playing of bagpipes and carrying of traditional arms were also banned.[21] Although the act was repealed in 1782, the damage to the clan social structure was complete. As chief: clansfolk became landlord: tenant the social transformation of the Highland region was under way. Clan lands now became private property and clan's folk became tenants to those who had formerly been clan chiefs. The area of the Highlands named Sutherland was one area in which 794,000 acres of previously clan-owned land became the property of the Countess of Sutherland.[22] In appropriating such land the Highland clearances led to widespread emigration; a migration of people that played a key role in the globalising of the games.

The late 18th and early 19th centuries witnessed a revival in Highland culture. Despite the ongoing emigration of Highlanders, various Highland Societies were created in order to preserve a traditional culture. This led to the creation of various Highland Gatherings that continue to exist today (for example the Northern Meeting, Braemar and Lonach). Icons that had become transgressive due to the act of proscription were now presented again. This period was one in which Highland landlords attached new meanings to old cultural icons.[23] The romantic literature associated with the likes of Walter Scott influenced the ceremonial use of Highland Dress.[24] Highland cultural identity was quickly becoming a Scottish cultural identity based on kitsch symbolism. This can perhaps be exemplified by the visit to Edinburgh of King George IV in 1822. In an attempt to further incorporate Scotland into the British state, the King dressed entirely in Highland dress.[25] This marked the beginning of a relationship between Highland culture and British monarchs.

The period between 1850 and 1920 has been positioned as the golden era in the development in the Highland games. Buoyed by the support of Queen Victoria, the games grew in popularity. This marked a process referred to as 'balmoralisation', the growing interconnection between the Queen's residence at Balmoral and the Braemar Highland Gathering. The Monarchy was influential in furthering the Highland games, but this occurred alongside the emergence of 'sporting landlords' who recreated land in the Highlands and often constituted the organising committee of Highland Gatherings.[26] These sporting landlords transformed farming land to sporting spaces for more lucrative endeavours such as deer hunting. Those who had previously worked the land suffered, with many either forced or coerced into emigration. The migration of these marginalised or aspirational families also meant that Scottish population growth stagnated.[27]

The popularity of the games in the 20th century faltered as the games struggled to adapt to wider social changes.[28] The continuation of traditional values became 'kitsch' in a surrounding society that had become more rational, bureaucratised and modern. Like various sports, the games became governed by bureaucracies that created standardised rules and records.[29] At the same time the Highland games underwent commodification, a process whereby a variety of commercial interests have, in some cases, turned particular gatherings into profit-making enterprises.[30] The games, in Scotland, have also been challenged by a growth in the awareness and representation of other global sports. Nevertheless, members of the royal family continue to attend the Braemar Highland Gathering and approximately 80 gatherings took place across Scotland in 2018.[31] This, however, only contributes a fraction of the games that took place across the world. How these games began is inextricably linked to the migration of Scots, a topic we will not address.

The Scottish diaspora and the games

Highland games are no longer simply a community festival taking place in the northern regions of Scotland. Events take place in nations that have seen substantial immigration by Scots. The history of Scots moving within the former British Empire is well known.[32] Briefly put, the second half of the 1700s saw transatlantic emigration to Canada and the US, while others were enticed to Australia for the profitability of untouched land.[33] The late 17th and early 18th century also marked a lesser known migratory path, often to other European nations such as Holland, Denmark, Sweden and what is now known as Belgium. These channels of emigration created a diaspora which, in celebrating its own cultural heritage, led to the creation of their own versions of the games around the world.[34]

Caledonian societies were often the driving force behind the creation of Highland games outside of Scotland. Initially many Caledonian societies excluded those locals that did not have Scottish ancestry.[35] Nevertheless, approximately 1200 of these societies were formed in the US between 1850 and 1914.[36] These groups led to the creation of around 125 US Highland games events by 1920.[37] By this point Caledonian Societies were much more inclusive, meaning that local Highland Gatherings were to be enjoyed by all, regardless of ethnic background.[38]

The mid-20th century saw a contraction in the number of games played. There were only around 25 games held annually within the 1960s.[39] Yet this was to rapidly turn around by the explosion of individuals, most often the descendants of Scots migrants, who took great interest in preserving a Scottish identity. By 2003, there were almost 230 games in the US and a further 70 held in Canada. Compared to the 80 or so games held in Scotland, North America contributes at least three times as many Highland games events each year.[40]

Across the Atlantic there are also approximately 130 games per year within continental Europe,[41] again dwarfing the number of games taking place within Scotland. Germany, the host of most continental European games, saw most of its expansion in the late 20th century.[42] There is little evidence to suggest that migration of Scots to continental Europe led to the creation of a Highland games scene a few centuries later. This is crucial in understanding the large variety that exists not only between North American and Scottish games, but also within continental Europe. It is these differences that we will now address.

Geographical Variation in the games

It is indisputable that common cultural icons and practices are shared across games events around the world. The wearing of Highland dress is universal, but variations also exists. The games held in Scotland continue to reproduce much of the traditions established from the late 18th and early 19th centuries. Most Scottish games are held in the months of July and August, differing greatly in size.[43] The biggest games are held at Cowal, where around 20,000–23,000 spectators attend annually.[44] In 2018 approximately 80 Highland games were due to take place in Scotland, down from the 96 scheduled in 2007 and the 117 organised for 2000.[45] Most games events fall under the remit of the Scottish Highland games Association (SHGA), a body that provides documentation of basic rules across a range of sporting disciplines.[46] The heavy athletics events in Scotland take place either as individual competition at a singular event or as a championship format using a range of events. For example, the Braemar games does not have an overall championship competition, while the Cowal games has championship titles and a standalone caber competition.[47] The games played in North America have championship events as standard.

The games held in North America are sanctioned and officiated by levels of governing associations. This oversight is necessary for the preservation of safety, integrity, and competitiveness, often through the standardisation and moderation of rules. An example of a highly influential body is the North American Scottish games Association (NASGA), which works to ensure that athletes are competing with standardised equipment. All implements must be the same dimensions and constructed of approved material. Aids for suitable substances worn on the hands

Figure 41.1   Terri Ventress, three times Masters World Champion.
Photo by Laurence Ventress

such as gloves, tape, sticky must be standardised for all competitions. The size and shape of the throwing area, the method of scoring, the order of events and even the process for recording and sharing the breaking of records are all subject to the same rules.[48]

In contrast to the games in Scotland, the North American rules stipulate that a Scottish heavy events competition must have at least five events.[49] However, the geographical vastness of North America means that a variety of governing bodies exist, each having their own vagaries around the rules of competition.[50] Nevertheless, most North American competitions are held across a variety of age, weight and experience categories. Men and women are divided into A, B and C classes based on experience. Weight categories, for men under 200 lb and women below 150 lb, exist to offer competition for those at a physical disadvantage (see image). Meanwhile, games in Scotland tend to have simple categories for men and women, with some ancillary groupings for young or local athletes. The North American heavy athletics also feature an event that is rarely played in Scotland. The sheaf toss involves the vertical tossing of a bundle of straw. Weighing around 9 kg for men and 4.5 kg for women, the sheaf is thrown over a raised bar that is heightened after each successful attempt.[51]

Whereas athletes in Scotland and North America compete alone, most continental European games draw upon a team-based structure consisting of groups of four to six.[52] Unique events litter the continental European games, often reflecting local icons and customs. In Bressuire, France a 12.8kg champagne cork is thrown, while the Alpen games in Austria play 'kilted soccer'.[53] Away from the festival environment, a range of European enterprises offer team building exercises that involve participating in Highland games events.[54] Most European games organisers have little or no Scottish heritage, instead creating inspired events with local touches.[55] As in Scotland and North America, the magnitude of continental European games differs greatly. The largest games are likely to be the Peine Highland Gathering, close to Hanover, Germany. In 2009 it was estimated that around 20,000 spectators had attended the event; a number that rivals that of the biggest games in Scotland.[56] The Highland games globally is splintered by these geographical variations, but it has also been transformed by wider social changes. The inclusion of previously marginalised groups will now be discussed.

The games and inclusivity

The construction of the games as we know it today, mainly through the 18th and 19th centuries, was determined by a clan structure that was undeniably patriarchal. The 'clan', a Gaelic word for family or children, were led by male chiefs who gained their power via kinship rather than ownership of local lands. The chief was understood to be 'the natural leader or father of his people'.[57] The games space has largely followed these gendered dynamics with most participants being young males. Yet the late 20th and early 21st centuries has witnessed a change in gender relations across both sport and wider society.[58] The Highland games have not been left behind in these social changes.

In North America, the prevalence of female athletes in heavy events has grown immensely. Despite being significantly behind the development of the men's games, Canada first hosted a women's competition in 1995.[59] In the US, the introduction of women appears to date back to the 1980s.[60] The women's games in the US are bigger than in Canada and within the United States it is not uncommon for events to offer Women's A and B level categories. Though in the interest of time, competition classes are sometimes under-enrolled and are therefore combined with scores kept separate. There has been some concern around sexism within the Highland games overall[61] and within its women's heavy athletics in particular.[62] Concerns have included the lack of attention given to the women's Game, the spatial and chronological locating of women's competition and also the media representations of female athletes. In Scotland it is rare to see women throwing in Highland games and it appears that the growth of the women's Game is also limited in continental Europe. Although female spectators still outnumber female participants, the European games do offer women a chance to partake in either mixed or all-female teams.[63]

Another area in which the games have expanded is in its provision of competition for older athletes. Dedicated Masters World Championships (MWGs) have run annually since

2001, with a variety of countries hosting the event. The US has hosted most MWGs at 12, while Scotland has accommodated the event 3 times. Canada, Iceland and Germany have all held the MWGs once.[64] Competition follows the North American format of competition with multiple events adding up to an overall standing. The championships offer competition across a range of age categories, with the oldest athletes participating in the over 80s category. Competition among the men under 50 years of age is also divided into 'heavies' and those under 200 lb in weight. The last games to be hosted in Scotland took place in Inverness during 2014. Here 126 men and 34 women participated in the event, representing 12 different nations. Only 17 athletes registered as residing in Scotland, while the majority of athletes travelled from the United States (107). Almost 80% of the women competing at the 2014 MWGs came from the US and no women residing in Scotland took part.[65] This reinforces the notion that the women's games have seen its biggest development within North America.

Elsewhere, one argument suggests that the growth of a Masters movement is one face of liberalisation that has occurred within the games.[66] Facing many of the challenges present in the mid to late 20th century, the encouragement of women and older adults to the games is a necessity in a surrounding culture that offers new possibilities for both groups. The Masters Highland games athletes transgress more enfeebling discourses that situate ageing bodies as frail and dependant.[67] Extending the games to these groups has also brought about new logics to the practice of playing in the games. Participation can be seen as challenging both gendered and aged stereotypes.[68] These social changes have led to what could be described as a pluralism of rationales for participation; a topic that we will now explore.

Taking part in the games

Understanding the rationales behind participation in the Highland games is an underdeveloped area of research on the Highland games. Much research on this topic understands the games as a way of preserving culture and heritage.[69] Historical accounts have often taken this line and suggested that spectatorship and participation at Highland games is simply about reproducing and protecting a diasporic identity. Research into tourism has also examined the phenomenon, exploring ideas such as cultural authenticity.[70] The perception of authenticity around cultural icons has been established as a key component of heritage tourism and is perceived as one attraction of the games. Authenticity has also been explored through the examination of North Americans completing genealogical research that legitimises a link to Scotland and the Highlands.[71] This takes a role within the Masters' community where an interesting relationship exists between genealogical research and participation in the games.[72] Some athletes had performed heritage research prior to beginning a career in the Highland games, a phenomenon that to some extent can be understood as a performance of national identity.[73] Others had been inspired by the games community to undertake further research.[74]

Other athletes have little or no connection to Scotland or its diasporic population. Within the Masters community it was established that many athletes transitioned comfortably from other sporting disciplines.[75] Many athletes had backgrounds in track and field athletics or in bodybuilding/powerlifting. The ease of this transition between sports is facilitated by the similarities between the ways in which the body is used across each activity. These sports are connected by a shared bodily hexis; an embodiment that occupies bodily dispositions that stretch across these sporting disciplines.[76]

Enactments of these shared practices are sometimes facilitated by the organisation of the games itself. One growing trend is the hybridisation of the traditional Scottish heavy events with other strength events such as ones derived from the World's Strongest Man competitions. It is also becoming a popular choice for event organisers and promoters, with the added spectacle potentially drawing in more spectators. One example of this is the Luss Highland games, held near Loch Lomond. Here athletes can compete in the typical Highland games events but also a strongman competition.[77] This format also features at the Topeka Classic Strength Festival in Kansas, USA.[78] This offers a competitive platform for many athletes who would otherwise compete at different venues across their various sports.

Conclusion

This chapter has tracked a variety of developments that have occurred within the Highland games. First, a social history of the games in Scotland located the development of the games in its origin nation. Highlighting the lack of credible evidence on the origins of the games, the creation of what we know as the Highland games took place in the late 18th and early 19th centuries. The golden era of the games came during the late 1800s; made famous in some part by the advocacy of Queen Victoria. The 20th century provided a series of challenges for the Highland games, with the modernisation and rationalisation of Scottish society seen as incompatible with the Highland tradition.

Secondly, this history and the wider social developments of the Scottish Highlands led to a migration of people to various parts of the world. This migration provided the framework for the globalising of the games. The nations of Australia, Canada and the US all created Highland games events as a result of initial migration and the reflexivity of those with Scottish ancestry. Although a small Scottish diaspora does exist within continental Europe, the development of the games there was divorced from such migratory patterns.

Thirdly, some of the vagaries of the games in each location have been described. North America hosts the most games events throughout the year and has also created a standardised framework with which to play the sport. European games have a much more pluralistic approach to the games, with competitions often differing through the inclusion of local, regional or sub-national cultures. The games in Scotland continues in the same vain as it did through its formalisation in the early 1800s.

Fourthly, we have explored some of the wider social changes that have been embraced by some of the Highland games. Women, while still being in the minority of participants, have developed their sport with slowly growing numbers. Older athletes have also been embraced by the games. Developing from the early 2000s, World Championships for Masters athletes have been held at a variety of locations across the world. The inclusion of both women and older adults can be seen as a form of liberalisation in the face of the wider social changes brought about in the late 20th and early 21st centuries.

Finally we explored some of the rationales for participation. Beyond merely celebrating Scottish heritage, culture and customs, the games mean different things to different people. Many athletes incorporated the sport into a wider sport and physical activity career, one that often included participation in track and field athletics or other strength based sports (powerlifting, bodybuilding). This variety of rationales is fitting, given that the sport itself has developed at different rates and in different ways from its original formation in the late 1700s.

Notes

1 G. Jarvie and J. Burnett, *Sport, Scotland and the Scots* (East Linton: Tuckwell, 2000), 128–142
2 'Shot Put', retrieved from: www.iaaf.org/disciplines/throws/shot-put (accessed 15 November 2018)

3 'Hammer Throw', retrieved from www.scottishheavyathletics.com/hammer.html (accessed 7 November 2018).

4 Ibid.

5 Jarvie and Burnett, *Sport, Scotland and the Scots*, 128–142.

6 'Specific rules relating to tradition Scottish Heavy Events at Amateur Highland Games' *Scottish Athletics* Retrieved from: www.scottishathletics.org.uk/wp-content/uploads/2014/04/Specific-Rules-Relating-to-Traditional-Scottish-Heavy-Events-at-Amateur-Highland-Games.pdf (accessed 13 November 2018).

7 'Scottish History Made: Caber Tossing World Record Set in Inverness', retrieved from www.guinnessworldrecords.com/news/2014/9/scottish-history-made-most-people-caber-tossing-simultaneously-world-record-set-in-inverness-60499 (accessed 7 November 2018).

8 'Fergus Scottish Festival Reclaims Caber Toss Guinness World Record', retrieved from www.wellingtonadvertiser.com/comments/index.cfm?articleID=27376 (accessed 7 November 2018).

9 G. Jarvie, *Highland Games: The Making of the Myth* (Edinburgh: Edinburgh University Press, 1991).

10 Ibid., 2–11.

11 See the works of I. Colquhoun and H. Machell, *Highland Gatherings* (London: Heath Cranton, 1927); D.P. Webster, *Scottish Highland Games* (Glasgow: Collins, 1959); and D.P. Webster and LE, Richardson, *The World History of Highland Games* (Edinburgh: Luath, 2011).

12 Jarvie, *Highland Games*, 14–32.

13 Ibid.

14 Ibid., 28–30.

15 Ibid.

16 I. Brown, *From Tartan to Tartanry: Scottish Culture, History and Myth* (Edinburgh: Edinburgh University Press, 2010).

17 This is explored both by H. Trevor-Roper, 'The Invention of Tradition: The Highland Tradition of Scotland', in E. Hobsbawm and T. Ranger (eds), *The Invention of Tradition.* (Cambridge: Cambridge University Press, 1983), and J.T. Dunbar, *History of Highland Dress* (Edinburgh: Oliver & Boyd, 1962).

18 D. McCrone, *The New Sociology of Scotland* (London: Sage, 2017).

19 Jarvie, *Highland Games*, 16–22.

20 D.P. Webster and L.E. Richardson, *The World History of Highland Games* (Edinburgh: Luath, 2011).

21 D. Stewart, *Sketches the Highlanders of Scotland* (Edinburgh, 1822).

22 K. Marx, 'The Duchess of Sutherland and Slavery' *The People's Paper 12* (1853), 45.

23 Jarvie, *Highland Games*, 43–61.

24 I.F. Grant, *Highland Folk Ways* (London: Routledge & Kegan, 1961).

25 Jarvie, *Highland Games*, 59

26 Ibid., 75.

27 M. Fry, The Scottish Diaspora and the Empire. In M. Leith and D. Sim (eds), *The Modern Scottish Diaspora: Contemporary Debates and Perspectives* (Edinburgh: Edinburgh University Press, 2014), 32–46

28 Jarvie, *Highland Games*, 81–100.

29 E. Dunning and K. Sheard, 'Barbarians', in *Gentlemen and Players: A Sociological Study of the Development of Rugby Football* (Oxford: Martin Robertson & Co, 1979).

30 Jarvie, *Highland Games*, 86.

31 Visit Scotland, 'Highland Games', retrieved from www.visitscotland.com/see-do/events/highland-games (accessed 2 November 2018)

32 T.M. Devine, *Scotland's Empire: The Origins of the Global Diaspora* (London: Penguin, 2012).

33 M. Fry, The Scottish Diaspora and the Empire. In M. Leith M. and D. Sim (eds), *The Modern Scottish Diaspora: Contemporary Debates and Perspectives* (Edinburgh: Edinburgh University Press, 2014), 32–46.

34 M. Brewster, J. Connell and SJ. Page, 'The Scottish Highland Games: Evolution, Development and Role as a Community Event'. *Current Issues in Tourism* 1, 12 (2009) 271–293.

35 K. Sullivan, 'Scots by Association: Clubs and Societies in the Scottish Diaspora', in M. Leith and D. Sim (eds), *The Modern Scottish Diaspora: Contemporary Debates and Perspectives* (Edinburgh: Edinburgh University Press, 2014), 47–63.

36 T.M. Devine, *To the Ends of the Earth: Scotland's Diaspora, 1750–2010.* (London: Penguin, 2011).

37 C. Ray, 'Transatlantic Scots and Ethnicity', in C. Ray and J. Hunter (eds), *Transatlantic Scots* (Alabama: University of Alabama Press, 2005), 21–47.

38 See the examples within Sullivan, 'Scots by Association', and G. Redmond, *The Caledonian Games in Nineteenth-Century America.* (Rutherford, NJ: Fairleigh Dickinson University Press, 1971).

39 Ray, 'Transatlantic Scots and Ethnicity', 21–47.

40 Ibid.

41 D. Hesse, *Warrior Dreams: Playing Scotsmen in Mainland Europe.* (Oxford: Oxford University Press, 2014), 108–129.

42 Ibid.

43 Brewster et al., 'The Scottish Highland Games', 271–293.

44 A difference in the estimations of attendance at Cowal exists between the organisers themselves and the press. The Scotsman suggests the figure is closer to 20,000, while the Cowal Gathering website suggests 23,000: 'A Guide to the 2018 Highland Games in Scotland and Why You Should Go to One of Them', retrieved from www.scotsman.com/news/a-guide-to-the-2018-highland-games-in-scotland-and-why-you-should-go-to-one-of-them-1-4721528 (accessed 6 November 2018), and 'About the Event', retrieved from www.cowalgathering.com/event-guide/about/ (accessed 6 November 2018)

45 The figure for 2007 can be taken from Brewster et al., 'The Scottish Highland Games', 271–293. The earlier number comes from: E. Lothian, 'Tourism Games and the Commodification of Tradition', in J. Horne (ed.), *Leisure Cultures, Consumption and Commodification* (Eastbourne: LSA Publications, 2001).

46 'Competition Rules', Retrieved from: www.shga.co.uk/competition-rules.php (accessed 9 November 2018).

47 From the Braemar results, athletes compete across individual disciplines: 'Braemar Gathering, Events', retrieved from www.braemargathering.org/events (accessed 9 November 2018). From Cowal, the Games offers results on overall championships and a standalone caber competition: 'Cowal Gathering', retrieved from www.cowalgathering.com/results/heavy-athletics (accessed 9 November 2018).

48 North American Scottish Games Association, 'Rules', retrieved from www.nasgaweb.com/rules.asp (accessed 9 November 2018).

49 This rule is rule 1 of the general rules for all events and can be found at: 'North American Scottish Games Association: Rules', retrieved from www.nasgaweb.com/rules.asp (accessed 9 November 2018).

50 An overview of these differences comes from M. McVey, 'Comparing the Rule Sets: NASGA Based vs Others', retrieved from www.heavyeventsjudging.org/comparingrulesets/nasgavsothers/ (accessed 9 November 2018).

51 Scottish Heavy Athletics, 'Sheaf Toss', retrieved from www.scottishheavyathletics.com/sheaf.html (accessed 9 November 2018).

52 D. Hesse, *Warrior Dreams: Playing Scotsmen in Mainland Europe* (Oxford: Oxford University Press, 2014), 108–129.

53 Ibid.

54 Ibid.

55 Ibid.

56 C. Davies, 'Families Flock to Germany's Highland Games', 3 May 2009, retrieved from www.theguardian.com/world/2009/may/03/highland-games-peine-germany (accessed 9 November 2018)

57 Jarvie, *Highland Games*, 33.

58 R. Jeanes, L. Hills and T. Kay, 'Women, Sport and Gender Inequity', in B. Houlihan and D. Malcolm (eds), *Sport and Society* (London: Sage, 2016), 134–156.

59 J.C. Freeman-Gibb, 'Women's Involvement in Highland Games Heavy Events: A Hope and Strengths Perspective' (2016). Electronic Theses and Dissertations. 5820. https://scholar.uwindsor.ca/etd/5820

60 D.P. Webster and L.E. Richardson, *The World History of Highland Games* (Edinburgh: Luath, 2011), 231–235.

61 B. Borland, 'Highland Games across Scotland Accused of Sexism', 18 February 2018, retrieved from www.express.co.uk/news/uk/920384/Highland-Games-Dufftown-Scotland-sexism-feminist-website-accusation (Accessed 08 November 2018)

62 The suggestion of sexism faced by the women's athletes can be found in Webster and Richardson, *World History of Highland Games*; Freeman-Gibb, '*Women's Involvement in Highland Games Heavy Events*; and also in J. Bowness, *Physical Activity in Later Life : A Phenomenology of Ageing Men and Women in the Masters Highland Games* (London: British Library EThOS, 2017).

63 D. Hesse, *Warrior Dreams: Playing Scotsmen in Mainland Europe* (Oxford: Oxford University Press, 2014), 116.

64 Bowness, *Physical Activity in Later Life.*

65 Ibid.

66 Ibid.

67 Ibid.

68 Ibid.

69 G. Jarvie, 'The North American Émigré, Highland Games and social capital in international communities', in C. Ray (ed.), *Transatlantic Scots* (Tuscaloosa, AL: University of Alabama Press, 2005), 198–214.

70 D. Chhabra, R. Healy and E. Sills, 'Staged Authenticity and Heritage Tourism', *Annals of Tourism Research* 30, 3 (2003), 702–719.

71 P. Basu, *Highland Homecomings: Genealogy and Heritage Tourism in the Scottish Diaspora.* (Routledge: London, 2007).

72 Bowness, *Physical Activity in Later Life*, 174–212.

73 T. Edensor, *National Identity, Popular Culture and Everyday Life.* (Oxford: Berg, 2002).

74 Bowness, *Physical Activity in Later Life*, 174–212.

75 Ibid., 136–173.

76 Ibid., 168–174. See the use of Bourdieusian social theory and the concept of bodily hexis.

77 Luss Highland Games, 'Event Schedule', retrieved from www.lusshighlandgames.co.uk/event-schedule (accessed 12 November 2018).

78 Topeka Strength Classic Festival, 'About', retrieved from www.topekagames.com/about (accessed 15 November 2018)

Index

Note: Page locators in *italic* refer to figures and page locators in **bold** refer to tables.

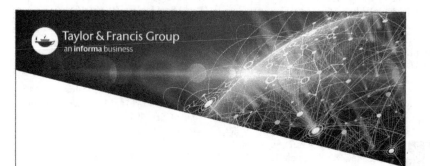